DATE DUE

~~ill 1841752~~	
~~WVU 3 01 05~~	

ESSAYS ON THE OCCASION OF THE SEVENTIETH ANNIVERSARY OF THE DROPSIE UNIVERSITY

ESSAYS ON THE OCCASION OF THE SEVENTIETH ANNIVERSARY OF THE DROPSIE UNIVERSITY

(1909-1979)

Edited by Abraham I. Katsh
and Leon Nemoy

Published by
THE DROPSIE UNIVERSITY
Philadelphia, PA 19132 U.S.A.

Library of Congress Catalog Number: 79-88348

Printed in the United States of America

ISBN 0-9602686-0-X

This volume is dedicated to
the memory of Professor Solomon Zeitlin ז"ל
(died December 28, 1976)

Professor Solomon Zeitlin, who originally headed this project, was an alumnus and teacher of The Dropsie University for six decades. His scholarship was original and profound, his teaching stimulating and challenging. His friendships were widespread and enduring. The results of his scholarship are incorporated in hundreds of articles and in a number of monographs. The effectiveness of his teaching is witnessed by numerous disciples who carry forward his tradition of earnest research. His friendship, however, must remain a personal and precious memory. The contributors to this volume and everyone associated with Dropsie University express herewith their profound sense of loss. The memory of Solomon Zeitlin will surely continue to serve as a blessing for future generations of scholars.

CONTENTS

INTRODUCTION

Moses Aaron Dropsie, Philadelphia lawyer, had a vision—the establishment of an institution of higher learning that would be nonsectarian and nontheological, and devoted solely to the study of Hebrew, Biblical and Rabbinic literature, the Middle East, and cognate fields. As such, it would be the first of its kind in America.

In his will, made public after his death in 1905, he wrote: "My primary object is that as far as possible every branch of knowledge shall be taught in the said college requisite to the attainment of mature scholarship in Hebrew and cognate learning, with which would be conducted original investigation and research." In a word, a school concerned with *Torah Lishmah*, learning for its own sake, protected by the widest academic freedom and pursued by scholars who would be admitted without distinction as to color, sex, or creed. The research, untrammeled by any doctrine, dogma, or bias, would be in accordance with the objective and critical methodology of detached inquiry fostered by the *Wissenschaft des Judentums* school.

By one of those not-so-rare coincidences of history, an institution similar to Dropsie was opened in 1908 in St. Petersburg, Russia, by the scholarly Jewish philanthropist, Baron David Guenzburg. Among the students in that academy were Professor Solomon Zeitlin, to whose memory this volume is dedicated, and Zalman Shazar, third President of the State of Israel. On November 1, 1970, when Dropsie University conferred an honorary doctorate on President Shazar, the late President noted this coincidence, as well as the unique significance of the school:

> "The Institution founded by Baron Guenzburg in Petrograd was cruelly cut down by the regime in Russia which has suppressed Jewish culture within that country and in countries under its influence. For the searing agony of that loss there can be no atonement, not even in Russia's contribution to the rescue of thousands of Jews from Nazi extermination nor in the significant and deeply appreciated aid it gave to the establishment of Israel's statehood. The fate of the American "twin" was very different: organically intertwined with the growing and developing American Jewish community, Dropsie, too, grew and developed. Exposed to all the dangers that threaten the community, it has also benefited from the human and national opportunities open to the community.
>
> "In its realization, the beautiful dream of the blind advocate named Moses Aaron Dropsie bears witness to his extraordinarily clear vision. His decision that the institution be nonsectarian was characteristic of his time, but he was ahead of his time in his insistence on scientific objectivity and nonaffiliation with any of the religious trends in Jewry. Indeed, at a recent conference of the Leo Baeck Institute held in Jerusalem, Professor Gershom Scholem pointed out that he knew of only

> two schools of Jewish higher learning in the Diaspora which were purely academic and free from theological influence and connection: Dropsie University and the Petrograd course of Baron Guenzburg."

The new postgraduate instituion of higher learning, organized in 1907, was granted a charter on June 6, 1909, under the name of "The Dropsie College for Hebrew and Cognate Learning." When it opened in 1909 it had two major departments of Bible and rabbinics; shortly thereafter the Department of Cognate Languages was added, followed by the Department of History in 1913. Additional departments and divisions were established soon thereafter. In 1969 the name was officially changed to "The Dropsie University."

Since its inception, Dropsie University has had only four presidents. Dr. Cyrus Adler occupied that office from the establishments of the College until his death in 1940. He was succeeded by Dr. Abraham A. Neuman, who had been professor of history and was associated with Dropsie in various capacities since 1913. Dr. Neuman served in the presidency until 1965 and on the Board of Governors until his death in 1970. Between 1965 and 1967 the late Solomon Satinsky and Dr. Samuel J. Ajl served as acting presidents. On November 26, 1967, Dr. Abraham I. Katsh, a Dropsie alumnus, was inaugurated as third president. Upon his retirement in 1976, Dr. Leon J. Perelman, Chairman of the Executive Committee and member of the Board of Governors, served first as acting president, and in 1978 was elected President.

Dropsie University, albeit a small institution, is motivated by a majestic mission: to inspire Jewish scholarly creativity in the United States. The late Dr. Frederic K. Miller, former Commissioner of Higher Education of the Commonwealth of Pennsylvania, said at the commencement exercises on June 3, 1969:

> "The temptation is indeed strong to alter the traditional nature of many institutions. Unlimited growth of student enrollment; unrestricted duplication of programs and curricula; increased involvement in community and state problems to the detriment of students; all of these and more are constant temptations for the expenditure of time, effort, and budget. It is worthwhile to say again that among all Pennsylvania institutions, The Dropsie College has been unique. It has accpeted the mission of a strong, small graduate institution, with well-defined but limited aims and objectives. It has indeed, 'held high the torch' of research and scholarship in a unique way. Your uniqueness is to be cherished, your singleness of purpose should be preserved, and the insistence upon the highest kind of scholarship should be strengthened."

Dropsie University has indeed held true to its original tasks. It has never sought to enlist a large student body purely for the sake of numbers. It has rather appealed to those students who are willing to devote their lives to scholarship. The specialized approach, which permits free interaction between teacher and student, is in the classic tradition of true scholarly inquiry. Visiting scholars continue close relationships with students long after the end of their stay, and it should be kept in mind that Dropsie's students come from all parts of the world. Minimum requirement for all faculty is the earned doctorate. In addition, faculty status is reserved only for those who specialize in Hebraica, Judaica, Near Eastern studies, and cognate fields.

As a specialized graduate university, the organization of disciplines in Dropsie is not affected by interdepartmental rivalries or "empire building." As a result, Dropsie University may indeed be an "ivory tower," but it is one with commitment and motivation. Its scholars delve deeply into the sources of historical knowledge, test conventional and accepted hypotheses, and lay the groundwork for fresh insights and judgments. In the context of the comparative study of Western culture and world religions, Hebrew literature offers the student a broader perspective for understanding man's ongoing dialogue with God. The pursuit of truth for its own sake frequently turns out to be directly relevant to the deepest concerns of every age.

For over seventy years Dropsie has attracted and produced the finest scholars, researchers, and educators. Its alumni can be found in all major institutions of learning here and abroad. In the last eight years, seventy students in the field of Hebrew and Middle East scholarship were graduated and are now occupying positions throughout the world. The University's president, professors, and students have lectured extensively in numerous colleges and universities here and abroad. This outreach includes many exhibits, as well as the loan of Dropsie's rare archival treasures for display in the exhibits of other institutions. Conversely, each year has seen renowned scholars and statesmen coming to Dropsie University to deliver lectures which are open to the general public. These lectures serve not only specialized students and scholars but also the cultural life of the community in a most significant way.

The Joseph and Sally Handleman Communications Center for the Study of Man's Humanity was opened in 1970 as a component part of Dropsie University. The aim of the Center is to study the role played by communications as an instrument for research in humanity, and to gain an understanding of the impact of communications in shaping human attitudes and behavior. In addition, the University has utilized the Center as a vehicle for public dissemination of the research results of Dropsie's scholars.

Thus, in 1973, a colloquium on the Holocaust was co-sponsored with Villanova University. The printed record of this all-day colloquium, one of the first to be held in our country on that subject, has been distributed to institutions, libraries, and individuals throughout the world. Papers read at the colloquium included accounts of spiritual resistance by two survivors of the Holocaust, as well as studies of the sources and origins of Hitlerian anti-Semitism, and of the role of anti-Jewish teachings throughout the centuries.

For three summers, from 1970 to 1973, Dropsie University joined with Harvard, Drew, Drake, Duke, Princeton, and Minnesota Universities, under the auspices of the American Schools of Oriental Research and directed by Professor Eric M. Meyers, in an archeological expedition at Khirbet Shema in Israel, where the ruins of an ancient synagogue were uncovered. Khirbet Shema is a Galilean town of the Second Temple period which lasted through the Roman and Byzantine Ages. It is located at Meiron, ten miles west of Safed, in an area known to have been populated by Jews and Christians in the early centuries of the Common Era. The student volunteers who participated in the dig were guided by experienced teachers expert in the intricacies of transforming archeological excavation into living history.

As can be seen from the foregoing, Dropsie University cooperates fully with institutions and university departments for mutual objectives. A reciprocal agreement for student exchange at the graduate level between Temple University and Dropsie permits full-time graduate students enrolled at either institution to take courses at the other without additional fees and without formal transfer of credits. Certain academic requirements, of course, must be met. Similar arrangements exist with the University of Pennsylvania.

The degree of Doctor of Philosophy is the principal degree offered by Dropsie University.

Since 1975 the Jewish Academy of Arts and Sciences has moved from New York to the Handleman Center of Dropsie. Founded in 1927 as an honor society of Jews who had attained distinction in the arts, sciences, and professions, the Academy's main objective is to encourage and stimulate the interchange of views on all branches of scholarship and learning, with particular reference to those bearing on Jewish life and thought.

The Academy has enjoyed the leadership of the following scholars who have served as presidents of the JAAS: Drs. Henry Keller, Morris Raphael Cohen, Chaim Tchernowitz and Leo Jung. Its objectives are: to encourage and promote the advancement of the arts, sciences, and all other branches of knowledge; to encourage the interchange of views in all fields of learning, with particular reference to those bearing on Jewish life and thought; to cultivate and maintain friendly intercourse among its members and fellows; to foster research and publication, and to establish sound relations with other academies, societies, and institutions of learning throughout the world.

Dropsie University has been closely linked with scholarship and archeological research in the State of Israel. Not only have prime ministers, ambassadors, and Knesset members come to the University to deliver important addresses, but the University has gone to Jerusalem to stage a special convocation at which an honorary degree of Doctor of Laws was conferred upon the late President Zalman Shazar. Dropsie also sponsored, jointly with the World Jewish Bible Society in Jerusalem, the publication of a *Festschrift* in honor of President Shazar, edited by Dr. Zeitlin and David Ben-Gurion. Israeli archeologists and academicians have been featured in public lectures at Dropsie, including such eminent personalities as Professors Yigal Yadin, Benjamin Mazar, Jehoshaphat Harkavy, and Joseph Bazak.

Of special significance for Dropsie University in its training of scholars for work with original sources is the Abraham I. Katsh Center for Manuscript Research:

> "The student who has never undergone the discipline given by the editing of an ancient text or the writing of a serious commentary to an ancient classic, where the smallest detail has its meaning . . . will never acquire that sense of responsibility and scientific conscience which alone go to make the real scholar."*

Thus wrote the late Professor Solomon Schechter. Moreover, there is no doubt that the acquisition of primary sources is essential in fulfilling our comprehension of many unresolved scholarly issues. However, acquisition must be followed by preservation, systematization, and use. To this end, the Center has been established to further the study of Genizah documents and other rare manuscripts.

The Abraham I. Katsh Center has made it possible to initiate and continue the microfilming and preparation of an annotated catalogue of the five major Hebraica Libraries in the U.S.S.R., Hungary, and Poland. The Dropsie University possesses the only microfilm collection of the holdings of these Libraries, which include (a) the Baron David Guenzburg Collection in the Lenin Library in Moscow; (b) the Antonin Genizah Collection in the Saltykov-Shchedrin Library in Leningrad; (c) the Friedland Collection in the Oriental Institute of the Asiatic Peoples at the Leningrad Academy of Sciences; (d) some of the Firkowitch (First and Second) Collections in the Saltykov-Shchedrin Public Library in Leningrad; and (e) The David Kaufmann Collection in the Academy of Sciences in Budapest, Hungary, and the Jewish Historical Society in Warsaw, Poland.

The major share of the Guenzburg Collection in our possession is rich in several important fields. Among the most notable are Bible, Mishnah, Talmud, Responsa, Codes, Liturgy, Linguistics, Lexicography, Poetry, Kabbalah and Mysticism, Philosophy, History, Medicine, and Science. It

* A. I. Katsh, The Mission of The Dropsie University, Philadelphia, 1976, p. 15.

also contains unpublished manuscripts by the great scholars of the 18th and 19th centuries. Because of the destruction of all centers of learning during the Hitler era, this material is extremely rare. Unlike manuscripts of any era during the Middle Ages which may have duplicates in European libraries (generally with significant variants), Genizah fragments consist of only one copy. The microfilm collection was acquired by President Katsh during six visits to Russia in 1956–76, several of which were supported by the American Council of Learned Societies and the Rockefeller Foundation. This collection is now available to Western scholars for the first time.

The library at Dropsie, which now contains over 115,000 volumes, is particularly rich in publications on Biblical and post-Biblical learning, Semitic languages, Jewish history, Assyriology, and Egyptology, and contains special collections in the areas of Jewish education, Israel, and the Middle East.

> "The Library also includes the collections of Isaac Leeser; the Hebrew collection of Joshua L. Cohen, M.D., of Baltimore; the valuable collection of Dr. Eduard Glaser, well-known for his travels in Arabia; a selection from the library of Judge Mayer Sulzberger; and the library of Professor Max L. Margolis, which is deposited in the Biblical lecture room and is especially rich in books on the Bible and its versions. Professor Solomon L. Skoss bequeathed to the University a collection of photostats of rare Judeo-Arabic manuscripts from many parts of the world, particularly valuable and helpful to scholars because they bear Professor Skoss's identifications of time, place, and authorship. The University has received from the library of Professor Leo L. Honor a collection of books on Hebrew Literature, Jewish education, and history. More recently, it has also acquired the Abraham A. Neuman valuable collection of books dealing with Jewish history; rare Bibles from the late Dr. Herman Blum; the archives of the late B. Z. Goldberg, dealing with the American Jewish Labor Movement; and the Judaica and Hebraica collection of the late Sol Satinsky. A special collection of Americana has been set up recently as a result of a grant from Mr. David Rose, on the occasion of the 100th anniversary of the arrival of the Rose family in the United States."**

The library contains also 450 fragments from the Cairo Genizah in Hebrew and Arabic, in addition to the Katsh microfilm material; 255 Oriental manuscripts in Arabic, Ethiopic, Hebrew, Samaritan, Coptic, Persian, Sanskrit, and Turkish; some fragments of Coptic papyri; 32 incunabula; 290 16th century books, and other rarities.

The Dropsie University publication program merits a special word here. During the 1940's Dropsie inaugurated a new series of translations of the

**The Mission of The Dropsie University, p. 14.

Apocrypha and the Pseudepigrapha, those products of Jewish creativity in the twilight period between the closing of the Hebrew Biblical canon and the dawn of Christianity. There is no doubt that their ideas, although rejected by normative Judaism, left their mark upon the Talmud and the Midrash, and especially upon Christian doctrine. Dropsie University continues to sponsor this project, seven volumes of which have already been published: First Book of Maccabees, Letter to Aristeas, Third and Fourth Books of Maccabees, Second Book of Maccabees, Book of Wisdom, Book of Tobit, and Book of Judith.

Dropsie University continues to publish the *Jewish Quarterly Review*, which had been published originally in Cambridge, England from 1888 to 1909 under the editorial guidance of the late Claude G. Montefiore and Israel Abrahams. Transferred to Dropsie, it resumed publication in 1910 under the editorship of Dr. Cyrus Adler and Dr. Solomon Schechter. Since 1940 it was edited first by Dr. Abraham Neuman, then by Dr. Neuman jointly with Dr. Zeitlin, then by Dr. Zeitlin alone, and subsequently by Dr. Katsh and Dr. Zeitlin, with Dr. Solomon Grayzel as book review editor and Dr. Leon Nemoy as literary editor.

In this connection it would not be amiss to cite from a report made by a Middle States Evaluation Team in May, 1977:

> "Dropsie University remains an amazingly vital ganglion of Hebrew and cognate studies. Beyond any question this is due to the unusual constellation of scholars assembled on its small 15-man faculty. Almost all are distinguished specialists in their respective fields, and more often than not, they are recognized authorities in more than one field. The leading four or five scholars on the faculty rank among the giants of contemporary scholarship in the realm of Hebrew and cognate learning. Their breath-taking array of publications . . . and the respect in which they are held by scholars in secular disciplines, as well as in the academies of other religions, continually reinforce the reputation that Dropsie has always enjoyed for the highest academic probity and productivity. No better single indication of the academic achievement of this unusual institution can be found than the continued high level of its renowned publication, the *Jewish Quarterly Review*, one of the handful of outstanding scientific journals of scholarship in Hebrew and cognate learning."

We have said at the outset that Dropsie University is a sort of ivory tower. Of what possible use to the world is an ivory tower, especially at a time when that world seems to be falling apart or about to explode? What do the ancient books and manuscripts studied here have to do with the problems that bedevil us today? The answer lies in the truth which is at the foundation of all ivory towers: in order to understand the forces that shape our present and our future, we must understand what has gone before. In that respect Dropsie is not merely a place where scholars decipher manuscripts, but also a center where human beings study humanity. That was the dream of its founder. Clearly he did not wish that vision to remain his alone. We must make it ours.

We wish to extend our thanks to all the scholars who contributed to this volume, as well as to the Board of Governors of The Dropsie University, and to all who participated in its preparation.

Abraham I. Katsh
Leon Nemoy

R. Jacob Tam's Stringent Criticism of R. Meshullam of Melun, in its Historical Setting

By IRVING A. AGUS
Yeshiva University

IN THE *Sefer haYashar* OF R. Jacob Tam are included several of his letters to R. Meshullam B. Nathan and to the community of Melun, in which he sharply criticizes R. Meshullam for many of his decisions in ritual law, and for his manner of expounding certain Talmudic passages, often on the basis of faulty, textual emendations.[1] Some of R. Meshullam's novel expositions resulted in no changes in law, or in religious conduct. Thus he advocated a textual change in the statement of R. Joshua, *Menahot* 65b (who attempted to prove that the holiday of *Shabuot* ought to be forty-nine days after the first day of Passover), from "the *Torah* said; 'count days and sanctify the New-Moon,' to" count years and sanctify the Jubilee year."[2] At one time he explained to his students the reason for not listing, in the Pentateuch, the sin-offering of the New Moon among the sacrifices of New-Year's Day.[3] At another time he changed the explanation of R. Nachman bar Yitzchak (*B.M.* 38a, that fruit deposited with a person may not be sold by the depositee even when it begins to deteriorate) from "since its owner might have declared it to be *Terumah* or *Maaser* on fruit he kept elsewhere," to ". . . declared it to be *Terumat Maaser* on fruit he kept elsewhere."[4] Similarly, in *Ketuboth* 5a, he changed the reading: "lest he [the bridegroom, to entertain his guests,] slaughter a young bird [on the Sabbath]," to "lest he slaughter a bird on that day."[5]

These textual changes introduced by R. Meshullam merely affected the meaning of the Talmudic passages referred to, but did not involve any changes in law or custom. Nevertheless R. Tam criticized R. Meshullam sharply, and warned him that a person willfully introducing textual changes in the Talmud was cursed in Heaven and would be exposed to the fires of hell.[6]

Much stronger was his reaction to the textual emendations and novel interpretations of R. Meshullam that led to differences in law or conduct.

[1] See *Sefer haYashar*, edited by F. Rosenthal, Berlin 1898, henceforth cited as *SHYR*, nos. 43–50.

[2] See *ibid.*, p. 74.

[3] See *ibid.*

[4] *Ibid.*, pp. 78 f.; also, pp. 85 f.

[5] *Ibid.*, pp. 88 f.

[6] *Ibid.*, p. 75.

Thus the latter asserted that "the fiftieth year," the Jubilee, was a year apart, and was not included in the following "week of years" (*Nedarim*, 61a); that a Jubilee cycle thus consisted of fifty years; and that in the statement of R. Huna (*A.Z.* 9b, describing the manner of calculating the position of a year in the seven-year cycle) the words: "from every century two years should be subtracted," be deleted.[7] This emendation would change the position of each year in the seven-year cycle and the determination of the year in which debts are cancelled. He also ruled that vinegar—as well as wine produced from unripe grapes—did not become "forbidden" when touched by a Gentile;[8] that a person ritually unclean might immerse himself in a natural spring and thus become clean, even when there was not enough water in that spring to cover his entire body;[9] and that a woman whose seventh day after menstruation fell on a Friday night, wash herself immediately before the Sabbath and next morning, immerse herself in a ritual bath.[10]

R. Meshullam also instituted in his community that on a holiday, when no more than five men were to be called up to read the required portion of the Torah and a sixth man to read the special portion, called *Maftir*—taken from Numbers, chapters 28 or 29—that the fifth person read that special portion, and the sixth person repeat the same portion (similar to the procedure of an ordinary Sabbath).[11] Furthermore, he instructed the women not to recite any blessing when they lighted the Sabbath candles;[12] he ruled that, at wedding ceremonies, the betrothal blessings and the marriage blessings be recited on one cup of wine,[13] and that the third meal on the Sabbath be eaten late in the afternoon, after the *Minchah*-service.[14] All these rulings were at variance with the practices and decisions of the authorities respected by R. Tam.

When the latter first heard general rumors about these novel teachings expounded in Melun and ascribed to R. Meshullam, he refused to believe that a man of such high calibre would be so reckless in introducing textual emendations and in ruling contrary to accepted law and practice. He wrote

[7] *Ibid.*, pp. 76 f.

[8] *Ibid.*, pp. 79 f., and 87 f.

[9] *Ibid.*, p. 90.

[10] *Ibid.*, p. 80. See also p. 88, the very sharp reaction of R. Tam who curses anyone who will follow the ruling of R. Meshullam.

[11] *Ibid.*, p. 81.

[12] *Ibid.*, p. 92.

[13] *Ibid.*, p. 82.

[14] *Ibid.*, p. 84.

[15] In the *Sefer haYashar* the correspondence between R. Tam and R. Meshullam is not entered in the proper order; nor are the letters of the latter fully preserved. There is no doubt that at first R. Tam wrote to the community of Melon (no. 45); then came the letter of R. Meshullam (no. 43), the answer to which is no. 44. *Cf.*, however, E. E. Urbach, *The Tosaphists: Their History, Writings and Methods* (Hebrew), Jerusalem 1955, pp. 62–3.

to the community of Melun[15] about the disquieting rumors he had heard, explained why the new teachings were wrong, and asked that the practice be stopped. R. Meshullam, then wrote to R. Tam. He stated exactly what he had taught on the subjects mentioned by the latter and tried to prove the truth of his opinions, his textual emendations, and his rulings. The controversy that ensued was very sharp and very acrimonious. R. Tam demanded that R. Meshullam stop his practice of arbitrarily emending the text of the Talmud,[16] and that he reverse himself on the actions he had taken—otherwise the former would be forced to denounce him at special communal assemblies,[17] to threaten to ban anyone who would follow his rulings, and to warn the women, albeit "in a mild tone," that they do not practice his irresponsible leniencies.[18] He strongly condemned R. Meshullam's emendations and even ridiculed his opinions (saying: "a child knows better than that," and: "anyone hearing your explanations would laugh at them").[19]

Why did R. Tam so sharply criticize the opinions and acts of an outstanding scholar that he himself, in his letter to the community of Melun,[20] refers to him with the title Rabbenu? What drove R. Tam to use such acrimonious language, such condemning terms, even outright threats, merely because a scholar dared differ with him?

We are tempted to look for the answer to these questions in the character of R. Tam; to assume that it was his high opinion of himself that drove him to use such sharp language against those who dared differ with him.[21] Some modern scholars pointed to the fact that even though R. Tam denounced so sharply those who dared amend the text of the Talmud, he himself resorted to such emendations on innumerable occasions.[22] Apparently, therefore, it was the character of R. Tam that drove him to condemn others for practices that he himself was guilty of.

It is highly improbable, however, that a man of the calibre of R. Tam would be so strongly dominated by his emotions. One must, therefore,

[16] See *SHYR*, p. 86: "arbitrary emendations are signs of ignorance and stupidity. . . ."

[17] See *ibid.*, p. 88: "Cursed be those who listen to you . . . and if they will not pay attention to us, we shall pronounce the ban against them in all our communities." *Cf.* also p. 90.

[18] See *ibid.*

[19] *Ibid.*, pp. 76, 81, and 82; see especially end of p. 93, and of p. 97.

[20] *Ibid.*, p. 84. *Cf.* also the Responsum of R. Tam to R. Meshullam (V. Aptowitzer, *Mabo l'Sepher Rabiyah*, Jerusalem 1938, p. 303) where the former addresses the latter with respect.

[21] See E. E. Urbach, *op. cit.*, p. 55, where he briefly reviews the evaluations of the character of R. Tam. V. Aptowitzer, *op. cit.*, p. 359, attempts to understand the reactions of R. Tam on the basis of his character, but finally admits that he could not find the solution to this problem.

[22] See J. H. Weiss, *Dor Dor veDorshov*, Vilna 1911, vol. IV, p. 301; V. Aptowitzer, *op. cit.*, p. 359.

endeavor to uncover the exact situation that he found himself in, and the compelling forces of the moment that drove him to react in the manner described. To illustrate the difference in approach between ascribing the reactions of R. Tam to quirks of his character, and endeavoring fully to understand the situation he found himself in that determined his actions—let us review the following case:[23] The husband of a certain young lady apostatized and subsequently was induced to give her a Jewish divorce. After the divorce-document was written and delivered to her, witnesses came before R. Yom Tob B. Judah, a relative of R. Tam, and testified to some irregularities in the signing of the document (the document was allegedly signed after it was delivered). It was also discovered that the Gentile name of the apostate was not included in the document. Whereupon R. Yom Tob declared that the divorce was void and that the young lady was still a married woman. When R. Tam learned about the situation, he wrote a letter to R. Yom Tob, condemning his action, in very strong terms. The reaction of Professor V. Aptowitzer[24] to this action of R. Tam, was: "We can understand R. Tam's [acerbity] in his relation with R. Meshullam [of Melun]—he hated amenders [of the text of the Talmud]—but what was the sin and what the transgression of his relative R. Yom Tob who [merely] refused to change the custom [of his day], introduced no textual emendations, but, according to R. Tam, made a mistake in applying the proper law to this case? Oh, what [sharp] phrases and what [condemning] expressions R. Tam uses in writing to R. Yom Tob!"

Little did Prof. Aptowitzer realize what untold suffering and what pain the action of R. Yom Tob inflicted on the young woman and on her relatives. For she was thus condemned to be an *agunah*, an abandoned wife—who could not marry anyone until she receives a second divorce. She was still young—R. Tam advises her father "to marry her to anyone he desire," an expression used regarding young daughters—and usually under such circumstances the chances of a woman persuading her apostate husband to give her a second divorce was quite slim. (R. Tam accuses R. Yom Tob of causing the woman to become an *agunah*).[25] The religious overmeticulousness of R. Yom Tob has thus caused the young woman untold suffering. R. Tam, on the other hand, was very sensitive to the vulnerability of

[23] See *SHYR*, nos. 25 and 26.

[24] See V. Aptowitzer, *ibid.*

[25] See *SHYR*, p. 42. No. 36 is a letter R. Tam wrote to the father of the woman. Note the meticulousness of R. Tam in answering every possible objection one could raise to the validity of the divorce. He was writing to a layman, and yet he tried so hard to assure the father of the validity of the divorce. He even advised him to write and deliver a second document before the husband changed his mind. This can only be explained in the light of the conditions of that day, that a woman, the validity of whose divorce was questioned, was exposed to tremendous suffering; the slightest doubt on the legality of such a woman to remarry would make her life unbearable.

divorced women and to the pain and suffering that could be caused to them by irresponsible persons who raised doubts on the legality of their divorces. Thus he went to great lengths in order to pass "an ordinance of the communities" prohibiting anyone from expressing doubts on the legality of a divorce after the action was completed.[26] Obviously, he was quite justified in his sharp criticism of the actions of R. Yom Tob.

The altercation between R. Tam and R. Meshullam also can be understood only in the light of the compelling conditions of that day. It was the radical change in the method of study of Talmudic law, caused by the devastation of the highly erudite communities of the Rhineland, in the year 1096, that was mainly responsible for the sharpness of tone of the above described controversy. Before the First Crusade, all knowledge of Jewish law and custom—in Italy, Germany and France—was derived almost exclusively "from the mouth of one's teacher." Students learned from their teachers the exact wording of every statement of the Talmud, the final decision in controversial matters, and all ritual practices—usually without seeing or examining the written text of the Talmud on which the information was based.[27] For even great scholars relied, for their source of knowledge of Jewish law, not on written texts but mainly on the studied accuracy with which their teachers had transmitted to them the oral traditions, called *Shemuot*,[28] of the scholars of the earlier generations.[29]

It is true that these teachers spent a great deal of time and effort in order to explain to their students how the legal principles and ceremonial customs, they were teaching them, were logically embedded in the statements of the Talmud. Nevertheless, accurate tradition rather than logical deduction, was still the dominant factor in their method of arriving at a correct decision in law and custom. For the determination of the exact wording of each Talmudic statement, was itself dependant mainly on accurately memorized traditions. Books, therefore, as sources of knowledge of Jewish law, were of secondary importance.

In the tenth and eleventh centuries, the greatest scholars of Ashkenazic Jewry lived in the communities of the Rhineland, and their knowledge of the oral traditions of that Jewry—their *Shemuot*—was considered most

[26] See Louis Finkelstein, *Jewish Self-Government in the Middle Ages*, New York, 1924, pp. 44 f., and 105 f.

[27] See I. A. Agus, *The Heroic Age of Franco-German Jewry*, New York 1969, pp, 321–31; *cf. also ibid.*, "The Oral Traditions of Pre-Crusade Ashkenazic Jewry," *Studies and Essays in Honor of Abraham A. Neuman*, Philadelphia 1962, pp. 1–16.

[28] See *ibid.*, pp. 322–25.

[29] *Cf.* I. A. Agus, *Urban Civilization in Pre-Crusade Europe*, New York 1965, p. 542. "Thus, since such ruling is not to be found in the Talmud, but is derived through logical reasoning—I prefer the logic of the words of R. Leon, words he transferred to me in the process of learning; for he was a remarkable sage in his generation, and his words should not be disputed . . . Gershom, b. R. Judah."

reliable. In the first quarter of the eleventh century, therefore, students flocked to Mainz from all parts of Europe, in order to study under R. Gershom, R. Eliezer the Great and their colleagues.[30] They came to study under these great scholars not because these teachers were remarkably brilliant—outstanding geniuses—but because it was known that they had mastered fully the oral traditions, the *Shemuot*, of the greatest scholars of the previous generation. However, in the widespread massacres of the summer of 1096, massacres that brought destruction to the most scholarly communities of Ashkenazic Jewry, the greatest students of the most devoted pupils of R. Gershom and R. Eliezer, were killed. The line of transmission of oral tradition, was thus irreparably broken—causing a most radical change in the system of learning and in the method of arriving at decisions in questions of law and ritual.[31]

Suddenly the method of learning of a thousand years, underwent a most radical change. From being almost exclusively concentrated on the ear and on innumerable verbal repetitions (to insure the total memorization of the *Shemuot*)—it now became eye-centered and greatly dependant on logical analysis and deduction. From deriving all knowledge from a human being, the learning process became centered on notes, on books, and on logical derivations.[32] The main task of the scholars of the twelfth century was: to reconstruct the knowledge of the true meaning of the Talmudic text, of the law and of custom, of the great scholars of the previous century—a knowledge that was so sadly shattered by the massacres of the First Crusade and the slaughter of the devoted scholars of the Rhineland. The only scholar of stature who survived this slaughter—a scholar who had received his knowledge of oral traditions of Ashkenazic Jewry from the mouth of the most devoted students of R. Gershom and R. Eliezer—was Rashi, a very busy vine grower and wine manufacturer of Troyes. In the next nine years Rashi made available to hundreds of copyists his latest revision of the notes he had taken in the yeshivot of Worms and Mainz; and in a short time these notes became the most widely accepted exposition of the text of the Talmud.[33] Brief notes of other students of the scholars of Mainz and Worms, of the pre-crusade period, also became very important as authoritative guides to an understanding of the Talmud, and they too were widely copied.[34] All notes, all books, all collections of written decisions and Re-

[30] See I. A. Agus, "Rabbinic Scholarship in Northern Europe," *The World History of the Jewish People*, second series, vol. II, Tel Aviv 1966, pp. 189–248.

[31] See *ibid.*, pp. 210–222.

[32] See Agus, *The Heroic Age of Franco-German Jewry*, pp. 329 f.

[33] See Agus, "Rashi and his School," *The World History of the Jewish People*, pp. 210–39.

[34] See Abraham Epstein, "Der Gerschom Meor haGola Zugeschriebenen Talmud Kommentar," *Festschrift . . . Moritz Steinschneider*, 1896; J. N. Epstein, "The Commentaries of R. Jehudah b. Nathan and the Commentaries of Worms (Hebrew)," *Tarbitz*, IV, 1932, pp. 11 ff.

sponsa—even books that were composed in Babylonia and in North Africa—suddenly became very important to the Franco-German Scholars engaged in the above-described task of reconstruction.

In this effort at reconstruction the following elements became important: a) The oral traditions, the notes, and the opinions of scholars of Mainz, Worms, Cologne and Spires, who have survived the First Crusade. Such Scholars were: Rashi, his sons-in-law, the sons of R. Machir, R. Kalonymus the Elder and R. Isaac B. Asher, (both of Spires).[35] b) Widespread practices and customs that originally must have been based on authentic traditions.[36] c) The commentary on the Talmud of R. Hananel of Kairwan—based on the accurate traditions of his teachers of Italy, the original homeland of the scholarship of Ashkenazic Jewry—and the work of his outstanding student, R. Isaac Alfasi, that also incorporated these traditions.[37] d) Books composed by the Geonim of Babylonia, such as the *Halakot Gedolot* and the *Siddur of R. Amrom*.[38] e) Old manuscripts of the Talmud that contained many accurate readings on which Ashkenazic scholarship of the pre-crusade period was based.[39]

The most important element in this process of reconstruction, however, was the human mind that had to evaluate the evidence contained in these sources and, by a leap of genius, arrive at a correct knowledge of the pre-crusade traditions. Scholars possessing that spark of genius could do wonders in truly rediscovering lost or forgotten ideas and principles. In the Jewish world of the twelfth century, such men would be highly honored, would attract outstanding students to their schools, and would be addressed with the honorific title "Rabbi." The great danger was, however, that this high honor accorded to truly gifted scholars, provided a very strong incentive to scholars lacking that spark of genius recklessly to propound new ideas, propose many textual emendations, and advocate novel and more lenient

[35] See V. Aptowitzer, *Mabo*, pp. 369 f., 390 f., 395 ff.; A. Epstein, "Introduction to *Maasei haGeonim* (Hebrew)." *Maasei haGeonim*, Berlin, 1909. See also *SHYR*, p. 83: "R. Gershom, our teachers from Bari . . . and R. Solomon derived his knowledge from them;" *ibid.*, p. 85: "for we drink the waters of R. Solomon;" which means: we derive our knowledge of Jewish law from R. Solomon.

[36] See *ibid.*, pp. 80–1, 84–5, 99–100; and especially p. 101: "our custom is the authentic Law."

[37] See *Sefer haYashar*, ed. Vienna 1810, p. 10b, end of no. 59: "There are no older books than [the oral traditions contained in the commentary of] R. Hananel." See also *SHYR*, pp. 83, 88, and especially p. 89: "see the reading of R. Hananel . . . and that of R. Isaac Alfasi, his student; for their reading [of the text of the Talmud], is correct and authentic. There are places where R. Hananel adopted a harsh ruling . . . and in rare instances his explanations and his logic are not correct; but his *Shemuot* (i. e., his oral traditions) are always authentic."

[38] See *ibid.*, pp. 80–2, 88, 90, 97–101.

[39] See "Introduction of R. Jacob Tam," *Sefer haYashar*, Vienna 1810, p. IV; *ibid.*, p. 10b.

practices and customs, in order that they too, be accorded the respect and honor of their more talented colleagues.[40]

The old manuscripts (element e), therefore—whether of the Talmud itself or of the writings of post-Talmudic scholars—presented a very serious problem to the scholars of this period. For manuscripts usually contain errors, often in very crucial statements.[41] The students of the great schools of the Rhineland, of the pre-crusade period, had retained the knowledge of the exact wording of many parts of the Talmud. When they were faced with faulty readings in an old manuscript, they were forced to point out such errors by using the phrase *hakha garsinan*, which originally meant: "this is how we recite by heart the exact wording of this statement." The implication was, of course, that they had learned that "exact wording of the statement" from the mouth of their teachers, or that the laws and principles they learned from these teachers must have been based on such a reading. Many students, however, began to think that the phrase *hakha garsinan* meant: "this is the preferred reading." They often thought, therefore, that a scholar used that phrase even when he willfully amended the text merely on logical grounds (i. e. arbitrary emendations) to make the text fit his personal interpretation of the law. The great scholars therefore, by informing the public (in writing) of the traditionally transmitted wording of the text of the Talmud, and especially by establishing the correct text through the process of reconstruction, they were opening the door to second-rate scholars who would introduce emendations of the text based on faulty logic.

It was for this reason that R. Tam was so highly critical of those scholars who arbitrarily amended the text of the Talmud. He wrote his *Sefer haYashar* specifically for the purpose of reconstructing many parts of the traditionally transmitted knowledge of Jewish-law—part of which reconstruction was based on the oral tradition of the exact wording of the text of the Talmud. In order that his establishing of the exact text be not used as an excuse for "arbitrary emendations," he drew the attention of the readers to the fact that "R. Gershom, the Light of the Exile, cursed all those who dared amend the text [of the Talmud]." In fact his entire introduction[42] to his *Sefer haYashar*, is devoted to a sharp criticism of such amenders and, especially, of those scholars, who were so convinced of the truth of their "arbitrary emendations" that they would introduce their changes in the very text of the old manuscript, thus obliterating any trace of the original reading.[43] Such an amender would thus destroy a bit of accurate knowledge that had survived the destruction caused by the First Crusade; and his wrongfully

[40] R. Tam accused R. Meshullam that his interpretations and emendations were made "in order that he be addressed as Rabbi." See *SHYR*, p. 105; *cf.* p. 101 (no. 11).

[41] See "Introduction of R. Jacob Tam," *Sefer haYashar*, Vienna 1810, p. IV.

[42] See *ibid.*; *cf.* Meir Friedman, *Sifre*, Vienna 1864, Introduction, p. III.

[43] See *SHYR*, p. 105.

amended manuscript would become a stumbling block to future scholars. The very fact that one of the main reasons that drove R. Tam to write his *Sefer haYashar*, was to correct the damage done by reckless textual emendations, proves that the problems posed by such "reckless emendations," in this period, were very grave indeed.[44] We can fully understand, therefore, why the reaction of R. Tam to the emendations of R. Meshullam, was so sharp.

Furthermore, the serious loss of the knowledge of the oral traditions of the pre-crusade period, led some twelfth century scholars to adopt the mistaken idea that these oral traditions were concentrated exclusively on the Talmud; that the process of reconstructing the knowledge of law and custom that had been contained in these traditions, must be limited to a study of the Talmud itself; and that there existed no other source of information.[44] This, too, was a very dangerous notion, since this principle would invalidate many legal provisions and religious practices known to, and practiced by, Ashkenazic Jewry—not mentioned, or hinted at, in the Talmud—even though they had been preserved by oral tradition as the teachings and practices of the sages of old. Were some scholars to adopt this idea—espoused by R. Meshullam—they would thus be led to abrogate many laws and customs practiced by their fathers for many centuries. This would cause a very serious split in Jewish ranks, the consequences of which would be very sad indeed.[45]

These are the reasons, therefore, that in his controversy with R. Meshullam, R. Tam stressed the following three principles: a) Rashi was the most outstanding pupil of the great students of R. Gershom and of R. Eliezer the Great, who had survived the holocaust of the year 1096; thus he retained the most accurate knowledge of the oral traditions of these great scholars. European Jewry, therefore, should follow the teachings, the interpretations and the decisions of Rashi and of his school.[46] b) Old manuscripts of the Talmud contain very valuable information on the exact wording of the original text. To introduce arbitrary changes and corrections in these manuscripts, is a very grave sin; for what appears to one scholar to be a faulty reading, may one day be proven by another scholar (on the basis of a profound study of parallel passages in other parts of the Talmud) to be the correct reading. A scholar is permitted to suggest to his students, or in his writings, that a certain reading is faulty and that another reading is to be preferred; but he should never dare introduce the readings he preferred, in the text itself.[47] c) The knowledge of Jewish law and custom is not

[44] See *ibid.*, pp. 81 f., 85, 87, and 99.

[45] Hence the appeal of R. Tam to the community of Melun, *ibid.*, p. 85: "Do not allow that schismatic groups appear in our kingdom."

[46] See *ibid.*, pp. 83, 85, 87, 89, and 100.

[47] See "Introduction of R. Jacob Tam" to *Sefer haYashar*, Vienna 1810, p. IV.

derived exclusively from the Talmud. For part of that knowledge had survived in the *Shemuot* and the traditions of the great scholars of the previous generations, as well as in the books of the Geonim, and even in the Midrashim.[48] Before a person may dare to change a law or a custom, he must consult the great teachers of his generation, teachers who have studied carefully all these sources of information.[49]

From an historical point of view, therefore, R. Tam was quite justified in his sharp criticism of the teachings, the activities, and the decisions of R. Meshullam.

[48] See *SHYR*, pp. 81, 85, 87, 88, and 99.
[49] See *ibid.*, p. 101, no. 11.

Continuing Creativity in Maimonides' Philosophy

By JACOB B. AGUS
The Dropsie University

MAIMONIDES' CONCEPTION OF God appears to be austere, remote and forbidding. He elaborated the historical notion of Negative Attributes in a way which seemed to rob it of religious import.[1]

He stressed that of God we can know only what He is not. God is not a physical being, moving within space, neither is He subject to influences from others, for He transcends the flow of time. We can approach Him most nearly by intellectual reasoning, but then He eludes the grasp of our intellect as well. Even such basic attributes as "wise, powerful and volitional" can be ascribed to Him only in a negativistic way—He is not not-wise, not not-strong, not incapable of willing. (*Guide of the Perplexed*, I, 59, 60).

Attributes of action, that is, qualities inferred from the operation of nature, may indeed be postulated of Him, but then, it would seem that no more could be said of Him than could be inferred from the ordinary operations of nature (I, 53). He is "good," because life is on the whole more pleasant than painful (III, 10); He is compassionate because all living things seem to be endowed with all that they need for survival (III, 12). But, He does not break the chains of causality in response to human pleas, or in order to save the righteous from destruction (III, 27).

In medieval as in modern times, Orthodox pietists condemned Maimonides' way of overcoming the crudities of anthropomorphism as a snare and a delusion. Is there any sense in praying to a God, who cannot be placated by supplications; who does not soften the cold and indifferent physical laws of the universe by His gracious intervention; who remains impassive in the face of "the righteous suffering and the wicked prospering?"[2]

To be sure, Maimonides introduces the "leap of faith" as a decisive factor in affirming the doctrine of *creatio ex nihilo* (II, 25). He demonstrates that the Aristotelian argument for the eternity of the cosmos is no more convincing than the contrary argument proving the creation of the cosmos at some moment in the past. In view of the scales of reasoning being equally

[1] The critics stated "that a being who cannot be comprehended by their thoughts and of Whom they cannot form a rational image, so that He can only be described by negations, does not exist at all." Iggeret Hakenaot, printed in *Kovez Teshuvot Ha-Rambam*, Lipsia, 1859, cited in the introduction.

[2] For a review of the Maimonidean controversy, see N. Brüll, "Die Polemik für u. gegen Maimuni," *Jahrbücher für T. Geschichte u. Literatur*, vol. IV. Also J. Sarachek, *Faith and Reason, The Conflict over the Rationalism of Maimonides*, New York 1935.

balanced, he opts for creation, "in order to make the Torah possible." But, he does not make use of this pragmatic "will to believe" in order to prove the reality of a personal God. On the contrary, he castigates the theologians who design the world to suit their preconceived notions, instead of deducing ideas from the harsh, unyielding data of reality (I, 71). Divine creation makes it possible for us to allow that some biblical miracles did indeed take place, in reality, not merely in a dream, having been built into the unvarying causal chain of the cosmos in the moment of creation (II, 19). But, as to the concept of God, we are left with the strict injunction not to attribute to Him either wrath or compassion, either resentment of the evil ways of men or forgiveness for their sins should they repent.[3]

* * *

David Kaufmann suggests that the *via negativa* is calculated to deepen man's apprehension of the incomprehensibility of God's Will. Its religious import is to impress upon us our human littleness and God's remoteness.[4]

However, Maimonides insists on the *comprehensibility* in principle of all the *mizvot*. And his goal is not the fear of God, but the love of Him. He ranks the ritual commandments below the inner truths of Torah, which lead through the activity of man's intellect directly to the Active Reason, and beyond it to God.

The various *mizvot* of the Torah are indeed designed to instill "the fear of God" in the hearts of the Israelites, as well as to promote the ethical perfection of the individual and of the "divine society" (III, 27). But, the purpose of the inner secrets of the Torah is to teach the love of God.

"Consider how it is explicitly stated for your benefit that the intention of *all the words of this Law* is one end, namely, *that thou mayest fear the Name*, and so on . . . As for the opinions that the Torah teaches us—namely, the apprehension of His Being and His unity, may He be exalted—these opinions teach us love, as we have explained several times. For these two ends, namely, *love* and *fear*, are achieved through two things: love through the opinions taught by the Law, which include the apprehension of His Being as He,

[3] In his *Iggeret Tehiyat Hametim*, he distinguishes between the miracle which breaks with "customary nature" and the one which defies reason.
וכבר בארנו ב"מורה נבוכים," בדברנו בחדוש העולם, שעם אמונת חדוש העולם יתחייב בהכרח שיהיו המופתים כולם אפשריים, ולזה יהיה גם כן תחית המתים אפשרי, וכל אפשר שיבא בו הגדת הנביא נאמין ולא נצטרך לפרשו, ולא נוציאהו מפשוטו. ואמנם נצטרך לפרש הדבר שפשוטו נמנע, כהגשמת השם, אבל האפשרי יעמוד כאשר הוא. ואשר ישתדל ויפרש תחית המתים עד שלא יהיה שם שוב הנפש לגוף. אמנם יעשה זה בהאמינו שהוא נמנע מצד השכל, לא ממנהג הטבע . . . (קבץ תשובות, רמב"ם)

[4] David Kaufmann, *Geschichte der Attributenlehre in der Jüdischen Religionsphilosophie des Mittelalters*, Gotha, Friedrich Andreas Perthes, 1877, pp. 471–501.

[5] A'had Ha'am maintained in his justly famous essay on Maimonides, "Shilton Hasekhel," that the latter was a pure rationalist.

may He be exalted, is in truth; while *fear* is achieved by means of all actions prescribed by the Law, as we have explained. Understand this summary" (*Guide* III, 52, Pines' tr. p. 630).

The final exhortation of this section is manifestly a summons to understand the hidden meaning of the entire book, which cannot be disclosed to the general public. Only the saintly philosophers can learn to pierce through the literal teaching of Torah and to reach the heights of metaphysical speculation. It follows that they, and they alone, can learn to "love" God, in the double sense of intellectual contemplation and whole-souled devotion. For it is "the intellect that overflows toward us and is the bond between us and Him, may He be exalted. Just as we apprehend Him by means of that light which He caused to overflow toward us—as it says, 'in Thy light do we see light' " (Psalms 36, 1) (*Guide*, III, 52).

The overflow of the divine intellect comes only to those who attain the highest level of moral and intellectual perfection. As Afudi points out in his commentary on this chapter, the love of God is reached through "true wisdom."

Doubtless, Maimonides was aware of Halevi's contention that "the God of Abraham, Isaac and Jacob" elicits impassioned yearning and personal love from His worshippers, while "the God of Aristotle" leaves them cold ("Kuzari," IV, 16). Throughout the *Guide*, Maimonides polemizes against Halevi and against all the naively pious who imagine that they can approach God either through emotions or through ritual actions. He insists that "it is pure thought deriving from the perfection of the intellect that leads to that impassioned love (*hoshek*) of God, may He be exalted, and as the intellect increases in strength, its light and its joy in what it has conceived are increased" (III, 51). Does he then shut the door to the love of God, and hence to the goal of human life for the majority of the Jewish community?—We note, too, that the counterpart to man's love of God, namely, God's love for man, is inseparable from the same intellectual overflow, for in God, reason, will and power are one.[5] Does Maimonides then deny God's love for the people of Israel, reserving it solely for the saintly philosophers of all

"Whoever knows in what esteem our ancestors of that period held the study of the Torah will not be surprised that many wise men and rabbis were driven to the conclusion that 'this Chapter was not written by the Master, or if it was, it should be suppressed, or best of all, burned.' "

"Poor, simple men! They did not see that this chapter (III, 51) could not be either suppressed or burned except in company with all the other chapters of Maimonides' system . . ." (See commentary of Narboni on III, 51).

A'had Ha'am maintained also that Maimonides was impelled to write the *Guide*, not out of religious feeling, since "religious emotion certainly gained nothing" from his efforts, but only by "the national sentiment."

An English translation by Leon Simon of A'had Ha'am's essay is included in the reprint by Arno Press of the *Maimonides Octocentennial Series*.

nations, and for them only in rare moments of sudden illumination? Such an inference would contradict all that we know of his life's work.

Maimonides set out to reconcile the teaching of Torah with the doctrines of the scientific philosophers, chiefly Aristotle. Did he then achieve his goal by a laborious process of "interpretation," whereby the Aristotelian philosophy was shown to be the true and inner intention of the Torah, while its explicit instructions were meant only for the untutored masses?—Such a solution is ruled out by our knowledge of Maimonides' boundless devotion to Torah, and to Jewish people, wherever they lived.

The difficulty is compounded when we reflect on the fact that, to Maimonides, divine Providence seems to be limited to the philosophers and prophets, whose mind is open to the overflow of Active Reason, and even in the case of these pious sages, the protective guidance of God is restricted to those moments when they are actually enraptured in meditation (III, 51). He allows that the Patriarchs and Moses managed to cling to God, even when they went about their daily tasks. It is this suggestion that Israel Baal Shem Tov turned into the cornerstone of his teaching—namely, to train the body to attend to normal activities, while the soul is totally embraced in the ecstasy of the impassioned love of God (*Tsavoat Horivosh*, ed. Talpiot, 1951, p. 227). However, Maimonides specifically ruled out this possibility for virtually all men, by stating that one like himself cannot aspire to reach that exalted state.[6]

Indeed, Maimonides consistently exempted Moses and the Patriarch Abraham from the generality of mankind. With these exemptions from the range of Providence, it follows that all events are governed by the nexus of cause and effect. Can we then conclude that the universe is a physical mechanism, indifferent to human weal and woe? Did Maimonides himself subscribe to the view that he himself condemns as the essence of heresy, *leth din veleth dayan*? (Vayikra Rabb. 28). If God is conceived only through the *via negativa*, it is hardly possible to dispute this conclusion.

* * *

I. Husik blandly assumed that by asserting the supremacy of divine freedom in the original creation, Maimonides had managed to justify not merely the miracles mentioned in Scriptures but also petitional prayer and divine responsiveness to human needs. Husik goes so far as to describe Maimonides' concept of God as "personal."[7]

So wide-ranging a deduction from the doctrine of creation is belied by

[6] Pines points out that the Arabic phrase can be construed to say—"someone like myself cannot aspire to guide others with a view to their achieving this rank" (Pines, *op. cit.*, p. 624).

[7] "Mechanical necessity as a universal explanation of phenomena would exclude free will and the efficacy of prayer as ordinarily understood . . . A miracle is a discontinuity

Maimonides' explicit disavowal of the belief that God listens to prayer, listing it among the "necessary" in contrast to the "true" beliefs (*Guide*, III, 28).

Julius Guttmann is undecided concerning the range of Providence in the Maimonidean world. Commenting on the inferences to be drawn from the doctrine of *creatio ex nihilo*, he points out that Maimonides might have concluded that God interfered regularly in the course of events, breaking into the physical chain of cause and effect in accord with His higher purpose. If He created the cosmos at one time, why not assume a succession of creative acts, miracles and wonders, interrupting the course of nature? But, Guttmann insists, Maimonides stays far from such naive views of popular belief. In particular, he distances himself from this view in his commentary on the *Mishnah*, where he teaches that the miracles were imbedded in the natural course of events at creation, and that all extraordinary events flow out of the immanent forces which were imbedded in nature at the time it was created.[8] "It seems that in the *Guide of the Perplexed* he no longer adheres to this extremist view which disallows any intervention of God within the course of nature, maintaining that such interventions are not breaches of the causal nexus, but that they are embraced in the original plan of the Deity."

If Maimonides believed in a succession of acts of creation, he would not have restricted the range of Providence, as we have seen, and he would not have insisted that the messianic redeemer would come in the normal course of history (Hilchot Melochin, end). In his notes, Guttmann casts doubt upon his own interpretation in the text (*ibid.*, p. 392, note 451).

Since Maimonides assumed that the cosmos was created through the Perfect Wisdom of God, he was compelled to conclude that no tinkering with its basic mechanism was needed in order for it to function, excepting only those actions which were specifically foretold in the Torah. Maimonides goes to some pains to show that the miracles performed by Moses were in a class by themselves. Decisive for the final import of God's attributes is the nature of Providence, and direct Providence was conceivable to him only for those prophets and pious philosophers whose intellect received the divine overflow (*Guide*, III, 18).

Maimonides' contradictory views on the nature of Divine Providence were noticed already by his first translator, Samuel Ibn Tibbon.[9] In his letter to the author, Ibn Tibbon pointed out the difficulty of reconciling the views expressed in III, 17, where Providence is described in the spirit of tradition, as operating in accord with the moral law, with the opinions

in the laws of nature brought to pass on a special occasion by a personal being *in response to a prayer* or in order to realize a given purpose" (I. Husik, "Medieval Jewish Philosophy," Macmillan, 1930, p. 274. italics, mine).

[8] J. Guttmann, *Haphilosophia shel Hayahadut*, Jerusalem, 1951, p. 158.

[9] Z. Diesendruck, *Hebrew Union College Annual*, 11, pp. 341–366.

expressed in III, 23, where the problem of Job is answered by the assertion that true felicity, which is the knowledge of God, is always available to the pious, and with the thoughts presented in III, 51, where Providence is said to be related solely to intellection. Guttman maintains that, in view of these contradictions, the least innovative view should be followed.

But, it would seem that Maimonides would not have covered his traces by deliberate contradictions, if he had intended only to state the traditional view, that God governs the world according to the law of Justice.[10] Indeed, Maimonides boldly separates himself from the prevailing view among the rabbis (III, 17).

S. B. Urbach resorts to some forced interpretations in order to safeguard the orthodoxy of Maimonides. In a note he writes,

"Maimonides asserts the reality of Providence in maintaining that a pattern of reward and punishment for individuals was built into the normal course of human affairs, and the intellectual bond is only a technical instrument, which makes possible the manifestation of this Providence . . . And it is grievous mistake when some scholars write that 'not ethical considerations but the range of the intellect of people alone determines the nature of Divine Providence' . . ."[11]

Samuel Atlas, argues against Guttmann's notion that Maimonides changed his view of Providence in the *Guide*. The fact is that Maimonides quotes the same midrashim in the *Guide* (II, 19) as in his commentary on the Mishnah. "Perfection and divine intervention are incompatible; they constitute a contradiction in terms . . ." Miracles, therefore, are pre-ordained deviations from natural law, which were built into the course of nature, at creation, and it is only the time of their occurrence that was revealed to the prophets.[12]

* * *

Leo Strauss has expressed the view that Maimonides belongs in the company of those medieval philosophers whose primary interest was political. Their real philosophy was imparted only to a select few, while their public writings were designed to foster a well-regulated, well-disciplined society. Hence, we may assume that the real philosophy of Maimonides was worlds apart from the plain meaning of the *Guide*.[13]

Strauss did not undertake to spell out the real philosophy of Maimonides.

[10] J. Guttmann, *op. cit.*, p. 392, note 453.

[11] Simha Bunim Urbach, *Amudai Hamahshavah Hayisrealit*, Jerusalem, 1956, vol. 4, p. 401.

[12] S. Atlas, "Moses in the Philosophy of Maimonides, Spinoza, and Solomon Maimon, *Hebrew Union College Annual*, XXV, p. 374.

[13] Leo Straus, "On Abravanel's Philosophy and Political Thinking," *Spinoza's Critique of Religion*. See also J. Guttmann, *op. cit.*, p. 394, note 476.

However, another scholar, Jacob Becker, did not hesitate to carry this insight to its logical conclusion. In a brilliant, introductory study, he calls attention to the distinction between "true beliefs" (*emunot amitiot*) אמונות אמיתיות and "necessary beliefs" (*emunot hekhrohiot*) אמונות הכרחיות—the latter being dogmas "necessary for the abolition of reciprocal wrongdoing or for the acquisition of a noble moral quality, as for instance, the belief that He, may He be exalted, has a violent anger against those who do injustice . . . or that He responds instantaneously to the prayer of someone wronged or deceived . . ." (*Guide*, III, 28)

Maimonides himself warns time and again that his true teaching is both concealed and revealed in the *Guide*. He set out to instruct the would-be philosophers, without hurting the naive piety of those who are not properly prepared for the dangerous flights of metaphysical speculation (*Guide*, Introduction). He claimed to reveal the mysteries of which the Mishnah speaks—מעשה בראשית (*maaseh bereshit*) and מעשה מרכבה (*maaseh merkavah*), the works of creation and of providence. Such mysteries could not be revealed to the general public, only to one or two worthy scholars in a generation (Hagigah 12b).

Becker concludes that the entire web of religious attitudes, beliefs and practices in Judaism was, to Maimonides, merely the outer garment, while his real thought formed a consistent, philosophical system, best expounded by Aristotle, but which, he believed, was derived originally from Moses and the prophets. In this view, all contradictions are resolved, easily; in our view, this reconciliation is achieved all too easily.

As we have pointed out, Maimonides' personal integrity hardly squares with so jaundiced a view of the dichotomies in his thought. We cannot but assume that he saw an inner coherence between the true ideas, the "golden apple" in his metaphor, and the external pattern of deeds and opinions, the filigreed silver that encased the true philosophy (*Guide*, Introduction).

In our view, the so called "necessary truths" were only popular versions of ethereal concepts; hence, they were true in intention, even if in content they were so only in a qualified way. The best example of this relationship is the relation of the dogma of bodily resurrection to the belief in immortality, as described in the Eight Chapters. If we view his works as a whole, we see that in his popular works, Maimonides describes a steady ascent to the truth of speculation. He does not speak of an abyss between two categories of Jews, but of a unitary Torah-community.

Nor does he propound the doctrine of "two truths" which the Parisian Averroists later espoused.[14]

In Becker's view, the cleavage in the *Guide* between the truths of phi-

[14] In medieval Jewish philosophy, this doctrine was maintained by Isaac Albalag, in *De-ot Haphilosophim*.

losophy and the popular religion is so wide and deep as to be totally unbridgeable. It is the "necessary truths" and the laws of the Talmud that Maimonides has in mind when he writes, "For only truth pleases, may He be exalted, and only that which is false angers Him. Your opinions and thoughts should not become confused so that you believe in incorrect opinions that are very remote from the truth and you regard them as Law. For the Laws are absolute truths if they are understood in the way they ought to be" (*Guide*, II, 47).[15]

Becker assumes that the Thirteen Principles of Faith sum up the beliefs of the popular religion, while the truths of philosophy are only three—God's unity, His incorporeality and His eternity.[16]

These three ideas can, of course, be reached only through the *via negativa*. However, they were revealed to Moses "in the cleft of the rock," and through his prophetic successors this teaching was conveyed to the Greek philosophers (I, 71). In Becker's interpretation of Maimonides, the personality of Moses is exalted to the point of attaining a "superhuman" status.

"The entire trend of Maimonides' philosophy flows out of his deep conviction that Moses attained a level that is superhuman, supernatural, divine—'he became pure reason."

"The foundation of the *Guide*, which I revealed in this study, is based upon this basic thought—the deification of Moses."[17]

From our standpoint, the radical conclusions of Becker are totally unacceptable. The entire impetus of philosophic thought is against the radical exemption of any one person or any one experience from the laws of logic and structure of being. In our view, the dogma which Maimonides lays down concerning the unique character of Mosaic prophecy was itself rooted in the Torah and promulgated for the same reason, namely, the need of providing stability to the Jewish community. That dogma is therefore in itself a "necessary belief," rather than a "true belief." Yet, as will be shown later, in this dogma, as in all "necessary beliefs," there is an intimate correspondence between the assertion that Mosaic prophecy was unique and its actual functioning as such in the history of mankind.

We can treat as a merely "necessary truth" that which Maimonides himself so categorizes or so suggests—for example, the resurrection of the dead—but not immortality and not the advent of the Messiah.[18]

However, both Strauss and Becker were impelled to suggest radical solutions to the puzzles in the *Guide* by the apparent poverty of Maimonides' conception of the Deity, Who is reached only through the *via negativa*.

[15] J. Becker, *Mishnato Hafilosofit shel Horambam*, Tel Aviv, 1957, p. 47.

[16] Becker, *op. cit.*, p. 48, *Guide*, III, 28.

[17] Becker, *op. cit.*, p. 129.

[18] Bodily resurrection is expressly reinterpreted in the Eight Chapters. In the *Guide*, II, 27, it is referred to as the belief of those who interpret the Midrashim literally.

* * *

We propose herein that the key to the *Guide* was actually the intention of Maimonides to open an affirmative way to God, a *via eminentia*, that would result in a rebirth of Israel and the nations of the world. The *via negativa* was already an accepted doctrine in his day; his contribution was to stimulate interest in the affirmative aspects of Divine Providence.

Four scholars have pointed the way to this interpretation:

Harry A. Wolfson—"While excluding God from knowable universal qualities, the attributes affirm of Him some unknowable qualities, peculiar to Himself, and identical with His essence."[19] In a later article, Wolfson states that Maimonides employed the negative attributes as a way "of justifying the affirmative form in which certain terms must be predicated."[20]

Z. Diesendruck, in his *Die Teleologie bei Maimonides*, refers to "the neo-vitalistic trends in recent philosophy" for an understanding of Maimonides' attempt to relate the purpose of creation to the noblest goal of human life.[21]

Prof. Solomon Zeitlin, pointed out in his book on Maimonides that the massive labors of Maimonides were future-oriented, toward the establishment of a constitution for Israel reborn.

Prof. Israel Efros brought to the study of the *Guide* his own central insight that the affirmative and negative dimensions of the Jewish religious experience were basically inseparable—*kavod* and *kadosh.*

In his view, Maimonides saw God as an Artist who blended Wisdom and Will in a continuous series of creations.[22]

* * *

The abyss between Maimonides' two major works—his *Code* and his *Guide*—is a grand demonstration of the gap between the two philosophies of life that he aimed to overcome. The *Code* is a faithful transcription of the entire Oral Law, without any concession to the claims of reason. So, the sacrificial system is included as a pattern for the future, not merely as an expression of "Divine Cunning," in weaning the Israelites from the practices of ancient pagans.[23] By the same token, the *Guide* follows, on the whole, the logical direction of speculative philosophy, concluding in the famous parable (III, 51), where the philosophers of all nations are ranked far ahead of the Talmudists.

[19] *JQR*, New Series, VII, 22.

[20] "Ginzberg Jubilee Volume," pp. 411–46.

[21] *Hebrew Union College Annual*, V (1928), pp. 415–534.

[22] I. Efros, *Haphilosophia Hayehudit Bimai Habenayim*, Devir, 5727, I, p. 204.

[23] It is interesting to note that Rabad, Maimonides' critic, a mystic in the Kabbalistic tradition, foresaw an ethereal transmutation of the sacrificial regimen. "This has been revealed to me by God's mysterious instruction to those who fear Him." Salo W. Baron, *A Social and Religious History of the Jews*, VIII, p. 41 and note 45, p. 292.

But, with consummate skill, Maimonides proceeds to close the manifest gap, by including in the *Guide*, the reasons for the Commandments, and inserting his philosophical principles into the Code not only at its beginning, where it is clearly stated, but also at its end, where its significance in projecting a new philosophy of history was not generally noticed.

Insofar as the reasons for the Commandments are concerned, the striking fact is that he did not resort to the usual device of justifying all the *mizvot* on the ground that they were given by God, Who knows best. He insists that they represent God's "Wisdom," as well as His Will; therefore, they must be transparent to human reason. Furthermore, he introduced the concepts of Primary Intention, Secondary Intention and "divine cunning," הערמה האלהית (III, 32), thereby establishing the historical context for the assaying of the import of the *mizvot*. For this latter emphasis, there was no precedent at all in Jewish philosophy, and he opened himself up to the bitter criticism of all traditionalists. Evidently, this "historical" approach was not a secondary afterthought in his mind, but a central implication of his conception of the course of Jewish and human history.

In fact, the *Code*, for all its detailed description of a static and unvarying law, also stresses both the dynamic and historical aspects of Judaism in projecting the messianic era as a necessary outgrowth of the regular forces operative in history.

The first book of the *Code*, *Sefer Hamada*, was always recognized as a summation of Maimonides' philosophy. Those who attacked the *Guide* generally included this book in their condemnation. But, the intimate connection between the first book of the *Code* and the last chapters, depicting the messianic future, was not previously recognized.

Let us first note the reinterpretation of the messianic hope that Maimonides offers in the last chapters of the *Code*. The messianic era, he claims, will eventuate out of the regular course of history, without any supernatural intervention.

"Do not imagine that in the days of the Messiah anything will be changed in the operation of the universe, or that there will be any innovation in the works of creation."[24] Maimonides cited the dictum of the Babylonian teacher, Samuel, that "in the days of the Messiah, all that will be changed is the suppression of governments." But, then, Samuel and other teachers deferred the domain of total redemption to the appearance of *Olam haba*, when this cosmos will come to an end, and a new form of human life will come into being, along with the bodily resurrection of the dead. An apocalyptic *Eschaton* is assumed in Talmudic literature. In Maimonides' view, *olam haba* is the post-mortem state of the souls of the philosophical saints ("Eight Chapters"). And the doctrine of the resurrection of the dead

[24] *Code*, Hilchot Melachim, XII, 1.

is altogether scorned in the *Guide* (II, 27). At most, it might be regarded as a "necessary belief," calculated to please the vulgar, in accordance with his reasoning in the "Eight Chapters." In sum, the Messianic Era will grow out of the horizontal course of history, not through a sudden interruption, or a vertical entrance of the Divine into the affairs of mankind.

Still, Maimonides was neither a naturalistic philosopher nor a rationalistic believer in progress a la the nineteenth century liberals. The source of ethical progress was, in his view, the persistent thrust of the Divine Power and Wisdom, which are manifested in the operation of the Holy Spirit and prophecy. He was liberal enough to recognize that this Divine nisus operated among the Christians and the Moslems, as well as within Jewry, since these religions promulgated faith in God and devotion to the ethic of Holy Scripture.[25] But, the Torah-society was for him the unique instrument of Divine guidance for all men, since "all of existence is like one living organism" (I, 71). Hence, the task of readying the Jewish community for its central role in the course of redemption.

To be sure, the Jewish people generally cannot possibly aspire to the rank of prophecy, but they can provide the social matrix for the emergence of prophets and men inspired by the Holy Spirit. Here is where his organismic view of society became central. All the cosmos is as one organism (I, 72), with the saints and the philosophers bringing down the renewing vitality of Divine Power to the society of mankind. And within the body of mankind, the Torah-society is a similarly constituted organism. Since the Holy Spirit stimulates statesmanship and inventiveness as well as devotion to the common good, we can readily acknowledge its significance for the advance of all the aspects of human culture. Indeed, the rebirth of the Jewish people and the revitalization of the human order are interdependent. The Messiah himself is both a universal prophet and the King of Israel reborn.[26] His advent depends on the general progress of humanity and on the resurgence of the prophetic genius, in all its manifestations.

But is there any hope for the reemergence of prophecy, either in Israel or among the nations? Maimonides, unlike Halevi, did not confine the gift of prophecy either to the people of Israel or to the land of Israel (*Kusari*, I, 93–103). All that the Israelites lacked basically was peace of mind (II, 36). However, as he saw it, the Talmudists circle around the "palace of the King," without daring to enter through its portals, by way of philosophic meditation (III, 51). It was necessary for him to compile the *Code*, which renders superfluous the study of other works, in order to channel the intellectual energy of Jewish people first toward secular disciplines, and second, to the unflagging ardor of philosophic meditation, culminating in the rhapsodic states of the Holy Spirit (*Code*, Introduction). The preoccupa-

[25] Hilchot Melachim, X, 12, the uncensored Constantinople edition.
[26] *Iggeret Teman*, edition Goldman, p. 96.

tion of Jewish savants with the perplexing casuistry of the Talmud prevented them from devoting themselves completely to the contemplation of the great truths—the problems of creation and providence.

As to Jewish society generally, the first book of the *Code* is intended to acquaint them with the elementary principles of philosophical speculation. "What is the right way to the love of God and the fear of Him?" His answer is to contemplate the wondrous works of creation, recognizing His Infinite Wisdom, so that we be transported by the ecstasy of His Glory, and then be moved to reflect on our human frailty and finitude, and that we tremble in fear (*Sefer Hamada*, I, 2).

Here, then, there is no attempt to approach God by way of *mizvot*, but through intellectual meditation, as explained in the *Guide* (III, 52).

Intellectual contemplation must be based upon the attainment of perfection in one's moral qualities. These in turn are described in the terms of philosophy—the happy medium between two extremes and "the imitation of God" (Hilkhot Deot, I, 4, 6). The latter principle, mentioned by Plato in *Theaetetus*, is manifestly contrary to the entire trend of Maimonidean thought. If we cannot ascribe to God any anthropomorphic qualities, how can we emulate His ways? Maimonides replies that the prophets attributed such qualities to God, for tactical reasons, in order to recommend the corresponding human virtues for imitation.[27] This dialectical twist might appear to be a *tour de force*, but it is really central to the Maimonidean philosophy. The goal of life is to attain "the nearness of God," as much as possible—first through moral training, then through intellectual disciplines, and finally by means of philosophical meditation. The imitation of God, in this sense, implies these three aspects of the unending quest, which is inspirational and prophetic in character.[28]

Second, the essence of the Divine influence, consists in the bestowal of wisdom and redemptive power to ever greater circles of humanity. Just as God is outgoing, with His "Goodness renewing daily the works of creation," so the recipient of the Divine power is driven to share his bounty with others. He is charged with the task of bringing more and more people to the high levels of devotion and inspiration that he has attained. The recipient of God's "flow" must undertake to bring *hesed*, steadfast love, and *zedek*, charity, as well as *mishpat*, justice, into the affairs of society (III, 54).

It follows that the inspired statesman and philosopher becomes an in-

[27] Hilchot Deot, I, 6.

"ועל דרך זו קראו הנביאים לאל בכל אותן הכנויים, ארך אפים . . . להודיע שהן דרכים טובים וישרים, וחייב אדם להנהיג עצמו בהן ולהדמות אליו כפי כחו."

[28] In *Guide*, I, 69, Maimonides speaks of the purpose of all existence as being the imitation of His Being. Z. Diesendruck sees in the concluding sentences of this chapter the final summation of Maimonides' teleology—the purpose of creation is to make possible man's free *imitatio Dei*. Man can rise "above nature." *Op. cit.*, pp. 530, 533.

strument of divine redemption within the course of history, helping to perfect human society, step by step, toward the climax of the messianic era.

This redemptive power, deriving from God through the Active Reason, is manifested in many and diverse ways that all can see, though God in Himself transcends our grasp. Human culture, in its esthetic forms as well as in its industrial arts, is reinvigorated by the impact of Divine energy upon the imaginative faculties of poets, artists, inventors and statesmen (II, 45). So culture and religion go hand in hand. The dynamic guidance of prophets is the key factor in the organization of an ideal society, one that promotes the intellectual climate of the community as well as its moral and esthetic disciplines (II, 38 and 40). But the esthetic and industrial arts are also produced by the Divine redeeming power and they are essential for the building of the noble society of the future. In a very real sense, Maimonides propounded a philosophy of universal culture, as well as of universal history, under the guise of an interpretation of biblical symbolism. His theological terminology served to conceal his broad-gauged humanism; indeed, his plea is for a manysided renaissance of culture, with the revived genius of prophecy at its heart.

But the impassioned humanism of Maimonides was not obtained at the cost of interpreting away the landmarks of Torah. On the contrary, he believed that he uncovered the original dimensions and full meaning of Torah. His philosophy remained theocentric, with the doctrine of *creatio ex nihilo* at its heart. All creation continues to be directly dependent upon the Creator—this thesis was to him not an abstract proposition, but the living core of his ardent piety (I, 69). For the purpose of man's life is "the apprehension of true opinions and clinging to the divine reason that flows toward him" (III, 8). השגת דעת אמיתי בכל דבר, והדבק בשכל האלהי השופע עליו. This "Divine Reason" is inseparable from His Power, in the operation of Providence, which directs the lives of great men as well as the entire human race. אאמין שההשגחה נמשכת אחר השכל ומדובקת בו. His philosophy remained Israel-centric, in that a society patterned after the Torah is alone calculated to serve as the nucleus of mankind redeemed.

* * *

To recognize the new horizons of the Maimonidean philosophy, we have to give full weight to the two degrees of inspiration that he considers to be pre-prophetic.

The first degree is that known in our literature as *ruah hakodesh.* But in the scheme of Maimonides, it is purged of theurgic or magical implications. Instead, the term is given a broad, secular denotation.

"The first of the degrees of prophecy consists in the fact that an individual receives divine help (עזר אלהי) that moves and activates him to a great, righteous and important action—such as the deliverance of a community of virtuous people from a community of wicked people, or the deliverance of a virtuous and great man, or the conferring of benefits on numerous people או השפיע טוב על אנשים רבים (literally, 'making good overflow')" (Pines' trans. *Guide*, II, 45, p. 196).[29]

If we bear this definition of *ruah hakodesh* in mind when we read of the Divine Overflow affecting only the imaginative faculty, we recognize its broad, secular implications.

"If again the overflow reaches only the imaginative faculty, the defect of the rational faculty deriving either from its original natural disposition or from insufficiency of training, this is characteristic of those who govern cities, while being the legislators, the soothsayers, the augurs and the dreamers of veridical dreams. All those who do extraordinary things by means of strange devices and secret arts, and withal are not men of science, belong likewise to this third class."

Here, then is a description of skill in statesmanship and industrial inventiveness, as inclusive as one could possibly express in the last decade of the twelfth century.

The second degree of pre-prophetic inspiration is attained when some orators or authors are moved to compose great literary works. They experience the feeling of being seized by a superior power—"That another force has come upon him and made him speak . . . concerning governmental or divine matters."[30]

Maimonides includes in this category the wisdom and poetic works in the Bible. Their authors did not attain the double perfection of both the imaginative and the rational faculties. The imaginative faculty includes an intuitive power, which predisposes its possessor to anticipate future events.[31]

29 We note that the "Messiahs of Israel," impelled by the Holy Spirit, may not always succeed in their endeavors. Samson and Saul failed in the end, though they were successful initially. So, in the last chapter of his *Code*, Maimonides describes Bar Kochba as a paradigmatic messiah, though his enterprise ended in a terrible catastrophe. Similarly, in his *Iggeret Teman*, he speaks reverently of a pseudo-messianic prophet in the days of his father, concluding, "may his memory be blessed." Similarly in Bergson's *Creative Evolution*, the élan vital does not always succeed. *Iggeret Teman*, edition Solomon Goldman, 1950, p. 112. *Iggrot Harambam*, edition "Rishonim," Tel Aviv, 1951, p. 195. Maimonides mentions this enthusiast as a *hassid*, in his responsa (*Kovetz Teshuvot*, I, 26).

30 Pines' interpretation of "another force" as being different from the one operative in the first degree is illogical. The Divine flow is always the same. The differences are due to the variations of the receptive faculties. "Another force" is simply the subjective feeling of the recipient, since on this level, he is fully awake and conscious. The imaginative faculty makes one attribute inner experiences to external stimuli (II, 36. Pines, p. 379). Ibn Tibbon's translation reads: שימצא האדם כאילו ענין אחד חל עליו וכח אחד התחדש וישימהו לדבר. Al Harizi's translation agrees with this interpretation.

31 Pines' translation of the Hebrew, *Koah homeshaer*, as "the faculty of divination" is rendered by Friedlander as "an intuitive faculty," which is the meaning that best fits the context.

It is important to note that the two pre-prophetic degrees of inspiration are of a general, human character. "It is a part of the wisdom of the deity with regard to the permanence of the species . . ." (II, 40) — that is, the human race — that statesmen, legislators and governors should arise to impose laws upon their respective communities. If those laws do not take account of the need to develop speculative perfection, they belong to the class of *nomoi* — that is, they were designed by the impact of the Active Reason upon men "who are perfect only in their imaginative faculty" (II, 40, Pines', p. 384).

We note that Maimonides distinguishes between the laws of pagans and those of cultured people (II. 39) — only the latter were the product of pre-prophetic, divine inspiration. But, all of mankind is a species that Providence seeks to preserve, even as it preserves all biological species by means of instincts. While man is not the purpose of all creation, he is the most perfect of all creation, and his perfection is in the future (III, 13). כי הכונה האחרונה הוא הגיע השלמות. ומבואר הוא שהשלם שאפשר מציאותו מזה החמר הוא האדם. Divine inspiration, in its pre-prophetic levels takes the place of instincts, pre-disposing some to be governed, others to govern (II, 37). The latter fall into various categories — poets, statesmen, inventors, artists, and at their best, prophets. So prophecy is not a unique quality, but a blending of all other qualities, in their right proportions (II, 36). It follows that religion is the perfect harmonization of all of man's capacities (II, 39). It generates the various facets of culture and imposes a celestial harmony upon the conflicting forces in society.

* * *

From all the above, there emerges the outline of a philosophy that strikes a responsive chord in the hearts of moderns. We might describe it as panentheistic, in contrast to the pantheism of Spinoza. Nature is in God, but God is beyond nature. God works through the laws of nature, but He also supplements them by fresh infusions of spiritual power. Yet reason and the quest of truth are the surest guides to His nearness. "For only truth pleases Him and only falsehood angers Him" (II, 47). He imparts of His creative power most fully to prophets and fragmentarily also to philosophers and statesmen, inventors and poets. In this manner, He impels human society to ever greater heights of moral and intellectual achievement. Ultimately, the messianic world of moral and physical perfection will come into being, as a result of these successive upward thrusts.

But while the dynamic, creative energy of Divine Providence cannot be forced, it can be tapped with great assurance that it will be forthcoming. When a morally disciplined person, with a refined imagination and a keen intellect, achieves the climax of philosophical intuition, then "almost surely" the good God will not withhold prophecy from him (II, 32). Maimonides differs from both the Orthodox, who describe prophecy as a divine fiat, and the philosophers who consider it a purely human achievement. Since God is freedom, the entrance of His Reason and Will into the mind of man cannot be subject to the mechanical laws of necessity. Since He is also good, eager to bestow goodness, He will surely bestow the prize of prophecy upon the deserving ones. As a result of this antinomy, we can only prepare ourselves for the occasional thrusts of divine power, especially insofar as they affect those of us who can only qualify for preprophetic bounties.[32]

In assimilating prophecy to speculative perfection, on the one hand, and to all phases of culture, on the other hand, Maimonides created a theory of secular culture and progress, that is reminiscent of such modern panentheists as Bergson, Alexander, Whitehead and Hartshorne. While "the origin of species" was outside his ken, he saw the continuous creativity of Divine Providence in the course of human history, for "the final intention is to bring about perfection" (III, 13). He did not merely combine religion and philosophy; he created a religious philosophy in which prayer and meditation were organically related to all the domains of secular culture. The revival of prophecy was essential to the progress of mankind as a whole, and he expanded the horizons of prophecy far beyond their biblical limitations.

Far from being a divided soul, or a manipulative philosopher, Maimonides was a thoroughly systematic thinker and pietist—at once the noblest exponent of Judaism and a prophet of humanity redeemed.

Maimonides' image of the cosmos was so vastly different than ours that we fail to note its similarity to what Hartshorne calls the "convergent classical philosophy." In his view, the earth was the center of all creation, with a series of "spheres," surrounding it. The "spheres" were composed out of a heavenly matter that was not subject to corruption, and they moved in circular fashion in order to articulate their love and knowledge of God. Each sphere was endowed with its own Intelligence. God Himself transcended all spheres (I, 71); and by means of the sphere of Active Reason, He continued to bestow the thrusts of His creative energy upon those individuals whose personalities had become receptive to His power. Furthermore, all living things were marked by the quality of purposiveness, in so far as their matter was capable of receiving the imprint of His Being (III, 19). All birds and animals manifest an inherent wisdom and an intricate network of interdependence. Indeed, the purposiveness of life is the noblest proof of the existence of God, for all living beings are impelled by the longing to imitate Him (I, 69): ותכלית הכל גם כן ההדמות בשלמותו, כפי היכלת....

Here, then, is a cosmos, that is truly one organism, and the soul of its

[32] See Afudi, II, 32, who assumes dissimulation on the part of Maimonides. וכדי שלא יראה שסברותנו כסברת הפילוסוף המוחלט, שם זה החלוף, ואם אינו כן כפי האמתות.

soul is God. From Him comes the power that sustains life in all the species of plant and animal life and, in the case of mankind, the preprophetic and prophetic forces that impel human society to the perfection of the messianic era. Even death is "very good" in this perspective of continuous spiritual growth (III, 10). In a world where God is the Goal as well as the Source of all existence, it is but natural that the purpose of man's life should be, "to reach for truth in all things and to cling to the reason of God that streams upon him" (III, 8).

We recall that Leibnitz was led to postulate that ours is "the best of all possible worlds," since it was designed by the Perfect Being. To Maimonides, "the best of all possible worlds" for man was still in the future, and God was steadily propelling mankind upward and toward that goal. Even while insisting on His negative attributes, Maimonides suggests this goal when he asserts that he can think of no better metaphor for God acting upon His world than that of "a captain in the ship" (I, 58). Rather than make use of the rabbinic image of the Master of the Palace (Baal Habirah) (Genesis Rabba 39, 1), he prefers the dynamic image of the Captain in a ship, leading His charges closer and closer to the haven of perfection.

It is through the proliferation of divine wisdom and creative energy that all rivalries and hatreds will be overcome and the messianic era will dawn (III, 11).

The perfection of humanity in the days of the Messiah will be entirely "natural," as Maimonides takes pains to clarity in his *Code*. But this "natural" consummation is assured, because of the several ways in which the Divine nisus penetrates this earthly world.[33]

[33] Alvin J. Reines, in his *Maimonides and Abrabanel on Prophecy* (Cincinnati, 1970), describes Maimonides' religion as "naturalistic." He claims that Maimonides regarded "prophecy as a natural event" (XXXI). He disputes the notion "that the special divine will plays a role in every occurrence of prophecy." He takes issue with Diesendruck, who maintained that prophecy is the direct creation of God. (S. Diesendruck, "Maimonides Lehre des Prophetie" in *Jewish Studies in Memory of Israel Abrahams*, Vienna, 1927).

From our analysis, it appears that the categories of "natural" and "supernatural" do not apply to the universe of Maimonides. God's role in prophecy is not a capricious act of will that is totally undetermined. It is not a new act of *creatio ex nihilo*, but a thrust toward greater perfection and rationality. The contrast between the terms, natural-supernatural and immanent-transcendent, is great indeed. In the latter case, there is a persistent, creative drive, rising by degrees from the lower pole of reality that is Matter to God, Who is the "Purpose of all purposes" (III, 13). As Diesendruck points out, Maimonides expanded the role of purpose in the cosmos far beyond its range in Aristotle. Z. Diesendruck, "Hatachlit Vehataarim Betorat Harambam," *Tarbitz*, I, p. 106.

In our view, the Jewish philosophy of history, which Maimonides reinterpreted in the sense of a continuous drive toward perfection in human history, transformed his understanding of the relation of God to mankind. The remote God of Aristotle became a dynamic Presence, ever ready to inspire those who open their hearts and minds to Him, prodding the human race with "wily graciousness" (*heᶜormo heᵓelohit*) (III, 32) toward messianic fulfillment.

Nature (*teva*), on its lowest levels, is totally mechanical and invariant. On a higher cosmic level, we encounter the complexities of organic life, which derive intelligent guidance from God. The complexity of structure in the eye cannot be due to fortuitous mechanical configurations (III, 19). "Nature is not endowed with intellect and the capacity for goverance . . . according to us, it is the act of an intelligent being." Organic life is then more than "nature," though at times Maimonides continues to speak of living beings as instances of nature's wisdom—"If you consider the divine actions—I mean to say the natural actions—the deity's wily graciousness and wisdom, as shown in the creation of living beings . . ." (III, 32, Pines' translation, p. 525).

There is no clear dividing line between the "natural" and the divine, but a steady ascent from Matter to God, from the simplest events in inanimate nature to the highest reaches of the prophetic personalities.

Above the level of animal life, the human race is more open to the constant "flow" of Divine power. Mankind was denied the sure guidance of invariant instincts, and humans differ in abilities and opinions. To survive, the society of mankind had to be sustained even in pagan or primitive times by preprophetic and pseudo-prophetic leaders, who managed to impose an order of some sort upon the undisciplined multitude (II, 40). Even the "Sabeans," or pagans, were governed by rulers and "diviners," whose gifts were imaginative and non-rational. The divine "flow" in their case was minimally rational and largely intuitive (III, 38).

On a still higher level, Providence operated in human society through the agency of statesmen, who worked out systematic laws for the governance of men, the so called *nomoi* of the Greeks and Romans. Here, the effect of the pre-prophetic divine power was manifested not merely in the relative rationality of the *nomoi*, but also in the readiness of cultured peoples to abide by these laws. For, as we have noted, the submission of people to government is an effect of a Divine incursion into society. Other consequences of preprophetic inspiration are the various inventions and artifacts which serve to enhance the quality of human life (II, 45, first degree) (II, 37).

The emergence of prophets, like Abraham, impelled humanity to a still higher level, but then only individuals were directly affected by the Patriarchs. The critical moment in the advance of humanity toward perfection occurred at Sinai, when Moses concluded the covenant with the people of Israel.

The prophecy of Moses was devoid of any imaginative elements. It was therefore in a class by itself. Yet he, too, was only human and when he was deeply anguished by the disaster that followed the report of the spies, he declined in his imaginative perfection, and for many years in the wilderness he failed to attain the noblest heights of prophecy (II, 36). For prophecy is the reception of God's *nisus* toward perfection and completeness. Hence, one must be perfect in all respects—physically, intuitively or imaginatively, morally and rationally.

Maimondes had to rank the prophecy of Moses far beyond that of other prophets, in keeping with the teaching of the Torah itself, and in order to foreclose the possibility of the Mosaic law being superseded by the laws of Jesus or Mohammed. As we noted earlier, this is an instance of a "necessary belief" (III, 32). Still, he makes a special point of stressing the exceptional character of "the miracles" performed by Moses—they were done "before the eyes of all Israel" (II, 35). In view of Maimonides' insistence that all miracles were embedded into the invariant nexus of the laws of nature (II, 25), this reference to the testimony of all Israel appears strange at first glance. Halevi employed this argument to prove the truth of the Jewish faith as against the claims of other religions. But Maimonides is not interested in this argument in the *Guide*. In general, he plays down the range and the persuasive power of miracles.

Manifestly, the presence of all Israel at Sinai was all-important to him, as proof of the divine potency of Mosaic prophecy. The divine flow that comes to the prophet compels him to disseminate his message (II, 37); at the same time, the divine power predisposes the people to listen to the prophet and to obey his message (II, 40). The role of the prophet is, after all, to satisfy the human need for inner coherence in society. The readiness "to be governed" is as important as the courage and intuitive power that statesmen need in order to govern.

So, at Sinai, the Israelites attained only the rational understanding of the first two Commandments; they heard a mighty voice and saw impressive sights. But, they did not attain the rank of prophecy and did not hear "the voice of God," as it were. But they were filled with the passive consequence of prophecy—the readiness to obey and follow the teaching of God through Moses. So they assented in the famous words, *na'ase venishma*. There was only one Torah and that was the Torah of Moses (II, 39). For if a thing is the most perfect of its kind, other things must be less perfect, "either through excess or defect."

The prophets who came after Moses called upon the people to be faithful to the Torah of Moses. So it is the assembly of the Israelites at Sinai that conveys to us the meaning of history. The prophet and the people stand as one before God, with the prophet attaining the highest degree of human openness to the Thought and Will of God, and the people dedicating themselves to live in accord with the Torah revealed to the prophet.

The prophet's vision, at its highest potential, and the humble obedience of the people were jointly solemnized in the covenant. The messianic era will achieve the fulfillment of the Sinaitic covenant, involving the whole of mankind in a renewed bond between prophetic-philosophical vision and popular obedience. Until that day, the virtue of obedience will be fostered by the Israelites through the observance of the Oral Law, as formulated in the *Code*, and the embers of prophecy will be nurtured and protected by the saintly philosophers of all monotheistic faiths.

Here, then, the *Code* (*Yad Hahazakah*), in all its many-faceted complexity, and the *Guide*, in all its abstract rationality, converge to reveal the two aspects of Judaism—the infinite quest of the philosophers and prophets, on the one hand, and on the other, the balanced, harmonious way of the Israelites, in the first place, and ultimately of mankind.

In all these levels of the entrance of Divine power into human life, we cannot draw a line between the "natural" and the "supernatural," since the Divine power is the source of all purposiveness in nature, and there is a gradual ascent of beings on the cosmic ladder extending from inanimate nature to the Torah-society. Indeed, Maimonides writes of Torah as being both natural and not natural (II, 40). "Therefore, I say that the Law, although it is not natural, enters into what is natural. It is a part of the wisdom of the deity with regard to the permanence of this species of which He has willed the existence, that He put it into its nature that individuals belonging to it should have the faculty of ruling" (Pines' translation, p. 382): ולזה אומר שזאת התורה, אע׳פ שאינה טבעית, יש לה מבוא בענין הטבעי.

Maimonides' philosophy is dualistic, in the sense that all things are composed of Matter and Form, with Matter being the source of imperfection—hence, of evil (II, 14). A righteous person might encounter many troubles, on account of the matter in his body, which the Lord cannot change.[34]

Maimonides designates Matter as Satan, but Satan is not a selfexistent force, cunning and malicious.[35] There is no hell, much less an inferno of eternal fire for Satan to preside over. The wicked, whose potential higher soul was never actualized, simply disintegrate at death. But the philosophical saints can actualize their potential rational soul and thereby attain immortality.

[34] Shem Tov's summation in III, 14.
ויקרה לצדיק כפי חמרו רעות, והשם יתעלה לא יוכל לשנות מה שהוא נמנע, ואינו לאות בכחו.

[35] David Neumark in his *Toldot Hophilosophia Beyisroel* (Jerusalem, 1971, III, pp. 341–418), maintains that Maimonides eliminated matter altogether from his view of reality. Neumark describes Maimonides' philosophy as an anticipation of the neo-Kantian, "critical" philosophy. In our judgment, his interpretation is unconvincing.

[36] We have referred to the two last paragraphs of Maimonides' *Code* "Hilchot Melachim," Constantinople, uncensored edition. A translation of these paragraphs is printed in Twersky's "A Maimonides Reader," pp. 226, 227.

Maimonides' universalism is expressed also in his famous letter to R. Hisdai Halevi, *Kovetz Teshuvot Horambam*, Lipsia, 1859, II, no. 24.
ומה ששאלת את האומות, הוי יודע דרחמנא לבא בעי, ואחר כונת הלב הם הדברים... ועל כן אמרו חכמי האמת... חסידי אומות העולם, אם השיגו מה שראוי להשיג מידיעת הבורא ית׳ והתקינו נפשם במדות הטובות... בודאי הוא מבני העוה׳ב.

In this world, Satan cannot long delay the ultimate attainment of human perfection.[36] For the divine *nisus* in its two preprophetic stages is at work among Christians and Moslems, as well as Jews, impelling mankind to the *Eschaton* through the processes of history.

Some Traditional Principles in Biblical Exegesis

By WILLIAM CHOMSKY
The Dropsie University

THE PURPOSE OF this article is to point up some traditional principles of biblical exegesis employed in the Talmud and by medieval Jewish commentators, which may facilitate the interpretation of biblical passages puzzling modern commentators. To this end an extension of these principles is hereby suggested, and examples are offered, which are by no means exhaustive.

A. *Syntactical Transposition*

Inversion of letters, especially words, even phrases, is a common phenomenon in languages.[1] Indeed, in the Hebrew Bible, many verses make sense only when interpreted on the principle of inversion. This was already recognized by the talmudic sages. The classical example is ונר אלהים טרם יכבה ושמואל שוכב בהיכל ה' (Isa. 3:3), where the sages regard the possibility of Samuel's "sleeping in the temple of the Lord" as inappropriate and inconceivable. Hence the transposition of בהיכל ה' is recommended, so that the verse could be rendered "and the lamp of the Lord was not yet gone out in the temple of the Lord."[2] Numerous other such instances of inversion are quoted in the Talmud.[3] Extensive use of this principle was made by the medieval grammarians and commentators, especially Ibn Janaḥ[4] and David Kimḥi.[5] To a lesser extent it was applied also by Saadia,[6] Dunash,[7] Rashi,[8] Ibn Ezra,[9] and Ramban.[10] Most of these interpretations have unfortunately not been utilized by modern commentators and translators.

There are, however, some instances where the application of the principle of inversion could clear up some exegetical difficulties, which escaped the attention of the talmudic and medieval scholars. In Gen. 6:16, for example, the expression תכלנה מלמעלה makes no sense. Speiser in his commentary,

[1] *Cf.* Jespersen, O., *Essentials of English Grammar*, 101 ff.
[2] B. Kid., 78b.
[3] See Levi, J., s. v., סרס; also Bacher, W., *Terminologia*, I and II, s. v., סרס.
[4] *Cf. Rikma*, ed. Wilensky, 224 f.; 395–368.
[5] *Mikhlol*, ed. Lyk, 89b–191a.
[6] Commentary to Prov. 1:19.
[7] *Teshubot against Menahem*, 97.
[8] See Shereshevsky, E., *Gratz College Anniversary*, vol., 1971.
[9] Commentary to Lev. 19:24; also Bacher's *Abraham Ibn Ezra als Grammätiker*, 140 f.
[10] Commentary to Gen. 2:3.

ad loc., declares: "The specific detail remains obscure." However, Arnold Ehrlich plausibly suggests that the word מלמעלה should be transposed and placed after לתבה. The meaning of the verse would then be clarified: The window (צהר) should, accordingly, be placed on the top of the ark and should be a cubit wide. The use of צהר in the fem. (תכלנה) presents no problem, according to Ehrlich, since its synonym (חלון) also occurs in the Bible in the feminine (Ezek. 41:16).[11]

Another case where the principle of inversion might be applied is in Prov. 24:5, where the construction and meaning of the first half of the verse (גבר חכם בעז) are unclear. Commentators have added little to their clarification. However, the transposition of the prefixed particle ב from the third to the first word would render the expression meaningful and parallel to the second half of the verse. One could clearly find in it a source for Lord Bacon's famous dictum: "Knowledge (or wisdom) is power." Similarly, the reading in Isa. 21:1 מספר גבורי קשת is preferable to the masoretic reading מספר קשת גברי.

Transposition is sometimes carried over one or more verses, e. g., Gen. 24:29–30, where the phrase ויבא אל האיש in verse 30 should logically follow immediately after the end of the preceding verse. Examples of such remote inversions are not rare and are quoted by Ibn Janaḥ and Kimḥi,[12] as well as by Ibn Ezra.[13]

It may be interesting to add that cases of inversion may be found also in Mishnaic Hebrew, e .g., Aboth 1:3, where the expression שלא על מנת לקבל פרס in our texts should probably be read על מנת שלא לקבל פרס, as in the Cairo Geniza manuscript, edited by Professor Abraham I. Katsh.[14]

B. *Paronomasia*

Words similar in sound but different in meaning (paronomasia) are often employed in language with the object of heightening the effect of an expression. Such usages, or plays upon words, are of frequent occurrence in the Bible and were already noted by the early medieval commentators Rashi[15] and Radak[16] and were designated by them by the term לשון נופל על לשון, which may be traced back to the Midrash.[17] But an even earlier medieval grammarian, Jonah Ibn Janaḥ (995–1050), construes the verb in Jer. 4:1

[11] See מקרא כפשוטו, 19 f.
[12] *Op. cit.* (Ibn Janaḥ, 362–68).
[13] *Cf.* Bacher's *Ibn Ezra, etc.*, 140, note 23.
[14] ק"א, מוסד הרב קוק, גנזי משנה.
[15] Num. 21:9, Mic. 1:10.
[16] Commentary, Isa. 57:6, Jer. 48:2, Mic. 1:13.
[17] Bresh. Rabba 18:6.

and 8:4, where it occurs twice in each verse, as a case of paronomasia: the first instance in the usual sense of "return" and the second, in the sense of "persistence," "continuation."[18]

But there are numerous instances of paronomasia in the Bible which escaped the attention of the medieval commentators and scholars. Many obscurities in biblical passages could be obviated by the application of this principle. Indeed, a 19th century scholar, Mordecai Dobesh, collected a considerable list of biblical passages, where this principle seems to operate.[19] Although some of the examples adduced by him may seem far-fetched and open to challenge, in many of the passages quoted the evidence of paronomasia is quite evident.

There are, however, some additional instances, where obscurities in the biblical passages could vanish by the application of this principle. A glaring example is the sarcastic use of the verb נשׂא and the noun משׂא by the prophet Jeremiah in two different meanings (23:33–39). Another example is the use of משמני as in the preceding מטל in Gen. 27:28 and 39, apparently in two different meanings, according to Speiser,[20] where in the first instance the prefixed particle מ is partitive, while in the second it is privative (far from). Speiser rejects the rendering of the particle מ in the latter instance in the sense of "without," by some translators as "not sanctioned by established Heb. usage." But the use of this particle in the negative sense is not uncommon in the Bible.[21]

Further examples of paronomasia in the Bible may be cited, such as the use of נשא in Gen. 40:13 and 19 (ישא... מ), Exod. 32:18, where the two forms עֲנוֹת (shouting) are followed by the monograph עַנּוֹת (injury), Judg. 15:16, where the word חמור is to be interpreted in two different meanings,[22] Isa. 32:7 (כלי כליו), and the like. Incidentally, one may cite as a talmudic example of paronomasia the familiar dictum: בשלשה דברים האדם ניכר בכוסו בכיסו ובכעסו.[23]

C. *From Generalization to Specification*

Some troublesome biblical passages, which have puzzled medieval and modern commentators could readily be resolved by applying the principle of proceeding "from the general to the specific" (מכלל ופרט). This is one of

[18] *Op. cit.*
[19] *Heḥalutz*, II, 1853, 94–99.
[20] See Commentary, *ad loc.*
[21] *Cf.* Brockelmann, Carl, *Hebraishe Syntax*, 109 f.
[22] See Rashi and Radak, *ad loc.*
[23] Er. 35:

the thirteen rules by means of which the Torah is to be interpreted according to the tannaitic sages (Introduction to Sifra). A biblical passage may be introduced, according to this rule, by a general term, which is then followed by specifics.

Some medieval and many modern commentators, for example, prefer to regard the first verse in Genesis as a dependent clause, even though a change in the traditional vocalization is thereby necessitated, for a variety of reasons.[24] But U. Cassuto convincingly disputes the validity of these reasons and suggests that this verse be construed as an independent statement serving as an introductory generalization, of which the following verses in the chapter constitute the specifics.[25] The phrase **את השמים ואת הארץ** need not be taken literally; it should rather be interpreted as a hendiadys, like **תהו ובהו**, **טוב ורע**, in the sense of "everything." The first verse, as well as the whole chapter may have been designed as a protesting rejection of the Mesopotamian polytheistic account of creation, involving the battle of the gods, Marduk and Tiamat.[26]

Similarly, in the same chapter, verse 11, the commentators are uncertain about the meaning of the word **דשא**. "Seed-bearing plants" and "fruit-trees" are familiar components of vegetation, but what sort of growth is **דשא**? Cassuto again plausibly suggests that **דֶשא** is a general term "vegetation," while the "seed-bearing plants" and the "fruit trees" are the particulars.[27]

The account of the theophany in Genesis, chapter 18 is rather confusing. According to the first verse Yahweh appeared alone to Abraham. In the following verses we are told about the visitation of "three men." This looks like a contradiction. The only plausible explanation in this case is that the first verse is a general statement, which is followed by a specific description of the manner in which Yahweh appeared. This is precisely the explanation offered by the Rashbam, *ad loc.* "From the biblical viewpoint, it is nothing supernatural for three divine beings, in the form of men, to visit Abraham, who entertained them in good bedouin fashion . . ."[28]

A problem of duplication confronts the biblical commentators in Genesis, chapter 37, vv. 21 f. The verb **ויצלהו** indicates that Reuben saved Joseph, but what follows is merely an account of a suggested plan by Reuben to save him. Most of the commentators ignore the problem, while Speiser, *ad loc.*, takes the verb in a conative sense ("he tried, attempted to save him"). This strained interpretation is, however, unnecessary. The difficulty can be easily removed by the application of the principle "from the general to the specific," i. e., Reuben saved him as follows: he said (to himself): "We should

[24] *Cf.* Rashi and Speiser, *ad loc.*

[25] See **מאדם עד נח**, 10.

[26] *Cf. ANET*, ed. by Pritchard, James B., 31 ff.

[27] *Op. cit.*, 23 f.

[28] *Cf.* Gordon, Cyrus H., *Old Testament Times*, 106.

not take his life . . ." Reuben earnestly planned "to save him from their hands and to restore him to his father." But unfortunately his plan miscarried.[29]

[29] According to the Rashbam's ingenious and plausible interpretation of verse 28, the brothers did not sell Joseph, as is generally maintained. When they sat down to eat at some distance from the pit, where Joseph was placed, they noticed a caravan of Ishmaelites approaching, and Judah suggested that they sell him to the Ishmaelites. But in the meanwhile an unobserved caravan of Midianite traders reached the pit, lifted the crying boy, sold him to the passing Ishmaelites, who brought him to Egypt. This interpretation explains the Midianite-Ishmaelite confusion, as well as the consternation of Reuben when he returned to rescue Joseph and did not find him in the pit.

Dr. Chomsky, Professor of Hebrew Language at The Dropsie University from 1956, died July 19, 1977.

The Fictions of Measurements

By HAIM H. COHN
The Supreme Court, Israel

In Memoriam Moshe Silberg.

I.

By a legal fiction, something is "deemed"[1] to be what it is not, in order that a legal norm may become applicable to it which otherwise it would not be. The falsity is freely admitted, and it is justified whether as a *Notluege*,[2] that is, a white lie dictated by necessity, or as an artifice, innocent in itself, to facilitate the play and speed of mental processes.[3] It is, of course, not only the law that operates with fictions: *fictiones rationis* have always been an integral part of logic, and no mathematics are conceivable without the fictions of suppositions or of imaginary quantities. Indeed, because of the prevalence of fictions in mathematics, legal fictions have aptly been called "the algebra of the law."[4] And if this metaphor applies to legal fictions in general, all the more must it apply to one special category of legal fictions, namely, the fictions of numerical and metrical standards and measurements.

There is nothing new in the cognition that numerical and metrical standards set by law are mere fictions.[5] Nobody ever brought that point home in a more poignant manner than R. Yirmiya with his pertinent—or impertinent—questions prompted by the arbitrariness of such standards.[6] And the answers that were given to him (when he was given answers and not, for his impertinence, summarily thrown out of the academy),[7] virtually confirmed his premiss that all those numerical and metrical standards set by the Sages were binding in law, irrespective of whether or not they were or could be based on any factual or scientific data. They were held to be binding, not because they were or could be based on any such data, but notwithstanding the fact that they could not be so based. Far from purporting to lay down scientifically established facts or figures, they were in the nature of purely normative regulations: it is true that these regulations were often

[1] The phonetic resemblance between the English "deem" and the Hebrew and Aramaic "*damah*" is striking to the lay ear but has no etymological basis.

[2] Ihering, Geist des Roemischen Rechts (9th ed., Reprint Aalen 1968), Vol. 4, p. 305.

[3] Jones, Historical Introduction to the Theory of Law (Oxford 1956), p. 166.

[4] Tourtoulon, Philosophy in the Development of the Law (1922), quoted by Frank, Law and the Modern Mind (Anchor Books ed., 1963), p. 344, n. 10.

[5] Frank, *op. cit.*, p. 179.

[6] Rosh Hashanah 13a; Soṭah 16b; Bava Bathra 23b. And see Silberg, Kushyotav shel R. Yirmiya—Shitta o Offee? (Jerusalem 1965). The same line of questioning is reported of R. Shimon in Mishnah Menahoth XII 4 and of Abaye in Kethuvoth 104a.

[7] Bava Bathra 23b. He was later readmitted: *ibid.*, 165b.

given an appearance *as if* they were grounded on actual fact, but whether this was done in order to render the norm more palatable, or to reflect the practical wisdom behind it, no such appearance can derogate from the fictitious character of the norm. Nor does it affect their fictitious character that they are sometimes expressed as "estimates,"[8] or sometimes as average or "statistical"[9] norms: indeed, one of the elements of all estimation and averaging is the (legitimate) suppression of accuracy in the individual case and the substitution for it of discretionary or statistical conclusions of more general validity.

Fictions introduced for normative and regulatory purposes are, according to the classification first suggested by Ihering,[10] of two kinds: analogous or historical fictions, and dogmatic fictions. The former owe their name to the fact that a given norm is already ("historically") in existence, and is analogically extended to apply to circumstances not covered by it but fictitiously subsumed under it. An example of such a fiction, in the realm of measurements, from talmudical law is that for the applicability of certain norms two days are deemed to be one long day.[11] Where, however, a fiction is created not in order to subsume new circumstances under existing norms, but in order to render cognizable the scope of applicability of a new norm, we speak of a dogmatic fiction: here the fiction is introduced for the purpose of facilitating the realisation of the legal image of the norm.[12] Most of the numerical and metrical standards of the law are dogmatic fictions: it is by setting the fictional standard that the norm acquires its content and dimension; without it the norm has no "measurable" scope or application at all.

It has also been said of legal fictions that they reduce mental fatigue:[13] if, instead of having these numerical and metrical fictions handed to us ready-made on a platter, we would in each individual case have to make the necessary estimates or measurements ourselves, not only would there be no end to litigation, but the mental exertion involved would in most cases be out of all proportion to the cause at issue. In some cases, such mental exertion may lead to accurate results; but in very many instances are human estimates and measurements liable to be wrong: *errare humanum est.* The dogmatic fictions, providing us with ready-made and normative estimates and measurements, enable us—and, *qua* binding law, even compel us—to shift any potential responsibility for our own unavoidable errors unto the legislators who relieved us by their fictions of our cause to err. The talmudic legislators succeeded to go a step further and shift their responsibility for

[8] The term *Shiᶜur*, measure or measurement, is derived from the verb *Shaᶜer*, estimate, appraise. See text at nn. 17–20, *infra*.

[9] Silberg, Principia Talmudica (Hebrew) (Jerusalem 1961), p. 51.

[10] Ihering, *op. cit.*, Vol. 4, pp. 302 ff.

[11] Bezah 30b.

[12] "*Erleichterung der juristischen Vorstellung*": Ihering, *op. cit.*, Vol. 4, p. 308.

[13] Tourtoulon, *loc. cit.*, at n. 4, *supra*.

their own (perhaps also unavoidable) errors in their legislative and fictional estimates and measurements, unto earliest and most sacrosanct Mosaic tradition or inspiration.[14]

Ever since the legitimacy of fictions was recognized in legal theory, it was axiomatic that no fiction ought to be introduced into law unless it was necessary, and suitable, for the promotion of justice and equity: *in fictione iuris semper aequitas existit.*[15] In the language of Blackstone: "These fictions of law, though at first they may startle the student, he will find upon further consideration to be highly beneficial and useful, especially as this maxim is ever invariably observed, that no fiction shall extend to work an injury—its proper operation being to prevent a mischief or remedy an inconvenience that might result from the general rule of law."[16] While the fictions of standards and measurements are ostensibly neutral or technical, and have no apparent bearing on loftier notions of justice and equity, it will be shown—at least insofar as Jewish law is concerned—that even they were intended and calculated to minimize the rigor of the law and provide a spacious arena for the free play of individual rights and interests. There is inherent in every fiction of measurement some limitation—the fictional and normative measurement excluding, as it were, any measure in excess thereof; and the norm to which the fictional measurement applies, is thus automatically restricted in its application to within the boundaries of the measurement. Any such restriction of a prohibitive norm is beneficial to all those to whom the prohibition applies; and any such restriction of a permissive norm is beneficial to all those whose rights might be affected by the permission. As the formalistic rules of criminal procedure have been called the *magna charta* of persons accused of crime, so the formalistic fictions of standards and measurements are a bulwark which the law has erected to protect the individual from undue infringements of his liberties.

II.

The normative measurements ("*Shi'urin*") of talmudic law are, in many places, said to have been *estimated* by the Sages ("*Shi'aru Hakhamim*")—the term for measurement being, indeed, a derivative of the term for estimate. These estimates were by no means arbitrary: if they were not founded on actual research data, at any rate they may be presumed to have flowed from practical experience and observation. Thus, it was "estimated" that the capacity of the human oesophagus was not more than two olives, or, according to another view, one hen's egg[17]—presumably because it so

[14] ᶜEruvin 41; Sukkah 5b. And see text at n. 30, *infra*.

[15] Coke on Littleton 150. In the language of Bartolus (Commentaries on Digesta 41.3.15, No. 67): *fictio cessat ubi cessat aequitas*.

[16] Commentaries on the Laws of England (London 1746), Vol. 3, p. 43.

[17] Kerithoth 14a; Yoma 80a.

happened that somebody was demonstrated or reported to have that capacity. Or, when the question arose from what distance was a man in duty bound to rescue "the ass of him that hateth thee"[18] or his "brother's ox or his sheep,"[19] the distance was "estimated" at 266 and 2/3 cubits[20]—presumably because somebody had been observed to see and clearly discern from that distance. But even if these figures (and many like them) were founded on practical experience, good care was taken that they should be known and described as "estimates" only: however binding in law these figures became in the context of the norm in which they were incorporated, they remained in the nature of "estimates" which might or might not, in any particular case, represent factual truth. And for their quality as binding norms it was quite sufficient that they were "estimates": the truth of the matter in the particular case became wholly irrelevant.

We find the Sages "estimating" measurements also for nonnormative purposes: when the prayers of Honi, the Circle-Drawer, were granted and rain poured down from heaven, the Sages estimated that there was no drop of rain which did not contain at least one lug of water.[21] Not that they measured the drops—they estimated what they saw, and gave their figure as a mere estimate.[22] If they did so where they had the evidence of their own eyes, all the more would they do so where they had to rely on the experience of others.

The classical example for a normative estimate of measurement is the measure of the quantity of water required for the *Mikveh*: forty se'ah, that is, a square cubit to the height of three cubits.[23] Here, too, common experience appeared to prove that this quantity of water would suffice to enable an average man to immerse. Had a lesser quantity been estimated, much inconvenience might have been caused to a good many persons who could not comfortably effect the immersion; had a larger quantity been estimated, a burden would have been imposed on builders and operators of *Mikva'ot* which the average needs would not have justified. The quantity "estimated" as the final and binding rule became law, not because of the accuracy of the estimate, but inspite of its possible inaccuracy.

Or, consider the dispute which was the cause of R. Yirmiya's expulsion from the academy: the mishnaic rule is that a young dove found within fifty cubits from the dovecote, belongs to the owner of the cote; if found beyond fifty cubits, it belongs to the finder.[24] It was later explained that the rule

[18] Exod. 23:5.

[19] Deut. 22:1.

[20] Bava Meziʿaʾ 33a.

[21] Taʿanith 23a.

[22] This estimate did apparently not satisfy the Aggadist: an anonymous addendum raises the amount of water in each drop of rain to a barrelful: *ibid.*

[23] Rosh Hashanah 13a; Ḥagigah 11a; Kethuvoth 104a; Menahoth 103b.

[24] Bava Bathra II 6.

applied to doves so young that they were just learning to walk and move, and no such dove could move for any distance exceeding fifty cubits.[25] Whether this measure was also founded on observation of animal life, or whether it was just an arbitrary estimate, at any rate there is a *ratio legis* to be discerned: on the one hand, the rights of the owner must be protected; on the other hand, the owner's rights were not to be stretched in such a way as to affect the right of the public to acquire property in ownerless goods. As a matter of legislative policy, it was considered less injurious for the owner to lose a stray dove than for the public to be deprived of finders' rights. To dispense a measure of justice to both, some distance had to be "estimated" to limit the expansion of the owner's *dominium*—and it did not really matter whether that estimate was or was not zoologically correct.

The same reasoning applies to most, if not all, estimated measurements to be found in the Talmud: by fixing minimum quantities, for instance, below which the partaking of forbidden food is not prohibited,[26] or below which no uncleanness is incurred,[27] the burden of the onerous—and originally quite unrestricted—laws was relieved, with a view to protecting as far as possible the general public in its purity and legality.

From a legal and legislative point of view, the questions of R. Yirmiya appear therefore wholly irrelevant: it would, indeed, have made no difference, if instead of fifty cubits a distance of sixty or forty cubits had been "estimated" for the purpose of the rule in respect of stray doves; some distance had to be fixed for attaining the legislative purpose; and the only relevant consideration is whether the final "estimate" attained that purpose.

We find some measurements which, rather than "estimated," were fixed with the particular legislative purpose in mind: thus, for instance, the width of a private way was fixed at four cubits, so that a loaden donkey may comfortably pass;[28] or, the heights of a *Sukka* was limited to twenty cubits, so that a man should feel he lives in a *Sukka* and not in a house, and that his abode is temporary and not permanent.[29]

It is highly significant that all the measurements of talmudic law were proclaimed to stem from Moses himself ("*Halakha leMoshe miSinai*").[30] The common feature of this kind of Mosaic rules is that there is no authority to be found for them, either by literal or by analogical interpretation of the Written Law,[31] and so the authority is vested in them by talmudic proclamation. The effect of the elevation of a rule to Mosaic authority is that there can be no dispute over the rule: the lack of any derivation from biblical

[25] Bava Bathra 23b.
[26] Ḥagigah 11a; Nazir 52a.
[27] Kerithoth 15a; Shabbath 70b, 80b.
[28] Bava Bathra 99b–100a.
[29] Sukkah 2a.
[30] ᶜEruvin 4a; Sukkah 5b. And *cf.* Maimonides, Maᶜakhalot Assurot 14,2.
[31] Maimonides, Introduction to Mishna Commentary.

sources, as well as the lack of any logical foundation, expose these rules to easy attack as being unreasonable, ineffective, or superfluous; and it is to immunize them from such attack that they were clothed with unassailability.[32] [33]

The more authoritative and conclusive the normative measurements were declared to be, the greater is the surprise to detect in them an inherent flexibility. I know of no other system of law in which numerical and metrical standards set by law were so adaptable to particular circumstances, as some of the measurements of talmudic law were prescribed to be.

The most widespread measurement, the cubit, may serve as a good example. Its very definition, as the length of the lower arm from the elbow to the top of the middle finger,[34] indicates a necessity of marginal differentiations, according to the differences between the sizes of men. But an uncertain standard would serve no legislative purpose, and for the sake of certainty and justice the varying measurements had here, too, to be averaged; indeed, the individual cubit became (with one exception to which I shall revert) irrelevant for practical purposes. Still, it was found that one single measure of cubit would not be suitable for all purposes; and a verse in which two different kinds of cubit were juxtaposed,[35] was called in aid to justify setting up differently sized cubits for different purposes.[36] Thus, we find "large cubits" and "small cubits" and "medium cubits,"[37] each with functions of its own allotted to it; and we find different measures of cubits named according to their various functions, such as "building-cubits," "tools-cubits,"[38] "mixture-cubits,"[39] or "sacred cubits."[40] While the average and most common cubit was named also the Cubit of Moses, as if derived from Mosaic tradition,[41] a larger cubit was named after that great metropolis, the Cubit of Shushan the Capital.[42]

An instance where in one contract different measures of cubits were prescribed, is worthy of mention: contractors for temple works had to deliver in large cubits but were paid according to small cubits, "so as not to tempt them into embezzlement."[43]

[32] Although the proclamation of Mosaic authority for measurements is reported to have been made in the name of Rav (3rd cent.), the questions ascribed to R. Yirmiya were made two generations later—which may perhaps account for the vehement resentment they aroused.

[33] The question is disputed whether these rules are to be classified as Written (*MideOrajta*) or Oral (*MideRabbanan*) Law, the former being in cases of doubt strictly and the latter liberally interpreted. While a dictum to the effect that all doubts in respect of measurement norms are to be strictly determined (Ḥullin 55a; Niddah 58b), is uncontested, it has not been adopted in the Maimonidean code, the Maimonidean view being that all rules proclaimed as *Halakha leMoshe miSinai* are to be classified as Oral Law only (Responsa, ed. Freimann, 166).

[34] Kethuvoth 5b and Rashi, *ad loc.*

[35] Ezek. 43:13.

[36] Menaḥoth 97a–b, Tossefta Kelim Mezi^ca^ɔ VI 13.

While opinions differed what the measurements of the various different cubits should respectively be, there was general consensus that each must have a certain and well-defined measurement. Within the framework of such certain and well-defined cubits, however, we find many shades and varieties, as if to remind the unyielding arithmetics of the ever changing interplay of the diversities of life. We discover "laughing cubits" and "dejected cubits,"[44] "ample cubits" and "narrow cubits,"[45] "noble cubits" and "constrained cubits,"[46] poetry getting the better of measurements! While the laughing and the dejected cubits might have been regarded as self-explanatory, pains were taken to point out that when a man opened his mouth laughingly, the size of his mouth grew larger, whereas in dejection a man would tightly close his lips and appear reduced in size.[47] In one instance, where a measure of cubits was prescribed for a given purpose, it was expressly laid down as a proviso that the cubits should not be stereotyped, but that they should be laughing or dejected, ample or narrow, as circumstances may require.[48]

There is one exceptional case where the law expressly provided for the individualization of measurements. The zone within which a person was allowed to move freely around and carry his belongings on the *Shabbat*, was fixed as a circuit of four cubits; and the question arose, whether the four cubits were to be measured by one of the existing and predefined yardsticks, or whether they ought to tally with the individual size of the person concerned—for if they were to be measured by objective standards, what will become of Og, King of Bashan? (Og is reported to have measured nine cubits in length and four cubits in breadth).[49] In the ensuing discussion, R. Papa is reported to have issued a stern warning against too much formalism in the law; and the problem was solved by preferring the individual to the formalistic and objective measurements. The objection that then the rule should not be expressed in terms of "four cubits" at all, but should simply state "according to what each person is like," was met with

[37] ᶜEruvin 3b, 4b; Mishnah Kelim XVII 9–10.

[38] Menahoth 97a.

[39] Eruvin 4a.

[40] Eruvin 48a.

[41] Mishnah Kelim XVII 9; and see Rashi ad Behorot 44a, q. v., *Amma shel Kodesh.*

[42] Mishnah Kelim, *ibid.*

[43] Mishnah Kelim, *ibid.*; Menahoth 98a; Maimonides, Meᶜilah 8,5.

[44] Mishnah Sheqalim VI 4; ᶜEruvin 3b; Sukkah 4a; Maimonides, Shabbath 17,36 and Kilᵓayim 8,12.

[45] ᶜEruvin 48a; Asheri ad ᶜEruvin IV 11.

[46] Ezek. 41:8; Maimonides, Shabbath 17,36.

[47] Rashi ad Sukkah 7a; ᶜArukh, q. v., *Sahak.*

[48] ᶜEruvin 4a and Rashi *ad loc.*

[49] Deut. 3:11.

the rejoinder that a dwarf should in any case be entitled to his four cubits[50]—the measurement being thus established as a minimum standard only.

III.

The fiictional character of the prescribed measurements and some of the underlying reasons for their enactment, are well illustrated by a debate on what should happen to surpluses where the quantities prescribed were in excess of actual requirements. The mishnaic rule provided for a fixed quantity of oil to be used everyday for lighting the temple chandelier; and opinions were divided whether the quantities prescribed for each day were to be taken as absolute, the quantity prescribed being by law set aside for the one particular day only, or whether the quantity fixed by law was to be regarded only as a means to an end, and if not used up on that particular day could be put to use on some other day. Although the measure of oil needed to light the temple could probably be pre-calculated with great accuracy, not only because the volume and capacity of all lighting implements were matters of law, but also because the experience of daily lighting would provide conclusive statistics—it appears that the quantities of oil needed for the purpose were preferred to be fixed in "ample" or "noble" measure, and so the surplus problem could arise. Those scholars who held that any surplus had to be thrown away, did not, however, adduce as their reason the absoluteness and exclusiveness of the daily ration as imposed by the measurement norm; they were not prompted by any formalistic subservience to the letter of the standard set by law. They gave as their reason for not storing away any such surplus of oil, that there should be no poverty where splendour reigns—implying that the *ratio* for fixing "ample" and "noble" measures for this purpose was to conform to the magnificence of the temple. On the other hand, those who held that any surplus ought to be held over for the next day, in no way insinuated that the measurements as fixed by law were not absolutely binding: what they gave as the *ratio legis* was that the law protects property and shuns waste: the law has always to be interpreted and applied in a manner that would involve the least expense and the greatest economy.[51]

These rationalizations, however superimposed they may be on the original norm, bear witness to the existence of ulterior motives, wherever a fictional measurement is made into law. If justice and equity have always been acclaimed as motives for legal fictions in general, we may perhaps particularize in respect of numerical and metrical fictions, to the effect that they are motivated by the desire, and by the necessity, to strike a just balance between public and private interests in all matters in which the

50 ᶜEruvin 48a.
51 Menahoth 89a.

lack of legal standards would lead to encroachments on either side. In essence, these fictions of measurement are but the performance, on the legislative plane, of the general duty to do justice, and not to do unrighteousness, in meteyard, in weight, or in measure.[52] It was observed that meteyard, weights and measures were preceded in this verse by *Mishpat*, meaning judgment or law, although the prohibition not to do unrighteousness in judgment had been laid down before:[53] to indicate that a judgment is involved in every measurement, and the measurer is called a judge.[54] The same applies, *a fortiori*, to legislative measurements, where the judgment involved would affect not only the party concerned but the general public. It is a policy judgment, the policy being to do justice to the greatest possible number and avoid injustice from the greatest possible number.

While the legislative measurements have perforce to be fictional, and may hence afford the luxury of flexibility, the individual measurements used in daily commerce msut be absolutely "just":[55] no measure may be in your possession which is excessive or deficient even by an iota;[56] nor may you have divers weights, using one for the one and another for the other person.[57] Nothing is so abhorrent to God as dishonest and inaccurate measurements,[58] nor can you endure long as an economic society unless your weights and measures are completely honest.[59] But it is in this context of the absolutely accurate measurements that we are admonished to observe "all the laws" and "and all the norms"[60]—to remind us that there are normative measurements which have to be observed as a matter of law, notwithstanding their possible inaccuracy and their fictionality.

[52] Lev. 19:35.
[53] Lev. 19:15.
[54] Sifra, Kedoshim, Cap. 8.
[55] Lev. 19:36; Deut. 25:15.
[56] Bava Bathra 89b.
[57] Deut. 25:13–14.
[58] Deut. 25:16.
[59] Deut. 25:15.
[60] Lev. 19:37.

Once More, The Messiah

By MORTON S. ENSLIN
The Dropsie University

In both Jewish and Christian thinking the word *Messiah* as a definite title for one specifically designated office has come to be a very important, even central, term. A not unnatural question arises as to when and under what circumstances did a word originally not a title or even a noun, but rather an adjective, always coupled with a noun expressed or clearly understood, come to undergo this change. Discussions of the word, both as an adjective and eventually as a noun, have been many and with radically different verdicts, but too frequently the basic query as to the precise time and occasion for the transformation has been clouded by the too easy assumption, natural in a religion which considers itself one of revelation from a God whose purposes never change, that what is the case now always has been; in a word, that the situation at the beginning of the second Christian century had been the situation a hundred years before. Into this pit of confusion many, including highly competent and properly respected historians, have not infrequently slipped.

That in the days of Hadrian Bar Kokhba in his revolt against Rome and attempt to reestablish his nation laid claim to the title in its now definite sense as the expected deliverer who would overthrow the impious heathen and restore the throne of David, as God long since had promised would be the case, is certain. His claim, although contested by some, was increasingly supported by many aghast at the report circulating in Jerusalem of Rome's intent to build a heathen city on the ruins of the eternal city of David and to ban the God-commanded rite of circumcision. That Bar Kokhba did make such a claim, with the use of a title, Messiah, which scandalized Christians as a glaring challenge to their crucified Lord whom they had come to reverence under that name, now in its Greek form Christ, is not to be disputed.

But it must be stressed that this is the first time in Jewish history, at least so far as we have any clear-cut evidence, that this claim had been made and accepted. Constant and unwarranted use of that title, with the remark that this rebel or that had been so regarded and had so regarded himself, have been made but without support save the confidence of the later writer who so read in and then out his conclusion. One such figure who has frequently been so cast by those discussing the incident, without the support of actual evidence, is Judas of Galilee (called by Josephus "a Gaulonite of a city whose name was Gamala),"[1] who was one of many to

[1] Josephus, *Ant*. 18,1,1 (4).

rise in armed opposition to Rome's decision in C.E. 6 to turn the ethnarchy of Archelaus into a Roman province. That Judas, presumably the son of Hezekiah whom Herod had executed years before, did attempt such a revolt is certain. But the notion that he considered himself or was so regarded by his fellows as the Messiah is supported by no evidence other than the opinion of those who write about the incident. And the same may be said of all the others over the years who are today regarded too easily in this light.[2]

The first point to be observed is that in the Old Testament and the Apocrypha the term Messiah is, as has been remarked above, always an adjective, not a noun. It is used of various individuals or groups of individuals including kings, high priests, patriarchs, the nation itself, even Cyrus of Persia. And it always reflects the basic confidence of Judaism that what is done is done by God, sometimes directly, sometimes by those whom he has chosen and especially blessed for the task. Thus the common phrase, applied to widely different figures, is "anointed of the Lord" (מְשִׁיחַ יְיָ), that is, chosen, approved, blessed, consecrated by God himself to the particular function or status.

The origin of this figure of speech indicating divine selection and approval by the term "anointed" is a consequence of Hebrew practice where the use of oil was a basic part of the ceremony of king-making. Pouring oil on the head of the king was presumably originally definitely an act of religious veneration. So also in the case of the priests, eventually to be regarded and styled "high priests." In Exodus 29 it is prescribed that the anointing oil be poured on the head after the ceremony of robing. With this background the use of this specific term to indicate God's approval, choice, and blessing not unnaturally continued even after the actual practice of pouring the consecrating oil ceased.

This practice, so meaningful in Hebrew circles, was unknown in the Greco-Roman world. The Greek translation of משיח was χριστός. But to the Greek the connotation was very different. It was far from descriptive of king- or priest-making. Rather, oil was a remedy for the relief of pain or a cosmetic. Thus ὁ χριστός would naturally suggest an invalid smeared with medicated oil or a fop prettied up with paint and powder. Thus, although there is a very real problem as to how this term first came to be applied to Jesus of Nazareth, we can be very sure that it was the result of Jewish, not Greco-Roman, practice. It should not be forgotten that once the group eventually came to find itself in the Greek world the word χριστός speedily lost any earlier descriptive sense and became easily part of the proper name, *Jesus Christ.* Instead of the designation "the Christ," which was sure to suggest to unsympathetic hearers "the smeared one" or "the

[2] In the eyes of many Christians Jesus of Nazareth did make such a claim. With this possible exception (see below) the statement holds.

perfumed one," a different title became necessary and was speedily found, viz., ὁ κύριος, the Lord.

In view of the seeming absence of evidence that at the time of the ministry of Jesus (ca. C.E. 30) the word משיח had become the specific designation of any figure, past, present, or to come, the popular use today of the term, "the Messianic hope," to describe the expectation of future blessedness which every pious Jew was expecting is most unfortunate and misleading. The term suggests two emphases, both of which are unwarranted. First it suggests that there was *one* expectation and only one of the coming time or era of happy blessedness to which every Jew looked with confidence. That in Jewish eyes what may properly be styled the golden age was not in the past but yet to come is certain. God's promise to Abraham was sure to be fulfilled. The verdict of the years had been hard to take: the break-up of the Davidic kingdom; the fall first of Israel, then of Judah; the destruction of the Temple and the bondage in Babylonia; the disillusioning certainty under Persian rule that the confidently expected restoration was not to be their portion; defeat and subjection under a series of gentile lords, Alexander and his successors the Ptolemies and the Seleucids; the overthrow of the Hasmonean kingdom, which had proved a pyramid set upon it apex, at the hands of Rome. This was a sad commentary upon God's promise to their father Abraham. These were inescapable facts, but the hope was still certain. God has not, can not forget or violate his promise. Ours, not his, is the cause of the long delay. Not yet are we ready for the fulfillment of the promise which will mean our eventual triumph and universal responsibility. When God sees that we are ready, his promise will become reality. Our sad fate is but the consequence of the Almighty's wise purpose and plan: "Whom the Lord loveth, he chasteneth and scourgeth every son whom he receiveth." He is burning out the dross, refining the gold. When that painful process is over, we shall enter in. Our golden age will dawn.

That this view was universally held by every Jew, proud to call himself such, in the days of the Christian beginnings is certain. But that is far different from saying that there was but one form in which every pious Jew held this expectation. Judaism is, and always has been, a religion of doing rather than of believing. Obedience to the Law, not orthodoxy of belief, has long been central. Nowhere is this quality more evident than in the universally held hopes for the future. Many and divergent are the forms in which this all-pervading confidence was to be realized. Thus to style it "*the* Messianic hope," as if all saw alike, is totally wrong and sadly misleading.

And second, "the *Messianic* hope" throws into unwarranted prominence the figure of the coming one styled "the Messiah." As already remarked, at the time of the Christian beginnings there was no such figure in popular thought and parlance. Nor is it to be objected that this is an unjustified overinsistence on terms; that regardless of how he was to be styled, the universal expectation and hope centered in the coming of one of the house of David who would shatter the gentile tyrants and their tyranny, would reestablish and take his place upon David's throne. This notion, still widespread in popular—and often in what is regarded scholarly—literature, that the Jewish expectation at the time of the Christian beginnings was limited to anticipation of a leader in wars of liberation and conquest, is entirely unwarranted. That at a later time this was the form the expectation had come to assume is very true. Bar Kokhba is an evidence of it. The Targums reflect it in their so often faulty understanding of the Scripture they seek to explain.[3]

That this form of expectation, at times in Jewish history, may have been heatedly voiced is probable. That it was to the fore when Cyrus brought the Babylonian captivity to an end is not unlikely. Now a scion of David will sit again, in accord with God's own promise,[4] upon his restored throne. The expectation speedily died as it became only too evident what was the real intent of Cyrus, whom a perfervid imagination had seen as God's own choice to restore his dispersed people. As the years passed, with Israel forced to become a church with a high priest at its head instead of a nation with a king upon his throne, less and less did the warloving leader in wars of liberation and conquest loom large in universal thinking. A few, to be loosely styled "home rulists," may have sought to keep it alive, but as the years passed, to the more sober-minded the miracles which God had wrought for the benefit of the campaigns of Joshua and Gideon seemed unlikely to be repeated against the legions of Rome.

In the days of Augustus and Tiberius the nation was enjoying far more liberty and self-rule than it had during the reign of the last of their own kings. Memories of the bloodthirsty Alexander Janneus and the utter domination, even if occasionally marked by benevolent interludes, of Herod must have been very effective blinders on eyes looking for another king. They had had their fill of kings. Of course Rome was an outrageous interloper, with a Caesar venturing to sit upon a throne reserved for God Almighty. But after all, despite all pious and religious rhetoric, those of balance and down-to-earth judgment must have known that they were, at least in God's interim, better off under Rome than under their own kings. And the not infrequent delegations to Rome to urge direct Roman control instead of that by Herod's sons is not to be overlooked.

[3] A targum interprets Isa. 42:1, "Behold, my servant, whom I uphold; my chosen, in whom my soul delighteth," with the words, "Behold, my servant the Anointed (Messiah), my Chosen in whom my word (i. e., I myself) delights." That this was the meaning of the author or of his contemporaries is certainly most improbable.

[4] *Cf.* II Sam. 7:16; I Chron. 17:14, 26 f.

Rome was a remarkably cautious and astute mistress. Her governors were directed to allow the provinces as much freedom from irksome control as possible. In Judea the governor stayed in Caesarea, coming to Jerusalem only occasionally to be sure that the holy days did not become dangerous holidays. The Sanhedrin was in essential control. Local religious practices and prejudices were scrupulously safeguarded. Taxes, while high, were under severe audit, with the governor receiving a fixed salary and not allowed to enrich himself at the expense of the provinces as had earlier been the case before Augustus had rectified danger-provoking abuses. And a large part of the taxes went for the betterment of the provinces.

I am far from suggesting that Rome's policy reflected anything to be styled benevolence or loving-kindness. It was down-to-earth practicality and common sense. Rome might never rival Greece in the realm of literature and speculative learning, but she was a past mistress in the realm of good government. Well did Augustus and Tiberius know the practical value of policies which prevented native differences and prejudices becoming cause of unrest and rebellion, and their governors well knew the consequences to them personally of failure to follow the emperor's lead. Their later successors —Gaius, Claudius, Nero—proved less astute, and antipathies which had been kept under control through the clear evidence of advantages enjoyed turned into disastrous rebellion.

Undoubtedly there were some in Judea who minimized all this and sought to provoke their fellows to violence. This was nothing new. Always there had been some so striving. To style them "Zealots" and to see their origin as a new consequence of Judas of Galilee's futile effort is a most misleading modern fantasy. They were there, but were far from influential. When, as the years passed, and abuses due to mismanagement became more and more offensive, this unorganized group of radicals may well have become increasingly influential. The act of making the kingdom of the popular Agrippa, at the time of his death, once more a Roman province may well have been a cause of increasing difficulty for the local procurator. Emperors like Gaius, Claudius, and Nero were far less skilled than had been Augustus and Tiberius in avoiding costly rebellion. But what was to happen toward the end of the first century is far from what was happening several decades earlier.

Thus, at the time of the Christian beginnings, to see all dreams for the future in terms of a leader in war and rebellion, whatever might be his title at that moment, is definitely contrary to the evidence which we have and to sober conclusions drawn from that data. So to limit dreams of the future to the expectation of a monarch and restored monarchy subsequent to the bashing in of the heads of the heathen is almost grotesquely unwarranted. In large blocks of Jewish thinking there is no place for any coming ruler save God alone. To meet this embarrassing fact champions have been forced, as George Foot Moore sardonically remarked, to invent the phrase "messianic age without a messiah."[5]

But in addition, together with what may be soberly styled Jewish hope for the future, with its many forms and details of expectation, there was a very different train of ideas, basically not Jewish or even Hebrew in origin, but seemingly in essence Persian, and which had been gradually adopted and thereby made Jewish as the years had elapsed. In contrast to the Jewish expectations of a golden age on this earth when God saw the nation ready, the Persian concept was a future grand cataclysm which would bring the present evil age to a close. The world would be literally consumed by fire to purge it from evil. The righteous would rise to take their place in the glorious new age. Judgment would be held, and men's fates settled by a great supernatural judge, Shaoshyant, God's special representative. In the days we are considering, this figure, Shaoshyant, was apparently styled in Jewish speech Son of man (*bar nasha*), i. e., The Man, due to a phrase taken over from the book of Daniel. This term is peculiarly liable to misinterpretation. He was not a human being as *son of man* would seem to suggest. Rather he was a supernatural angelic being.[6] Eventually in Jewish thinking these two utterly dissimilar types of expectation came to be combined and reconciled the one to the other. How far this had taken place at the time of the ministry of Jesus is uncertain. But one thing is reasonably certain. Eventually Jesus came to be regarded by his followers after his death as Son of man and also as the anointed son of David. Thus by what seems good mathematics—two things equal to the same thing are equal to each other—the two originally different and cluttered sets of notions came to be combined and made one.

Against this background of thought and expression the long-debated question of the views and claims of Jesus of Nazareth may well be reconsidered. During the past seventy-five years of argument and debate there has been a steadily increasing doubt that Jesus viewed himself as, and claimed to be, the Messiah. Earlier scholars, such as Renan and Bousset, were sure that he had made the claim, even though they frankly conceded it seemed remote from his own expectation. Rather, they contended, since the coming of the Messiah was the one concern preeminent over all others in the thought and passionate hope of Israel, it was unavoidable for any leader, hoping to gain a following, to avoid such a claim. If, as I have argued in earlier paragraphs, this fancied all-central expectation was still to be born, there seems little reason to assume that Jesus laid claim to a task which in no wise seemed akin to his purpose and interest. Thus to the query,

[5] G. F. Moore, *Judaism*, II, p. 327.

[6] The popular description of Jesus by Christian preachers and theologians, "both Son of man and Son of God, that is, both human and divine," is a grotesque example of misunderstanding.

"Did Jesus make claim to be the Messiah?" the only reasonable answer would seem to be a definite No.

With regard to the related query, "Did he claim to be the expected Son of man, the supernatural being expected to set up and preside over the coming Judgment?" the situation is greatly different. This figure was expected, and no responsible critic can exclude constant references to him from the words attributed to Jesus. The one note that is central in words attributed to him is the certain and immediate end of the present evil age, and the dawn of the new Age to Come, which he seems to have designated the "kingdom of God or heaven." To remove this certainty from Jesus' speech and to seek to attribute it to later misguided followers who mistakenly read it back to their crucified and risen Lord is to remove the one central foundation of what may be conveniently, if proleptically, styled the Christian beginnings. And without that foundation the whole structure collapses. Furthermore, another indisputable certainty is the amazingly persistent confidence of his first followers in him and his, to them certain, support and blessing by God who had sent him for his task. Only so can their confidence, despite the crushing verdict of the cross, be explained. Thus to see them radically altering his God-inspired word is most unlikely.

While interest in a restored throne of David seems remote from the thinking and announcement of Jesus, the immediacy of the dawn of the kingdom of God is central. God's agent for that all-central event was this supernatural agent, dubbed "The Man." That this phrase, *bar nasha*, was constantly on Jesus' lips, despite its denial by some earlier critics, such as Lietzmann, seems certain. The only question is: "Did Jesus claim to be this figure or was he content to herald his advent?" I have sought,[7] along with other scholars, to indicate my reason for feeling that the latter is the case and that the phrasing in the gospel reports reflects the earliest answer to the question which the crucifixion made imperative: "Who, then, was he?" In a word, the query which now stands awkwardly in the gospel narrative, "Who do men say that I am?" and Peter's reply, "Thou art the Christ,"[8] may well be a paraphrase of this early postcrucifixion query, "Who, then, was he?", and the resultant confident response: "He was and is the Son of man of whom he constantly spoke; in our blindness we thought he was speaking of another."[9]

Surely this conjecture would simplify a tangled complex of problems. It would preserve intact the nature and content of Jesus' message. It would

[7] M. S. Enslin, *The Prophet from Nazareth*, pp. 137–146; *cf. Christian Beginnings*, pp. 161–163.

[8] Mark 8:27 ff.; Matt. 16:13–23; Luke 9:18–22.

[9] *Cf.* my article, "The Date of Peter's Confession" in *Quantulacumque—Studies Presented to Kirsopp Lake*, pp. 117–122; also, "And That He Hath Been Raised," in *JQR*, 43,1 (1952), pp. 27–56.

free him from the otherwise scarcely avoidable diagnosis of serious mental imbalance of a flesh-and-blood man considering himself a supernatural angelic figure. It would avoid the awkwardness of seeing his followers caught in the strange dilemma of believing him especially blest and sent by God to proclaim a message which they were now unhesitatingly altering, even actually inventing and seeking to make his. It would suggest that the transformation of John the Baptist, an independent and widely esteemed preacher, into a voice content to herald the advent of his greater successor, is but a reflection of Jesus the prophet's heralding the advent of his successor whom he was insistently proclaiming, the Son of man, soon to appear and consummate God's long-promised and equally long-delayed promise for which Israel had been waiting. In addition, it may even throw light on that other problem, "When and why did the term משיח become a definite and specific title?"

One detail too often minimized is the mention of "prophecy" and "prophet" in connection with Jesus in the gospel stories. They seem primitive touches which have escaped editorial alteration. At the dinner to which Simon the Pharisee had invited him and during which Jesus had been anointed by the sinful woman, his host indignantly exclaims, "This man, *if he were a prophet*, would have perceived. . . ."[10] In the Markan account of the insulting horseplay, "And some began to spit on him, and to cover his face, and to buffet him," is their demand," *Prophesy*!"[11] Both Matthew and Luke expand this brutal demand by adding the to them clarifying words, "Who is he that struck thee?"[12] Certainly the natural conclusion is that both the epithet" "prophet" and the demand "Prophesy!" are sneering taunts reflecting and ridiculing his claim to be a prophet, and thus clearly suggest that the earliest appraisal of Jesus, both by those to whom he spoke and by him himself, was that he was a prophet sent by God. In the thinking of Judaism at the time of the Christian beginnings the age of revelation by prophetic agency had ended when the Spirit was withdrawn. Whereas of old God had declared his will through men especially chosen and had fitted them to be his mouthpiece, now his will was known and knowable through the Law, in which his complete and entire revelation was to be found. Although God no longer commonly spoke through the prophets—"When the last prophets, Haggai, Zechariah, and Malachi died, the holy spirit ceased out of Israel"[13]—it was occasionally possible to hear communications

[10] Luke 7:39.

[11] Mark 14:65.

[12] Matt. 26:68; Luke 22:64. Mark had presumably meant by the sneering demand, "Give us a sample of your prophesying," a gibe parallel to the cruel taunt to the exiles in Ps. 137:13. Matthew's not infrequent attempts to make clear to his readers a statement in Mark which he fears they may misunderstand often indicate that the misunderstanding was his own.

[13] Tos. Soṭah 13,2.

from God by means of a mysterious voice. Examples of this mysterious voice are to be seen in such stories as the ominous word to Nebuchadrezzar,[14] or the word at the baptism of Jesus,[15] at the transfiguration,[16] and at the time of climax, heralded by the coming of the Greeks.[17]

More than that was the confident expectation that in the future once again God would speak directly through the mouth of his prophet. None less than Moses himself had announced this: "Yahweh thy God will raise up unto thee a prophet from the midst of thee, of thy brethren, like unto me; unto him ye shall hearken."[18] That this promise was ever overlooked or forgotten is not to be imagined. Certainly it lay back of Judas the Maccabee's cautious decision to lay the defiled stones of the altar aside until a prophet should arise who could answer what to Judas the soldier was uncertain.[19] In the speeches of Peter[20] and Stephen[21] Moses' word is quoted, and there can be little doubt that it is seen as fulfilled in Jesus. That this is a post-crucifixion discovery appears to me most unlikely. Rather it is highly probable that it was the firm confidence, frankly announced, of Jesus himself that not only was he a prophet sent by God to utter his word, but that he was *the* prophet whom Moses had announced, and that his divinely given message was the climaxing announcement that at long last God's promise to Israel was to be made real in the spectacular coming of the new age, the age to come, the kingdom of God, to enter which men were to bend every effort.

Im my judgment this indicates that Jesus is to be seen as a thoroughgoing apocalyptist. He did not make his proclamation in written form as had a Daniel, an Enoch, or an Ezra, but his message was essentially of the same sort: The promised day of the Lord is at hand. God's plan will be finally established, his promise fulfilled, his honor vindicated. Even now the clock has struck. Apocalypticism, as it had come to be colored and modified once it had come to be understood and accepted by a sizable portion of the Jewish world, was in a real sense the opposite of the older prophecy. A Micaiah, a Jeremiah, an Amos had announced the certain doom of a sinful and blind-eyed nation. They had fulminated and written when the nation was too prosperous for its own good. In the interim the situation had changed. Disasters had befallen Israel. The head once held high was in the dust. But though right was on the scaffold, wrong upon the throne, God stood within the shadows keeping watch upon his own. In what may

[14] Dan. 4:31 f.
[15] Mark 1:11; Matt. 3:17; Luke 3:22.
[16] Mark 9:7; Matt. 17:5; Luke 9:35.
[17] John 12:28.
[18] Deut. 18:15.
[19] I Macc. 4:46.
[20] Acts 3:22.
[21] Acts 7:37.

be hazarded as the Jewish adoption and adaptation of this alien sort of thought a definitely patriotic emphasis had become central. In the age to come Israel would find the fulfillment of God's promise to Abraham.

Two additional consequences of such a type of thought and confidence are not to be overlooked. The man who essayed the role of sounding forth God's clarion call—in a word, the prophet—was convinced that his position was unique. God had definitely called him, empowered him with his spirit in a way not shared by his fellows, and had very literally put his word on the prophet's tongue. In a word, in Jewish idiom he was God's anointed, chosen, blest, prophet, endowed by God for his task. The prophet himself must be firmly convinced of this and thus ready to style himself as "anointed by the Lord"; and his hearers, if they are to hearken and pay heed, must share that confidence of his divine election, that is, "anointing." When the prophet spoke, it was God who was speaking. What might sound like impossible arrogance was not such. The demands and certainties were not the prophet's. He was simply giving utterance to God, who had chosen him and made him his mouthpiece. Many attempts have been made to explain such a conviction as an abnormal pathological obsession, and various diagnoses have been proposed. It is certain that they saw visions, had mental experiences far from what we style "normal." But it also must be said that in men, as in lamps, a wick turned too high, though it yields smoke, may still give an intense light.

A second consequence or characteristic of apocalyptic experience and expression, which had become the new prophetism, is that there always seems to have been some tragic action or event which convinced the author that now the hour had come. What led a Daniel, an Enoch, an Ezra, a John to feel that the last moment had come, that at any instant the cataclysm would result? Occasionally it is reasonably clear: for "Daniel" the outrage of Antiochus Epiphanes was the "abomination of desolation." Nothing could ever exceed it. The *end* must be at hand. What seemed to the author so certain, must, he was sure, seem so to God. The same may be hazarded in the case of the "Little Apocalypse" now preserved, at least in substantial part, in Mark 13. The unbelievable effrontery of Gaius to demand setting *his* image in the Temple's Holy of Holies must be the last straw on the already overheavy pile, thus indicating the end and spurring the author to sound his call. In a word, the apocalyptist is an alarmist. He may well have magnified an especial abuse to a degree not shared by all or even most of his fellows. When we view Jesus as a "prophet" of that sort, convinced that the moment for proclamation of the word of God has finally come, the question is natural, if not insistent: "What led him to this conviction, not only that the final hour had come, but that he was uniquely selected, 'anointed' by God to announce it?" The answer, "God did it," is no answer at all to the historian, who insistently, if reverently, seeks to answer what is to him the immediately consequent question, "How?"

In the case of Jesus the evidence is scanty in the eyes of the historian, although the theologian may find a sonorous "God did it" quite sufficient. I have ventured to suggest that the solution here may be found in the story of John the Baptist. That that story as we have it shows clear evidence of Christian editorship and reworking appears to me very probable and to be explained as a deliberate attempt to bring him into the Christian saga as the God-sent herald of his greater successor Jesus. I have sought to justify this assumption and need not here repeat what is now in print.[22] Although the two figures, John and Jesus, had had no immediate contacts or fellowship, the murder of the one by the Roman governor in nearby Tiberias may well have served as the tocsin that convinced Jesus that this awful crime was the concluding note of the prelude. The drama was now to begin.

In the light of this background, to those to whom these suggestions may seem worth considering, the hitherto baffling connection of the word "Christ" with Jesus becomes intelligible. It was not a title as such; it had nothing to do with the activity of a warrior king, be he of the line of David or Hezekiah. Rather it is the verdict, unavoidable by any devout Jew who approved the claim that this figure who had appeared at long last, as Moses had predicted he would, had not so acted on his own initiative. Here, as everywhere else, what is done is done by Yahweh. Thus it was inevitable that the descriptive "anointed," that is, approved, endorsed, selected, should be natural, both on the lips of Jesus as the guarantee of the rightness of his word, and on the lips of his enthusiastic hearers. He was, of course, "the long-expected anointed prophet of the Lord," or in crisper speech which meant this and only this, "the anointed of the Lord."

As time passed and other rungs were added to the rapidly lengthening ladder now styled "christology," the same confidence continued. All this was God's act, not the invention of man. With the confidence of his early followers that both he and his movement were of course included in God's all-inclusive revelation, it is not surprising that evidence was increasingly found predicting the advent of God's anointed, with little caution to keep the discovered references in their original compass. "Touch not mine anointed and do my prophets no harm,"[23] as the psalmist sang, might well in Christian eyes have seemed a clear reference to their Lord.

As already suggested, once the movement had spread into the outside world this Jewish figure of speech, with "anointed" the simple equivalent of appointed or God-approved, tended to become misleading if not definitely unacceptable. For some χριστός could be played on as χρηστός, but gradually the difficulty was more satisfactorily removed by simply giving

[22] *Cf.* "John and Jesus" in *ZNW*, 66 (1975), pp. 1–18; "Once Again: John the Baptist," in *Religion in Life*, 27,4 (1958), pp. 557–566.

[23] Ps. 105:15; I Chron. 16:22.

it up as a title and instead making it a part of the name, Jesus Christ or Christ Jesus.

If this argument seems solid, it would appear to follow that the phrase "the anointed" as a sort of title had become well-established in what we may call Christian usage before it came to the fore in Jewish speech in a very different sense. As more and more the pot of Jewish unrest at Rome's control came to the stage of boiling; as the wise provisions of Augustus and Tiberius lessened in the hands of their successors; as the procurators were forced by the growing unrest to be more severe and restrictive; as not unnaturally fuel was fed to the flames by the transformation of Agrippa's kingdom once more into a Roman province—it was not unnatural that the demands of the more belligerent advocates of rebellion, the home rulists or "fourth philosophy," who had earlier been unsuccessful in gaining support from their more influential and worldly-wise fellows, became more acceptable. The outbreak of war against Rome and its tragic consequences of destruction to city, Temple, and pride simply increased the blaze. When repeated and garbled rumors of Hadrian's intent to turn Zion into a heathen and godless Aelia Capitolina were spread about, the long-expected outbreak occurred. The longing for a Jewish king able and eager to destroy the godless heathen captors, which for the past fifty years had been increasing, with the early emphasis in the days of Cyrus of a Davidic scion in restored control, which had speedily proved short-lived and subsequently almost completely dormant, once more became alive. In a word, the expectation now, as it had not been a half-century earlier, was for the appearance of a God-appointed, that is, "anointed," figure. And Bar Kokhba seemed the answer. He claimed to be and was enthusiastically accepted by many as the Messiah, long-expected, now appeared.

During these years of developing confusion, the results of which are clear, but with many points of the development most uncertain, there can be little question but what Christian thinking was affected. They already had one whom they had come to reverence as God's Anointed. It is highly probable that along with the growing demands of their Jewish neighbors, Christians automatically felt these expectations already had been met in their crucified and resurrected Lord. When "son of David" came to be of increasing concern in Jewish circles as essential to any claim to the title משיח or χριστός, Christians met the challenge. There is little certainty, perhaps even little probability that actually Jesus of Nazareth was of Davidic stock. This lack was seemingly made a Jewish jeer at Christian claims, and apparently was first met by the Christian insistence[24] that Davidic birth was not, as their opponents maintained, essential to the claim of being "the anointed." A second and far more effective Christian answer was the insistence that actually Jesus was of Davidic stock, as was proved

[24] Mark 12:35–37; Matt. 22:41–46; Luke 20:41–44.

by the genealogies and birth stories which the later Matthew and Luke provided.

Thus it is not surprising that to the claims and demands made by Bar Kokhba and now endorsed by many influential Jews, Christians were forced to make a negative reply. Despite any desire which some Christians of Jewish stock and ancestry might have had to give this champion their support, they could not, for so to do would be to deny their Lord who for long had so properly borne that title which could not be shared with another. In consequence Christians were treated with especial cruelty by Bar Kokhba. Here may well be seen the last stage of the "parting of the ways" between Synagogue and Church which had for many decades been becoming increasingly divided.

Many details in this singularly tangled skein of hopes and expectations remain uncertain. To many readers, almost certainly Jewish and Christian alike, some of the suggestions which to me appear not improbable, at least worth considering, will be dismissed as fanciful if not actually perverse. Although for the sake of clarity and in the hope that they may be considered, even if thereafter dismissed, they may seem to have been expressed too baldly and with little or no seeming attention to the studies of other scholars in which possible support or openly expressed denial might be found, I must insist that so far as I am competent to judge they are not in violation of what may be regarded soberly as actual evidence. They are frankly hypothetical, but to the historian hypotheses, not facts of mathematical certainty, are very regularly his safest, at times his only, answer, unless he be also a theologian for whom uncertainties are apparently far less common or even embarrassing.

כלי נתר Egyptian Faience or Glazeware

By LOUIS FINKELSTEIN
The Jewish Theological Seminary

THE TERM כלי נתר OCCURS in Rabbinic works infrequently: in the Mishna in two contexts, in *Tosefta* in one; in *Sifra*, in three; in *Sifre Zutta* in one; in the *Babylonian Talmud* in three (one a quotation from *Mishna Kelim*); on rare occasions in *Yerushalmi*; and in the Minor Tractates. These utensils, it may be presumed, therefore, were not widely used. They were, apparently, what might now be called luxury items, concerning which few ritual problems arose.[1]

The most significant norm regarding them is that stated in Mishna *Kelim* 2.1, where we are told that כלי נתר have the same status as earthenware, so far as the laws of purity there discussed are concerned. They

[1] I was greatly assisted in the research leading to this article by my friend, Rabbi Joseph Kappah of Jerusalem; my beloved son-in-law, Professor Jacob Katzenstein, also of Jerusalem; and Professor Saul Weinberg of The University of Missouri. The study would have been impossible without the facilities of the Library of the Jewish Theological Seminary of America, and the generosity of its Librarian, Professor Menahem Schmelzer, as well as the kindness of the Librarians of Union Theological Seminary and Columbia University.

The mss. of the *Sifra* to which reference is made in this article were photographed and collected on my behalf by the American Council of Learned Societies, the photographs being deposited in the Library of Congress, and generously made available to me. I have to thank the officials of the Bodleian Library, the Library of Cambridge University, the British Library, and the Librarian and staff of the Vatican Library and those of the Biblioteca Palatina in Parma for their permission to have the mss. of the *Sifra* in their possession photographed for me. In preparation for a forthcoming edition of the *Sifra*, I have been able to use these mss., as well as those of the Jewish Theological Seminary of America. Before the Second World War, the Librarian and staff of the Jewish Theological Seminary of Breslau (alas, no longer in existence), gave permission to have the Ms. of the *Sifra* in their possession, photographed for me. That manuscript is now in the Library of the Jewish Theological Seminary of America. Rabbi Joseph Kappah, in addition to other assistance, had his own ms. of *Sifra* photographed for me. Professor Alexander Scheiber of Budapest was able to obtain for me photographs of the manuscript of the portion of the *Sifra* found in Statni Zidovski Museum in Prague, for which I am grateful to him and the staff of the institution.

Dr. A. I. Katsh, President of Dropsie University, was able to obtain photographs of *Yalkut Talmud Torah*, by R. Jacob of Sicily, which includes large sections of the *Sifra*, from the Baron David Guenzburg collection in Moscow, and I have to thank him for his kindness in making them available to me.

I am particularly grateful to the staff of the Metropolitan Museum of Art for their kind assistance, and their permission to examine the specimens of Egyptian faience in their great collection; and the staff of the British Museum for permission to examine their collection. My former secretary, Mrs. Nancy Nesvet, assisted me greatly in some aspects of this research; and for this, I record my gratitude to her.

become defiled if a source of impurity comes within their confines (even though it does not touch them); if they are defiled, they defile food or drink within their confines, although not in contact with them; they defile food or liquids which are in contact with them from the outside, but they cannot be defiled from the outside through contact with contaminated material.[2]

According to *Tosefta Kelim*, *Baba Qamma* 2.1, p. 570, this view was held only by the School of Hillel. The School of Shammai held that such vessels were defiled if a source of impurity was in contact with them from outside.

According to *Yer. Kilaim* 8.5, 31c, the Shammaites took this stringent view because they were uncertain about the proper classification of כלי נתר.[3]

According to *Pirqe Rabbenu ha-Qadosh*, ed. S. Schoenblum, p. 15b, also, the status of כלי נתר was one of six matters, concerning which no decision was reached.

In *Sifre Zutta*, 19.15, p. 310, it is assumed that כלי נתר and earthenware vessels have the same status, so far as rule discussed there is concerned. However, in the parallel passage in Sifre *Numbers* 126, p. 163, no mention is made of כלי נתר.

In *Sifra Shemini*, *par*. 7.1, ed. Weiss 53c, in a comment on the biblical statement (Lev. 11:33) that any earthenware vessel into which the dead body of a "creeping thing" falls, becomes defiled, the *vav* in the word for "*and* any earthenware vessel"[4] is interpreted as suggesting that the same rule applied to כלי נתר.

In *Sifra Zabim*, *par*. 3.1, ed. Weiss 77a, the *vav* in the word "*and* an earthenware vessel" (Lev. 15:12) is similarly interpreted to suggest that the rule there stated, applied also to כלי נתר.

These remarks in *Sifra* follow, of course, the method of R. Akiba, who interpreted the letter *vav* in such instances to suggest that some other object,

[2] This is the interpretation of the passage by Maimonides, and is followed by Ch. Albeck in his commentary.

[3] I owe this reference to my learned colleague, Professor Saul Lieberman.

[4] See comment of R. Samuel Strashun on *B. Shabbat* 16b, where he points out that *Sifra* infers the inclusion of the כלי נתר not from the use of the word *kol*, "any," but from the use of the *vav*.

[5] Wine owned by pagans, or put in their charge, or even touched by them, was forbidden for Jews to drink or even to use in any way, because the pagans might have intended it for idolatrous purposes. Anything so intended was forbidden to Jews to use in any way (Mishna *Aboda Zara* 2.1). The rule was extended to apply even to wine belonging to a Jew but entrusted to a pagan (*B. Aboda Zara* 31a). Similarly all wine prepared by Gentiles was forbidden. The Talmud is quite frank about the reason for this last extension of the law—it was intended to prevent socializing which might lead to intermarriage. Because of the prohibition against the use of wine belonging to pagans, earthenware containers in which it was stored were forbidden; and even if the containers belonged to a pagan, and the wine stored in them to a Jew, both the wine and the containers were held to be forbidden (Mishna *Aboda Zara* 2.4). The reason for this rule was that the containers, having been used first by a pagan, to whom they belonged, presumably absorbed some of

in addition to the one specifically mentioned in the text, was subject to the rule stated.

It is not surprising, therefore, to find in *Sifra* the same comment, in connection with the verse (Lev. 6:21), commanding that an earthenware vessel in which the meat of a sin-offering was cooked, be broken. There, too, a *vav* is added to the *kli*, "vessel." See *Sifra Ẓav, pereq* 7.1, ed. Weiss 32d.

The norm cited in *Sifra Ẓutta*, also occurs in Mishna *Kelim* 10.1.

In the Babylonian Talmud, Mishna *Kelim* 2.1 is quoted in *Shabbat* 16a. In *B. Aboda Ẓara* 33a, we are told that earthenware containers bought from pagans, and which had been used by them for wine,[5] may be used by Jews only if they have been filled with fresh water, changed each day, for three days, so as to remove any trace of the wine of the pagans. On the other hand (*ibid.* 33b), R. Yosena said in the name of R. Ammi that כלי נתר purchased from pagans, and which the pagans had used for wine, could never be purified.

At this point, the Talmud asks "What are כלי נתר?" R. Yose b. Abin (who had been born and had matured in the Holy Land, but had come to Babylonia) replied: "Vessels made out of [earth dug from] a mine of alum." This passage will have to be discussed at some length below.

In *B. Niddah* 17a, R. Johanan asserted that כלי נתר have the same status as metalware so far as the rule stated there is concerned.[6] The rule is that one who drinks liquids which have been mixed with water, and thus prepared for drinking, but were permitted to remain overnight, risks his life. The implication is, of course, that it is forbidden to drink such liquids, for one must not put one's life in danger. Rab Judah in the name of Samuel held that the rule applied only to liquids kept in metalware. R. Johanan apparently agreed with this opinion; but said that so far as this rule was

his wine in their sides; and this wine might be washed out by any liquid put into the containers afterward. However, many leniencies were introduced in regard to containers. They could be "purified" by filling them with fresh water for three days in succession. It might be assumed that the water kept in them day after day would wash out any wine absorbed in the walls of the containers. They were also purified if kept for a year without being used. In the course of that time, the wine absorbed in the walls of the containers would have become so dry that it could no longer be washed out by liquids put into the containers.

[6] Perhaps R. Johanan came to this conclusion because of the statement regarding כלי נתר in *Tosefta Kelim, loc. cit.* There the Shammaites held, as remarked above, that these utensils are defiled if touched by a source of impurity from the outside. That must mean that they have the status of metalware in some respects. Although R. Johanan himself held (*Yer. Kilaim* 8.5, 31c) that the Shammaites asserted this view, only because of their uncertainty regarding the status of כלי נתר, he apparently believed that where life is in danger, even the slightest possibility of peril must be taken into account; and therefore although the law followed the view of the Hillelites while the Shammaite view itself was based not on certainty but on doubt, R. Johanan held that one who drank mixed liquids left overnight in כלי נתר did wrong.

concerned, כלי נתר were to be considered like metalware. The rule but not the comment of R. Johanan, is quoted in *Masseket Derek Erez* chap. 11 (see *Mesiktot Derek Erez*, ed. M. Higger, p. 308).

The issue of what כלי נתר are, was the subject of a well-known controversy between Maimonides, and earlier commentators.[7]

According to the Geonic commentary on *Toharot*, *Kelim* 2.1, ed. J. N. Epstein, p. 8, the term refers to utensils made of material *held together* by alum, alum being described as occurring in tiny crystals, which when dissolved in a dye, act as a mordant, preventing the dye from ever fading.[8]

By "held together," the commentator evidently meant that the earthenware was glazed with alum, which fortified it.

While the Geonim described כלי נתר only as utensils, the materials of which *were held together* by alum, some commentators and lexicographers, including Ibn Janah, interpreted נתר as meaning *alum* (Ibn Janah, *Sefer ha-Shorashim*, s.v. נתר) and therefore interpreted כלי נתר as vessels made of alum. R. David Kimhi, in his dictionary, cites this as a possible interpretation (see his *Sefer ha-Shorashim*, s.v. נתר).

Ibn Janah presumably based his interpretation on the remark of R. Yose b. Abin in *B. Aboda Zara*, *loc. cit.* The same interpretation is cited by R. Hananel in his commentary on *B. Aboda Zara*, *loc. cit.*, as one opinion; and in *Aruk*, s.v. חפר and צרף.

Maimonides objected vigorously to this interpretation. He wrote in his commentary on Mishna *Kelim* 2.1 (ed. J. Kappah, p. 55): "כלי נתר are natron vessels. [Natron] is a soft stone, blue in color,[9] which is readily dissolved in water, and is used for washing one's hair and garments. Indeed the Sages mention it among materials used for washing נתר ובורית קימוניא ואשלג (Mishna *Niddah* 9.6). The manufacture of כלי נתר is quite common among us of the far west (i. e. Moorish Spain and Morocco). But their manufacture is a difficult (art), because they (i. e. the makers of כלי נתר) knead the נתר, making bottles for water out of it, like those made of earthenware. But the material cannot endure [great] heat, as earthenware does, because if the heat is too great, the vessel disintegrates and is ruined. On the other hand, if the fire does not reach all the parts of this utensil

[7] Although *Yer. Shabbat* 9.5, 12b, clearly defines נתר as natron, the mediaeval authorities were by no means in agreement regarding this identification. In *B. Niddah* 62a, a distinction is drawn between two types of נתר, that coming from Alexandria and that coming from Antipatris, in Judea itself. See Responsa of R. Simeon b. Zemah Duran, *Tashbez*, I, responsum 28.

[8] For the use of alum as a mordant in ancient Egypt, see A. Lucas, *Ancient Materials and Industries*, fourth ed., edited and revised by J. R. Harris, London 1962, p. 259. See also *Index*, under *alum*. The view of the Geonic commentary is also that of *Halakot Gedolot*, ed. Venice, p. 123b.

[9] Natron is naturally white; see Noble, *op. cit.*, p. 437. The faience articles made of it would be white if no copper sulphate, giving the object its blue color, were present. The

[equally], the material emerges raw; and, in that event, when water is put into it, it dissolves, and is ruined. These vessels are used for drinking water, because the water becomes very enjoyable and it gets a fragrant odor, which refreshes the sick and those who suffer from stomach trouble.[10] Because of this (i. e., the fact that the vessels need some heat in all their parts, but not too much heat in any part), only few craftsmen can make them, in such a way that the vessel emerges blue in color, like the raw material, and yet has been sufficiently fired, so that water will not dissolve it. And they also cannot be made, except with very thin sides, the thickness of the sides being almost like that of pages of paper.[11] For if it should be thicker than that, the fire [which heats it] will not warm the inside because of the weakness of the fire [which is used for it]. And in the same manner of manufacture is that of the vessels which we call אנג'באר. That is like נתר, but its color is bright red, and so is [the color of] the vessels made of it. Those vessels are also used for drinking water. And because these vessels are not completely fired, for the firing does not change their appearance (i. e. their color) but the appearance of the utensils whether raw or fired is the same, it might have seemed to us that they are to be considered [unfired] vessels made of clay, which are not subject to defilement.[12] Therefore, we are taught that since originally they are clay, but have been subjected to firing, although the fire is not intense, their status is that of [fired] earthenware . . . I have described this matter at such great length so that you may see the matter clearly, and so that the truth may become evident. [I have done this] because everyone who has commented on these words, and whose [comments] have reached me, explains כלי נתר as alum vessels. But Heaven knows how much I wonder what one who says this is imagining. For it is in accord neither with experience nor tradition—that it is possible to make a vessel out of alum. There is no doubt, that one who says this has never seen alum. Even if we should suppose, that [he has in mind] one who has dug alum in a mine, and that the alum [under consideration] is a large [alum] stone, out of which one made a utensil, that would not be suitable for anything, as it is. And [even] if we suppose this [i. e., the mining of a large alum stone], it [the utensil] would not be subject

material which Maimonides examined was therefore not pure natron, but natron containing copper sulphate.

[10] According to Rabbi Joseph Kappah (private communication) the faience articles now used in Yemen have the same characteristics. However, Egyptian faience in the Metropolitan Museum of Art in New York, which I examined, has no fragrance whatever. I am told this is true of all Egyptian faience.

[11] The specimens of Egyptian faience which I have examined, while all quite small, have sides considerably thicker than paper. Apparently, in Arabic times, a more sophisticated form of manufacture made possible the creation of these articles with very thin sides.

[12] Vessels made of clay or mud were not subject to defilement unless fired. (See Mishna *Kelim* 10.1, and commentaries there.)

to defilement, for then it would merely be an earthen vessel [not fired], which is not subject to defilement, as will be explained."

(It is difficult to understand why Maimonides did not take into consideration the kind of vessel described in the Geonic commentary, which consisted of clay, glazed with alum, to re-inforce the clay; and was, of course, fired in the usual manner. Perhaps he thought that such vessels needed no special designation. They were simply fired earthenware.)

Whatever may have been the strength or weakness of the interpretation of כלי נתר which reached Maimonides, and was that of Ibn Janah, and was cited by R. Hananel and others, the author of the Geonic commentary on *Toharot* knew very well what alum was, and described some of its properties with precision.[13] It was evident to the author of the Geonic commentary, that the containers called כלי נתר in *B. Aboda Zara* 33b, had to have a constituent which was a mordant; and that because the mordant made dyes fast and permanent, it would have the same effect on wine stains. Alum was such a substance. He concluded that the כלי נתר discussed in *B. Aboda Zara* 33b were containers, which were *held together*, i. e., glazed, with alum. When wine was poured into such containers, some of it adhered to the alum glaze, and left an indelible stain, which could not be washed away in any manner. Therefore, while simple earthenware bottles, used for wine of pagans, could be purified through change of water over three days, containers for which alum was used, could never be purified, if they had contained wine of pagans. The stain of the wine in contact with the alum would be indelible.

The Geonic author of the commentary on *Toharot* apparently reasoned that since כלי נתר in *B. Aboda Zara* 33b, were utensils made of earth containing alum, presumably that was also true of the term everywhere, including Mishna *Kelim* 2.1. Because of the interpretation given in the Talmud, he concluded that the Mishna was discussing only glazed containers with an alum content. Thus he presumed that נתר was used in the term כלי נתר in a derivative sense; for he elsewhere described נתר as natron (*Commentary of the Geonim on Toharot*, ed. J. N. Epstein, p. 114).

The Gaon (like other authorities) saw no inconsistency in this interpretation of נתר as natron, and of כלי נתר as earthenware with an alum glaze. The word נתר, they apparently held, could be used both for natron and bauxite, as special kinds of earth. But according to them, כלי נתר always meant vessels with an alum glaze.

On the other hand, Maimonides was writing on the basis of his observations in his country and time. The method of manufacture of the utensils to which he referred was still in use in Yemen in our time, when Rabbi

[13] For example, its use as a mordant; see above.

[14] See M. Rostovtzeff, *The Social and Economic History of the Hellenistic World*, Oxford 1941, *Index* under *Faience*; and *Enzyklopedia Miqrait*, V, col. 278.

Joseph Kappah lived there, as he states in his notes to his edition and translation of the commentary of Maimonides, *loc. cit.*; and as he confirmed in private correspondence with me.

While one can hardly presume the manner of manufacture of natron vessels in Moorish Spain or Morocco in the twelfth century was precisely identical with that used a thousand years earlier in Egypt, some similarities between the utensils described by Maimonides as well as their mode of manufacture and those of Egyptian faience are striking. Egyptian faience, too, was of natron, and often the utensils were blue. They were small utensils, beads, amulets, chalices, cosmetic jars, etc. The process of manufacture lent itself primarily to diminutive objects (see Joseph Veach Noble, *American Journal of Archaeology* LXXIII (1969), pp. 435 ff.). However, unlike medieval faience, Egyptian faience articles were not *covered* with glazing material. The material was *self-glazing* (see Noble, *op. cit.*). It is generally believed that the "faience" of Moorish Spain and of Morocco was a highly sophisticated development of the type used in ancient Egypt. Indeed the ancient Egyptian method of manufacture of faience was still in use as late as the fourteenth century (see A. V. Lucas, *Ancient Egyptian Materials and Industries*, p. 157).

There can be little doubt, therefore, that Maimonides is right in identifying the כלי נתר of the Mishna as natron vessels, although it must be emphasized that utensils precisely like those described by Maimonides were apparently unknown in ancient times. The Egyptian faience articles surviving have no fragrance, such as those used in Maimonides' time had; and their sides are by no means as thin as paper. The manufacturers of glazed articles had introduced, in the course of the millennium before Maimonides, new methods, and created a new type of vessel.

Yet the name *natron* itself employed for the ancient vessels indicates the use of that material. Probably the natron vessels used in ancient Israel were imported from Egypt, where they were manufactured.[14]

While R. Hananel in his commentary, cited above, quoted authorities who identified כלי נתר as alum vessels, he apparently felt uncertain about that identification. Therefore, he said merely, "Some explain" the term in that manner. Living in North Africa, he was probably acquainted with vessels made of natron, and may have concluded that they were possibly what the Mishna and kindred works meant by כלי נתר. However, he felt obliged also to record the variant interpretation based on the statements in *B. Aboda Zara* 33b.

Rashi, on the other hand, like the Geonim, realized that the rule set down in *B. Aboda Zara* 33b referred to utensils containing an admixture of alum, and not to vessels made of alum.

That Rashi was well acquainted with the nature of alum is clear from his comment on another passage in the same context in *B. Aboda Zara* 33b.

There we are told that "Rab Zebid said, 'Glazed ware (which had been used by a pagan to contain wine), if white or black may be used (i. e. after the prescribed cleansing). If yellow, it may not be used' " (i. e. cannot be purified). Apparently, the reason for R. Zebid's ruling was that the yellow glaze derived from its alum content, and alum is a mordant. Rashi interprets the word used by R. Zebid for "glaze" to mean "glaze with a lead content." Glaze containing lead was used in Egypt in ancient times and apparently became increasingly common with the passage of time (see A. V. Lucas, *op. cit.*, pp. 157 ff.). Thus Rashi holds that a glazed vessel with an alum content which had been used by pagans for wine was forever forbidden. (For other interpretations of R. Zebid's statement, see below p. 72).

The view of R. Ammi and R. Zebid was rejected by Amemar, who held that all glazeware may be purified in the same manner as earthenware. Apparently, it was the view of Amemar that the stains retained in glazeware containing alum were completely absorbed in the material, and could not be exuded into any liquid poured into the containers later. Any wine not so absorbed could be rinsed away through pouring fresh water into the container, changing the water each day for three days.

In the light of the statements by R. Ammi and R. Zebid, Rashi interpreted כלי נתר in the Talmudic passage in *Aboda Zara* 33b as referring to vessels made of "*the ground* from which alum is dug." The same explanation was offered by R. Samson of Sens and by R. Asher b. Yehiel in their commentaries on Mishna *Kelim* 2.1.

However, Rashi himself, in his commentary on *B. Shabbat* 16a, where Mishna *Kelim* 2.1 is quoted, defined נתר simply as "a sort of white earth." Apparently, Rashi considered the term כלי נתר a generic one for vessels made of salts, including both natron and alum. In each passage, the word had to be explained according to the context. In *B. Aboda Zara* 33b, it meant "earth containing alum"; in Mishna *Kelim* 2.1, and related passages, it meant natron.

Maimonides' criticism of the interpretation of Mishna *Kelim* 2.1, which reached him, did not, of course, at all apply to the interpretation of the Geonim in the Commentary on *Toharot* nor to that of Rashi.

R. Obadiah of Bertinoro realized this fact. Hence, despite his great reverence for Maimonides, he interpreted Mishna *Kelim* 2.1, in accordance with the views of R. Samson of Sens, and in accordance with the clear implications of the passage in *B. Aboda Zara* 33b.

He apparently did not realize the force of Rashi's brief comment in his commentary on *B. Shabbat* 16a, where he described נתר as being made "of a kind of white earth," without suggesting that this white earth was either bauxite or natron, both of which might be so described.

J. N. Epstein also evidently recognized (in his notes) the distinction between the interpretation given in the Geonic Commentary on *Toharot*, p. 8, and that which Maimonides rejected. However, R. Yom Tob Lipman Heller in *Tosefot Yom Tob*, *Kelim* 2.1, identified the interpretation given R. Obadiah Bertinoro (and taken from R. Samson of Sens) with that opposed by Maimonides. So did R. Solomon Adeni in his commentary (*Meleket Shelomoh*), *ad loc.* But the precise significance of Rashi's language was recognized by R. Gershon Hanoch, the author of the commentary *Sidre Toharah*, *Kelim*, *loc. cit.*

Tosafot, *Aboda Zara* 33b, apparently bearing in mind Rashi's comment on כלי נתר in *B. Shabbat* 16a as well as in *B. Aboda Zara* 33b, concluded that there were two types of כלי נתר. In Mishna *Kelim* 2.1, the term כלי נתר means utensils made of natron; in *B. Abodah Zara* 33b, it means utensils consisting of material having some alum content. Apparently, this is precisely how Rashi understood the passages.

However, the identification of כלי נתר as natron vessels, and therefore as Egyptian faience, made the passage in *Sifra Zav*, *pereq* 7.1, ed. Weiss 32d, dealing with the verse in Leviticus, where vessels in which the meat of a sin-offering was cooked are discussed, quite unintelligible for Maimonides; since, as is clear from his description, the natron utensils of his day were as little fit for cooking purposes as the Egyptian faience a thousand years earlier. Both would disintegrate in the heat. Neither was manufactured for use except as chalices, ornaments and small containers. Yet the passage in *Sifra* is found in every surviving text (except Ms. Oxford, which lacks two whole pages of this part of the work). Maimonides almost certainly had it in his text of *Sifra*, for it is included in Ms. Assemani 31, the readings of which generally agree with those of Maimonides; and in the Yemenite *midrashim* (*Midrash Ha-Gadol*, and *Midrash ha-Biyyur*).

Maimonides, naturally aware of this difficulty, clearly took it for granted that the passage in *Sifra Zav*, the language of which is identical with that in *Sifra Shemini* and *Zabim*, was inserted only under the influence of those passages, as often happens in tannaitic *midrashim*. Therefore, while in his Code, he cited the statement that natron vessels are subject to the same rules as earthenware vessels, so far as the law of purity is concerned (*Yad*, *Hilkot Kelim*, chap. 1, end), he made no mention of natron vessels in his discussion of the law dealing with the meat of a sin-offering which was cooked (*Yad*, *Hilkot Ma'ase ha-Qorbanot* 8.11).

Maimonides seems to have encountered equal difficulty in his interpretation of Mishna *Kelim* 10.1. That passage deals with the rules derived from Num. 19:14: "This is the law: when a man dieth in a tent . . . every open vessel which hath no covering close-bound upon it is unclean." From this verse, the Rabbinic authorities deduced a series of very complicated rules.

They limited the rule under discussion to vessels, which could not be defiled at all or could not be defiled from outside; for obviously if the vessel could be defiled from outside, whether it had a "covering close-bound" on it or not was irrelevant. Thus, the rule applied primarily to earthenware, which cannot be defiled from outside, and to vessels made of the skin or bones of a fish and other material, which are not susceptible to defilement at all. It was further held that such vessels not only do not become defiled, but because of that fact, nothing contained in them could be defiled.

According to Mishna *Kelim* 10.1 this rule, applying to earthenware vessels, applied also to כלי נתר. The same extension is made in *Sifre Zutta* 19.15, p. 310, as observed above. However, it is difficult to envisage a natron vessel, with a "covering closebound." Natron vessels were either ornaments, not used to contain anything, or open chalices or small bowls. Hence, Maimonides in his commentary on Mishna *Kelim* 10.1, resorted to unusual circumlocution. After discussing several types of containers which protected their contents from defilement, if they were in the same room with a corpse, "and also earthenware vessels, and all vessels *which are associated with earthenware vessels*, that is natron vessels" have the same quality, namely that they protect their contents against defilement, if they are in the same room with a corpse. The prolixity of Maimonides in this instance might be considered less significant, were it not for the fact that in his Code, when discussing this rule, he omits all mention of natron vessels (see *Yad. Hilkot Tumat Met* 21.1).

In this omission, he follows *Sifre* Numbers 126, p. 163, which also makes no reference to כלי נתר in its comment on Numbers 19.15, where the rule is stated.

Maimonides apparently rejected, as a misunderstanding, the discussion in *B. Aboda Zara*, 33b, where כלי נתר are clearly identified (as Rashi and *Aruk* suggest) with vessels made of earth containing alum. Hence he ignored R. Yosena's statement there in the name of R. Ammi, making no mention of it in his Code. (On the other hand, he interpreted the statement of R. Zebid, as Rashi did, namely as referring to a glaze containing lead; and asserting that yellow glaze made a vessel permanently forbidden. However, he does not explain the difference. See *Yad*, *Hilkot Ma-'akalot 'Asurot* 11.19. This decision followed that of the Talmud in *B. Ketubot* 107b.)

However, accepting the interpretation of כלי נתר by Maimonides as correct, the remark of R. Ammi and the discussion in the Talmud based upon it, in *B. Aboda Zara* 33b, still remains to be explained. It is on the face of it astonishing that in that passage, the Talmud should suddenly ask, "What are כלי נתר?" since the term occurs in the Mishna, *loc. cit.* Why was the question raised only in connection with the norm stated by R. Yosena in the name of R. Ammi? The answer appears to be that the term כלי נתר in the statement of R. Yosena could not refer to natron vessels, for natron vessels would not have a status different from that of earthenware in regard to the problem of wine belonging to pagans. Why should כלי נתר, which were held subject to the same rules as earthenware in regard to the laws of purity, be subject to a more stringent rule than earthenware in regard to the law forbidding the use of containers of wine bought from pagans? R. Jose b. Abin explained that the כלי נתר of which R. Yosena spoke in the name of R. Ammi were vessels made of earth deriving from a mine of alum. It was reasonable for them to be subject to a special rule concerning the wine of pagans, because alum is a mordant.

But why did R. Yosena and his teacher, R. Ammi, call these vessels כלי נתר? They both lived in the Land of Israel, as R. Jose b. Abin did for many years, and they certainly had firm traditions concerning the utensils discussed in Mishna *Kelim* 2.1, and related tannatic sources. Presumably, so great a scholar as R. Ammi, had actually observed natron objects, in order thoroughly to understand the Mishna.

R. Ammi may have been perplexed (as Maimonides was, in his time) by the comment in *Sifra Ẓav*, *pereq* 7.1 which discusses the use of כלי נתר for cooking. As he knew that natron vessels could not be used for cooking, he concluded that כלי נתר must refer also to vessels made of some other material, such as bauxite. In that event, the term כלי נתר could be used to describe any glazed utensils, including those glazed with material containing alum.

Thus the difficulty in regard to the passage in *Sifra Ẓav* was resolved for R. Ammi and his disciples, and following them for the Geonim, Rashi and his disciples.

R. Hillel interpreted the passage in *Sifra Ẓav*, as dealing with vessels containing alum, or consisting of alum. Likewise, in the commentary on *Sifra*, erroneously ascribed R. Samson of Sens,[15] כלי נתר are defined (in the explanation of the passage in *Sifra Ẓav*) as vessels made of material containing alum. R. Hillel held that the כלי נתר mentioned in *Sifra Shemini*, *loc. cit.*, which were the same as those under discussion in Mishna *Kelim* 2.1, were made of bauxite. In this, he apparently disagreed with Rashi.

However, in the commentary ascribed to R. Samson, the question is raised, how to explain *Tosefta Kelim* 2.1, according to which the Shammaites held that כלי נתר, while falling under the norms of purity of earthenware, were also subject to those dealing with metalware. If כלי נתר everywhere

[15] That this commentary was erroneously ascribed to R. Samson of Sens was noted by R. Zadok of Lublin. (See his work, *Pri Ẓaddik*, *Bereshit*, 36c.) The late Dr. Chayyim Heller brought this fact and the reference to my attention, many years ago. It was independently noticed by Professor Saul Lieberman in *Tosefet Rishonim*, II, p. 295, and in his book *Sifre Ẓutta*, p. 1, note. He suggests, by inference, that the author of the commentary was the famous R. Moses b. Hisdai Taku. (He confirmed the identification in an oral communication to me.) See also J. L. Fischman, *Sefer Rashi*, p. 36.

meant utensils made of earth containing alum, one could understand the special norm cited in *B. Aboda Zara* 33b; but surely the law of purity governing metalware could not apply to them. The author offers the suggestion that these utensils must have been made somewhat differently from earthenware vessels, but does not say in what way. He also suggests the possibility that because the vessels were made of earth containing alum, "which is white, and therefore smooth," they might be considered metalware. The author apparently ascribed whiteness to bauxite, because Rashi in his commentary on *B. Shabbat* 16a, describes כלי נתר as being made of white material. But, as we have seen, Rashi in that passage was interpreting כלי נתר as natron vessels, distinguishing the כלי נתר of Mishna *Kelim* 2.1 from those discussed in *B. Aboda Zara* 33b.

It apparently did not occur to the author, as it did to Rashi, that the term כלי נתר might be used for different types of utensils, both natron vessels, and those made of bauxite; and that Mishna *Kelim* 2.1, like *Tosefta Kelim* 2.1, refers to natron vessels. Neither was this possibility considered by the author of the Geonic commentary on *Toharot*, or by R. Samson of Sens in his commentary on Mishna *Kelim* 2.1.

The analysis of the earlier sources thus suggests that the term כלי נתר was used in different senses by early Rabbinic authorities, and that it is this difference which underlay the various interpretations of the term by Maimonides and the Geonim. R. Ammi certainly used the term in the sense of glazed objects, not necessarily made of natron. The belief that כלי נתר were natron vessels was apparently held by the School of R. Akiba; hence their assertion that containers which were כלי נתר protected their contents from defilement, if they were in the same house with a corpse. That view is reflected in *Sifre Zutta* 19.15, and in Mishna *Kelim* 10.1. However, in the School of R. Ishmael, כלי נתר signified glazed vessels, some of which could be defiled from outside. Hence the passage in *Sifre* Numbers dealing with the same norm, and emanating from that School, makes no reference to כלי נתר. The earlier Hillelites also used the term in the sense of natron vessels, and held that natron vessels, being self-glazing, belong to the class of earthenware vessels in general. In the School of Shammai, the term was also used for glazed ware, some types of which contained metal. They therefore held that כלי נתר might be defiled if touched by a source of impurity from outside.

The Policy of the German Government towards Zionism, 1897-1918

By ISAIAH FRIEDMAN
Ben Gurion University

GERMAN INTEREST IN the Orient goes back to the forties of the XIX th Century, when Helmuth von Moltke, who later became a Count and a Field Marshall, travelled extensively in the Ottoman Empire. Moltke was the first German to recognize the importance of Palestine for German interests.[1] It fitted into his scheme of *Mitteleuropa* and of German expansion towards the highlands of Anatolia and Mesopotamia.[2] Although some years later he modified his views to comply with the official line of Chancellor Otto von Bismarck,[3] it would not be wrong to consider him as one of the principal forerunners of a number of German thinkers, economists and strategists, who propounded the idea of *Drang nach Osten*.[4]

There is abundant literature on Germany's penetration of the Orient, but its connection with the Jews is less well known. The more pronounced the drive to the East, the more emphatic became the protection afforded to German Jews and proteges in Palestine. "It was Germany's merit," Paul von Tischendorf, the Consul-General in Jerusalem, reported, "to be the

Glossary

A.A.A. Auswärtiges Amt Akten
C.Z.A. Central Zionist Archives, Jerusalem
E.A.C. Engeres Aktions-Comitee (Zionist Executive)
G.A.C. Grosses Aktions Comitee (Zionist Council)
P.E.C. Provisional Executive Committee for General Zionist Affairs (New York).

[1] Field Marshall Count Helmuth von Moltke, *Essays, Speeches and Memoirs* (Engl. trans. London, 1893), Vol. 1, pp. 274–96.

[2] Henry C. Meyer in his *Mitteleuropa in German Thought and Action, 1815–1945* (The Hague, 1955) credits Friedrich List as 'the oldest prophet of *Mitteleuropa*' (p. 11) and makes no mention of Moltke. The publication of Moltke's articles coincided with that of List's *The National System of Political Economy* (1841).

[3] Speech in the Imperial Diet, reproduced in *German Opinion on National Policy prior to July 1914*, Handbook prepared under the Direction of the Historical Section of the Foreign Office, No. 155, H.M.S.O., 1920.

[4] For a critical list of authors and publications which advocated this idea see Meyer, *op. cit.*, pp. 57–8, 95–102; G. W. Prothero, *German Policy before the War* (London, 1916), p. 39; Percy Evans Lewin, *The German Road to the East* (London, 1916), pp. 26–32; J. E. Barker, 'The Future of Asiatic Turkey,' *XIX Century and After* (June 1916), no. 472; Vladimir Jabotinsky, *Turkey and the War* (London, 1917), p. 56.

only European Power to advocate in 1893 the cancellation of the [Ottoman] decree prohibiting Jews from purchasing land."[5] But it was not until the eve of Wilhelm II's departure for the East in the autumn of 1898 that it looked for a while as if the Emperor intended to declare his protection of Jewish immigration and colonization in Palestine in earnest. Guided by his friend and mentor, Count zu Eulenburg, the Kaiser arrived at the conclusion that Turkey would benefit economically from Jewish settlement in Palestine, while Germany would gain a firm foothold in the Orient, simultaneously easing the solution of the Jewish problem. Wilhelm II's position was made clear in his letter to the Grand Duke of Baden, his uncle, dated September 29, 1898 in which he wrote:

> The fundamental idea of Zionism has always interested me and even aroused my sympathy. I have come to the conclusion that here we have to deal with a question of the most far-reaching importance. Therefore I have requested that cautious contact should be made with the promoters of this idea. I am willing to grant an audience to a Zionist deputation in Jerusalem on the occasion of our presence there.
>
> I am convinced that the settlement of the Holy Land by the wealthy and industrious people of Israel [Volk Israel] will bring unexampled prosperity and blessings to the Holy Land, which may do much to revive and develop Asia Minor. Such a settlement would bring millions into the purse of the Turks . . . and so gradually help to save the "Sick Man" from bankruptcy . . . The Turk will recover, getting his money without borrowing, and will be able to build his own highways and railways without foreign companies and then it would not be so easy to dismember Turkey.
>
> In addition, the energy and the creative powers and abilities of the tribe of Shem would be directed to more dignified purposes than the exploitation of Christians, and many Semites of the Social Democratic Party, who are stirring up opposition, will move eastwards, where more rewarding work will present itself . . . I know very well that nine-tenths of all Germans will be deeply shocked when they hear, at a later time, that I sympathize with the Zionists or even that I place them under my protection when they appeal to me.

Wilhelm then alluded to the story that "the Jews killed the Redeemer," but thought it was up to God himself to punish them, as he had done. However, he added, "neither the anti-Semites nor others including myself, were ordered or empowered to maltreat these people to the greater glory of God." These moral arguments the Kaiser reinforced with those of expediency.

[5] A.A.A., *Türkei*, Nr. 195, *Die Juden in Türkei*, K692/K175847–64 (hereafter *Türkei* 195), Tischedorf to Auswärtiges Amt, 19 June 1897.

> From the point of view of secular *Realpolitik*, the question cannot be ignored. In view of the gigantic power (very dangerous in a way) of international Jewish capital, would it not be an immense achievement for Germany, if the world of the Hebrews looked to her with gratitude? Everywhere the hydra of the most awful anti-Semitism raises its terrible and brutal head, and the Jews, full of anxiety, are ready to leave the countries where they are threatened to return to the Holy Land and look for protection and security. I shall intercede with the Sultan, for the Scripture says, "Make friends even with unjust Mammon" and "Be ye wise as serpents and harmless as doves."[6]

This extraordinary document sheds an interesting light on the Emperor's character and ideas. He was certainly not free from the religious prejudices which Adolph Stöcker and his Calvinist tutor G. E. Hinzpeter had implanted in him; but here his reaction to anti-Semitism was unusual. By proposing a constructive solution to the Jewish problem he seemed to stand out from most of its contemporaries, though obviously, without the impact of Herzl's memorandum (re-echoed partly in his letter), as well as Eulenburg's assistance, it is doubtful whether his conclusions would have been so far-reaching.

The Kaiser did receive Herzl in Constantinople on October 18, 1898 in the presence of his Foreign Minister, Bernard von Bülow. The Emperor listened attentively to Herzl's exposition and expressed confidence that the Zionists, with financial and human resources at their disposal, would be successful in their venture. But Bülow had different ideas. As his biographer noted, while recognizing Herzl's great literary talents, he was unable to work up any enthusiasm for his political ideas. Bülow was well aware of the hardships which the Jews in Eastern Europe had to endure, but was not convinced that mass emigration to Palestine would improve their lot. He also doubted whether Herzl's project could be applied to the German Jews, who were strongly attached to Germany and felt no need to rush into an unpromising and undefined venture in Palestine. Zionism, in Bülow's opinion, could at best attract the destitute, not the prosperous and educated among the Jews of Europe; but beggars were not capable of founding a state or even of colonizing it. He was also dubious about the attitude of the Turks.[7]

Bülow's scepticism amounted to veiled obstructiveness during the audience with the Emperor. The Foreign Minister contradicted Wilhelm II in

[6] Hermann and Bessie Ellern, *Herzl, Hechler the Grand Duke of Baden and the German Emperor, 1896–1904* (Tel Aviv, 1962) pp. 48–53, Wilhelm II to the Grand Duke of Baden, 29 Sept. 1898; see also Isaiah Friedman, *Germany, Turkey and Zionism, 1897–1918* (Oxford, 1977) pp. 65–8.

[7] Sigmund Münz, *Prince Bülow: The Statesman and Man*, English trans. (London, 1935), pp. 102–3. On Bülow's opinion of Herzl see his *Memoirs*, English trans. (London, 1931), ii, pp. 249–50.

every way he could except for using the little word "NO." However, the Emperor, who often allowed himself to be guided by his Minister, in this case supported Herzl and agreed that Zionism was a "completely natural" solution. He felt confident that he would be successful in persuading the Sultan of the feasibility of the project. However, this proved a misjudgement.[8]

Our evidence of Wilhelm II's encounter with Abdul Hamid is circumstantial, but it does not require much imagination to realize why "German protection of a Jewish chartered company" could not commend itself to the Sultan. For years Turkey had been struggling against the system of Capitulations, which provided the Europeans Powers with an instrument for meddling in her internal affairs. The spectre of a second Franco-Lebanon in the form of a Judeo-German Palestine was too alarming. Ahmed Tewfik, the Turkish Foreign Minister, who accompanied the Kaiser on his tour in Palestine, made it clear that "the Sultan would have nothing to do with Zionism and an independent Jewish kingdom." As a result Wilhelm lost his enthusiasm for Zionism. Tewfik was also reported to have declared at the time the Turks had settled their accounts with the Armenians in three days; with the Zionists it would take only three hours.[9]

Herzl may have been flattered when the Kaiser stopped for a while and chatted with him at the gates of Mikve-Israel, the agricultural school near Jaffa to the astonishment of the spectators watching the imperial procession on its way to Jerusalem. But the interview which Herzl had with the Legation Counsellot Klehmet, whom Bülow had brought with him from Berlin as his secretary, was discouraging.

During the second audience, which took place in Jerusalem on November 2, 1898, Wilhelm assured the Zionist deputation of his continued interest, but the conclusive statement which Herzl was so eagerly awaiting was not forthcoming, and the political aspect of the scheme was passed over. The Kaiser said "neither yes nor no," and Herzl inferred that his stock had depreciated. The official communique that was issued by the German news agency was colorless and disappointing.[10]

[8] Theodor Herzl, *The Complete Diaries of . . .*, ed. by Raphael Patai, trans. by Harry Zohn, 5 Vols. (New York, London, 1946), Vol. ii, pp. 726–34, 737. In his memoirs (written presumably in the early 1920s) Wilhelm attested that Herzl's account of his meeting in Constantinople was 'absolutely correct, reliable and praiseworthy.' Herzl impressed him as 'a clever and a highly intelligent figure with expressive eyes . . . an enthusiastic idealist,' who communicated his ideas in 'a captivating manner.' Wilhelm recalled that he agreed to recommend Herzl's plan to the Sultan. The latter, though not enthusiastic, assured the Kaiser that he would instruct his Ministers to inquire into the matter and report. (Excerpt from *Memoirs* of Wilhelm II published by Dr. Alex Bein (in German) in the *Festschrift* in honor of Dr. N. M. Gelber (Tel Aviv, 1963), p. 17.)

[9] I. Friedman, *op. cit.*, pp. 76–9.

[10] Herzl, *Diaries*, Vol. ii, pp. 743–4, 748–9, 754–7, 767; *The Memoirs of Max I. Bodenheimer: Prelude to Israel*, trans. to English (London, 1963), pp. 101–4; Prince Bernhard Bülow, *Memoirs*, trans. (London, 1931), vol. ii, p. 239.

In the Wilhelmstrasse it became clear that only by developing an attitude of sympathetic disinterestedness towards Turkey and by avoiding any policy which might be objectionable to her, might the peaceful German economic penetration of the East be possible. At the time when Georg von Siemens, the Director of the Deutsche Bank was negotiating to carry through the Anatolian and Baghdad railway projects, it was imperative that Germany steered clear of any scheme with a political complexion, such as Zionism definitely was.[11]

Yet, whatever motives compelled German diplomacy to dissociate itself from Zionism, interest in the Jewish settlement in Palestine continued. Like the French, the Germans were quick to realize the importance of dissemination of their language as an indispensable medium in the process of peaceful economic and cultural penetration and soon after discovered in the Jews its most suitable carriers. Moreover, the inherent weakness of the German *Drang* to the East was manifest in the absence of a German settlement in Turkey. Thus the element of security for the colossal capital investments, which only a planned colonization could have provided, was absent. This was, perhaps, why the Jewish colonies, expanding steadily in the teeth of Turkish opposition attracted the attention of the German diplomats. It was, however, not before the year of 1912 that the German Consulate and economists ascertained the latent potentialities in the Jewish settlement in Palestine for German interests. Once this was realized it was also clear that the driving force behind the Jewish colonization was the Zionist ideal. Thus, the German Government was presented for the first time with a dilemma as to the expediency of reaching an accomodation with the Zionist Organization.

With the revival of French claims to Syria and Palestine, the matter assumed greater urgency and when Freiherr von Wangenheim, the German Ambassador in Constantinople, learned that his French opposite number offered Ottoman Jewry French protection, he advised Berlin that it would be economically, culturally, and politically advantageous if Germany did the same.[12]

Rear Admiral Trummler, Commander of the German naval unit in the Mediterranean, evaluated the importance of the Jews from a different angle. On a reconnaissance mission along the eastern shores of the Mediterranean, he wished not only to examine harbor and railway facilities, as well as development projects, but also to ascertain the political aspirations of the local population. He found that the Arab nationalist movement in Syria was on a collision course with Turkey and that for this reason the Palestine Jews 100,000 strong deserved "special attention." He attached particular significance to the Zionists who aspired to the renaissance of the Jewish people in Palestine. He singled out their loyalty to the Turkish Government

[11] I. Friedman, *op. cit.*, pp. 73, 82, 86.
[12] *Ibid.*, pp. 154–5, 161–4.

which recently had become more favourably disposed to them—quite justly—because Turkey would "undoubtedly profit from the Jewish element." He envisaged that, "thanks to their business talent and the large investments of the Zionists . . . in the not too distant future, the Jewish population will achieve a national coherence, which will give it a special weight and importance in Palestine." These facts were also "of special significance for Germany because of the Jews "strong pro-German leanings." The majority of Palestinian Jews learned German as a foreign language; the projected Technical College in Haifa was to introduce German as its language of instruction, and the seat of the central office of the Zionist Organization was in Berlin. He thought it quite inevitable, therefore, that "in case of a split amongst the population [Arabs versus Jews], the German Jewish element would certainly welcome German protection." He concluded:

> Through the Jewish population in Palestine, Germany has undoubtedly the means to advance her interests, which in total would constitute such an important factor that any French claims to this rich and promising country should not come under discussion at all.[13]

Dr. Alfred Zimmermann, the newly appointed Under Secretary for Foreign Affairs, was impressed with Trummler's report and, as future events showed, was ready to act on his recommendations.

Such a line of thinking would not have been possible had not the Turkish Government altered their attitude towards the Jewish colonization in Palestine at that time. It was the confrontation with Arab demands for decentralization, intensified by Turkey's defeat during the Balkan wars, on the one hand, and the manifest loyalty of the Zionists on the other, that made Constantinople revise its policy. Some individuals among the Young Turks recognized the great economic and cultural value of their enterprise, responsible for the country's flowering, others wanted to exploit Zionism as a counterweight against the Arabs. Talaat Bey, the Minister of the Interior, was particularly friendly to the Zionists.[14] Restrictions on freedom of immigration and on other discriminatory ordinances in Palestine were abrogated and the newly appointed Governor, Mahdi Bey, was exceptionally obliging to the Jewish colonists.[15] Given these factors it would be fair to

[13] A.A.A., *Türkei*, 177, *Der Libanon (Syrien)*, Bd. 9 (copy in *Türkei*, 195, K176427–32). The report (31 May 1913) was made to the Kaiser as Commander-in-Chief but was deposited in the files of the Foreign Ministry.

[14] *Türkei*, 195, K176407–14, Loytved-Hardegg to A.A.A., 9 May 1913; K177300–46, memorandum by Brode, 26 August, 1915.

[15] C.Z.A., Z3/443, report by Tschlenow at the meeting of the Zionist Council, 23 Nov. 1913; Z3/449 report by Jacobson to the same, 7 June 1914; Richard Lichtheim, *She'ar Yashuv* (Tel Aviv, 1953), pp. 244–50; *idem*, *Rückkehr* (Stuttgart, 1970), pp. 222–6; *Sefer Hayovel L'Rishon L'Zion* (Hebrew) ed. D. Idelovitch (Rishon L'Zion, 1941), p. 405.

say that in the immediate period before the First World War there existed a possibility of potential identity of interests between Germany, Turkey and the Zionists. That such a combination did not come into being was largely due to the fact that the Palestinian Zionists, completely ignorant of Germany's true intentions, launched in the winter of 1913/14 an anti-German language struggle, the *Sprachenkampf.*[16]

It antagonized the German Consulate and deterred the *Auswärtiges Amt* from taking the clear-cut decision mooted some time earlier. However, once the controversy subsided, the Zionists regained their respectability and were believed to be a factor worthy of being taken into consideration within the framework of Germany's Ostpolitik. This might be deduced from the statement made by Ambassador von Wangenheim, to Richard Lichtheim, the Zionist representative in Constantinople. Wangenheim reassured Lichtheim of his great sympathy. Germany was in no position to commit herself politically, but within the limit of his capacity and unofficially he promised to render his support. He hinted that the idea of a benevolent treatment of the Zionists emanated from Berlin, and stated conclusively that, should the Zionists in Turkey be persecuted, he would do his best to protect them. Lichtheim gained the impression that Wangenheim was animated by "perfectly sincere sympathy," which stemmed from the conviction that the Zionists were able to do valuable work for Turkey and benefit Germany too by disseminating her cultural and economic influence in the Orient.[17] The ensuing months, after the outbreak of the War, gave Lichtheim ample opportunity to see how serious and sincere Wangenheim was.

On August 30, 1914, following the outbreak of the War, Zimmermann instructed Wangenheim "to see to it, if necessary, that the Palestine Jews, regardless of nationality, remain unmolested," and on November 3rd he added that "it would be very wise if the Turkish Government also tried to win the sympathies of international Jewry, especially in America, by an accomodating treatment of Zionism."[18]

The policy of protection proved invaluable for the preservation of the Yishuv during the War, when the attitude of the Turkish authorities suddenly changed. The resurgence of Turkish nationalism and the unilateral abrogation of the Capitulations, placed the non-Turkish minorities in a most unenviable position. In Palestine, it was Ahmed Djemal Pasha, the Commander of the IV th Army, and his subordinates who were responsible for initiating the policy of oppression and banishment. Djemal Pasha, who exercised authocratic powers, branded Zionism as a "revolutionary and

[16] On the *Sprachenkampf* see I. Friedman, *op. cit.*, Chap. 10.

[17] C.Z.A., Z3/11, Lichtheim to the E.A.C., 29 June 1914; Lichtheim, *She'ar Yashuv*, pp. 272–7; *idem*, *Rückkehr*, pp. 241–6.

[18] *Türkei*, 195, K176701–2, K176716–17, Sec. of State to Wangenheim, 30 August, 3 Nov. 1914, tel. no. 577, dis. no. 704.

anti-Turkish movement, which must be eradicated." His system of mass deportations would have brought the whole Jewish settlement to complete ruin had not the powerful intercessions by the German and American Embassies stopped him.

The Germans were naturally concerned lest they would be held indirectly responsible for the Turkish atrocities and indeed Entente propaganda tried to make the most of it. Count Heinrich Bernstorff, the German Ambassador in Washington, realized how important it was to keep Germany's slate clean. Propaganda played an important role in the general warfare strategy and among the limited number of friends Germany had in the U.S.A. was a considerable section of the influential Jewish population. The correct behaviour of the German Army in occupied Poland, when contrasted with Russia's humiliating treatment of the Jews and her black record in the past, as well as Germany's promise at the beginning of the War to extend protection to the Jews in Palestine, gave reasonable hope of attracting the sympathy of American Jewry. The Turkish anti-Jewish atrocities, however, acted like a thunderbolt and could have upset Ambassador Bernstorff's applecart. He therefore persistently insisted on the necessity of drawing the attention of the Turkish Government to the principles underlying German policy towards the Jews in general, and the Zionists in particular, in order to prevent dangerous Turkish practices in Palestine. Von Wangenheim did not need any prodding. He repeatedly intervened with the Turkish Government and was gratified to learn that Talaat Bey, the Minister of the Interior, had a complete understanding of the political importance of this question but it appeared that neither Talaat, nor the Grand Vizier, were able to curb Djemal Pasha, who exercised supreme, if not independent, power in Syria and Palestine.[19]

Wangenheim still had to be careful not to offend the susceptibilities of his touchy ally. The Germans had difficulties of their own with the Turks. After the abolition of the Capitulations, the Turks, proud of their newly acquired independence, disliked any foreign interference. The defeat of the Allied fleet in the Dardanelles made them feel contemptuous not only of their Christian foes but even of their Christian allies. Behind the façade of the aggressive Turkish nationalism there lingered yet a very acute suspicion of Germany's post-war designs. This was why the Germans had to move warily and to decline the Zionists' overtures for a more definite commitment to their cause. Yet, in spite of these limitations and the strained relationship with the Turks over the Armenian question, the German Government issued in November, 1915, instructions to the Consulate in Palestine of far-reaching importance. In this document, which was top secret, it was stated amongst other things, that it was "politically advisable to show a friendly attitude towards Zionism and its aims." The Consulate was instructed in cases of

[19] I. Friedman, *op. cit.*, pp. 197–204, 212–27.

need to help the Palestine Jews as far as possible by all practical means.[20]

Such a specific wording as "to show a friendly attitude towards Zionism and its aims," would in all probability have been regarded by the Turks as a flagrant violation of their prerogatives. However, if the German diplomats preferred to ignore the inherent implications of this directive, it shows that either they became convinced at last of the plausibility of the Zionist argument that there existed no incompatibility between Zionist and Turkish interests, or realized that promotion of Zionism was so important to Germany that in the event of a victory by the Central Powers, Turkey would be forced to submit to Germany's control even in domestic affairs. Whatever the case, for the Zionists, and for Lichtheim in particular, the Instructions heralded a signal victory.

The German Government would not have troubled to issue these Instructions unless moved by serious political considerations. First, it wished to strengthen the hands of the German Zionist leaders within the Zionist movement and reap maximum propaganda benefit. But the deeper motives for issuing the Instructions related to long-term considerations. After the outbreak of the War Germany was for the first time confronted with a Jewish problem outside her own boundaries. Military conquests brought her directly into contact with the Jewish masses in Eastern Europe. Within a few months about two million and by the end of 1915 over five million out of a total of six and a half million Russian Jews came under German domination. The Germans realized that Polish antagonism made the future of so large a Jewish community very insecure. In addition, as a result of deliberate maltreatment and cruel expulsions by the Tsarist regime, over one and a half million Jews were completely uprooted from their homes. A very serious refugee problem emerged and it was feared, both in official and unofficial circles, that many of the refugees would migrate westwards. To spare Germany this problem it was suggested that if the Central Powers were victorious, the German Government should prevail upon her Turkish ally to remove all restrictions on freedom of immigration to Palestine. No forcible transfer was contemplated, but here Zionism offered itself to meet the need.

This line was argued both in private and publicly. Thus, Dr. Paul Rohrbach, in an address to the Prussian Parliament on March 3, 1915, contended that it was the Zionist movement alone that could divert immigration of Jewish masses from Europe to Asia, because the attraction of a "free national life" in Palestine was the only factor that could outweigh any material inducements elsewhere. A national Jewish entity by no means clashed with Germany's *Weltpolitik* because parallel with the development of Hebrew civilization the Jews would be able to propagate German *Kultur*

[20] *Türkei*, 195, K177404–7, Metternich to Bethmann Hollweg, 22 Nov. 1915, dis. no. 603 and encls.

and commerce in the Orient. Rohrbach thought that the interests of national Jewry coincided with German rather than with British aspirations for, in contrast to Germany, the British were bent on the destruction of the Ottoman Empire and were fostering Arab ambitions in preference to those of the Zionists.[21]

Dr. Heinrich Brode, the German Vice-Consul in Jaffa, later Consul in Jerusalem, was more blunt. In a memorandum, dated August 26, 1915, he asserted that "Zionism would ensure that the millions of Jews for whom things were getting "too hot" in Russia would not as hitherto flood to the West, but immigrate to Palestine." However, in his "Geheime Bemerkungen" ("Secret Observations"), which he stressed, did not contradict his earlier statement, he found that Zionism deserved consideration, because it could make "a substantial contribution to the solution of the Jewish problem in Germany."

> The very idea that a Jew as a senior officer, or administrative official, might represent the authority of the State is somewhat repellent to our national feeling . . . As an homogenous national state, our tendency is to encourage assimilation of foreign minority groups [but] . . . since Jewish characteristics have shown themselves extraordinarily dominant in intermarriage, the question arises whether our *Volkstum* is able to digest such an increase without impairing its innate *Wesen*. From this point of view, Zionism must be welcomed by us almost as a deliverance. From the standpoint of a conscious anti-Semite one should even wish that, if possible, every Jew should deliberate on the consequences of Zionism in order to preserve our people from the excessive penetration of Oriental blood.[22]

From the observation of the Foreign Ministry that the memorandum did not reveal "any important new material," it may be inferred that Brode merely re-echoed established thinking in the Wilhelmstrasse. The licence that he took to voice anti-Semitic arguments in an official document is astonishing. Yet it would be incorrect to deduce that German policy towards Zionism was largely motivated by anti-Semitism. According to Dr. Victor Jacobson, one of the leading German Zionist leaders, Dr. Zimmermann the Under Secretary of State for Foreign Affairs, entertained "unlimited sympathy" for the Zionist ideal. Zimmermann intended to bring the issue before the future Peace Conference, but during the War, out of consideration for Turkey, any public association with the Zionists had to be discounted.

[21] *Die Jüdische Presse. Konservative Wochenschrift* (Mar. 1915) (cutting in *Türkei*, 195, K176917); *Jüdische Rundschau* (12 Mar. 1915), p. 87; Friedman, *op. cit.*, pp. 252–5.

[22] *Türkei*, 195, K177300–46, 'Memorandum über den Zionismus und Weltkrieg' (confidential); and 'Geheime Bemerkungen zu dem Memorandum,' encl. to dis. no. 76/1278.

"The main object" he told Jacobson, "is to preserve the Jewish settlement in Palestine unscarred until after the war. All the rest is *cura posterior.*"[23]

However, during the spring of 1917, with the information reaching Germany that the British were bent on capturing the Zionist movement, Zimmermann, now promoted to Foreign Minister, could no longer afford to play a waiting game. There is incontrovertible evidence to show that he intended to induce the Turkish Government to issue a joint or a simultaneous declaration in favour of unimpeded Jewish immigration and colonization of Palestine. He had good reason to be optimistic since the climate of opinion in Constantinople became more congenial for the Zionists than ever before. Talaat was appointed Grand Vizier and Djavid Bey, a crypto-Jew of the Dönmeh sect, re-entered the Cabinet as Finance Minister. Together they formed a formidable combination. From intercepted correspondence Zimmermann knew that, through Abram Elkus, the American Ambassador in Constantinople, they were conducting secret negotiations with Jacob Schiff for a certain *quid pro quo*. Talaat, even before the War was known to have favoured the Jewish colonization of Palestine and Zimmermann therefore thought that the time was ripe to prevail upon him to forestall the British. However, to Zimmermann's astonishment, Richard Kühlmann, newly appointed German Ambassador in Constantinople, refused categorically even to sound out the Turkish Ministers. Kühlmann feared that the declaration would warm up still further the cordial relations between Turkey and the United States and, since Germany's relations with America were strained at that time,this in his view was undesirable. The entry of the United States into the war against Germany in April, 1917, followed by Turkey's forced severance of diplomatic relations, killed finally the idea of a pro-Zionist declaration. With Zimmermann's resignation in August 1917 and Kühlmann's succession as Secretary of State for Foreign Affairs, prospects for an accomodation with the Zionists dimmed still further.[24]

In contrast to official circles, the German Press began to awaken to the importance of the problem. Thus the *Reichsbote* (May 2, 1917), a Junker weekly, pointed to the strategic importance of Palestine as a bridge between Asia and Africa. England, the paper maintained, was using Zionism to entrench herself in this vital area, and the Central Powers should appropriate the same weapon. "The establishment of a Jewish State under Turkish supremacy would be for us a measure of defence, just as the U-boat is the only possible reply to the English blockade." The *Allgemeine Anzeiger* (August 27, 1917) also asserted that the Palestine question had become an integral part of the Weltpolitik; by meeting Jewish demands, the Central Powers would render the Entente propaganda ineffective. Turkey would benefit economically and Germany would gain "a strong outpost" in the Near East.

[23] C.Z.A., Z3/58, Z3/61, Jacobson to Lichtheim, 9 March, 24, 26 Oct. 1916.
[24] I. Friedman, *op. cit.*, pp. 282–8, 294–5, 297–307, 328.

This thesis was re-echoed by the liberal *Vossische Zeitung*, the *Chemnitzer Volksstimme*, the *Düsseldorfer Generalanzeiger*, the *Leipziger Neueste Nachrichten*, the *Münchener Neueste Nachrichten*, and a score of other leading papers.

The German Press was studied carefully in German and British official circles. But it appears that it made an incomparably greater impact on the latter than on the former. In London it was assumed that if articles in the German Press of almost every political shade were speaking with the same voice then those articles must have been inspired and stimulated by the German Government and reflected its thinking. The British were under the firm impression that the Germans were courting the Zionists and might at any moment publicly identify themselves with the Zionist cause. How deep-rooted was this belief is shown by the fact that Balfour felt obliged to warn the War Cabinet that "the German Government was making great efforts to capture the sympathy of the Zionist Movement."[25] But, as documentary evidence shows, the British Government's concern lest they might be forestalled by the Germans was unfounded. During the late summer and autumn of 1917 the Wilhelmstrasse remained completely uninterested in suggestions made in various quarters that it come out openly in support of the Zionists.

Following the publication of the Balfour Declaration the German Press complained that the Central Powers "missed another opportunity of gaining the support of world Jewry."[26] The German Legation at Berne urged that there was still a great store of confidence in Germany's *Realpolitik* and that the sooner she made a pro-Zionist declaration the better. Matthias Erzberger, the powerful leader of the Zentrum party, also pressed hard and forwarded to the Foreign Ministry a draft declaration. All the same, Wilhelmstrasse maintained that it was in no position to make a unilateral declaration "without *full* consideration for Turkey."[27]

This attitude of *non-possumus* was conditioned by a firm belief that the Entente Powers were bent on the establishment of a Jewish state to deprive Turkey of an important province. With the Turco-German Treaty of Mutual Alliance being re-negotiated at that time, the Germans had to tread warily. One of Turkey's main ambitions was to secure from Germany a guarantee of her territorial integrity and sovereignty. The Turks apparently distrusted Germany also, fearing a German arrangement with the Entente Powers at Turkey's expense. Kühlmann was aware that, unless Germany dispelled

[25] Leonard Stein, *The Balfour Declaration* (London, 1961), pp. 516–7, 543–5; Isaiah Friedman, *The Question of Palestine, 1914–1918, British-Jewish-Arab Relations* (London, New York, 1973), pp. 244–5, 275–7, 286–7.

[26] For a summary of the reaction of the German Press to the Balfour Declaration see *Jüdische Rundschau*, Nr. 52 (28 Dec. 1917).

[27] *Türkei*, 195, K179917–23, Romberg to Hertling, 24 Nov. 1917, dis. no. 3611, and marginalia by Hertling, Richthofen and others; K179939–41, Erzberger to Kühlmann, 30 Nov. 1917.

these suspicions, "the pro-German regime in Turkey may collapse."[28] He therefore avoided any issue which smacked of separatism. However, with regard to Zionism he was mistaken. There was nothing in the text of the Balfour Declaration to indicate that Britain intended to tear Palestine away from Turkey, and the Zionists, with the exception of those in Britain, were quite content to realize their aspirations within the framework of Ottoman sovereignty. Kühlmann's judgement was based on erroneous information. The *Auswärtiges Amt* made the same blunder as the British did by taking the British press reports as a reflection of their adversaries official policy.

The German Government was unable, and from August 1917, after Kühlmann was appointed Foreign Minister unwilling, to rival the British. Yet it cannot be denied that it was chiefly owing to Germany's forceful intervention that the danger which hovered over the Palestinian Jews in 1917 was averted. The chief credit for this must go to Zimmermann. Had it not been for his singular determination nothing would have stopped Djemal Pasha from delivering a crippling blow to the Yishuv.

On March 27, 1917, following the British defeat at Gaza on the previous day, the Turkish local authorities ordered the total evacuation of the civilian population of Jaffa/Tel Aviv and its environs but, since the Arab population was hardly affected by the order and the Christian Germans were exempted, the German Consulate suspected that the only objective of the Turks was to annihilate the Jews. This impression was reinforced following the news of the British defeat at Gaza which invalidated the military justification for the evacuation. Yet, despite strong protests by the German and Austro-Hungarian Consulates, 9,000 Jews were deported. Tel Aviv remained a dead city.

Ten days after Jaffa's evacuation Djemal attempted to make a move on Jerusalem, although no military danger threatened the city. Friedrich Freiherr Kress von Kressenstein, the Chief of Staff, to whom the credit for repelling the British on the Gaza front was mainly due, thought that Djemal's intention bordered on the insane. "The evacuation of Jerusalem would have been a great tactical error and would have involved those concerned in terrifying hazards," he cabled the Military Attaché in Constantinople.

Zimmermann was more effective. On April 26, when he took the matter up with the High Command, he knew what he was doing. The military authorities had little use for diplomatic niceties and on their explicit instructions Enver Pasha, the Ottoman Minister of War, ordered Djemal to cancel the evacuation. Kress was delighted at the defeat of his arch-enemy; even more gratifying was the fact that Jerusalem, at least for the time being, was saved.

Entente propaganda made skillful use of the events in Palestine to blame

[28] *Deutschland*, 128, Nr. 5, Bd. 7, note on Talaat Pasha's visit to Berlin; also *Aide-Mémoire*, 23 Oct. 1917; Kühlmann to Grünau (G.H.Q.), 17 Nov. 1917.

not only the Turks but also the Germans. The news, particularly when described in an exaggerated form, alarmed Jews and non-Jews alike in all parts of the world. The matter was raised in the Reichstag and in the British Parliament. Even the Spanish Government, which was neutral, as well as the Vatican remonstrated with the Turks. The Sublime Porte also disapproved of any atrocities against the Jews. Foreign intervention and the unusual agitation in the Press all over the world had a restraining effect on Djemal but it seems that he was only biding his time. The discovery of the Aaron Aaronsohn spy-ring in October 1917 gave him a long-awaited opportunity to carry out his pernicious design. The ring, which was based on Zichron-Yaakov, was transmitting military information to Egypt in the hope that it would accelerate the British invasion and facilitate recognition of the Jewish claim to Palestine.

Nearly all Palestinian Jews had steered clear of any association with the Aaronsohn group; they felt instinctively that any act of disloyalty to the regime, let alone active assistance to the enemy, was bound to imperil the well-being of the whole community; however bitter they were against their Turkish overlord, no pretext was to be given which could be used against them. The lesson of the Armenian tragedy was well appreciated. In September all relations were severed, and espionage was repeatedly and openly condemned.

But although the majority of Jews were innocent, on November 8, 1917 Djemal summoned Jewish representatives to tell them that he considered all their people guilty of espionage. The Turkish Governor of Haifa warned that "all Jewish colonies will be turned into a heap of ruins." The very survival of the Yishuv now seemed in question. Fortunately, Djemal was recalled to Constantinople and General von Falkenhayn arrived in Jerusalem to take over the High Command of the Ottoman Army. We have some circumstantial evidence that, before leaving for the East, von Falkenhayn was summoned by the Kaiser and instructed to prevail upon Djemal to treat the Jews considerately. On this point von Falkenhayn discharged his mission admirably; only those individuals who were actually involved in espionage were imprisoned; the Jewish community as a whole was exculpated. On December 9th Jerusalem was captured by the British. To their surprise they found that with the exception of Jaffa the Jewish colonies had on the whole survived unscathed. Nor had the population in Jerusalem been bled white as might have been expected. The Zionist leaders duly expressed their deep appreciation of, and gratitude for, the German Government's energetic protection. Particularly moving was Dr. Jacob Thon's acknowledgement:

> . . . We would have suffered irreparable harm had the mighty hand of the German Government not protected us in the hour of danger. Altered circumstances will not make us forget this.

> . . . It was particularly fortunate that in the last critical days the supreme command was in the hands of General Falkenhayn. Had Djemal been responsible, he would, as he had so often threatened, have driven out the population . . . and turned the country into a ruin. We, and the rest of the population . . . must hold Falkenhayn in deep gratitude for having prevented the projected total evacuation and thus preserved the civil population from destruction.[29]

In contrast to Djemal, Talaat Pasha was much more sensitive of Turkey's reputation. On one occasion he gave an unequivocal reassurance to Ambassador Bernstorff: "We have done much harm to the Armenians but we shall do nothing to the Jews."[30] Now with Djemal Pasha bowing out of the scene Talaat was free to take a further step. On December 12, 1917 he received Dr. Julius Becker, a correspondent of the *Vossische Zeitung* and, while dismissing the Balfour Declaration as "*une blague*" pledged to support the Jewish settlement in Palestine and allow unrestricted immigration, though within the economic absorbtive capacity of the country.[31] This declaration enabled the German Government to follow suit. On January 5, 1918, von dem Bussche-Haddenhausen, the Under-Secretary of State, invited the Zionist leaders and made a similar declaration of sympathy.[32] Kühlmann too changed his attitude and gave his blessing to the Jewish delegation (Vereiningung jüdischer Organisationen Deutschlands) V.J.O.D., which had been invited by Talaat to visit Constantinople.[33] However, in spite of Talaat's genuine interest in satisfying the Jews, the results of the negotiations fell short of expectations. Late in 1918 the Turkish forces were beaten by the British and the Ottoman era in Asia came to a close.

No longer inhibited by the need to pay heed to Turkish susceptibilities, the German Government could now unreservedly come out in support of the Zionists. In April 1919, Count Brockdorff-Rantzau, who succeeded Kühlmann as Foreign Minister, declared himself to be in "fundamental agreement" with the Zionist programme which had been presented to the Peace Conference in Paris. It called for "the creation of such political, administrative, and economic conditions in Palestine that would secure its development

[29] The above is based on my article 'German Intervention on Behalf of the *Yishuv*, 1917,' published in Jan. 1971 issue of *Jewish Social Studies*, xxxiii, no. 1, 24–43.

[30] *Türkei*, 195, K179664, Bernstorff to A.A.A., 30 Oct. 1917, tel. no. 1345.

[31] C.Z.A., Z3/11, Becker's report to the E.A.C. (? undated, presumably early in Jan. 1918).

[32] *Norddeutsche Allgemeine Zeitung*, 6 Jan. 1918; *Jüdische Rundschau*, *Jüdische Presse* (11 Jan.).

[33] *Türkei*, 195, K180558, Kühlmann to E.A.C., and to Bernstorff, 10 June 1918 (copy in C.Z.A., Z 3/23). On the foundation of the V.J.O.D. see *Jüdische Rundschau*, Nr. 7 (15 Feb. 1918), pp. 49–50.

into an autonomous Commonwealth (Gemeinwesen)."[34] However, Germany was denied a say at the Peace Conference, while Britain emerged as the chief beneficiary. Germany should nevertheless be given due credit. She was the first European Power to assist the Zionists and protect their enterprise in Palestine. Had it not been for her persistent interventions with the Turkish Government (as well as those of the United States till April 1917), the Yishuv would not have survived. Although, following the Balfour Declaration, the limelight turned on Britain, the service rendered by Germany was of no less monentous import, for in a *judenrein* Palestine the later development of the Jewish National Home would have been very unlikely.

[34] A.A.A., *Geschäftsstelle für die Friedensverhandlungen Judenfrage. 1919.* L 381517, Bergen to the Office for Peace Negotiations, 22 Mar. 1919; L 381507, note, dated Mar. 1919 (confidential); L 381482–3, State Secretary to the Minister of the Interior, 25 Apr. 1919.

Notes on Isaiah

By THEODOR HERZL GASTER
The Dropsie University

1:31 וְהָיָה הֶחָסֹן לִנְעֹרֶת וּפֹעֲלוֹ לְנִיצוֹץ
וּבָעֲרוּ שְׁנֵיהֶם יַחְדָּו וְאֵין מְכַבֶּה

Neither the וּפָעֲלוֹ of LXX and Targum nor the ופעלכם of Vulgate and QIs[A] really removes the oddity of the expression. Taking חסן in the sense of *sturdy tree*, as in Amos 2:9, I would therefore suggest the simple emendation, וְיִפִי עָלָו *and its beauteous leaves* (*cf*. Ezek. 31:3, 8, 9). This yields an exquisite point: the shimmering, sunkissed leaves will now glow only with the sparks of a forest fire or a stroke of lightning.

8:14 וְהָיָה לְמִקְדָּשׁ וּלְאֶבֶן נֶגֶף וּלְצוּר מִכְשׁוֹל
לִשְׁנֵי בָתֵּי יִשְׂרָאֵל וגו׳

It is plain that למקדש does not chime with the sense of the verse, and the emendation לְמַקְשִׁיר scarcely improves matters. May not the true reading be simply וְהָיָה לָמוֹ קָדְשׁוֹ לְאֶבֶן וגו׳, the pronoun למו referring proleptically to שני בתי ישראל and the possessive suffix in קדשו to the העם הזה of vv. 11 and 12? (For the position of למו, which more often comes at the end of a clause, *cf*. Isa. 16:4; Pss. 58:5; 64:6; 119:165; Job 24:17.) Then צור should probably be vocalized צֹר, sharp pebble, although this would be intended, to be sure, as a pun on צור, for the prophet would be playing ironically on the use of צור and אבן (*cf*. Gen. 49:24) as epithets of deity:

> But what it (i. e. the impious people) holds holy will prove for them but a Stone over which they will trip and a Rock against which they will stumble.

9:10 וַיְשַׂגֵּב (l. וישגב) אֶת־צָרֵי רְצִין עָלָיו
וְאֶת־אֹיְבָיו יְסַכְסֵךְ

The verbs have a point which does not seem to have been appreciated. The stricken recalcitrants of the Northern Kingdom have responded to the disaster which has befallen them by crying out grandly (in v. 8 rd., with QIs[A], וַיָּרְעוּ for וידעו), 'Sycamores may have been felled, but we will replace them with cedars!' Taking up this image and applying it ironically, the prophet retorts: 'But what the LORD will cause to tower over them will be—not lofty cedars, but their foes; and he will tangle them—not in the criss-cross of verdant branches, but in the mesh of their enemies!' The verb יסכסך thus contains a subtle double entente, suggesting both (a) סוך, 'spur, incite', and (b) סכך, 'interweave'.

10:1 הוֹי הַחֹקְקִים חִקְקֵי*־אָוֶן וּמְכַתְּבִים עָמָל כִּתֵּבוּ

The reference, I suggest, is not to oppressive lawmakers, as usually understood, but to devious lawyers, who insert 'trick clauses' into deeds in order to defraud the poor and helpless of their rights and property. For חק in the sense of *legal stipulation cf.* Jer. 32:11. Note the effect of the succession of harsh gutturals, as though the prophet were virtually spitting at these miscreants. Approximately:

Fie on them who *d*raw up *d*evilish *d*eeds,
*scr*iveners who *scr*ibble *scr*abbled *scr*eeds!

* Perhaps, as affording a closer parallel to כתבו, we should read חִקְקוּ (=אשר חקקו).

10:4 בִּלְתִּי כָרַע תַּחַת אַסִּיר וְתַחַת הֲרוּגִים יִפֹּלוּ

Lagarde's over-ingenious בֵּלְתִּי כֹרַעַת חַת אֹסִיר (Beltis bends the knee, Osiris collapses) has now itself been brought to its knees. But, surely, no more is needed than simply to vocalize כָּרַע, to take תחת to mean *instead of*, and to construe יִפְּלוּ as = אשר יפלו:

So that you yourselves be not brought to your knees
in place of those you hold captive
and in place of those that fall murdered (at your hands).

10:12 וְהָיָה כִּי־יְבַצַּע אֲדֹנָי אֶת־כָּל־מַעֲשֵׂהוּ
בְּהַר צִיּוֹן וּבִירוּשָׁלִָם אֶפְקֹד עַל־פְּרִי־גֹדֶל לְבַב
מֶלֶךְ־אַשּׁוּר וְעַל־תִּפְאֶרֶת רוּם עֵינָיו

It seems to me that אדני is an incorrect gloss and that the subject is really מלך־אשור, i. e. Sennacherib, who indeed turned back, like Hannibal before Rome, at the very gates of Jerusalem; *cf.* 37:36–37. (The verb יבצע will then be inchoative, i. e. 'when he is about to consummate his exploits/operation'). This explanation enables us to retain MT's אפקד (Vulg. visitabo; 𝔗 אסער) instead of emending it (after LXX's ἐπάξει) to יפקד. —Furthermore, since תפארת here stands parallel to פרי, would it not be more plausible to derive it here from √פאר I (*cf.* Deut. 24:20; nouns פארה, פְּאָרָה) rather than from √פאר II, as is usually done? Tr. 'burgeoning'.

10:16 וְתַחַת כְּבֹדוֹ יֵקַד יְקֹד

Since, in the preceding verses, the prophet has been satirizing expressions used by Assyrian monarchs in their triumphal inscriptions and annals, and since it is now recognized that כבוד can also mean *nimbus, sheen,* is it not possible that this phrase satirizes Sennacherib's boasts about his *melammu,* or kingly 'lustre' (e. g. Taylor Cylinder, ii.35; iii.30), the word תחת then being understood in the sense of *instead of*? The meaning will then be:

and instead of his blazing glory
there will be a blazing fire.

This comports well with the following mention of the אור and להבה of Israel and Israel's God.

11:11 יוֹסִיף י׳ | שֵׁנִית יָדוֹ לִקְנוֹת אֶת־שְׁאָר עַמּוֹ

It is apparent that שנית (which so puzzled the Masoretes that they introduced the warning Paseq!) conceals the verb to which יוסיף is auxiliary and which is variously supplied—if only by paraphrase—in the Versions (LXX: προσθήσει . . . τοῦ δεῖξαι; Vulg.; adjiciet secundo). The emendation, שאת is, however, too facile, for so simple a word would scarcely have been corrupted into something virtually unintelligible, while שַׁנּוֹת*, after Arabic سني, 'be high', substitutes a word unparalleled elsewhere for what is normally expressed in Biblical Hebrew by הרים or נשא. Surely, the right reading is שַׁנֵּת, which occurs in the Elephantine papyri (AP 28.6; Brooklyn 5.3, 7; 8.6, 7, 9; *cf.* E. Kraeling. The Brooklyn Museum Aramaic Papyri [1953], 183) as a technical term (evidently a back-formation and loanword from Akkadian *šindu*) for marking or branding persons as chattels and which corresponds to the Akkadian *ritta šaṭāru* (*cf.* R. P. Dougherty, The Shirkûtu of Babylonian Deities [1923], 82 f.; A. L. Oppenheim, in BASOR 93 [1944], 14 f.). This accords perfectly with לקנות. (The suffix in ידו refers, of course, to שאר עמו, not to God, and the expression is paralleled by וזה יכתב ידו ליהוה in 44.5.)

14:12 נִגְדַּעְתָּ לָאָרֶץ חוֹלֵשׁ עַל־גּוֹיִם

(LXX: ὁ ἀποστέλλων [= השולח!] πρὸς πάντα τὰ ἔθνη; Vulg.: qui vulnerabis gentes; 𝔗 דהותא קטול בעממיא.)

For these notoriously difficult words, which have been variously interpreted, I suggest the emendation, עֱלִי חוֹלֵשׁ גּוֹיִם, 'Pestle that has been pounding (whole) nations,' taking חולש as equivalent by metathesis to Akkadian *ḫašālu,* Arabic حسل, Syr. ܚܫܠ. The picture is, of course, that of inflicting crushing defeats. A perfect parallel occurs in Jer. 50:23 (likewise addressed to the King of Babylon!):

אֵיךְ נִגְדַּע וַיִּשָּׁבֵר פַּטִּישׁ כָּל־הָאָרֶץ.

14:26 זֹאת הָעֵצָה הַיְּעוּצָה עַל־כָּל־הָאָרֶץ
וְזֹאת הַיָּד הַנְּטוּיָה עַל־כָּל־הַגּוֹיִם

This is usually taken to refer to God's designs, but does it not make for a more effective point if it be read as a jibe at the ambitions of Sennacherib, the ensuing verse being the prophet's retort:

So this is what has become of the scheme
devised against the whole earth,
this of the hand that was poised to strike
the nations all!
Aye, but when 'tis the LORD of Hosts
draws up the scheme,
when His is the hand that is poised to strike,
who can turn it back?

(Note that the traditional title, י׳ צבאות is here used with special point, as if to designate the LORD as the only effective commander-in-chief!)

15:9 כִּי מֵי דִימוֹן מָלְאוּ דָם
כִּי־אָשִׁית עַל־דִּימוֹן נוֹסָפוֹת

This is usually taken to mean that God will yet heap additional disasters on Dîmôn. But, seeing that מלאו is obviously used here in the specific sense of *be at floodtide* (*cf.* Akkadian *milû*; Mari, ARM iv.23.14 *nârum mali-ma*; *ibid.*, iii.9.5 *milum ša nârim*; Syr. ܡܠܬܐ;? so also Ps. 73:10 וּמֵי מָלֵא יִמָּצוּ לָמוֹ), may not נוספות have the meaning, 'additional waters, overflow,' thus continuing the metaphor?

ibid. לִפְלֵיטַת מוֹאָב אַרְיֵה וְלִשְׁאֵרִית אֲדָמָה

This oft-emended verse can make sense, I suggest, by the simple re-vocalization, וְלַשְּׁאֵרִית:

For those of Moab that escape
there will be lions (in wait),
and for those that are left behind
—only the (bare) soil!

The mention of the two different fates is then peculiarly effective.

19:13 פִּנַּת שְׁבָטֶיהָ

(LXX: κατὰ φυλάς; Vulg.: angulum populorum ejus; 𝔗: רבני פלכה).

Since this prophecy against Egypt contains several Egyptianisms by way of lending local color (see below), it may perhaps be suggested that פנת is here an imitation of Egyptian *ḳnb.t*, from *ḳnb*, 'cornerpiece, angle,' in the specific sense of 'bureaucracy, body of officials;' Anglicè, 'kingpins.'

⟦I append a rendering of the passage, vv. 1–15:

1 See, here comes the LORD
charioting swiftly[a] on a cloud,
headed for E g y p t !

No sooner will He appear
than E g y p t ' s idle idols
will be rocked upon their heels,
and E g y p t ' s heart dissolve in its breast.

2 I will incite[b] the E g y p t i a n s
against one another,
and they will be locked in battle
each man against his brother,
each man against his neighbor,
city against city,
kingdom against kingdom.

3 The spirit of E g y p t
will be emptied out of his breast,
and I will confound his design(s).
They will go seeking counsel
from (those) idle idols (of theirs),
from spooks and ghosts and warlocks.

4 But I will hand over[c] the E g y p t i a n s
to a harsh lord,
and a cruel king will bear rule over them,"
quoth the (only true) lord,[d]
the LORD of Hosts.

5 E g y p t ' s lake(s)[e] will be drained,
her River run dry and parched;

6 her waterways will reek,
the branches of the Nile
will dwindle and go dry.[f]

Rush and reed[g] will shrivel;
7 the sedges[h] beside the Nile,
there on the edge of the Nile,
and all that is sown beside the Nile
will wither and disappear,
blown on the wind.

8 The fishermen will moan,
and all the anglers in the Nile will mourn,
and all the trawlers languish.

9 They that *dress* the flax
will find themselves in dis*tress*;[i]
the women that card[j] and the men that weave
become white as sheets.[k]

10 The pillars of the realm[l]
will be pounded to dust;
all that construct the dams
themselves become sloughs of despond.[m]

11 AH, what dolts ye be,
ye princes there in Tanis,
Pharaoh's master-minds
who have given him such counsel
as has proven a counsel of folly!
How can you go saying to Pharaoh,
'Scion of ancient kings,
every man of us here
is a scion of sages!'

12 Where, then, are they now, (O Pharaoh,)
those master-minds of yours?
Pray let them tell you now
(for, surely, they should know!)
what plans the LORD of Hosts
has been drawing up against E g y p t !

13 Nay, they are proven dolts,
those princes there in Tanis;
proven dupes they are,
those princes there in Memphis,
Those kingpins of her tribes
have been leading Egypt astray.

14 The LORD has been brewing within them
a spirit to set men awhirl,
and they have led Egypt astray
in all that she has been doing,
reeling like a drunkard in his vomit.

15 And now there will be nothing that Egypt can do,
stricken like a beast from head to tail,
blasted like a plant bulb and stem![n]

---

a. The word קל must refer to the LORD, not to the cloud, since it is elsewhere used only of animate beings. Moreover, clouds are represented in Semitic literature as the chariots, not the steeds, of gods.

b. The Heb. verb וסכסכתי may, however, here have the meaning of *entangle*, which would comport more closely with the etymological meaning of the parallel ונלחמו (*cf.* Arabic لحم, *be interlocked*).

c. Heb. וסכרתי. The verb is usually explained as a variant of הסגיר *sensu* 'deliver up', or as a corruption of ומכרתי. But perhaps the prophet chose this odd form deliberately to suggest שכר, *be a hireling*, which would comport neatly with אדנים.

d. האדון here stands in pointed contrast to the mortal אדנים.

e. ים is here used in the sense of E. g., š3, Arabic بحر.

f. וחרבו seems to be a hypermetrical gloss.

g. סוף = E. g., *ṯwf*.

h. ערות = E. g., *ʿrw*.

i. This rendering is intended to reproduce the pun, פשתים . . . בוש. The latter here means, *be disappointed*.

j. Reading שְׂרֻקוֹת for שְׂרִיקוֹת.

k. Heb. חורי. Since the whole point of this passage is to describe the fate of Egypt's laborers and craftsmen in terms ironically applicable to their very products, the word חורי, *white stuff*, is clearly le mot juste, and the variant חָוָרוּ, 'grow pale', is a banal 'emendation.'

l. The following מְדֻכָּאִים shows that שתותיה must mean *pillars* or *bases*, rather than *spinners*. Moreover, the masc. form of מְדֻכָּאִים shows that the word is used metaphorically, to denote dignitaries, or persons of (seemingly) stable position.

m. Heb. כל־עשי שכר אגמי־נפש. I have preferred this traditional rendering because it accords neatly with אגמי נפש, if the latter be taken as a bold metaphor, connected with אגם, 'marsh, swamp,' i. e., spiritual morasses. Bunyan's 'slough of despond' would then best reproduce the sense. However, LXX and Pesh. read שֵׁכָר, which would then refer specifically to the drink called σίκερι made from barley grown beside the Nile (*cf.* Herodotus i. 77;

Diodorus Siculus, i. 34). In that case, אגמי would derive from √אגם, עגם, *be gloomy*, and the general sense would be, 'They that brew the cup that cheers will themselves be gloomy and glum.' But √עשה is nowhere used of preparing drinks.

n. The simile recurs at 9.13. I have filled it out, to convey the point.

24:15

עַל־כֵּן בָּאֻרִים כַּבְּדוּ י'

בְּאִיֵּי הַיָּם שֵׁם י'* אֱלֹהֵי יִשְׂרָאֵל

---

* dl. mtr. gr.

There is no need to emend בָּאֻרִים. First: it provides the perfect antithesis to עָרְבָה כָּל־שִׂמְחָה, 'all joy has met its dusk,' in v. 11: those that have fled to the islands smugly think themselves safe and sing their hallelujahs there where all is light! Second: it may be suggested that there is here an ironic allusion to the widespread belief in Isles of the Blest, situated where the sun either rises or sets and therefore bathed in light; *cf.* the Classical descriptions in Pindar, Ol. ii.68 f.; Diodorus, i.39; Valerius Flaccus, i.844 f., and for parallels, *cf.* T. H. Gaster, Myth, Legend and Custom in the Old Testament (1969), §§ 12–13; A. Graf, La leggende del paradiso terrestre (1878). Gilgamesh (v. 47) comes upon such a faery garden (*ḫiṣṣu*) where the sun rises, and there seems to be an allusion to it also in Ps. 36:7–10 (*cf.* especially, 10b: בְּאוֹרְךָ נִרְאֶה־אוֹר; Gaster, *op. cit.*, § 259). These islands are characterized by singing (*cf.* Euripides, *Hippolytus*, 741 f.; Valerius Flaccus, *loc. cit.*), and are the glorious abodes of the righteous and of heroes. (Note that in later Greek legend Achilles was said to have been translated to the isle of Leukē, i. e. 'Bright', variously located.) All this chimes perfectly with what the prophet says: the refugees sing at the top of their voices (vv. 14, 16) in regions of light situated in the islands (v. 15) at the far bourne of the earth (v. 16), and what they chant are the self-congratulatory words, צְבִי לַצַּדִּיק, which do not refer (as commonly interpreted) to God in the sense of 'Glory be to the Righteous One,' but mean simply, 'what beauty (radiance) the righteous enjoys!' and which evoke the prophet's prompt retort, 'But what I say is, Woe, woe! What hypocrites they are, what deep-dyed hypocrites!'

(v. 16:

וָאֹמַר רָזִי־לִי רָזִי־לִי אוֹי לִי בֹּגְדִים* בָּגָדוּ וּבֶגֶד† בּוֹגְדִים* בָּגָדוּ)

---

* Or read, LXX, with אוֹי לַבֹּגְדִים ? † ?rd. בֶּגֶד (dittogr.).

24:23 וְחָפְרָה הַלְּבָנָה וּבוֹשָׁה הַחַמָּה
כִּי־מָלַךְ י׳ צְבָאוֹת בְּהַר צִיּוֹן וּבִירוּשָׁלַםִ
וְנֶגֶד זְקֵנָיו כָּבוֹד

כבוד should here be understood in the not uncommon sense of *nimbus*, *sheen* (Akkadian *melammu*) of divinity. The meaning is:

When the LORD of Hosts has installed Himself as king
 on Mount Zion and in Jerusalem,
such a glow will stream o'er His court (lit. elders)
 that the moon will be put to shame,
 and the sun abashed.

26:16 י׳* בַּצַּר פְּקָדוּךָ צָקוּן לַחַשׁ מוּסָרְךָ לָמוֹ

* י׳ is an anacrusis extra metrum.

Locus conclamatus. But is it really so hopeless? צָקוּן is obviously needed to balance בַּצַּר, so that the common rendering, 'They poured out a whispered prayer'—at best, a pis aller—ruins the parallelism. We can, I think, make perfect sense by giving to לחש the not uncommon meaning, *magical spell*. The sense will then be:

LORD, when they were in straits,
 then they took thought of Thee [*cf*. Hos. 5:15];
hard-pressed though indeed they had been,
 Thy chastisement acted upon them (lit. was to them)
(like) a magical spell!

The 'magic' consisted in the fact—described in the ensuing verses—that men who had been dead to God, no better than corpses, sprang to new life and that the devastated earth was quickened as by the shimmering dew of morn. Whereas, aforetime, for all their travail, there had been no assurance of progeny, now the very shades seemed to have been revived!

In v. 19 the suffix in מֵתֶיךָ refers to God, i. e., 'men who were dead to Thee,' and that in נְבֵלָתִי to the prophet's own countrymen. This is shown by the fact that throughout the prophecy the 2nd. sg. suffixes refer uniformly to the LORD, never to the people. Hence, the verse is not (as usually interpreted) God's reassurance to the latter, but rather the prophet's exclamation of joy, addressed to them.

[[The following free rendering will bring out what I take to be the sense of the entire passage, vv. 13–19:

13 LORD, though other lords there be
have held us in their thrall,
Thee only will we celebrate
and on Thy name will call.

14 For they—they are but as the dead
which cannot come alive;
and, being naught but listless shades
which never can revive,
they lie beneath Thy punishment
extinct without a trace,
and all remembrance of their name,
O LORD, Thou dost efface;

15 while Thou Thyself art glorified;
this folk, at Thy command,
is grown apace; Thou spreadest far
the borders of its land.

16 LORD, when troubles pressed them, then
their minds to Thee were bent,
and now to a magic spell for them
is turned Thy chastisement.

17 Stricken by Thee we were, O LORD,
like them with child that cry
and writhe in agonies of birth
when that their time is nigh.

18 But though the throes had come on us,
naught bore we but the wind,
nor did there ever come to birth
new heirs for lost mankind,
nor for the devastated earth
could we salvation find.

19 Yet now, they that were dead to Thee
are sprung to life anew;
my countrymen that corpses were
are risen, for a dew,
a glinting dew has come to them,
like to the dew of morn,
and bathed the earth, and from it spring
the listless shades reborn!]]

27:7

בְּסַאסְּאָה בְּשַׁלְחָהּ תְּרִיבֶנָּה
הָגָה בְּרוּחוֹ הַקָּשָׁה בְּיוֹם קָדִים

Anyone with a modicum of sense or taste recognizes at once that to render בסאסאה (virtually, 'peck by peck,' if connected with סאה) as 'measure by measure' in a figurative sense is untenable. I suggest the following interpretation:

(*a*) סאסאה is onomatopoeic, like Latin *susurrus*, indicating the soughing of the wind.

(*b*) The suffix in בשלחהּ refers proleptically to רוחו, and the verb is employed in the same sense as in Ps. 104:30, תְּשַׁלַּח רוּחֲךָ.

(*c*) The subject of תריבנה is רוחו, and the suffix is that of the emphatic, as in תשברנה in v. 11, תרמסנה in 26:6, and תשלחנה in Judg. 5:26.

(*d*) הגה means *make a murmuring sound, rumble*, not *drive*, the subject being God.

Thus the meaning will be:

When He rumbles with His dire wind
what time He launches it
on a day of monsoon(s),
'tis but with a gentle soughing
that it vents itself on (lit. contends with) *him* (i. e. Israel).

29:22

לָכֵן כֹּה־אָמַר י׳ אֶל־בֵּית יַעֲקֹב
אֲשֶׁר פָּדָה אֶת־אַבְרָהָם
לֹא־עַתָּה יֵבוֹשׁ יַעֲקֹב
וְלֹא עַתָּה פָּנָיו יֶחֱוָרוּ
כִּי בִרְאֹתוֹ יְלָדָיו
מַעֲשֵׂה יָדַי בְּקִרְבּוֹ
יַקְדִּישׁוּ שְׁמִי
וְהִקְדִּישׁוּ אֶת־קְדוֹשׁ יַעֲקֹב
וְאֶת־אֱלֹהֵי יִשְׂרָאֵל יַעֲרִיצוּ

Just as God once redeemed Jacob's forebear, so will He now redeem his offspring. The suffix in בראתו is objective and refers proleptically to מעשה ידי, while in the final lines of the passage, יעקב and ישראל refer to the patriarch. Thus, the sense will be:

Wherefore, thus says the LORD,
    the same who redeemed Abraham,
unto the household of Jacob:
'Now need Jacob not feel ashamed
    and now need he not blench,
for when his offspring see it—
    (see) what I do in their (lit. his) midst,
they will know that I am there
in all My holiness,*
and they then will hold to be holy
    Him whom Jacob held holy,
and Him will they hold in awe
    whom Israel knew as his god.'

* Lit. will hold My name holy. The 'name' is the visible presence.

30:1 וְלִנְסֹךְ מַסֵּכָה וְלֹא רוּחִי
לְמַעַן סְפוֹת* חַטָּאת עַל־חַטָּאת

Is it too fanciful to suppose that the prophet is here playing on the word חוט, 'thread', the sense being:

weaving a tangled web
    which no spirit of Mine designed,
minded but to add *sin* to *sin*
    like *skein* to *skein*?

* Probably rd. סֶפֶת (from √יסף).

30:31 כִּי־מִקּוֹל י׳ יֵחַת אַשּׁוּר בַּשֵּׁבֶט יַכֶּה

To take בשבט יכה as referring to the LORD spoils the point. *Assyria*, which has been flailing around with its rod, will collapse at the mere sound of the LORD's voice!

31:2 וְגַם־הוּא חָכָם וַיָּבֵא רָע
וְאֶת־דְּבָרָיו לֹא הֵסִיר

These words occur in a prophecy denouncing Egypt. Accordingly, may not חכם here be a pointed jibe at the wizards of that land, the word being used in the specific sense which it bears in such passages as Gen. 41:8;

Exod. 7:11 (= Eg. *rḥ 'iḫ.t*)? The words וַיָּבֵא רַע will then allude to the working of 'black magic':

But He too is a master magician,
and (once before) brought ill-hap,
and when once He had cast His spell,
did not then reverse it.

The following יַטֶּה יָדוֹ (v. 3), though meaning primarily, 'will launch His attack,' may then also contain a subtle double entente, alluding at the same time to the magical gesture of extending the hand or wand (*cf.* Exod. 7:19; 8:1, 2, 12, 13; 14:16, 26, etc.).

31:6 שׁוּבוּ לַאֲשֶׁר הֶעְמִיקוּ סָרָה בְּנֵי יִשְׂרָאֵל

Is there here a play on words?

32:17 וְהָיָה מַעֲשֵׂה הַצְּדָקָה שָׁלוֹם וַעֲבֹדַת הַמִּשְׁפָּט* הַשְׁקֵט וָבֶטַח

* MT erroneously repeats הצדקה, but see the preceding verse.

This is usually rendered, 'the work of righteousness and the effect of justice,' but this misses the point. Justice, we are told, will make its home in the מדבר, or pasture-land, and righteousness (or lawfulness) will dwell in the כרמל, or region of orchards. Hence מעשה has the specific sense of עשה פרי and עבודה of עבודת האדמה, viz., yield and tilth.

33:8 הֵפֵר בְּרִית מָאַס עָרִים לֹא חָשַׁב אֱנוֹשׁ

For ערים QIs[A] has עדים. It should be noted, however, that this is not עֵדִים, *witnesses*, but the word עדי, *treaty*, *pact* (Akkadian *adû*) of the Sujin Inscription.—אנוש here bears the sense of Arabic أنس, 'human, social relations.'

33:18 לִבְּךָ יֶהְגֶּה אֵימָה אַיֵּה סֹפֵר אַיֵּה שֹׁקֵל וגו'

For אֵימָה I suggest אַיֵּמֹה = אַיֵּמוֹ, 'where are they (now)?'

38:20 יהוה לְהוֹשִׁיעֵנִי וּנְגִינוֹתַי נְנַגֵּן
כָּל־יְמֵי חַיֵּינוּ עַל־בֵּית י'

Metri gratia I propose להוש' <הָיָה לִי> יהוה—error through double haplography; *cf.* Jer. 15:20; 30:11; 42:11; Pss. 31:4; 71:3.—Then for the difficult עַל־בֵּית יְ׳ read (error again due to haplography) נַעֲלֶה בֵּית יְ׳, for *cf.*, in the very next verse, כִּי אֶעֱלֶה בֵּית יְ׳:

> The LORD <has been here> to save me,
> wherefore let us sing songs which I shall compose,
> make pilgrimages to His temple
> throughout our lives.

40:5 וְנִגְלָה כְּבוֹד יְ׳

Once more, כבוד means *sheen*. The sense is not that hills and ridges will lower themselves in deference to the LORD, but rather to permit an unobstructed view of His splendor as it emerges like the rising sun.

40:6 כָּל־הַבָּשָׂר חָצִיר וְכָל־חַסְדּוֹ כְּצִיץ הַשָּׂדֶה

H. L. Ginsberg (orally) has made a spirited defense of MT, claiming that what is meant is that man's loyalty is no more than fading grass. However, for חסדו LXX has δόξα, Vulg. gloria, 𝔗 תוקפא. Various emendations have been proposed, e.g. חסנו, חמדו, הדרו. Surely, what the context requires is חֶלְדּוֹ, *its continuance, permanence; cf.* Pss. 39:6; 89:48; Job 11:17; Arabic خلد.

43:13 גַּם־מִיּוֹם אֲנִי הוּא וְאֵין מִיָּדִי מַצִּיל
אֶפְעַל וּמִי יְשִׁיבֶנָּה

The word מיום is a notorious crux. LXX's ἀπ' ἀρχῆς, Vulgate's ab initio, and 𝔗's מעלמא are mere paraphrases. If, however, the passage be transcribed into 'Qumran script', the true reading at once emerges: by the loss of a single tag, the original אֲצַוֶּהוּ, was misread, אני הו(א). Hence render:

> Once I give the command,
> no one can snatch from My hand;
> when I act, who can reverse it?

כִּי־
57:1 מִפְּנֵי הָרָעָה נֶאֱסַף הַצַּדִּיק
יָבוֹא שָׁלוֹם יָנוּחוּ עַל־מִשְׁכְּבוֹתָם
הוֹלֵךְ נְכֹחוֹ

May not the first part of this verse be a popular tag, to which the second gives the prophet's rejoinder? Reading, with Graetz, יָנוּחַ עַל־מִשְׁכָּבוֹ תָּם

and giving to בוא the specific sense of *come home in the evening* (used both of men and of cattle), as in Arabic بَا and as occasionally in OT (e. g. Deut. 33:7; Zeph. 3:20) the meaning will be:

Although when evil wields its sway,
  righteous men are whisked away,
yet, the simple man who walks
  direct and straight ahead
comes safely home at last to lie
  tranquil on his bed.

57:13 בְּזַעֲקֵךְ יַצִּילֻךְ קִבּוּצַיִךְ

A subtle double entente: On the one hand, קִבּוּצַיִךְ, may be explained from two Ugaritic instances of *qbṣ in* the sense of a *company of 'shades or quasi-deified beings'* (*qbṣ rp'im*; III Krt iii.14, RŠ 34.126, 3.10) and, on the other, as in Mic. 1:7, in the sense of 'immoral gains which you have amassed.' A double rendering will best bring out the point:

When you cry out (in anguish),
let those idol hordes of yours
—yes, your idle hoards—
come to your rescue!

58:11 וְהִשְׂבִּיעַ בְּצַחְצָחוֹת נַפְשֶׁךָ
וְעַצְמֹתֶיךָ יַחֲלִיץ וְהָיִיתָ כְּגַן רָוֶה
וּכְמוֹצָא* מַיִם אֲשֶׁר לֹא־יְכַזְּבוּ מֵימָיו

* ? rd., metri gratia, וכְ<מו>מוֹצָא (haplogr.).

Taking צחצחות to mean *parched places*, I would interpret חלץ as equivalent, by metathesis, to Arabic خضل, *bedew*, thus continuing the metaphor.

61:2 לִקְרֹא שְׁנַת־רָצוֹן לי' וְיוֹם נָקָם לֵאלֹהֵינוּ

The meaning would seem to be improved if רצון be taken here (from רצה II, pay off) in the sense of *clearance of debts*. The LORD will play the role of a *go'el* in the year of jubilee:

to proclaim that this is the year
  when the LORD will settle accounts,
and the day when our God will take vengeance.

61:3 מַעֲטֵה תְהִלָּה תַּחַת רוּחַ כֵּהָה

The antithesis surely demands that תְּהִלָּה be here derived from √הלל I (= Ar. هلّ), *shine* (as again in Habakkuk 3.3) rather than from √הלל II, *praise*.

63:3 אֲנִי מְדַבֵּר בִּצְדָקָה רַב לְהוֹשִׁיעַ

For רַב we must read רָב (*cf.* Vulg. propugnator [LXX κρίσιν=ריב]), as more consonant with the context. The words צדקה and הושיע here carry the military nuance of *victory;*; *cf.* ישע/ישועה ‖ צדקה|/צדק, Isa. 45:8; 51:5, 6, 8; 56:1; 61:10; 65:6. *Cf.* also 45:21 אֵל צַדִּיק וּמוֹשִׁיעַ; Zech. 9:9. צַדִּיק וְנוֹשָׁע and, especially, Isa. 19:20 מוֹשִׁיעַ וָרָב.—The word מְדַבֵּר likewise bears the military nuance of *issue orders*, like Akkadian *qibita qabû*. Thus the sense is:

I am He
Who never gives a command
    but unto victory,
Who never takes up the fight
    but that He wins the day!

63:6 וְאָבוּס (וָא *l.*) עַמִּים בְּאַפִּי וַאֲשַׁכְּרֵם (וָא *l.*) בַּחֲמָתִי

The word ואשכרם is inapposite since it is the nations who are themselves the trodden grapes. Nor is the variant ואשברם any better, for שבר can scarcely describe the trampling. I would therefore suggest וָאֲכַשְּׁרֵם* 'and crushed them,' after Arabic كسر. The fact that this word does not recur in OT would readily have caused the corruption.

65:4 הַיֹּשְׁבִים בַּקְּבָרִים וּבַנְּצוּרִים יָלִינוּ

For בנצורים LXX has ἐν τοῖς σπηλαίοις; Vulg., in delubris idolorum, and 𝔗, paraphrastically, עם פגרי אנשא. Ehrlich has already suggested וּבֵין צֻרִים. As affording a better parallel, I would propose וּבֵין צְרִ<חִ>ים, 'and among vaults'; *cf.* I Sam. 13:6; Nabat. צריחא; Arabic ضريح.

NEB's 'keeping vigil all night long' is over-ingenious, for √נצר always contains the nuance of *guard*, *protect* and is never used of keeping a religious vigil.

66:11, 12, 14 לְמַעַן תִּינְקוּ וּשְׂבַעְתֶּם מִשֹּׁד (מִשֵּׁד *l.*) תַּנְחֻמֶיהָ
לְמַעַן תָּמֹצּוּ וְהִתְעַנַּגְתֶּם מִזִּיו כְּבוֹדָהּ

. . . .

וִינַקְתֶּם . . . .

וּרְאִיתֶם וְשָׂשׂ לִבְּכֶם וְעַצְמוֹתֵיכֶם כַּדֶּשֶׁא תִפְרַחְנָה

The context suggests that וראיתם should here be understood as = וּרְוִיתֶם. *Cp.* similarly 53:11 מֵעֲמַל נַפְשׁוֹ יִרְאֶה || יִשְׂבָּע בְּדַעְתּוֹ; Ps. 91:16 אֹרֶךְ יָמִים אַשְׂבִּיעֵהוּ || וְאַרְאֵהוּ בִּישׁוּעָתִי; *cf.* also Ps. 60:5 הִרְאִיתָה עַמְּךָ קָשָׁה || הִשְׁקִיתָנוּ יַיִן תַּרְעֵלָה.

66:24 וְיָצְאוּ וְרָאוּ

In view of the preceding יָבוֹא כָל־בָּשָׂר לְהִשְׁתַּחֲוֹת לְפָנַי, it seems to me that **יצא** here bears the technical nuance of *go out in a religious procession*, as in the Akkadian noun *ṣītu*.

ibid. כִּי תוֹלַעְתָּם לֹא תָמוּת וְאִשָּׁם לֹא תִכְבֶּה
וְהָיוּ דֵרָאוֹן לְכָל־בָּשָׂר

The usual rendering, 'Their worm shall not die nor their fire be quenched' misses the point, which is that what will meet their eyes is a pile of recent corpses—so recent that the worms will still be gnawing on them and the pyres still smouldering.—Note too the irony of the words לכל־בשר: the burning flesh will be a thing from which all *living* flesh will recoil in horror (*cf.* Arabic درأ).

Edom, Israel and Amos—An Unrecognized Source for Edomite History

By ROBERT GORDIS
Jewish Theological Seminary

Only those who were privileged to know Dr. Zeitlin intimately learned to love him for his personal qualities, his warm friendship and loyalty, and his genuine concern for the well-being of others. "He was my friend, faithful and just to me." This study in biblical history and literature is offered as a tribute to one of the great Jewish historians of the twentieth century.

The following works will be cited below by author and page:

James Barr, *Comparative Philology and The Text of the Old Testament* (Oxford, 1968); J. R. Bartlett, "The Rise and Fall of the Kingdom of Edom," *PEQ* (104), 1972, 26–37; Francis Brown, S. R. Driver, Charles A. Briggs, *A Hebrew and English Lexicon of the Old Testament* (Boston, New York: 1907) = BDB; S. R. Driver, *Introduction to the Literature of the Old Testament*, 12th edition (New York: Scribner, 1906); Otto Eissfeldt, *The Old Testament: An Introduction*, trans. by Peter R. Ackroyd (New York: Harper and Row, 1965); L. Finkelstein, *The Pharisees* (Philadelphia: Jewish Publication Society, 1938), 2 vols.; M. Fishbane, "The Treaty Background of Amos 1:11 and Related Matters," *JBL*, 89, 1970, 313–18; Gesenius-Kautzsch, *Hebräische Grammatik* (Leipzig: Vogel, 1888), 25th edition; N. Glueck, *The Other Side of the Jordan* (Phila.: JPSA, 1940); *idem*, art. "Edom" in *Encyclopedia Miqrait* (Jerusalem: Mosad Bialik, 1950), 91–98; *idem*, "*Ezion-Geber*," *BA* 29, 1965, 70–87; R. Gordis, "The Composition and Structure of Amos," in *Harvard Theological Review*, 33 (1944), 239–51, cited as Gordis, Composition, reprinted in R. Gordis, *Poets, Prophets and Sages: Essays in Biblical Interpretation* = *PPS* (Bloomington, Ind.: Indiana University Press, 1971), 217–229; *idem*, "The Heptad as an Element in Biblical and Rabbinic Style," in *JBL*, 62 (1943), 17–26, cited as Gordis, Heptad, reprinted in *PPS*, 95–103; *idem*, *The Word and The Book, Studies in Biblical Language and Literature* (New York: KTAV, 1976) = WB; M. Haran, "Observations of the Historical Background of Amos 1:2–2:6," in *Israel Exploration Journal*, 18, 4, 1968; W. R. Harper, *Amos and Hosea, International Critical Commentary* (New York: Scribners, 1905); A. S. Kapelrud, *Central Ideas in Amos* (Oslo: Oslo University Press, 1961); Y. Kaufmann, *Toledot Haʾemunah Hayisreʾelit* (Tel-Aviv: Mosad Bialik, 1937–56), 7 vols.; *idem*, *The Religion of Israel* (Chicago: University of Chicago Press, 1960), Eng. abridgment and translation by M. Greenberg; R. Kittel, ed., *Biblia Hebraica*, 4th edition (Stuttgart: Privileg. Würt. Bibelanstalt, 1937) = BH: E. Hammershaimb, *The Book of Amos—A Commentary*, trans. John Sturdy (Oxford: Basil Blackwell, 1970); L. Koehler and W. Baumgartner, *Lexicon in Veteris Testamenti Libros* (Leiden: Brill, 1951) = KB; H. McKeating, *The Books of Amos, Hosea and Micah*, Cambridge Bible Commentary (Cambridge University Press, 1971); *The New English Bible with the Apocrypha* (Oxford: Cambridge, 1970) = *NEB*; R. H. Pfeiffer, *Introduction to the Old Testament* (New York: Harper, 1948); J. B. Pritchard, *Ancient Near Eastern Texts Relating to the Old Testament* (Princeton, 1955), 2nd ed., cited as *ANET; Revised*

Standard Version; cited as *RSV*; W. M. W. Roth, "The Numerical Sequence X/X+1 in the Old Testament," *VT*, 12, 1962; Georg Sauer, *Die Sprüche Agurs, Untersuchungen zur Herkunft Verbreitung und Bedeutung einer biblischen Stilform* (BWANT 84, 1963); W. Schmidt, "Die Deuteronomistische Redaktion des Amosbuches," *ZAW*, 1965, 168–93; W. R. Smith, *Prophets of Israel* (Edinburgh, E. and T. Clark, 1902); N. H. Snaith, *Amos, Hosea and Micah* (London: Epworth Press, 1956); E. A. Speiser, *Genesis, Anchor Bible* (New York: Doubleday, 1964); James M. Ward, *Amos and Isaiah* (Nashville, New York: Abingdon, 1969); J. D. W. Watts, *Vision and Prophecy in Amos* (Leiden: Brill, 1958); Artur Weiser, *Das Buch der Zwölf kleinen Propheten* (ATD, 1963); *idem*, *Die Profetie des Amos* (Giessen: Töpelmann, 1929); H. W. Wolff, *Amos the Prophet, The Man and His Background*, trans. by F. R. Curley (Phila.: Fortress Press, 1973).

I

The relationship of Israel and Edom throughout history was both intimate and ambivalent. Always there was a consciousness of close kinship, but generally it was neutralized by an attitude of strong antagonism. Their mutual attitude is well symbolized by two roots used in *Genesis* in connection with Jacob during his contacts with Esau, וַיֵּאָבֵק "he wrestled with him,"[1] and וַיְחַבְּקֵהוּ "he embraced him."[2]

In point of fact, the entire relationship of Edom and Israel is epitomized in two oracles in *Genesis* involving Esau. When Rebecca, suffering the pains of a difficult pregnancy, "inquires of God," she is told:

"Two nations are in your womb,
two peoples at odds while still in your bosom.
But one people shall surpass the other
and the older shall serve the younger."[3]

The second oracle is Isaac's belated blessing of Esau:

"Your home shall be far from the earth's riches,
and the dew of heaven above.
By your sword you shall live,
and your brother you shall serve.
But as you grow restive,
you shall throw off his yoke from your neck."[4]

There are three implications in the first oracle: First, Jacob and Esau are closer than ordinary brothers, for they are twins. Second, Esau is older than Jacob. The inference is that Edom developed its state and government as a people before Israel, a conclusion expressly stated in the famous passage: "These are the kings who reigned in the land of Edom, before any king reigned over the Israelites."[5] Third, Jacob, the younger brother, will succeed to the prerogatives of the first-born. In national terms, Israel will have hegemony over Edom.

The second oracle adds two details: Edom will live in a basically barren area and be forced to earn his livelihood by preying upon the caravans going through his territory. Finally, there will be a time (or times) when Edom will be able to throw off the yoke of vassalage that Israel has imposed upon it. It is noteworthy that Edom is not being promised rule over Israel, only that the foreign overlordship will be terminated.

This ambivalent relationship of kinship-hostility characterized the subsequent history of the two peoples. The Israelites, wandering through the desert on the way to the Promised Land, were denied passage through Edom's territory, but no warlike measures were taken against Edom.[6] Glueck's excavations have revealed a network of fortifications on Edom's southern and eastern borders.[7] Hence an Israelite incursion into the land would have been difficult if not impossible.[8] When the same negative

[1] Gen. 32:25. The Midrash associates the verb also with Esau, since it identifies the man who wrestled with Jacob at night as שרו של עשו, "the tutelary angel of Esau" (*Mid. Gen. Rabba*, 77, 3).

[2] Gen. 33:4.

[3] Translation of Speiser, 193. He calls attention to the fact that in Akkadian law *māru rabū*, the elder son, received an inheritance double that of *māru seḫrū*—a practice Speiser equates with the law in Deut. 21:16 f. To be sure, the terms used in the biblical oracle and in Akkadian are identical, and both reflect the preferential position enjoyed by the first-born. However, the biblical law provides that the eldest son receive *pi šᵉnayim*, which really meant "two portions (out of three), i. e., two-thirds." Thus, if there were more than two sons, as was often the case, the eldest son received considerably more (66%) than twice the portion of any of his younger brothers. On this original meaning of the Hebrew idiom, which is clear from II Kings 2:9 and Zech. 13:8, see Gordis, WB, 344–46. The *Siphrē* on Deut. 21:17 is well aware of the original meaning of the phrase, but rejects it on Talmudic grounds in favor of the view that it means, "double that of the other brothers." This reduction in the share of the first-born is in line with the general development of rabbinic law in the direction of equality for underprivileged groups. *Cf.* L. Finkelstein, I, 284 f., 342 f.

To revert to the earlier, biblical period, the principle of preferential rights for the first-born was universal in the ancient Orient, but it took on different forms in Akkadian, Hurrian and Hebrew law. Thus, as Speiser points out, the rights of primogeniture could be set aside at will by the father in Hurrian law, while biblical law expressly forbids such action (Deut. 21:16 f.).

[4] Gen. 27:39 f. The translation is that of Speiser, 207 f. The Hebrew verb *tārīd* in 40c is difficult. It is generally rendered "wander restlessly, roam," with Arab. *raʾda* (*mediae waw*), "go to and fro," Akk. *rādu*, "tremble," Eth. *radda*, "run up or invade," adduced as cognates. *Cf.* Jer. 2:31. See BDB, 923b, KB, 876a.

[5] Gen. 36:31. Bartlett interprets "the kings" as being purely local rulers. See note 8.

[6] Num. 20:14–21.

[7] N. Glueck, *Encyclopedia Miqrait*, col. 90–98, *The Other Side of the Jordan* (New Haven, 1940), 50–113.

[8] On the basis of his excavations in the Negev, during the 1930s, Glueck formulated a history of the area which has been generally accepted. More recently, several elements of his reconstruction have come under challenge. Thus Bartlett, in his comprehensive paper cited above, differs on several important particulars: (A) He is critical of Glueck's view that Edom constituted a well-organized state from the 13th century onwards. He believes that there was no Edomite national unity in Edom before the middle of the 9th century,

response was received from Siḥon, king of the Amorites, he was attacked and destroyed.[9] While the Deuteronomic legislation excludes the Ammonites and the Moabites "from the community of the Lord," because "they did not meet you with bread and water on the way when you came forth out of Egypt," the Edomites, who had committed the same offense, were not given the same treatment. The reason undoubtedly inheres in the sense of close kinship of which Israel, at least, remained conscious: "You shall not abominate an Edomite for he is your brother . . . The children of the third generation that are born to them may enter the assembly of the Lord."[10]

However, the consciousness of kinship, then as now, was powerless to overcome the clash of military, political and economic interests. It impelled the kingdom of Judah constantly to seek to establish its rule over Edom. The difficulties in our historical sources, often fragmentary and obscure, are complicated by the frequent scribal confusion between ארם and אדום, *Reš* and *Daled* being virtually indistinguishable.

that its independence lasted a brief time, and that it became a significant power in the region only at the time when Babylonia became a threat to Judah, at the beginning of the 6th century. (B) He also maintains that Edomite trade expanded at that time and not, as Glueck believes, in the post-exilic period of the Nabateans. (C) Bartlett interprets the "kings" in Gen. 36:31 to be local rulers and therefore no evidence of an organized state. (D) He regards biblical references to Edom in Numbers and Deuteronomy as reflecting, not the conditions of the Exodus and the desert period, but the situation centuries later in David's period and beyond. (E) He maintains that it was the Egyptians, not the Israelites or the Judeans, and certainly not the Edomites, who were responsible for the mining operations at *Wadi ʾel Arabah.*

The last position has been energetically maintained by B. Rothenberg, whose more recent excavations in the Timna Valley have revealed remains of Egyptian temples going back to Sethos I (1318–04 B.C.E.) and Rameses III (1198–66 B.C.E.) one set over the other. Basing himself upon these discoveries, Rothenberg is now firmly convinced that it was the Egyptians who worked the copper mines and not the Israelites in Solomon's day (see "Notes and News," *PEQ*, 1969, 57–99 and *Illustrated London News*, November 16, 1969, 32–33 and November 29, 1969, 28–29). As late as 1962, Rothenberg confidently believed that the mines were Solomonic. For his earlier work in Timna see "Ancient Copper Industries in the Western Arabah, I" *PEQ*, 1962, 5–71. It is not difficult to understand why D. Harden (*The Phoenicians*, Harmondsworth, England, 1971) expresses some astonishment that pottery given a tenth-century date in 1962 is now transferred to a period centuries earlier.

With regard to Bartlett's other positions, it may be pointed out that he is constrained to give little credence to the authenticity of the references to Edom in Genesis, Numbers, and Deuteronomy. He also is compelled to argue a great deal from the silence of the sources and the absence of archaeological discoveries for his reconstruction of Edomite history. It is clear that the paucity of literary and historical data and the ambiguous character of a good deal of the archaeological findings make dogmatism on Edomite history very questionable. Important as these divergences between Glueck and his critics are, they do not affect the basic concerns of this paper.

[9] Num. 21:21 ff.

[10] Deut. 23:4, 8, 9.

Nevertheless, several major stages in the relationship of Judah and Edom may be reconstructed. David, whose efforts to expand the boundaries of his kingdom in all directions proved highly successful, won a major victory over Edom at *Gey' Melaḥ* (the Valley of Salt),[11] and then proceeded to set up prefects over all Edom, thus converting it into a province of Judah.

Glueck suggests that Solomon raised copper mining in the Arabah to the level of a national industry. Toward the end of Solomon's reign, when cracks in his empire began showing, various suppressed groups, both within Israel and without, attempted to revolt. Hadad, who was a scion of the royal Edomite line and had been a protegé of the Egyptian court throughout Solomon's reign (c. 973–933), apparently succeeded in throwing off the Judean yoke, or at least "in doing mischief to Solomon"[12] and establishing himself on the throne.

The period of Edomite independence or autonomy cannot have lasted very long. In the reign of Jehoshaphat (c. 875–851), a Judean prefect apparently had at least a measure of authority in Edom.[13] It is quite possible that the authority was more formal than substantive, for shortly thereafter, when Jehoshaphat was still on the throne of Judah, Jehoram of Israel, facing a revolt by Mesha, king of Moab, set out to subjugate the rebel with the kings of Judah and Edom as his allies.[14] That there could be a "king of

[11] II Sam. 8:13–14 and reading with the parallel in I Chron. 18:21, LXX, Peshita and all moderns, אֱדוֹם for אֲרָם. In I Kings 11:15–16, reference is made to the destruction of all males in Edom during David's reign. If this latter passage referred to a second war, the extent of the carnage would suggest two major campaigns within a few years, which is not likely. Probably the passages in *Samuel* and *Kings* preserve two divergent reports concerning David's successful subjugation of Edom.

In I Sam. 14:47, Saul is described as waging successful wars against all the surrounding peoples, Edom included. Bartlett suggests that the passage is a retroversion of the victories of David to Saul's reign. Saul's brief and checquered reign can hardly have encompassed so many far-flung campaigns.

[12] The account in I Kings 11:14–25 is unclear and the text in v. 25 is surely not in order. Probably because of another scribal confusion of אֲרָם and אֱדוֹם, a passage dealing with an Aramean revolt (vv. 23–24) has been introduced into the account of Hadad the Edomite's rebellion and has affected the text of v. 25, which refers to Edom. In LXX, vv. 23–24 are lacking and v. 25 follows immediately after v. 22. The v. in LXX reads: "So Ader (!) returned to his own country; this the evil which Ader did and he bitterly hated Israel and he reigned in the land of Edom."

[13] In I Kings 22:48, נִצָּב is surely to be read נְצִיב, "prefect," but evidently the verse has sustained additional damage, probably the loss of material. *RSV* renders: "There was no king in Edom, a deputy was king;" *NEB*, "only a viceroy of Jehoshaphat." Both renderings undoubtedly transmit the original sense of the passage, but effectively disguise the textual difficulty.

[14] II Kings 3:9, 10. M. Haran regards the phrase "king of Edom" (in 3:9) as a reference to the Judean commissioner over Edom (208, n. 19). This appears unlikely, especially in view of the reference to "these three kings" in v. 10. The solution proposed in the text above seems to us preferable.

Edom" side by side with a Judean prefect in the land is suggested by the situation prevalent during the Conquest of Canaan by the Israelites. As we know from Egyptian sources, Egypt held suzerainty over Palestine during the fourteenth, thirteenth and twelfth centuries. That this Egyptian Empire was not an empty claim is clear from the Tel-el-Amarna Inscriptions at the end of the fourteenth century, the Merneptah stele (1220 B.C.E.), and the records of Rameses III (1195–64), the last Pharaoh to hold sway over Palestine. Nevertheless, the book of *Joshua* consistently refers to "the kings" of the various cities in Canaan.[15]

Jehoshaphat's reign seems to have been marked by widespread revolts that involved the vassal states, Moab, Ammon and Edom, who attacked Ein Gedi in force.[16] After the rebels were repulsed by Judah, the Ammonites and the Moabites apparently turned savagely upon the Edomites, leaving a vast amount of booty for the Judeans.[17] On the other hand, the disaster that overtook Jehoshaphat's ships at Ezion-Geber, if it was not the result of a storm at sea, but took place in port, suggests that Edomite resistance was not totally crushed.[18]

Full independence was won by the Edomites in the reign of Jehoshaphat's son, Jehoram of Judah (c. 852–50 to 845–43 B.C.E.) with the Edomites setting up their own king.[19] As has always been customary in military communiques issued by combattants, the Hebrew account describes the battle as a victory for Judah, but actually the Judean infantry was put to rout. The victory dispatch is tempered by the information that Edom revolted against Judah "until this day."[20] Edom's independent status approximately a half century later (802 B.C.E.) is attested by the inscription of Adad Nirari III, who lists Edom among the tributaries of Assyria.[21]

Once again Edomite liberty did not last very long, perhaps because,

[15] See the list of "kings" in Josh. 12:9–24.

[16] See the elaborate and liturgically expanded account in II Chronicles, chap. 20. In v. 2, מֵאֲרָם is again to be read מֵאֱדוֹם, as clear from vv. 22 and 23 הַר שֵׂעִיר.

[17] II Chron. 20:22–26. The text of v. 23 is uncertain and the meaning is correspondingly unclear.

[18] See I Kings 22:49 f.; II Chron. 20:35 f.

[19] II Kings 8:20–22; II Chron. 21:8–10. In *Chronicles*, the phrase וַיָּנָס הָעָם לְאֹהָלָיו is omitted, but both writers refer twice to Edom's successful revolt (פָּשַׁע, וַיִּפְשַׁע אֱדוֹם).

[20] The phrase "to this day" is a frequent biblical formula, particularly in historical accounts, "denoting permanence of a name or a situation, or the result of an event" (BDB, s. v., יוֹם, 401a). The phrase naturally remained unchanged when the texts in which they occurred were incorporated *verbatim* into more comprehensive works, like *Kings* or *Chronicles*. Thus the Chronicler is surely not suggesting that Edom remained independent of Judah until the 3rd century B.C.E. when he was composing his work! Other instances where the phrase clearly signifies a limited time-span are Deut. 11:4; Josh. 4:9; 7:26; Judg. 6:24; I Sam. 6:18. The phrase, therefore, need not refer to the time of the final compilation of *Kings*, but it does indicate an extended period.

[21] *ANET*, 281.

though unable to enforce its claim to suzerainty, Judah never officially recognized Edom's complete independence. King Amaziah of Judah (798–780) defeated the Edomites, once again at the historic battleground of *Gey' Melaḥ*, inflicting ten thousand losses on them. He captured the city of Sela, which he added to Judean territory,[22] and renamed Yokteel. Evidently, Amaziah's victory over Edom encouraged him to attempt the annexation of Israelite territory in the north, but this brought swift retribution from Jehoash of Israel on the battlefield.[23] Amaziah's successor, Uzziah, built Elat and restored it to Judah.[24]

However, once again Edom proved restive. According to our extant sources, the seaport of Elat was restored to Edom by Rezin, king of Aram and ally of Pekaḥ of Israel during the Syro-Ephraimitic War (734 B.C.E.).[25] This step was evidently designed to win Edomite participation in the revolt against Assyria and to undermine the rule of Ahaz of Judah who had refused to join the West-Asian rebel alliance.

Our extant historical sources shed no light on the subsequent history of the Edomite kingdom until its final conquest by the Babylonians in the sixth century. It is a fair inference, however, that the Edomites retained a strong national consciousness and a correspondingly powerful hostility toward the Judeans. The last century and a half of the Judean state was marked by mounting difficulties, which the Edomites may well have exploited to regain their national independence. Their position must surely have improved sufficiently for Edomites to express their joy at the destruction of the Jewish state, and to practice cruelty upon the Judean refugees during the final agonies of the Holy City. For their attitude and actions, the prophetic and poetic books of the Bible castigate them severely.[26]

The subsequent history of Edom in the Hellenistic period is not our present concern. The Idumeans continued to be a source of irritation and danger to the Second Jewish Commonwealth, until John Hyrcanus conquered Aduram and Mareshah and compelled the Edomites to accept

[22] II Kings 14:7. In II Chron. 25:11–13, the victory is magnified and the 10,000 casualties are amplified by 10,000 captives who are said to have been hurled to their deaths from a crag (*hasselaᶜ*). Thus *Sela* is not treated as a nameplace by the Chronicler. Generally, but not universally, *Sela* is identified with the capital Petra. See Haran, 211 f. for objections to this identification.

[23] II Kings 14:8–14. II Chron. 25:11–24 fills in important details lacking in the earlier and briefer account.

[24] II Kings 14:22; II Chron. 26:2.

[25] II Kings 16:6. The use of the verb *hēšībh*, "restored," strongly supports reading לֶאֱדוֹם for לַאֲרָם in the first half of the verse. In the second half, the Masoretic rendering is וַאֲדוֹמִים, though some mss. register וארומים as the Kethib and ואדומים as the Qere. P and T read the word with a *Reš*, probably to bring it into line with Rezin, the king of Aram.

[26] See Jer. 49:7–22; Ezek. 25:12–14; 35:1–15; 36:5 ff.; Isa. 63:1–6; Obadiah; Mal. 1:1–4; Ps. 137:7; Lam. 4:21 f.

Judaism.[27] Perhaps they had their final and exquisite revenge when Herod, son of the Idumean Antipater, became king of the Jews by the grace of Rome. Edom then vanishes from the stage of history, leaving behind virtually no literary remains expressive of its religion and culture.[28]

II

This summary account of the data available on Edomite history should suffice to demonstrate that our biblical sources on Edom are fragmentary, frequently obscure, and partial in both senses of the term. It is, therefore, methodologically dubious to draw far-reaching inferences from silence in our extant sources or to delete or emend passages in biblical texts in order to make them conform with assumptions on Edomite history that are uncertain at best.

Thus, Amaziah's victory at *Gey' Hamelaḥ* is generally interpreted as meaning the total subjugation of Edom which lasted until Ahaz. Now it is taken for granted (a) that Amos did not begin to prophesy until long after Amaziah's victory, and (b) that the section on Edom (2:4–12) in Amos' great "Arraignment of the Nations" in the two opening chapters of his book which speaks of Edom as "pursuing his brother with the sword" (2:11),

[27] Josephus, *Antiquities* XIII, 9, 1; *War*, I, 2, 6.

[28] It is not totally irrelevant to comment briefly on the frequently encountered theory regarding the phenomenal "wisdom of the Edomites." Pfeiffer goes so far as to postulate a special document in *Genesis*, aside from J, E, and P, that he calls S (=Seir), to which he assigns the lion's share of the early narratives in Genesis. According to Pfeiffer, this source includes (a) the primeval mythological history of mankind (Genesis 2–11) and (b) the legendary history of Southern Palestine and Trans-Jordan (Genesis 14, 19, 34, 35, 36, 38). This Edomite source is credited with a "definite philosophy of history" which Pfeiffer proceeds to spell out in detail. He also assigns to the Edomite Wisdom literature "The Words of Agur" (Prov., chap. 30) and the book of *Job*.

Though the Pfeiffer hypothesis has not been widely accepted, "the wisdom of the Edomites" is almost a staple of biblical scholarship. Thus Wolff writes that "Their wisdom is often mentioned in the Old Testament." As proof he cites I Kings 5:10; Jer. 49:7; Obad. 1:8; and Job 2:11. Even if these four passages were relevant, they would not demonstrate that the wisdom of the Edomites is "often mentioned" in the Old Testament. Actually, I Kings 5:10 refers to "the wisdom of the sons of the East and the wisdom of Egypt." Extant Oriental Wisdom literature, Sumerian, Babylonian and Egyptian, makes it likely that the passage refers to the Wisdom literature of Mesopotamia and Egypt rather than to Edom. The phrase being general in character need not have the same meaning in every instance. In Isa. 11:14, *b^enei qedem* refers to Edom, Moab and Ammon. No Wisdom literature (and very little else) has survived of any of the three. Jer. 49:7 describes the destruction of Edom and then rhetorically asks whether there is any wisdom left in Edom to avert the threatened calamity. Obad. 1:8 f., which largely parallels the Jeremiah passage, speaks of the destruction of the political and military leadership, "the wise men and the mighty men," from whom alone Edom might have expected succor. Job 2:11 makes no reference at all to wisdom, Edomite or otherwise. The rabbinic phrase "mountains hanging by a hair" may well be applied to the theory of Edomite wisdom, which is, of course, difficult to disprove in view of the fact that no Edomite literature has survived.

refers to Judah as the victim. Since Edom is apparently enjoying independence and even victory over Judah, the pericope poses problems of authenticity and date. Several answers have been proposed:

1. Most scholars have assumed that the passage in Amos is late and reflects the hostility engendered by the cruelty toward the Judean refugees displayed by the Edomites after the destruction of Jerusalem in 586 B.C.E. The passage is, therefore, deleted as a post-exilic interpolation.[29]

There is, however, no authority in the manuscripts or in the Ancient Versions for excising the section. Moreover, this pericope cannot be evaluated in isolation from the entire passage in which it occurs. As will be noted below, there are significant general considerations that speak for the authenticity of the entire text in Amos.

2. Yehezkel Kaufmann believes that Amos used and embodied in his work an earlier prophetic scroll which contained this passage on Edom.[30] The section, therefore, goes back a century earlier, to the days of Jehoram, when the Edomites successfully rebelled against Judah and established their independence. Kaufmann assumes that the Edomites avenged themselves cruelly upon their erstwhile oppressors and it is this sin to which the prophet refers. There is, of course, no objective evidence either for the independent existence of such a scroll or for the assumed ferocity displayed by the Edomites in their successful bid for independence. Kaufmann's hypothesis with regard to Amos' use of a prophetic scroll a century older recalls his similar theory of the two Hoseas.[31]

[29] Most scholars who eliminate the section on Edom (1:11–12) also delete some or all of the sections on the Philistines (1:6–8), Tyre (1:9–10) and Judah (2:4–5).

The sections on Tyre, Philistia and Judah are deleted by J. Wellhausen, K. Marti, W. Sellin, W. Nowack, W. R. Smith, A. Kuenen, M. Lohr, W. R. Harper, E. Baumann, A. Weiser, R. Pfeiffer, 579, O. Eissfeldt, 400, W. H. Schmidt, "*Die Deuteronomistische Redaktion des Amosbuches*," *ZAW* 77 (1965), 174–178. E. Sellin, 165 f., after discussing the arguments for deleting the sections, concludes that there are no decisive grounds either in form or in content for rejecting them. He then proceeds to eliminate Tyre, Edom and Judah for metrical reasons.

The authenticity of some or all of these sections is defended by S. R. Driver, H. Gressmann, Th. H. Robinson, R. S. Cripps, and by more recent scholars like Kramer, Neher and Reventlow. See also V. Maag: *Text, Wortschatz und Begriffswelt des Buches Amos* (Leiden, 1951), 51; G. J. Botterweck: "*Zur Authentizität des Buches Amos*," *BZ*, 2 (1958), 179–180; E. Hammershaimb, 31–32. Kapelrud, 27, finds only the Edom section doubtful, the others authentic. Hammershaimb, 42, is skeptical about all the deletions. Snaith, 15, retains Edom and Judah. He believes that only Tyre is probably to be deleted, because the reference "He did not remember the covenant of brothers" has never been satisfactorily explained in the Tyre context. On this point, see our paper below. Ward, 99, very effectively rebuts the arguments against the authenticity of these sections, but declares that "the Judah oracle is admittedly 'vague' and deuteronomic, and therefore has the poorest claim to originality." On these arguments, see the text of our paper and notes 40 and 43.

[30] *Toledot*, VI, 56–92; *Religion*, 363–67.

[31] *Toledot*, VI, 93–146; *Religion*, 368–77.

3. M. Haran rightly finds both these approaches unsatisfactory. He proposes to solve the difficulty by assuming that the victories of Amaziah and Uzziah over Edom were by no means decisive and that they did not destroy Edomite independence. They merely meant the annexation of Sela (which Haran does not equate with Petra) and the securing of access to the sea for Judah through Elat. In his words:

> "Thus, Uzziah did not conquer Edom and it is doubtful whether he even fought any significant war against that country. At the same time, hatred and retained vengeance on the part of Edom toward Judah could continue to seethe long after Jehoram, precisely once Edom had attained its independence. The horrible defeat at *Gey' Melaḥ* could also very well only excite these feelings. Upon such a background—even when the Judean kings dominated the Red Sea coast—many a local outbreak and acts of 'pursuit with the sword' were apt to occur. Nothing appears to contradict that such were the circumstances during the early years of Jeroboam II, or a few years prior."[32]

However, Haran himself describes the military defeat at *Gey' Melaḥ* as "horrible." It was followed by the annexation of Sela, probably the capital city of Petra. For if it were an unimportant village, its capture would not have been singled out for mention nor would its name have been changed and the act recorded in our sources. Amaziah's subjugation of Edom was followed a little later by Uzziah's occupation of the major seaport Elat, which necessarily involved land-passage to the sea. All these elements do not suggest a limited victory for Judah. This is particularly true of Uzziah, who, together with Jeroboam II of Israel, restored the boundaries of the Davidic kingdom and whose military exploits are described in great detail.[33] That Uzziah would have left Edom unconquered on his southern flank is hardly likely.

We believe that the pericope on Edom must be examined within the broader context of the entire "Arraignment of the Nations," which makes reference to Edom in three other sections that deal with the Philistines, Tyre and Moab.[34] The form-critical and exegetical problems of the entire passage must be met before dealing with the historical issues involved.

III

With Amos, Hebrew literary prophecy emerges full grown on the stage of history. To be sure, his name is interpreted by the Rabbis as meaning "of heavy speech." The statement is echoed by Jerome, who calls him

[32] Haran, 211.
[33] II Chron. 26:1–15.
[34] Amos 1:6, 9; 2:2.

imperitus sermone sed non scientia.[35] Actually, Amos is a superb master of language and style, utilizing all the familiar rhetorical usages such as simile, metaphor and assonance, as well as two special devices that will be noted below, ascending numeration and the heptad.

The title (1:1) gives the occupation and origin of the prophet in Tekoa in Judah and indicates that he prophesied in the days of King Uzziah of Judah and Jeroboam II of Israel, "two years before the earthquake." Then comes a one-verse oracle, the first half of which evidently served as a succinct formulation of the prophetic calling. It was, therefore, taken up by his successors, occurring identically in Joel 4:16 and in very similar form in Jer. 25:30. The verse is an admirable motto and proem to the entire book of *Amos*;

"The Lord roars from Zion,
and utters his voice from Jerusalem;
the pastures of the shepherds mourn,
and the top of Carmel withers."

Its purpose seems to be to emphasize that though Amos' basic activity is directed to the Northern Kingdom, he speaks in the name of the God whose sanctuary is in Zion.

Amos has received the call to prophesy against Israel and to warn the large and prosperous Kingdom of the North of the doom that awaits it because of its rampant sins—personal immorality, social injustice, governmental corruption and the perversion of the idealism of the youth. The prophet refrains from launching immediately into his basic theme. Instead, he turns to the neighboring peoples, upbraiding them for their crimes and announcing their condign punishment. Displaying a remarkable knowledge of international affairs, the shepherd of Tekoa passes judgment on the actions of Aram, the Philistines, Tyre, Edom, Ammon, Moab and Judah.

This "Arraignment of the Nations" is a consummate example of the blending of form and content. Amos uses the very effective device of ascending numeration (or graduated numerical sequence) to heighten the effect of his words: "For three sins of . . . and for four, I shall not let it rest."[36] By passing in review the conduct of Israel's neighbors, Amos wins the favorable attention of his Israelite audience, which is only too delighted to hear the excoriation of their foes and the announcement of their imminent destruction.

But far more than psychological strategy is involved. The prophet is underscoring his fundamental faith that the one living God of righteousness

[35] *Midrash, Lev. R.*, sec. 10; *Midrash Koheleth Rabba*, sec. 1; *Yalqut Šimᵉoni* on Isaiah, sec. 307; Jerome, *Preface to Amos.*

[36] This rhetorical usage occurs primarily in Hebrew, but is attested also in the Ara-

holds sway over all nations. Years later Amos will declare that the Ethiopians, who were the object of widespread scorn, are on a par with Israel and that the hand of God is discernible in the migrations of all the nations no less than in the Exodus of the Israelites from Egypt.[37] As the God of righteousness, He will judge all nations equally by the standard of justice and humanity.

Suddenly the prophet turns upon his audience and applies the same formula to Israel. In far greater detail than is the case with the other nations he castigates their wrongdoings and announces the punishment that awaits them, "For three sins of Israel . . . and for four I shall not let it rest."

The same element of surprise was utilized decades later by Amos' spiritual disciple Isaiah in the "Song of the Vineyard." Here, the prophet begins to sing what is apparently a sad ballad of unrequited love, but suddenly it turns into a bitter complaint by God over the people's faithlessness.[38]

The authenticity and integrity of several sections of Amos' "Arraignment of the Nations" (aside from the passage on Edom), notably those on Tyre and Judah, have been challenged on grounds of content and style. The pericope on Judah has been pronounced an interpolation on three principal grounds: (1) The language is "deuteronomistic" in its reference to "Torah" and is therefore inappropriate for the prophet. (2) The sins charged against Judah are general rather than specific. (3) Amos is not concerned with Judah.

On analysis, these grounds do not appear convincing. (1) The term *tōrah*, "guidance, teaching," was by no means the exclusive property of one school of thought in ancient Israel. While very popular with Priestly writers, it occurs frequently in the Wisdom literature and the Psalms.[39] All the Prophets use the term to refer to their religious and ethical outlook.[40]

(2) The contention that the sins of Judah are not spelled out in detail has been countered by the observation that several of the sections, such as those on the Philistines, Tyre and Edom, are not specific either.[41] In any

maic text of *Ahiqar* and in Ugaritic. Virtually all numbers are represented: one-two (Ps. 62:12 f.); three-four (Prov. 30:15 f., 10 f., 21 ff., 29 ff.; Ben Sira 26 f.); six-seven (Prov. 6:16–19); nine-ten (B.S. 25:7–11). In all these passages, the writer proceeds to list a number of instances of the category being discussed which is identical with the higher figure. On Job 5:19–24, where the six-seven combination occurs, the discrepancy in the disasters listed is apparent rather than real. See Gordis, *The Book of Job, Commentary, New Translation and Special Studies* (New York: Jewish Theological Seminary, 1978) *ad loc.* Our passage in *Amos* is virtually the only case where the ascending numeration (three-four) is used loosely and where only one major sin is then specified. *Cf.* also Ps. 62:12 and Job 33:29, where the usage means "several." Wolff makes the plausible suggestion that in Prov. 30:18 f. and 29 ff.; B.S. 26:28; 25:7–11; 50:25 f., the writer is really concerned only with one phenomenon, the last one on his list, which alone involves human relations and that the earlier ones are introduced only to highlight the last one. See his excellent study 39 ff. and W. M. Roth, *passim.*

event, the brief general indictment of Judah is understandable for several reasons. Evidently, the recent history of Judah did not include a single heinous crime on the level of the physical cruelty charged against Aram, Ammon and Moab. Moreover, the sins of his own people with which the prophet was concerned were internal and social, rather than external and military. Finally, Judah is not the burden of Amos' message; he wishes to move on as quickly as possible to his basic theme, the conduct of Israel. On the other hand, Amos cannot pass over Judah in silence, if only because his audience, having heard his castigation of all the neighboring enemies of Israel, would expect some comment on Judah as well, especially since the Southern Kingdom was a foe almost as often as it was an ally of Israel.

(3) It was not merely in order to please his hearers that Amos included Judah in his "Arraignment of the Nations," His own world-view was involved. The omission of Judah would have been a glaring lacuna in his all-encompassing standard of equal justice.

Elsewhere[42] we have pointed out that the editing of the book of *Amos*, like that of the books of *Isaiah* and *Jeremiah*, follows the formula of A + H + B, that is to say, a first collection of prophecies (A), followed by historical traditions on the life and career of the prophet (H), completed by a second collection of prophecies (B). It is noteworthy that in the first section of Amos (A) (chapters 1–7:9), the prophet bends all his energies to the task of regenerating and thus saving Israel. On the other hand, all his references to Judah are brief and negative. Amos' hopes, however slight and tentative, were pinned on Israel. Then comes the historical material describing Amos' encounter with Amaziah at Bethel (H) (7:10–17). This is followed by Chapters 8 and 9. (C). These constitute a collection of later utterances following Amos' expulsion from Bethel. Having been denied the opportunity of speaking to the Northern Israelites, Amos despairs of any possibility of their repentance and restoration. He now transfers his hopes for the survival of his people to Judah, for it is this people alone, for all its imperfections, that is the exemplar of God's cause in a pagan world. It is

[37] Amos 9:7.

[38] Isa. 5:1–7.

[39] The term is the subject of an unpublished dissertation by S. H. Blank, *Das Wort Torah im A.T.* (Jena, 1925); see G. Östborn, *Tora in the Old Testament.*

[40] The term is very common in Isaiah of Jerusalem (1:10; 2:3; 5:24; 8:16, 20; 24:5; 30:9). It occurs in virtually every prophet from Hosea to Deutero-Isaiah and Malachi in the meaning of God's law of conduct for Israel and not as a term for a ritual or legal code. Isa. 42:4, 21, 24; 51:4; Jer. 6:19; 8:8; 44:23; Ezek. 44:24; Hos. 4:6; Mic. 4:25; Hab. 1:4; Zeph. 3:4; Hab. 2:11; Zech. 7:12; Mal. 2:7, 8, 9.

[41] Ward, *loc. cit.*

[42] See Gordis, Composition, *passim.*

striking and significant that all the references to Judah in section A are negative,[43] while the references in section C are favorable.[44]

Whether or not the inference we have drawn from the data for the structure of Amos is accepted, the extant text demonstrates what could be assumed *a priori*, that a Hebrew prophet would not be indifferent to the character and destiny of Judah. For Amos, as for all the biblical prophets and historians, there was only one people of Israel and the division of the kingdom was both a political crime and a sin against God. It may be added that a later post-exilic interpolation on Judah would more probably have been consolatory rather than condemnatory. In conclusion, the elimination of all references to Judah is rendered impossible in several instances by the poetic structure of the text.[45]

The sections on Tyre and Edom are deleted by many critics as later interpolations because they lack the closing formula **אמר ה'** (or **אמר ה' אלהים**) that occurs at the end of the sections on Aram, Philistia, Ammon and Moab. It is taken for granted that a poet or a prophet adopting a given literary formula will adhere to it exactly, without any variation. This assumption is questionable, since any writer worth his salt will seek to avoid monotony and create interest by introducing a measure of change. Hence, refrains in biblical poetry, while obviously repeated in order to add power and emphasis, will yet differ in detail for the sake of variety.[46] Actually, this principle of variety within a fixed pattern is exhibited by our passage itself. The closing formula is not identical; **אמר ה'** occurs in 1:5, and **אמר ה' אלהים** in 1:7, followed by **אמר ה'** twice more (1:15; 2:3).

In fact, the present text does possess a *regular pattern*. The closing formula is used in the first two instances, Aram and the Philistines (1:5, 8), is omitted in the next two, Tyre and Edom (1:9, 12), occurs once more in the two following, Ammon and Moab (1:15; 2:3), and is omitted in the final two, Judah and Israel (2:5).[47]

Finally, there is one other basic consideration that argues strongly in

[43] *Cf.* 3:1b; 5:5c; especially 6:1. I cannot understand Ward's statement 99, n. 4, that nowhere else is Judah mentioned in an oracle of Amos. The vocable "Judah" may not occur, but the references are clear. See Gordis, Composition, 219–22.

[44] *Cf.* 9:8 ff. See the discussion in Gordis, *op. cit.*

[45] Note especially 6:1, also 5:5c; 9.8b, and see Gordis, Composition.

[46] *Cf.*, e. g., Job 28:18 (תָּבוֹא), v. 20 (תִּמָּצֵא), Ps. 107:6 (וַיִּצְעֲקוּ), v. 13 (וַיִּזְעֲקוּ), v. 19 (וַיִּזְעֲקוּ), v. 28 (וַיִּצְעֲקוּ). *Baruch*, in the Apocrypha, has an opening refrain with variations in chap. 4. Thus, 4:5, "Take heart my people," v. 21, "Take heart my children," v. 27, "Take heart my children," v. 30, "Take heart, Jerusalem" (trans. *NEB*).

The changes in the refrain are not to be attributed to scribal error. Hebrew scribes are perfectly capable of repeating the identical formulation, as, e. g., in the tribal census (Num. 1:20 ff.) or the gifts of the princes (Num. 7:12 ff.).

[47] In the much longer pericope on Israel, the prophet twice uses **נְאֻם ה'** instead (2:11, 16).

favor of the authenticity of all the sections in the "Arraignment of the Nations." It is the presence of a *heptadic structure*, the use of seven units as an organizing principle without explicit reference to the number "seven."[48] Before approaching his basic subject, Israel, Amos reviews the actions of seven nations. We have called attention elsewhere to the heptad as a significant rhetorical pattern in the Hebrew Bible, Rabbinic literature and the New Testament.[49]

Moreover, the use of the heptad was apparently particularly congenial to Amos. In 3:3–7, we have a series of seven questions: (v. 3) a meeting of two men, (v. 4) the lion (2 instances), (v. 5) the bird in the trap (2 instances), (v. 6) the trumpet, (v. 7) the prophet.

In 4:6–13, the prophet enumerates a series of calamities, which also total seven in number: (1) hunger (v. 6), (2) drought (v. 7), (3) lack of drinking water (vv. 7, 8), (4) diseases of the crop (v. 9), (5) the locust (v. 9), (6) the plague (v. 10), (7) the earthquake (v. 11).[50]

In sum, the "Arraignment of the Nations" in its present form is a *datum*, while all suggested deletions are hypotheses with no textual support either in the manuscripts or the Ancient Versions. All considerations of content, structure and style support the authenticity of the entire passage.

IV

In view of the detailed critical scrutiny to which the first two chapters of *Amos* have been subjected, it is astonishing that a major difficulty has attracted relatively little attention. In describing the offenses of the Philistines, Amos uses the phrase עַל־הַגְלוֹתָם גָּלוּת שְׁלֵמָה לְהַסְגִּיר לֶאֱדוֹם, usually translated "because they carried into exile a whole people, to deliver them up to Edom." Tyre is charged with the same offence expressed in a slightly divergent form: עַל־הַסְגִּירָם גָּלוּת שְׁלֵמָה לֶאֱדוֹם rendered: "Because they delivered up a whole people to Edom."[51] It is universally taken for granted that the victims who were being sold into slavery to Edom were the inhabitants of Israel.

This view suffers from several major difficulties:

(1) There is the logistical problem of how Tyre, located north of Israel, would be able to sell slaves and have them transported to Edom, which lay inland south of Judah.

[48] An analogy may be found in the conventional rules for the sonnet in Western literature as consisting of precisely fourteen lines.

[49] See Gordis, Heptad, for the evidence of this widespread usage.

[50] My former student (now Professor) Abraham Karp of the University of Rochester, following up this insight, discovered other instances in *Amos*.

[51] The translations are those of *RSV*.

(2) The Philistines and the Phoenicians were the two great maritime trading nations of the ancient Orient. If they had slaves available for sale, their own ships plying the Mediterranean would obviously be the natural means of disposing of their cargo. There would be no reason for selling them to Edom, remote from the coast and virtually landlocked.

(3) The actual condition of Edom during this period was far removed from the role of large-scale slave-dealers. In the same passage, Amos charges Moab with "burning to lime the bones of the king of Edom," the ultimate indignity in the ancient world.

(4) Amos' career came during a period of great national prosperity and confidence, with two great kings on the throne, Uzziah in Israel and Jeroboam in Israel. This era hardly offers a suitable occasion for the mass enslavement of Israel. In fact, as is clear from our brief survey of Edomite history, there never was a time until perhaps shortly before the destruction of the Judean state by the Babylonians when the Edomites were sufficiently powerful to be in position to sell them into "total exile."

(5) Most fundamental of all, *it is incomprehensible that the prophet would indicate a relatively unimportant fact, the identity of the slave-dealers, but leave unstated a basic fact, the identity of the slaves themselves.* The parallel usually adduced in support of the accepted interpretation is Joel 3:6:

> The people of Judah and Jerusalem you have sold to the
> Greeks, removing them far from their own borders.

But this verse actually underscores the difficulty in our passage. Joel not only indicates the identity of the victims, but emphasizes the fact by placing it at the very beginning of the verse. It is noteworthy that in every other section Amos explicitly identifies the victims.[52]

That the slaves alluded to by Amos are the Israelites is generally taken for granted largely because of a theological assumption that is itself untenable—that Amos was interested only in sins committed against the Hebrews. This view is refuted by the pericope of Moab, whose sin was not directed either against Israel or Judah. But the subject is too basic to be determined by one brief passage.

That Amos would be directly concerned with the fortunes of his own kinsmen is entirely natural. His entire career, which required leaving his homeland and his normal activity, and courting unpopularity and exile, demonstrates Amos' deep love and concern for his entire people. Eissfeldt's summary judgment on Amos, *Bei ihm ist Gott alles, Israel nichts*, "For him God is everything, Israel, nothing," is impossible both on theological as well as on psychological grounds. As a spokesman for God, no Hebrew prophet could look with equanimity upon the total destruction of his people, which would mean the extinction of God's cause in a heathen world for

[52] See Amos 1:3, 11, 13; 2:1.

which Israel was the only spokesman, however imperfect. Moreover, no prophet could embark upon his calling and face scorn, ostracism and hatred, even persecution and death, unless actuated by a profound love for his people.

Because Amos was uncompromising in stressing the even-handed justice with which God deals with all nations, he has all too often been pictured as dour and unrelenting. Though not given to overt emotional expression like Hosea and his spiritual descendant Jeremiah, Amos, like his spiritual disciple Isaiah, is moved by a love and pity for his errant brethren, that is all the more profound because he does not wear his heart on his sleeve. Amos' love for his people is unmistakable in passage after passage:

> Hate evil, and love good, and establish justice in the gate;
> Perhaps the Lord, the God of hosts, will be gracious to the
> remnant of Joseph. (5:15)
>
> And I said:
>
> O Lord God, forgive, I beseech thee!
> How can Jacob stand? He is so small! (7:2)
>
> Then I said,
>
> O Lord God, cease, I beseech thee!
> How can Jacob stand? He is so small! (7:5)

Even when he announces the doom of the state, he declares that the people will not be destroyed:

> Behold, the eyes of the Lord God are upon the
> sinful kingdom,
> and I will destroy it from the face of the earth.
> But I will not completely destroy the house of Jacob,"
> says the Lord. (9:8)

Amos sees a process of selection winnowing out the sinful elements of Israel, and looks forward to a regenerated Remnant that would be restored under the legitimate rule of the house of David:

> For lo, I will command, and shake the house of Israel
> among all the nations, as one shakes with a sieve,
> but no pebble shall fall upon the earth.
> All the sinners of my people shall die by the sword,
> who say, 'Evil shall not overtake or meet us.'
> In that day I will raise up the booth of David that
> is fallen and repair its breaches,
> and raise up its ruins,
> and rebuild it as in the days of old. (9:9–11)

The doctrine of the Remnant becomes the foundation of Isaiah's faith and a staple of prophetic teaching. To be sure, the prophet has no sympathy with the widely held folk-belief that "the Day of the Lord" would bring automatic and inevitable victory to Israel over its foes. However, he does not reject the doctrine *in toto*, but reinterprets it as the day when evil, whatever its source, would be destroyed because righteousness is the only key to survival. It is therefore a prospect which Israel, having violated God's will, must confront with fear and foreboding, unless it re-orders its conduct before it is too late.

Similarly, Amos does not reject the closely related concept of Israel as the elect of God, but reinterprets it in terms of Israel's obligation to be loyal to God and the moral law. This he achieves by quoting the popular doctrine, to which he adds his unforgettable commentary:

> You only have I known of all the families of the earth;
> therefore I will punish you for all your iniquities. (3:2)

The folk-belief that Israel was the favorite of God was popularly supported by the memories of the Exodus from Egypt. Amos counters this comfortable notion by reminding his hearers that in God's eyes even the lowly Ethiopians are equal with Israel and that the migration of all nations is under His direction:

> Indeed, you are like the Ethiopians to me,
> O people of Israel, says the Lord.
> Surely I brought up Israel from the land of Egypt—
> but also the Philistines from Caphtor and the Arameans from Kir.
> (9:7)

Nevertheless, Amos does not downgrade the significance of the Exodus. On the contrary, Amos sees in it a historical experience of transcendental importance, for it served to consecrate the people of Israel to God's cause. Hence all the more heinous is their defection from this commitment:

> Yet I destroyed the Amorite before them,
> whose height was like the height of cedars,
> and who was as strong as the oaks;
> I destroyed his fruit above and his roots beneath.
>
> Also I brought you up out of the land of Egypt,
> and led you forty years in the wilderness,
> to possess the land of the Amorite.
>
> And I raised up some of your sons for prophets,
> and some of your young men for Nazirites.

Is it not so, O people of Israel?
says the Lord.
But you made the Nazirites drink wine,
and commanded the prophets, saying
'You shall not prophesy.' (2:9–12)

In sum, like all his great successors among the prophets of Israel, Amos was neither a "universalist" in the vulgar sense of the term, indifferent to his own people, nor a "particularist," interested in no other. Put differently, in a truer sense, Amos, like Isaiah of Jerusalem, was both a universalist and a particularist, a true "inter-nationalist" who saw his people playing a central role in the life of mankind. Nearly three millennia earlier, Amos anticipated the wise counsel of the American philosopher George Santayana, "A man should stand with his feet firmly planted in his own country, but his eyes should survey the world."

This excursus into Amos' theology has demonstrated that there are no *a priori* grounds for assuming that the victims of the slave-trade unspecified in the text could only be the Hebrews. On the other hand, there are compelling reasons for ruling this view out as impossible, as has been noted above.

Virtually the only scholar who has been conscious of some of the difficulties involved in identifying the slaves "sold to Edom" as Hebrews is M. Haran. He has proposed the following solution: In view of the general weakness of Edom throughout the period of the late monarchy and the logistical problem that would confront the Phoenicians and the Philistines in selling slaves to Edom, he suggests emending the references in Amos 1:6 and 1:9 from לֶאֱדוֹם to לַאֲרָם.[53] Thus the Syrians would be the purchasers of the Hebrew slaves sold by Tyre and the Philistines. To be sure, the emendation is slight because of the similarity of *Reš* and *Daled*. The confusion of "Aram" and "Edom" does occur in our biblical text, as has been noted, several times.

That there is no support for the change in manuscripts or the Ancient Versions is perhaps less important than several substantive drawbacks. While the emendation meets problems no. 1 and 3, it leaves unsolved three major difficulties: (4) When could a mass enslavement of the Israelites have taken place during the first half of the 8th century B.C.E., an era in which the country enjoyed unprecedented prosperity and wellbeing? (5) Why are the slave-traders identified but not the victims themselves? Moreover, question 2 also remains unanswered. In view of their access to the sea, would not the Phoenicians sell their slaves to more distant lands rather than only to Aram? In the case of the Philistines, there would be the additional difficulty for a people living on the southern coast of Palestine to transport slaves overland to Syria in the northeast.

[53] Haran, 203.

V

In view of all the considerations advanced, we wish to propose a new interpretation of the two passages. *We suggest that Amos does indicate the identity of the slaves sold by the Philistines and the Phoenicians and that the victims were the Edomites.* In both v. 6 and v. 9, which are synonymous, לֶאֱדוֹם is to be construed as the direct object of the infinitives הַגְלוֹתָם (v. 6) and הַסְגִּירָם (v. 9).

The two passages exhibit three syntactic traits that are authentically Hebraic, two of them actually being attested elsewhere in the book of *Amos*:

(1) The *Lamed Accusativus*, (לֶאֱדוֹם) often described as an "Aramaism," is a genuinely Hebraic construction. It belongs to the first category of "Aramaisms" so-called because it is common in Aramaic, but rare in Hebrew.[54] The *Lamed accusativus* is to be found in all periods of biblical Hebrew, though it becomes more common in later stages because of the growing influence of Aramaic. The construction occurs in לְשַׁחֵת לָעִיר, וְאָהַבְתָּ לְרֵעֲךָ כָּמוֹךָ, הָרְגוּ לְאַבְנֵר and often elsewhere.[55] It is to be met with in two other passages in Amos: וְאָכְלָה וְאֵין־מְכַבֶּה לְבֵית־אֵל "It will devour Bethel with none to quench it,"[56] and in 6:3 הַמְנַדִּים לְיוֹם רָע "Those who push off the day of evil."

(2) In both passages *the direct object* (לֶאֱדוֹם) *is held off to the end of the clause.* The same phenomenon occurs elsewhere in our book. Thus, in 6:14, כִּי הִנְנִי מֵקִים עֲלֵיכֶם בֵּית יִשְׂרָאֵל נְאֻם ה' אֱלֹהֵי צְבָאוֹת גּוֹי would usually be expressed כִּי הִנְנִי מֵקִים עֲלֵיכֶם גּוֹי וגו'. A less clear example occurs in 5:1: שִׁמְעוּ אֶת־הַדָּבָר הַזֶּה אֲשֶׁר אָנֹכִי נֹשֵׂא עֲלֵיכֶם קִינָה בֵּית יִשְׂרָאֵל. It would gen-

[54] There are four principal categories of Aramaisms that should be clearly distinguished, even though we are not always in position to assign a given instance to one or another type: (1) a word or usage belonging to Northwest Semitic, which was more frequent in Aramaic but less common in Hebrew, where it would be restricted to poetic and archaic use (like אָתָה, "come" and מִלֵּל, "speak"). (2) Words and usages that entered biblical Hebrew during the First Temple period because of contact by Hebrews with Arameans, particularly in Northern Israel (like רָעָה, "pursue, desire," Hos. 12:2, parallel to רדף). (3) Words and usages that entered Hebrew in the Bab. and Persian eras when Aramaic was the *lingua franca* of the Middle East and (4) words and idioms that entered into Hebrew during the Second Temple period where Jews spoke Aramaic in daily life and were deeply influenced by it in their literary works (as in Ecclesiastes and Esther). In spite of differences in formulation, our approach to "Aramaisms" (*JQR* 61, 1970, 103–116; WB, 13, is similar to that of Barr, 121 ff.

[55] The references are I Sam. 23:10; Lev. 19:18; II Sam. 3:30; Job 5:2. The *Lamed accusativus* occurs with many verbs ברך, גדל, זכר, חלק. The *Lamed* is used with our verb הגלה in I Chron. 5:26. The *Lamed Accusativus* is frequent with Hiphil verbs like הנחיל, הרגיז, הרבה, החיה, השגיא, הפתה and not rarely with verbs in other conjugations, like בזה, עזר, חרף, etc. See BDB, s. v., *Lamed*, sec. 3, 511b.

[56] The LXX reading of לְבֵית יִשְׂרָאֵל for לְבֵית־אֵל does not, of course, affect the syntax or the exegesis.

erally have been phrased: שִׁמְעוּ אֶת הַדָּבָר הַזֶּה קִינָה אֲשֶׁר אָנֹכִי נֹשֵׂא עֲלֵיכֶם בֵּית יִשְׂרָאֵל.

Another instance of this usage occurs in the passage already cited, 5:6, וְאָכְלָה וְאֵין מְכַבֶּה לְבֵית־אֵל equivalent to וְאָכְלָה לְבֵית־אֵל וְאֵין מְכַבֶּה.

(3) *The infinitive with Lamed in v. 6* (לְהַסְגִּיר) *is used loosely* to indicate its general area of reference in the clause in which it occurs. The usage is very frequent in biblical Hebrew, in all stages of the language.[57]

Hence, the final clause in Amos 1:6 is to be rendered literally, "Because they sent Edom into complete exile for sale," The parallel clause in v. 9 is to be rendered, "Because they sold Edom into complete exile."

The two pericopes on the Philistines and on Tyre, when read in conjunction with the section on Moab, suggest a major catastrophe in Edomite history that went beyond the confines of normal military defeat. The Moabites may well not have been the only adversary of Edom in this war, which ended with the ignominious burning of the Edomite king's remains. Evidently, hordes of prisoners were taken by the victors. They proved a source of lucrative trade for the mercantile Philistines and Phoenicians, who could dispose of them along the Mediterranean littoral.

It is noteworthy that Tyre is indicted on an additional charge, "they did not remember the covenant of brothers," a sin that is lacking in the case of the Philistines. That the Philistines were an alien people of a stock and culture different from the native inhabitants of Western Asia was always keenly felt. The Phoenicians, on the other hand, like the Moabites, the Ammonites and the Edomites, were kinsfolk culturally and religiously, speaking only slightly divergent dialects of Canaanite, a term which legitimately includes Hebrew as well as Ugaritic.[58] In ancient thought this relationship would be expressed as ethnic "brotherhood."

The memory of this calamity that befell Edom did not disappear quickly. In the closing chapter of the book, which emanates from the latest period in the Prophet's career, Amos still speaks of Judah's taking possession of "the remnant of Edom."[59]

In view of the fragmentary character of the information available to us on the history of Edom, the particular calamity to which Amos refers cannot be identified with certainty. Even the limited information available to us suggests that there were many vicissitudes in Edomite history, with defeats predominating over victories. That this particular catastrophe left

[57] Some examples are II Sam. 14:17 (לִשְׁאוֹל); 14:23 (לְהַלֵּל); Joel 2:26 (לְהַפְלִיא); I Chron. 12:8 (לְמַהֵר). On this use of the infinitive, see BDB, s. v., *Lamed*, sec. 7, 517a, who define the use as "limiting or qualifying the idea expressed by the principal verb and so resolvable sometimes into *so as to*, *to* and sometimes into *in respect of*, *in*."

[58] *Cf.* Isa. 19:18.

[59] Amos 9:12.

no record behind would be entirely understandable, since it may not have involved the active participation of Israel and Judah, for whatever reason. Perhaps additional discoveries in the future may bring to light sources that will shed light upon this disaster in Edomite history.

VI

However, it is possible that this major defeat of Edom, which brought in its wake the wholesale enslavement of the population, refers to the war of Amaziah, briefly narrated in the book of *Kings*. The death of ten thousand Edomites at *Gey' Hamelaḥ* mentioned in *Kings* suggests a victory of major proportions, as does the annexation of Sela and its change of name, symbolizing its total incorporation into Judah. Amos is concerned with presenting the prophetic philosophy of history, in accordance with which national wrong-doing leads to national disaster. Hence he refers to the sale of the Edomite prisoners on a mass scale by the rapacious Philistines and Tyrian slave-dealers and the cruel behavior of the Moabites, which was the height of impiety.[60] He makes no reference to Judah's participation in this war, either because he may have regarded the conflict as justified, or because his objective is to concentrate on the internal social sins of his people in the present.

It is true that the title at the head of the book refers to Amos' prophesying during the reign of Uzziah, "two years before the earthquake." For many reasons, few scholars today maintain the view that Amos prophesied only once, at one fixed point in time. There are substantial grounds for seeing in our book the literary remains of a much more extensive prophetic career.[61] The first fifteen years of the reign of Jeroboam II of Israel coincided with the reign of Amaziah.[62] The "Arraignment of the Nations" coming at the beginning of the book would, therefore, faithfully preserve one of his early prophecies. It was probably his inaugural vision, delivered after Amaziah's crushing victory, the consequences of which included the mass deportation of the Edomites and their being sold as slaves, as well as the burning of the remains of the Edomite king.

There may be some additional data in *Amos* with regard to this major catastrophe in Edomite history. In the pericope on Edom, the nation is charged:

עַל־רָדְפוֹ בַחֶרֶב אָחִיו   וְשִׁחֵת רַחֲמָיו
וַיִּטְרֹף לָעַד אַפּוֹ   וְעֶבְרָתוֹ שְׁמָרָה נֶצַח

[60] The heinous character of burning human remains was felt acutely in the ancient world. See Josh. 7:25; II Kings 23:16; Isa. 66:24; Josephus, *Antiquities* xvi, 7.

[61] See Gordis, Composition, *passim*.

[62] II Kings 14:17.

In stichs e and f וַיִּטְרֹף is emended to וַיִּטֹּר by virtually all scholars, and the two stichs are rendered, "He guarded his anger forever and his wrath he kept eternally."[63]

However, וְשִׁחֵת רַחֲמָיו remains difficult. It is generally rendered, "He cast off all pity," but the use of שִׁחֵת with an abstract noun as object is without warrant. In an interesting paper, M. Fishbane has proposed that רַחֲמָיו in our passage means, "ally, friend," on the basis of the Akkadian root *ra'amu*, which occurs in Mesopotamian treaty contexts.[64] Accordingly, he renders the passage:

> "For he pursued his brother with the sword,
> and utterly destroyed his allies/friends."

That the two nouns אח and רחם in our verse are parallel is an excellent suggestion, but it should, we believe, be modified for several reasons: 1) The proposed rendering raises a substantive difficulty arising from Edomite history that we have already encountered. It is highly unlikely that Edom was in position during the eighth century to "utterly destroy his allies." 2) Moreover, the parallelism would be enhanced by vocalizing the first noun as a plural אֶחָיו. רַחֲמָיו should be rendered as "friends," on the basis of the Semitic root, which is common in Aramaic,[65] but it is best to refer it to domestic enemies.[66] A civil war fought by various factions within the country is a more likely hypothesis than Edom's being able to destroy foreign allies or vassals. The small states of Western Asia were a buffer for centuries between the empires of the East and Egypt. Each power would stimulate the activity of local factions to support their respective causes, like the pro-Assyrian and pro-Babylonian parties that were ranged against

[63] Reading with Peshita, Vulgate and most moderns, and interpreting שָׁמְרָה as virtually containing a *mappiq* in the *He*. On נטר parallel to שמר, *cf.* Jer. 3:5.

[64] Fishbane, 315 ff.

[65] See the parallel use of אָח and רֵעַ (Lev. 18:16–18) and the feminine counterparts in אֲחוֹתִי רַעְיָתִי. (Cant. 5:2). The nouns רֵעַ and מֵרֵעַ are rendered by *rāḥēm* in the Targumim.

An explanation may be ventured for the enigmatic rendering of LXX for the clause וְשִׁחֵת רַחֲמָיו, which is translated καὶ ἐλυμήνατο μητέρα ἐπὶ γῆς, "He destroyed the mother, upon the ground (or, earth)." LXX here exhibits a rabbinic norm of interpretation *g^{e}zērāh šāwāh*, "the identical category," in which two biblical passages using the same term are regarded as referring to the same subject matter. The verb שחת, "destroy," especially in conjunction with רחם which suggests "womb," and hence "mother," reminds the translator of the sin of Onan in Gen. 38:9 שִׁחֵת אַרְצָה, "He destroyed his seed upon the ground." The rendering here of רַחֲמָיו as' 'mother" supports our proposed rendering of מרחם as מִרְחָם a noun meaning "mother" in Isa. 49:15 (note the parallelism with אִשָּׁה). See Gordis, WB, 7, 355.

[66] For many years, I have been presenting this interpretation of the passage in teaching Amos at the Jewish Theological Seminary. I repeated the suggestion at a public lecture before the *Hug Hamiqra* of the Hebrew University in Jerusalem in the spring of 1972, while I was serving as visiting professor of Bible there.

the pro-Egyptian parties in Judah during the days of Isaiah and Jeremiah. Such a civil conflict would invite foreign intervention and conquest by neighboring powers and might well lead to the spoliation of Edom and the enslavement of its population.

The major conclusions of this study may be set forth as follows:

1. The integrity and authenticity of the entire text of Amos' "Arraignment of the Nations" is supported by weighty considerations of style, structure and substance.

2. The passage contains four pericopes relating to Edom. They all supply valuable information regarding a major catastrophe that befell the kingdom of Edom, in the first half of the eighth century.

3. The sections on the Philistines and Tyre charge both peoples with engaging in an extensive slave-trade, in which Edom was not the perpetrator or the partner, but the victim and object. לֶאֱדוֹם in both pericopes is the direct object of the infinitives הַגְלוֹתָם and הַסְגִּירָם respectively.

4. The pericope on Edom's sin suggests the possibility that a bitter civil war within Edom may have prepared the way for its defeat by foreign foes and the selling of its population into slavery.

5. The major indignity visited upon the king of Edom's body indicates that the defeat was devastating, far beyond the norm.

6. In view of the fragmentary and frequently obscure references to Edom in our historical sources, it is not possible to identify with certainty the particular national disaster suffered by Edom.

7. It is likely, however, that the references in *Amos* relate to the Judean king Amaziah's victory at *Gey' Melaḥ*, which took place during the first decade and a half of the reign of Jeroboam II of Israel, the period during which Amos' prophetic career had its inception.

8. The "Arraignment of the Nations" is probably the first prophetic address by Amos, a conclusion supported by its position at the beginning of the book.

Echoes of Ebla

By CYRUS H. GORDON
New York University

ANY MAJOR DISCOVERY is likely to have wide repercussions on the broad field to which it is related. Such is the case with the extensive library of cuneiform tablets discovered by Paolo Matthiae, thirty-four miles south of Aleppo. Over 15,000 texts capable of being pronounced and translated, dating from the Early Bronze Age (specifically from about 2400 to 2250) are about to revolutionize ancient Near Eastern Studies. It is the purpose of this article to outline some of the questions that Ebla is reopening and to indicate provisionally the revaluation that is in store.[1]

The Ebla archives are all in the Sumerian script and about eighty percent in the Sumerian language. The remaining twenty percent is in the native Semitic language of Ebla. There is no fundamental problem of decipherment, for the Ebla texts define about 2,500 Eblaite words in the known Sumerian language and also provide bilingual Sumero-Eblaite grammatical paradigms. Many Eblaite and even Sumerian points require clarification in detail, but the phonetic value of the signs and the vocabulary and grammar of both languages are "knowns" to be handled by philologians rather than "unknowns" to be solved by cryptanalysts.

The Ebla material starts before the establishment of the Dynasty of Akkad by Sargon in the twenty-fourth century. This means that Syria (and not Sargonid Mesopotamia) is the first known source of Semitic inscriptions, and of bilingual school texts. The Ebla tablets mention southern cities such as Jerusalem, Gaza and (in the same order as they are listed in Genesis 14) the five towns named Sodom, Gomorrah, Admah, Zeboyim and Zoar.[2] Bronze Age Syria-Palestine nurtured a highly literate urban civilization.

Although traditions are not the same as history, archeology has taught us not to dismiss them automatically as myth and legend. They often preserve historic memories. Faith in Homer led to the excavation of Troy, Mycenae, Tiryns and Knossos. Faith in Scripture led to the unearthing of Nineveh, Babylon, Susa plus a host of buried cities in the Holy Land. Mesopotamian tablets record the establishment of Sumerian Empires stretch-

[1] The main published sources of information available to me at the time of writing (1 March 1977) are by Giovanni Pettinato: "Testi cuneiformi del 3. millennio in paleocananeo rinvenuti nella campagna 1974 a Tell Mardikh = Ebla," *Orientalia* 44, 1975, pp. 361–374; and "The Royal Archives of Tell Mardikh-Ebla," *Biblical Archeologist*, 39 (no. 2), May 1976, pp. 44–52. While this article was in proof, the following study with additional bibliography appeared: Ignace J. Gelb, "Thoughts about Ibla: A Preliminary Evaluation," *Syro-Mesopotamian Studies* I, 1, March 1977, pp. 3–30.

[2] I learned about the Ebla listing of these five towns from Pettinato's lectures in the U.S.A. during the latter part of 1976.

ing to the Mediterranean, not only in the reign of Lugalzaggesi of Uruk (whom Sargon vanquished) but also of Lugalannemundu of Adab, six generations earlier. There must be a kernel of truth in such traditions because Syria-Palestine (= Syria-Lebanon-Israel-Jordan) was intellectually Sumerianized well before 2400 as we know from Ebla. The presence of cuneiform scribes in Syria-Palestine owed more to commerce than to warfare, though trade was often spread, and protected, by armed personnel. Sumerian rulers like Lugalannemundu, as he is reflected in ancient Mesopotamian tradition, must have implanted Sumerianism in the West.

The Sumerians were accomplished intellectually and technologically. Theirs is the world's first known literature. Their technology embraced city planning, monumental architecture, elaborate irrigational developments, stone cutting and metallurgy. Since it is impossible to think of Sumerian civilization without skilled lapidaries and smiths, the Sumerians could not have originated in Sumer (southern Babylonia) which is devoid of all minerals: stone or metal. That land is formed solely of alluvial silt brought down by the Tigris and Euphrates Rivers. The Sumerians from the start had foreign sources of raw materials from several directions, to provide the stones and metals that their craftsmen required. Sumer provides a good illustration of the principle that "internationalism"[3] precedes all high local civilizations.

Sumerian is agglutinative and quite different structurally from the other languages of the Near East. The high frequency of monosyllabic homonyms (represented by the distinctive signs that are not confused in the script despite their identity as to consonants and vowels) suggests that they were distinguished tonally. Tonality characterizes Chinese and several other languages of East Asia. However, in spite of various suggestions, Sumerian still remains isolated from the other known languages of the world.

The Sumerians had contacts with other speech groups prior to the time of the earliest Sumerian inscriptions (ca. 3,000). The names of the rivers and many cities in Sumer go back to Neolithic or earlier times when now-lost languages were spoken including one that is termed "Proto-Euphratean." Contact with Semites is reflected by loanwords in early Sumerian texts.[4] Thus DAM-GAR in Sumerian means "merchant" and is derived from the Semitic root *m-k-r* "to sell or buy, engage in trade"; = Akkadian *tamkâr-* "merchant." Sumerian *silim* "peace" is borrowed from Semitic *s-l-m* (cf. *salâm-* "peace" in Arabic = Hebrew *šālôm*). Now the name of Jerusalem in the cuneiform tablets, starting with Ebla, is Uru-salim; the first element is *uru*, the Sumerian word for "city"; the second is Semitic,[5] though its root,

[3] This term is useful and expressive, even though it is strictly speaking inaccurate when applied to times prior to the rise of nationalism.

[4] See Arno Poebel, *Grundzüge der sumerischen Grammatik*, Rostock: privately printed, 1923, pp. 33–34.

as we have just noted, was borrowed quite early into Sumerian. Sumerian mercantilism seems to be responsible for naming Jerusalem deep in the Early Bronze Age.

Hebrew (along with other Semitic languages) has old Sumerian loan-words. For example, *hêkāl* "palace, temple" is derived from Sumerian É-GAL (É "house" + GAL "big"). Ugaritic *hkl* "palace, temple" shows that the Semites of Syria-Palestine had borrowed the word in pre-Israelite times. It is generally assumed that this word was borrowed via Akkadian *ekallu*. However, the Ebla tablets oblige us to consider whether such loan-words entered Northwest Semitic directly from Sumerian in Syria-Palestine.

It is debatable whether some words were borrowed into Semitic from Sumerian or vice versa. The same word for "chair" occurs in Sumerian as GU-ZA and in Hebrew as *kissê*ʾ (= Ugaritic *ksu*, Akkadian *kussû*). Scholars were once agreed that the Semites borrowed it from the Sumerians. Now some outstanding authorities believe it was the other way around.

A number of Hebrew words derived from Sumerian are well known. Sumerian EN-GAR "farmer" comes into Hebrew as *ʾikkâr*. Of the same formation is Sumerian NA(N)-GAR "carpenter" borrowed widely into the Semitic languages; e. g., Hebrew *naggâr* "carpenter." Though the Hebrew is by chance attested only in post-biblical records, we know from Ugaritic *ngr* "carpenter" that it entered Northwest Semitic dialects before the earliest biblical books.

Semitic nomina agentis of the *qaṭṭâl* type are patterned after Sumerian professional designations like NA(N)-GAR/*naggâr*. Thus Hebrew *ṭabbâḥ* "cook," *dayyân* "judge," *gannâb* "thief," etc. The so-called Canaanite shift of accented *â* to *ô* is not operative in this nominal formation. Accordingly, the Sumerian impact that introduced this formation (*qaṭṭâl*) took place after that shift had taken place in the parent language of Canaanite/Hebrew.

The land between Mesopotamia and Egypt was called Amurru by the Akkadians. How extensive Amurru (= the land of the "Amorites") was, is hard to say. It may have embraced the Syro-Arabian wilderness and all of Syria-Palestine. Scholars speak often enough of the Amorite language though the evidence for it is restricted to personal names in cuneiform texts. Yet the term "Amorite" is convenient on occasion for want of a better name.

By the early second millennium the Sumerian leadership of Mesopotamia was on the road to extinction and the new rulers were Semites of western or Amorite origin. Hammurapi's dynasty at Babylon was Amorite, and so were those of Šamši-Adad I of Assur, of Mari and of a host of other city states in Mesopotamia and north Syria. Something can be deduced from the

[5] "Salim" is here probably the god whose name is written *šlm* in Ugaritic; see Cyrus H. Gordon, *Ugaritic Textbook*, Rome: Pontifical Biblical Institute, 1965 and 1967, pp. 490–1 (no. 2424).

names of the Amorites. For example, the theophoric element in a number of Amorite names, is written Ya-we or Ya-ah-we, which is the divine name that appears in Hebrew as *yahwe* "Yahweh."

"Amorite" as a linguistic term might be applied to the interrelated dialects of Amurru. But there were so many such dialects that the term is more likely to spread confusion than provide clarity. Arguing whether Eblaite is a branch of Amorite is not likely to be productive. It is wiser to consider, for the time being at least, Eblaite as an independent Semitic language.

Eblaite has so many affinities with "East Semitic" Akkadian as well as with "West Semitic" Canaanite, that the presumed sharp distinction between "East" and "West" Semitic must be reconsidered. Moreover, Eblaite calls for a reassessment of the relationship between the Semitic languages and Egyptian. The literature reflects an understandable desire to establish a classification and nomenclature. Less defensible is the urge to adhere to antiquated schemes and terminology when new evidence changes the picture. It is for this reason that I broke with the "Canaanite" classification of Ugaritic. Instead of splitting hairs about the linguistic position of Ugaritic, it would be more constructive to bring Ugaritic to bear, as comprehensively as possible, and without prejudice, on the nature of the entire Semitic family. This is now the case with Eblaite too.

The fundamental relationship between Semitic and Egyptian is recognized by all who are acquainted with both fields and have put thought on the problem. At the same time, those who know most about it shy away from coming to grips with the problem because of its frustrating complexities. Egypto-Semitic interrelationship is a bottomless pit. Only new discoveries bearing on the question in a significant way warrant reopening the subject. Ebla is such a discovery.

One of the links that connect Egyptian with Semitic is the tense called the Old Perfective in Egyptian, but the Permansive in Akkadian. It is a suffix tense used with transitive verbs (often with a passive meaning) as well as with intransitives. For example, the Old Perfective *rdi-kwi* or *dd-kw(i)* "I was given, set, put" represents the same tense as the Permansive *nadn-â-ku* "I was given, set, put." That the Old Perfective and Permansive are of the same origin is well known.[6] But how can this be explained, with Akkadian on the eastern fringe and Egyptian on the western fringe of the Egypto-Semitic speech area? Geographical linguistics would maintain that the tense existed in "Primitive Egypto-Semitic" but that it was displaced by innovations emanating from the central area (Arabia-Syria). According to this approach, the isogloss survived in the marginal areas (extreme east and west) until both Akkadian and Egyptian were totally extinguished by speech forms from the Central area (i. e., first Canaanite and then Aramaic). Un-

[6] Alan Gardiner, *Egyptian Grammar*, 3rd ed., Oxford University Press, 1957, pp. 235–6.

fortunately, such reasoning gets us deeper and deeper into artificial hypotheses. First we have to set up the fictions of "Primitive Semitic" and of "Primitive Egyptian"; then we are forced to invent the pre-prehistoric "Primitive Egypto-Semitic." Ebla provides a more realistic, historic approach.

Throughout Early Bronze and probably earlier (i. e., before 3,000), Syria-Palestine was a dynamic area whose native language consisted of dialects akin to Eblaite. The area was already permeated with Mesopotamian linguistic and other cultural influences. Syria-Palestine served as a land-bridge actively connecting Egypt and Mesopotamia from at least Early Dynastic times. Akkado-Egyptian isoglosses can accordingly be attributable to the lively contacts between the Nile and Euphrates valleys attested at Early Bronze sites such as Ebla.

There are other striking isoglosses that link Akkadian and Egyptian. Both of them use a sibilant as the prefix to indicate the causative conjugation (*ś* in Egyptian, *š* in Akkadian) while Arabic employs ʾ-; Hebrew, *h*-; and Aramaic, both ʾ- and *h*- dialectally. Eblaite and Ugaritic, however, regularly use *š*-. There are vestiges, however, of the sibilant causative in Hebrew, Arabic and Aramaic (though in the latter many are borrowings from Akkadian). The dialects of Syria-Palestine with *š*-causatives thus link Mesopotamia and Egypt whose languages share the same feature.

Along with the *š*-causative are the third person pronouns in Akkadian and Egyptian versus Ugaritic, Hebrew, Aramaic and Arabic which employ *h*-. The Egyptian dependent pronouns *sw* "he" and *sy* "she" go with Akkadian *šū* "he" and *šī* "she" versus Ugaritic-Hebrew-Aramaic-Arabic *huw*(*a*) "he" and *hiy*(*a*) "she."[7] In Old and Middle Egyptian there is an epicene form *swt* "he, she" with final *-t*. The Qumran Hebrew forms spelled *hwʾh* "he" and *hyʾh* "she" apparently reflect an earlier final *-t*. In any case, the oblique forms *hwt* "him" and *hyt* "her" in Ugaritic, and *šuâti* "him" and *šiâti* "her" in Akkadian preserve the *-t*. Curiously, Old and Middle Egyptian *swt* covers "he" and "she"; and similarly Old Babylonian *šuâti* "him" and "her" covers both genders. These epicene pronouns have an analogue in Hebrew. In the consonantal text of the Pentateuch both "he" and "she" are written *hwʾ*. This feature of the Pentateuch creates problems. The epicene pronoun for "he, she" pervades the Pentateuch (and only the Pentateuch) regardless of the hypothetical source (J, E, D, P), whether early or late. The counterparts of this epicene pronoun are limited to the

[7] To keep the discussion clear, I have refrained from citing all the cognates. However, at this juncture it is worth pointing out an interesting suggestion of Gotthelf Bergsträsser (*Einführung in die semitischen Sprachen*, Munich: Max Hueber Verlag, 1928, p. 8) that in Primitive Semitic "he" was *huʾa* while "she" was *šiʾa*. Note the distinction made in the Mehri dialect of South Arabia, in which *he* is "he" but *si* is "she" (*ibid.*, p. 127). The resemblance to the English pronouns "he" and "she" is striking, if only accidental.

early stages of Egyptian and Akkadian, which suggests an early redaction of the entire Pentateuch embracing all of its sources.

Another isogloss shared by Akkadian and Egyptian is the first person singular independent pronoun "I"; the Egyptian is written *ink* (Coptic *anok*), while the Akkadian is *anâku*. The other Semitic languages lack the final *-k*, except for Hebrew (*ʾânôkī* and *ʾanī*) and Ugaritic (*ank* and *an*) which have both.

Mesopotamian contacts with Egypt in early Sumerian times, when Egyptian culture was in a formative stage, have long been known. For instance, the intertwined serpentine necks of mythical beasts on such early Egyptian objects as the Narmer palette have been rightly connected with Sumerian art. The appearance of seal cylinders in Egypt is also correctly attributed to Mesopotamia influence. The stepped form of the earliest monumental pyramid in Egypt (built by Imhotep at Saqqara for the Third Dynasty Pharaoh Joser) recalls the ziggurats of Sumer. The title *ensi* of Sumerian rulers has been suggested as the origin of the Egyptian title *nsw* "King of Upper Egypt." It would be easy to compile a long list of probable Sumerian affinities with early Egypt.

Suffice it to note that Syria-Palestine was the meeting ground of Mesopotamian and Egyptian forces from prehistoric times through subsequent ages that are documented in writing as well as archeologically. Moreover, Syria-Palestine was not merely a link between two civilized areas. In its own right it could boast of a high, creative culture, that contributed significantly to the rise of influential civilizations on various segments of Syria-Palestine. The Hebraic and Phoenician civilizations, in the forms we know them, are relatively late. Ugarit precedes both of them and illuminates their origins. It is too soon fully to evaluate Ebla which antedates the flowering of Ugarit by a thousand years, because hardly any of the huge Ebla archives has been published. Yet some conclusions can now be drawn:

Syria-Palestine was already a creative urban region connecting Egypt and Mesopotamia in the Early Bronze Age. The Mesopotamian and Egyptian factors imbedded in Syro-Palestinian (including Hebrew) civilization stem largely from the Early Bronze synthesis and not entirely from later periods such as the ages of the Hyksos, Bondage, Babylonian Exile, etc. Intellectual internationalism is first attested in Syria-Palestine where bilingual education was fostered at Bronze Age Ebla with lexica and grammars. The classical medium of that culture was Sumerian, whose impact can be felt in the pre-Hebraic literature of Syria-Palestine, to say nothing of the Bible itself.

The linguistic affinities of Eblaite, going now with "East Semitic Akkadian" and now with "Northwest Semitic Canaanite" reopens the classification of the Semitic languages. Still more basically, it calls for a fuller integration of Egyptian into the Semitic languages. The term "Egypto-

Semitic" is as misleading as "Indo-Hittite" (which proves to be an unnecessary complication once Hittite is treated as an Indo-European language).

There is no longer any hard and fast line of demarcation between "East" and "West" Semitic; nor can we go on employing "South" in classifying the Semitic languages. The unsatisfactory character of the usual classifications is highlighted by the fact that as thorough a scholar as Arthur Ungnad abandoned them[8] and decided to group Ethiopic with Akkadian as East Semitic.[9] An understandable reason for this decision is the fact that Ethiopic and Akkadian have two varieties of the prefix tense in the simple conjugation; one with, and the other without, a vowel between the first and second consonants of the root. By basing classifications on selected criteria one can "prove" anything. But the far southwestern location of Ethiopia makes the "East" Semitic classification of Ethiopic meaningless.

Until the time is ripe for setting up a more realistic classification, we can at least divest ourselves of the arbitrary and mistaken features of current classifications, and pave the way for something better.

There are differences of opinion as to the main path of the early Mesopotamian impact (around the Jemdat Nasr Period) on Egypt (just before the First Dynasty). There are two possible routes: via the Indian Ocean and Red Sea, or overland through Syria-Palestine.[10] The discoveries at Ebla tip the scales in favor of the overland road.

[8] In his *Syrische Grammatik* (Munich: Oskar Beck) of 1913 (p. 1) Ungnad follows the conventional classification.

[9] In his *Grammatik des Akkadischen* (Munich: Biederstein Verlag) dated 1949, Ungnad groups the "South Arabs" (which includes the Ethiopians) with the Akkadians as East Semites.

[10] For a summary of the problem and the evidence, see Alan Gardiner, *Egypt of the Pharaohs*, Oxford: Clarendon Press, 1961 (paperback ed., 1964), pp. 396–398.

Comparative Semitics—A Premature Obituary[1]

By M. H. GOSHEN-GOTTSTEIN
The Hebrew University, Jerusalem

THIS PAPER IS one of a series of attempts to understand some major aspects of the history of Semitic Studies in post-Renaissance Europe. In a way, it focuses on issues contrasting, yet complementary, to those dealt with in a paper on the rise of Hebrew Studies and their comparative background, five centuries ago.[2] The task of the historian of a discipline is but to try and understand the past; but the historian who is also intimately involved in day-to-day work may wish, from time to time, to move from past to present and even to project into the future. Gaining a different perspective of the past and discerning trends which lead into the present may, perhaps, enable us to think of the future in somewhat different terms.

It is hardly a coincidence that in the academic setup of today Departments of Semitics are almost extinct.[3] To be sure, much of the traditional subject matter has found its way into reorganized units of Near Eastern Languages, or the like. This change of terminology reflects attitudes of discipline and interest as well as of University politics, public appeal and finances. If it would not sound so banal one could almost say that Semitic Studies are not what they used to be.

Even a quantitative inquiry comparing the type of scholarly output in Comparative Semitic linguistics in major journals, like *ZDMG*, around the turn of the century, with what is being published in today's journals would

[1] An earlier and shortened version of this paper was read at the annual meeting of the American Oriental Society in April 1977, as an invited paper. Certain other aspects were examined in a paper read before the Fifth Annual meeting of the North American Conference on Afroasiatic Linguistics which will be published elsewhere. Both papers try, in different ways, to gain a broader perspective of Comparative Semitics in the past and to suggest some directions for the future.

For centuries Hebrew has been the center of Comparative Semitics, and the two fields remain intimately linked. On many occasions over the past decades aspects of this connection have been studied under the auspices of Dropsie University and in the pages of the *Jewish Quarterly Review*. It is with memories of that past that I continue this tradition in this special volume also published by Dropsie University.

[2] I have lectured on this subject at various institutions during my stay in the States in the academic year 1976–77. Most of the issues referred to in my lectures are scheduled to be discussed at length in my forthcoming history: *Hebrew Studies and the Bible* I: *Theology, Humanism and the Rise of Semitic Philology, 1470–1670.*

[3] I am not sure whether even one such Department has survived in the United States. A few remain on the Continent, in England and in Israel.

come up with findings which would correlate with a widespread malaise felt by most students of Semitics. Comparative Semitic linguistics seems to have gone out of business. The state of the art seems to be frozen almost where it was left in the beginning of this century, as summed up by Brockelmann—with only relatively minor adjustments. Students of Semitics being, anyway, few and far between, hardly anyone who remains interested in this field dares to move into the comparative area. It used to be the feeling of beginners that everything worthwhile has already been said and that one should move to different fields since nothing can be done. This seems to have become the reaction of more seasoned scholars who have acquiesced in the unspoken judgment that Comparative Semitics is more dead than alive.[4]

The historian of Semitic Studies has no difficulty to suggest a good many reasons—apart from heaving a deep sigh about bad times, materialistic students, generative conquests, computor-happy generation, tape-recorder dialectology, etc. For four centuries Semitic Studies were intimately related to *Philologia Sacra.*[5] Or, if you will: it was the central position of Hebrew Studies that kept the flame of Semitics burning—in many shapes—since the first fullfledged comparative outline of Semitic grammar was written by Canini in mid-16th century. Again, Hebrew was at the center of 17th century parallelistic grammars and dictionaries (see note 13), strengthened by an ideology which regarded Hebrew as the mother language. Even when the "mother-daughter" relation seesawed in theological ideology and pseudo-prehistory allowed for the de facto preeminence of Arabic as a result of Schultens' work (see note 15), Hebrew remained the *raison d'être* of Semitics. As long as the study of Semitics was the study of Church-Culture languages,[6] the entire structure of Comparative Semitics could revolve around that seesaw relationship between Hebrew and Arabic, right into the late 19th century.

To be sure, Accadian had entered the scene by then. The kind of Comparative Semitics exemplified by Brockelmann's masterly catalogue—the *Grundriss*—took notice of the existence of the then newly discovered Semitic

[4] The chapter on Semitics contributed by H. Polotsky in *The World History of the Jewish People* I, 1 (1964) 99 f. is hardly an ordered survey of the field. But it contains some important observations on the specific subject dealt with here.

[5] In my scheme of periodization the post-medieval period starts in the last decades of the 15th century. Semitics started very slowly to free itself from that symbiotic embrace at the end of last century. To be sure, there remains the problem of differences between various subfields of Semitics. *Cf.* meanwhile my remarks in "Some thoughts on Syriac Studies in the Twentieth Century," *Proceedings of the 27th International Congress of Orientalists* (1971) 141.

[6] The literary "Church-Culture" languages became part of Humanistic knowledge during the first half of the 16th century. Apart from Hebrew, these were Aramaic, Arabic, Ethiopic. That body of languages was studied more and more intensively as time went by. Only the advent, in the 19th century, of Assyriology and Arabic dialectology changed the nature of the material studied by Semitists.

language. It was the notice given to an intruder who had upset the clear traditional model—it would lead us too far on this occasion to deal with that attitude as expressed by the greatest Semitist of the outgoing 19th century, i. e. Theodor Nöldeke. Yet once the impact of Accadian had truly settled in the post-Delitzsch generation—things were never the same again, and Comparative Semitics never regained a center of gravity. This, of course, is not unrelated to the fact that later "comparative grammars" are hardly more than adjusted minor rewrites of Brockelmann.

It should, however, not be overlooked that Brockelmann's attempt was far from being what later scholars made it to be. Even if we disregard the syntax, most sections of his *Grundriss* were not at all comparative-historical in the full 19th century meaning of the idea. More often than we care to admit the sections registered parallel facts side by side, without an attempt at connection, evaluation, etc. Only if we contrast the method with that practiced in that generation in the kindred field of Comparative Hebrew linguistics according to the tradition of the Stade-school can we appreciate fully the retreat beaten by Brockelmann—no doubt because of the problems he saw and the caution he practiced. I do not think I exaggerate very much if I suggest that Brockelmann unwittingly heralded the end of 19th century Comparative Semitics and at least turned partly back towards polyglot parallelistic registration.[7]

This major internal development might not have gone as far as it did without certain external events. The academic specialization of our century was bound to exercise a centrifugal effect on Semitic Studies. Scholars tended more and more to shy away from speculative structures and general statements and to opt for mastery of subfields which can be studied intensively and for which all the facts are known. Like other fields of historical-philological inquiry, Semitics tended to disintegrate into ever more refined subspecializations. The specialist in Assyriology, Islamic sciences, Christian Orient etc. knew both less and more than his 19th century predecessor. Even if he was—by profession and interest—a linguist, he tended to develop his field of specialization rather from within—often in conscious rebellion against comparativism. If you take the sum total of dissertations written during the past generation in the various fields of Semitic linguistics, it

[7] The methodological contrast between comparative-(pre)historical Hebrew linguistics—from Ewald via Stade to Bauer-Leander—and the "registration" type of Brockelmann's comprehensive *Grundriss* cannot be gone into here. There is little historization in Brockelmann's comparativism and hardly any functionalism or comparative weighing of options. It remains often hardly more than a well-ordered file index—much nearer to the method employed in his other great achievement, the *History of Arabic Literature*, than one is usually ready to admit. To be sure, there are differences of treatment between different sections in phonology, morphology and syntax, but only a relatively small number of sections emerges as properly historical-comparative.

becomes obvious that anti-comparativism has almost become a virtue.[8] The enticing new possibilities of dialect research, structural description, generative restatement etc. have effectively used up most of the scarce manpower. Once a young scholar has made his mark in a field like, say, Arabic dialectology, he will hardly ever get out. After all, there is objective justification to concentrate your efforts on issues which can be studied without lack of material, where you can control information, where you are not reduced to speculation. Small wonder that an entire generation has come to regard Comparative Semitics with suspicion—often justifiedly so in view of certain practices.

This paper does not intend to exhaust all the possible reasons for what has happened. But the historian of Semitic Studies cannot ignore the ideological component in the downfall of comparativism: the collapse of the positivistic picture of 19th century historicism robbed comparativism of its most potent justification. *Ursprache* and pedigree-model had been discarded. The substitute offered by a more cautious, less self-confident, generation proved too weak an incentive for comparativism. Historicism had overplayed its hand—like theology. What point remained there in playing the game of retrojection, in working out relationships and correlations, when the structure seemed to be built on sand?

It would, however, by wrong to conclude that comparativism has disappeared altogether. The opposite is the case. Whereas the phenomenon needs to be studied in detail, the facts are telling. Those who are inclined towards comparative exercises have found a large new field of activity. For almost a century we are aware of almost all the major facts which form the basis for Hamito-Semitic comparisons.[9] Yet at the very time when Semitic Comparativism is almost at a standstill, Hamito-Semitics is flourishing. Those few facts known and agreed upon have become the object of continuous reformulation as if they were new discoveries[10]—and on that basis

[8] When structural techniques caught up with Semitic linguistics after World War II, the methodological "revolution" tended to create an almost anti-comparative mood. As fads go, the hey-days of structuralism are over; but certain misinterpretations of its message are still with us.

[9] By the beginning of this century Reinisch had completed his major studies. *Cf.* especially his *Das persönliche Fürwort und die Verbalflexion in den Chamito-semitischen Sprachen* (1909). I am not entirely convinced that change of terminology (Afro-Asiatic) is a change of substance. I suspect that there might even be some political undercurrent.

[10] I am referring to the Cohen-Roessler-Thacker-Vycichl types of Hamito-Semitic comparisons. I have to admit that I have little understanding for the recent more radical Africanization. I should make it clear that I am not concerned at the moment with the correctness of a model that transcends Semitics, but with the practical possibility of using such knowledge meaningfully for Comparative Semitics—beyond the few often-discussed basic facts. It will be my contention that Afro-Asiatics has de facto stifled Comparative Semitic inquiry to a considerable extent, precisely by opening the door beyond manageability.

the claim is voiced that Comparative Semitics can only succeed within the framework of Hamito-Semitics.

There is little doubt that part of this curious phenomenon is due to genuine search for new facts, to a wish to get out of the cul-de-sac of traditional Comparative Semitics. But we cannot be sure that there are not some less healthy components. We have already alluded to the fact that Semitic reconstructions of the late 19th century did not always bear up under the methodological scrutiny of junggrammatical procedures. Much of what seemed assured fact had to be discarded, and comparativism in its classical form often lost out. It was defeated on both flanks, as it were: by the suspiciousness of anti-comparativism and by the zeal of hyper-comparativism. Those whose inclination went towards comparative adventures were all too ready to move into the beckoning pastures of Hamito-Semitics where strict methods could not be enforced, by the very nature of the material. Precisely because Comparative Semitics had become hesitant to offer more than individual proto-Semitic retrojections, precisely because it had become questionable to suggest entire proto-Semitic paradigms, etc. and comparison had been reduced anyway to atomistic reflections, it was not difficult to supply that kind of comparativism from the "enlarged" field of Hamito-Semitics. Be that as it may, the classical Nöldeke-Brockelmann type of Comparative Semitics turned out to be the loser.

This is enough for the moment by way of an obituary for Comparative Semitics. I should now like to develop some points of an argument in another direction—again, this is hardly more than an outline of what should be argued in detail.

It was the fate of Comparative Semitics to become, during the 19th century, the functional equivalent of other fields of comparative linguistics—notably Indo-European.[11] It is common knowledge that its history is different. It is not so well appreciated that to ignore the previous stages may mean to misjudge the present—and, perhaps, the future. It is the ups and downs of a thousand years of changing methods and points of view that prevent us from being too impressed by the fact that a certain type of inquiry seems to have run its course and to yield little further fruit.

It was the medieval symbiosis of Hebrew, Arabic and Aramaic that provided one happy set of circumstances to launch Comparative Semitics.[12]

[11] A less generous way of formulating the issue would be to suggest that in the second half of the 19th century Semitists tried to keep up with the advancement of the then comparatively recent discipline of Indo-European linguistics. In a way, this phenomenon was reenacted, when Semitics went structuralist—after World War II.

[12] I am concerned with methodological comparisons, not with sporadic insights such as contained, for instances, in midrashic literature. In the framework of a paper in this volume we are well advised to remember that in the past generation much important work on Comparative Hebrew linguistics in Saadyanic times was connected with the name of Solomon Skoss of Dropsie.

The newly discovered languages in the Renaissance-Humanist environment of 1500-1550 provided another matrix.[13] Again, the changing *Weltbild* after Leibnitz and Spinoza[14] made it possible that the pseudo-prehistoric construction of Schultens[15] could have the revolutionizing effect which started the era of pan-Arabism in Comparative Semitics in the first half of the 18th century—long before it is usually said to have started.

Put differently: *Wissenschaftsgeschichte* teaches us the simple fact that there existed different brands and types of Comparative Semitics, before it encountered the methodological advances in the newly established neighbouring discipline of Indo-European linguistics in the 19th century. This must suffice for now to remind us of the fact that we have got used to identifying a particular brand of Comparative Semitics with the entire field. To be sure, it is central to the way we were taught to think and work. But, perhaps, deepening our historical perspective might help us to evaluate our reaction if we are led to believe that Comparative Semitics—as a whole—is dead.[16]

[13] A considerable amount of monographic study in the volume mentioned above, n. 2, will deal with the developments in Comparative Semitics between 1550 and 1700. That stage is characterized by the attempt of Canini's *Institutiones* (1554). In my model of delineating the stages within the first period of the revival of Hebrew Studies in Renaissance times, Canini opens stage three—following the stages of Pellican-Reuchlin and of Muenster. The parallelistic-contrastive-polyglot type of Comparative Semitics is exemplified by names like Schindler, deDieu, Guichard, Cruciger, Hottinger—all of them almost forgotten. To be sure, all that achievement in Comparative Semitics is directly built on the basis laid by the Antwerp Polyglot—just as later on the *Lexicon Orientale* of Castellus was linked to Walton's enterprise.

It is only fair to stress that whereas a fully developed type of Comparative Semitics came into being in that period, Indo-European Studies had to boast little more than some forerunners. Even so, previous stages of Indo-European linguistics are often underestimated. *Cf.* the recent remarks of G. J. Metcalf "The Indo-European Hypothesis in the 16th and 17th centuries," in Dell Hymes (ed), *Studies in the History of Linguistics*: Traditions and Paradigms (1974) 233 f.

[14] Both philosophers were deeply concerned with the problem of Hebrew as the universal "mother-tongue" and, in a way, the study of Hebrew was not only influenced by the change but also contributed to it. The correspondence between Leibnitz and Ludolf is worth renewed study.

[15] The positing of a paleo-Hebrew language, to which all theologically relevant statements are made to refer and which may be recovered by Arabic, is the single most ingenious hypothesis in the history of Semitic Studies between 1550 and 1800. To be sure, Schultens too had his predecessors. But he evolved a new brand of Comparative Semitics almost singlehandedly—largely for the use of etymology. Were practitioners of Semitic linguistics better acquainted with the history of their discipline, they would appreciate that the notorious pan-Arabism of the 19th century is the direct result of Schultens' life work. The amazing duplicity of development in Ben Yehuda's ideology—almost two centuries later—will be gone into elsewhere.

[16] At this point it should be obvious that what I am trying to explore is the possibility of continued methodological pluralism in Comparative Semitics—once we have realized its changing character in the past. This methodological exploration is quite distinct from

Again, we shall have to ask ourselves whether what seems like lack of movement in the field of Comparative Semitics, as we know it, may be connected to the fact that in spite of all protests to the contrary it has remained Hebrew-Arabic centered. Take away Biblical Hebrew as the major *explicandum*[17] and push Arabic out of the center without substituting Accadian truly and fully—and the entire structure seems to collapse.

I have tried to argue these points from various directions in order to ask ourselves: are we facing something else than what we think we are? Even within the limited area of historical-comparative Semitics in its 19th century phase we may not yet have begun to digest the facts—let alone be in a position where everything has been said. Those facts came too late, as it were, to influence profoundly our standard post-Brockelmann teaching.[18] Far from having reached the end of the road and being dead, historical-comparative studies wait to be revived. Since the beginning of our century the facts of Accadian, ESA, Ugaritic etc., have been added to the existing picture as a kind of patchwork afterthought. The Semitist may have some reason to blame many distinguished students of Accadian whose attitude was far from helpful.[19] But the basic duty was his. We have not even tried to explore the heuristic possibilities of a non-Arabistic model in the reconstruction of Semitic systems—disclaimers notwithstanding. The perennial preoccupation with the one and only subject, the relationship between the East and West Semitic verbal systems, is the exception to the rule—not the rule itself. That was the only point where Accadian forced the Comparativist to rethink his position—with remarkably little success.

Hence: even if we were to start afresh to rethink Comparative Semitics on the typological lines of 19th century thought, there is no end to what must be done. And just in time: there is a good chance that the scholars of the 21st century will have to re-do the job—in light of Ebla and possible other finds from the third millennium.

attempts in the field of general linguistics, such as J. Ellis, *Towards a general comparative Linguistics* (The Hague, 1966).

[17] It is no coincidence that only Biblical Hebrew (and Aramaic) were ever treated as the target of proper comparative (pre)historic inquiry. The academic fate of the study of Hebrew is part and parcel of the story. Students of Arabic, Accadian etc. learned to get along with the barest minimum of comparative insights. In this context *cf.* also the chapter on "The History of the Bible-text and Comparative Semitics" in my *Text and Language in Bible and Qumran* (1960) 156 f.

[18] A theme to be developed is my claim that some major attempts at synthesis conceived in the late 19th century came at a point before epoch-making new facts could be assimilated. Hence 20th century scholars have tried ever since to struggle with the tension between an insufficient yet convenient model and the facts to be accommodated.

[19] Many Assyriologists of the past generation acted out an almost oedipal rebellion against anything connected with Hebrew Studies. It may well take a generation before the balance is redressed.

The corpse is kicking in all directions—little reason to issue a certificate of death.

We may go one step further. I have already remarked on the fact that the 19th century brand of Comparative Semitics was geared to prehistoric retrojections—since discredited. The reaction to the collapse of pedigree and *Ursprache* models has been almost total evasion of reconstruction. The Semitist has become extremely defensive when he ventures into Proto-Semitic. As suggested, he even shies away from attempting a paradigm.[20] I am not suggesting a return to Proto-Semitic *Aggada*-exercises á la Schleicher. But Comparative Semitics stands to gain if the heuristic value of retrojections is explored anew on a completely different scale.[21]

This, however, is not the entire thrust of this paper. I am trying to get at something more fundamental in light of what I have suggested for the past: the rejuvenation of Comparative Semitics on a broader, pluralistic, basis. The details for various types will have to be worked out carefully. For the moment we must be content with some general hints.

We shall deal at present with only two types of what to me seem to be emerging types of Comparative Semitics. One of these—if I am allowed to mention this—is of particular interest to me, because it has been growing almost unwilled by myself, right in my backyard.[22] These types are not intended to exclude others, nor are they meant to supersede or usurp the place of traditional Comparative Semitics. What I am suggesting is that we sensitize ourselves to additional possibilities of concentrations, to new questions and new answers. Just as we have now come to realize that there was more than one type in the past we should appreciate pluralism in the future. Just as we have learned during the past generation to allow for different types of noncomparative linguistics, we must now get used to different types of comparative linguistics. Different questions are being asked—different

[20] Bergstraesser's famous chapter in his *Einfuehrung in die semitischen Sprachen*—half a century ago—was the last audacious exercise in that direction. For my bias against atomistic comparative linguistics *cf.* especially p. xiv; 97 f. in the volume mentioned in n. 17.

[21] My "System of Verbal Stems in the Classical Semitic Languages," *Proceedings of the International Conference on Semitic Studies* 1965 (1969) 70 f. should be regarded as an attempt to practice this kind of inquiry.

[22] The method has been developed for a quarter of a century in classroom teaching, but this is the first attempt to argue some of the theoretical aspects common to all such explorations. Problems have been discussed until now in different frameworks. *Cf.* the Introduction to my *Medieval Hebrew Syntax and Vocabulary as influenced by Arabic* (1951) and the series on *Medieval Translations and Translators* (for an inventory *cf.* the forthcoming instalment in a Festschrift dedicated to Alexander Altmann). For different angles *cf.* my textbooks on *Aramaic Bible Versions*, *Medieval Hebrew Texts* and *Aḥiqar*. Note also my *Hebrew and Semitic Languages: an Outline Introduction* (1965) 25. The recent thesis written under my direction by Iddo Avinery on the Syntax of the Peshitta Pentateuch develops yet another aspect.

answers are given, and different scholars should feel free to explore the possibilities of each type.

The first type is what I call for the time being systemic-contrastive, taking up certain cues from 17th century contrastive parallelistic Semitics and developing them into new directions. The study of Semitics has been characterized in the past by the predominance of culture languages functioning in some kind of symbiosis. Because of shared culture values, the same content was expressed in different languages, some of them intimately related. Problems of translation techniques are not the invention of Semitists and the contact situations encountered are not unique. But various aspects of comparativism can be seen in a new light if the same contents is rendered into related yet different languages: Hebrew into different dialects of Aramaic, Aramaic (Syriac) into Arabic, Arabic into Hebrew. The problems are known from various subfields of Semitic philologies—we just have to get used to see them as a whole. You encounter them in the study of Bible versions, in medieval Hebrew-Arabic philology, in wisdom tales retold, back and forth, from Aramaic into Arabic and vice versa. Take together the methodic advances and observations made over the past decades in the study of the language in fields such as Targum and Peshitta, Sa'adya's *Tafsīr*, Tibbonite versions, recensions of Aḥiqar etc.—and you realize what we are trying to get at: the systematizing of insights achieved into a new type of Comparative Semitic inquiry.[23]

The nearer related the languages, the more outstanding the structure of different choices. What seems to be equally extant according to the cataloguing paragraph in a Brockelmann "Comparative Syntax," is obviously avoided in one dialect while preferred in another. Why would the translator avoid a construction which is suggested by the source language and whose parallel we would expect to be employed in the target-language? How do syntactic alternatives really function when you have what amounts to a limited control situation? Why will one Aramaic language express, say, the contents of emphasising the non-predicate by enclitic *-hu*, whereas the other will cleft the sentence? Why will the translator shift the object systematically into another position, when the syntactic description which we have at our disposal at present does not tell us anything about a possible problem. I am not concerned with instances of translation techniques—those have been studied elsewhere. I am exploring the problem whether we can extend the limits of Comparative Semitics—and how. What additional brand can be developed, if we try to study structures and functions in controlled contrasts—given the fact that the necessity to express the contents exactly

[23] I should like to make us aware that certain techniques go back to about 1600 and can be discerned, for instances, in unpublished manuscripts of nobody less than Scaliger himself.

keeps the variables down to a minimum. Can we forge tools that will allow us to get at the "innere Sprachform" of the classical Semitic languages in a way which was not possible according to the 19th century type of syntax—simply because one did not ask those questions?

It should be obvious that different types of Comparative Semitics are neither mutually exclusive nor complementary—they may be overlapping or hardly touching each other. The type just described will be helpful only in the study of areas where the basic conditions of widespread translations are met. But it can penetrate where the 19th century type never got a foothold, i. e., in the study of syntax and semantics.

I should like to suggest, finally, another type which should be explored within this pluralistic framework. For the moment I shall call it: formulaic-equivational. This type would not deal with data gained by actual translations, but would try to evaluate the possibilities inherent in the procedure of applying mental retranslations. Put differently: The exegesis in the field of Cananite, Ugaritic, Aramaic epigraphy etc., has much benefited from the procedure of looking for interdialectal calques and common idioms. This procedure has also been carried into intra-Accadian textual exegesis. I am referring to the method in which certain procedures used by Haupt and Landsberger have been systematically applied in recent years by Held.[24] Again, what has been applied until now for the understanding of individual textual stretches might be relevant within a new pluralistic typology of Comparative Semitics.

I trust I have made it clear that I do not accept the contention that the 19th century brand of Comparative Semitics is dead. It does not command any more its old exclusive position, but its techniques are there to stay and to develop. The body of language to be analyzed grows steadily, and even new horizons may open up if we manage to push the boundaries back into the third millennium. But, over and beyond that, the main thrust of the suggestions is that we must learn from the past in order to become aware of the possibilities of pluralism for future enrichment of research. In a way, a certain dimension of depth lost to Comparative Semitics when the idea of a proto-language was practically discarded, can now be regained, if different types of comparative inquiry can be made to function side by side.

An obituary for Comparative Semitics?—Premature, indeed.

[24] I do not think that participants are necessarily the most reliable witnesses. But for the sake of future historians of Semitic linguistics I would say that although Held and myself started out by learning from the same teachers some thirty five years ago, our development of new techniques does not result from a common source. I would also assume that Held is less interested than myself in aspects of the history of methodology of Comparative Semitics.

Popes, Jews, and Inquisition

from "Sicut" to "Turbato"

By SOLOMON GRAYZEL
The Dropsie University

THIS ESSAY[1] DEALS with the status of the Jews in western and central Europe in relation to the Church, as that relationship evolved in the course of the 12th and 13th centuries. It attemps to show 1) how the effectiveness of the more or less permissive and clearly defensive bull *Sicut Judaeis* was eroded, since it no longer fitted the conditions that came into being during the 12th century; 2) that the new spirit, essentially suspicious and aggressive, was reflected in the discussions of the theologians of these two centuries as they formulated and defined the theory of "the plenitude of power" which they claimed for the papacy; 3) that this new spirit animated the bull *Turbato corde*, issued and re-issued in the second half of the 13th century at the request of the Inquisition of the Middle Ages;[2] and that 4) nevertheless, something of the *Sicut* attitude remained, and the popes occasionally con-

[1] This essay is concerned mainly with the 12th and 13th centuries. It is my hope, God willing, to continue the discussion into the 14th century in another study. Research for this essay was made possible by funds provided by the generosity of Mr. D. Hays Solis-Cohen, the Fred J. Rosenau Foundation, and the A. L. and Jennie L. Luria Foundation. I am very grateful for their help. I offer my thanks also for the courtesies extended to me by the Archivio Segreto Vaticano and by the authorities at the Library of the University of Pennsylvania, especially by its Lea Library.

[2] One cannot, in the course of writing a brief essay on an important subject, refer to all the books consulted. Yet these may be the very books that stimulated interest and provided basic information. I therefore list a few of them here:

S. W. Baron, *A Social and Religious History of the Jews*, 2nd edition, Columbia University Press and the Jewish Publication Society, 1962 ff., vols. IX to XI = Baron, *History*.

Peter Browe, *Die Judenmission im Mittelalter und die Päpste*, Rome 1942 = Browe, *JM*.

James Parkes, *The Conflict of the Church and the Synagogue*, London 1934 = Parkes, *Conflict*; *idem*, *The Jew in the Medieval Community*, London 1938 = Parkes, *Community*.

Other works, dealing with the Inquisition of the Middle Ages, are listed below, in n.77.

Some other volumes, the names of which occur frequently in abbreviated form, are the following:

Baer I = F.(Y) Baer, *Die Juden in Christlichen Spanien, Aragonien.*

Baer II = *idem*, *Die Juden in Christlichen Spanien, Kastilien.*

ChJ = S. Grayzel, *The Church and the Jews in the 13th Century*, Philadelphia 1933.

CJC = *Corpus Juris Canonici*, ed. E. Friedberg, Leipzig 1879–1881.

MGH = *Monumenta Germaniae Historica.*

Potthast = *Regesta Pontificum Romanorum*, 2 vols., Berlin 1874–5.

Raynald. = Raynaldus, Odoricus, *Annales ecclesiastici.*

Stern, *UB* = Moritz Stern, *Urkundliche Beiträge über die Stellung der Päpste zu den Juden*, Kiel 1893.

The customary abbreviations have been used for periodicals:

JJS = *Journal of Jewish Studies.*

tinued the policy of protecting the Jews, sometimes even restraining the Inquisition. On the whole, however, the new attitude was to characterize Christian-Jewish relations for centuries to come.

Sicut represented the attitude of the Church as that attitude evolved in the early Middle Ages. Ever since the days of Constantine, the Jews occupied an anomalous position in Christendom. On the one hand, since they denied the essential Christian belief in Jesus as Savior, they had to be considered heretics, more dangerous than pagans.[3] On the other hand, their right to live among Christians had been recognized by the early Christian emperors and by almost all the early theologians. The emperors found them economically useful,[4] and the theologians assigned to them a prominent place in the drama of Christian salvation. Augustine himself defined their position in terms of limited toleration:[5] they were not to be killed, but they were to be dispersed and degraded.

In actual fact, the situation worked out almost as Augustine had suggested. Efforts to convert the Jews did not cease, and such efforts were sometimes accompanied by force. They were deprived of some of the rights they had enjoyed under the pagan emperors, but enough remained to maintain them in their Jewishness during the turbulent era of the barbarian invasions. Pope Gregory I (590–604) enunciated a policy on this aspect of the situation. In a number of letters to various princes and prelates,[6] he expressed the

JQR = *Jewish Quarterly Review*.
HUCA = *Hebrew Union College Annual*.
MGWJ = *Monatschrift für die Geschichte und Wissenschaft der Juden*.
PAAJR = *Proceedings of the American Academy for Jewish Research*.
REJ = *Revue des Etudes Juives*.

[3] Ambrose, in his commentary on Psalm 37 (Migne, *PL* 14, col. 1062), argues that the Jews, having rejected Jesus, ceased to be. *Cf.* Jean Juster, *Les Juifs dans l'Empire Romain* (Paris 1914), I, 177 ff.; 272, n. 1.

[4] Juster, *ibid.*, I, 209 ff., points to the numerical importance of the Empire's Jews, and pp. 235 ff. to the maintenance of the privileges which had been granted them by the pagan emperors. *Cf.* Grayzel, "The Jews and Roman Law," *JQR*, 59 (1968), 93–117.

[5] *Cf.* Augustine's comment on Ps. 59 (58):10–12; also *City of God*, Bk. 18, ch. 46 (Everyman's Library edition, II, 221):

> "Some may say that the sibyl's prophecies which concern the Jews are but fictions of the Christians. But that suffices us which we have from the books of our enemies . . . that they preserve it for us against their wills . . . in every corner of the world, as that prophecy of the psalm which they themselves do read foretells them: . . . *Slay them not, lest my people forget it, but scatter them abroad with Thy power*. . . . So it were nothing to say, *Slay them not*, but that he adds, *scatter them abroad*; for if they were not dispersed throughout the whole world with their scriptures, the Church would lack their testimonies concerning those prophecies fulfilled in our Messiah."

[6] For the text of Gregory's letters see *MGH*, Epistolae, I and II. Their Jewish references are discussed by Solomon Katz, "Pope Gregory the Great and the Jews," *JQR*,

view that conversion by force was contrary to the divine will; suasion alone was the proper method and kindness the proper expression of Christian faith; that within the limitations of Roman Law, Jews were entitled to live their lives and observe their religion in peace.[7] On the whole, except for the Visigothic experience of the 7th century,[8] and a few other instances of intolerance during the next four centuries:[9] the Jewish condition remained more or less in accord with the views of Gregory.[10] Local councils and a number of churchmen continued to urge further restrictions on Jewish life; but even they never thought of introducing such repressive measures without the consent of the civil government.[11]

24 (1933–4), 113–36; and by Parkes, *Conflict*, pp. 210–20; see also the summaries provided by B. Blumenkranz, *Les auteurs chrétiens latins du Moyen Age* (Paris 1963), pp. 73–80.

[7] *MGH*, Reg. Greg. I, Bk. I, 34, March 16, 591; Jaffe 1104:

> "... Hos enim qui a Christiana religione discordant, mansuetudine, benignitate, admonendo, suadendo ad unitatem fidei necesse est congregare. ..."

His letter to the Bishop of Palermo, *ibid.*, Bk. 8, 25, June 598; Jaffe 1514, is the one that begins with the words *Sicut Judaeis*. Only its first sentence and the sentiments were copied later.

[8] For the Visigothic experience of the Jews in Spain see Bernard S. Bachrach, "A Reassessment of Visigothic Jewish Policy, 580–711," *American Historical Review*, 78 (1973), 11–34; also Parkes, *Conflict*, pp. 345–70.

[9] A number of anti-Jewish outbreaks occurred in various parts of Western Europe in the course of these centuries down to the First Crusade. They are described by B. Blumenkranz, "The Roman Church and the Jews," *The Dark Ages*, ed. by Cecil Roth (Tel Aviv 1966), pp. 69–99; Cecil Roth, "Italy," *ibid.*, pp. 100–121; S. Schwarzfuchs, "France and Germany under the Carolingians," *ibid.*, pp. 122–42; *idem*, "France under the Early Capets," *ibid.*, pp. 142–61; Blumenkranz, "Germany," *ibid.*, pp. 162–74.

[10] Pope Leo VII (937–939) was asked by the Archbishop of Mainz what to do with the Jews who refused to join the Church. The pope replied, in what he must have considered to be the spirit of Gregory—expulsion was apparently then not considered an act of compulsion—that he must first try to persuade: "... si autem credere noluerint, de civitatibus vestris cum nostra auctoritate illos expellite. Per virtutem autem et sine illorum voluntate nolite eos baptizare." Migne, *PL*, 132, col. 1083; Aronius, *Regensten zur Geschichter der Juden im fränkischen und deutschen Reiche bis zum Jahre 1273* (Berlin 1902), no. 125; Jaffe 2766: *Diebus vitae*. There is also the story of Pope John XVIII (1004–1009) sending a special emissary to save the Jews of Normandy: *cf.* V. Zimmermann, *Papsturkunden*, no. 1018. Above all, we have the expressed gratification of Pope Alexander II in 1065 that the prince of Benevento refused to force Jews into Christianity (S. Loewenfeld, *Epistolae Pontificium Romanorum ineditae* (Leipzig 1885), p. 52, no. 105), and to Viscount Berengarius of Narbonne (Jaffe 4528), as well as to other bishops, for defending the Jews against the knights on their way to aid in the reconquest of Spain (Migne, *PL*, 146, col. 1386; Mansi, XIX, 964).

[11] On the efforts of Bishops Agobard and Amulo of Lyons and their colleagues to have the Carolingian emperors impose further restrictions on the Jews, see *Agobardi Lugdunensis Archiepiscopi Epistolae*, *MGH*, Epistolae, V, 164, 199 f., 239 f.; Arthur J. Zuckerman, "The Political Uses of Theology, the Conflict of Bishop Agobard and the Jews of Lyons," *Studies in Medieval Culture*, III, ed. by J. R. Sommerfeldt for the Medieval Institute, Western Michigan University, 1970, pp. 23–51; Blumenkranz, *Les Auteurs*, pp. 152 ff. *Cf.* also Aronius, *Regesten*, nos. 84–97.

Equally significant was the attitude following the attacks upon the Jews in the Rhineland at the beginning of the First Crusade. There were bishops who were ready to protect the Jews, until it became obvious that the mob of crusaders could not be stayed. The attackers left behind a considerable number of dead and a number of forced converts. The following year, in 1097, Emperor Henry IV permitted the converts to return to Judaism.[12] Pope Urban II, who had initiated the crusade, had not spoken out against the rioters and now voiced no objection to the return to Judaism of the forced converts. The one who did object was the so-called Clement III, the anti-pope of the day: he declared the reversion to Judaism to be contrary to Canon Law.[13]

The need of the Jews for additional protection was so patent at the beginning of the 12th century that Emperor Henry IV included them in the country-wide peace proclaimed in 1103 at Mainz.[14] The Jews must have appealed to the pope as well, perhaps through the Jewish community in Rome. But it was not until some twenty years after the *Landfrieden* of Mainz that Pope Calixtus II (1119–1124) issued the famous Bull of Protection, *Sicut Judaeis*.[15]

[12] Reversion to Judaism was permitted by the early Christian emperors: *cf.* Theodosian Code (*ThC*) XVI.8.23. In later centuries, down to the First Crusade, there is also little evidence that reversion was punished, although it was of course frowned upon, except in Visigothic Spain (see next note). Even a century later, when, at the time of Richard's coronation, Benedict of York was forcibly converted, the archbishop of Canterbury permitted his reversion to Judaism (*cf.* Joseph Jacobs, *The Jews of Angevin England* [London 1893], p. 106). Henry IV's permission to revert to Judaism is discussed by Parkes, *Community* (2nd ed., New York 1976), pp. 79 f.; Aronius, *Regesten*, no. 203. *Cf.* Browe, *JM*, pp. 252 ff. Sara Schiffmann, "Heinrich IV. Verhältniss zu den Juden zur Zeit des ersten Kreuzzuges," *Zeitschrift für die Geschichte der Juden in Deutschland*, 1931, 39–58, esp. p. 50.

[13] "Relatum est nobis a quibusdam quod Judaeis baptizatis, nescio qua ratione . . .": Philip Jaffe, *Monumenta Bamburgensis* (vol. V of Bibliotheca rerum Germanicarum), p. 75, no. 90; Aronius, *Regesten*, no. 204; Jaffe 5339 [4013]. The reference to this being prohibited by Canon Law—"secundum canonicam sanctionem"—can refer only to the IV Council of Toledo (Dec. 633) and to the inclusion of the same attitude in subsequent canons of various Church councils. No papal expression and no universally accepted code of Canon Law was as yet in existence to prohibit reversion to Judaism.

[14] For the Landfrieden of Mainz in 1103, see Aronius, *Regesten*, no. 210. The Jews were taken under imperial protection, along with churches, clerics, monks, laymen, merchants, and women. This automatically deprived them of the right of self-defense, that is, the right to carry weapons. In a sense this had social disadvantages: *cf.* Kisch, *The Jews in Medieval Germany* (Chicago 1949), pp. 140 ff. It led before long to the evolution of the concept of the Jews as *servi camerae*.

[15] For a discussion of *Sicut* see Grayzel, "The Papal Bull *Sicut Judaeis*," *Studies and Essays in Honor of Abraham A. Neuman*, ed. by Meir Ben-Horin, Bernard D. Weinryb, and Solomon Zeitlin (Philadelphia 1962), pp. 243–280. There, on pp. 244 ff., the Bull is given in full. It is also given in Grayzel, *ChJ* (2nd ed., New York 1966), p. 92, no. 5, with the addition by Pope Innocent III (Potthast 834, *Licet perfidia*). *Cf.* Baron, *History*, IV, 7 f.; J. R. Marcus, *The Jew in the Medieval World*, (Cincinnati 1938), pp. 152 f., with the addition by Gregory X.

The entire introductory sentence of Pope Calixtus' *Sicut* echoes the Gregorian attitude, thereby indicating that the pope of the 12th century was following in the footsteps of the pope of the sixth. Moreover, Pope Calixtus did not address his Bull to any one bishop or to any specified local authority; he addressed it "To all the Christian Faithful," urging them in effect to recognize the right of the Jews to live peacefully in their midst. The introductory statement made two points: 1) Since there were limits to what was permitted the Jews, there should be limits to what was forbidden them. 2) The pope says that, although they remain obstinately insistent on their Jewish beliefs, nevertheless he, the pope, out of Christian kindness, grants the protection for which they asked.[16] The Bull then goes on to enumerate the areas in which protection is extended: No one must be converted to Christianity by force, for a conversion which is not voluntary is not trustworthy.[17] No Jew should be put to death excepting by decision of the local judicial authorities. Nor must a Jew be harmed in body or property.[18] The prevailing good customs regarding the Jews in any land ought not to be changed.[19] There had apparently been frequent instances of desecration of Jewish cemeteries; the miscreants must be punished.[20] The Bull concludes, however, on a disturbing note, namely, that it applies only to such Jews as are not guilty of plotting to subvert the Christian faith.[21] Reasonable enough under the then prevailing circumstances, the clause, perhaps unintentionally, suggested a method for counteracting the spirit and content of the entire document.

There can be little doubt that, as an exhortation to Christian piety, *Sicut* prevented many a riot and some hostile legislation. Yet it seems clear in retrospect that the Bull spoke to a state of affairs that did not long continue. The 12th century witnessed many changes in European society. It

[16] "Sicut Judaeis non debet esse licentia in synagogis suis ultra permissum est lege presumere, ita in his que eis concessa sunt nullum debet prejudicium sustinere. Nos ergo licet in sua magis velint duritia perdurare quam prophetarum verba et suarum scripturarum arcana cognoscere atque ad Christianae fidei et salutis notitiam pervenire, quia tamen defensionem nostram et auxilium postulant, ex Christianae pietatis mansuetudine [At this point, succeeding issues of the Bull mentioned the names of all or most of the predecessors who had issued it.], ipsorum petitionem admittimus eisque protectionis nostre clypeum indulgemus."

[17] "Statuimus etiam ut nullus Christianus invitos vel nolentes eos ad baptismum per violentiam venire compellat. . . . Veram quippe Christianitatis fidem habere non creditur qui ad Christianorum baptisma non spontaneus sed invitus cognoscitur pervenire."

[18] "Nullus etiam Christianus eorum personas sine judicio potestatis terrae vulnerare aut occidere vel suas pecunias auferre presumat."

[19] "aut bonas quas hactenus in ea qua habitant regione habuerint consuetudines immutare."

[20] ". . . decernimus ut nemo cemetarium Judeorum mutilare vel minuere audeat, sive obtentu pecunie corpora humata effodere."

[21] "Eos autem dumtaxat huius protectionis presidio volumus communiri qui nihil machinari presumpserint in subversionem fidei Christianae."

saw the growth of cities and the rise of a Christian middle class. It saw, consequently, the reduction of the Jews to a lower economic status and their increasing reliance on moneylending as an occupation.[22] In the religious aspects of 12th century life, changes were also in the making. There was no let-up in crusade preaching, with its concomitant stirring of religious fervor,[23] one indirect consequence of which was the myth of Ritual Murder. Above all, for the purpose of this discussion, it must be noted that the Church became better organized and more centralized. In the course of the 12th century, theologians and canonists were deeply involved in the discussion of the proper relationship between the pope and the secular rulers, that is, between Church and State. A corollary of that relationship was that between the Church and the Jews.[24]

It may be well to speculate, at this point, on the spirit in which *Sicut* was issued by succeeding popes. One has the feeling—it can be no more than that at present—that, judging merely from the paucity of other defensive papal statements in the second half of the 12th century, the re-issuance of *Sicut* was still considered an effective defense of the Jewish population. In the 13th century, on the other hand, the need for fairly frequent defensive utterances appears to indicate that *Sicut* could no longer be considered effective. Its re-issuance by most 13th-century popes seems to be a gesture, a formality, part of the ceremonial connected with the official entrance of the pope into the Eternal City. This impression is strengthened by the fact that three of the 13th-century popes considered it necessary, probably at the urgent appeal of the Jews, to add a statement to the official wording of *Sicut* dealing with the Ritual Murder charges.[25] In the 14th century, in the Avignon period, the issuance of *Sicut* went out of style. Only two popes of that period issued it: Clement VI (July 4, 1348) in its original form, while a few months later he issued a longer, more specific letter of protection to warn Christians that Jews must not be accused of causing the Black Death

22 *Cf.* Robert S. Lopez, *The Commercial Revolution of the Middle Ages, 950–1350* (New York, Prentice-Hall, 1971), esp. pp. 121 f.

23 During the Second Crusade, 1144 and for a few following years, Pope Eugenius III was not heard from when the Jews of Germany were again in danger, but Bernard of Clairvaux did intervene in their behalf. See his letter to Henry, Archbishop of Mainz (1146) in Bruno James, *The Letters of Bernard of Clairvaux* (Chicago 1953), pp. 465 f., no. 465.

24 *Cf.* S. W. Baron, "Plenitude of Apostolic Power and Medieval Jewish Serfdom" (Hebrew), *Sefer Yobel leYitzhak Baer* (Jerusalem 1960), pp. 102–124; *idem*, "Medieval Nationalism and Jewish Serfdom," *Studies and Essays in Honor of Abraham A. Neuman* (Philadelphia, Dropsie College 1962), pp. 17–48; Kisch, *Germany*, 145–53. *Cf.* also Walter Ullmann, *The Growth of Papal Government in the Middle Ages*, I (London 1962), ch. 13, pp. 413–446.

25 Innocent IV in 1247; Gregory X in 1272; Martin IV in 1281. The additions are noted in the essay in the Neuman *Studies*, pp. 258–61. They are also discussed below.

26 Reg. Vat. 187, 20v–21r has the two Bulls: *Quamvis perfidiam* as no. 105, and *Sicut* as

by poisoning the drinking water.[26] On June 7, 1365, Pope Urban V likewise issued the traditional *Sicut*, directed to the Jews of Avignon, for reasons which cannot be specified.[26a] It was issued in the 15th century by Pope Martin V, on February 20, 1422.[27] It began with the usual wording, and went on to warn the monks to stop arousing the populace against the Jews. Finally, a *Sicut* was issued by Pope Eugenius IV (January 25, 1432), which turned into an order that the Jews in the State of the Church must not be burdened to excess with exactions of all kinds.[28] Clearly, the document on which popes and Jews at first relied as a means of protection lost its efficacy sometime during the 13th century. When and how did this change take place?

The turning point seems to have been the *Sicut* issued by Innocent III (September 15, 1199). He made no changes in the by then already traditional text; he did, however, add a prefatory statement. He thought it necessary to explain that he took the Bull seriously because it reflected the theological principle enunciated by Augustine, namely, that the Jews should not be oppressed too severely, since they bear witness to the truth of Christianity.[29] Even more than the need for the appendices mentioned above, this statement by Innocent III shows that, barely eighty years after its origin, the *Sicut* Bull was reduced to little more than an exhortation that, for the sake of tradition, Christians ought not to kill the Jews in their midst, even though their presence is intolerable.[30] The same view was taken by most of Innocent's successors. They saw no contradiction between issuing *Sicut* and urging action directly contrary to its letter and spirit. For to their

no. 106. Raynald, a.a. 1348 #33, runs them together. Both were occasioned by the charge that the Black Death was due to the Jews poisoning the drinking water, and *Quamvis* urges the prelates to fight against the charge. *Quamvis* is given in full in A. Lang, *Acta Salzburgo-Aquilajensia*, I (Graz 1903), pp. 300 f.

[26a] Reg. Vat. 254, fol. 34r.; *Bull. Rom.* III, 22, 327. Clement VII of the Avignon succession issued a Bull on October 18, 1379, which begins like a *Sicut* but continues as a defense of the Jews of Avignon against a compulsory change of residence (Reg. Avin. 215, fol. 158 r-v). He issued the usual *Sicut* on November 12, 1393 (Reg. Avin. 273, fol. 354r.).

[27] Félix Vernet, "Le Pape Martin V et les Juifs," *Revue des questions historiques*, LI (1892), 373–423, lists a number of Bulls issued by Pope Martin that began with the phrase *Sicut Judaeis*, and even listed preceding popes who issued a *Sicut*, but soon went off into matters of immediate moment to the Jews. So no. 9 of his appended list (p. 411) is given by Raynald, a.a. 1419 #2. So too no. 24, given at Rome on February 20, 1422, is the one cited by Moritz Stern, *UB*, pp. 31 ff., and quoted by Raynald, a.a. 1422 #36.

[28] The Bull is given in full in Stern, *UB*, p. 43, no. 34.

[29] The few lines read as follows: "Licet perfidia Judaeorum sit multipliciter reprobanda, quia tamen per eos fides nostra veraciter comprobatur, non sunt a fidelibus graviter opprimendi. . . . quam ipsi non intelligentes, in libris suis intelligentibus representant." *Cf.* Neuman, *Studies*, p. 256; *ChJ*, p. 92; Potthast, 834.

[30] Innocent III, *Etsi Judeos*, to the Archbishop of Sens and the Bishop of Paris, July 15, 1205: ungrateful and untrustworthy as they are, "pietas Christiana receptet et sustineat cohabitationem illorum." Potthast 2565; *ChJ*, pp. 114 ff., no. 18; Decr. Greg. IX, Lib. V, tit. 6, c. xiii (Friedberg, II, col. 775).

minds there was no contradiction; they were acting in the spirit of their age, which—as we shall see—did not tolerate religious deviation and which some moderns have, for that very reason, admiringly called "The Age of Faith." People of that age did in fact consider the mere repetition of *Sicut* as an act of grace, an example of *mansuetudo* or *pietas Christiana.*

The primary appeal of *Sicut* was for the safety of the Jews in life and property and for their privilege of observing their religion unless they chose to abandon it of their own free will.[31] Decretalists and popes continued to insist that conversion must be voluntary, but with a difference. Gratian (*ca.* 1140), who laid the foundation for official Canon Law, chose to emphasize, not the nature or the degree of force used in converting Jews, but rather the sanctity of the formula spoken while they were being baptized. He said:[32]

> ". . . Therefore they are not to be induced to conversion by force, but by the use of their judgment. Those, however, who had already been compelled—as happened in the days of the very religious prince, Sisebut—inasmuch as by accepting the grace of baptism they had become associated with the divine sacraments, . . . it is only proper that they be compelled to retain the faith they had accepted, whether by force or necessity, lest the name of the Lord be blasphemed and the faith they had assumed be considered vile and contemptible."

Gratian's ruling was, of course, not yet official. But whatever doubts remained on the subject of the converts' reversion to their original faith were removed by Innocent III in 1201.[33] The Archbishop of Arles, ap-

[31] See above, nn. 16 and 17.

[32] "Ergo non vi, sed libera arbitrii facultate ut convertantur suadendi sunt, non potius impellendi. Qui autem jampridem ad Christianitatem coacti sunt, (sicut factum est temporibus religiosissimi principis Sisebuti), quia iam constat eos sacramentis divinis associatos et baptismi gratiam suscepisse, et crismate unctos esse, et corporis Domini extitisse participes, oportet ut fidem, quam vi vel necessitate susceperint tenere cogantur, ne nomen Domini blasphemetur et fidem quam susceperunt vilis ac contemptibilis habeatur." Gratian, *Decreti*, part I, distinctio XLV, c. 5 (Friedberg, I, col. 162).

This is a quotation from IV Toledo (633), as transmitted by Ivo of Chartres (Mansi, X, 633). It is to be noted that the council took place after Sisebut's death. He had tried to convert the Jews by force, without benefit of a council, about 613. The IV Toledo was more lenient than "the very religious" Prince Sisebut had been. *Cf.* S. Katz, *The Jews in the Visigothic Kingdoms of Spain and Gaul* (Cambridge, Mass. 1937), p. 12.

[33] *Maiores ecclesiae*: Potthast 1479; *Decr. Greg. IX*, Lib. III, tit. 42, c. iii; *ChJ*, p. 100, no. 12: ". . . Verum id est religioni Christiane contrarium ut semper invitus et penitus contradicens ad recipiendam et servandam Christianitatem aliquis compellatur. Propter quod inter invitum et invitum, coactum et coactum, alii non absurde disinguunt, quod is qui terroribus atque suppliciis violenter attrahitur, et ne detrimentum incurrat Baptismi suscipit sacramentum (sicut et qui ficte ad Baptismum accedit) characterem suscipit Christianitatis impressum, et ipse tamquam conditionaliter volens, licet absolute non

parently faced with an actual situation, was not sure that Gratian's decision was correct; he may have recognized the conflict between Gratian and the statement in *Sicut*. He therefore turned to Pope Innocent with a series of questions on doubtful baptisms: of a person baptized while asleep, of an infant baptized without the consent of its parents, and of a baptism under compulsion. To the last instance the pope replied practically in the words of Gratian and of IV Toledo. A distinction should be made, he said, between people who, when under compulsion, objected vocally and continuously, and such as objected inwardly or not insistently; the baptism of the latter is valid and they must be compelled to remain Christians. "It is better to object unmistakably than to consent in the slightest degree." Considering that, at that time, almost all conversions from Judaism were the result of riots, with the knife literally at the Jew's throat, it is difficult to see how Innocent's view, and its ultimate inclusion in the *Corpus Juris Canonici*,[34] can be anything but a negation of *Sicut*. Indeed, it all but made rioting a holy endeavor. For every riot took its toll, both of those who protested insistently, even unto death, and of those who refused martyrdom and soon became subject to inquisitional investigation.[35]

A related problem, one on which Church opinion varied through the years, concerned the infant children of Jews. *Sicut* said nothing about children; the subject had not been broached at the time of the Bull's first issuance. Perhaps humaneness was then more important than theology. In the 13th century it occurred to some theologians that to leave children under the authority of unbelieving parents was to endanger their souls.[36] Consequently, they suggested that, since Christian princes claimed the Jews as

velit, cogendus est ad observantiam fidei Christiane, in quo casu debet intelligi decretum Concilii Toletani . . . habeatur. Ille vero qui numquam consentit, sed potius contradicit, nec rem nec characterem suscipit sacramenti; quia plus est expresse contradicere quam minime consentire. . . ."

[34] The reference to *CJC* was given above, in the preceding note. How unquestioningly the attitude was accepted is clear from its surprising defense by Thomas Aquinas (*Summa*, Bk. II, pt. II, qu. 10, art. 8). One should remember, however, that Aquinas was not justifying the existing Canon Law as much as setting it forth rationally. It may be considered subjective on the part of a Jew to feel that Aquinas' argument on this point is unconvincing, but it does appear unworthy for a man of his intellectual stature to offer the following comparison: "sicut vovere est voluntatis, reddere autem est necessitatis, ita accipere fidem est voluntatis, sed tenere iam acceptam est necessitatis." Making a voluntary promise and choosing between life and death are not comparable situations. In time, of course, force itself came to be justified. See Browe, *JM*, pp. 237–51, esp. 239.

[35] A number of instances will be cited below, notably the one in Southern Italy, the one at La Marche in France, and the one in Rome in 1290. *Cf.* respectively nn. 125, 127, and 107. The pious prospect of making converts could serve as an excuse.

[36] The statement in Gratian reads: "Judeorum filios vel filias, ne parentum ultra involvantur erroribus, ab eorum consortio separari decernimus, deputatos . . ." either to monasteries or to God-fearing Christians from whom they might learn the ways of Chris-

their slaves, they could and should take away their children and have them baptized. Thomas Aquinas, however, after listing the arguments for doing so, rejected the idea on several interesting grounds.[37] Nothing of the kind had ever been done by important Christians, either emperors or theologians.[38] If the baptized children remained with their parents, there was always the possibility that the parents might influence them and that their Christianity might become doubtful. Above all, Aquinas argued in a long introduction to his objections, the removal of children from their parents was contrary to Natural Law which is equivalent to Divine Law.[39] Duns Scotus, in the generation following that of Aquinas, took issue with him on this point: God's rights over the child are superior to the rights of the parents.[40] As for those who argued that to take children away from their parents was to use force in conversion of the parents, the answer was that only the Church could define the meaning of the term "force."

It may be noted in this connection that one of the popes in the second half of the 13th century—it may have been Clement IV (1265–1268)[41]—took a stand against the baptism of a child. He wrote to a certain bishop

tianity. It seems to apply to Jewish children of whatever age and already converted under whatever circumstances. *Decreti*, II, Causa XXVIII, qu. 1, c. xi. This statement, too, is traceable back to Visigothic precedent, that of King Reccared and III Toledo (589); *cf.* Mansi, IX, col. 996 #14. For a discussion of the subject see Mario Condorelli, *I fondamenti giuridici della tolleranza religiosa* (Milan 1960), pp. 103–04; Guido Kisch, "Toleranz und Menschenwuerde," *Judentum im Mittlealter* (Miscellanea Mediaevalia, 4), (Berlin 1966), 1–36, esp. 17 ff.

[37] *Summa*, Bk. II, pt. ii, qu. 10, art. 11.

[38] Aquinas properly omits the Visigothic examples, since Recarred's edict was directed against children of a mixed relationship, and that of Egica (XVII Toledo, 694; Mansi, XII, 101–03) represented a conversion by force of both children and adults.

[39] *Ibid.*: "Alia vero ratio est quia repugnat iustitiae naturali. Filius enim naturaliter est aliquid patris. . . . Unde contra iustitiam naturalem esset si puer, antequam habeat usum rationis, sit sub cura patris, vel de eo aliquid ordinetur invitis parentibus." The third point in his refutation is, therefore, "quod Iudaei sunt servi principum servitute civili, quae non excludit ordinem iuris naturalis vel divini."

[40] Duns Scotus said, "Nam in parvulo Deus habet maius jus dominii quam parentes." *Cf.* The Kisch essay mentioned above, p. 18. Ultimately this view prevailed over that of Aquinas, at least in practice. No one raised his voice in criticism of King Manoel of Portugal when, in 1497, he took all Jewish children away from their parents and had them baptized in order to retain the parents in Portugal.

[41] The document on which this is based comes from the Vatican Archive, Armarium XXXI, no. 72, fol. 232 r., no. 2360. It was published in full by me, "Jewish References in a 13th Century Formulary," *JQR*, XLVI (1955), pp. 61–63. The attribution to Pope Clement IV is conjectural, since offhand it strikes one as out of character. In the Formulary, however, it is located following a number of other Bulls by that pope. The Formulary does not identify the authors of the Bulls. This Bull (*Cum de tam*), says in part: "Verum sicut interdicta est eis seducendi Christianos audacia . . . sic ad fidem non sunt inviti cogendi. . . . Sane lacrimabili nobis Eleazar-Judaeus cum quaestione monstravit quod clericus tuae diocesis filiam suam septennem par pedisecam eius seduci faciens at abduci,

ordering him to have a child that had been abducted returned to its parents. He offered two reasons for the return of the child, a girl of seven: a) the father offered to let her remain a Christian; b) not to return the child would give some critics an opening for maligning the Church.

The imposition of the Jewish Badge by the IV Lateran Council was also contrary to the urging of *Sicut*, which states that no change ought to be made in the customs of a land which Jews inhabit.[42] No one could have taken seriously the charge of immorality by which the imposition of the Badge was justified. Instances of immorality between Jews and Christians no doubt occurred, but to involve all the Jews was patently absurd.[43] It was more likely to have been intended, as both Jews and Christians understood it from the first, to further social and commercial separation, exactly the sort of thing the early *Sicuts* were meant to prevent. Since the enforcement of the Badge was not in the hands of the Church, the civil governments sometimes did and sometimes did not enforce it, depending apparently on the personal and financial influence of the Jews concerned.[44]

eam renitentem ad quosdam monasterium asportavit; et cum a domino terre, ad predicti Judei querimoniam, quereretur, idem clericus ad partes alias transferri fecit eandem; et sic pater querens eam et non inveniens paterno discruiratur affectu. Quare nobis humiliter supplicavit ut eam sibi liberam restitui faceremus, non curaturus si demum ad religionem transire voluerit fidei Christiane." The pope orders the guilty cleric's superior to see that the child is brought back and restored to her father.

[42] Above, n. 19. There is no convincing evidence that a Badge had been imposed on the Jews anywhere in Europe before the IV Lateran Council in 1215.

[43] The justification offered at the IV Latern Council for the imposition of the Badge, implying that Moses had ordered the Jews to be distinguishable in their clothing and that therefore Jews ought not complain about it, was obviously merely a turn of the screw: the Badge was hardly equivalent to *tsitsit* as described in Num. 15:37–41. The justification for the Badge from the Christian point of view was apparently meant to be insulting. The idea that Jews were prone to fornication may have been derived from the Vulgate translation of the Hebrew word *zonim* as *fornicatores*. For the canons of the Council *cf. Decr. Greg. IX*, Lib. V, tit. 19, c. v; Mansi, XXII, 1055; *ChJ*, pp. 308 f. *Cf.* Kisch, *Germany*, p. 205 and notes on the punishment of fornication between Jews and Christians; but it does not help in estimating its frequency.

[44] After 1215, there was a steady flow of papal letters to various princes to remind them of their new obligation to enforce the rule of the Badge. For the first half of the 13th century see *ChJ*, s. v., "Badge." The Jews naturally tried to free themselves from the degrading sign; they at first succeeded by bribing or otherwise prevailing upon the local governments to lower their visibility. Their economic usefulness was crucial in this respect: *cf.* Robert Anchel, *Les Juifs de France* (Paris 1946), p. 120. On September 3, 1258, Pope Alexander IV reminded the Duke Hugh of Burgundy and Count Charles of Anjou and the Provence, brother of King Louis IX, of their obligation to impose the Badge, to refrain from appointing Jews to public office, and to burn the Talmud. *Cf. In sacro generali*, among the documents published by I. Loeb, *REJ*, I (1880), 116 f. A similar letter was sent also to King Louis (Archives Nationales, L 252, no. 178), which speaks of the Badge and of the appointment of Jews to office, but not of the Talmud, probably because King Louis had been zealous enough in that regard. *Cf.* the Council of Beziers, May 6, 1255, Mansi XXIII.882; *ChJ*, 336–37.

Still another indication of the waning influence of *Sicut* were the two attacks on the Talmud during the 13th century. There is no need to go into the oft-told story of the charges against the Talmud, its trial, condemnation, and its burning in Paris in 1242. Gregory IX's widely circulated letter in 1239[45] made no secret of his hope that the elimination of the Talmud would expedite the conversion of the Jews and of his horror at the blasphemies it contained.[46] But it was the aftermath of the trial that showed the erosion of *Sicut*. More copies of the Talmud and of other rabbinic works seem to have been found and confiscated in the years that followed. Thereupon the Jews managed to persuade Pope Innocent IV (1243–1254) that these books were essential for their understanding and observance of Judaism, a right which *Sicut* conceded. Certainly the books were no danger to Christendom, since very few Christians could read them. The pope, in general not unfavorably disposed to the Jews, was ready to order the books returned to them. But Odo of Chateauroux, his legate to France, voiced strong objection. "The Jewish teachers of the Kingdom of France," he said, "told a falsehood to Your Holiness and to the venerable fathers, the cardinals, when they claimed that, without these books, which in Hebrew are called Talmud, they could not understand the Bible and other ordinances of their faith."[47] It was perhaps not to be expected that Bishop Odo, considering the mentality of his day, would not realize the effrontery of his remark that he knew better than the Jews what they needed for the practice of their own religion. But Pope Innocent knew better; yet he too failed to realize that, by changing his mind about the return of the books, he was interfering with the right of the Jews to observe Judaism, which had long been theirs and which *Sicut* granted.

The results of the Paris disputation were not lost on the Dominicans of

[45] *Si vera sunt*, June 9 and 10, 1239; Potthast 10759, 10776, 10768; *ChJ*, pp. 239 ff. See also *ibid.*, no. 95, ordering the Bishop of Paris to distribute the letter among the French prelates. Among princes, the letter was sent to the kings of France, England, Aragon, Navarre, Castile, Leon, and Portugal.

[46] ". . . in qua tot abusiones et nefaria continentur quod pudori referentibus et audientibus sunt horrori. Cum igitur hec dicatur esse causa precipua que Judeos tenet in sua perfidia obstinatos . . ." The best contemporary outline of the accusations and of the Paris manuscript Latin 16558 is to be found in Ch. Merchavia, *Ha'talmud be're'i ha'natsrut* (Jerusalem 1970), chs. 12 and 13, pp. 249–315. See also Isidore Loeb, "La Controverse de 1240 sur le Talmud," *REJ*, I (1880), 247–61; II (1881), 248–70; III (1881), 39–57. *Cf.* Baron, *History*, IX, 66 ff.

[47] For Innocent's attitude see Walter Ullmann, *Medieval Papalism*, p. 122. For Pope Innocent IV's change of mind, see his letter to the King of France, *Ad instar*, August 12, 1247, Denifle, *Chartularium*, I, 201, no. 172; with the argument of Odo of Chateauroux attached, in *ChJ*, pp. 275–80: "Unde manifestum est magistros Judeorum regni Francie nuper falsitatem Sanctitati vestre, et venerabilibus patribus dominis cardinalibus, suggesisse dicentes quod sine illis libris, qui Hebraice Talmut dicuntur, Bibliam et alia instituta sue legis secundum fidem ipsorum intelligere nequeunt."

Aragon. King James I of Aragon (1213–1276) had not reacted to the papal letter about the Talmud in 1239; indeed, he was getting along very well with the Jews of his dominions. It seemed clear to the Dominicans of Aragon that they should do no less than had been done at Paris. But to arrange a trial on Aragonese soil, they needed a learned ex-Jew like Nicolas Donin. About 1260, they were joined by a convert named Paul, and he assured them that he could surpass Donin's achievement, that he could prove that the Talmud, not only contained blasphemies against Christianity, but also contained proof of the truth of Christianity.[48] The most respected Dominican of that day was Raymond of Peñaforte,[49] an experienced polemicist, an expert in Canon Law, and a person highly regarded by King James. Pressure was therefore brought on the king to arrange a public disputation on the Talmud.[50] To oppose Paul Christian the monks prevailed on the king to compel the participation of Nahmanides (Moses ben Nahman), at the time the foremost talmudic scholar in Aragon. The disputation took place in Barcelona on July 20 to 27, 1263.[51]

Again the course of the disputation is less important for our purpose than its aftermath: the efforts made by the monks to curtail the freedom of the Jews to observe their religion as they used to. The Dominicans naturally proclaimed the result of the disputation as a victory for their side.[52] Shortly thereafter, undoubtedly at the insistence of the friars, the king issued a number of edicts. One was addressed to the royal officers, commanding them to aid the Dominicans by compelling Muslims and Jews to listen to conversionary sermons.[53] Another royal command ordered the Jews to erase

[48] For changes in the approach to Christian-Jewish polemics see Amos Funkenstein, "Changes in the Patterns of Christian anti-Jewish Polemics in the 12th Century," (Hebrew with English summary), *Zion*, XXXIII (1968), 125–44; and *idem*, "Basic Types of Christian anti-Jewish Polemics in the Later Middle Ages," *Viator*, II (1971), 375–82.

[49] For Raymond of Peñaforte see A. Lukyn-Williams, *Adversus Judaeos* (Cambridge Univ. Press, 1935), pp. 241–48.

[50] Martin A. Cohen, "Reflections on the Text and Context of the Disputation of Barcelona," *HUC Annual*, XXXV (1964), 157–92, speaks of the political intrigues by which the king was forced to permit, and participate in, the disputation.

[51] In addition to the references given above, attention must be called to the following: Heinrich Denifle, "Quellen zur Disputation Pablos Christiani mit Mose Nachmani zu Barcelona 1263," *Historisches Jahrbuch der Goerres Gesellschaft*, VIII (1887), 225–44, containing many of the documents connected with the disputation and its aftermath; Cecil Roth, "The Disputation of Barcelona (1263)," *Harvard Theological Review*, 43 (Apr. 1950), 117–44; Y. Baer, "A Review of the Disputations of R. Yechiel of Paris and of R. Moses ben Nachman," (Hebrew), *Tarbits*, II (1931–2), 172–87; Jose M. Millas Vallicrosa, "Sobre las fuentes documentales de la controversia de Barcelona en el año 1263," *Anales de la Universidad de Barcelona, memorias y communicaciones*, 1940, 25–43.

[52] The official Latin report in Denifle, *op. cit.*, pp. 231 ff.

[53] On August 26th, just about a month after the end of the disputation, the king addressed the bailiffs, judges and other local officials: "Dicimus et mandamus vobis quod

or remove from their books whatever blasphemies the Dominicans might point out to them or which they themselves knew to be there.[54] It is noteworthy that Maimonides' *Mishneh Torah* merited a separate edict—it was to be burned wherever the monks found it, since it spoke of the messiah in terms unacceptable to Christianity.[55]

The Jews, in their turn, reacted by pointing out to the king the effect that these decrees were having on their persons and on their faith. In a matter of months, the king modified his decrees. Since the Jews were physically endangered when they left their own quarters to listen to the Christian sermons, the king agreed that they did not have to go outside their district. Moreover, if the friars came into the Jewish quarter to preach, they should be accompanied, not by a mob, but by only ten respectable men.[56] Also, the Jews did not have to erase passages that they themselves deemed blasphemous; they could wait until the monks pointed out such passages to them, and they could then defend such passages and take an oath that they were not meant in the sense in which the monks understood them.[57] Such was the royal compromise; it did not deny censorship, but set limits to it; it did not abolish conversionary preaching, but curtailed its use for stirring riots.

cum fratres ordinis fratrum predicatorum venerint ad vos et Judaeis vel Sarracenis voluerint predicare, ipsos fratres benigne recipiatis, et inducatis Judeos et Sarracenos, tan pueros quam senes viros et mulieres et, si necesse fuerit, compellatis, ut coram ipsis fratribus, ubi et quando et quomodo ipsi voluerint, conveniant et verba ipsorum sub silencio audiant diligenter . . .:" *ibid.*, pp. 234 f., no. 2. *Ibid.*, pp. 235 f., no. 4 is a special order to the Jews to give close attention to the preaching and the arguments of Brother Paul the Christian whenever he comes to them to argue against Judaism.

[54] *Ibid.*, p. 236, no. 5: ". . . mandamus universis Judeis . . . quod quascunque blasfemias contra ipsum Dominum nostrum Jhesum Christum et matrem suam beatam Mariam virginem gloriosam in libris vestris vel quibuscunque scriptis inveneritis, per vos ipsos vel qui vobis significati fuerint vel hostensi per fratrem Paulum Christiani ordinis fratrum predicatorum viva voce vel litteris, cum consilio fratris Raymundi de Pennaforti et fratris A. Segarra eiusdem ordinis, scindatis omnino de libris vestris intra spacium trium mensium . . ." If this is not done, the books are to be burned and the Jews heavily fined.

[55] *Ibid.*, p. 235, no. 3: ". . . libros qui vocantur Soffrim, compositos a quondam Judeo qui vocabatur Moyses filius Maimon egipciacus, sive de Alcayra, Jhesu Christi blasfemias continentes . . ." If they do not hand these books over for destruction, the Jews are to be punished severely. The word *soffrim* is an obvious misreading of *Shofetim*, the last book in the *Mishneh Torah* of Maimonides which concludes with a description of the Jewish concept of the Messiah and the Messianic Era completely at variance with the Christian idea.

[56] Francisco de Bofarull y Sans, *Jaime I y los Judios* (Barcelona 1910), pp. 76 f., no. lxxiii: ". . . quod non teneamini ire ad abscultandam predicationem alicuius fratris . . . extra vestra calla judaica. . . . Et si predicti fratres vel alii intus synagogas vos voluerint predicare non veniant ad ipsas synagogas cum multitudine . . ." (Oct. 1268). *Cf.* Denifle, p. 237, no. 6.

[57] Denifle, *ibid.*, p. 238, no. 7: ". . . quod non teneamini aliquid de ipsis libris levare nec dampnare per penam . . . donec per fratrum Paulum vel per alium sint vobis ostensa capitula dictarum blasfemiarum, . . . si ea excusare potestis non fore blasfemia . . . ad

But the greatest disappointment for the Dominicans was connected with Nahmanides. He disappeared from view for over a year following the disputation, perhaps for safety's sake. He had, in the meantime, composed a book in which he gave his version of the argument; and according to it he had had the better of it.[58] This infuriated the Dominicans, and they complained to the king, who apparently gave them little satisfaction.[59] Thereupon, they sent Paul Christian to Rome to submit their case to the pope.

Late in the year 1266, Pope Clement IV wrote to King James in what must be described as highly critical terms.[60] After recalling the king's great services to Christendom in having conquered so much territory from the Muslims, the pope enumerates the king's misdeeds: first in permitting so much freedom to the conquered Muslims, and, secondly, giving so much leeway to the Jews. With papal claims to supreme authority clearly in mind, Pope Clement asserts that it is for the pope, not the king, to decide what privileges Jews are to enjoy.[61] The letter concludes with a demand that the king punish the man who, after the disputation with Brother Paul, wrote a book full of falsehoods and had it widely distributed. Such insolence deserves chastisement, though not such as might endanger life and limb.[62]

cognitionem et iudicium super hoc assignatorum a nobis . . . non teneamini dampnare aliquid vel levare de eisdem. . . ." This was issued as early as March 1264; in 1268 another royal order freed the Jews from taking cognizance of accusations of blasphemy in rabbinic literature not agreed to by the royal court: Bofarull, *ibid.*, p. 78, no. lxxv, "quod non teneamini respondere alicui vel aliquibus personis in aliquibus petitionibus quas vobis moneant super aliquibus que asserant in libris vestris ebrayicis contra fidem nostram continere . . . Et quod de hoc simus Nos vel nostri, et non alii . . ."

[58] The essays cited above (n. 51) discuss the relative trustworthiness of the official Latin report (given in Denifle, *ibid.*, pp. 231 ff.) and the report composed by Nahmanides. Denifle naturally says that Nahmanides lied. Baer (and *cf.* Millas Vallicrosa) points out that the official report puts into Nahmanides' mouth words that he could not possibly have said: e. g., admitting that the Messiah had already come. Roth argues that 1) the claim of victory by both sides was to have been expected; 2) Nahmanides could express himself in writing more openly and more forcefully than he could during the debate when he, of necessity, had to guard his speech.

[59] The meeting is described in Bofarull, p. 67, no. liii. Raymond de Peñaforte, A. de Segarra, and Paul Christian formed the committee of Dominicans come to accuse Nahmanides of having committed blasphemy by the publication of his report. King James told them that the punishment he had fixed was a two-year exile and the burning of the report: ". . . volebamus ipsum Judeum per sentenciam exilare de terra nostra per duos annos et facere comburi libros qui scripti erant . . . quam quidem sentenciam dicti fratres predicatores admittere nullo voluerunt." Thereupon, the king in effect dismissed the case.

[60] *Agit nec immerito*, Potthast 19911; E. Jordan, *Les Registres de Clement IV*, p. 334, no. 848; Denifle, *ibid.*, pp. 240 ff., no. 9.

[61] ". . . ipsos in aliquo non extollas, sed in quantum concessa eis a Sede Apostolica privilegia patiuntur. . . ."

[62] ". . . Sed illius precipue castiges audaciam qui de disputatione quam in tua presencia cum dilecto filio, religioso viro, fratre Paulo de ordine predicatorum habuerat,

Since this last phrase was the one used by the Inquisition when it relaxed a condemned heretic to the secular arm, it seems to suggest that the punishment was to be most severe. In any event, Nahmanides, warned—possibly through the king—of impending trouble and perhaps unwilling to embarrass the friendly king, left his native country and spent his few remaining years in the Holy Land.

The above-mentioned letter had been dispatched to King James by the hand of Paul Christian. It produced no results. The king's relaxation of his various edicts and the flight of Nahmanides deprived the Dominicans of whatever triumph they had expected to gain from the disputation. Not only was the Talmud not burned, as it had been in Paris, but the Jews were now permitted to challenge every accusation levelled against it.[63] This is apparently why Paul was again sent to Rome, and why, barely half a year later, Pope Clement sent another vigorous letter to King James, seconded this time by one of like tenor addressed to the prelates of Aragon.[64]

This second Bull begins with invective against the Jews reminiscent of the one issued by Innocent III in 1205 about the Jews of Champagne.[65] It continues with accusations against the Talmud, as in Gregory IX's Bulls of 1239.[66] And it concludes with instructions that the talmudic books be confiscated and examined by a commission which was to include Paul, in order to make sure that the books contained no blasphemies. Only such books may be restored to the Jews as contained no falsehoods and no insults to Christianity.[67] There is no evidence that King James complied.

Whatever the two dramatic trials of rabbinic literature achieved in terms of degrading Judaism and the Jews in the opinion of Christians, they

multis confictis adjectisque mendaciis librum composuisse dicitur, . . . Cuius ausum temerarium sic debite censura iustitie, absque tamen mortis periculo et membrorum mutilatione, castiget ut quid excessus meruerit districtionis severitas manifestet . . ."

63 *Cf.* n. 57 above. The Jews were apparently willing to grant that some passages in the Talmud could be interpreted in a sense offensive to Christians and agreed to expunge them.

64 *Damnabili perfidia*, July 15, 1267; Potthast 20081; Coll. Doat 32, fol. 11r.–15r.; Sbaralea, *Bullarium Franciscanum*, III, 123 f.; Ripoll, *Bullarium Ordinis FF. Predicatorum*, I, 487.

65 *Etsi Judeos*, addressed to the Archbishop of Sens and the Bishop of Paris; Potthast 2526; *ChJ*, pp. 114 ff., no. 18. See above, n. 30.

66 *Si vera sunt*, addressed to the prelates of France; Potthast 10759; *ChJ*, pp. 240 ff., nos. 96 ff. See above, n. 45.

67 ". . . ut a Judeis tibi et eis (i. e., his barons and officers) subditis totum Talmud cum suis additionibus et expositionibus, et omnes eorum libros, ipsis faciatis liberaliter exhiberi, quibus exhibitis, illos ex eis qui de textu Biblie fuerint et alios de quibus nulla sit dubitatio quod blasphemias vel errores contineant, seu etiam falsitatem, Judeis restituant supradictis." Other books are to be kept under seal in a safe place until the pope decides what is to be done with them. Great care should be taken that the confiscation is carried out "ita prudenter et caute quod id ubicumque contingat fieri simul et eodem tempore fiat, ne Judeorum ipsorum fallacia dictos libros quomodolibet valeat occultare."

made meaningless the Church's promise in *Sicut* to leave Judaism entirely to the Jews. And if the attempt to deprive the Jews of the Talmud largely failed in Spain in 1263, it did not stop attacks on, and burnings of, the Talmud in later years.[68]

What then remained of *Sicut* in the second half of the 13th century? Practically little more was left than that living Jews, when all was peaceful around them, could not be compelled to accept baptism, and that dead Jews might remain in their cemeteries undisturbed. Even the reason why Jews were to be permitted to dwell in the midst of Christians was beginning to undergo a change of emphasis. Innocent III and his 13th century successors still relied on Augustine's remark about the need for Jews as witnesses of Christian truth; later popes stressed that part of the remark which emphasized the desirability of degrading them.[68a] If they were at all conscious of the effects of their actions, they naturally blamed everything on the Jews—their blindness, their stubbornness, their hatred of Christianity, its symbols and its beliefs.[68b]

One of the chief issues in the 12th and 13th centuries was the question of jurisdiction: did the Church or the State possess supreme authority? Could a pope have authority over an emperor, not only in the latter's status as a Christian, but also in his capacity as civil ruler?[69] One of the complicating aspects of this situation—though certainly a lesser one—was the ancient Christian tradition affecting the ecclesiastical jurisdiction over the Jews, or any other non-Christian.

It was traced back to a statement by Paul in I Cor. 5:12–13: "For what

Paul is to have a voice in deciding about the books: "Ad hoc autem dilectus filius Frater Paulus, dictu Christianus . . . lator presentium . . . tum quia ex Judeis trahens originem et inter eos litteris hebraicis competenter instructus linguam novit et legem antiquam ac illorum errores, tum etiam quia de sacro fonte renatus zelum habet fidei Catholice . . ." It is noteworthy that nothing is said in this Bull about burning the rabbinic books. Conceivably Paul presented to the pope his case in favor of bargaining with the Jews for the degree and the nature of a censorship that would be favorable to him—and to Christianity.

[68] A Christian scholar's report on Christianity and the Talmud is Peter Browe, S.J., "Die religiöse Duldung der Juden im Mittelalter," *Archiv für katholisches Kirchenrecht*, 118 (1938), 1–76, esp. 42 ff.

[68a] *Cf.* Kenneth R. Stow, *Catholic Thought and Papal Jewry Policy, 1555–1593* (New York 1977), pp. 92 and *passim.*

[68b] *Cf.* Browe, *Judenmission*, pp. 267–310, summarizing the failure of the missionary policy.

[69] The problem has naturally produced an extensive literature. Among the books which touch upon the Jewish aspect are: R. W. and A. J. Carlyle, *A History of Medieval Political Theory in the West* (London 1928), V, esp. ch. V, 318–54; John A. Watt, *The Theory of Papal Monarchy in the 13th Century*, London 1965; Walter Ullmann, *Medieval Papalism* (London 1949), and his *Growth of Papal Government in the Middle Ages* (London 1953). On the Jewish aspect, see the Baron essays cited above, in n. 24.

have I to do to judge them that are without (*qui foris sunt*)? Do not ye judge them that are within? But them that are without God judgeth." According to Augustine, this meant abstention from judging those who are not under Christian law, whom the Church could not discipline. The canonist Gratian quotes Augustine and accepts his view.[70] Innocent III likewise fell back on this principle in dealing with a case of divorce involving a non-Christian.[71]

On the basis of this *foris* principle, the Church could not interfere with Jews at all. Matters spiritual fell directly into this category; as to material matters, they were the concern of civil law and local civil authorities. An ecclesiastic could deal with nonreligious matters only if he was at the same time the civil ruler, as happened fairly often. Yet there was always the problem of a Jew violating a Church regulation, like failing to pay the tithe on property which had once belonged to a Christian, or treating a cleric with disrespect, or not wearing the Badge. In such cases, if the local civil ruler refused to punish the recalcitrant Jew, the Church resorted to indirect punishment, that is, to threatening with excommunication those Christians who refused to suspend their social and economic relations with the Jew or Jews involved. This method, called *judicium Judaeorum*, was so common and had been used for so long that the term came to be applied to situations that had nothing to do with Jews.[72]

It galled the decretalists and the canonists of the 13th century to see limitations placed on the authority of the pope. Even though *foris* was of Biblical origin, they sought and found a Biblical argument to supersede it. Since all God's creatures were God's flock over whom Peter has been placed as shepherd,[73] the pope, being Peter's successor, has unquestionable authority over secular rulers. Now Jews were subservient to these rulers and

[70] ". . . ab his qui non sunt sui juris, in quos nequit disciplina exerceri." Causa XXIII, qu. 4, 17: quoted from Mario Cordorelli, *I fondamenti juridici della toleranza religiosa*, Milan 1960, p. 24, n. 13.

[71] Innocent III, in *CJC*, Lib. X, tit. 8, c. 4, 19, *de divortiis*.

[72] A number of such instances are offered in *ChJ*, s. v., "Boycott." See *ibid.*, pp. 250 f., no. 103. The earliest use of this method appears to have been mentioned by Raoul Glaber in the 11th century; *cf.* B. Blumenkranz, *Les auteurs Chrétiens Latins du Moyen Age* (The Hague 1963), p. 258; see also Urban IV, on May 2, 1262, in the case of a quarrel among Christians, in Jean Giraud, *Les registres d'Urbain IV*, no. 2900. But no case can be found of a reigning prince being excommunicated solely because he violated a Church law in connection with Jews: *cf.* the long-drawn-out argument with Alfonso III of Portugal: E. Jordan, *Les registres de Clement IV*, 236, no. 669, c. 1265, and Raynaldus, a.a. 1273 #26. The method was more effective when applied locally.

[73] John 21:16–17; *cf.* Ezek. 34:16–17. From the fact that Jesus entrusted his sheep to Peter, "apparet quod papa (as Peter's successor) super omnes habet jurisdictionem et potestatem de jure, licet non de facto." God's sheep includes all His creations, believers as well as non-believers. Quoted from Condorelli, *op. cit.*, p. 25, citing Sinibaldus Fieschi (Innocent IV) in his *Decretalium Commentaria. Cf.* Pietro Gismondi, *Ephemerides Juris Canonici*, III (1947), p. 21. n. 4, Ullmann, *Med. Papalism*, p. 119; Carlyle, *op. cit.*, V, 323, n. 2.

therefore came under ecclesiastical authority. This conclusion was drawn by Sinibaldus Fieschi (Pope Innocent IV) in the commentary which he prepared on the decretals which the learned Raymond de Peñaforte had prepared for Gregory IX. There are three situations, Pope Innocent declared in his commentary, so basic to the welfare of Christianity as to supersede the rule of *foris* and bring Jews under the direct jurisdiction of the Church: Granted that he could not force unbelievers to convert, the pope could nevertheless force them to listen to conversionary sermons intended to lead them from ignorance to truth.[74] Secondly, he could punish them when they violated the laws of nature: for example, when they led immoral lives by cohabiting with Christians.[75] Thirdly, the pope could order them punished when they acted against divine law, as when they blasphemed against Christianity, or even when they violated their own law and were not punished for it by their own religious guides.[76] It seems, however, that in all such cases the pope was willing to work through the territorial princes.

Thus, in the days of Innocent IV, the middle of the 13th century, the attempt to extend ecclesiastical jurisdiction to the Jews was still theory. Even the condemnation of the Talmud depended for its execution on the civil government. The princes were still far from willing to relinquish their full authority over their Jews. But the idea of a dominant Church was to bear fruit in time, if not in most respects, certainly with respect to lowering the status of the Jews.[76a] That status fell increasingly under Church definition as the economic position of the Jews declined, as the attitude of the princes to them changed, and as the propaganda of the friars penetrated ever wider circles of the Christian population.

Broad Church jurisdiction over Jews was achieved through the Inquisition. This new organization came into being as a result of the heresies

[74] "Licet non debeant infideles cogi ad fidem . . . tamen mandare potest papa infidelibus quod admittant predicatores Evangelii in terris sue jurisdictionis . . . si ipsi prohibent predicatores predicare peccant, et ideo puniendi sunt." Condorelli, p. 125.

[75] ". . . si contra legem naturae facit, potest licite puniri per papam." The example offered is that of the city of Sodom, in which, according to the story of Lot (Genesis 19), immorality prevailed. The immorality indicated among Jews is cohabiting with Christians. Condorelli, *op. cit.*, p. 126.

[76] "Item Judaeos potest judicare papa si contra legem Evangelii faciunt in moralibus, si eorum prelati eos non puniunt, et eodem modo si hereses circa suam legem inveniant; et hac ratione motus papa Gregorius et Innocentius mandaverunt comburi libros talium in quibus multe continebantur hereses . . ." Condorelli, *op. cit.*, 127 f.; Carlyle, *op. cit.*, V, 323, n. 2.

[76a] For a description of the Church attitude toward the Jews when the attitude reached its nadir, in the late 16th century, when the divine purpose in keeping the Jews alive was interpreted as meant solely to test the zeal of Christians in working for their conversion, *cf.* Kenneth R. Stow, *Catholic Thought and Papal Jewry Policy, 1555–1593* (JTSA, New York 1977). The book reached me too late for more extensive use. The only echo of *Sicut* that one finds in it is the continued frowning on outright physical force.

rampant in southern France at the end of the 12th and in the 13th centuries. The crusade that Innocent III organized against the Albigenses and the other heretical sects laid waste the province, but did not destroy the heresies, exponents of which now spread through Central France and Northern Italy. The Dominican and Franciscan Orders were organized for the specific purpose of combatting heresy by preaching and example; but their progress by these methods was understandably slow. Gregory IX, in the early 1230's, therefore, decided to attack the problem more directly and vigorously. The searching out of heretics was taken out of the hands of the bishops, where it had rested until then, and was transferred to investigating committees appointed from among the members of the Mendicant Orders. It was expected that these committees of inquiry, or inquisitors, under the direct control of, and responsible to, the pope, would be more effective in ferreting out the heretics and punishing them.[77] Not even the princes who were most jealous of their rights and jurisdiction could object. After all, heresy was considered equivalent to treason—worse, since it was treason against God—and treason merited the severest kind of punishment.[78] From its very beginning the Inquisition proved efficient. Whenever it wanted additional powers, it turned to the pope and was rarely refused.[79] By the 1260's, it was in full bloom.

From the first, the powers of the inquisitors extended, not only to practicing heretics, but also to those who sympathized with them, or pro-

[77] The following, among a great many other works on the subject, offer the essential information on the establishment and functioning of the Inquisition of the Middle Ages: Henry Charles Lea, *The Inquisition of the Middle Ages*, 3 vols. (New York 1887). The introduction to an edition published in 1963, by Walter Ullmann, is very useful. Jean Giraud, *Histoire de l'Inquisition du Moyen Age*, 2 vols. (Paris 1935). C. Douais, *Documents pour servire a l'histoire de l'inquisition dans le Languedoc*, 2 vols. (Paris 1900). M. J. Vidal, *Bullaire de l'inquisition française au XIVe siecle* (Paris 1913). Useful shorter works are: R. W. Emery, *Heresy and Inquisition in Narbonne* (New York 1941); A. C. Shannon, *The Popes and Heresy in the 13th Century* (Villanova 1949). Useful as a summary of the Inquisition's evolution is the chapter by Tuberville in *Cambridge Medieval History*, VI. The following are of special interest to the Jewish aspect of the Inquisition's activities: L. I. Newman, *Jewish Influence on Christian Reform Movements* (New York 1923). J. H. Yerushalmi, "The Inquisition and the Jews of France in the Time of Bernard Gui," *Harvard Theological Review*, 63 (1970), 317–76. S. W. Baron, *A Social and Religious History of the Jews*, IX (1965), 1–134 and the notes to these pages.

[78] The trend to severity began in the 12th century. In 1220, Frederick II's constitution for his Sicilian kingdom decreed, "ut vivi in conspectu populi comburantur." The attitude was adopted and repeated by a number of popes. As is generally known, the Church condemned and, if the condemnation involved a sentence of death, handed the guilty persons over ("relaxed") to the State for execution. *Cf.* Ullmann, *Med. Papalism*, p. 252; Lea, I, 541 ff.; *Cambridge Med. Hist.*, VI, 716 ff. Lea, *ibid.*, 549 ff., points out that actual executions were comparatively few; the terror which the Inquisition inspired was due rather to the confiscations, the torture, and the imprisonment. On heresy as treason, see also Kisch, *Germany*, pp. 199, 203.

tected them, or received them in their homes (*fautores*, *protectatores*, *receptatores*).[80] The wide circle of those whom the Inquisition could consider suspect must have included many who were quite innocent of heresy. Nor did the procedures of the Inquisition inspire confidence, since there was hardly a chance for defense, and punishment was severe.[81] One must conclude that inquisitors were none too popular in any community. In the course of the 13th century, there were a few popular uprisings against the Inquisition and some assassinations of inquisitors. Pope Urban IV (1261–1264) found it necessary to declare null and void any regulation by a local authority that stood in the way of the Inquisition's work. His successor, Clement IV, required local officials to take an oath that they will not impede its work.[82] It would be hardly surprising, therefore, if Jews threatened by the Inquisition, whether as reverts to Judaism or as aids to any such, took advantage of the Inquisition's unpopularity in whatever way they could. But they occasioned thereby the issuance of a fateful Bull directed against them.

The great majority of those accused of heresy by the Inquisition of the Middle Ages were undoubtedly of non-Jewish origin. But there certainly were some Jews who, having been caught in a riot and been baptized under duress, tried to return to the faith of their fathers or to observe it to whatever extent they could or dared.[83] From the viewpoint of the Inquisition, they

[79] The entire series of papal regulations in *Sexti Decret.* V, tit. ii, *de Hereticis*, extending from Gregory IX to Boniface VIII, is of this nature. Several areas of activity were apparently omitted deliberately: e. g., the enforcement of the Jewish Badge was, for practical reasons, left to local civil authorities: *cf.* Ullmann, *Med. Papalism*, pp. 122 f. The war against the Talmud, like the two public disputations discussed above, was left to the Mendicant Orders; at least in the 13th century the Inquisition took no direct part in it. The practice of usury was a difficult subject to class with heresy, even where Christians were concerned. Alexander IV, in 1260, in answer to a question of the extent of their jurisdiction, replied to inquisitors in Italy that they could consider it heresy if the accused claimed that Christianity permitted usury, but not when they merely practiced it. Eventually, however, the Inquisition did find ways of prosecuting Jewish moneylenders. *Cf.* Alexander IV, *Quod super nonnullis*, Potthast 17745.

[80] H. C. Lea, I, 461, defines the concept as "Receivers and defenders—those who showed hospitality, gave alms, or sheltered or assisted heretics in any way, or neglected to denounce them to the authorities."

[81] H. C. Lea, I, 360 ff., 450 ff. G. G. Coulton, *Inquisition and Liberty* (London 1938), ch. 18, pp. 192–99. Innocent IV, in 1243, Potthast 11083; Ripoll, I, 118, no. 2, urged the inquisitors to act: "sicut eidem negotio expedire videretis, tam contra hereticos, credentes, fautores, receptatores, et defensores eorum quam contra alios ipsi negotio adversantes." Also in 1254: Potthast 15473; Ripoll, I, 252, no. 342, to Inquisitors in Lombardy. Their aids included the "familiars," who spied and informed. The interrogations were carried on in secret and torture was permitted. Names of informers and witnesses were not revealed.

[82] Urban IV, *Sexti Decr.*, V, tit. 2, c. ix; Clement IV, *ibid.*, c. xi.

[83] The problem was, of course, not new. Jews had reverted to Judaism before and the State had them severely punished. *Cf.* Bouquet, *Recueill des Historiens*, XVI, 8: Louis VII

had "not been precisely coerced," so that their baptism was valid.[84] The convert, however, knew better, and so did his relatives and friends. They may have hidden him (or her) until he could be smuggled out to a foreign land where he might resume the practice of Judaism.[85] If that is what happened, the local inquisitor spared no effort to locate the escapee. The simplest means was to hale a Jewish relative or friend before the inquisitional court and by threat or some other means extort the required information.[86] Or a pious or hostile Christian neighbor might accuse a Jew of harboring a suspicious guest.[87] In any event, there were openings for an inquisitor to claim jurisdiction over individual Jews and occasionally over entire communities.

Still another consideration must be kept in mind when discussing reversions to Judaism. Christian princes had always been especially jealous of their control of Jews who were their *servi camerae*. The conversion of a Jew meant the loss of control over his possessions and income. Consequently the conversion of a Jew led to the confiscation of his property by the prince, who sometimes handed it back to the convert's Jewish relatives so that they might continue to make profit out of it for the prince. The Church had always protested against the resulting impoverishment of the convert.[88]

in 1144, during the period of the Second Crusade: "Statuimus igitur . . . ut deinceps quicumque Judeorum per baptismi gratiam in Christo renati ad suae vetustatis errorem revolare presumpserint, in toto regno nostro remanere audeant, et si capi poterint, vel capitali damnentur judicio vel membrorum portione multentur." Louis VII was a contemporary of Gratian (see above n. 32). But there is no record of the frequency with which this edict was applied; there was as yet no Inquisition to enforce it.

[84] *Cf.* Innocent III's *Maiores*, above, n. 33.

[85] Pope Honorius IV, in his *Nimis*, addressed to John Pekham, Archbishop of Canterbury, in 1285, Potthast 22290–1; M. Prou, *Les registres d'Honorius IV*, cols 76 f. and 88 f., nos. 96–97, did not know which was worse, a converted Jew continuing to practice Judaism in the very parish where he had been baptized or one going to places where he would not be recognized in order to revert to Judaism there, always with the aid of other Jews. Such organizations for mutual help and assistance in escaping to foreign parts functioned among non-Jewish heretics in various countries: *cf.* Jean Guireaud, *Histoire de l'Inquisition de Moyen Age*, II, 251 ff.

[86] A case in point is the Inquisitional document discussed by Joseph Shatzmiller, "L'Inquisition et les Juifs de Provence au XIIIe Siecle," *Provence Historique*, fascicules 93 et 94. The family of Abraham de Grasse is accused of aiding his step-daughter to revert to Judaism after her baptism. He had to clear himself of this accusation twice, and did so apparently at considerable cost.

[87] *Cf.* Nicolas IV in 1288: Potthast 22846; Douais, *Documents*, I, xxxi. It addresses all Christians, urging them to confess to their priests if they become aware of a heretic or of anyone extending aid to a heretic. The names of witnesses against them were not divulged to the accused: Gregory X, 1273: *Prae cunctis*, Ripoll, I, 512, no. 12. On the nature of some witnesses, see Lea, I, 434; Tuberville, *Camb. Med. Hist.*, VI, 722.

[88] The III Lateran, in 1179, c. 26: ". . . principibus vel potestatibus eorundem locorum sub poena excommunicationis injungimus ut portionem hereditatis et bonorum suorum ex integro eis faciant exhiberi." Pope Innocent IV, in 1245, praised James of

Now, however, in the case of most reverts to Judaism, the property had already been lost in the riot which had brought about the baptism, or been otherwise disposed of, often to the benefit of the prince. The usual prince might, therefore, not object to action by the Inquisition against converts under suspicion of reversion, since the prince was losing nothing by it. But he would object strenuously to the inquisitor's accusing, arresting, and imposing a heavy fine on unbaptized Jews on the charge of being *fautores*. The subject will necessarily come up again. But what has to be said at this point is that this kind of interference by princes, added to the difficulties interposed by the principle of *foris*, probably prompted the inquisitors to turn to the pope with a request for further aid.

On July 27, 1267, barely two weeks after having dispatched the bull *Damnabili*[89] to King James of Aragon, Pope Clement IV issued his *Turbato corde*:[90]

> "With a troubled heart we relate what we have heard: A number of bad Christians have abandoned the true Christian faith and wickedly transferred themselves to the rites of the Jews. This is obviously the more reprehensible since it makes it possible for the most holy name

Aragon for having done just that; at least, he ordered it done in an edict which Pope Innocent repeated: *Ea que*, Potthast 10822; *ChJ*, pp. 254, no. 105. For a discussion of the subject, *cf.* Browe, *Judenmission*, pp. 185 ff.

[89] See above n. 64. This proximity in time may have prompted Cecil Roth's assertion that *Turbato* was an outgrowth of *Damnabili* and the situation there described. If there was such a relationship, it was not necessarily close. (*Cf.* Roth's essay in *HTR*, XLIII (1950), p. 143, discussed above.

[90] The Bull, addressed to the Dominican and Franciscan friars now, or in the future to be, appointed as inquisitors of heresy, reads:

> "Turbato corde audivimus et narramus quod quamplurimi Christiani, veritatem Catholice fidei abnegantes, se ad ritum Judaicum damnabiliter transtulerunt; quod tanto magis reprobum fore dignoscitur quanto ex hoc nomen Christi sanctissimum quadam familiari hostilitate securius blasphematur. Cum autem huic pesti damnabili, que, sicut accepimus, non sine subversione predictae fidei nimis excrescit, congruis et festinis deceat remediis obviari: Universitati vestrae per apostolica scripta mandamus quatenus, infra terminos vobis ad inquirendum contra hereticos auctoritate Sedis Apostolicae designatos, super premissis, tam per Christianos quam etiam per Judaeos inquisita diligenter et solicite veritate, contra Christianos quos talia inveneritis commisisse tanquam contra hereticos procedatis, Judaeos autem, qui Christianos utriusque sexus ad eorum ritum execrabilem hactenus induxerunt aut inveneritis de caetero inducentes poena debita puniatis. Contradictores per censuram ecclesiasticam, appelatione postposita, compescendo; invocato ad hoc, si opus fuerit, auxilio brachii secularis.
>
> Datum Viterbii, vi Kalendas Augusti, anno tertio."

Potthast 20095; Sbaralea, *Bull. Francisc.*, III, 126; Fond Doat XXXI, fol. 328r.–333v.; Browe, *Judenmission*, p. 258; also Armarium XXXI, 72, fol. 238r. In a general way, the contents of *Turbato* had been covered by Alexander IV in what we have in *Sexti Decret.*, Lib. V, tit. II, c. 2.

of Christ to be more safely blasphemed by enemies out of his own household. We have been informed, moreover, that this is not without injurious effect on the said faith, and it should therefore be countered by means of quick and appropriate remedies.

"We order your organization (*universitati vestrae*), within the territories entrusted to you by the Apostolic See for searching out heretics, to make diligent and thorough inquiry into the above, through Christians as well as through Jews. Against Christians whom you find guilty of the above you shall proceed as against heretics. Upon Jews whom you may find guilty of having induced Christians of either sex to join their execrable rites, or whom you may find doing so in the future, you shall impose fitting punishment. By means of appropriate ecclesiastical censure you shall silence all who oppose you. If necessary, you may call on the secular arm."

It is not surprising that the Inquisition asked several succeding popes for a reissue of this Bull. But it is interesting that the succeeding issues[91] were slightly but significantly modified. The Inquisition apparently felt that the above-cited form did not cover two important points: It did not specify that the chief problem was with converts from Judaism and with Jews who tried to draw them back into the Jewish faith; and it did not openly say that Jews were trying to subvert the faith of born Christians. When *Turbato* was repeated, it began as follows:[92]

"With a troubled heart we relate what we have heard: Not only are certain converts from the error of Jewish blindness to the light of the Christian faith known to have reverted to their former false belief, but

[91] By Gregory X on March 1, 1274; and by Nicolas IV on September 5, 1288, and September 9, 1290. It is possible that it was also issued by Martin IV, as indicated in Fond Doat 37, 193 ff., and consequently by Ulysse Robert, "Catalogue d'Actes Relatifs aux Juifs," in *REJ*, III (1881), 218, no. 53. The difficulty is with the date, March 1; a coincidence with the date of issue by Gregory X; besides, March 1, 1281, was only a short time after Martin's election and before his coronation. The *Bullaria* and the *Registres* compiled by Olivier-Martin do not list a *Turbato* by Pope Martin. Conceivably, a copy of the Gregory Bull could have been forwarded to some French inquisitors in 1281, with the consent of the newly-elected pope. See the next note.

[92] The Gregory X issue: Potthast 20724, 20798; Ripoll, I, 517, no. 19; Sbaralea, III, 213. Nicolas IV issue: Potthast 23391, *cf.* 22795; Sbaralea, V, 234; Fond Doat 32, fol, 193r.–194v.; *Registres de Nicolas IV*, by E. Langlois, p. 62, no. 322, and p. 511, no. 3186, Wadding, *Annales Minorum*, a.a. 1290 #7, explains the re-issue by saying that the pope was concerned about similar conditions in Germany. *Cf.* Kisch, *Germany*, pp. 463 f. A summary, credited to Boniface VIII, in *CJC*, Sixt., V, tit. II, c. 13.

"Turbato corde audivimus et narramus quod non solum quidam de Judaicae caecitatis errore ad lumen fidei Christianae conversi ad priorem reversi esse perfidiam dignoscuntur, verum etiam quamplurimi Christiani, veritatem Catholicae fidei abnegantes, se damnabiliter ad ritum Judaicum transtulerunt. . . ."

even [born] Christians, denying the true Catholic faith, have wickedly transferred themselves to the rites of Judaism. . . ."

There were thus four categories of person over whom the Inquisition sought and was given authority: born Jews who had been baptized and the Jews who presumably helped them to return to Judaism, and born Christians who were attracted to Judaism, and the Jews who allegedly lured them into the Jewish religion. There was, to be sure, a fifth category, of Jews who laid themselves open to the charge of blasphemy by retaining copies of the Talmud in their possession. But at least in the 13th century the Inquisition did not bother with these or other acts of alleged blasphemy by Jews, such as the charge of desecrating the Host levelled against them in Paris in 1290.[93] Local clergy and friars were active in Host desecration charges. As to the Talmud, that charge continued to be raised sporadically, whenever the Church reminded itself of the subject.[94] Besides, it involved entire communities, whereas for the time being the Inquisition was concerned only with individual Jews.

Before turning to the charge that Jews aided baptized but repentant Jews, it is necessary to examine the charge that they actively engaged in the proselytization of born Christians. It is impossible to estimate the

[93] Boniface VIII, July 17, 1295: *Petitio dilecti*, Potthast 24139; D. Michel Félibien. *Histoire de la Ville de Paris* (Paris 1725), III, 296 f.; G. Digard *et al.*, *Registres de Boniface VIII*, col. 156, no. 441. Raynald, a.a. 1290 #54, tells the story of the Host desecration by a Jew; whose house was thereupon destroyed by a mob. A number of other accounts of the miracle are given in the *Recueil des Historiens*, XX, 658; XXI, 127, 132; XXII, 32–33; also *MGH*, XXV, 578. The papal letter speaks of the Jew trying to stab the wafer and then putting it in boiling water. The pope grants the request of a citizen of Paris to establish a chapel in the place where the Jew had resided. This Host desecration is discussed by Peter Browe, "Die Hostienschändungen der Juden im Mittelalter," *Römische Quartalschrift*, XXXIV, 167–97, esp. pp. 180 ff. In another essay—"Die Eucharistenwunder des Mittelalters," *Breslauer Studien zur historischen Theologie*, n.F., 4 (1938), 128–39, 162–65—Browe described the annual procession which took place in Paris, in honor of the miracle, down to the 15th century, *ibid.*, 131 ff. There is no evidence that the Inquisition had any part in this.

[94] There is no indication that the Inquisition was concerned directly with the Talmud during the second half of the 13th century. It has already been shown above that it had no direct share in the public disputations. The Inquisition is not mentioned in the Bulls which Alexander IV sent on September 3, 1258, to Hugh IV, Duke of Burgundy, and to Charles, Count of Anjou and the Provence: *In sacro generali*: Archives Nationales, L 252, no. 178; *cf.* Isidore Loeb, in *REJ*, I (1880), 116, no. 2. A similar letter was sent at the same time to Louis IX of France, which, Loeb failed to notice, did not contain any reference to the prohibition of the Talmud. The omission was probably due to the fact that the pious king was himself very much concerned with this matter. (*Cf.* the Council of Beziers in 1255, in *ChJ*, p. 336.) Nor was the Inquisition directly involved in the attack on the Talmud in Southern Italy by the greedy convert Manoforte, ca. 1270, of whom we shall speak later. The Inquisition was not mentioned in the orders sent by Philip IV in 1299 to his officials in Southern France, which included an attack on those *libros damnatos*: Fond Doat 37, fol. 246v.–247v.; Saige, *Les Juifs de Languedoc*, p. 235, no. 20.

number of Christians who adopted Judaism in the course of the centuries when the Inquisition of the Middle Ages was active.[95] Such action was fraught with great danger for both convert and converter.[96] Consequently when it did take place, it was either kept secret or became notorious. Certainly there were more instances of this than became known. Yet even if the actual number was tenfold that known, it would hardly have justified the frequency and the expressions of outrage with which several popes made the charge in terms that lead one to believe that conversions of born Christians was a real problem for the Church.

What appears to have been really involved was the matter of social contact between Christians and Jews. An explicit illustration of how Jews led Christians to "Judaize" may be seen in the letter which Pope Honorius IV (1285–1287) addressed to John Peckham of Canterbury and to other English prelates in 1286.[97] Among the misdeeds of which the Jews were accused—teaching the Talmud to their children, employing Christian domestics, cursing Christianity in their prayers, luring ex-Jews back to Judaism—was the charge that they[98]

[95] Louis I. Newman, *Jewish Influence on Christian Reform Movements* (New York 1925), esp. pp. 393–430, seems to exaggerate the influence. Benzion Wacholder, "Cases of Proselytizing in Tosafoth Responsa," *JQR*, 51 (1961), 288–315, offers no specific instances. Both cover a good many generations. See also B. Blumenkranz, "Jüdische und Christliche Konvertiten," *Judentum im Mittelalter* (Berlin 1966), pp. 264–82; and Baron, *History*, IX, 57 and 266, n. 3. A. Paschovsky, *Der Passauer Anonymus* (*MGH SS*, vol. 22, Stuttgart, 1968) p. 152, mentions two clerics who adopted Judaism, One of them was the brother of a prelate, who had become a Jew for love of a Jewish woman. He returned to Christianity after having been castrated by order of his brother. This can hardly be called a case of Jewish proselytization. Moreover, the story sounds like an *exemplum* used in a sermon, not a real case.

[96] From early times proselytization of Christians by Jews was punished severely (*CTh.*, 16.8.6). The cases of Bado-Eleazar ca. 840 and of Andreas-Obadiah ca. 1102, indicate that a Christian convert to Judaism had to fear for his life if he did not flee to Muslim territory (*cf.* Blumenkranz, *op. cit.*, pp. 266 ff. and 269 ff.). Cecil Roth, *History of the Jews in England* (Oxford 1941), pp. 41 and 83, speaks of two cases in England, both of which ended in execution. The *Siete Partidas* of Alfonso X of Castile, VII, tit. 24, *ley* 7, speaks of a Christian who converts to Judaism and ordains that he is to be executed for it, as one would execute a heretic, and his property is to be dealt with as the property of a heretic. One must assume that this law included also ex-Jews who had reverted to Judaism, since the *Siete Partidas* does not mention this contingency elsewhere. That the problem of reversion to Judaism was not unknown is evident from a number of measures taken by previous kings of Castile. (*Cf.* Browe, *Judenmission*, p. 165.)

[97] *Cf.* n. 85 above; also Grayzel, "Bishop to Bishop I," in *Gratz College Anniversary Volume* (Philadelphia 1971), 131–45.

[98] "Non omittit Judaeorum ipsorum nequitia quin fidei orthodoxae cultores quolibet die Sabbati ac aliis solempnitatibus eorundem invitet ac instanter inducat ut in synagogis suis ipsorum officium audiant, illudque juxta sui ritus consuetudinem sollempnizent, rotulo involuto membranis . . . reverenciam exhibentes, quemobrem plerique christicole cum Judaeis pariter judaizant. . . ."

"miss no opportunity to invite followers of the orthosox faith to attend services in their synagogues on Sabbaths and on other solemn occasions, when they observe their rites in accordance with their customs, when they show reverence to their parchment scroll in which their Law is written. On such occasions many Christians Judaize along with the Jews. . . ."

In the same letter one finds additional information—doubtless also given the pope by the archbishop—that Christians in the England of that day visited Jewish homes, where they ate and drank. This too was considered dangerous, because it was bound to lead to discussions of religion, an action forbidden by Canon Law except to those especially equipped for it.[99] This Bull, and others which charge deliberate proselytization efforts by Jews, leave the clear impression that the term "to Judaize" meant to associate with Jews, and not necessarily to become one of them. The danger was a potential one.[100]

Other papal pronouncements fortify this impression. Thus the bull *Damnabili*[101] sent to the prelates of the Provence and Toulouse in December, 1267, begins the list of Jewish misdeeds with a statement that the Jews lure simple Christian souls into their damnable rites, and proceeds to illustrate the charge by listing their employment of Christian domestics, not wearing the Badge, and failing to obey other canonical restrictions on Jewish life. Two other papal letters, both sent by Nicolas IV on January 28, 1290, urged the prelates of southern France and the civil authorities of the Comtat Venaissin to cooperate with the inquisitors in their search for baptized

[99] The prohibition of eating with Jews goes back to the Council of Elvira (ca. 306): Mansi, II, 14, par. 50. The prohibition for laymen to discuss religion publicly or privately is recorded, in the name of Pope Alexander IV, in *CJC, Sexti Decret.*, Lib. V, tit. ii, c. 2, #1. An example of the fast spreading attitude against socializing with Jews out of fear for Christianity is the order of an English bishop (1286) forbidding his parishioners to accept an invitation to a Jewish wedding: "ut sic fidei Christianae, cuius hostes gratis existunt, detrahere valeant et sinistra simplicibus predicare:" *Registrum Recardi de Swinfield*, ed. W. W. Capes (London 1909), pp. 120 ff. Baron, in his *History*, IX, 57 f., brings another example of how Christians felt the Jews were corrupting Christianity. Louis I. Newman, *Jewish Influence on Christian Reform Movements*, esp. 360–430, and 393 ff. on proselytization, makes some exaggerated claims. But the fears of the Christians cannot be completely discounted.

[100] "Cum itaque non sit tam pestilens et periculosus morbus aliquatenus contemnendus, ne, quod absit, relictus neglectui tractu temporis invalescat." On Judaism as "contagious," see also Ullmann, *Med. Papalism*, p. 254.

[101] This *Damnabili*, not the one sent earlier in 1267 to the king of Aragon, was addressed to the prelates of Poitou, Toulouse, and the Provence. It is to be found in Fond Doat, 32, fol. 4r.–7r.; For some of the background see Emile Camau, *La Provence à travers les siecles*, III, 466–75. The relevant sentence is: "Nam, ut dolentes audivimus et penitus reprobamus, Christianos utriusque sexus simplices ad suum ritum dampnabilem retrahere moliuntur. . . ."

Jews who reverted to Judaism and for Jews who came to their aid. Such Jews, the pope said, were also active among born Christians and made every effort to infect them with heresy.[102] A month later, the pope wrote to the inquisitors of the same provinces, instructing them vigorously to pursue these destroyers of the faith, be they Jews or Christians.[103]

It is not difficult to understand why the cooperation of the bishops had not been forthcoming. They had, from the first, resented the Inquisition's intrusion into an area which had previously been theirs, not to mention the matter of income from fines and confiscations. The inclusion of the Jews in the Inquisition's range of activity made for further dissatisfaction. Indeed, the quarrel between the episcopal and inquisitional branches of the Church were to continue the occupy the attention of the Ecumenical Council of Vienne in 1311–1312.[104] As to the differences between the Inquisition and the civil governments, it has been spoken of already and will be again below. These differences may have reached a critical stage about 1290. In any event, the Inquisition found that its hold could be strengthened on suspected converts from Judaism, especially if its attack could be fortified by an accusation that Jews were carrying on active propaganda among born Christians.[105] It was self-serving propaganda, and it resulted in increasing hostility between Christians and Jews.

There can be little doubt, however, that under the definition of "force" which the Church had adopted, the problem posed by converts from Judaism

[102] *Attendite fratres*, addressed to the prelates and abbots of Aix, Arles, and Embrun: Potthast 23170; Sbaralea, IV, 131, no. 209; Reg. Vat. 44, fol. 284 r.-v.; *Inter innumerabiles*, Reg. Vat., *ibid.*; Langlois, *Les registres de Nicolas IV*, no. 2029. Since a good part of both documents is identical, the same sentence occurs in both: ". . . ac ipsi Judaei, nostrae fidei corruptores, conversos et baptizatos de ipsis ad fidem nostram, immo ipsos etiam Christianos, inficere et apostatare pro posse nituntur, in contumeliam fidei Christianae."

[103] *Ad augmentum*, addressed to the iniquisitors of Aix, Arles, and Embrun, on February 20, 1290: Potthast 23185; Reg. Vat. 44, fol. 294v.: Langlois, *Registres*, nos. 2124–5; Raynald, vol. XIV, a.a. 1290 #49. "Et si quos tales inveneritis Christianos, cuiuscumque conditionis aut status existant . . . etiam si Judaei vel Christiani esse noscuntur, qui eis talia suadeant . . ."

[104] *Cf.* Council of Vienne, 1311–1312, *Conciliorum Oecumenicorum Decreta*, 1962, pp. 356 ff., 26; *cf.* Lea, II, 96.

[105] There is evidence that, after *Turbato*, the Inquisition extended its activity concerning Jews, for example, the prosecution of Jews on a charge of mistreating converts: G. Opitz, "Ueber zwei Codices zum Inquisitionsprozess," in *Quellen u. Forschungen aus italienischen Archiven*, 8 (1937–38), p. 103. Wadding reports for 1290 that Pope Nicolas became so concerned about the spread of heresy and Judaism in Palestine that he ordered the patriarch of Jerusalem to appoint a special inquisitor there (a.a. 1290 #2). In the second half of the 13th century, the belief became widespread that the time of the Antichrist was approaching, partly as a result of Jewish and heretical activity in subversion of Christianity: A. Paschovsky, *Der Passauer Anonymus*, p. 158.

was real. They would not, or could not, completely and suddenly break with the faith of their fathers. A number of papal letters illustrate how this problem manifested itself. One such letter [106] speaks of a riot which occurred in the county of La Marche, in central France, about 1280. A number of Jews chose baptism rather than death, and they naturally asked that their infant children also be baptized. Subsequently, the riot over, they wanted to return to Judaism. The inquisitors thereupon imprisoned them and kept them in their jail for over a year. But the Jews steadfastly refused to adhere to Christianity. The inquisitors, perhaps impressed by such persistence, turned to the pope for guidance. The pope replied that they should be treated as heretics. For they had not been strictly speaking forced into conversion (*non precise coacti*), as seemed clear from the fact that they had of their own free will offered their children for baptism.[107]

Another letter[108] of Pope Nicolas IV lists the activities by which the disloyalty of the converts might be recognized. Addressing the inquisitors of the provinces whose prelates he had urged a few months earlier[109] to cooperate in the search for secret Judaizers, he speaks of their suspicious actions. In times of personal crisis, they bring candles and lamps to the synagogue and make special offerings there. They hold vigils, especially on the Sabbath, that the sick may regain their health, that the shipwrecked may reach a safe port, that women in childbirth may come through safely, that the sterile may be blessed with children. They show reverence to the

[106] *Sicut nobis* by Pope Nicolas IV, May 7, 1288. Fond Doat 37, fol. 191r.–192r. gives it as by Nicolas III, also dated as of the nones of May, in his first year, while fol. 206r.–208r. gives it again, presumably for Nicolas IV. The document is therefore listed twice in Ulysse Robert's catalogue in *REJ*, III (1981), 217, no. 50 and 219, no. 62. Consequently, Joshua Starr (*Speculum*, XXI [1946], 205, n. 15) and Guido Kisch, (*Germany*, pp. 463 f., n. 101), and myself as well (*ChJ*, p. 15, n. 15) credited it to Nicolas III, re-issued by Nicolas IV. But there is nothing in the document that would call for a re-issue. The date, moreover, is suspicious on several counts. On the whole, it appears more reasonable to attribute the Bull to Nicolas IV.

[107] "Dudum in Comitatu Marchiae contra [Judaeos] inibi commorantes per Christianos illarum partium persecutionis insurgente procella, plures ex dictis Judaeis metu mortis . . . non tamen absolute seu precise coacti, se baptizari fecerunt; aliqui ipsorum quibusdam infantibus lactentibus filiis suis et consaguineis baptismum conferri per huius metum illatum ipsis modo simili permisserunt . . . Postmodum vero predicti taliter baptizati sacramentum baptizmatis . . . dampnabiliter contempnentes . . . ad caecitatem Judaicam redierant; propter quod inquisitores hereticae pravitatis tunc in Regno Francie . . . eos capi fecerunt et carcerali custodiae mancipari. . . . Sed sibi predictam excommunicationis sententiam et squalores carceris per annum et amplius contemptibiliter sustinuerunt animis induratis ad Christianam fidem redire penitus denegantes. The pope concludes that the inquisitors must proceed against them "as against heretics."

[108] For references see n. 103 above: *Ad augmentum*.

[109] *Attendite fratres*. For references see n. 102 above.

Scroll of the Law as though it were an idol. Against these the inquisitors were granted permission to proceed as against heretics and idol worshipers.[110]

In fact, one might spend a lifetime unsuspected of judaizing and reveal his true inclinations when on the point of death. This was the case in Southern Burgundy (the later Franche Comté). On the surface it appeared that the Inquisition had nothing to do in that province; no Jews lived there, nor any known ex-Jews. Yet in 1267, the inquisitors, while searching the neighborhood for Waldensians, were informed about residents of the province who, on their deathbed, had confessed to their Jewish sympathies. The inquisitors promptly informed Pope Clement IV; he in turn wrote to Jean de Salins, Count of Burgundy, to say that it was his duty to let the inquisitors operate in his territory.[111] Not only was it probable that there were Judaizers among the living, but according to the rules of the Inquisition, it could disinter the dead, confiscate what property they had bequeathed to their children, and impose serious penalties and restrictions on them.[112]

As already mentioned, the attitude of suspicion toward converts spilled over into suspicion of any Jew who might have been in contact with a convert.[113] Such a Jew, accused of aiding an ex-Jew to revert to Judaism, was more defenseless against his accusers than any outright heretic, who could conceivably obtain favorable testimony from a credible Christian. A Jew accused of being a *fautor* had only one recourse: he could appeal to his overlord. Not that the princes were lacking in piety—they were simply protecting their rights and, quite directly, their property. For if found guilty, the Jew's property would, in large measure, be taken by the Inquisition in fines or outright confiscation.[114]

Instances of such protection can be cited for almost every country after the issuance of *Turbato*. Even before the issuance of this Bull, as already

110 "... quamplures sacri baptizatis fonte renati ... dum languorum afflictionibus et tribulationum periculis a Domino visitantur, ad Judaici ritus vanum auxilium errando recurrunt, in synagoga Judaeorum lampades et candelas tenentes accensas et oblationes inibi facientes, vigilias quoque die precipue sabbati protrahunt, ut infirmi recuperent sanitatem, naufrangantes ad portum salutis pervenissent, existentes in partu absque periculo pariant, et steriles prolis fecunditate letentur; ibi pro his et aliis suffragia implorantes dicti ritus, rotulo quasi per idolatriae modum nefarium devotionis et reverentiae signa patentia exhibendo. . . ."

111 Clement IV, *Professionis Christianae*, August 17, 1267, addressed to Jean de Salins: Jean Delois, *Speculum Inquisitionis Bisuntinae* (Dôle 1628), pp. 229–31. Another letter about aid to the Inquisition had been written on July 6, 1267: *ibid.*—*Prae cunctis*, pp. 165–72: Potthast 20064; but it makes no mention of Jews. In *Professionis* the Pope says he had been informed "quod multos in locis tibi subjectis et adjacentibus crimen heretici pravitatis infecit . . . tamquam in tenebris et umbra mortis positi caecitatis Judaice veteram et corruptam damnabiliter induunt." In a note, Delois says that there were no known Jews in that province at that time. *Cf.* J. Morey, "Les Juifs en Franche Comté au XIVe siecle," *REJ*, VII (1883), 3; also Leon Gauthiers, *Memoires . . . du Jura*, 9me serie, III, 91.

112 *Cf. Sexti Decret.*, Lib. V, tit. ii, c. 2. Confiscation was part of the regular punishment

noted, King James I of Aragon took all matters connected with the Barcelona disputation out of the hands of the Church.[115] In 1275, the same king threatened to impose a heavy fine on aynone, layman or cleric, who cited the Jews of Perpingnan (then part of his domain) before an ecclesiastical court, as long as they were willing to appear before a royal court.[116] A day later, he informed the Jews of Southern France—those under his rule—that, unless his officers agreed to the contrary, they were under no obligation to change their places of residence because of an ecclesiastical order.[117] He even took the charge of blasphemy out of the hands of the Church.[118] James' son, Peter III, in September 1284, ordered his officials to make the inquisitors stop investigating certain Jews on a charge of having opened their doors to some converts. If these Jews are to be punished, he said, he will do the punishing.[119] Peter's son, James II, expressed himself in the same

for heresy: *cf.* Lea, I, 501 ff. It naturally became desirable to condemn a heretic *post mortem*, so that his property might be confiscated.

[113] *Cf.* above, nn. 80 and 86.

[114] The Inquisition of the Middle Ages was never established in England. The bishops did not want it—with the possible exception of Archbishop Pekham of Canterbury—because they were aware of the resentment against it on the part of the continental bishops. Nor did Henry III or Edward I want to have it interfere with their subjects, especially with the Jews, whose property they considered their own. Edward's attitude is revealed in the discussion of it in H. G. Richardson, *The English Jewry under Angevin Kings* (London 1960), pp. 223 ff., especially in his relations to the Jews of Gascony which was then under his rule.

[115] *Cf.* above, n. 59. See the very interesting and, for the time, very liberal charter which King James I of Aragon gave to the Jews of Lerida in 1268 (reprinted by James Parkes in his *The Jew in the Medieval Community*, pp. 403 f.). He there unmistakably asserts his authority as against interference by Church and Inquisition. He would enforce the Church's viewpoint regarding blasphemy in Jewish books, the erection of new and ornate synagogues, or the preaching of conversionary sermons, but it must all be done under his direction and with his consent. He concludes by saying: "Concedimus etiam vobis et vestris quod super aliquibus non possit vobis fieri aliqua innovatio."

[116] Regné, "Catalogue des Actes," etc., *REJ*, 62 (1912), 62, no. 625.

[117] *Ibid.*, p. 63, no. 630.

[118] In this respect he emulated and outdid Edward I of England: *Calendar of Close Rolls*, 1272–9, 529–30, 565–6. There blasphemy was a capital offense. James I of Aragon, not only claimed it as under his own jurisdiction, but also pardoned a number of Jews, although the evidence against them might elsewhere have been considered strong. *Cf.* F. de Bofarull y Sans, *Los Judios en el territorio de Barcelona* (Barcelona 1910), no. 49, which is understandable if it really refers to a charge of blasphemy (in 1265) against Nahmanides in connection with the disputation, but no. 60 presents a more puzzling case. No matter what the antecedent quarrels within the family of the accused, and no matter how valuable the accused was as a royal official, he would scarcely have been freed by an ecclesiastical court when his own family accused him of blasphemy against the cross. *Cf.* Regné, *REJ*, 61 (1911), p. 24, no. 354.

[119] Regné, "Catalogue," *REJ*, 65 (1913), p. 76, no. 1101: the rights of the Jews and their property must be protected; p. 204, no. 1206: the Dominicans must not prosecute the Jews of Barcelona on the charge of having aided ex-Jews to revert to Judaism.

vein to inquisitors in 1292: "Since," he said, "Jews are not of the Catholic faith or under Catholic law, if they do anything against the law, he will punish them, not they."[120]

The French royal attitude was essentially no different. There were few differences between king and Inquisition under the pious Louis IX; the king sympathized with the Inquisition, and the inquisitors were careful with the king. But the situation took a different turn under the self-willed Philip IV (the Fair), Louis's grandson. Philip repeatedly opposed the claims of the Inquisition where Jews were concerned. Not that he had any special affection for Jews—he was to expel them from his territory in 1306 because he badly needed their confiscated money and property. His interest in them was purely financial, and his personal authority and jurisdictional rights were more important. In 1287, he ordered his officers and his seneschal in Carcassonne not to permit the molestation of his Jews, whose synagogue and cemetery were endangered.[121] He was furious when, in 1288 in the city of Troyes, thirteen Jews were haled before a clerical tribunal, tortured and executed on a charge of Ritual Murder, all of this being done without informing him or his officers.[122] In 1293, he again ordered his seneschal in the Provence not to permit the molestation of Jews without the civil authority's consent. To be sure, he included in this order a copy of *Turbato* Bull and ordered the seneschal to observe its contents, though without permitting this to result in the arrest and punishment of Jews.[123] The obvious double-talk can only be explained by assuming that the king would tolerate Inquisitional jurisdiction over baptized Jews if their baptism could be proved, but not the imprisonment or fining of Jews on the charge of having been *fautores*. In 1299, however, King Philip's sentiments appear to

[120] On June 20, 1292, James II ordered the inquisitors not to concern themselves with the Jews of Gerona, since they were not subject to Catholic law: "cum non sint de fide seu lege catholica; et si aliquo excesserint contra legem, sint per nos puniendi." *Cf.* Baer, I, 148, no. 133, He also promised to see to it that converts are not harmed or persecuted by their former coreligionists; *cf.* Rubio y Lluch, *Documentos per la historia de la cultura Catalana*, II, no. 12. But anyone accused of aiding a convert to return to Judaism had to be brought before his court: Baer, *ibid.*, nos. 164 and 168. *Cf.* also J. L. Shneidman, *REJ*, 121 (1962), 49–58.

[121] Gustave Saige, *Les Juifs de Languedoc anterieurement au XIVe Siecle*, p. 249, no. 6.

[122] Arsène Darmsteter, "L'autodafé de Troyes," *REJ*, II, 199–247, esp. p. 246. The court that tried the 13 unfortunate Jews may not have been inquisitional, but it probably consisted of monks and clerics. This may have resulted in the order forbidding Churchmen to take money from Jews as fines or to imprison them. Boutaric, *Actes de Parlement*, I, 414; Saige, *op. cit.*, pp. 233–6. *Cf.* Robert Chazan, *Medieval Jewry in Northern France* (Baltimore 1975), pp. 180 ff.

[123] Douais, in his *Documents*, I, 228, was so eager to show that Philip IV cooperated with the Inquisition that he failed to note the king's tergiversations in accordance with his political needs. In 1291, the king ordered his seneschal, Simon Brisetête, to protect the Jews in all their privileges regarding synagogues, bodily injury, and excessive fines (Saige,

have undergone a marked change. This was in the midst of his quarrel with Pope Boniface VIII, when the king wanted to appear more papal than the pope. He now accused the Jews of everything that the most zealous inquisitor could have thought of. But in 1302, he reverted to his original stand and would not permit inquisitors to molest his Jews in matters which were no concern of theirs, such as usury, blasphemy, or magic. Four years later, he expelled the Jews for reasons which had nothing to do with Church or Inquisition.

Still another example of protection against the Inquisition extended to the Jews by their princes is the attitude of Charles I, king of the Two Sicilies, and duke of several provinces in South-Eastern and Western France. He obviously had a freer hand in his French territories than in his Italian kingdom, where he was the vassal of the pope. That he could use his income from France to maintain himself in Italy may serve to explain his actions. But he yielded to his Jewish subjects by freeing them from the Badge, probably in return for a substantial payment. In 1276, he took a strong stand against the inquisitors in the Provence who had imprisoned a number of Jews, extorted money from them in fines, imposed an unusually large Badge on them, and subjected one of them to torture. He warned the inquisitors in no uncertain terms that they must not exercize any jurisdiction over his Jews.[124] In his Sicilian kingdom, on the other hand, Charles could not but encourage the anti-Jewish activities instigated by Manoforte in 1267.[125]

op. cit., 223 f.). In 1293, when his quarrel with the pope had not yet gone very far, Philip appeared willing to follow *Turbato*, though certainly not all the way, for he ordered his seneschal, at the same time: "et si sit super his aliquid dubium vel obscurum, ad captionem predictorum (accused Jews) nostra curia inconsulta non procedatis" (Saige, *ibid.*, 231 f.; Fond Doat 37, 239v.–240v.; 241r.–245r.). In 1299, Philip IV charged that they build new synagogues, protect heretics, sing too loudly at their services, study the Talmud, and seduce simple-minded Christians into having themselves circumcised (Saige, *ibid.*, 235 f.). In 1302, the quarrel with the pope practically won, the king reverted to protecting his Jews (*Ordonances des rois de France*, I, 346; *REJ*, 2 (1881), 31, no. 15; Chazan, *op. cit.*, p. 177).

124 Charles I of Sicily to his officials in the Provence, March 26, 1276: He had heard that Brother Bertrand Rocca and his fellow inquisitor in the Provence "plura gravamina indebite et injuste Judaeis nostris Provinciae intulerunt, auferendo illis magnam pecuniae summam, que nostra erat et ad nostram curiam pertinebat; imponendo quoque aliquibus ex eisdem magna signa et insolita, et quosdam ponendo in carcere, et alia plura mala et gravia fecerunt eisdem et cotidie facere moliuntur." He had consulted some of his learned friends—he was in Rome at the time—and they told him that he was within his rights to put a stop to all this. *Cf.* Papon, *Histoire Générale de Provence*, III, Preuves, pp. XXXII–XXXIII.

125 Manoforte of Trani was a convert who, in 1267, initiated a conversionary campaign and a confiscation of rabbinic books. As a reward King Charles I assigned to him a substantial sum from the income of the Jewish dyeing establishments, a Jewish monopoly. *Cf.* G. del Giudice, *Codex diplomaticus del regno di Carlo I* (Naples 1863), pp. 314 ff.; D. A.

Charles I's son, Charles II, however, either out of personal ineptitude or, because as a vassal of the pope he could not oppose the Inquisition, did not even try to defend the Jews. Under pressure from the inquisitors, and perhaps also of the townsmen of his French provinces of Maine and Anjou, he expelled the Jews from these provinces,[126] though not from the Provence. At the same time, the inquisitors proved too much for him in Naples as well. Here conversion was soon followed by regret, and regret by inquisition, so that a flourishing Jewish community was almost totally destroyed.[127] Before long, churches in Southern Italy were complaining of impoverishment due to lack of income from Jewish sources.[128]

To summarize: whether inquisitors would have much or any authority over unbaptized Jews depended on the sovereign's character and on the local political and economic situation. To be sure, the sovereign was unreliable and could change his attitude from day to day; but at least he could not be suspected of malevolence, since the presence of Jews as his *servi camerae* was to his advantage. The dread which the Inquisition inspired, by the end of the 13th century, is evident from the fact that a certain Arnold Déjean, newly appointed inquisitor in Pamiers, felt called upon to reassure the Jews, as some of his predecessors had done. It is not the condescending tone of the brief document that calls for comment—the Jews must already have been used to *hauteur*—but the very need for assurance. In effect, the document promised nothing; it said only that, if they conducted themselves "acceptably," they would be treated acceptably. The body of the document reads as follows:[129]

Cassuto, "Destruction of the South Italian Yeshibot in the 13th Century," *Studies in Memory of Asher Gulak and Samuel Stern* (Hebrew) (Jerusalem 1942), pp. 137–52, esp. 141 f.; Joshua Starr, "The Mass Conversion of Jews in Southern Italy, 1290–1293," *Speculum*, XXI (1946), pp. 203–11; N. Ferrorelli, *Gli Ebrei nell'Italia Meridionale* (Bologna 1915), pp. 53 ff. It is well to remember that this was during the reign of Pope Clement IV, a firm believer in conversion of Jews and in the destruction of rabbinic literature.

126 On the expulsions from the French provinces, see Lucien Lazard, "Les Juifs de Touraine," *REJ*, 17 (1888), 210–34, esp. 225, no. VI (December 1288); also Leon Brunschvicg, "Les Juifs d'Angers et de pays Angevin," *REJ*, 29 (1894), 229–41.

127 For the events in the Kingdom of Naples from 1290 to 1294, see the essays by Cassuto and Starr, as well as the references in the volume by Ferrorelli, listed in n. 125, above. They estimate the number of converts at about 8,000. Since many of these soon regretted their conversion, the inquisitors had much to do, both with the suspected neophytes and with the remaining Jews accused of aiding the former to continue their practice of Judaism in secret.

128 See the complaint of Bartholomeo, Bishop-Elect of Trani, in 1328, to which Pope John XXII replied by asking the inquisitors in South Italy to refrain from prosecuting and impoverishing the converts and the Jews for a period of two years, so that the Jews can have some means from which the Church of Trani might draw income. Since the bishop had undertaken to punish the culprits, they may move against such only at the bishop's request. John XXII, *Petitio dilecti*: Mollat, *Lettres communes de Jean XXII*, no.40234; Eubel, *Bullarium Franciscanum*, V, 338, no. 700 n.: Grayzel, "References to the Jews in the Correspondence of John XXII," *HUC Annual*, XXIII (1950–1), 73 f., no. 33.

"In view of the fact that the Catholic Church, hopeful and confident that God will remove the veil from your hearts, supports your presence and tolerates your rites, therefore, we, following in the footsteps of our predecessors, grant the following to your collectivity (*universitati vestrae*): You may live and conduct yourselves acceptably in manner and custom, just as the Jews of Narbonne are permitted to live and conduct themselves. We, for our part, have no intention of imposing upon you any serious or unusual innovations. We grant you this by these letters, and we affix our seal in witness of the above."

There were occasions when the popes themselves had to restrain the zeal of the inquisitors, and sometimes of other clerics and lay Christians as well. When a Jewish community pressed its complaint—whatever form that pressure might have taken, since it was never easy and always expensive to get the pope's attention—the complaint was investigated and, if found justified, the guilty party was ordered to desist. That the first order was not always effective is proved by the fact that later popes had to repeat it. One source of complaint was that Jews—sometimes even converted Jews—would be summoned to answer charges against them, not before the court in the place where they lived, but before one at some considerable distance. Sometimes this was done out of malice, to annoy or to increase the defendant's expense; usually it was done to get him to appear in a court away from the customary civil jurisdiction. A number of popes recognized the unfairness of such action, and they tried to stop it.[130]

[129] The document is taken from *Histoire generale de Languedoc*, X, Preuves, col. 347 f.: "Frater Arnaldus Johannis, de Ordine Fratrum Predicatorum, inquisitor heretice pravitatis in Appamiarum diocesi auctoritate apostolica deputatus, universis et singulis Judaeis in predicta Appamiarum diocesi commorantibus spiritum consilii sanioris et viam agnoscere veritatis. Considerantes quod Ecclesia catholica, habens spes et fiduciam quod Deus auferat velamen de cordibus vestris, statum vestrum sustinet et habet in tollerantia ritus vestros, predecessorum nostrorum vestigiis inherantes, universitati vestre tenore presentium duximus concedendum ut positis vivere, esse et conversari secundum modum et usitationem tollerabilem, sicut in Narbonensi provincia Judaei communiter conversari et vivere permittuntur; non enim intendimus vobis facere aliquas graves et insolitas novitates. Concendentes vobis presentes litteras, sigillo nostro sigillatas in testimonium premissorum. Datum Appamiis, dominica secunda in quadragesima, anno Domini MCCXCVII." *Cf.* J. M. Vidal, *Le tribunal d'Inquisition de Pamiers* (Toulouse 1906), pp. 66 f.; Fond Doat XXXVII, fol. 160r.

[130] Alexander IV protected converted Jews against this kind of chicanery in his Bull *Ex parte vestra*, December 9, 1255: C. Bourel de la Roncière *et al.*, *Registres d'Alexandre IV*, no. 957. Nicolas IV protested against such violations of justice three times within six days, all the letters being addressed to officials in the Comtat Venaissin: *Sicut ad nostrum*, November 5, 1290, addressed to all the inhabitants of the Comtat (*Registres* 3574), *Intellecto dudum*: November 6, to the Bishop of Carpentras (*Registres* 3575), *Ut ex gratia*: November 9, 1290, addressed to the inhabitants, assuring them that he wants to protect their liberties (*Registres* 3573). In all cases the culprits mentioned were clerics as well as laymen, and the sufferers were Jews and non-Jews. It was evidently a common practice; for Ed-

A much more serious situation was that connected with witnesses to charges of Ritual Murder. The number of such accusations, with all their murderous consequences, increased appallingly during the German interregnum (1250–1272) and continued thereafter. In 1272, Pope Gregory X issued a *Sicut* to which he appended a long statement refuting the charge and accusing enemies of the Jews of trumping it up in order to extort money from the Jews or profiting otherwise.[131] Since this papal exhortation obviously was doing no good, Pope Martin IV, issued in 1281 a *Sicut* the most important part of which was not its stereotyped wording, but a paragraph designed to limit inimical and inquisitional activity. It made the following points: Witnesses against Jews must take a solemn oath; they must be made to understand that, if they failed to substantiate their charges, they would suffer the fate their victims would have suffered if the charges had been proved. Finally, Pope Martin said that a Jew should not be accused of encouraging a convert to return to Judaism if all that was known was that the two had been engaged in conversation.[132] Neither Gregory's refutation nor Martin's suggestion is known to have served its purpose; accusations of Ritual Murder have continued down into modern times.[133]

A part of the inquisitional procedure which some of the popes recognized as unfair to Jews (and to others) derived from the right of the inquisitors not to divulge the names of witnesses hostile to the accused. The right had been granted as far back as Innocent IV and Alexander IV, that is, in the 1250's. The excuse for secrecy in so delicate a situation was the danger to the accuser and to his witnesses, since the accused might be a "powerful person" and might be able to cause harm to his opponents.[134] But the with-

ward I of England strongly objected to it being practiced in his French province of Gascony. *Cf. Foedera*, II (a. 1281), p. 180.

[131] Gregory X's *Sicut*, with its addition on the subject of Ritual Murder, has been reproduced many times: Potthast 20915: Stern, *Urkundliche Beiträge* (Kiel 1893), no. 1, pp. 5 ff.; and *idem*, *Päpstliche Bullen über die Blutbeschuldigung* (Munich 1900), pp. 18 ff.; G. Bondy and F. Dworsky, *Zur Geschichte der Juden in Boehmen* (Prague 1906), I, 32 ff. Grayzel, in *Studies and Essays . . . A. A. Neuman* (Philadelphia 1962), pp. 269 f. The last-named essay also has the addition on the subject by Innocent IV (p. 258).

[132] The *Sicut* by Martin IV in B. and G. Lagumina, *Codice diplomatico dei Giudei di Sicilia*, I, 117, no. 81. The pope orders that no inquisitor or any other official shall detain a Jew on the testimony of anyone: "sed ille qui eos accusaverit det et prestet ydoniam fidejussoriam . . . et si legitime non probaverit de quo accusatus est, quod accusator teneatur ad illam poenam sicut accusatus est teneretur . . . et si aliquis Judaeus baptizatus haberet aliquam familiaritatem cum aliquo alio Judaeo . . . quod non teneatur ad poenam aliquam." How much grief would have been saved had this order been adhered to!

[133] *Cf. The Ritual Murder Libel and the Jew*, edited by Cecil Roth (London 1935); it contains much of the material referred to above.

[134] *Sexti Decret.* Lib. V, tit. ii, c. 20: "Jubemus tamen quod, si accusatoribus vel testibus in causa haeresis intervenientibus . . . propter potentiam personarum contra quas inquiritur, videant episcopus vel inquisitores grave periculum imminere si contingat fieri

holding of such crucial information obviously put the accused at a great disadvantage. He had to guess who his accusers might be, what they could have said about him, and why. But this very guessing was useful to the inquisitors; as a result of it they could spread their net ever wider. The inquisitors' powers in this respect was somewhat limited later, as a result of complaints from non-Jewish sources, by a requirement that the names of witnesses should be revealed to a number of reliable persons, though still not to the accused. The limitation was imposed as a possible answer to the widespread charge that the Inquisition, by causing the accused to reveal the names of his possible enemies, was really on a perpetual "fishing expedition" for more accusers and witnesses against him.

Down to the end of the 13th century the Jews were still considered *potentes*. Any Jew could be forced to appear before the inquisitional court, and without being told of any specific charge or by whom it had been lodged, be put on trial, with his life or at least his possessions in jeopardy. One cannot tell how long or how often the Jews had protested. At long last, Boniface VIII, in 1299, issued a Bull[135] by which he granted that Jews, even the wealthy ones among them, could hardly be called "powerful." The Bull tells the Jews of Rome, to whom it was addressed, that they may demand that the inquisitors reveal to them the names of the witnesses against them. If there is any suspicion that the Jew in question is unduly influential, the matter should be referred to the pope.

A reputable Jewish historical work connects Pope Boniface's action with the tragic incident that had taken place in Rome the year before.[136] The entire Jewish community was endangered by an accusation, presumably of having tried to persuade converts to return to Judaism. The converts could well have been from among those who had fallen victim to the riots and pressures of some years previously in Southern Italy. Whatever the accusation and whoever was involved, Elias de Pomis, a highly respected leader of the Roman Jewish community, took the blame upon himself and as a result was burned at the stake.

publicationem nominum eorundem, ipsorum nomina non publice sed secreto . . . aliquibus aliis personis . . . exprimantur." For earlier regulations in that direction, by Innocent IV and Alexander IV, see *Layette du Tresor des Chartes*, III, nos. 4112, 4113, 4221.

135 Boniface VIII, June 13, 1299: *Exhibita nobis*, G. Digard *et al.*, *Les Registres de Boniface VIII*, II, 412, no. 3063. On July 7, 1299, the same Bull was sent also to the Jews of the County Venaissin: *ibid.*, no. 3215. "Inquisitores tamen . . . vos asserentes potentes, publicationem huiusmodi vobis aliquando facere denegant, sicque vobis ex hoc debite defensionis facultas subtrahitur. . . . Nos autem, considerantes imbecillitatem vestram et propterea vos, etiam si divitiis habundetis, impotentum numero ascribentes, volumus ut tanquam impotentibus predicti inquisitores . . . vobis predictam publicationem faciant." In cases of doubt, the pope is to be consulted.

136 H. Vogelstein und P. Rieger, *Geschichte der Juden in Rom* (Berlin 1896), I, 256 f.

It was clear by the end of the 13th century that failure to protect the weak from one threatening danger lays them open to others. The reign of Pope Nicholas IV (1288–1292) is instructive in this respect. In 1288, and again in 1290, he reissued *Turbato*,[137] the first time to the Inquisition in general, the second to the inquisitors in the Romagna, which was more directly under his control. In that same year 1290, he urged Churchmen in France to cooperate with the Inquisition, and he repeated the charge that Jews were actively proselyitizing among born Christians.[138] For a century now, Judaism was being called a threat and the Jews a malicious lot. Should the pope have been surprised when laymen and clerics anywhere made Jewish life as difficult as they could?[139] This dual and contradictory approach to their Jewish problem should have been clear to the popes long before this. In 1290, Pope Nicolas IV felt constrained to address to his vicar in Rome an eloquent appeal for moderation on the part of the Roman population. Mother Church, he said, prays for the veil to be lifted from the hearts of the Jews; yet Churchmen are guilty of making Christianity odious to them. Pope Nicholas therefore asks his vicar to make sure that justice is done to the Jews.[140]

But that was the spirit of *Sicut*. Unfortunately for both sides the spirit of *Turbato* had replaced it.

137 See note 92, above.

138 See note 102, above.

139 See note 130, above.

140 Nicolas IV, January 30, 1291: *Orat mater*, Potthast 23541, A. Theiner, *Codex diplomaticus domini temporalis S. Sedis*, I, 315, no. 486. "Orat mater ecclesia pro subducendo velamine de cordibus Judaeorum et de ipsorum oculis squamis caecitatis eductis Christum illuminati agnoscant, candorem lucis eterne; propter quod ipsa ecclesia non tolerat patienter ut Judaeos injuriis vel jacturis indebite afficiant Christiani nominis professores. Nuper siquidem sinagoga Judaeorum de Urbe nobis insinuate admodum flebili patefecit quod nonnulli clerici de predicta Urbe manus infestationis extendentes pontice in eos ipsos gravare exactionibus gravibus afficere injuriis et in bonis suis graviter molestare non cessant; quare ipsi pressi tam infestis angustiis humiliter implorarunt super hoc presidium apostolice pietatis. Nos, itaque attendentes, quod mansuetudinem christianam non decet in Judaeos molestiis et insolentiis excandere, ac propterea volentes ut ipsi apostolice clementie favore protecti contra injustitiam non vexantur, discretioni tue per apostolica scripta mandamus quatinus prefatos Judaeos non permittas super hiis a talibus indebite molestari. Molestatores huiusmodi per censuram ecclesiasticam, appellatione postposita, compescendo. Datum apud Urbemveterem, III Kalendas Februarii, Pontificatus nostri anno tertio."

The Jubilees Calendar and The 'Days of Assembly'*

By SIDNEY B. HOENIG
The Dropsie University

MONDAY, THURSDAY AND Saturday are known in tannaitic literature as the "days of assembly."[1] Ezra the Scribe, it is noted, had decreed these days to be designated for the reading of the Torah and the convening of the judicial courts.[2] In probing this tradition, the Talmud surmises that the implementation of these days as 'days of assembly' is much older; it attributes it to unnamed "prophets."[3] This Talmudic contention, similar to the basic Mekhilta version,[4] is derived from an interpretation of Exod. 15:23:[5] " 'They (the Israelites) went without water for three days in the desert.' . . . The prophets among them arose and ordained that they read (the Torah) on the Sabbath day, and abstain on the first day (Sunday) and read on the second (i. e., Monday). They refrained on Tuesday and Wednesday and read on Thursday, and again refrained on the eve of the Sabbath (i. e., Friday), so that they should not wait (literally "sleep") three days without Torah."

This explanation of not permitting three days to pass without reading the Torah, as based on a comparison to water, may immediately be recognized as homiletical;[6] it gives no clear historic reason for the origin of the days of Assembly.

* Research on this paper was made possible by a National Endowment for Humanities Fellowship Grant for Independent Study and Research, 1975–1976.

[1] Megillah 1:1, 2: כפרים מקדימים ליום הכניסה *ibid.*, 1:3: מקום שנכנסים בשני ובחמישי. See explanation by Rashi, Megillah 2a top. For Sabbath assembly see Jos. *Vita* 277, *Ag. Ap.* II 175 and *Ant.* XVI.43: "we give every seventh day over to the study of our customs and law . . ." Also, Philo, *De Opificio Mundi* XLIII, 128: ". . . to keep a seventh day holy . . . and giving their time to the one sole object of philosophy . . ."

[2] Bava Qamma 82a: עשרה תקנות תקן עזרא שקורין במנחה בשבת וקורין בשני ובחמישי ודנין בשני ובחמישי. *Cf.* Yer. Megillah 75a: עזרה התקין לישראל שיהו קורין בתורה בשני ובחמישי. See S. Zeitlin, "Takkanot Ezra," *JQR*, VIII, 1 (July 1917), 61.

[3] *Ibid.* ועמדו נביאים שביניהם. See next note.

[4] Mekhilta Beshallah, Tractate Vayassa, Exodus 15 (Lauterbach ed., II, 89): דורשי רשומות אמרו לא מצאו דברי תורה שנמשלו למים ומנין לדברי תורה שהן משולים במים שנאמר הוי כל צמא לכו למים לפי שפרשו מדברי תורה שלשת ימים לכך מרדו לפיכך התקינו הזקנים והנביאים שיהיו קורין בתורה בשבת בשני ובחמישי הא כיצד קורין בשבת ומפסיקין לאחר שבת וקורין בשני ומפסיקין בשלישי וברביעי וקורין בחמישי ומפסיקין בערב שבת. *Cf.* reading in Bava Qamma 82a.

[5] וילכו שלשת ימים במדבר ולא מצאו מים.

[6] For the homilies of the *Dorshe Reshumot*, among which the above is included, see S. B. Hoenig, *Rabbinics and Research; The Scholarship of Dr. Bernard Revel* (Yeshiva University Press (New York 1968), pp. 110 ff.

The suggestion that Monday, Thursday and Saturday were chosen because they are "days of mercy"[7] likewise cannot be accepted as imparting an historic provenance.

One might perhaps logically explain the choice of these particular days from an economic purview, noting the mode of daily living and activity. The days before (i. e., Friday) and after the Sabbath (i. e., Sunday) were not convenient for assembly because of their proximity to the day of rest. Hence Monday and Thursday were chosen, for such arrangement would also provide for two days of uninterrupted activity, on Tuesday and Wednesday. This notion no doubt lies beneath the concept that the days of assembly were also the "market days."[8] Therefore they were also suitable for reading the Torah[9] and ajudicating cases,[10] since the populace gathered in the villages.

The record noted above that the determination of these days as days of assembly were set by earlier 'prophets' suggests however a still earlier tradition, before the time of Ezra.[11] Such a notion may be corroborated by an analysis of the calendar of the Book of Jubilees and the important days listed therein.

The basic feature of the Book of Jubilees is given in Chapter VI:32 ff.:[12]

> And command thou the Children of Israel that they observe the years according to this reckoning—three hundred and sixty-four days and (these) will constitute a complete year, and they will not disturb its

[7] Tosafoth Bava Qamma 82a, s. v., כדי. The query is וא"ת מ"ש שתיקנו שני וחמישי, and quoting a Midrash that Moses ascended Mount Sinai on a Thursday to receive the Torah and descended on a Monday; ולפי שהיה עת רצון באותה עליה וירידה קבעו בשני וחמישי. The Midrash quoted is found in Tanḥuma (Buber, p. 94) on Gen. 19:24: ומנין סמכו הדורות שיהו מתענין בשני ובחמישי אלא כשעשו ישראל אותה מעשה עלה משה בחמישי וירד בשני . . . . The commentary on Ein Yakov, Bava Qamma 82a explains the query: דיותר היה להם לתקן בג׳ וד׳ שבג׳ נאמרו בו ב׳ פעמים כי טוב ובד׳ שבו נתלו המאורות רמז לאור התורה. Other reasons given, as based on Gen. 2:4: ב׳ ה בראם and Isa. 56:6: דרשו ב׳ ה׳ מצאו are similarly only quaint explanations rendered by the liturgic book *Mattei Moshe*, ס׳ ריט.

[8] See, e. g., Megillah 2a: חכמים הקילו על הכפרים להיות מקדימין ליום הכניסה כדי שיספקו מים ומזון לאחיהם שבכרכים. *Cf.* G. F. Moore, *Judaism* II, 296: "Ezra is said to have prescribed the readings on market days (Monday and Thursday) . . ."

[9] Megillah 3:6: בשני ובחמישי ובשבת במנחה קורין כסדרן.

[10] Ketuvoth 1:1: שפעמים בשבת בתי דינין יושבין בעיירות ביום השני וביום החמישי, and Bava Qamma 82a: ודנין בב׳ ובה׳.

[11] *Cf.* Maimonides, *Yad*, Hilkhoth Tefillah 12: משה רבינו תיקן להם לישראל שיהו קורין בתורה ברבים בשבת ובשני ובחמישי בשחרית כדי שלא ישהו שלשת ימים בלא שמיעת תורה ועזרא תיקן שיהו קורין כן במנחה בכל שבת משום יושבי קרנות וגם הוא תיקן שיהו קורין בשני בחמישי שלשה בני אדם ולא יקראו פחות מעשרה פסוקים. Thus Maimonides attributes the Monday and Thursday readings to antiquity—to Moses. *Cf.* also explanation in Bava Qamma 82a.

[12] See Charles, *Book of Jubilees* (1902), 56 and in his *Apocrypha and Pseudepigrapha* (1903) II, 23.

> time from its days and from its feasts; for everything will fall out in them according to their testimony and they will not leave out any day nor disturb any feasts.

Scholars agree that the Jubilees calendar is a solar one. Nevertheless various suggestions have been proposed for its calendation:

a. 12 months of 30 days each, plus four intercalary days.[13]
b. 13 months of 28 days each.[14]
c. 12 months of 28 days each with the addition of a week after every season of 91 days.[15]
d. Utilization of two calendars—a civil one of 12 months and an ecclesiastical of 13[16] for the observance of the festivals, thus combining *a* and *b*.

These suggestions however may be discounted[17] because the Jubilees calendar is a very simple one. It notes that the year had four seasons;

> each had 13 weeks; from one to another (passed) their memorial, from the first to the second, and from the second to the third and from the third to the fourth. And all the days of the commandment will be two and fifty weeks of days, and these will make the entire year complete.[18]

[13] This would be parallel to the Egyptian calendar. *Cf.* O. Neugebauer, *The Exact Sciences in Antiquity*² (Providence, R. I., 1957), p. 81; Richard A. Parker, *The Calendar of Ancient Egypt* (1950).

[14] Frankel, *MGWJ* 1856, pp. 311–316; 380–400. Refuted by B. Beer in *Das Buch der Jubilaean und sein Verhaltniss zu den Midraschim* (Leipzig, 1856) and "Noch ein Wort über das Buch der Jubilaean," (1857).

[15] G. Box, *The Book of Jubilees* (London, 1917; Reprinted Cleveland 1964).

[16] A. Eppstein, *REJ* XXII (1890), pp. 10–13. Charles, *op. cit.*, p. LXVIII and pp. 55–56 accepts this, noting ". . . this theory is the best solution of the problem yet offered."

[17] Refutation may be here considered for each theory: (a) The four intercalary days were not added at the end of the year as in the Egyptian calendar. (See below and also note 22) *Cf.* J. Finegan, *Handbook of Biblical Chronology* (Princeton 1964), pp. 24–25. (b) Jubilees IV.17 mentions the "signs of heaven (the zodiac) according to the order of their months" and also XXV.16, the 12 sons of Jacob "according to the number of months of the year." (c) The account of the Deluge records 150 days for five months (*cf.* Gen. 7:24). According to Box it should be more than 154 days. *Cf.* Zeitlin, "Jubilees" (*JQR*, 30 [1939]) and in his *Studies in the Early History of Judaism* Vol. II (Ktav, New York), p. 142. (d) The Book of Jubilees would not use two calendars (even though among the Egyptians there was both a civil solar calendar and also an ecclesiastical lunar one) because the order of the festivals as ordained by Noah (VI, 32) is definitely only according to a solar calendar.

The various theories cited above were given by the scholars only in their attempt to prove that the Festival of Shevuʾoth occurred 50 days after the offering of the ʾOmer. But Jubilees is not at all concerned with such ceremony, observance or reckoning. *Cf.* Zeitlin *op. cit.*, p. 142.

[18] Jubilees VI.29–30.

It is apparent that each season[19] consisted of 91[20] days or 13 weeks (13 × 7), and the four seasons comprised the fulness of the Jubilee solar year. The arrangement for each season was on the basis of three months, following the sequence of 30, 30 and 31 days.[21] Where the Egyptian calendar added the intercalary days at the end of the year,[22] the Jubilees system was to add after every seasonal period.[23] This additional day in the third month of the season facilitated and completed the totality of 91 days or full 13 weeks.

It also kept the days of the week intact based upon the reckoning of the first week of creation, and set the scheme whereby all holidays occurred on the same day of the week throughout the years.[24]

It has been generally accepted that each season (or the Jubilee calendar at large) started with Sunday as the first day of the week in its full reckoning.[25] Accordingly, the beginnings of the three consecutive months in each season and the most important days therein would be in sequence Sunday, Tuesday and Thursday. The Feast of Passover (1/14) would then be on a Saturday; the Day of Atonement (7/10) on a Tuesday; Feast of Tabernacles (7/15) on a Sunday and Feast of Weeks (3/15) on a Thursday.

Such arrangement seems improbable because according to this calculation (of a Sunday beginning the calendation), Jacob made his journey to

[19] Though it is not specified in *Jubilees* a seasonal arrangement was no doubt related to the vernal and autumnal equinoxes and the summer and winter solstices. *Cf.* Finegan, *op. cit.*, p. 53. The affinity to I Enoch 72.9 would suggest that "the calendar year must have been considered as beginning at the vernal equinox."

[20] These are the *Tekufot* which are still reckoned today despite the fact that the present calendar is a lunar-solar one and the *Tekufot* refer basically to the beginnings of the solar seasons. The reason for its retention is for the recital of the prayers for rain, the blessing of the sun (*kiddush hahamah*) every 28th year, and for the determination of Passover within the period of the vernal equinox (Deut. 16:1: שמור את חדש האביב ועשית פסח למועד חדש האביב, amd Sukkot in the time of the autumnal equinox: Exod. 23:16, וחג האסיף בצאת השנה; Exod. 34:22, וחג האסיף תקופת השנה. The Targum renders it במסקא דשתא parallel to Exod. 23:16. See *Jewish Encyclopedia*, "Tekufah," Vol. 12, p. 76; also *Encyclopedia Judaica*, "Calendar," Vol. 5, pp. 46–47. See also Finegan, *op. cit.*, p. 44, section 81 on "tekufot" and A. Spier, *Comprehensive Hebrew Calendar* (1952, Behrman House Publishers, New York), p. 223.

[21] Suggestions that the months of the season were in sequence of (a) 30, 31, 30 days, or (b) 31, 30, 30 days would not affect the same week-days for the festivals occurring in the first and the seventh months, e. g., 1/14 — Passover, and 7/10 — Day of Atonement. But see below for the exact calendrical reckoning of 3 months of 30, 30, 31 days (adding the last day) for the specific purpose of establishing the season of 91 days.

[22] Finegan, *op. cit.*, p. 24, especially note 2. See above notes 13, 17.

[23] The Jubilee calendar had 364 days. *Cf.* also *IDB*, p. 487 (s. v., calendar). On the problem of an extra day in the biblical calendar beyond the 364 days (91 x 4), see S. Zeitlin, "Some States of the Jewish Calendar" reprinted in his *Studies* I, p. 183, and S. B. Hoenig, "Sabbatical Years and the Year of Jubilee, *JQR* (Jan 1969) p. 222.

[24] *Ibid.*, Zeitlin, *Studies* I, p. 185.

[25] *Cf.* views of S. Zeitlin, Epstein, Box, Charles, Finegan and others cited above.

Gilead on a *Sabbath* (1/21).[26] This would indeed be contrary to the notion of strict observance of the Sabbath delineated in the book of Jubilees.[27]

The discovery of the Qumran Scrolls has brought forth a new interpretation of *Jubilees*. Mme A. Jaubert has suggested that there was a heterodox calendar in which Wednesday was the outstanding day and the beginning of the calendar.[28] This notion has attracted the attention of

[26] Jubilees XXIX.5.

[27] Jubilees, chapter 50 ff., especially 50.12 "not to go on a journey."

[28] A. Jaubert, *La Date de la Cene Calendrier biblique et liturgie chretienne* (in English—*The Date of the Last Supper. The Biblical Calendar and Christian Liturgy*, Abba House, Staten Island (New York, 1965).

To support her theory Mme Jaubert adds in an Appendix (II, pp. 129 ff.) "Texts relating to a solar cycle of 28 years, beginning on Wednesday in Judaism." These texts are taken from Bab. Talmud Berakhoth 59b quoting Abaye (4th century), *Pirke d'Rabbi Eliezer* (*PRE*) (8th century) and Al-Biruni's *Chronology* (10th century); she concludes therefrom (p. 135) "the existence of a broad, common Jewish base for a calendar beginning on Wednesday."

On examination one finds that these late texts relate to the Tekufah cycle (See *JE*, Vol. 11, 591, s. v., "Sun, Blessing of") and the ceremony to commemorate the birth of the sun (believed to have occurred on the Wednesday eve of creation). It is noted especially (see *PRE*, Friedlander's translation, pp. 35–36) that the first Tekufah of Nisan took place at the beginning of the hours of Saturn (i. e., on the eve of the fourth day at 6 PM, Tuesday night). This is also recorded, e. g., in ברייתא דשמואל הקטן. (see M. Kasher, *Torah Shelemah on Genesis*, p. 135 (קלה): והחכמים הסכימו כדברי הכלדיים ואמרו תחלת בריית המאורות חמה ולבנה שניהם נבראו בתחלת טלה בחלק ראשון בתחלת ליל ד׳ ובחלק האמור כאן אחד משלשים במזל. In the commentary on Maimonides in *Hilkhot Kiddush ha-hamah*, chap. 10 it is noted: והחמה בראה הקב״ה בראש טלה [i. e., Aries (vernal equinox)] בתחילת ליל ד׳. (i. e., Saturn hour) אבל הירח נברא בסוף מזל דגים (i. e., Pisces) שבתחילת הבריאה קדמה החמה ללבנה ט׳ תרמ״ב. *PRE* also writes: "All the stars and constellations were created at the beginning of the fourth day, one luminary did not precede the other except by the period of two-thirds of an hour. Therefore every motion of the sun is done with deliberation and every motion of the moon is done quickly (since the sun was created just before the moon)."

On this basis it was generally believed and accepted that the Tekufah cycle of 28 years begins again at the beginning of the fourth day in the hour of Saturn, in the hour when the sun was created. *Cf.* also Finegan, *op. cit.*, p. 44: "The Tequfah of Nisan which began at the vernal equinox when the sun enters the constellation of Aries."

Jaubert (p. 24) also asserts: "The justification for beginning the year on the fourth day of the week (Wednesday) is the fact that the stars were created on the fourth day. For it is precisely when the stars began to regulate the course of time that the days, the months and cycles of festivals began to run. If then the year is to begin on Wednesday in Jubilees, the Pasch (15/1) also falls on a Wednesday."

It is evident that the determination of the Tekufah cycle is based on calculations made by the Amoraim Samuel and Rav Ada (See *JE*, s. v., *Calendar*). Their prime purpose was the conciliation of the lunar-solar calendar. Hence these various texts which utilize the lunar-solar reckoning cannot be applied to the Book of Jubilees which is based strictly on a precise solar reckoning. Jubilees stresses the sunrise as the beginning of the day, and does not fit into any notion of the sun being created in the first hour of the preceding night. (Interestingly, even in Jewish observance, the ceremony of the Tekufah 28 yr. cycle be-many scholars who accepted it outright.[29] Driver, for instance, noted that "the only day of the week on which the patriarchs never do travel is the fourth day, i.e. Wednesday . . ."[30] This, according to the proposal of these scholars, was the sectarian Sabbath—a distinct feature of the book of Jubilees and of Qumran. Careful examination of the text however will negate this notion.[31] It is recorded that Jacob "passed over the Jabbok in the ninth month on the *eleventh* thereof."[32] According to the Jaubert calendation 9/11 would be precisely on a Wednesday! Use of the Latin version of Jubilees which does not give the definite day of the month but reads "*in mense nono transivit Jaboc et undecim filii eius* cannot be accepted as authentic above the Ethiopic version[33] which mentions specifically the "eleventh" of the month. Were the Latin version correct it would have copied the entire biblical verse of Gen. 32:23[34] which mentions not only the *eleven* children of Jacob who crossed the Jabbok with him but also his two wives and two maidservants. It is the general practice of the author of Jubilees to mention within his context the exact month and day of the month therein;[35] accordingly the Ethiopic text of Jubilees is superior.[36] The

gins in the morning, though the Tekufah calculation no more applies. (See *JE*, s. v., "Tekufah.")

It is likewise known that the Tekufah of Nisan (the vernal equinox) itself varies in cycles of 4 years, according to present Jewish calculations. It may occur at: (a) 6 PM in the first year, (b) 12 PM—the 2nd year (c) then 6 AM and (d) 12 noon (See Spier, *op. cit.* (note 20 above) and W. Feldman, *Rabbinical Mathematics and Astronomy* (London 1931) pp. 199 ff. (reprinted Hermon Press, New York 1965).

The next beginning of the 28 year cycle, Tekufah Nisan, will occur on Nisan 4, 5741 (April 8, 1981) at 6 A.M.

Accordingly, these late texts and the variations appertaining to the Tekufah cycle and the lunar-solar reckoning cannot at all be utilized for a "Wednesday" beginning. It would only mean that the day begins in the evening as positively asserted by Jaubert, p. 133: "The point of departure is still the beginning of the night of Wednesday." Such application does not apply to the Jubilees solar calendar wherein sunrise is the point of departure. Reliance on *PRE* for proof of a solar calendation in Jubilees is also not at all acceptable, especially when it speaks in an anachronistic manner of "intercalations by Adam" (see *PRE*, chap 8, p. 152, in Friedlander's translation).

The proof of *sunrise* as the point of departure may be substantiated also from XII Patriarchs, verse 69 (in the Cambridge Aramaic Fragment):—"Kohath (son of Levi) was born on 1/1 at *sunrise*."

For the exact day of week for 1/1, see below.

[29] Finegan, *op. cit.*, 53; *Interpreters Dictionary of Bible* (*IDB*) I, 487b, s. v., "Calendar."

[30] G. R. Driver, *The Judean Scrolls* (Oxford 1965), p. 321.

[31] See the analysis in my "Sectarian Scrolls," *JQR*, LIX, 1 (July 1968) 49–50, and "Qumran Fantasies," *JQR*, LXIII, 3 (Jan. 1973), 299.

[32] Jubilees XXIX. 13.

[33] *Cf.* Charles's *Ethiopic Version of the Hebrew Book of Jubilees* (Oxford 1895), 106.

[34] ויקח את שתי נשיו ואת שתי שפחותיו ואת אחד עשר ילדיו ויעבר את מעבר יבק.

[35] E. g., in the same chapter, Jubilees XXIX.5—"in the first month on the twenty-first thereof; "in the third month on the thirteenth thereof. See also list of events below.

calendrical notion of Mme Jaubert that "D (the 4th day of the week) is the Sabbath"[37] and of Professor Driver that "in Jubilees the place of the Sabbath is taken by Wednesday"[38] is thus definitely negated.[39] The inaccuracy of the Jaubert calendar has also been demonstrated by M. Testuz.[40]

It is here suggested that in the Jubilees solar calendar the first day of the first month (irrespective of the arrangement of the *week* which is based on the creation story)[41] always began on a Thursday. In other words, the week[42] always began on a Sunday and the seventh day of the week was always the Sabbath. But, in the reckoning of months and seasons, the first day of the calendrical reckoning started with the fifth day—i. e. Thursday.[43] It is well known that the sequence of the week-days has never been altered, whereas the arrangement of the months, and the counting of the years and their start have been often variously set.[44]

It is understandable that to have any sort of calendation the requisites are the instruments therefor. These in ancient days as well as today are the celestial luminaries.[45] Both the Bible and Jubilees note that the creation of the sun and moon occurred on the fourth day of the week—Wednesday. Thus we read in Jubilees.[46]

> And on the fourth day He created the sun and the moon and the stars and set them in the firmament of the heaven to give light upon all the earth and to rule over the day and the night and divide the light from the darkness. And God *appointed the sun to be a great sign* on the earth for days and for sabbaths and for months and for feasts and

[36] *Cf.* Charles, *op. cit.*, p. XXVII: "This version is most accurate and trustworthy and indeed as a rule servilely literal."

[37] Jaubert, *op. cit.*, p. 27.

[38] Driver, *op. cit.* (note 30), p. 322.

[39] *Cf.* Hoenig, "Qumran Fantasies" (note 31) p. 299.

[40] M. Testuz, *Les Idées Religieuses de Livre des Jubilees* (1960).

[41] Genesis, chap 1. The Sabbath is the 7th day in the reckoning of the week. See Gen. 2:1. In rabbinic terminology it is called שבת בראשית. *Cf.* Menaḥoth 66a: – תספור לך ספירה תלויה בבית דין יצתה שבת בראשית שספירתה בכל אדם. ממחרת השבת .... אתה אומר ממחרת יו"ט או שאינו אלא ממחרת שבת בראשית. The early recital of the Psalms indicates the works of the six days of creation. *Cf.* Rosh Hashanah 31a.

[42] *Cf.* Finegan, *op. cit.*, p. 15, "The Week" and S. B. Hoenig, "A Jewish Reaction to Calendar Reform," *Tradition*, Vol. 7, 1 (Winter 1964–5), p. 16.

[43] *Cf.* Rosh Hashanah 30b: תמיד של ראש השנה שחרית קרב כהלכתו במוסף מהו אומר הרנינו לאלקים עוזנו, which is Psalm 81. See below notes 97 and 99.

[44] On the change of the calendar throughout the centuries see Finegan, *op. cit.*, and S. Zeitlin, "Some Stages of the Jewish Calendar" (*SAJ Review* 1929), reprinted in *Studies* I, pp. 183 ff.

[45] See Finegan, p. 7: "units of time were associated with the celestial bodies." *Cf.* also J. Van Goudever, *Biblical Chronology* (Leiden 1959), pp. vii, 62 ff.

[46] Jubilees II.8–9.

for years and for sabbaths of years and for jubilees and for all seasons of the years.

Whereas in Genesis[47] both the sun and moon are designated: "let *them* be for signs and for seasons and for days and years . . .", Jubilees deliberately stresses only "the *sun* to be a great sign upon the earth . . .", thereby indicating specifically use of a solar calendar.

The mention in Jubilees of the creation of the sun and the moon and the stars . . . to give light upon the earth and to rule over the day and the night and divide the light from the darkness,"[48] though the "sun is the sign," implies the setting forth first, of the sun[49] and then, the moon for the full count, i. e. first daytime and then the night followed it.[50] Only when the luminaries—sun and moon-completed their task for determination of a full day could the implementation of the "sign" for reckoning "days, seasons, etc." be undertaken. This means that only after having both luminaries as signs or instruments of setting both the daytime and nighttime, could the first count be made. This then began on Thursday—sunrise—the fifth day of the week,[51] which ultimately became the first day of reckoning the solar calendar.

The Jubilee Calendar therefore, for every recurring season of 91 days (three months), on the basis of 30, 30, 31 days, would be as detailed below:

Months	Sun	M	Tu	W	Th	F	Sat
					1	2	3
I	4	5	6	7	8	9	10
4–7–10	11	12	13	14	15	16	17
	18	19	20	21	22	23	24
	25	26	27	28	29	30	1
	2	3	4	5	6	7	8
II	9	10	11	12	13	14	15
5–8–11	16	17	18	19	20	21	22
	23	24	25	26	27	28	29
	30	1	2	3	4	5	6
	7	8	9	10	11	12	13
III	14	15	16	17	18	19	29
6–9–12	21	22	23	24	25	26	27
	28	29	30	31			

Jubilees especially notes:[52]

[47] Gen. 1:14.

[48] See note 46 above.

[49] The notion that the sun and moon were created on Tuesday night as given in *PRE*, chap 7, is a late concept based on the rabbinic solar-lunar calendation.

[50] See S. Zeitlin, "The Beginning of the Jewish Day," *JQR*, XXXVI, 4 (April 1946) p. 404.

[51] See Tamid 7.4 on the liturgic use of היום יום ה׳ בשבת in tannaitic literature.

[52] Jubilees VI 23 ff.

> "And on the new moon of the first month and on the new moon of the fourth month and on the new moon of the seventh month and on the new moon of the tenth month are the *days of remembrances* and the days of the seasons in the four divisions of the year. These are written and ordained as a testimony for ever.

The phrase 'new moon'[53] is not to be taken literally. It simply means, in the solar calendation, the beginning of the new month, as a translation of *Rosh Hodesh.*[54] The beginnings of the first, fourth, seventh and tenth months were the days of remembrance. These began always on a Thursday. The

[53] Even in a solar calendar the word *month*—derived from moon—is used. Thus the Bible which follows a solar calendar (see my "Sabbatical Years and the Year of Jubilee," *JQR*, LIX (Jan 1969) p. 224) has I Kings 6:37: ירח זיו; *ibid.*, 6:38: ירח בול; *ibid.*, 8:2: ירח איתנים; Zech. 11:8: בירח אחד. In Greek *μήνη* is *moon* and *μην* is *month.* ירח is both *moon*, וירח (שמש) and *month* as in Deut. 21:13 ירח ימים. The Latin has *primo die* for חדש. *Cf.* Jaubert, *op. cit.*, p. 28.

The solar calendar reckoning of a month of 30 *days* may be seen in Gen. 7:11; 8:3–4; Num. 20:29: ויבכו את אהרן שלשים יום; Deut. 21:13: ירח ימים; 34:8: ויבכו את משה שלשים יום. The year of 12 months is also evident in I Kings 4:7: . . . . לשלמה שנים עשר נצבים וכלכלו את המלך ואת ביתו חדש בשנה יהיה כל אחד לכלכל. I Chron. 27:1–15 has mention of 12 months of service: והיוצאת חדש בחדש לכל חדשי השנה.

Further evidence for a biblical solar calendar may be found in II Sam. 11:1: ויהי לתשובת השנה לעת צאת המלכים. This is interpreted as "the season (beginning) of the year when kings go out to battle." This would be the spring and accords with the description of Bath-sheba bathing on the roof, seen by David, narrated in the same chapter.

Similarly in Jer. 36:22: והמלך יושב בית החרף בחדש התשיעי ואת האח לפני מבערת.

The portrayal of the 9th month as being in the winter (the present Kislev) corroborates the biblical count of the year as beginning in the spring, which is according to the solar reckoning. *Cf.* Exod. 12:2: החדש הזה לכם ראש חדשים ראשון הוא לכם לחדשי השנה.

It is to be pointed out that wherever the Bible gives an added explanation of identity of a particular month it is evident that a change had occurred. Thus in I Kings 6:1: בחדש זו הוא החדש השני. The Canaanite nomenclature Ziv was already obsolete and had to be identified by the Hebrew numeral which was the biblical mode. On the other hand, in the post-exilic books as Esther and Zechariah the identification indicates a change from the Hebrew biblical numeral mode to the new Babylonian count. Hence, e. g., Zech. 1:7: לעשתי עשר חדש הוא חדש שבט, and Esther 2:16: בחדש העשירי הוא חדש טבת, or Esther 3:7: בחדש הראשון הוא חדש ניסן. The old mode of reckoning had ended and the new nomenclature based on the Babylonian calendar was the new mode. The lunar-solar calendar now displaced the old biblical calendation.

Apparently at this time the opposition to the new calendar was voiced by the Book of Jubilees which sought to maintain the old solar calendation. Hence the Book of Jubilees was probably written in this era. A suggestion had been made that the solar calendar was that of Northern Israel; perhaps the Book of Jubilees was composed by one of the stock of Northern Israel living in Judea. See, e. g., II Chron. 30:25 (describing the Passover celebration of Hezekiah): וישמחו כל קהל יהודה וכל הקהל הבאים מישראל והגרים באים מארץ ישראל והיושבים ביהודה. *Cf.* Abba Hillel Silver, "The Lunar and Solar Calendars in Ancient Israel," *Essays in honor of Solomon B. Freehof* (Pittsburgh 1964), pp. 300–309.

[54] The word חדש likewise is both *month* (renewal of days) and the *new moon* as in Psalm 81: תקעו בחדש שופר.

2nd, 5th, 8th, 11th months started always on a Saturday and the 3rd, 6th, 9th and 12th months began on a Monday. Thus in the Jubilee calendar the sequence of the beginning of the months in each season of three months (91 days) were Thursday, Saturday and Monday. These are the traditional "days of assembly." As such one may surmise that the later choice of these particular week-days as "days of Assembly" was based on a tradition of their importance in antiquity, serving as the beginning days of the various months in each season. The significance of the Rosh Hodesh later diminished[55] as a special holiday even when the lunar-solar calendar was adopted, but the significance of these three weekdays on which the Rosh Hodesh had first occurred in the solar calendar was not lost. The reason may have been forgotten but the factual significances always remained.

A further detailed probing of Jubilees, in which stress is made of the date of any event in a particular month, will especially reveal the significance of the Thursday, Saturday and Monday triad. Below is the full listing of recorded events:

Text in Jubilees	Event	Month	Date	Week Day
1:1	Moses ascended onto the mount	3	16	Tues.
3:17	Adam and Eve sinned	2	17	Mon.
3:32	The Expulsion from the Garden	4	1	Thurs.
5:22 (also 6:25)	Noah was commanded to make the Ark	1	1	Thurs.
5:23	Noah entered the Ark . . .	2	1	Sat.
	till the sixteenth	2	16	Sun.
	The ark was closed without	2	17	Mon.
5:29 (also 6:26)	The fountains of the great deep were closed	4	1	Thurs.
(")	The water began to descend into the deep below	7	1	Thurs.
5:30 (also 6:27)	The tops of the mountain were visible	10	1	Thurs.
	The earth became visible	1	1	Thurs.
5:31	The earth was dry	2	17	Mon.
5:32	Noah opened the ark	2	27	Thurs.

[55] The importance of the Rosh Hodesh—new moon—in biblical days is recognizable as in Isa. 66:23: מדי חדש בחדשו ומדי שבת בשבתו, and II Kings 4:23: היום לא חדש ולא שבת. Earlier sources mention חדש before שבת. In rabbinic tradition work is permitted on the new moon. *Cf.* Megillah 22b: ושאין בו ביטול מלאכה לעם כגון ראשי חדשים. See also Ḥagigah 18a: ראש חדש יוכיח שיש בו קרבן מוסף ומותר בעשיית מלאכה. *Cf.* Tosafot, *ad loc.* s. v., ר"ח.

Generally the term חדש is used, not ראש חדש, as I Sam. 20:18: ומחר חדש; Isa. 1:13: חדש ושבת קרא מקרא; Amos 8:5: מתי יעבר החדש והשבת; Hos. 2:13: והשבעתי כל משושה חגה חדשה ושבתה וכל מועדה; Ezek. 46:3: והשתחוו עם הארץ בשבתות ובחדשים. An exception is Num. 10:10: וביום שמחתכם ובמועדיכם ובראשי חדשיכם.

Text in Jubilees	Event	Month	Date	Week Day
6:1	Noah went forth from the ark	3	1	Mon.
6:17	Noah celebrated the Covenant	3	15	Mon.
6:23	The day of remembrance	1	1	Thurs.
	The day of remembrance	4	1	Thurs.
	The day of remembrance	7	1	Thurs.
	The day of remembrance	10	1	Thurs.
7:2	Noah kept his wine for celebration	1	1	Thurs.
12:16	Abram observes the star to determine the future	7	1	Thurs.
13:8	Abram built an altar and offered sacrifice	1	1	Thurs.
14:1	The promise to Abraham	3	1	Mon.
14:10	Abram offers sacrifice celebrating the Covenant	3	15	Mon.
15:1	Abram celebrates feasts of first fruits	3	15	Mon.
16:1	Abram again receives promise of a son	4	1	Thurs.
16:11	Abram moved and dwelt at the well of the Oath	5	15	Sat.
16:12	Sarah conceived	6	15	Mon.
16:13	Isaac was born	3	15	Mon.
16:14	Isaac was circumcised on 8th day	3	22	Mon.
16:21	Abraham instituted celebration of Feast of Tabernacles	7	15	Thurs.
17:15	Proposal to test Abram	1	12	Mon.
18:1	3 days later—the binding of Isaac	1	14	Wed.
18:18	Abraham's celebration of a week long festival of joy	1	15–21	Thurs.
24:22	God's Vision to Isaac	1	1	Thurs.
27:19	Jacob's dream at Bethel	1	1	Thurs.
28:11	Birth of Reuben	9	14	Sun.
28:13	Birth of Simeon	10	21	Wed.
28:14	Birth of Levi	1	1	Thurs.
28:15	Birth of Judah	3	15	Mon.
28:18	Birth of Dan	6	9	Tues.
28:19	Birth of Naftali	7	5	Mon.
28:20	Birth of Gad	8	12	Wed.
28:21	Birth of Asher	11	2	Sun.
28:22	Birth of Issachar	5	4	Tues.
28:23	Birth of Zebulun and Dinah	7	7	Wed.
28:24	Birth of Joseph	4	1	Thurs.
29:5	Jacob turned his face to Gilead	1	21	Wed.
29:5	Laban overtook Jacob	3	13	Sat.
29:7	Jacob made a feast for Laban	3	15	Mon.
29:13	Jacob passed over Jabok	9	11	Thurs.
29:16	Jacob sent gifts to his parents 4 times a year	1,4,7,10	1	Thurs.
31:3	Jacob went up to Bethel	7	1	Thurs.
32:2	Jacob gave tithe	7	14	Wed.

Text in Jubilees	Event	Month	Date	Week Day
32:4	Jacob offered sacrifice	7	15	Thurs.
32:16	Jacob was called Israel	7	22	Thurs.
32:27	Jacob instituted celebration of the *Additional* Day	7	22	Thurs.
32:30	Deborah, Rebecca's nurse died	7	23	Fri.
32:33	Birth of Benjamin	8	11	Tues.
33:1	Jacob went to his father	10	1	Thurs.
34:18	The Institution of the Day of Atonement	7	10	Sat.
44:1	Jacob went to the well of the Oath	3	1	Mon.
	Jacob offered sacrifice	3	7	Sun.
	Jacob celebrated festival of first fruits, waited 7 day	3	15	Mon.
44:5	God assured Jacob not to fear going to Egypt	3	16	Tues.
	Israel went to Egypt	3	16	Tues.
45:1	Jacob came to Egypt and meets Joseph	4	1	Thurs.
49:1	The Observance of Passover	1	14	Wed.

A study of the above table of events demonstrates that most of the activities of the patriarchs as recorded in Jubilees occurred on Thursdays (There is a list of 30 items). As already seen, these were the Days of Remembrance, but included in the Thursday category are also the beginning of the Feast of Tabernacles (7/15) for seven days, instituted by Abraham,[56] and the "Additional Day" (7/22) instituted by Jacob.[57] Next in importance was Monday (16 items). The birth of Levi[58] (representing priesthood) and of Joseph[59] (paragon of righteousness) were on a Thursday. Judah[60] (bearer of the kingdom) was born on a Monday.* The less prominent sons of Jacob were born on insignificant week-days, according to Jubilees.[60a]

[56] Jubilees XV.20. Though the date 7/15 is not mentioned here, the inference is from v. 21: He built booths for himself and for his servants on this festival and he was the first to celebrate the feast of tabernacles on earth.

The date is apparent from the mention that Jacob added a day to the festival. See next note.

[57] Jubilees XXXII.27: And he (Jacob) celebrated there yet another day and he sacrificed thereon according to all that he sacrificed in former days and called its name *Addition* for this day was added and the former days he called the *Feast*.

This corresponds to the terminology of the Rabbis in the Mishnah in designating Sukkot as the Feast, חג. *Cf.* Rosh Hashanah 1.1 בחג נידונין על המים. Apparently the term חג, Feast, was already used profusely even before the Return, when Jubilees was written.

The special aspect of the Additional (eighth) day, though it is biblical (Num. 29:35) can be seen in Sukkah 4.1: ההלל והשמחה שמנה, and Sukkah 48a: כיצד מלמד שחייב, אדם בהלל ובשמחה ובכבוד יו"ט האחרון של חג כשאר ימות החג.

[58] Jubilees XXVIII.14.

[59] Jubilees XXVIII.24.

[60] Jubilees XXVIII.15.

Saturday was designated as the Sabbath day of rest.[61] On it too was set the Day of Atonement (7/10) as a remembrance of Jacob's mourning over Joseph.[62] This specification is stressed despite the fact that Jubilees generally forbids gloom and fasting on the Sabbath day.[63]

Interestingly, there are recorded occasions of travel on the Sabbath despite the Jubilees injunction against it. Abraham went to the Well of Oaths (5/15)[64] and Laban overtook Jacob (3/13)[65] on the Sabbath day. The explanation for these variations is simply that the Sabbath was given to Jacob;[66] it was not observed by anyone before him. Thus Noah prepared to enter the Ark (2/1) on the Sabbath for it is noted:[67] "he entered till the sixteenth. This was Sunday. The Ark was closed on the 17th—Monday. It is stressed too that the Sabbath was not given to Gentiles[68] and hence the injunction did not apply to Laban, as it is recorded:

> There were two and twenty heads of mankind from Adam to Jacob and two and twenty kinds of work were made until the seventh day; this is blessed and holy; and the former also is blessed and holy; and this one serves with that one for sanctification and blessing. And to this (Jacob and his seed) it was granted that they should always be the blessed and the holy ones of the first testimony and law, even as He had sanctified and blessed the Sabbath day on the seventh day.[69]

[60a] Though Naftali is also recorded as born on a Monday 7/5 Midrash Tadshe has 3/5—a Friday. This is one of its exceptions, for Jubilees and Midrash Tadshe generally agree.

[61] See above note 41.

[62] Jubilees XXXIV.18.

[63] Jubilees II.21: . . . "They should keep the Sabbath with us on the seventh day to eat and to drink . . ., and Jubilees L.10: "For great is the hour which the Lord has given to Israel that they should eat and drink and be satisfied on this festival day. Also L.12–13: "whoever fasts . . . on the Sabbath shall die."

[64] Jubilees XVI.11.

[65] Jubilees XXIX.5.

[66] Jubilees II.20: "And I have chosen the seed of Jacob from among all that I have seen and have written him down as thy first born son and have sanctified him unto My self for ever and ever and I will teach them the Sabbath day, that they may keep the Sabbath thereon from all work."

It is interesting to note that rabbinic tradition also recognized that the Sabbath was first given to Jacob; *cf.* Shabbath 118a: א״ר יוחנן משום רבי יוסי כל המענג את השבת נותנין לו נחלה בלי מצרים שנא׳ אז תתענג על ה׳ . . . והאכלתיך נחלת יעקב. So also Bereshit Rabbah 11.8: ר׳ יחנן בשם ר״י בר חלפתא אמר, אברהם שאין כתוב בו שמירת שבת ירש את העולם במדה שנא׳ קום התהלך בארץ לארכה ולרחבה אבל יעקב שכתוב בו שמירת שבת שנ׳ ויחן את פני העיר (ברא׳ לג) נכנס עם דמדומי חמה וקבע תחומין מבעוד יום.

[67] Jubilees V.23.

[68] Jubilees II.31: ". . . He did not sanctify all peoples and nations to keep the Sabbath thereon, but Israel alone; them alone he permitted to eat and drink and to keep the Sabbath thereon on the earth." *Cf.* also, II.19.

[69] Jubilees II.23–24.

Abraham is credited with the institution of the Feast of Tabernacles[70] and Noah with the Feast of Oaths (*Shevuot*),[71] but only to Jacob—Israel is assigned the institution of the Sabbath.[72]

The exceptional distinction of Saturday, in abstinence of any labor for Israel, is carried through in Jubilees even to the point that no births are recorded as occurring on the Sabbath day.[73]

A study of the other days (besides the Monday, Thursday, Saturday triad) likewise reveals some interesting features:

Wednesday (recorded 7 times) was the day of the binding of Isaac (1/14).[74] It became later a day of historic import—the Passover, but Jubilees already gives this day prominence long before the Exodus event. Jubilees indeed makes full mention of the slaying of the first born of Egypt, when God "passed by all the children of Israel,"[75] but the 14th day of the first month was long before that event already a festive day; followed by a week of joy; as recorded:[76]

> And he (Abraham) celebrated this festival, seven days with joy, and he called it the *festival of the Lord* according to the seven days during which he went and returned in peace. And accordingly has it been ordained and written on the heavenly tables regarding Israel and its seed that they should observe this festival *seven* days with the *joy of fesitval.*

In its chapter on the observance and regulations of the Passover, Jubilees notes:[77]

> And do thou Moses command the children of Israel to observe the ordinances of the Passover as it was commanded unto thee; declare thou unto them every year and the day of its days and the *festival of unleavened bread*, that they should eat unleavened bread seven days and that they should observe its festival . . .

[70] Jubilees XV.21. See above note 56.

[71] Jubilees VI.17–22. After being instituted by Noah, Abraham (XIV.10; XV.1) and Jacob (XLIV.1) also observe this festival occurring on 3/15, known also as the Festival of first fruits. Isaac and Jacob were born on this date.

[72] Jubilees II.20. See note 66.

[73] See list of births in table, above. Charles (*op. cit.*, p. 171) notes that Dan was born on 9/6. This would be on a Saturday. Apparently this is a typographical error, for Jubilees follows a distinct pattern of strict observance on the Sabbath; even no intercourse was permitted on that day. *Cf.* Jubilees, Chap L. See also A. Epstein, *Midrash Tadshe* VIII in his מקדמוניות היהודים, II, p. 151, קנא, where the reading is דן נולד בט׳ לחדש השישי. This is 6/9, a Tuesday.

[74] Jubilees XVIII.1.

[75] Jubilees XLIX. ff.

[76] Jubilees XVIII.18. It was not called the Festival of Matzot till the time of the Exodus.

[77] Jubilees XLIX.22.

A distinction is made here between the Festival of Passover and the Festival of the Unleavened Bread.[78] This is similar to the delineation in the Bible[79] and in Josephus.[80] The main point is that in Jubilees Isaac was the precursor of the sacrificial Paschal lamb, the event occurring on Wednesday (1/14). The following week-long celebration is first observed by Abraham, but naturally no mention is made of unleavened bread until the story of the Exodus in Chapters 48 and 49.[81]

With reference to events on Wednesday, it is recorded that "Jacob rose early in the morning in the 14th of this month . . . and gave tithes of all."[82] This was on Wednesday (7/14), for the next day was the beginning of the Festival of Tabernacles (7/15). Thus Jacob tithed *before* the Festival[83] which began on Thursday. Likewise it is noted that Jacob turned to Gilead on 1/21.[84] This would be on the last day of the Festival of joy of seven days as celebrated by Abraham, as noted above.[85] Did Jacob travel on the last day of the Festival? The text notes he "turned toward Gilead" which is interpreted as "planning;"[86] hence there is no evidence of actual travel by Jacob on this Festival day.

Tuesday is evident twice in Jubilees but it is only in connection with the Festival of the Covenant which, according to our calendar, was always on a Monday. We find that Moses ascended the mountain the *day after* the Festival of the First Fruits;[87] that is, on 3/16—Tuesday and also Israel (Jacob) went down to Egypt[88] on 3/16—Tuesday which was the *day after* the Festival of Oaths.

As to Friday—the only allusion to it is in connection with the death of Deborah, Rebecca's nurse.[89] This occurred on 7/23, but it was on the *day after* the Additional Day instituted by Jacob, on a Thursday, 7/22.[90] Thus the mention of Tuesday and Friday is only to stress that they occurred *after* an important Festival day.

[78] *Cf.* also my "Duration of the Festival of Matzot," *JQR*, XLIX (April 1959), 271 ff.

[79] **פסח**, Lev. 23:5; Num. 28:16; **חג המצות**, Lev. 23:6; Num. 28:17.

[80] Ant. 3.9.5 (248–9).

[81] See above note 76.

[82] Jubilees XXXII.2.

[83] Bezah 5.2: **ולא מגביהין תרומה והמעשר כל אלו ביום טוב אמרו קל וחומר בשבת.** Hence tithing was performed on the eve of the Sabbath and holidays. *Cf.* Shabbath 2.7: **שלשה דברים צריך אדם לומר בתוך ביתו ערב שבת עם חשכה עשרתם הדליקו את הנר ספק חשכה ספק לא חשכה אין מעשרין את הודאי.**

[84] Jubilees XXIX.5.

[85] Jubilees XVIII.18.

[86] *Cf.* M. Testuz, *op. cit.* (see note 40, above): Je pense que l'auteur veut dire que Jacob "tourne son attention" vers Gilead.

[87] Jubilees I.1.

[88] Jubilees XLIV.8.

[89] Jubilees XXXII.30. See above, note 60a.

[90] Jubilees XXXII.27. See above, note 57.

Sunday is recorded as the day Noah finally entered the Ark[91] (2/16); the ark was closed on 2/17,[92] *Monday*. Mention is also made that Jacob offered sacrifice at the Well of the Oath on Sunday, 3/7,[93] waiting there seven days for a vision from God and then celebrating the Feast of Oaths on *Monday*, 3/15.[94] The stress again is on the importance of Monday.

Though the Book of Jubilees is unique in its ascribing the origin of the Festivals and their delineation on particular days of the week it may nevertheless be seen that at times there are allusions to these same days and dates even in biblical phraseology and rabbinic traditions. Thus the assignment of the Day of Atonement, 7/10, to Saturday is cognate to this day being called in the Bible "the Sabbath of Sabbaths."[95] In like manner the first day of the seventh month is alluded to as a day of remembrance.[96] Whereas the other three days of Remembrance in Jubilees fell into obsolescence, that of the seventh month attained biblically and rabbinically special consideration. As seen, this day of remembrance was on a Thursday; in rabbinic tradition it was fixed that the same Psalm, 81, is to be recited on Thursdays[97] and also for the New Year, 7/1,[98] demonstrating thereby the close affinity.[99]

It has been noted that the binding of Isaac and the day of the Paschal sacrifice were assigned to Wednesday. This is also in conformity with rab-

[91] Jubilees V.23.

[92] *Ibid.*

[93] Jubilees XLIV.1.

[94] Jubilees XLIV. 3–4.

[95] The expression שבת שבתון is used only for the seventh day, and for the Day of Atonement (Lev. 16:31; Lev. 23:32) which also occurred on the Sabbath day. The full phrase שבת שבתון is not used for any other festivals, though שבתון alone (resting) is used in Lev. 23:24 for Sukkot: ביום הראשון שבתון וביום השמיני שבתון. The phrase שבתון is also used for 7/1 (Lev. 23:24); for Sukkot, 7/15 (the first day) and the eighth day (7/21) but we do not find שבת שבתון utilized except for the Sabbath day (the occurrence on the 7th day) and the *seventh* year.

Kirkisani notes the views of a sectarian group led by one Mishawayh who "asserted that the feast of Passover must always begin on Thursday, so that the day of Atonement might fall on the Sabbath, since it is called Lev. 23:32 שבת שבתון, meaning according to him a double Sabbath—one of the regular sabbath and the other, the sabbath of Atonement . . ." See L. Nemoy's translation of "Al-Qirqisani's Account of the Jewish Sects," *HUCA*, VII (1930) p. 300. Also see Graetz-Shaffer, *History* (Hebrew), Vol. III, in the addendum by A. Harkavay, לקורות הכתות בישראל, p. 509 [רו]. See also *Ginze Schechter*, Vol. II, p. 495 in the section מספרי הלכה של הקראים הקדמונים, p. 495: צאו וחשבו פסח באי הארץ הלא נפל יום חמישי במרץ. *Cf.* also B. Dinur, תולדות ישראל: ישראל בגולה, Vol. I, 2, p. 270, note 17—about Rosh Hashanah on Wednesday. See also Schreiner, "Les Juifs dans al-Biruni," (ca. 1048) *REJ*, XII (1886), 258–266.

[96] יום הזכרון is only a rabbinic term. It is זכרון תרועה that is biblical (Lev. 23:24). See the note in my "Origins of the Rosh Hashanah Liturgy," 75th Anniversary Volume of *JQR*, p. 313, n. 7.

[97] Tamid 7.4.

[98] See above note 43.

[99] See my "Origins of the Rosh Hashanah Liturgy," *op. cit.*, 330. See above note 96.

binic tradition that the offering of the paschal lamb before the Exodus event was on a Wednesday, and that the actual departure from Egypt was on a Thursday.[100] These similarities in dating therefore are not to be discounted.

In all, ancient traditions retained the significance of the particular week days—the Monday, Thursday and Saturday triad as well as other datings recorded in Jubilees. When Christianity became dominant, instead of the Monday-Thursday-Saturday tradition which originated in Jubilees and was strengthened by rabbinic observance, the week-days of importance became Sunday, Wednesday and Friday.[101] Christian tradition found its theological sources in Sunday—the Lord's Day,[102] Wednesday—Ash Day, and Friday—the Day of the Crucifixion. These days, chosen on the basis of events of the Passion,[103] thus differentiated[104] from the Jewish practice[105] of regarding the ancient days of *Assembly* (M, Th, S) as the days of the week of real significance in the calendar.

[100] Seder ᶜOlam Rabbah, chap 5: בי"ד בו שחטו ישראל את פסחיהן ויום רביעי היה. This is according to the Oxford MSs and כת"י רס"ט. See Ratner's edition, p. 23, n. 10. This is corroborated by Shabbath 87b: ניסן שבו יצאו ישראל ממצרים בי"ד שחטו פסחיהם ובט"ו יצאו . . . ואותו היום חמישי בשבת היה. Tosafot *ad loc.*, s. v., ואותו יום remarks: וא"כ ברביעי שחטו פסחיהם ונמצא בשבת שעברה לקחו פסחיהם שאז היה בעשור לחדש. . . . These correspond to the Jubilees datings.

Similarly the Talmudic tradition *ad loc.*, notes: ויסעו מאלים ויבואו כל עדת בני ישראל וגו' בחמשה עשר יום לחדש השני ואותו היום שבת היה. Thus 2/15 was also on the Sabbath. *Cf.* also Midrash Tehillim 104.16 and the note of W. G. Braude, *Psalms*, Vol. II, p. 505 (copying H. Freedman's note in translation of Genesis Rabbah, Soncino, p. 41) that "the Exodus took place . . . on a Thursday. See also *PRE*, chap IX: בה' יצאו אבותנו ממצרים.

[101] On the Christian week and the significance of Sunday, Wednesday and Friday see "*Dictionary of Christ and Gospels*, I, 251, s. v., "Calendar, the Christian."

[102] *Cf.* Lord's Day—Rev. 1:10. Pertaining to the Resurrection John 20:6 mentions "the first day of the week."

[103] Luke 18:12 mentions the practice of Pharisaic fasting twice a week." M. S. Enslin, *Christian Beginnings* (Harper & Bros. 1938) p. 116, notes commenting on Luke 18:12: "Nor was fasting a requirement as is often supposed. The canting hypocrite portrayed in the Gospel (Luke 18:12) with his smug "I fast twice in the week" . . . has tended to give a quite erroneous view here. Fasting on Monday and Thursday was often practiced but was entirely voluntary and an act of uncommon piety . . ." *Cf.* also I. Abrahams, *Studies in Pharisaism and the Gospels*, I, 125 (Ktav, New York).

The basic sources may be seen in the following: *Clement Stromata*, Book VII, sec. 12, p. 461: "He (the true Gnostic) knows also the enigmas of the fasting of those days. I mean the *Fourth* and the *Preparation*. *Cf.* also *The Apostolical Constitutions*, Book V, section XV, p. 134:

> But he commanded us to fast on the *fourth* and *sixth* days of the week; the former on account of His being betrayed and the latter on account of His passion. But he appointed us to break our fast on the seventh day at the cock-crowing but to fast on the Sabbath day. Not that the Sabbath day is a day of fasting, being the rest from the creation, but because we ought to fast on this one Sabbath only, while on this day the creator was under the earth.

The *Shepherd* of Hermas (*ca.* 140) applies the name "station" to fasting (Similitude V.1). This apparently is derived from the tannaitic term *ma^camad*—מעמד (*Cf.* S. B. Hoenig, "Historical Inquiries: Heber ᶜIr," *JQR*, XLVIII, 2 [Oct. 1957], 134). According to a talmudic text, those who observed the *maᶜamadot* fasted (Taᶜanith 4:3: ואנשי מעמד היו מתענין; *cf.* Taᶜanith 27b, Yer. Taᶜanith 68b). The angel speaking to Hermas recommends almsgiving equal to the price of the food saved in fasting (Similitude V.3). This is, also, in accord with the talmudic maxim, אגרא דתעניתא צדקתא, "The merit of a fast-day is in the charity given" (Berakhot 6b). Later usage of *statio*, in addition to stations of penitents, referred to 'stations of the cross' (*cf.* S. Hastings, *Encyclopedia of Religion and Ethics*, Vol. XI, s. v., "Stations," p. 855).

See also *Tertullian*, Vol. III, "On Fasting," Chap. XIV, p. 147:

> Why do we devote to stations the *fourth* and *sixth* days of the week, and to fasts the "*preparation day*?" Anyhow you sometimes continue your station even over the Sabbath,—a day never to be kept as a fast except at the passover season . . .

[104] *Didache 8.1*:

> Your fasts must not take place at the same time as those of the hypocrites. They fast on Monday and Thursday, you are to fast on Wednesday and Friday

See full discussion in A. Jaubert, *op. cit.*, pp. 53–54: "Wednesday, Friday and Sunday, these are the liturgical days of the primitive Christian community." Sunday = Lord's Day (Rev. 1:10) and the day of the Eucharistic assembly (Acts 20:7).

The early Christians who set Sunday as the Sabbath day of rest did not change the order of the days of the week. The sequence of the week was never disturbed. *Cf.*, e. g., *The Apostolic Constitutions*, Book II, ch XLVII, p. 75: Let your judicatures be held on the *second* day of the week . . . having an interval till the *Sabbath* . . . to reduce those to peace . . . against the *Lord's day*.

[105] Many customs of significance developed for the Monday and Thursday traditions, particularly fasting on those days of the week (Saturday was not a day of fast; *cf.* Midrash Tanḥuma וירא, p. 24: והשבת נתנה לישראל לקדושה לענג ולמנוחה ולא לצער. Hence we find the following aspects: Tos. Taᶜanith 2.4 (Lieberman ed., 330) יום שני וחמישי הודחו לתענית צבור ובהן בתי דינין יושבין בעיירות ובהן נכנסין לבתי כנסיות וקורין. The Tosefta thus notes 3 features for Monday and Thursday:

a. Fasting
b. Court sessions
c. Torah reading

Other sources are in Yer. Pesaḥim 30d and Taᶜanith 64c: מנהג בתרייא ובחמשתא אינו מנהג עד יתפני תעניתא מנהג. "A custom (of not working) on M and Th is inept, but (to refrain) until after a fast is a practise." Hence we read in Bab. Talmud Taᶜanith 12a about one's conduct on these days: יחיד שקבל עליו שני וחמשי של כל השנה כולה ואירעו בו ימים טובים הכתובין במגילה תענית וכו'.

In a late addendum to the scholion of Megillat Taᶜanith [see Warsaw ed. (5634; lithographed New York, 5720)]: ועוד גזרו רבותינו שיהו מתענים בה' וה' מפני שלשה דברים על חרבן הבית ועל תורה שנשרפה ועל חרפת השם ולעתיד לבא עתיד הקב"ה להפכה לששון ולשמחה. See also the late Tractate Soferim 21.3: והתלמידים מתענין בו בשני וחמשי מפני חלול השם ומפני כבוד (התורה) [ההיכל] שנשרף. Brüll gathered all of the sources of Jewish and non-Jewish fasting on Monday and Thursday in המגיד, XII, pp. 310. 317; XIII, 23, 47: See also S. Krauss, *JQR* OS VI, 235; L. Ginzberg, *Ginze Schechter* I, 483, 548; and G. Alon, *Tarbiz* IV, 285. See also full discussion and references in S. Lieberman, *Tosefta Kifshuta* V (Moed) p. 1083.

Similarly it was suggested that these days were significant for health; *cf.* Shabbath 129b: מי שיש לו זכות אבות יקיז בב' ובה'.

Interestingly it is also mentioned in *PRE*, chap 4 and in Genesis Rabbah I.3 and III.8 that the angels were created on the 2nd day (according to R. Johanan) or on the 5th (according to Rabbi Haninah). Herein one perceives again the significance attached to 'Monday and Thursday.' Whereas Jubilees records the creation of the angels on the first day, the Rabbis opposed this notion, for they sought to demonstrate that God was alone on the *first* day; hence the usage of the phrase יום אחד instead of יום ראשון, to demonstrate the unity or oneness (אחד) of God. See Genesis Rabbah 3:11: א״ר יודן שבו היה הקב״ה יחידי בעולמו. *Cf.* Rashi on Gen. 1:5: יום אחד לפי סדר לשון הפרשה היה לו לכתוב יום ראשון כמו שכתוב בשאר ימים..... למה כתב אחד לפי שהיה יחיד בעולמו שלא נבראו המלאכים עד יום שני כך מפורש בב״ר.

The Gracious Power of the Pietists

By LEO JUNG
Yeshiva University, New York

I

TWO EXPERIENCES HAVE caused me to choose this subject:

One was a meeting with the venerable head of the Habbad movement, a towering personality, initiating and maintaining its educational institutions on three continents.

The other was a Sabbath-morning service in a New York *Shtibel*. The service consisted of three hours of conversation occasionally interrupted by prayer. Every five minutes a fist pounded the Bimah demanding quiet. Children of all ages were dancing and playing around the Shtibel. I was ready to condemn them for lack of reverence, but then I became aware of their genuine piety and a feeling of warm companionship among the worshippers. Suddenly I recalled the Sage's advice: "Do not judge your neighbor *ad shetagia* (until you have labored yourself down) to his position."

What caused the change of my attitude was the etymological dictionary. I realized that the root of *Shtibel* is the German word *Stube* which means: a room in a family home. In such atmosphere, everything—prayer, conversation, infant's play and frequent cries of *SHA SHA* are perfectly natural, hence legitimate.

The Shtibel was not meant to be a synagogue, a communal house of worship, but merely a room in the home with the normal program of family life. Recent reading revealed the fascinating fact that a modern Jewish philosopher—Franz Rosenzweig—about to convert to Christianity, found himself by accident at a Sabbath service in a Shtibel. He was so impressed by its piety that he decided to seek the way home, to become a *Ba'al Teshuvah* (a penitent Jew).

What does *Hassid* mean? Essentially it stands for a person of kindness or devotion. Of the Lord of the Universe it is said that He is "חסיד בכל מעשיו (gracious and kindly in all His works)." A Hassid is one who endeavors to live up to the three 'R's of Judaism: Reverence, Righteousness and Rahamanut (mother-love, unselfish love).

What is *Hassidism*—as a movement, as a philosophy of life, as an organization? Jewish history will supply the answer to this question. Our national task is to be a Kingdom of Priests and through living up to the challenge of being a holy nation (גוי קדוש) to be God's ambassadors to a heathen world, the source of universal conscience, hence very unpopular. Stiff-necked in our loyalty to Torah, we paid the price of our timeless challenge through two millennia of suffering from *Rish'ut* (antisemitic affliction).

Rish'ut was begotten and developed by the misinterpretation of the New Testament by Popes, Cardinals, Bishops, Lutheran preachers and—in our own time—by Hitler, Eichman, Coughlin, Streicher, Moslim politicians and the heartless leaders and writers of the Soviets.

II

There are two types of Gentile anti-semites: The first: Rats waiting for a chance to rob, rape and murder. The second: The majority—victims of hate propaganda from the pulpit and often at mother's knee, unconscious inheritors of millennia of Christian anti-Jewish traditions. But there is also a glorious minority in genuine sympathy with the Jewish people, who kept protesting Christian violence, defamation, theological inhumanity. We have known and appreciated them—from Reuchlin to Lessing, from Tolstoy to Malcolm Hay, to Pope John the XXIII—all of them working for the humanization of humanity in conscious accord with our Torah, our Prophets and the Sages of the Talmud.

III

This essentially is the record of almost two thousand years of trouble endured by the people of Israel, throughout Europe, Asia, Africa and part of America.

There were three types of Jewish reaction to Rish'ut:

There were and are hopeless optimists, hardboiled egoists, or blind super-patriots who deliberately ignored the signs of trouble as long as their family or business seemed unaffected.

A second group, small in number, were the groaners and sighers whose contribution to the Jewish problems of the time was completely negative. They felt they were doing their duty by condemning the "wicked Goyim," by wailing in private or public.

The majority were and are the élite, who fought Rish'ut, who planned and promoted escape of its victims, who sacrificed to help our brothers. At the same time, in every country where they had an opportunity to do so, these genuine Jews worked for the peace and welfare of all of its inhabitants.

IV

There were very few peaceful periods for our people. From the eleventh century's crusaders with their religious madness—indulging in wholesale murder and robbing of all non-Christians—Jews were fleeing from Western and Central Europe to the East. There they were welcomed as agents or merchants, to become—in reality—serfs of kings, dukes and knights. Nowhere were our folk safe. All over Europe they were hated, branded as "Zhids," "Verdammte Juden," "Sale Juives."

A most terrible period commenced with 1648, at the end of The Thirty Years' War between Catholics and Protestants, a shocking example of sustained inhumanity.

The countries to which our people had escaped, Poland and Volhynia, soon knew dreadful pogroms. For Jews there were only two ways out: Baptism or flight back to the West.

The pogrom of Nemirov resulted in 10,000 victims. In the same year, devilish Chmielnitzky and his abominable gangs could boast of 100,000 murdered Jewish men, women and children.

That we survived, some as helpless victims, others as heroes and saints, verified the Psalmist's promise: "המה כרעו ונפלו ואנחנו קמנו ונתעודד (they bent down in defeat but we stayed upright and survived)." We did not merely survive, we remained upright, pious, noble and generous.

In 1946, at the end of the Second World War, I had an inspiring example of such Jewish heroes and saints. My wife and I were summering at Arosa in Switzerland, when we heard of a group of D.P.s (displaced persons, victims of Hitler) who were afflicted with Tuberculosis. They had found refuge in nearby Davos' Hospital—Etania, a fine Jewish institute for persons suffering from that disease. I decided to visit them. There were some twenty men whom the glorious sun of Davos had painted with apparently wholesome red cheeks, but the devoted loyal physician told me that this was superficial; their lungs were badly affected.

At their request, I arranged a *Siyyum* (conclusion of a Talmudic tractate). As I looked at them I suddenly felt dreadful and said to them: "I am not a rabbi from New York, I am not doctor or professor Jung—as you have been told—I am your brother. Tell me, please, what I can do for you!"

Their leader, Hayyim Raphael Hurowitz, replied: "During the five years in Buchenwalde, we suffered dreadful physical and emotional torture. But what pained us most was total absence of Humashim, Tanakh, Mishnayot, Gemorot. If you could send us some of these sacred books, we should be profoundly grateful." I responded: "I am not merely promising to do so, I am cabling my secretary to go tomorrow to a מוכר ספרים (bookseller) in New York, with the order to send you the required books and also a one-volume Talmud."

We went back to our hotel and next morning, at breakfast, the mail came in. As I opened the first letter and began to read it, my wife called out: "What is the matter with you? You are white in your face!" I handed her the letter from Hayyim Raphael Hurowitz. It read: "It was wonderful to have you visit us, to call yourself our brother, to promise us to cable for the books we begged for. But I owe you an explanation: During the five years in Buchenwalde, though we suffered dreadfully, none of us uttered one word against" "הקדוש ברוך הוא (The Holy One, blessed be He)." But our hearts were very bitter. We, therefore, do not deserve those Holy books. Kindly send us some מוסר ספרים (books of moral and spiritual instruction) so that we can make our peace with the Lord before enjoying the holy books which you promised us."

A few days later, before returning to Zurich, I decided to visit the patients at Davos again. They had gone for a walk and I managed to meet them, greet them and sought to shake hands with all of them. They all responded, with the exception of one man who would not offer me his hand. When I asked whether I had offended him, I was told that his malady had progressed to the point where he could not move his hands. Hayyim Raphael Hurowitz attended to him as a nurse cares for a newborn baby, washing him, feeding him, comforting him.

These were the Hassidic saints among the concentration camp victims. But I also met others whose faith had been shattered and whose values had been destroyed by the unimaginable sufferings during the years in Buchenwalde and elsewhere in Hitler's empire.

V

1648 had been interpreted by students of Kabbalah on the basis of Gematriotic* ingenuity as the year of the appearance of the Messiah. As the year passed without his appearance, they did not allow their hope to be dimmed. In their deadly plight they prayed, yearned, longed for the Messiah to end the Galut, to bring them to the Holy Land.

But new enemies had arisen from within the camp of Israel.

VI

The False Messiahs

The most notorious among them was Shabbatai Tzevi (1626—1676). Born in Smyrna, he died in Albania. A student of mysticism, especially of the Book of Zohar, he was convinced that he was the Messiah, that he was to free his people and write a chapter of peace and welfare. Fine looking, impressive, eloquent, he may—at the beginning of his career—have been self-deceived. He travelled from Salonika to Cairo, to Constantinople and to Jerusalem.

Although excommunicated by the rabbis, his charismatic personality made him proclaimed and acclaimed by multitudes. His Messianic fervor

* The use of Hebrew letters for their numerical value and homiletical interpretation based thereon.

seemed the only hope for his destitute, desperate followers. He was even accepted by some great rabbis. In Amsterdam, I saw a book of Halakhah (Jewish Law) whose title page read: "בשנה ראשונה של אדוננו מלכנו משיחנו שבתי צבי. (In the first year of our Master, King and Messiah, Shabbatai Tzevi)."

He travelled all over Europe, to North Africa and returned to Turkey. He lived in luxury, was finally suspected and imprisoned by the Turks and converted to Islam. His new name was *Mehemed Effendi*.

VII

Jacob L. Frank (1726–1791)

In spite of Shabbatai Tzevi's treacherous conversion, there were a number of stubborn adherents to his promise and personality.

There came an even greater affliction: Jacob Leibowitz Frank—a scoundrel from youth who saw and managed a role both significant and gainful. His employer had taken him to Constantinople where he met the *Doenmehs*, the remnant of Shabbatai Tzevi's followers. On his trip to Poland, Frank was hailed as the new Messiah. He was not ashamed to engage in the company of secret, licentious groups which were apprehended by the police and whose fate (imprisonment) he escaped because of his Turkish citizenship.

At the age of thirty, in 1756, he was excommunicated. But this condemnation led him but into ever deeper personal disgrace, rendering his record abysmal indeed. Abusing his acquaintance with Archbishop Dombrowsky of Lemberg, he arranged (through him) some forced disputations with Catholic leaders. At these conferences, Jews were prevented from proper reactions to attack on our faith because criticism of the church would involve dreadful punishment for them. Frank's slanderous defamation actually led to the burning of the Talmud. He reached his moral nadir by actual assertion that the church's horrible blood-libel was true (that Jews use the blood of Christian infants for the baking of Matzot).

In 1759, together with one thousand of his followers, Frank converted to Catholicism. Frank lived in immoral luxury, enriched by countless gifts from his followers, and continued his evil work in the castle he had bought in Hessen (Germany).

In these years, our folk were physically down, spiritually shaken, financially on the lowest level. Scholars escaped despair by concentrating on learning and producing mentally fascinating, but actually uninfluential, volumes of rabbinic literature.

Jews were not permitted to live in the cities and especially the *Dorfjuden* (inhabitants of the Shtetl) were oppressed, ignorant, poorest in spirit and forsaken.

The miracle of their survival came through *Israel Baal Shem Tov*.

VIII

Israel Baal Shem Tov was the son of poor, pious parents. His father provided his Hebrew teaching but Israel, from an early age, was also a student of nature. He found God not only in man but also by observing beasts, birds and plants in woods and vales.

First as a *Belfer* (originally German "Behelfer," i. e., assistant to the teacher of the Talmud Torah), he mingled with all, the poor, the ignorant and especially with the sinners. He sought them out and taught them lovingly by simple lessons, with stories and anecdotes. His accent was always on *love*.

Every Jew, no matter how oppressed, destitute or defamed, according to the teaching of the Besht (*B*aal *S*hem *T*ov), was part of the *Shekhinah* (Divine Presence). The Besht actually recreated the personality of his followers. He was opposed to asceticism, to fasting and to the condemnation of sinners. His teaching persists to this day.

I recall a lesson with my beloved teacher, the sainted Rav Kook, who in 1915, in the middle of a Talmud discourse, said to his faithful disciples—the sainted Isidore Epstein and myself: "The worst Jewish *Apikores* (heretic) has so much קדושה (holiness) in him that when I think of it, my eyes fill with tears of pride and gratitude." We had too much respect to express our astonishment at that statement. Thirty years later its full meaning dawned on me.

The occasion was an endeavor to aid the Yeshivah Farm Settlement of Mount Kisco, populated by a hundred Jewish souls who had escaped concentration camps. Their leader, Rabbi Weismandel, had managed to jump out of a death-train to Auschwitz, unable to save his wife and children who were destined for extermination. He organized underground aid for our hapless people. In 1945 he came to Hamburg on the way to the United States. Their visas to our beloved America were to lapse in ten days. Their only chance to escape forced return to Hitler's hell depended upon an immediate trip, with first class tickets, on a boat leaving two days later for New York. The group was blessed by the Joint Distribution Committee's chairman, Paul Baerwald, who agreed to provide those tickets (the only ones available for that trip) to prevent their being shipped back to Eastern Europe.

The gift of the generous Israel Rogosin, of blessed memory, enabled them to buy the Brewster estate in Mount Kisco. Originally it was inhabited by a millionaire's family and their servants, twenty persons in all; it was now destined as an ultimate home for one hundred (seventy-three adults and twenty-seven children). To provide essential hygienic facilities, a great deal of money was necessary. Assimilationist Jews in Mount Kisco turned their backs on the people with *peyot* and outlandish garb, apparently unwilling to be considered their relatives. The Center Family and other personal friends went out of their way to supply aid. Mrs. Hansom Baldwin, the wife of the military correspondent to The New York Times, did glorious, steadfast work, providing aid through the local Christian ministry against the Zoning Laws which endangered the Yeshivah's right to be located there. In that moment of genuine danger, there arose—in the form of Billy Rose—the answer, the explanation, the realization of Rav Kook's statement. Mr. Rose had few Jewish religious interests. But somewhere, under many layers of ashes, there was a Jewish spark waiting to blaze into a tremendous flame. He not only provided considerable financial help but, I was told, went from family to family of his neighbors, successfully involving them in constructive, generous participation in the work of Yeshivah Farm Settlement.

The Besht taught his followers the benefit of enthusiastic community service. The dancing (hora) of the modern *Halutz* is a derivative of the Saint's institution. His deathless optimism caused the ecstasy of the average Hassidic prayer.

The three major virtues taught by Hassidism were: שמחה (joyous, personal devotion in all religious work from prayer to fellowship), שפלות (humility which would look upon one's own record with proper self-criticism and allow generous comradeship to one's fellow Jew and fellow-man). דבקות (fervid attachment to our Father in Heaven) is the third quality preached and practiced by the Besht's followers.

Through mutual love, with every fellow-Jew, these happy servants of God created, maintained, and spread the music of their soul.

The Besht's influence was as profound as it became widespread and it helped greatly to overcome the evil wrought by Shabbatai Tzevi and Jacob Frank. There was however, an abiding dilemma which called for constant attention. It was a constant strain between overwhelming, passionate awaiting of the Messiah and—because of the confusing and destructive effect of the work of the two nefarious pretenders—Hassidism's paramount determination to prohibit even the mention of any Messianic hope. The masses of our people felt the agony. Their learned leaders clung to their studies to avoid any contribution to, or indication of similar yearning for, ימות המשיח (the days of the Messiah).

IX

Besht Hassidism began to gain new adherents through the Besht's disciple, the Maggid of Mezeritch, who won over many תלמידי חכמים (rabbinic scholars). But the emphasis of the Hassidim on intimate, fervent, personal preparedness for prayer, their accent on a lesser significance of definite hours of worship, their utterly novel enthusiams, brought about enmity. On these grounds in particular did Lithuanian scholars find fault with גדולים (Hassidic rabbinic authorities). It was the Gaon of Vilna who was disturbed by Hassidic accent on spontaneous private worship as against organized congregational programs at definite times. There emerged a sad fratricidal strife, actually ending in mutual book-burning.

Although the two great disciples of the Besht-Rabbi Bunim of Pshysha and Rabbi Yitzhak of Worka—fought emotionalism and stressed intellectual effort and especially the study of the Talmud, the abandonment of preoccupation with Kabbalah and, above all, the obligation to keep one's piety inconspicuous, the battle between the two major factions would not cease.

True, there was the inspiring example of the Hassidic Rebbe, the Tzaddik. He was not a Rav with a diploma, but a hereditary, selfless friend, counsellor and ideal leader. There was the sublime intellectual aloofness of the passionate teacher, the Kotzker Rabbi Mendel. There were many courts, some veritable palaces, others simple homes of dedicated Rebbes: the Gerrer, the Alexander, the Bobover, but all these assets notwithstanding, the battle between Hassidim and *Mitnagdim* (their opponents) threatened genuine disaster. It was avoided only by the almost miraculous new enemy from within.

That great danger arose from the reaction of some folk to the political emancipation in France and Germany. It bred and encouraged *Maskilim*—intellectuals—assimilationist Jews, to whom submerging in the new hope of the promised universal freedom and opportunity seemed the ultimate goal.

Emunah (faith), *Torah* and *Mitzvah* became old-fashioned to the Maskilim, useless values to be discarded in the dazzling new chapter of European history. These Maskilim attracted confused youth bereft of the understanding of Jewish faith, ignorant of Jewish teaching and above all of the towering moral qualities as harvest of a life in accord with the Mitzvot and the lessons of Jewish history.

Suddenly Hassidim and מתנגדים (Mitnagdim) realized that they must unite against the new movement—which preached and promoted intermarriage and encouraged irreligious super-patriotism.

I met such two-hundred-percent German and French Jews in their native country and in the United States, even as I had encounters with some Jewish super-enthusiastic socialists and communists, victims of similar illusions. I recall, in the late 20's, an almost tragic meeting with a Boston lady whom I tried to interest in Beth Jacob, the endeavor to supply Jewish education to Jewish girls in Eastern Europe. Associated with the National Council of Jewish Women, she admired my interest and work for the daughters of what she called "foreigners in Poland." When I protested to say that these foreigners are her and my own brothers and sisters, she was astonished and hurt.

X

Most significant today are the Habbad Hassidim. They use דעה, בינה והשכל (knowledge, intuition and common sense), combining passionate attachment to Torah and warm sentiment with moving interest in the welfare of every individual Jew and Jewess.

The following may serve as an illustration. The last but one great leader of the movement, the sainted Rav Joseph Schnayersohn, had commenced his work in the United States with an inspiring address at our Center. For decades we used to run an annual Melave Malke dinner as a virtual Center institution. When the Rebbe was very sick in Paris, he wrote me a letter couched in loving terms, begging my pardon and asking that I help Mrs. Halperin of East Broadway who found herself in financial straits, to get a position at the Beth Abraham Home in the Bronx.

When in 1951 I had started the Joint Distribution Committee's endeavor to provide vocational guidance for Yeshivah Bahurim in the Holy Land—so as to enable them eventually to feed their families as against the all too frequent utter poverty of Israeli scholars—it was Habbad leadership which enthusiastically endorsed the effort and actually, without delay, established in Lod the first such institution: a carpentry school for Yeshivah Bahurim. A few years later came another amazing achievement which I was privileged to observe at Meknes in Morocco. In some manner, the Rebbe had discovered that the youth in that city grew up without proper Torah education. He considered it his duty to open a Yeshivah for them. I met them, they spoke a difficult French and a very simple Arabic. When the Rebbe decided that they must have a Yeshivah, he managed to import teachers from Soviet Russia who spoke a difficult Russian and—what was to the local Jews a more foreign tongue—Yiddish. I found that the Yeshivah was working successfully and, through the help of the J.D.C., its esthetic and hygienic imperfections were soon overcome.

I had occasion to observe Habbad's missionaries work for Judaism on four continents, also at Harvard and Cambridge Universities, among many others. Habbad is a combination of Torah study, infinite בטחון (trust in God) and hard work of extraordinary dedication. The present Rebbe is a University graduate, a great למדן (scholar), a bold leader and a self-sacrificing teacher of students of all ages.

XI

In conclusion, may I offer you some stories which will help to explain the blissful influence of Hassidism throughout the centuries of its existence. One is the answer to a question about the stork. In Hebrew the stork is called חסידה in Latin—"Pia Avis," both meaning—pious bird. In both languages the name is a tribute to the exceeding loving care of the mother bird of its brood, the young ones. "Why then is the stork an עוף טמא an unclean bird that may not be eaten?" the Rebbe was asked. His answer was: "It is unclean because it is interested *only* in its own little ones."

Of the revered Sassower Rebbe it was reported that once he came very late to the Kol Nidre service and, to the astonishment of his reverent congregation, he explained that on the way to the House of Worship he had heard a baby cry. The mother, sure that it would stay asleep, had left for the service. He felt that he could not possibly ignore that poor infant and he took it in his arms, comforted it, made it fall asleep before going to Shul.

Rabbi Levi Yitzhak of Berditchev was one of the boldest defenders of his flock. There are endless stories about his infinite kindness. One had to do with a young man violating the Sabbath in public. When the Rebbe asked whether he knew what he was doing, the bold youth answered: "Yes." Whereupon Levi Yitzhak addressed himself to the Lord, saying: "How wonderful are Thy people! Even when they go utterly wrong, they have the courage to admit their transgression."

In a moment of keenest despair, the Berditchever did not hesitate to explain the plural in the term *Yom Hakippurim* by pleading: "It is a day of two cases of forgiveness. Heavenly Father, please—as You in Your mercy will forgive our past sins, we shall—with all our heart—forgive You the persecutions, the defamations, the agony which we constantly undergo in our effort to be loyal to Thy Torah."

What is the message of Hassidism to the Jews of our time? "As for our enemies, our 'revenge' is unchanging: They afflict us, but we survive them, Brethren! Don't ever be frantic with terror! Stand up and prepare defense, attack, and never neglect steadfast work in the Lord's vineyard."

It is hope and love based on faith which will bring to our people אתחלתא דאתחלתא דגאולה the beginning of the beginning of redemption for Israel, and for all His children the abiding humanization of humanity.

Unpublished Cairo Genizah Talmudic Fragments from the Antonin Collection in the Saltykov-Shchedrin Library in Leningrad

By ABRAHAM I. KATSH
The Dropsie University

FOR CENTURIES PRIOR to World War I, Jewish intellectuals and scholars collected rare manuscripts on Judaica and Hebraica, which for a long time have been serving as a vitalizing force in the perpetuation and growth of Jewish cultural and religious life.

These treasures were the property not only of academies but also of private individuals. As a result of the first World War and the Russian Revolution all private collections disappeared and only those in the libraries remained. How to obtain microfilms of these rare manuscripts presently unavailable to scholars outside the U.S.S.R. was my main concern when I first visited Russia in August of 1956, and subsequently on six additional occasions, the last one in November, of 1978.

In the Oriental Institute of the Academy of Sciences in Leningrad, I met a number of distinguished scholars in Hebrew and Islamic studies who not only train other specialists but devote much of their time and energy to the discovery of vital information from their magnificent resources.

In addition, the Oriental Institute publishes annually a scholarly magazine in which research is described and recorded.

The Oriental Institute houses a number of collections of manuscripts, one of the more outstanding being the Friedland collection. This collection is rich in Biblical commentaries, linguistic material, extensive Karaitic literature, Kabbalah, and valuable documents dealing with the history of Russian and Oriental Jewish communities. The Institute also possesses a handwritten descriptive catalogue in four volumes, arranged by the late Russian scholar Jonah Ginzburg, which has been recently revised for publication.

In the Public library in Leningrad I examined the famous Firkovitch collection. Abraham Firkovitch came from the Crimean peninsula, and in his zeal to prove that the Karaites had been settled in the Crimea for a much longer period than previously accepted, traveled to Cairo and elsewhere in the Middle East and succeeded in bringing together the largest collection of Hebrew, Samaritan, and early Karaitic manuscripts in the world. The Leningrad library bought a part of the Firkovitch collection in 1876 and the balance after his death.

The second Firkovitch collection is not only extensive but also extremely valuable. It contains 159 scrolls on parchment and leather, about 1,000 Hebrew manuscripts, and over 2,000 Arabic manuscripts. In addition, it includes over 1,500 manuscripts of the Hebrew Bible and Biblical fragments. At least fourteen of these, dated from 929 to 1121, have for the most part the text as fixed by Aaron ben Asher, the greatest Masoretic authority who lived in the first half of the tenth century.

The Leningrad Library also houses the Antonin collection, consisting of about 1,200 fragments from the Cairo Genizah which were brought together by Antonin, a Russian Archimandrite stationed in Jerusalem. Other Library collections include the archives of noted Hebrew scholars and writers such as Israel Zinberg, David Maggid, A. D. Gottlober and others.

In the Lenin Library in Moscow, I examined a two-volume catalogue of the Baron David Guenzburg collection and microfilmed a large number of them. This collection consists of about 6,000 manuscripts and fragments, many of them originally belonging to the collections of Joseph Josel Guenzburg and his children. The Guenzburg items deal with lexicography, Judaeo-Arabic and Aramaic commentaries on the Bible, Genizah liturgy, medieval Hebrew literature, responsa, Talmudic and Karaitic works, and literature dealing with Shabbethai Zevi, Kabbalah, and mysticism.

All told, there are between fifteen and twenty thousand Hebrew manuscripts and fragments in the libraries of Leningrad and Moscow alone. While in the U.S.S.R. I also learned of other valuable collections in Kiev, Odessa, and Vilna. In the estimation of the scholars there, the U.S.S.R. possesses close to 50,000 Hebrew manuscripts and fragments.

In my books *Ginze Mishnah*[1] and *Ginze Talmud Babli*[2] I presented the Mishnaic and Talmudic fragments from the Cairo Genizah now in the Antonin Collection in the Saltykov-Shchedrin Public Library in Leningrad. The material, when compared with the printed text and other sources, shows innumerable significant variants.

Originally a church, the building in Fostat (Old Cairo), where the Genizah was discovered, was transformed in 616 C.E. into a synagogue, where successive generations stored away sacred and secular material in a concealed chamber. The term Genizah comes from the Hebrew root *ganaz*

[1] Abraham I. Katsh, *Ginze Mishnah*, One Hundred and Fifty-nine Fragments from the Cairo Genizah in the Saltykov-Shchedrin Library in Leningrad, Appearing for the First Time with an Introduction, Notes, and Variants. Jerusalem, Mosad-Harav Kook, 1970.

[2] Abraham I. Katsh, *Ginze Talmud Babli*, One Hundred and Eighty-One Fragments from the Cairo Genizah in the Saltykov-Shchedrin Library in Leningrad, Appearing for the First Time with an Introduction, Notes, and Variants. Jerusalem, R. Mass, 1977.

(Arabic *janaza*), "to store away" or "to hide." The Jewish people's love for knowledge made them revere their learned books as sacred. Thus when a book could no longer be used, the people reacted to the battered pages as they would to a human corpse, and protected them from defilement by storing them away or burying them.

The use of the holy tongue, Hebrew, was not confined to sacred literature alone. Among the Jews, Hebrew was always a living tongue. They used Hebrew for personal letters, for keeping accounts, for composing love songs, and for other secular affairs. All legal documents, such as leases, contracts, marriage settlements, bills of divorce, and court decisions were drawn up in the sacred tongue or at least written in Hebrew letters. Happily for scholarship, the Genizah not only included sacred or semisacred books but also provided a refuge for a class of writing that never aspired to the dignity of sacred books and is today of tremendous importance for the study of hitherto unknown Jewish historical data.

Prior to Dr. Schechter's historic visit to Egypt (1896–97), which has since become an epoch-making event in the history of Jewish scholarship,[3] the Fostat synagogue was visited by an uncle of Heinrich Heine, Simon Geldern, in 1753; by Jacob Saphir, of what was then Palestine, in 1864; by S. A. Wertheimer; by Abraham Firkovitch, of the Crimea, in 1865; by E. N. Adler, of England, in 1888 and 1896; by Dr. Cyrus Adler in 1891; by Archimandrite Antonin, and others.

There is hardly a branch of Jewish learning that has not been enriched by the discovery of the Cairo Genizah treasures. We now know much about the Gaonic period of which very little was known to us before the Genizah discovery, especially from the Moslem conquest to the first Crusade. The Genizah shows clearly that Jerusalem was the seat of a school presided over by Geonim who made every effort to vie with the heads of the famous Babylonian academies of Sura and Pumbeditha.

Though significant studies have already appeared of documents from this Genizah, especially by Professor S. D. Goitein,[4] the bulk of it is dis-

[3] Alexander Marx, "The Importance of the Genizah for Jewish History," *PAAJR*, 16 (1946/47), pp. 183–04; Paul Kahle, *The Cairo Genizah* (London, 1960); Solomon Schechter, *Studies in Judaism*, 2nd Series (Philadelphia, 1908), pp. 12–30; Norman Bentwich, *Solomon Schechter* (Philadelphia, 1948), pp. 126–63.

[4] S. D. Goitein, *Records from the Cairo Genizah* (Philadelphia, 1960); *Jewish Education in Muslim Countries* (Jerusalem, 1962); *A Mediterranean Society* (Berkeley, 1971); Jacob Mann, *The Jews in Egypt and in Palestine under the Fatimid Caliphs* (New York, 1970); *Texts and Studies*, 2 vols. (Philadelphia, 1931–35); Louis Ginsberg, *Genizah Studies*, 3 vols. (Philadelphia, 1928–29); S. Assaf, *Gaonic Responsa* (Hebrew) (Jerusalem, 1928–33); E. N. Adler, *About Hebrew Manuscripts* (Oxford, 1950). Saul Lieberman, *The Tosefta* (New York, 1955).

persed among many libraries and private collections[5] and is still waiting to be deciphered, organized, edited, and published.

The noted scholar Professor David Kaufmann of Hungary has referred to the Genizah discovery as "the hidden light." Professor Schechter correctly states that "the collections from the Genizah consist not of volumes but of loose sheets each of them with a history of its own" and each requiring thorough study and examination.

Professor Jacob Mann was indeed right in stating that "I believe I am not exaggerating in saying that volumes of the size of Rabbinowicz's *Dikduke Soferim* could easily be written on each (Talmudic) tractate by utilizing all the material found in the Genizah, as well, of course, as all the variants found in the Gaonic literature made accessible to the scholarly world since Rabbinowicz published his great work."[6]

The Antonin Genizah Collection was acquired by the Russian Archimandrite Antonin Kapustin, who lived in Jerusalem from 1865 until his death in 1894. While in Jerusalem, Antonin was engaged mostly in archaeology. When he learned about the Cairo Genizah discovery he set out to secure a goodly share of it for himself. Being among the first on the scene, he was able to acquire a choice selection of the material. The Antonin material had been inaccessible to western scholars, except for a privileged few.[7]

[5] See A. I. Katsh, *Catalogue of Microfilms of the USSR Hebraica Collection*, Part I (New York, 1957); *Ginze Rusiyah*, Part II (New York, 1958); K. B. Starkova, *Forty Years of Semitic Studies in the USSR* (Russian), Publications of the Oriental Institute of the Academy of Sciences, XXV, 1960, pp. 263–77; I. I. Guenzburg, *Hebrew Manuscript Collection at the Oriental Institute of the Academy of Sciences* (Russian), a report submitted in 1936; Neubauer-Cowley, *Catalogue of the Hebrew Manuscripts in the Bodleian Library, II* (Oxford, 1906); B. Halper, *Descriptive Catalogue of the Genizah Fragments in Philadelphia*, 1924; R. Gottheil and W. H. Worrell, *Fragments from the Cairo Genizah in the Freer Collection* (New York, 1927), R. Gergely, ed., *Microcard Catalogue of the Kaufmann Collection* (Budapest, 1959); E. E. Urbach, Ba'alei ha-Tosafot (Jerusalem, 1956); S. Löwinger and A. Scheiber, *Ginze Kaufmann*, vol. 1 (Budapest, 1949); S. Abramson, *Bamerkazim Uva-tefutzot Bitkufat Ha-geonim* (Jerusalem, 1965).

[6] Jacob Mann, "The Genizah," *The Menorah Journal*, vol. VII, No. 5 (1921), 198–308. See also my article in the *Proceedings of the 25th International Oriental Congress*, held in Moscow, 1962, pp. 421–30.

[7] Solomon Skoss, Jacob Mann, A. E. Harkavy, and Simhah Assaf.

The Antonin Collection occupies a prominent position not so much in quantity as in quality,[8] and could be compared in significance with the much larger Genizah collections in England and America. It represents practically all branches of Jewish scholarship. Many items supply fragments hitherto missing in other collections and some are supplied with vowel-points and occasionally with accents.

Many of the Talmudic Genizah fragments are of early date, contain the Babylonian superlinear punctuation, and seem to have been written at a time when the Talmud was studied by oral transmission and not from written books.[9]

I wish to note that some of my visits to the U.S.S.R. were aided by grants from the Rockefeller Foundation and the American Council of Learned Societies. As a result, I succeeded in publishing the only complete catalogue of the Antonin Collection available at present.[10]

This article deals with thirty-two examples of unpublished Talmudic Genizah fragments, compared with the printed Romm text, the Munich codex, the Rif (Isaac ben Jacob Alfasi, 1013–1103), the Rosh (Rabbi Asher ben Jehiel, 1250–1327), *Diḳduḳe Soferim*, Tosafot, and others.[11]

[8] About the uniqueness of the Antonin Collection, A. E. Harkavy, in 1899, wrote the following: "The Hebrew and Arabic fragments of the Archimandrite Antonin Collection are from the identical source as the second collection of Firkovitch, namely, 'the Genizah' in Egypt, and they supplement each other greatly. Together they do honor to the Royal Public Library." A. E. Harkavy, *Report of the Royal Public Library for the Year 1889* (St. Petersburg, 1903), pp. 75–87 (in Russian). Similarly, the late Professor S. Assaf wrote:

״יד חוקר לא טפלה באוסף זה עד הזמן האחרון חוץ מרא״א הרכבי ז״ל שפרסם דברים
שונים ממנו והודיע על טיבם של קצת פרגמנטים הכלולים בו. עיקר הקושי שיש בשימוש
כתה״י שבלנינגרד הוא שעד היום לא נדפס מהם שום קטלוג, ואין איש יודע ידיעה ברורה
מכתה״י הנמצאים שם״. ״תשובות הגאונים מתוך הגניזה״, ירושלים תרפ״ט:

"Scholars other than (Harkavy) published some extracts and described the nature of some of the fragments included in it. The major difficulty involved in the use of the manuscripts in Leningrad is the lack of a catalogue, and no one knows exactly what the contents of the collection are. S. Assaf, *Gaonic Responsa from the Geniza* (Jerusalem, 1928, Introduction).

[9] S. Krauss, "Outdoor Teachings in Talmudic Times," *JJS*, I (1948), 82–84.

[10] Abraham I. Katsh, *The Antonin Genizah in the Saltykov-Shchedrin Public Library in Leningrad* (New York, 1963).

[11] For abbreviations in this article I have used G (for Genizah), M (for the Munich codex), DS (for *Diḳduḳe Soferim*), R (for Rosh), Ri (for Rif), Y (for Yalquṭ), Rd (for Rid), Rt (for Ritba), Rb (for Ramban), Rs (for Rashba), Me (for Meiri), B (for Berlin edition), and T (for Tosafot). The English translation is mostly from the Soncino edition.

I have compared the variants not only with the printed text and the internal evidence but also with Rabbinic authorities and others. In their efforts to present a better and proper rendering of a Talmudic text, the Rabbinic authorities seem to indicate that they were aware of such material since their references agree with our Genizah fragments.[12]

Kethuboth 29a
Printed Text:

קטנה מבת שלש שנים ויום אחד

A small female child from the age of three years and one day (until the time when she becomes mature, the fine applies to her).[1]

According to G (the fine applies to her) if she is a small female child one day old.[2]

קטנה מבת יום אחד

[1] *Cf.* Deut. 22:9 re "fine." See also M, TR, Rd, R.

[2] See Ḥulin 26b . . . and Rashi . . .

ד"ה הכי גרסינן קטנה מבת יום אחד עד שתביא שתי שערות יש לה מכר ואין לה קנס וחכמים אומרים קטנה בת ג' שנים שהיא ראויה לביאה יש לה קנס.

Kethuboth 29a
Printed Text:

The following paragraph which appears in G is missing in the printed text.[1]

רב יעקב בר נפתלי משמיה דראבינא מתני אמ' רב נחמן אמ' רבא בר אבוה ר' מאיר חיא

[1] The G statement also appears in M.

Kethuboth 29b
Printed Text:

נערה נערה הנערה

[12] *Cf.* Rabbi S. J. Zevin in his introduction to the (Tractate Ketubot I), Institute for the Complete Israeli Talmud, Jerusalem, 1972.

"... ענין גדול זה לברר הנוסחאות של התלמוד עסקו בו כל הראשונים בספריהם, ובייחוד רש"י, המביא תדיר: ה"ג = הכי גרסינן, וכוונתו להכריע בין הנוסחאות, וכן הלכו בדרך זו כמה מגדולי האחרונים כגון: המהרש"ל והב"ח והגר"א והגרי"ב, והדברים ידועים. אולם הם הכריעו כגירסא והגיהו, אבל מי מאתנו יקח עליו אחריות כזאת להכריע בין הגירסאות או להגיע מדעתו; ולפיכך תפקידנו בעיקר לאסוף הנוסחאות בכדי לדעתן, ולהבין על ידן בהירות שינוי הדעות בין מפרשי התלמוד הראשונים, שמימיהם אנו שותים ...".

maiden, maiden, the maiden.[1]

G renders it

נער נער הנער

lad, lad, the lad.[2]

---

[1] *Cf.* M. In T, Rd the rendering is נער נערה הנערה. In Rt the rendering is נער הנער הנערה.

[2] RS renders it as G.

Kethuboth 34b
Printed Text:

היתה פרה שאולה לו וטבחה בשבת פטור.

. . . If he had a cow that he had borrowed and he slaughtered it[1] on the Sabbath he is free.[2]

G renders it in different language:

היתה פרה שאולה לו וטבחה בשבת פטור שאם אין גניבה אין טביחה ואין מכירה[3]

---

[1] And thus stole it.

[2] From paying the fine. For the theft and the desecration of the Sabbath by the slaughtering were committed simultaneously; *cf.* M, Rashi, and Rt.
ולא גרסינן שאם אין גניבה אין טביחה ואין מכירה דגבי שואל לא שייך לא כפל ולא ארבעה וחמשה וכו׳. ולא גרסינן שאם אין גניבה אין איסור טביחה ואין מכירה דבשאלה ליכא וה׳ ע״כ.

[3] *Cf.* שטה מקובצת and RS.
והרא״ח ז״ל גריס לה ומפרש כגון שטען השואל שהוא שומר וטוען טענת גנב ונשבע ואשתכח בתר הכי דשואל הוא דאילו בחול מחייב ד׳ וה׳ ובשבת פטור שאם אין גניבה וכו׳

Kethuboth 35b
Printed Text

רב חייא

R. Hiyya.

According to G,[1]

רב אדא בר אהבה

---

[1] Same in M.

Kethuboth 35b
Printed Text:

הניחא אי סבר לה כרבי יוחנן הוא נמי מתרץ לה כרבי יוחנן אלא אי סבר
כריש לקיש היכי מתריץ לה[1]

. . . . It would be all right if he would hold like R. Johanan,[2] (for) he would then explain it[3] like R. Johanan. But if he holds like Resh Lakish[4]

G renders it as follows:

הניחא אי סבר לה כר' שמע' בן בן לקיש הוא נמי מתריץ לה כר' שמע' בן
לקיש אלא אי סבר לה כר' יוחנן היכי מתריץ לה

---

[1] *Cf.* M.
[2] *Cf.* Mishnah on this case, and also Kethuboth 32b and 34b.
[3] I. e., the Mishnah.
[4] *Cf.* 34b: even if no lashes are inflicted, there is still a liability to lashes and there is no payment.

Kethuboth 67b
Printed Text:

ליטרא בשר משל עופות

Our Rabbis taught: It once happened that the people of Upper Galilee bought for a poor member of a good family of Sepphoris[1] a pound of meat every day.[2] 'A pound of meat!' What is the greatness in this? R. Huna replied: (It was) a pound of fowl's meat.[3]

G's rendition is as follows:

ליטרא מוח של עופות[4]

---

[1] A town on one of the Upper Galilean mountains; *cf.* Meg. 6a and Judg. 1:30.
[2] *Cf.* Peʾah 4.
[3] Which was very expensive; *cf.* Rashi.
[4] Same in Venice edition: ליטרא בשר מוח עופות.

Kethuboth 107b
Printed Text:

מעשה בא לפני רבי בבית שערים ולא פסק לה מזונות לפני רבי ישמעאל
בציפורי ופסק לה מזונות אמר רבי יוחנן מה ראה רבי שלא פסק לה

Such a case was submitted to Rabbi at Beth Shearim and he did not grant her (the woman) any maintenance.[1] (While in a similar case which was submitted) to R. Ishmael at Sepphoris,[2] (the latter) granted her an allowance for her maintenance. Said R. Johanan: What reason could Rabbi see for not granting her an allowance?

According to G, the case was submitted to Rabbi in Beth Shearim and he *did* grant her maintenance, while R. Ishmael of Sepphoris refused to grant her maintenance. Said Rabbi, "What reason could R. Ishmael see for not granting an allowance?"

מעשה בא לפני ר' בבית שערים ופסק לה מזונות לפני ר' ישמעאל בר ר' יוסי בציפורין ולא פסק לה מזונות... א' ר' מה ראה ר' ישמעאל שלא פסק לה

[1] Out of the estate of her absent husband.

[2] At one time the capital of Galilee.

Kethuboth 108a
Printed Text:

ורבא אמר אפילו תימא רבנן הכא במאי עסקינן שלוה על מנת שלא לפרוע בשלמא רבא לא אמר כרב אושעיא דקמוקים לה כרבנן

Raba, however, replied: The ruling may be said (to agree even with the view of) the Rabbis,[1] for here we are dealing (with the case of a man) who borrowed money on the condition that he will not repay it (except when he is inclined to do so).[2] It is well that Raba does not give the same reply as R. Oshaia, since (he wishes) the ruling to agree with the opinion of the Rabbis.

The rendering of G is as follows:

רבא אמ' אפילו תימר כדברי הכל הכא במאי עסיקנן במלוה את חבירו על מנת שלא לפרוע בשלמא רבא לא אמ' כרב הושעיא דקא מוקים ליה כדברי הכל[3]

[1] Who hold a man liable for any expenses anyone may have incurred on his behalf.

[2] Since the creditor in such circumstances can never exact payment from the debtor, any man who repays it confers no real benefit upon the latter.

[3] Same in M.

Kethuboth 108b
Printed Text:

נימא תהיו תיובתא דר' חייא בר אבא דאמר ר' חייא בר אבא אמר ר' יוחנן

Must it consequently be presumed that this presents an objection against a ruling of R. Hiyya bar Abba? For R. Hiyya bar Abba ruled . . .[1]

G renders it as follows:

לימא תיהוי תיובתא דרב נחמן אמר שמואל דא' רב נחמן אמר שמואל

[1] M, Rd agree with the text.

Kethuboth 111a
Printed Text:

מתיב ר' אבא בר ממל

R. Abba b. Memel objected.[1]

According to G,

איתיבי רב בבא בר ממר לר' אלעזר

[1] *Cf.* M and Y.

Kethuboth 111a
Printed Text:

ואלא הכתיב נבלתי יקומון ההוא בנפלים הוא דכתיב ורבי אבא בר ממל
האי נותן נשמה לעם עליה מאי עביד ליה מיבעי לכדרבי אבהו דאמר
רבי אבהו אפילו שפחה כנענית שבא"י מובטח שהיא בת העולם הבא

That was written in reference to miscarriages.[1] Now as to R. Abba bar Memel, what (is the application) he makes of the text, *He that giveth breath unto the people upon it*? He requires it for (an exposition) like that of R. Abbahu, who stated: Even a Canaanite bondwoman who (lives) in the Land of Israel is assured of a place in the world to come.[2]

G's rendering is as follows:

ואידך האי לעם עליה מבעי ליה לכדרבי חייא בר אבא דא' א' ר' חייא
בר אבא אפילו שפחה שבארץ יש' מבטח לה שהיא בן העולם הבא

[1] They too will be resurrected, but only in the Land of Israel.
[2] *Cf.* M and Y.

Kethuboth 111a
Printed Text:

ורוח להולכים בה א"ר ירמיה בר אבא א"ר יוחנן כל המהלך ארבע אמות
בארץ ישראל מובטח לו שהוא בן העולם הבא

And spirit to them that work therein[1] (teaches), said R. Jeremiah bar Abba in the name of R. Johanan, that whoever walks four cubits in the Land of Israel is assured of a place in the world to come.[2]

G's rendering is as follows:

ור' אלעזר האי נבלתי מאי מוקי לה מוקים לה דנפלים

[1] Isa. 42:5.
[2] *Cf.* M and Y.

Kethuboth 111a
Printed Text

ישיבה שאין בה סמיכה עמידה שיש בה סמיכה נוחה הימנה

Standing is better than sitting when one has nothing to lean against.[1]

According to G,

עמידה וישיבה סמיכה נוחה ממנה

[1] *Cf.* M.

Kethuboth 111b
Printed Text

הקדוש ברוך הוא מביא רוח מבית גנזיו ומנשבה עליה ומשרה את סלתה

The Holy One, blessed be He, will bring a wind from his treasure houses, which He will cause to blow upon it. This will loosen its fine flour.[1]

According to G, the text is rendered differently:

הקב"ה מוציא רוח מאוצרותיו ומנשבת בה ומושרות את פירותיה

[1] M renders it as follows: הקב"ה מוציא מבית גנזיו ומשרי' את סלתה.

Giṭṭin 51a
Printed Text

שני שוורין קשורין מצאת והלה אומר מצאתי והחזרתי לך אחד מהן הרי זה נשבע

"You found two oxen tied together," and the other says, "I did so find, and I restored to you one of them," he has to take an oath.[1]

G renders the statement as follows:

שני שורים קשורין מצאתי לך והחזרתי לך אחד מהן והלה אומ' לא החזרת לי הרי זה נשבע

"I found you two oxen tied together, and returned one of them to you." But the other says, "You did not return to me," he has to take an oath.[2]

[1] M renders it as follows:
שני כיסין קשורין מצאת לי והל' או' מצאתי לי והחזרתי לך אחד מהן הל' או' לא החזרת לי הרי זה נשבע

[2] Same in T of Rd.

Giṭṭin 52a
Printed Text:

ומכרי׳ להן בהמה עבדים ושפחות בתים וכרמים להאכיל אבל לא להניח
ומוכרין להן פירות יינות שמנים וסלתות להאכיל אבל לא להניח

(Guardians) can also sell on their (orphan's) behalf cattle, slaves, male and female, houses, fields, and vineyards, in order to purchase food with the money but not to put it aside. They can also sell for them produce, wine, oil, and flour to purchase other food with the money, but not to set it aside.[1]

G renders the first part and omits the second:

ומוכרין להן בהמה עבדים ושפחות בתים וכרמים להאכיל אבל לא להניח[2]

[1] *Cf.* M and Rt:
ומוכרין להן שמני׳ וסלתות להאכיל אבל לא להניח ומוכרין להן בהמ׳ עבדים ושפחו׳
ושדו׳ וכרמים להאכיל אבל לא להניח

[2] Same in T of Rd, Ri and R.

Giṭṭin 52b
Printed Text:

אפוטרופוס דמפסיד מסלקינן ליה דאיתמר אפוטרופא דמפסיד רב הונא
אמר רב מסלקינן ליה דבי רבי שילא אמרי לא מסלקינן ליה והלכתא
מסלקינן ליה

If a guardian spoils the orphan's property, we remove him. For it has been stated, 'If a guardian spoils the property, R. Huna says in the name of Rab that we remove him, while the School of R. Shilah says that we do not remove him.' The law, however, is that we remove him.[1]

G abbreviates the entire statement and renders it as follows:

אפטרופא דמפסיד מסלקינן ליה והילכתא מסלקינן ליה

If a guardian spoils the orphan's property, we remove him. And the law is that we remove him.[2]

[1] *Cf.* M, R, and Ri.
[2] Same in T of Rd.

BḲ 116a
Printed Text:

כי מטא זמניה דרב ספרא שדר ליה חמרא ולא אכליה

A similar case happened with R. Safra when he was going along with a caravan. A lion followed them,[1] and every evening they had to abandon to it (in turn) an ass of each of them, which it ate. When the turn[2] of R. Safra came, and he gave the ass to the lion, it did not eat it.[3]

G renders it as follows:

כי מטא ההוא יומא דשדו חמרא דרב ספרא לא אתא[4]

---

[1] To guard them against robbers and wild beasts.

[2] I. e., the time.

[3] *Cf.* M.

[4] Similar rendering in Ri, B:

ההיא אורתא דמטי גבי רב ספרא שדויה ניהליה לחמריה לא אתיא אריא

Cf. DS:

כי מטא ההוא ליליא דרב ספרא שדו ליה חמרא דרב ספרא ולא אתא אריא.

BḲ 116b
Printed Text:

ורשאין הספנים להתנות שכל מי שאבדה לו ספינה יעמיד לו ספינה אחרת אבדה לו בכוסיא אין מעמידין[1]

The mariners are entitled to stipulate that one who loses his boat should be provided with another boat. If this was caused by his fault, they would not have to provide him with another boat.

According to G,

ורשאין הספנין להתנות כל משתאבד לו ספינה נעמיד לו ספינה.

---

[1] *Cf.* B, M, Ri and R: שלא בכוסיא מעמידין לו.

BḲ 117a
Printed Text:

הוו פרסאי דלא קפדי אשפיכות דמים והשתא איכא יוונאי דקפדו אש"ד ואמרי מרדין מרדין

But now the Persians,[1] who are particular regarding bloodshed, are here, and they will certainly say, "Murder, murder."[2]

G renders it:

יונאין לא קפיד אדמא הידנא פרסאי דקפיד אדמא[3]

---

[1] According to M, "the Greeks."

[2] Or "rebellion."

[3] *Cf.* B, M, DS:

דיונא הוא דלא קפדי אשפיכות דמים האידנא מלכותא דפרסאי היא וקפדי אשפיכות דמים

BḲ 117b
Printed Text:

דן את הדין זיכה את החייב וחייב את הזכאי[1]

where a judge in deciding (a certain case), declared innocent the person who was really liable, or made liable the person who was really innocent.

The rendering of G is as follows:

דן את הדין חייב את הזכיי וזיכה את החייב

[1] Same in M and B.

BḲ 117b
Printed Text:

דאקדים ואסיק חמרא למברא קמי דסליקו אינשי במברא בעי לאטבועי אתא ההוא גברא מלח ליה לחמרא דההוא גברא

A certain man managed to get his ass on to a ferry boat before the people in the boat had got out on the shore. The boat was in danger of sinking, so a certain person came along and pushed that man's ass over into the river, where it drowned. [1]

G renders it as follows:

דהוה קא סלקי אינשי למברא הוה קא מסיק הוא ח . . . דמטבעו אינשי מלה בה חד מיניהו ובחמריה[2]

[1] *Cf.* M:
דקדים חמרי׳ למעב׳ מקמי דסליקו אינשי ממעבר׳ בעי למטבע מבר׳ דחיוה ההו׳ חמר׳

[2] *Cf.* B agreeing with G:
דהוה קא מסיק אינשי למעברא הוה קא מסיק הוא חמאריה הוה בעי דניטבעו אינשי מלא ביה חד מיניהו בחמאריה

See also DS and הגהות הב״ח in Ri:
נ״ב גירסת אלפס ישן ההוא גברא דהוו קא סלקי אינשי למעברא הוה קא מסיק חמריא קא בעי למיטבע כו׳

BḲ 117b
Printed Text:

רודף שהיה רודף אחר חבירו להורגו ושיבר את הכלים בין של נרדף בין של כל אדם

If a man was pursuing another with the intention of killing him, and in his course broke utensils, whether they belonged to the pursued or to any other person, he would be exempt, for he was at that time[1] . . .

According to G,

רודף שהיה רודף אחר חבירו להורגו ושיבר את הכלים בין של רודף בין של נרדף בין של כל אדם[2]

[1] I. e., threatening to endanger human life, which involves a capital liability during the continuance of the threat; *cf.* Exod. 22:1 and B. Sanh. 8a. See also M, B and Ri.
[2] *Cf.* R.

Hullin 7b
Printed Text:

בכה רבי ואמר מה בחייהן כך

The Rabbi wept and said, "If this is (the power of the righteous) in their lifetime, (how great must it be after their death)."[1]

G renders it as follows:

בכה רבי ואמר אשריהם צדיקים ומה בחייהם . . .

The rabbi wept and said, "Happy are the righteous! If this is so in their lifetime[2] . . .

[1] *Cf.* M.
[2] *Cf.* DS: מה צדיקים בחייהם.

Ḥullin 8a
Printed Text:

(The following question was raised):

ליבן שפוד והכה בו משום שחין נידון

If one made a spit red-hot and struck with it, is the resulting wound (which turned into leprosy) to be regarded as a boil?[1]

G renders it as follows:

ליבן שפוד והכה בו משום שפוד הוא נידון

If one made a spit red-hot and struck with it, because of the spit it is regarded . . .

[1] *Cf.* Lev. 13:18–28. See also M.

Ḥullin 8a
Printed Text:

ואיזהו מכוה נכוה בגחלת ברמץ בסיד רותח בגפסית רותח ובכל דבר
הבא מחמת האור לאתויי חמי האור

And what is a burning? A burn caused by a live coal or hot ashes, or boiling lime or boiling gypsium, or any burn that is caused by fire, including a burn caused by water heated with fire.[1]

The rendering of G is as follows:

איזו היא מכוה נכוה בגחלת ברמץ בסיד רותח ובכל דבר שהוא מחמת
האור לאיתויי חמי טיביריה

What is it? A burning caused by a live coal, or hot ashes, or boiling lime, or anything that is caused by fire including the water of Tiberias.

---

[1] *Cf.* M.

Ḥullin 13b
Printed Text:

נכרים שבחוצה לארץ לאו עובדי עבודת כוכבים הן

The gentiles outside the Land of Israel are not idol worshipers.[1]

G's rendering is as follows:

גוים שבחוצה לארץ לאו עובדי עבודה זרה בטהרה הן

---

[1] *Cf.* M.

Ḥullin 17b
Printed Text:

... צריכא בדיקא אבישרא ואטופרא דאתלתא רוחתא – צריכא בדיקה
אבישרא ואטופרא ואתלתא רוחתא אמר ליה אבישרא ואטופרא אמרי
ואתלתא רוחתא לא אמרי איכא דאמרי אבישרא ואטופרא ואתלתא רוחתא
אמרי[1]

R. Pappa ruled that it (the knife) must be examined with the flesh of the finger and with the fingernail, and the examination must be of the three edges (of the knife).[2] . . . Rabina said it must be examined with the flesh and the nail on the three edges. R. Ashi replied: "I said, 'With the flesh and the nail but not on the three edges.' " Another version reads: R. Ashi replied, I said, 'With the flesh and the nail on the three edges.' "

---

[1] M states likewise with a few variants.

[2] The sharp edge and also the sides of this edge must be examined.

According to G,

צריכא אטופרא ואבישרא ואתלת רוחאתא – צריכא אטופרא ואבישרא ואתלת רוחאתא אמ' ליה אטופרא ואבישרא אמר אתלת רוחאתא לא אמר ואיכא דאמרי אטופרא ואבישרא ואתלת רוחאתא אמרי

Ḥullin 46a
Printed Text

בעי רבי ירמיה

R. Jeremiah raised the point.[1]

According to G,

בעי רבי אשי

R. Ashi raised the point.[2]

---

[1] *Cf.* M.
[2] *Cf.* RG, and Me.

Ḥullin 48b
Printed Text:

בעי רב הונא בריה דרב יהושע

R. Huna son of R. Joshua raised the point.[1]

According to G,
R. Jeremiah raised the point.

בעי ר' ירמיה

---

[1] *Cf.* M.

Niddah 20a
Printed Text:

רבי עקיבא אומר מבקעת יודפת רבי יוסי אומר מבקעת סכני רבי שמעון אומר אף מבקעת גנוסר

R. Akiba said: From the valley of Jotapata.[1] R. Jose said: From the valley of Sikni.[2] R. Simeon said: Also from the valley of Gennesaret.[3]

G renders it as follows:

ר' יהודה אומר מבקעת ידובת ר' יוסי אומר מבקעת סכני ר' שמעון בן אלעזר אומר משום רבי מאיר אף בקעת ים גינוסר[4]

---

[1] A fortress in Galilee.
[2] North of Jotapata.
[3] In Lower Galilee.
[4] *Cf.* M and R. Elijah of Vilna, who agree with G.

The Interrelationship Between Jews, Christians, Moslems, and Others, as Reflected in Arabic Proverbs

By SHIMON L. KHAYYAT
The Dropsie University

THE STUDY WHICH appears in the following pages is based on a group of proverbs collected by me over the past twenty years. My main sources are: oral communications by Iraqi Jews who came to Israel after 1950; manuscript collections of proverbs compiled by Jews, Christians, and Moslems, chiefly at the end of the nineteenth and at the beginning of the twentieth century; rare pamphlets written in Hebrew or Arabic characters, published in the East during the last seventy years; periodicals in Arabic and in European languages containing articles on Arabic folklore; printed collections of proverbs which appeared in the East and in Europe; and finally, interviews with Jews and non-Jews of Oriental origin now living in Europe and America.

The following proverbs are arranged according to the country of origin. For each proverb, the existent parallel proverb is given; comparisons with classical Arabic literature are made only when necessary, and the same applies to parallels from non-Arabic sources.

I. *IRAQ*

1. miṯil ṣalāt il-yahūd, nuṣṣ kufur w-nuṣṣ ġalaṭ:

"Like the prayer of the Jews—half heresy and half error."

Cf. Ḥanafī, II, 77, no. 1983.

The Egyptian version is "zayy qirāyt il-yahūd tiltēnhā kidb": "Like the prayer of the Jews—two-thirds of it is false."

Cf. Taymūr, no. 1498.

One might mention here the story of the two Moslem guards who were walking in a Jewish neighborhood in Baghdad during the Jewish service in the synagogue. When they heard the Jews repeatedly saying, "barūx hū u-barūx šemō" ("Blessed be He, and blessed be His name"), one of the guards asked the other, "What do they mean?" His friend, proud of his expertise in the Hebrew language acquired during his long service in this neighborhood, translated the prayer into the Moslem dialect as follows: "yā barġūṯ farrix čima," meaning "O flea, give birth to a mushroom!"

The proverb refers in general to someone whose word is usually unreliable.

2. mitil mā gāl il-xāxām, il-sana sana:

"Like the Rabbi said, this year will be some year!"

Cf. Hanafī, I, 206, no. 958; II, 82, no. 2016. Dulayshī, II, 122, no. 1028.

It is related that when New Year's Day arrived, an Iraqi rabbi said to his community, "This year will be some year!" When the year turned out to be excellent indeed, he said, "Did I not tell you so? Did I not prophesy thus to you?" The following year he told them again, "This year will be some year!" When the plague struck them in that year, he said again, "Didn't I tell you so?"

This proverb concerns something which may be interpreted in more than one way; it ridicules a person who claims the gift of prophecy, and then tries to justify himself when events disprove his predictions.

3. yhūdī xaybar;
mitil yahud xaybar:

"Like the Jews of Haybar."

Cf. Ḥanafī, II, 87, no. 2047; Takrītī, IV, no. 2739; Freyḥa, II, no. 4242.

This proverb deals with someone who causes damage and then disappears. It is also used to describe people who provoke violent enmity.

Khaybar is a region in Arabia which was settled by Jews, who were numerous, rich, and well fortified. The prophet Muhammad decided to attack them two years after his campaign against the Jewish tribes of Naḏir and Qurayḏa. In the seventh year after the Hijra, in the month Ğumāda I, he led his troops against the Jews of Khaybar and besieged them for twenty days, until they surrendered.

A humiliated person is called xaybarī, "a Khaybarite."

4. māydat banī ʾIsrāʾīl:

"The table of the Sons of Israel."

Cf. Ḥanafī, II, 57, no. 1863.

This is a nickname for people who are so gluttonous that they would not be satiated even if God sent them a table of food from heaven. Some think that the "table of the Sons of Israel" refers to the table which Jesus asked God to send down from heaven for the wedding feast at Cana.

Cf. John 6:5–14; Luke 9:13 f.; Matthew 14:17 f.; Mark 6:38 f.; Qurʾān 5:112–115.

Cf. the Maghribi proverb, "ṣendūq bnī Isrāʾīl," "the trunk of the Sons of Israel." Ben Cheneb, 2591.

Concerning the description of the table of the Israelites, see al-*Mustaṭraf*, I, 211.

5. mūsa tbarra minnā w-mḥammad mā ᶜurafā:

"Moses freed himself from him, and Muhammad did not know him."

Cf. Ḥanafī II, 119, no. 2231.

This is said of an unstable person who changes his mind every day, and as a result loses his old friends and does not gain new ones. The source of this proverb is believed to be the story of a Jew who was converted to Islam and died a few days later.

6. nām ᶜind il-naṣāra wkull ᶜind ilyhūd:

"Sleep at the Christian's house, and eat at the Jew's house."

Cf. Ḥanafī, II, 138, no. 2325; Yahūda, no. 148; *Baghdādiyyāt*, III, 69.

This is said of the stinginess of the Christian who provides security for his guest, as opposed to the generosity of the Jew who provides no such security. Moslems are permitted to eat at the house of a Jew, since Jewish law forbids the flesh of swine. The proverb clearly expresses, however, the Moslem's distrust of the Jew, which might have been enhanced by the Christian blood libel.

This proverb refers also to the absence of common dietary laws between Moslems and Christians.

I have heard the Druze in Israel express this proverb in the following form:

tġadda ᶜind il-mislim, tᶜašša ᶜind il-yahūdī, w-nām ᶜind il-masiḥī:

"Eat your breakfast in a Moslem's house, eat your supper in a Jew's house, and sleep in a Christian's house."

The Maghribis say: "en-nṣāra nᶜas fī frāšum lā tākul mākletum, l-ihūd kul mākletum la tnᶜas fī frāšum": "Sleep on the Christians' couch but do not eat their food; eat the Jews' food but do not sleep on their couch."

Cf. Westermarck, 467; Yahūda I, 148; Flamand, p. 117.

Cf. Champion, p. 329, no. 304: "Sup with the Jew, but sleep in the house of the Christian."

7. niyyālu il-yākil il-kiġġāṯ bsinn mislim:

"Fortunate is the man who eats leeks with Moslem teeth."

Cf. Ḥanafī II, 148, no. 2393.

This Moslem proverb is couched in the Judaeo-Iraqi dialect, in order to ridicule the Jew. It is said that leeks have great nutritional value but hurt the teeth, and the Moslem represents the Jew as claiming that it is best to eat leeks with Moslem teeth, so that the eater will gain maximum benefit without incurring any damage at all. The implication is that Jews are cunning and unscrupulous in business relationships.

8. hāḏa sabtak yā yhūdī:

"This is your Sabbath, O Jew!"

Cf. Ḥanafī, II, 169, no. 2501.

This is said of something as obligatory as the Jews' keeping the Sabbath.

9. yhūdī wsabbat:

"A Jew who keeps the Sabbath."

Cf. Ḥanafī, II, 234, no. 2840.

This refers to the close connection which exists between two things, and the efforts made to insure this connection, and is usually directed to the man who would like to speak but keeps silent.

10. halsabit brugbat hal-yhūdī.

"This Sabbath is hung around the Jew's neck."

Cf. Ḥanafī, II, 172, no. 2523; Dabbāġ, I, 221; Dulayshī, II, 103, no. 980.

Another version of this proverb is: "il-sabit brugbat yhūd," referring to something inescapable, or to someone who cannot release himself from a bad habit.

The Egyptian version is: "daxal il-sabt fī ᶜēn il-yahūdī": "The Sabbath has entered into the very eye of the Jew."

Cf. Zayyāt, p. 21; Yahūda, II, no. 2364; Bāǧūrī, p. 80; ᵓAbu Farrāǧ, p. 230, no. 1105.

The commandment of keeping the Sabbath is very important to the Jews, who are not allowed to light a fire, to cook, or to buy anything, since they are not allowed to use money on Saturday. Some Jews therefore used to ask their Moslem neighbors to light lamps for them on Friday night or during Saturday.

This proverb entered literary Arabic in a poem by the Iraqi poet, ᵓIbrahīm al-Wāᶜiḏ̣, in which he says: wa-mahmā kān minnī min taġāḏ̣in/ faᵓinna al-sabta fī ᶜunqi al-yahūdī: "Even if I pretend not to see it/ behold the Sabbath is hung on the Jew's neck." See Dabbāġ, I, 221.

11. ᵓil-sabt sbūt:

"Sabbath is for rest."

Cf. Dulayshī, II, 104, no. 982.

Saturday is the day on which markets were closed because it is a Jewish holy day, and this was a mark of the Jewish control of trade in Iraq. It was because of this control that many persons used to put off their business until after Saturday, since shops and banks were closed on that day.

It is related that the Palestinian refugees who came to Iraq after the Israeli War of Independence in 1948, walked along al-Rashid Street on Saturday. Observing that all the shops were closed, they asked jokingly, "Are we back in Tel-Aviv again?"

12. lā dinyā walā ᵓāxra mit̠il mgādī il-yahūd:

"Like the Jews, (they enjoy) neither this world nor the next."

Cf. Ḥanafī, II, 190, no. 2605; Yahūda, no. 1701; Dabbāġ, II, 416; ᵓAmīn, p. 67; Freyḥa, no. 3619; Taymūr, no. 1492. ᶜAbbūd, p. 202, no. 4240; Ǧuhaymān, III, 99, no. 2206; Bāǧūri, p. 90, ᵓAbu-Farrāǧ, p. 253, no. 1228; Shaᶜlān, p. 243; Burton, p. 342, no. 11.

The Egyptian version is "Zayy fuqrā il-yahūd, lā dunyā walā dīn": "Like poor Jews—neither world(ly goods) nor religious (bliss)."

This proverb is indicative of the economic status of the Jews in some Eastern countries, where the majority of them are poor. It is based on the Moslems' belief that Jews have no part in the next world. Thus, while rich Jews have plenty of good things, and thus at least a part in this world, poor Jews have nothing of worldly goods in this world and no Paradise in the next.

A man unfortunate in his religion as well as in his daily life is implicit here as well.

The Maghribi version is "Kefᵓīr l-ihūd lā dīn la deniā": "Like the poor of the Jews—having neither religious bliss nor worldly goods."

Cf. Ben Cheneb, 1463.

13. yhūdī ᵓabu bēḏ̣a:

"The Jew who owns an egg."

Cf. Ḥanafī, II, 233, no. 2836; *Baghdādiyyāt*, III, p. 45.

This refers to one who is very stingy and also has good business sense. The prototype of this proverb is supposedly a man who owned only one egg. He sold it and bought with the proceeds something else. He then continued buying and selling until he became a great merchant and a rich man.

Cf. the Hungarian proverb: "Nothing is worse than a poor Jew, lean pork, or a drunken woman."

Cf. Champion, p. 198, no. 161.

14. yhūdi ṭāliᶜ min ᶜīda, magrūd il yugaᶜ bīda.

"The Jew has finished his holiday—woe unto him who falls into his hands."

Cf. Ḥanafī, II, 233, no. 2837; Ben-ᶜAmi, no. 40.

The Moroccans say: "ᵓida xaraz lihūdī min ᶜidū wil būh man ṭāḥ fidū": "When the Jew completes his holiday, woe unto him who falls into his hands."

This refers to one who meets a greedy person and asks him for money. Since Jews do no work during their holidays, once they finish celebrating them, they are held to be eager to do business and earn the profit that might have escaped them during the holidays. The day after the holiday the Jew has no money left, and therefore insists on the payment of debts due to him.

15. yhūdī mzallaf:

"A Jew with sidelocks."

Cf. Ḥanafī, II, 233, no. 2838; Dabbāġ, II, 507.

A nickname for a corrupt and lying man. This proverb is applied not only to a Jew but also to a Moslem who cheats others in business and refuses to compromise in money matters.

Cf. the English idiom "to Jew down," to beat down the seller's price.

It also shows that Jews in Iraq used to wear long side-curls as a symbol of religious piety.

16. il-yahūdī min yiflas ydawwir dfātir ᶜittag:

"A bankrupt Jew searches through his old account books."

Cf. Ḥanafī, II, 233, no. 2839; Kirmilī, p. 131; Taymūr, no. 2546; Dabbāġ, I, 57, II, 507; Sassoon, p. 196; Qiṣṣa, p. 14; Maydānī (Beirut), I, 119; Shaᶜlān, p. 243; Yahūda, I, no. 460; ᵓAbu Farrāg, p. 177, no. 815.

See also Claud Field, *A Dictionary of Oriental Quotations* (*Arabic and Persian*), London, 1911, p. 127: "Idha ᵓftakara ᵓlyahūdiyyu nadhara fī ḥisābihi ᵓlᶜatīq" (Arab proverb), "When the Jew grows poor, he looks into his old accounts," hoping to recover old forgotten or overlooked debts due to him.

17. miṯil ᶜarzūlat il-yahūd kull šī mᶜallag bīhā:

"Like the tabernacle of the Jews—everything is hung upon it."

Cf. Ḥanafī, II, 252.

This is the description of a room or shop on the walls of which are hung many things; sometimes there is a connection between them, and sometimes there is none. If the latter is true, this proverb is used. The tabernacle of the Jews is the booth constructed for the festival of Tabernacles, in which are hung fruits, pictures, etc.

18. ᶜīsa b-dīna w-mūsa b-dīna:

"Jesus has his religion, and Moses has his."

Cf. Dulayshī, II, 279, no. 1406.

Cf. the Egyptian proverb "kull ᵓinsān ᶜala dīna," "Every man according to his religion." People of the book should not be forced to become Muslims. See ᵓUstāḏ, vol. 1, no. 15, 29/11/1892: "Lā ᵓikrāh fī al-dīn": "There may be no compulsion in religion."

See Qurᵓān 2:256.

19. hīčī ṣār ᶜal-yahūdī wmāt:

"This is what happened to the Jew, and he died."

Cf. Takrītī, IV, no. 2491; Freyḥa, no. 4082.

This is said of a man struck down by catastrophe, and is used in jest when questioning someone about something trivial. The Jew is supposed to be easily frightened. The proverb refers also to a man who is easily stopped by obstacles.

Cf. the Lebanese idiom "hēk ṣāb il yahūdī wmāt": "So it happened to the Jew and he died."

20. ykūn ᶜumrak miṯil badan il-yahūdī:

"May your life be (as long) as the body (garment) of the Jew."

Cf. Yahūda, no. 1491; *Qiṣṣa*, p. 2.

When a Jew made a new garment, he first wore it for many years on holy days and Saturdays. Afterwards he wore it on weekdays, and at last, when it became soiled and faded, he turned it inside out and wore it again first on Saturdays and after that on weekdays. When it finally became shabby, he gave it to his young son.

In this proverb the word "body" is used as a metaphor for garment.

21. ᵓaš qāl qalbak, ḥisqēl, min ṭaqqit il-ṭiqqāqa? :

"What did your heart say, Ezekiel, when the gun went off?"

Ḥesqēl, Ezekiel, is one of the most common names among Iraqi Jews. The proverb is based on an anecdote purporting to show the cowardice of Jews, especially when faced with firearms. A variant of this proverb is " ᵓēš qāl qalbak sāsōn min ṭaqqit il-ṭiqqāqa?" (Variant: a(l)-tufqāya = Turkish word meaning gun): "What did your heart say, Sasson, when the gun went off?"

Cf. Ḥanafī, I, 42, no. 116; Dulayshī, I, 64, no. 120.

Cf. the Polish proverb, "Be as fearful as the Jew who fears a rifle," Bystron, p. 173.

22. ʾaxaff min dīn mōšī:

"Weaker than the religion of Moses."

Cf. Dabbāġ I, 35; *Ǧamhara*, no. 209.

The Moslems believe that the Jewish religion is weak and claim that this is due to the Jews' alleged falsification of the Torah. In a wider sense the proverb is applied to things which are damaged quickly and are weak or false. It is also used in reference to a thin and weak cloth which is easily frayed.

A variant of this proverb is " ʾaḏ̣ʿaf min dīn ḥisqēl," "Weaker than the religion of Ezekiel."

Cf. *Ǧamhara*, no. 209.

The Hispano-Arabic proverb says: " ʾaraqqa min dīn yahūdī," "Weaker than the religion of a Jew." Ahwānī, 298, no. 13.

23. il bqalbī bqalbī:

"Whatever is in my heart, is in my heart (forever)."

Cf. Ḥanafī, II, 250, *Ǧamhara*, p. 302, no. 602, *Ḥadāʾiq*, II, 169, no. 2000.

A story is told of a Jew who was converted to Islam and wore the turban of Moslem merchants. Twenty years later he passed by a synagogue and saw that the path was well kept and birds were singing inside the synagogue. He walked on facing the synagogue and said "lā tʿaynēn ʿlayyī il bqalbī bqalbī," "Do not look at my external appearance; whatever is in my heart, is in my heart."

The proverb describes a person who cannot hide what is in his heart. Compare the Egyptian idiom " ʾillī fī il-qalb fī l-qalb yā kinīsa," "What is in the heart, is in the heart, O Church."

Cf. Taymūr, no. 323.

Another variation is "qālu yā knīsa ʾaslimī qālit ʾillī fī l-qalb fī l-qalb," "They said, O Church, become Moslem; she answered, Whatever is in the heart, is in the heart."

Cf. Taymūr, no. 2204.

Another variation is "yā knīsit il-rabb ʾillī fī l-qalb fī l-qalb," "O Church of God, whatever is in the heart, is in the heart"; Taymur, no. 3093.

The proverb expresses the idea that the Church is never really forgotten by apostate Christians. Although they no longer demonstrate their allegiance to the Church, neither do they show hatred for her, because in their hearts they still cherish her. People should be judged by what is in their hearts and not by what is seen externally. The idiom is used of someone who is ostensibly a convert to Islam, but still retains his original religion in his heart.

The same idea is expressed in the Maltese proverb "Ix-xita wix-xemx, qed jitghammed Lhudi (or: twieled Tork)," "When it rains while the sun is shining, a Jew is being baptized (or: a Turk is born)."

Simultaneous rain and sunshine is considered curious and unusual by many people.

Cf. Aquilina, XLV (89), p. 530.

24. ᵓalif darbūnat yahūdī bgalba:

"A thousand Jewish alleyes are in his heart."

Cf. *Ǧamhara*, I, no. 639.

This proverb expresses resentment towards the Jews by the idiom "darbūnat il-yahūdī," "a Jewish alley," and is applied to one whose behavior is bad.

Compare the Moroccan idiom "ṭwīl w-xāwī kīf darb ᵓil-yahūd," "Long and narrow like the alley of the Jews."

Cf. *Taṭwān*, no. 349.

Said of a person thought to possess great knowledge, power, and honor, although known facts prove the contrary.

25. ᵓalif yahūdī bgabr mislim w-ᵓalif mislim bgabr yhūdī:

"A thousand Jews in a Moslem grave, and a thousand Moslems in a Jewish grave."

Cf. *Ǧamhara*, I, no. 661.

The proverb suggests that the religion of a person is no proof of his being either good or bad. His character is determined by his behavior and his attitude toward others. If his behavior is good, and he upholds the rights of others and observes the laws of the permitted and the prohibited, especially in matters of trade and business, he is considered an honest man. If the opposite is true, he is considered evil. If it happens that a Jew is good and honest, it is as if he were buried in a Moslem grave. If the evil man is a Moslem, it is as if he were buried in a Jewish grave, for, according to the Moslems, a Jewish grave is unclean.

26. ᵓil yrīd yḏayyiᶜ rūḥa, xall yimšī biᶜgūd il-yahūd:

"He who wants to hide himself, let him walk in the Jewish quarter."

Cf. *Ǧamhara*, I, no. 908; Kirmilī, p. 131.

If a Moslem who has committed a crime or sin takes refuge with his parents or other members of his family, the police will look for him among these people. There is also the danger that one of the victims of the culprit's crime will tell the police about his hiding place, and he will most likely be apprehended. However, if the culprit hides in the Jewish quarter, the police will not think of finding him there, as it is not a likely place for a criminal. The Moslem culprit knew that the Jews would not dare to betray him to the police, and that therefore he had a good chance to go scot-free. This proverb is applied to a person who seeks a secure hiding place.

27. ᵓamal il-yahūd bil-ᵓabāᶜir:

"The Jews' hope (for success) is in the camel."

Cf. Ḥanafī, I, 66, no. 242; *Ǧamhara*, p. 994.

There is also a proverb to the contrary, because the Jews do not care for camels and are not allowed to eat their flesh. There is no known instance of a Jew dealing in camels or owning camel caravans. This proverb is used to express sore disappointment. This proverb is used ironically, because the last thing Jews depend upon is the camel. Jews in Arab countries did not own camels; when they needed to use camels in caravans, they would rent them from Moslems.

28. ᵓunfux! bāčir ᶜarāfā māl yhūd:

"Blow—tomorrow is the eve of the Jews' holiday."

Cf. *Ǧamhara*, no. 1104; Ḥanafī, I, 71, no. 273.

Before Passover Iraqi Jews gather their copper dishes together and take them to the tinker (a Moslem occupation) for polishing. These dishes would pile up in the tinker's shop, while he puts off taking care of them. However, just before the onset of Passover he would exert himself to do the job and would encourage his assistants by quoting the proverb, "Blow—tomorrow is the eve of the Jews' holiday," meaning, "Get on with this job, even though it cannot be finished in time." The proverb is said of a person who hastens to do something when it is already too late.

29. ᵓukul ᶜind il-yahūd wnām ᶜind il-naṣāra:

"Eat with Jews, and sleep with Christians."

Cf. *Ǧamhara*, no. 523.

Bahgdādiyyāt, III, 69; Tikrītī, I, no. 284; Dabbāġ, II, 568; Freytag, III, 1; Westermarck, no. 467.

Cf. the Lebanese variant "kull min ᵓakl il-yahūdī w-bāt ᶜind il-naṣrānī," "Eat of the Jews' food, and spend the night with the Christian"; cf. Freyḥa, I, nos. 1174, 1175; Qurᵓan 5:82: "Certainly you will find the most violent of people in enmity to those who believe (to be) the Jews and those who are idolaters. And you will constantly find the nearest in friendship to those who believe (to be) those who say, We are Christians. This is because there are priests and monks among them and because they do not behave proudly." This verse speaks of the better side of the Christian religion, and affords convincing proof of the universal character of the religion of Islam, which does not deprecate goodness even when manifested in a people openly inimical to it.

This proverb advises the Moslem to eat in Jewish homes but to sleep in Christian homes, because Jewish food is permissible to Moslems, whereas Christians eat pork which is forbidden, and it may happen that the Moslem would be offered pork and would eat it without knowing that it was swine's flesh. The Moslem is advised to sleep in Christian homes because of their security, since in other respects Christians are closer to Moslems than Jews. Muhammad did not allow Moslems to sleep in Jewish homes, because Jews were thought to be perfidious and might attack the Moslem while he is asleep.

Some interpret the proverb to mean that if the Moslem sleeps at the Christian's home and is attacked by another Moslem, and if he claims that the attacker was Moslem because he was circumcised, he will be believed, since his Christian host is surely uncircumcised. However, if the Moslem sleeps in a Jewish home and is attacked there by another Moslem, and if he claims that the attacker was a Moslem because he was circumcised, he cannot prove the truth of his accusation, since his Jewish host is also circumcised. He therefore cannot be secure from attack by another Moslem if he stays in a Jewish house.

From this one must conclude that Jewish houses were occasionally attacked by Moslems.

30. ᵓafraġ(u) min fuᵓādi ᵓummi mūsā:

"More carefree than the heart of ᵓumm Musa."

Cf. Ḥanafī, I, 46, no. 139; Maydānī, II, 25. Zamakhsharī, I, 271, no. 1138; Ǧuhaymān, I, 70, no. 146; *Ḥadāᵓiq*, II, 5, no. 1347.

This refers to the heart of Moses' mother, Jochebed, and is said of a mother who does not have to worry about her son.

In the classical proverbs included in Maidani's anthology great honor is shown to the Jewish forefathers, far less in the proverbs ascribed to the Muwalladūn and others.

This idiom is mentioned in the Qurᵓan as a metonym for anxiety and worry. See Qurᵓān 28:9: "And the heart (or: the mind) of the mother of Moses became void (of patience or of anxiety)."

31. ᶜInd il-yhūdī ᶜaḏāb il-ṇiṣġānī ḥasanī:

"To the Jew the chastisement of the Christian is a good (deed)."

Cf. Kirmilī, p. 70.

Compare this proverb with the proverb popular among the Moslems of Mosul: " ᶜaḏāb il-mislim ḥasanī," "To chastise a Moslem is a good (deed)." Cf. Dabbāġ, I, 268.

Said of the one who deals with a procrastinator.

32. qahwī balā dixxān, yhūdī balā xāxām, maǧlis balā doryān:

"Coffee without smoking, a Jew without a Rabbi, a meeting without Duryān."

Cf. Kirmilī, p. 87; Shuqayr, p. 37.

This proverb refers to things which are inseparable. It seems that this is a Christian proverb, because the name Duryān might refer to the proper name of a very famous entertainer. However, the main proof that the proverb is Christian is its language, which is typically Christian; cf. the ᵓimāla in "qahwī."

33. il-mislim b-sēfū, wil-naṣġānī b-ṣinᶜitū, wil-yhūdī b-ḥilitū:

"The Moslem (earns a living) by his sword, the Christian by his craft, and the Jew by his cunning."

Cf. Kirmilī, p. 110.

This proverb classifies the three communities in Iraq according to the manner in which they make a living.

The Moslem version reads: "il-mislim b-qiwwitū, wil-naṣġānī b-ṣinᶜitū wil-yhūdī b-ḥilitū."

Dabbāġ, II, 584. This variant is popular among the Moslems of Mosul.

The Moslem earns a living by his physical strength—he does physical work, and is known for his bravery. The Christian is known for his craftsmanship, while the Jew is famous for his lying, slyness, and deception.

Cf. the Iraqi proverb " ᶜa-ttarnīnē wᶜa-ttarnīnē," "With the tarnīnē song."

The story back of this proverb is that a Moslem from Mosul went on a trip with Satan. Because of the length of the journey Satan suggested that each one carry the other while the latter is singing a short song. First Satan was carried by the Mosuli, and after Satan finished his song, he carried the Mosuli. The latter, while carried by Satan, started to sing the above-cited verse but would not finish it. Satan, fed up with him and wanting to put him down, asked, "Are you finished with your singing?" The Mosuli replied that he had finished only one part of the song and would now begin the next part reading " ᶜa-ttarninē wᶜa-ttarnīnē." At this, Satan threw the Mosuli down.

The proverb is said to refer to the cunning and shrewdness of the Mosulis, and may be illustrated by the proverb " ᶜāšir il-wāwī wla tᶜāšir il-miṣlāwī," "Live with a fox, but do not live with a Mosuli."

The stereotype of the cheating Jew is reflected in many proverbs. The German says, "Willst du 'nen Juden betrügen, musst Du ein Jude sein," "If you would cheat a Jew, you must be a Jew yourself." See Bohn, p. 188.

Polish proverbs read: "The Jew will cheat the German, the Devil will cheat the Jew, the Russian will cheat the Devil, and he in turn will be cheated by a woman"; "A Jew would not be a Jew if he were not a cheat." Of an accomplished cheat it is said, "He can cheat a Jew." See Byrston, pp. 168–169.

34. ġabbinā ᵓaḥabbna wiᶜṭāna maṭaġ, wil-mislim min ᶜindū qalbū infaṭaġ:

"Our God loved us and gave us rain, and the Moslem split his own heart."

Cf. Kirmilī, p. 80.

This is said by Jews on the feast of Tabernacles, as a curse against the Moslem, wishing that he would suffer hunger while Jews enjoy abundance, expressed in this proverb by the word "rain."

35. ġibbinānu (ġibbōnu) ᶜala laḥm il-smīn, w-ṭalaᶜ ḥaḏḏ il-msilmīn:

"We raised him on fat meat, but he followed the lot of the Moslems."

Cf. Kirmilī, p. 80; *Qiṣṣa*, p. 13.

Said of a person from an illustrous family who falls in love with a Moslem woman.

These two proverbs are used by Jews in referring to Moslems and Christians.

36. ṯimm il-yhūdī ğayyif:

"The mouth of the Jew stinks."

Cf. Dabbāġ, I, 140.

Refers to the Jew who utters many curses and blasphemies; people are afraid of his curses.

37. Ḥazqalā:

"Ezekiel."

Cf. Dabbāġ, I, 161.

"Ḥazqalā" is the proper name Ezekiel (the name borne by one of the Biblical prophets) used as a term for a miser. The appellation means that a person has become like a Jew as regards miserliness.

38. ḥaṣġit mōšī ᶜala ṭaġbūšī:

"Like the sorrow of Moses, because of the loss of old shoes."

Cf. Dabbāġ, I, 163.

Said by a malicious person when one struck by a disaster had previously wronged him; the meaning is, "I hope you will never recover, and will be like Moses, who was sorrowful because of the loss of his shoes.

The proper name Mōšī is a metonymy for a Jew who deals in second-hand goods; "ṭaġbūšī" is an Aramaic loanword meaning "old shoe."

39. ḥīlat yhūdī:

"The Jew's trickery."

Cf. Dabbāġ, I, 171.

Said of someone who is skillful in tricks, deceitful, and cunning.

40. ṣār ᶜāṣūr[1]:

"It becomes forbidden (meat)."

Cf. Dabbāġ, I, 241.

The proverb refers to unclean meat which Jews are not permitted to eat, as opposed to the kosher meat which is permitted. The Baghdadi Jews called the former "ṭaref." An animal with an organic defect is forbidden for consumption. The Jewish slaughterer must examine the inner organs of fowl and sheep. If he finds the liver attached to the animal's back, its flesh is forbidden. If the liver is not attached to the animal's back, its flesh is kosher.

Said of someone with whom one is forbidden to deal, because of his bad behavior.

Cf. the classical proverb "ṣūrat ḥawḍ, man yaḏūqhā yabṣiq," "Like standing water—he who tastes it, will spit it out."

Said of a person whose relatives and neighbors keep their distance from him, because of his bad behavior.

[1] Note that in this Hebrew word the letter ᵓalef is pronounced ᶜayin in the Moslem dialect of Iraq.

41. ᶜumrū mā naṣaḥ mislim w-ᶜumrū mā kasar sabtū:

"All his life he never advised a Moslem, and all his life he never violated his Sabbath."

Cf. Dabbāġ, I, 281.

42. ᵓil-kufur mullā wāḥda:

"All infidels are of the same religion."

Cf. Dabbāġ, II, 325.

The proverb means that all unbelievers cooperate against the Moslems, even though they belong to different religions. Said of people who are equally evil. This is similar to the social solidarity which is common among the Moslem tribes, and is known as ᶜaṣabiyya.[2]

[2] Note that this phenomenon was very developed during the Umayyad period. See ᵓIbn Khaldūn, *Muqaddima*, English translation F. Rosenthal, I, 313.

43. lā maᶜa mūsā baqa walā maᶜa muḥammad iltaqa:
"He did not stay with Moses, nor did he meet with Muhammad."

Cf. Dabbāġ, II, 353; Jewett, no. 252.

The source of this proverb is the story of a Jew who wanted to follow Muḥammad in order to become a Moslem, and went forth to meet him but died on the way.

Said of a person who missed both possibilities. Dabbaġ claims that the Jew of the story was accepted as a Moslem, on the basis of Qurᵓān 4:100: "Whoso migrateth for the cause of Allah will find much refuge and abundance in the earth, and whoso forsaketh his home a fugitive unto Allah and His messenger, and death overtaketh him, his reward is then incumbent on Allah. Allah is ever forgiving, merciful."

44. mā ḥubban li-mūsā, baġḏ̣ata li-farᶜawn:

"Not out of love for Moses, but out of hate for Pharaoh."

Cf. Dabbāġ, II, 399; Ḥanafī, II, 122, no. 2241.

The Pharaoh referred to is the one who reigned during the time of Moses. Said of a good deed inspired by a selfish motive.

45. mit̠l il-yahūdī wil-tamattuᶜ.

"Like a Jew and like the Tamattuᶜ."

Cf. Dabbāġ, II, 405.

The Ottoman government had an income tax called "tamattuᶜ." The Jew would come to the tax office with his money in his pocket, but would not pay it immediately. Instead he would begin by asking for compassion and a reduction of the tax, claiming that he was poor and had to support a family, and offering other excuses. The tax clerks knew that it was all a trick and would proceed to beat him and slap his face. Each time they struck him, he would give them a little money towards the required tax, until he paid out the entire sum, after having been unmercifully beaten and deeply humiliated.

Said generally of someone who postpones paying his debts.

46. migrāš māl yhūd:

"A Midrash of the Jews."

Cf. Dabbāġ, II, 428.

The word "migrāš" is a bastardization of "midrāš," a homiletic commentary on Scripture.

Said of a noisy place and of noise in general. Cf. also the poem of Samuel Hannagid in which he satirizes teachers and students of Bible and Talmud (Dīwān of Samuel Hannagid, ed. Yarden, Jerusalem, 1966, p. 229).

47. yā mūsā ˀinta w-rabbak:

"O Moses! You and your God!"

Cf. Dabbāġ, II, 472.

Connected with that the Jews said to Moses according to Qurˀan 5:24: "They said: O Moses! We will never enter (the land) while they are in it. So go thou and thy Lord and fight. We will sit here."

Said of a coward.

48. ydawwiġ ᶜala ᶜaṣāt mūsā.

"He looks for Moses' staff."

Cf. Dabbāġ, II, 490.

It is a common belief among Moslems in Mosul that it is the custom of the Jews to look for Moses' staff in the open spaces every Saturday, because the Jews believe that it will be the means for their restoration and the gathering of their scattered remnants. Dabbaġ conjectures that the reason for their walking about so much on Saturday is their stinginess, because they prefer to walk about rather than sit in coffee houses where they would have to pay for the refreshments.

Said of anyone who is unemployed and is looking for work.

49. waqaᶜ b-niᶜmit banī ˀIsrāˀīl:

"The prosperity of the Israelites fell to him."

Cf. Dabbāġ, II, 591; Nūrī, II, 124, no. 12.

This is a reference to the prosperity which God brought to the Israelites with manna, quails, water from the rock, and a table from heaven. Said of someone who has a good chance to gain prosperity and an easy living.

Cf. the proverb common in Kuwait: "niᶜmat banī ˀIsrāˀīl." "Prosperity of the Israelites."

Cf. Nūrī, II, 124, no. 12.

50. yāxiḏ min ġās ᶜīsa w-yxallī b-ġās mūsa:

"He takes from Jesus' head and puts into Moses' head."

Cf. Dabbāġ, II, 593.

Said of someone who does not plan his actions properly. Rather, he makes connections among other people in his own interest, for example, borrows from one in order to pay the other, or takes from the third in order to give to the fourth. In this way he enmeshes himself in a net of unpleasant things which handicap him and prevent him from being successful.

51. lixalf mitil bōl il-ğamal:

"(Walking) backwards, like the urine of the camel."

Cf. Yahūda, no. 1864. Ḥanafī, II, 63, no. 1899; ᵓAbū Farrāğ, p. 246, no. 1179; Ğuhaymān, III, 91, no. 2189; Landberg, p. 311, no. 29; Maidānī (Beirut), p. 352. Said mockingly about the Jewish people, who supposedly never go forward, but only backward. According to popular belief, the camel's stream of urine is directed to the rear.

52. yhūdī mā kisar sabtā, ᶜumra mā nāč martā.

"A Jew never breaks his Sabbath, nor does he ever have intercourse with his wife on that day."

Although Jewish law does not forbid intercourse on the Sabbath, the Moslem-Iraqi proverb is unaware of it, or perhaps is meant to be ironical.

53. wib-tiwālī ᵓillēl ᵓanṣub ᶜazā hwāy ğīrānī kulhā yhūd maḥḥad bičā wyāy.

"At the end of the night, I mourned and sorrowed; but all my neighbors are Jews, and none of them wept with me."

A rhymed Moslem-Iraqi proverb, criticizing the alleged selfishness of the Jews. Even when the worst misfortune befalls a neighbor—a death in his family—they refuse to help.

54. mā baᶜd il-kufur ᵓillā il-dalāl.

"There is nothing after infidelity but falsehood."

Cf. Ḥanafī, II, 44, no. 1784.

Said of someone who is morally depraved and miserable as well.

55. mākū ᶜugb il-kufur ḏanib:

"After infidelity there is no sin."

Cf. Ḥanafī, II, 53, no. 1838; Ğuhaymān, II, 263, no. 1926.

Said in strong criticism of infidelity.

56. miṯḻ ᵓibn il-rāwandī, yᶜallim il-nās ᶜal-ṣalāt w-huwwa mā yṣallī.

"Like Ibn al-Rawandī, he teaches the people to pray while he himself does not pray."

Cf. Ḥanafī, II, 60, no. 1885.

Said of someone who does not practice what he asks and even forces other people to do, or does not benefit from the knowledge which he possesses or the wisdom which he has acquired, so that he leads other people but misleads himself. Ibn al-Rawandī was a famous heretic.

57. manārt il-čifil:

"The Minaret of Kifl."

Cf. Ḥanafī, II, 103, no. 2126.

Said of stubborn persons who deny known facts. It is said that the Iraqi Jews claimed that the holy tomb called "al-čifil," located in the city of al-Kifl, between Hilla and Kufa, belonged to them. However, the Iraqi Moslems have always claimed that this tomb is a mosque with a minaret that can be clearly seen. A delegation from Constantinople came to examine the matter, but the Jews bribed them, and the delegates "proved" in their report that there was no such minaret.

58. min qāmat ᶜaṣāt mūsā.

"Since the time that Moses' staff stood up."

Cf. Ḥanafī, II, 111, no. 2177.

Said of a matter which has been settled and judgment passed, referring to outdated things. The meaning is that the matter had been settled already in the time of Moses, when his staff stood up and proved the falsehood of the magicians by devouring their snakes.

59. il-nās ᶜala dīn mulūkhum:

"People profess the same religion as their king."

Cf. Ḥanafī, II, 136, no. 2316; Ǧuhaymān, III, 178, no. 2428.

Said about the proneness of people to imitate their leaders and follow in their ways, right or wrong.

Cf. the Hebrew saying: "dīnā de-malkhūta dīnā" (B. Ned. 28), "The law of the state is law (obligatory)."

60. yā mūsā ᵓinta w-rabbak:

"O Moses, you and your God!"

Cf. Ḥanafī, II, 207, no. 2689.

Said of one who is entangled in a difficulty and cannot find someone to help him out of it. The origin is Qurᵓān 5:24.

Cf. the variant " ᵓinta w-rabbak yā mūsā," "You and your God, O Moses!"

Cf. Ḥanafī, I, 67, no. 253.

Said also of someone who hopes to be successful, or ironically of one who is always unsuccessful.

See above, no. 47.

61. ᵓinfix, il-ǧanna mū xān ǧġān.

"Blow! The Garden of Eden is not the Ǧġān-market."

Cf. Ḥanafī, I, 72, no. 274.

The Ǧġān-market was a big market in Baghdad, and was the center for Jewish goldsmiths. The word is corrupted from "čigāla," the family name of the builder of the market, Sinān-pāsha ᵓal čgāla, who was governor of Baghdad and built the market in A.H. 999 (1590/91 C.E.). It was destroyed in the year 1929 and was replaced by a market of cloth merchants.

Said of giving good things to only certain people while withholding them from others.

The source of this proverb is the popular story of a Jewish goldsmith who had a shop in the "xān ǧġan." He was asked by his young servant who was working the bellows, "Master, do the Jews enter the Garden of Eden?" The master replied, "Don't you know, stupid, that the Garden of Eden belongs to the Jews?" After more hard and tiring work, the servant once more asked his master, "What about the Christians?" The master replied, "They will rot in the corridor of the Garden of Eden and back of its door." When the servant then asked a third question, "What about the Moslems?", the goldsmith shouted this proverb at his servant, thus ordering him to concentrate on doing his work and cease asking such questions, because the Garden of Eden is not like "xān ǧġan," a common market which everyone could enter, and which was open to the public.

62. čam slēmān bi-slēmān?:

"How many Solomons after Solomon?"

Cf. Ḥanafī, I, 139, no. 595.

Said of rulers over states and countries. Solomon here refers to King Solomon whose royal power was greater than any other king's.

63. dāyir ᶜakka w-makka wi-gbūr il-yahūd:

"He visited Acre, Mecca, and the tombs of the Jews."

Cf. Ḥanafī, I, 172, no. 772.

Said of someone who is an expert in human affairs and human character; also said of shifty ramblers.

64. ᶜaṣāt mūsā bi-ǧġāmūsa:

"Moses' staff is on the water buffalo."

Cf. Ḥanafī, I, 256, no. 1238.

Said of a thing which accidentally happens to be true.

65. ᶜīsa ᵓintičal ᶜalā mūsā, w-ḏ̣āᶜat il-ǧāmūsa:

"Jesus relied on Moses, meanwhile the water buffalo perished."

Cf. Ḥanafī, I, 271, no. 1320.

Said of worthless people who rely on each other, while important things are lost and serious damage is done.

66. qismat nabbiy ᵓaḷḷa mūsā:

"The division of Moses the prophet of God."

Cf. Ḥanafī, I, 293, no. 1426.

Said of an unfair division. The source of this proverb is the story of two men who came to Moses with a camel and asked him to divide it between them. He asked them whether they wanted a division according to God or according to Moses, and both chose God's division. Moses then severed the camel's neck and gave to the one the head and to the other the body, saying that this was God's division.

Cf. the Hispano-Arabic proverb cited by ᵓIbn ᶜĀṣim of Granada at the beginning of the 9th century A.H. (15th century C.E.): "qismat ḥunāns, al-niṣfu lī w-al-nisfu baynī wa-baynaka, "The division of Ḥunāns: one half for me, and the other half divided between me and you."

67. il-kufr bi-mḥalla ᶜbāda:

"Atheism in its place is a form of divine worship."

Cf. Ḥanafī, I, 302, no. 1473.

Said of an evil deed excused by the need for it.

Cf. the English "The end justifies the means."

68. kulman ᶜalā dīna ᵓaḷḷa yᶜīna:

"God helps everyone who has his own religion."

Cf. Ḥanafī, I, 311, no. 1532.

God helps all who worship Him, regardless of their religious differences.

This seems to be a reply to one who asks a member of another religion to change his faith so that God might help him: God's help is a matter of His wish and mercy, and cannot be secured by such tricks as exchanging one monotheistic religion for another.

Cf. the Egyptian saying "kul ᵓinsān ᶜala dīnū." "Everyone acts according to his own religion."

ᵓ*Ustāḏ*, vol. I, no. 15,360,29.11.1892.

69. yhūdī w-mā yṣallī dyāya xēr minnā:

"A Jew who does not pray—even a hen is better than he."

An Iraqi-Moslem proverb which I heard from an old woman. The language of the proverb shows that it originated in the city of Basra, in southern Iraq—in this dialect ğ becomes y. According to this proverb, a Jew should be a pious man and observe his religion, for which he will be respected by his Arab neighbors. If the Jew fails to do so, even a hen is better than he, because Iraqi people believe that even a hen worships God, when she raises her head while drinking water to thank Him for providing for her needs.

70. ᶜugb il-sabit laḥḥad yiğī:

"After Saturday comes Sunday."

Used by Iraqi Moslems as a threat against Christians, meaning that after the Moslems finish with the Jews, they will take care of the Christians. And indeed this was the procedure in Iraq: after the Jews were hounded by the Moslems during the 1950's and forced to leave Iraq, came the turn of the Christians, who likewise tried to flee Iraq because of such persecution. It should be noted that some of these emigrant Christians settled in the United States; see *Detroit News* of 12/5/1976, where in a letter to the editor Riyāḏ Ğirğis says: "The situation of the Christian citizens in Iraq is similar to that of the Jews who lived in Iraq till the '50's, namely the Christians are secondary citizens."

Cf. the Egyptian proverb "man qadam (a)l-sabt ylāqī a(l)-ḥadd ᵓuddamu," "Whoever crosses Saturday will see Sunday in front of him."

Cf. ᶜAbd al-Salām, p. 20.

71. ᶜabālak nāsi.

"You think of him as a Nasī (prince)."

Another version is "sāg lī rayyis māl yhūd," "He acts like the chief of the Jews."

Said by the Jews of themselves, describing a person who boasts much and is very proud of himself, although he actually is nothing special. The Nasi in Iraq was the chief of the local Jewish notables and lay leaders. The beginning of this dignitary's position is shrouded in darkness. We find records and names of Nesiim in Baghdad during the Gaonic period, and during the Ottoman and British periods the Nasi was selected from among the wealthy members of the community, and acted as chief banker or a kind of finance minister to the governor of Baghdad. See Sassoon, *History*, pp. 122 ff.; Ganīma, *Nuzha*, p. 173; Ben Yaᶜḳōv, *Yehūdē Babēl*, p. 109.

72. ᵓağallak ᵓaḻḻāh yahūdī:

"May God give you greatness, O Jew!"

Used by the Iraqi Moslems about thirty years ago whenever a Jew passed through public places which were crowded with Moslems. The person who knew that the man approaching was a Jew would warn his friend by using this saying, particularly in coffee houses which were frequented by Moslems.

However, since the verb ǧll may also have the opposite meaning "to humiliate," the proverb may also be rendered "May God humiliate you, O Jew!"

It should be mentioned here that Jewish children in Moslem elementary schools were not permitted to study the Qurʾān, and were ordered by the teacher to leave the classroom until the Qurʾān session was finished.

73. tikram yhūdī:

"In your honor, O Jew!"

Used about thirty years ago in Iraq whenever a Moslem introduced a Jewish friend to another Moslem, as an apology for doing so. Afterwards used whenever a Jew was presented to a Moslem company.

74. il-gōy min qāl yiḥǧim lak ḥiḍḍiġ lū qiṭin:

"When the Moslem tells you he would cup you, prepare cotton for him."

Used by Jews, and meaning that when a Moslem decides to do something, he is determined to do it, and Jews should prepare themselves for this action, whatever the result of it may be. In order to illustrate this proverb it is necessary to cite a story connected with another idiom, "ḥag ḍāyiᶜ," "Lost justice."

Each Saturday two very good friends, a Moslem and a Jew, would go for a walk and would return together. One Saturday the Moslem asked the Jew to go for their usual walk. When they arrived at a desolate place, the Moslem suddenly turned to his friend, saying, "A thought has come to my mind." When the Jew asked, "What is it, my dear friend?", the Moslem replied, "I have decided to kill you!" The Jew, shocked, tried to elicit the reason for this decision, but the Moslem cut him short and forthwith killed the Jew. Before the Jew was slain, however, he looked for a witness to his slaying, but finding none, asked a bird which he espied in the sky to be his witness. The Jew's wife waited anxiously for her husband's return, and when Saturday night arrived and her husband had not showed up, she went to inquire of his friend the Moslem. The latter pretended that he had returned with her husband in the afternoon as usual and did not know what had happened to him. The worst of the matter was that at the time of her husband's disappearance, the Jew's wife was three months pregnant. When she gave birth to a son, not knowing what to call him, she named him "Justice lost." The boy grew up, and his playmates wondered at his name. One day, while he was playing, the Caliph of Iraq, disguised as a peasant, walked by and was surprised to hear the name "Justice lost." He asked to see the boy, and inquired about the reason for his name. Since the boy did not know the answer, he brought the Caliph to his mother, who told the disguised Caliph all that had happened. The Caliph kept the matter in his mind and went back to his palace. In the meantime, the Moslem returned out of curiosity to the place where he had killed the Jew. To his surprise, he saw there a big fig tree whose fruit was red. The season being winter, he thought it would be a good idea to bring this unusual fruit to the Caliph, and the Caliph received his gift graciously and rewarded him richly. After the man left, the Caliph tried to eat the figs, but to his vast surprise, whenever he opened a fig, blood oozed out of it. The Caliph commanded that the person who had brought the figs be called back, and in the Caliph's presence the Moslem did not deny that he had slain the Jew. The Caliph thereupon summoned the Jew's widow to confront the killer. To her surprise, she realized that the guilty one was her husband's best friend. The Caliph thereupon gave her choice of either slaying the killer or accepting monetary compensation. She chose slaying the killer, and thus justice was finally served.

75. māy il-dōm:

"Weekday's water."

Said by one Jew to another to warn him to keep quiet if a Moslem should join the company. Although in the Judaeo-Iraqi dialect *dom* means weekday, the Jew is referring to the Hebrew word *dom*, "Be quiet!"

76. sabit b-rugbat yhūd:

"Sabbath is in the neck of the Jews."

Cf. Dulayshī, II, 103, no. 980.

Iraqi Jews rested on Saturday and refrained from all labor, e. g., they did not cook or even light the fire, and ate food kept on the fire overnight since Friday evening.

Jews had kept the Sabbath since the giving of the Scriptures to Moses, and according to Jewish tradition, God created the world from Sunday through Friday, and on the seventh day He rested (Gen. 2:1–2).

Said of people forced to do things which they cannot avoid doing, as is the case of the Sabbath which is tied to the neck of Jews.

Also said of one who should fulfill some responsibilities from which he cannot run away, or someone who is umemployed for a long time.

This proverb was used by the famous Iraqi poet Maʿrūf al-Ruṣāfī when he said "fanaḥnu ʾunāsun lam nazal fī baṭālatin/kaʾannā yahūdun kullu ayyāminā sabtu," "We are people who, still unemployed, are as Jews—all our days are Saturdays."

77. il-sabit ᶜawwād:

"Sabbath is repeated."

Cf. Dulayshī, II, 104, no. 981.

The proverb means that everything which one does on one Saturday will be done again the following Saturday, whether it is a good or bad thing. Said to forbid bad deeds and to encourage good deeds on Saturday.

78. ᶜalā hāmān yā furᶜūn?:

"Do you put one over on Haman, O Pharaoh?"

Cf. Dulayshī, II, 266, no. 1371; Ǧuhaymān, II, 149, no. 1334.

Refers to the Pharaoh who gathered magicians in order to defeat Moses, but, they came to believe in the God of Moses and Aaron.

According to Islamic tradition, Haman was the minister and adviser of Pharaoh. The proverb asks: "O Pharaoh, do you want to hide your secrets from Haman? Do you want to pretend to knowledge and power without him? He is the one who knows all your secrets and has taught you all the things which you did not know."

Said of one who pretends to be more than he is and to have knowledge and power, in front of one who knows him very well and is aware of all his weaknesses.

Cf. Quʾrān 40:36–37: "And Pharaoh said: O Haman! Build a tower for me that haply I may search the roads, the roads of the heavens, and may look upon the God of Moses, though verily I think him a liar."

79. ṣabur ʾayyūb ᶜalā balwāh:

"The endurance of Job for his calamity."

Cf. Dulayshī, II, 170, no. 1150; Nūrī, I, 185, no. 2; Ǧuhaymān, III, 254, no. 2629.

Refers to the prophet Job who is mentioned in the Old Testament.

Said of someone who endures his calamities like Job whom God tested him by afflicting him with misfortunes and calamities. Also said of someone who suffers a great deal of anxiety and worry.

80. ʾib-baṭin kāfir walā ḥadir ḥāfir:

"In the stomach of the infidel and not under the animal's hoof."

Cf. Dulayshī, I, 20, no. 15; Ḥanafī, I, 91, no. 354; Nūrī, I, 72, no. 12.

The proverb advises, if food is already cooked, give it even to an infidel, because he is a human being like you, and do not throw it down to be trodden by the hooves of animals.

Largely said to encourage feeding the hungry and to prohibit throwing food out.

81. ğannat il-kāfir bil-dinyā:

"The Garden of Eden of the infidel is in this world."

Cf. Dulayshī, I, 229, no. 487; Ğuhaymān, II, 274, no. 1679.

The proverb means that the infidel does not believe in the existence of an Everlasting Abode, nor in the coming of the Day of Reckoning. He believes, rather, that men should pursue the comfort and happiness of this world. This and nothing else represents the Garden of Eden to the infidel. Therefore God might let him enjoy himself in this world, because God will not grant him the comfort of the Everlasting Abode.

Said of one overly proud of transitory luxuries enjoyed in this world, who denies the Everlasting Abode and its eternal happiness.

82. yā sabtī yā mā ksiġtōk, qallū yā mā hġamtu bētak w-inta mā tiᶜġif:

"O my Sabbath, how many times have I desecrated you—he told him—how many times have I destroyed your home, and you even did not know of it!"

Cf. *Qiṣṣa*, p. 9.

Said by Iraqi Jews of their fellow Jews who do not keep the Sabbath, to tell them that God in heaven knows everything, and they cannot cheat Him; they do not keep the laws of the Sabbat, and God knows it. He will punish them unbeknownst to them.

83. li-yhūdī a(l)-tāli yġīnū (a)l-ᶜaqil ᶜiqib mā yinnahib yshawwik (i)l-ḥāyit:

"To the Jew wisdom comes at the end—after he is robbed, he puts brambles on the wall."

Cf. *Qiṣṣa*, p. 10; Sassoon, 195, no. 2.

Said by Iraqi Jews of themselves, to describe the way in which a Jew protects his property against robbers too late.

84. ysabbit:

"He keeps the Sabbath."

Cf. Dabbāġ, II, p. 491.

Refers to a person who behaves like a Jew on the Sabbath, i. e., does not work, carry money, cook, light a fire, or even smoke a cigarette. Used by Moslems to refer especially to lazy people. It reminds us of the Hebrew saying popular among Iraqi Jews; "shabbāth wa-yinafāsh," "It is the Sabbath, and he rests."

Bibliography

BIBLIOGRAPHY

ᶜAbbūd: Saᶜīd ᶜAbbūd ᵓAshqar, *Kitāb* al-Ṭurfa al-bāhiğa fī al-ᵓamthāl wal-ḥikam al-ᶜArabiyya al-dāriğa, Jerusalem, 1933.

ᵓAbū Farrāğ: Farağ al-sayyid Farağ, ᵓAbū Farrāğ, *Qālū fī al-ᵓamthāl*, Alexandria, 1970.

ᵓAhwānī: ᶜAbd al-ᶜAzīz al-ᵓAhwānī, " ᵓAmthāl al-ᶜāmma fī al-ᵓandalus," in: *ᵓIlā Tāha Ḥussayn* fī ᶜīd mīlādihi al-sabᶜīn, ed. ᶜAbd al-Raḥmān Badawī, Cairo, 1962, pp. 235–367.

ᵓAmīn: ᵓAḥmad ᵓAmin, *Qāmūs al-ᶜādāt wal-taqālīd wal-taᶜābīr al-Miṣriyyah*, Cairo, 1953.

Aquilina: *A Comparative Dictionary of Maltese Proverbs: compiled by Joseph Aquilina*, Malta, 1972.

Bāğūrī: ᵓIbrāhīm Bāğūrī, *ᵓAmthāl al-mutakalllimīn min ᶜawāmm al-Miṣriyyīn*, Cairo, (n.d.).

Baghdādiyyāt: ᶜAzīz Ğāsim al-Ḥağğiyya, *Baghdādiyyāt*, Baghdad, 1973, 3 vols.

Ben ᶜAmī: Y. Ben-ᶜAmī, "; ᵓElef we-ᵓeḥād piṯgamīm yehudiyyīm min Marōḳo," in: Folklore Research Center Publications, I, Jerusalem, 1970, pp. 35–148.

Ben Cheneb: M. Ben-Cheneb, *Proverbes arabes de lᵓAlgerie et du Maghreb*, Paris, 1905–07.

Ben-Yaᶜḳōv: Abraham Ben-Yaᶜḳōv, *Tōldōt yehūdē Bābēl*, Jerusalem, 1966.

Bohn: Henry G. Bohn, *A Polyglot of Foreign Proverbs, German, Dutch, etc. . . . with English Translation and General Index*, London, 1968.

Burton: R. F. Burton: "Proverbia communia Syriaca," *JRAS*, 5 (1870), pp. 338–366.

Bystron: Jan Bystron, *Przyslowia polskie*, Krakow, 1933.

Champion: *Racial Proverbs, a Selection ot the World's Proverbs Arranged Linguistically by Selwyn Gurney Champion, M. D.* London, 1938.

Dabbāġ: ᶜAbd al-Khāliq al-Dabbāġ al-Hadalī, *Muᶜğam ᵓamthāl al-Mawṣil al-ᶜAmmiyyah*, Mosul, 1956.

Dulayshī: ᶜAbd al-Laṭīf al-Dulayshī, *al-ᵓAmthāl al-shaᶜbiyya fī al-Baṣrah*, Baghdad, 1968–72, 2 vols.

Field: Claud Field, *A Dictionary of Oriental Quotations (Arabic and Persian)*, London, 1911.

Flamand: P. Flammand, *Quelques manifestations de l'esprit populaire des juiveries du Sud-Marocain*, Casablanca, 1960.

Freytag: Georg Freytag, *Arabum proverbia*, Bonn, 1838–43, 3 vols.

Freyḥa: ᵓAnīs Freyḥa, *al-ᵓAmthāl al-ᶜāmmiyyah al-Lubnāniyyah ᶜan rās al-matan*, Beirut, 1953.

Ǧamhara: ᶜAbd al-Raḥmān al-Takrītī, *Ǧamharat al-ᵓamthāl al-Baghdādiyya*, I, Baghdad, 1971.
Ġanīma: Yusuf Ġanīma, *Nuzhat al-mushtāq fī tārīkh yahūd al-ᶜIrāq*, Baghdad, 1924.
Ǧuhaymān: ᶜAbd al-Karīm al-Ǧuhaymān, *al-ᵓAmthal al-shaᶜbiyyah fī qalb Ǧazīrat al-ᶜArab*, Beirut, 1383 (A.H.), 1970, 3 vols.
Ḥadāᵓiq: Fāᵓiqah Ḥusayn Rāghib, *Ḥadāᵓiq al-ᵓamthāl al-ᶜāmmiyyah*, Cairo, 1943, 2 vols.
Ḥanafī: Ǧalāl al-Ḥanafī, *al-ᵓAmthāl al-Baghdādiyyah*, Baghdad, 1962–64, 2 vols.
Jewett: J. R. Jewett, "Arabic proverbs and proverbial phrases, "*JAOS*, 15 (1893), pp. 28–120.
Kirmilī: Anistās M. al-kirmilī, *al-ᵓAmthāl al-ᶜIrāqiyyah* (ms.).
Landberg: Carlo Landberg, *Proverbes et dictons de la province de Syrie*, Paris, 1883.
Maydānī: ᵓAbū al-Faḍl ᵓAḥmad ᵓibn Muḥammad al-Nisābūrī al-Maydānī, *Maǧmaᶜ al-ᵓamthāl*, Cairo, 1310 (A.H.), Beirut, 1961.
Mustaṭraf: Muḥammad ᵓibn Aḥmad al-Abshīhī, *al-Mustaṭraf fī kull fann mustaḍraṭ*, Cairo (n.d.).
Nūrī: ᶜAbd ᵓAḷḷah al-Nūrī, *al-ᵓAmthāl al-dāriǧah fī al-Kuwayt*, Beirut, 1965.
Qiṣṣa: *Qiṣṣat ᵓahl al-mathal*, Baghdad (n.d.).
ᶜAbd al-Salām: Ḥasan ᶜAbd al-Salām, *al-Mathal al-sāᵓir wa sulūk al-ᵓinsān*, Cairo, 1970.
Sassoon: D. S. Sassoon, *A History of the Jews in Baghdad*, Letchworth, 1949.
Shaᶜlān: ᵓIbrāhīm Shaᶜlān, *al-Shaᶜb al-Miṣrī fī ᵓamthālihi al-ᶜāmmiyyah*, Cairo, 1972.
Shuqayr: Naᶜūm, Shuqayr, *ᵓAmthāl al-ᶜAwāmm fī Miṣr wa al-Sūdān wa al-Shām*, Cairo, 1894.
Takrītī: ᶜAbd al-Raḥmān al-Takrītī, *al-ᵓAmthāl al-Baghdādiyya al-muqārana*, Baghdad, 1966–69, 4 vols.
Taṭwān: ᶜAbd al-Munᶜim sayyid ᶜAbd al-ᶜAlī, *Lahǧat shamāl al-Maghrib, Taṭwān, wa mā ḥawlahā*, Cairo, 1968.
Taymūr: ᵓAḥmad Taymūr, *al-ᵓAmthāl al-ᶜāmmiyyah*, Cairo, 1970.
ᵓUstād̲: *al-ᵓUstād̲, ǧarīda ᶜilmiyya tahd̲ibiyya fukāhiyya; al-ᵓUstād̲, a Literary Periodical Edited Once a Week by ᶜAbd Aḷḷah al-Nadīm al-ᵓIdrīsī*, Cairo, 1892 (established 1310 A.H.).
Westermarck: E. Westermarck, *Wit and Wisdom in Morocco*, London, 1930.
Yahūda: Y. B. Yahūda, *Mishlē ᶜArāb*, Jerusalem, 1932, 2 vols.
Zamakhsharī: ᵓAbu al-Qāsim Ǧār ᵓAḷḷah Maḥmūd ᵓibn ᶜUmar al-Zamakhsharī, *al-Mustaqṣā min ᵓamthāl al-ᶜArab*, I, Haydarabad, 1962.
Zayyāt: Muḥammad al-Zayyāt, *ᵓAᶜǧab mā fī nawādir al-zamān*, Cairo (n.d.).

The Contribution of German Jews to Law and Jurisprudence

A Summary Survey

By GUIDO KISCH
University of Basel, Switzerland

LIKE OTHER NATIONS the Jews always had their own law and their own jurisprudence. Throughout their history law and religion were intimately bound together. The study of the most important law sources, the Bible, Talmud, and rabbinical decisions, was earnestly fostered within the sphere of Jewish life. That is why Jewish law survived the downfall of the Jewish state. While the impact of the Decalogue on mankind cannot be overestimated and the Scriptures in general served as the basis of the law of the Church, post-biblical Jewish law remained to the greatest extent an internal feature of the life and history of the Jewish people.

On the other hand, the Jews came into superficial contact with the legal systems of other nations in whose midst they had to live and to whose political rule they were subordinated as passive subjects. These systems of law first assumed practical significance for them as objects of study when, in the nineteenth century, the State granting them emancipation placed under its control almost every field of activity of these its new citizens. From that time on, Jewish law lost its validity among a considerable number of emancipated Jews. It remained in practice solely among orthodox Jews who faithfully adhered to the way of life and to the law of their forbears, while among the greater part of Jewish citizens ancient Jewish law ceased to be practiced with their complete acceptance into and their accommodation to European civilization. Therefore, it was quite natural that henceforth the Jews should occupy and acquaint themselves with the laws of the states in which they were now living as recognized citizens of equal or almost equal rights. Consequently, the relationship of the Jews to general legal science became a problem worthy of consideration.

They participated early in the study of secular law and in the administration of justice in the various states of their residence. Their role in the legal profession became particularly great in Central Europe, where they lived in large numbers and where they were first emancipated. As early as the eighteenth century they were officially admitted to the study of law in Austrian universities. Raphael Joel of Wolin, Bohemia, was the first Jew to receive the degree of Doctor of Law in an Austrian university (Prague) in

1790.[1] He was also the first Jew to be admitted to the bar in Austria. The various states of which the German Reich was composed, followed only later and slowly.[2] As late as the eighteen-forties Levin Goldschmidt, who became a famous jurist, professor of law at the university of Berlin, member of the Supreme Court of the German Reich, was still barred from the study of law for which he was fervently longing, and had to begin with the study of medicine.[3] He was admitted to the lawschool only when in 1848 the situation changed and more favorable conditions emerged also for the Jews.

Restrictions against their participation in all fields of law were removed in Central Europe as late as the middle and during the second half of the nineteenth century. From that time on, Jews were represented in all juridical professions.[4] They played an active and even important part as practicing lawyers; many of them achieved a national or international reputation.

Their participation in and contribution to legal science, theory and literature—to which alone attention is to be directed in the following pages—was also very considerable. This will be proved by a few outstanding examples. Within the limits of a contribution to a jubilee and memorial volume an exhaustive study of the problem is obviously not possible. A comprehensive scholarly treatment of this interesting phenomenon in both general legal and Jewish history is a desideratum.[5]

Of the early Jewish professors who taught law in German universities first to be mentioned is Eduard Gans (1797–1839), the learned Hegelian and one of the leading adversaries of Friedrich Carl von Savigny,[6] the head

[1] Guido Kisch, *Die Prager Universität und die Juden 1348–1848* (Mährisch-Ostrau, 1935) (2nd. ed. Amsterdam, 1970), pp. 55–60, 108, n. 366, 177–199.

[2] Consult: Guido Kisch, "Universitätsgeschichte und jüdische Familienforschung," in *Jüdische Familienforschung*, X (1934), 566–574, 598–602 (also separate edition); G. Kisch, *Die Universitäten und die Juden* (Philosophie und Geschichte, vol. 77), (Tübingen, 1961); Monika Richarz, *Der Eintritt der Juden in die akademischen Berufe 1678–1848* (Tübingen, 1974), with full bibliography.

[3] Levin Goldschmidt, *Ein Lebensbild in Briefen* (Berlin, 1898), pp. 8, 10, letters to his parents of October 9 and November 17, 1847. On the other hand, Eduard Gans (see *infra*, note 6) was admitted to the study of law in Göttingen in 1817; in 1818 he changed to Heidelberg where he achieved the doctor's degree in 1819; see Hanns Günther Reissner, *Eduard Gans: Ein Leben im Vormärz* (Tübingen, 1965), pp. 41, 44 f.

[4] Consult: Monika Richarz, *op. cit.*, above n. 2; Robert M. W. Kempner, "Jüdische Juristen in Deutschland," in *Recht und Politik, Vierteljahrshefte für Rechts- und Verwaltungspolitik*, VII (1971), 112–118, 173–174, the most recent statistical survey arranged according to the various juridical professions; Hugo Sinzheimer, *Jüdische Klassiker der deutschen Rechtswissenschaft* (Amsterdam, 1938; 2nd. ed. Frankfurt a. M., 1953, with a *Geleitwort* by Franz Böhm); reviews by G. Kisch in *Social Research*, V (New York, 1938), 496–499, and by Helen Silving in *The American Journal of Comparative Law*, IV (1955), 292–297; Horst Göppinger, *Der Nationalsozialismus und die jüdischen Juristen: Die Verfolgung der Juristen jüdischer Abstammung durch den Nationalsozialismus* (Villingen, 1963); E. G. Lowenthal, *Bewährung im Untergang*, 2nd. ed. (Stuttgart, 1966); Ernest Hamburger, *Juden im öffentlichen Leben*

of the Historical School of Law. His main work was *Das Erbrecht in weltgeschichtlicher Entwicklung* (The Law of Inheritance in World-Historical Development, 4 vols., Berlin and Tübingen 1824–1835, unfinished); it was only recently reprinted.

Friedrich Julius Stahl (1802–1861; original name: Jolson)[7]—another Hegelian, the intellectual founder of the Christian conservative political doctrine in Prussia, prominent also in Lutheran ecclesiastical affairs—opposed, as elimination of experience, the abstract philosophy of the unhistorical rationalism of natural law of the eighteenth century, which claimed to be the true, unchangeable law. The foundation of his juristic and political thought was laid in his two-volume work, *Die Philosophie des Rechts nach geschichtlicher Ansicht* (The Philosophy of Law Based on History; Heidelberg, 1837; 4 editions until 1870, reprinted Tübingen, 1926). In the second volume, entitled *Rechts- und Staatslehre auf der Grundlage christlicher Weltanschauung*, he elevated theology to the central point of philosophy. Stahl became the undisputed leader of the Conservative Party in Prussia in the period of reaction after 1848. His *Die Kirchenverfassung nach Lehre und Recht der Protestanten* (The Constitution of the Church According to Protestant Doctrine and Law, Erlangen, 1840) had a second edition in 1862.

In contrast to the politically active and polemically engaged Stahl, Wilhelm Eduard Wilda (1800–1856, originally Seligmann)[8] was quietly devoted to research in the history of law. He published the basic work on the history of Germanic criminal law (*Das Strafrecht der Germanen*, Halle,

Deutschlands (Tübingen, 1968). Of older general works: Roderich Stintzing and Ernst Landsberg, *Geschichte der deutschen Rechtswissenschaft*, 6 vols. (München and Leipzig, 1880–1910).—When no special biographical literature is given on the individual personalities to be mentioned hereafter, one has to turn to the well-known general and Jewish encyclopedias.

[5] Some contributions are found in the aforementioned works. See furthermore: Guido Kisch, *Judentaufen* (Berlin, 1973); Ernst J. Cohn, "Three Jewish Lawyers of Germany," in *Year Book of the Leo Baeck Institute*, XVII (London, 1972), 155–178; E. J. Cohn, "Der Fall Opet," in *Festschrift für Wilhelm Wengler zum 65. Geburtstag* (Berlin, 1973), 211–234.

[6] H. G. Reissner's (quoted *supra*, note 3) most recent biography of Gans deals mainly with Gans as philosopher, politician, and co-founder of the "Verein für Cultur und Wissenschaft der Juden"; but unfortunately it does not do justice to Gans as a jurist and to his achievements in the science of law; *cf.* Landsberg, *Geschichte der deutschen Rechtswissenschaft*, III 2, pp. 354–369; Hermann Lübbe, "Eduard Gans," in *Neue Deutsche Biographie*, VI (1964), p. 63; Horst Schröder, "Zum Gedenken an Eduard Gans," in *Wissenschaftliche Zeitschrift der Humboldt-Universität zu Berlin, Gesellschafts- und sprachwissenschaftliche Reihe*, XIII (1964), 515–522 (written from the point of view of Marxism); G. Kisch in *Zeitschrift der Savigny-Stiftung für Rechtsgeschichte* (Roman. Abt.), LXXVII (1960), 401 (quoted hereafter as ZRG.(R); (G) = Germ. Abt.).

[7] Gerhard Masur, *Friedrich Julius Stahl: Geschichte seines Lebens*, I (Berlin, 1930).

[8] G. Kisch, "Wilhelm Eduard Wilda," in *Mitteldeutsche Lebensbilder*, V (Magdeburg, 1930), 339–352.

1842), which is still not obsolete. Another of his important contributions to the history of German law is *Das Gildenwesen im Mittelalter* (The Guilds in the Middle Ages, Halle, 1831).

It cannot be passed over silently that these three scholars had embraced the Christian religion. Although in the second half of the nineteenth century conversion, officially or unofficially, still was made a prerequisite to the admission to the academic career, we find several personalities of moral strength who withstood that enticement. A considerable number of Jewish jurists achieved prominence as teachers and scholars in German universities without conversion.

The above mentioned Levin Goldschmidt (1829–1897)[9] was internationally recognized as the founder of and greatest authority on the modern science of commercial law during the nineteenth century in Germany and perhaps in the world. In 1858 he founded the still flourishing *Zeitschrift für das gesamte Handelsrecht.*

Emil Albert Friedberg (1837–1910, baptized)[10] acquired a reputation as a leading scholar in canon law. He published the modern standard edition of the Canon Law Code, *Corpus juris canonici* (2 volumes, Leipzig 1879–1881), in which he provided a critical commentary on the texts of the laws in force until now in the Catholic Church. Of his works the *Lehrbuch des katholischen und evangelischen Kirchenrechts* (Leipzig, 1879, numerous editions since) was translated into several languages.

Paul Laband (1838–1918, baptized),[11] the most representative teacher of public law in imperial Germany, conceived public law as a pure legal discipline, setting aside political and sociological factors. By following this course he became the true founder of the so-called "conceptual jurisprudence" (*Begriffsjurisprudenz*) in public law. His main work, *Das Staatsrecht des Deutschen Reiches* (Tübingen, 1876–1882, originally 3, later 4 volumes) went, up to 1919, into seven editions.

Georg Jellinek (1851–1911, baptized),[12] son of the famous Viennese rabbi and preacher, was the author of several classical works on political theory, among them: *System der subjectiven öffentlichen Rechte* (System of Subjective Public Law, Freiburg, 1892), *Die Erklärung der Menschen- und Bürgerrechte* (The Declaration of the Rights of Man and the Citizen, Leipzig, 1895), and *Allgemeine Staatslehre* (The General Theory of the State, Berlin,

[9] Levin Goldschmidt, *Ein Lebensbild in Briefen* (Berlin, 1898); L. Goldschmidt, *Vermischte Schriften* (2 vols., Berlin, 1901).

[10] Emil Sehling, in *Deutsche Zeitschrift für Kirchenrecht*, XX (1910), I–VIII.

[11] Paul Laband, *Lebenserinnerungen.* Als Handschrift gedruckt. Ed. by Wilhelm Bruck (Berlin, 1918); Walter Wilhelm, *Zur juristischen Methodenlehre im 19. Jahrhundert: Die Herkunft der Methode Paul Labands.* (Frankfurter wissenschaftliche Beiträge, vol. 14, Frankfurt, 1958).

[12] Georg Jellinek, *Ausgewählte Schriften und Reden*, ed. by Walter Jellinek, 2 vols. (Berlin, 1911).

1900). In these works, he combined the sociology of the state with the science of public law. All these voluminous works went through several editions, were translated into many languages, and also strongly influenced foreign scholarship.

Otto Lenel's (1849–1935, baptized)[13] masterly reconstruction of the *Edictum perpetuum* (Leipzig, 1883) and the edition of the *Palingenesia juris civilis* (2 vols., Leipzig, 1889) made the entire bulk of the ancient Roman laws and legal literature easily accessible to scholars.

This line of outstanding professors of law at German universities and authors of epochmaking works in juridical literature, Jews or of Jewish origin, could be continued *in extenso*. This, however, would go beyond the limits set to the present essay. Hence, only a few remarkable names with a brief description of their achievements in the history of German law and jurisprudence should still be mentioned. However, the omission of some names of significance should not be interpreted as a lower valuation of or even discrimination against these personalities.[14]

Ernst Landsberg (1860–1927),[15] was author of the voluminous and authoritative History of German Jurisprudence (*Geschichte der deutschen Rechtswissenschaft im 18. und 19. Jahrhundert*, 4 vols., Munich and Berlin, 1898–1910). Felix Liebermann (1851–1925),[16] a brother of the famous painter, prepared the classical edition of Anglo-Saxon laws (*Die Gesetze der Angelsachsen*, 3 vols., Halle a.S., 1903–1916). Victor Ehrenberg (1851–1929, baptized),[17] was the pioneer "father of German insurance law" and editor of the *Handbuch des gesamten Handelsrechts* (13 vols., Leipzig, 1913–1922). Max Conrat (Cohn, 1848–1911)[18] and Hermann U. Kantorowicz (1877–1940, baptized),[19] were both masters in the history of Roman law of the

[13] Otto Lenel, "Selbstbiographie," in Hans Planitz (ed.), *Die Rechtswissenschaft der Gegenwart in Selbstdarstellungen*, I (Leipzig, 1924), pp. 133–152.

[14] Jewish scholars in law of other German-speaking countries, such as of Austria for example, were, in principle, excluded from this study. On Austrian Jewish jurists see Franz Kobler, "The Contribution of Austrian Jews to Jurisprudence," in Josef Fraenkel (ed.), *The Jews of Austria* (London, 1967), pp. 25–40.

[15] Fritz Schulz, "Ernst Landsberg," in ZRG (R), 48 (1928), pp. 1 ff.; *Gedächtnisschrift für Professor Dr. Ernst Landsberg* (Bonn, 1953).

[16] Ernst Heymann, "Felix Liebermann," in ZRG.(G), 46 (1926), pp. XXIII–XXXIX.

[17] Victor Ehrenberg, "Selbstbiographie," in Planitz, *op. cit.*, pp. 59–85; G. Kisch, *Judentaufen* (Berlin, 1973), pp. 33–35.

[18] Hermann U. Kantorowicz, "Max Conrat (Cohn) und die mediävistische Forschung," in ZRG.(R), 33 (1912), pp. 417–483. His main work: *Geschichte der Quellen und Literatur des römischen Rechts im früheren Mittelalter* (Leipzig, 1891).

[19] Adolf Berger, "Hermann Ulrich Kantorowicz," in ZRG. (R), 68 (1951), pp. 624–633. His main works: *Albertus Gandinus*, 2 vols. (Berlin, 1907, 1926); Gnaeus Flavius [pseud.], *Der Kampf um die Rechtswissenschaft* (Heidelberg, 1906); *Thomas Diplovatatius: De claris iuris consultis* (Berlin, 1919).

Middle Ages. Max Pappenheim (1860–1934),[20] was author of the *Handbuch des Seerechts* (2 vols., Leipzig, 1906, 1918), and authority on German maritime law. Otto Opet (1866–1941),[21] published a very large work entitled *Deutsches Theaterrecht* (Berlin, 1887), which dealt exhaustively with all the many legal topics that may arise in what is called today show business. It remained authoritative for nearly half a century.

Hermann Staub's (1856–1904) Commentary to the German Code of Commercial Law (1891, 11th ed. 1921) set the methodological pattern for all modern German and Austrian law commentaries. Friedrich Stein (1859–1923, originally Goldstein, baptized) is to be credited with a similar achievement in the field of civil procedure.

The two leading legal periodicals that appeared in Germany prior to 1933 were edited by Jews: the semi-weekly, *Deutsche Juristenzeitung*, by Otto Liebmann (1865–1942); and the widely disseminated weekly, *Juristische Wochenschrift*, the journal for practicing attorneys, by Julius Magnus (1867–1944).

This list of distinguished Jewish jurists, whose works were influential on legal theory and practice in Germany prior to 1933 and are still in use today in from time to time revised editions, is by far not complete. Merely a few more names of distinction should be mentioned (arranged alphabetically), whose bearers were compelled to emigrate by the Nazi government, but achieved eminence even in foreign law in England and the United States of America: Eberhard Bruck, Max Gruenhut, Max Hachenburg, Ernst Levy, Karl Loewenstein, Albrecht Mendelssohn-Bartholdy, Arthur Nussbaum, Fritz Pringsheim, Ernst Rabel, Max Rheinstein, Fritz Schulz, Hans Julius Wolff, Martin Wolff.

The question has been raised whether inherited talent, a "specifically Jewish mentality" ("*jüdischer Geist*"), has led to the comparatively vigorous participation of Jews in law and jurisprudence. The attitude of antisemites toward Jewish lawyers was (and still is) based on this unproven assertion. It was particularly strong in the Nazi-Reich. Hugo Sinzheimer, a noted

[20] Karl August Eckhardt, "Max Pappenheim," in ZRG.(G), 55 (1935), pp. XIII–XXIV; Ernst J. Cohn, "Three Jewish Lawyers of Germany," in *Leo Baeck Year Book*, XVII (London, 1972), pp. 163–170.

[21] Ernst J. Cohn, *op. cit.*, pp. 170–186; E. J. Cohn, "Der Fall Opet," in *Festschrift für Wilhelm Wengler zum 65. Geburtstag* (Berlin, 1973), pp. 211–234.

[22] See *supra*, note 4, particularly the reviews quoted there.

[23] So Kobler, *op. cit.* (*supra*, note 14), p. 25. In the same vein Karl Fees, "Die Juden in der Jurisprudenz," in *Menorah*, IX (Vienna-Berlin, 1931), pp. 9 f.: "So ist die jüdische Intelligenz, durch Generationen hindurch mit dem Talmud und den Regeln der Auslegungskunst als dem höchsten geistigen Gute vertraut und in den Künsten dieser Dialektik in einer Art und Weise geschult, welche von keinem anderen Volke erreicht wird. In der Dialektik, der Kunst der Gesetzesauslegung in Wort und Schrift ist eine der hervorragendsten Eigenschaften der jüdischen Juristen zu sehen. Hier liegt auch ein Grund dafür, dass die jüdischen Juristen sich der Tätigkeit in ihrer überwiegenden Mehrheit

German-Jewish jurist, in 1938 published a book, *Jüdische Klassiker der deutschen Rechtswissenschaft* (Jewish Classics of German Jurisprudence), to disprove that hypothesis.[22] He offered twelve carefully selected and painstakingly elaborated biographies of outstanding German-Jewish lawyers as proof that the work of these men was "neither specific nor Jewish," but rather was produced solely by a truly scientific spirit.

However, even among Jewish scholars the opinion has been advanced that—although hardly any links between Jewish and Western legal thought can be proven—"the Jews' strong sense of justice, deeply rooted in Judaism, their training in the interpretation of [Jewish] law [i. e. Bible, Talmud, postbiblical rabbinic law] gave a powerful impulse to the desire to play an active part in the administration of justice as well as in all branches of jurisprudence."[23] Similarly a reputed English-Jewish professor of law, Arthur L. Goodhart, maintains: "The Jewish people have always been known as The People of The Law. The Old Testament is, as everyone knows, a repository of law, containing both legislative provisions and legal precedents. . . . Even more strictly legal is the Talmud, that vast storehouse of Jewish learning. . . . It is not surprising therefore that the Jews have made important contributions to legal thought in most of the countries of the modern world. . . . I do not think it is improper to point out how great a contribution they have made to one of the major forces of civilization—the English Common Law."[24]

With regard to this doctrine attention may be called to the following facts.

All the jurists enumerated above were eminent scholars in their special fields. Only some of them were steadfast in refusing to sever their connection with Judaism; the greater part was, as converts always are, unfriendly or even inimical to their former religion. But even those who did not leave their fold, were what can be called "marginal Jews." In general, they were not ready to take a leading part in the Jewish community. They were trying to find what they believed to be a "wider sphere" of work: to render services to their country, to scholarship, to humanity rather than to the Jewish community.[25] Very few had any relationship to Judaism or to the Jewish

zuwenden, bei welcher sie ihre natürliche dialektische Begabung am besten anwenden und zu ihrem und dem Vorteile des Rechts verwerten können, zu der Rechtsanwaltschaft. . . . Mit der Dialektik, der Kunst der Auslegung, das ist der Auseinanderlegung, hängt ein weiterer Zug jüdischen Wesens zusammen, welcher für die gesamte Wissenschaft, insonderheit aber für die Rechtswissenschaft von grösster Bedeutung in positivem und negativem Sinne ist; es ist die analytische Begabung des jüdischen Menschen." *Cf.* the reviews by G. Kisch and H. Silving quoted *supra*, note 4.

[24] Goodhart, *Five Jewish Lawyers of the Common Law* (London, 1949), pp. 1, 66. *Cf.* the competent critical review by Emil Weitzner in *Jewish Social Studies*, XIII (1951), 263 f., who contradicts "the grouping of the five as Jewish lawyers rather than as lawyers *per se*." He asks: "Were the five actually influenced by their Jewishness and, if so, how?"

[25] *Cf.* E. J. Cohn, "Three Jewish Lawyers of Germany" (*supra*, note 5), pp. 155, 176.

community. Exceptions prove the rule. Well known is the historical open letter that Levin Goldschmidt, "the Lord Mansfield of the German Law Merchant," as he was called (Helen Silving), addressed in 1881 at the height of the first antisemitic wave in Germany to the historian, Professor Heinrich von Treitschke of Berlin University, the protagonist of the doctrine of the "Germanic-Christian State."[26] Julius Magnus served on the Board of the Jewish community of Berlin and was active in the promotion of the Hebrew University.[27] Arthur Nussbaum, a professed agnostic, published a penetrating inquiry into the "ritual murder" trial of Leopold Hilsner, based on the records of the trial and a profound knowledge of modern criminal psychology.[28] He definitely established the fact that Hilsner was the victim of a judicial murder, and directed the attention of the jurists of the world to this fact.

These are exceptions indeed. As a rule, these men were wholly ignorant of Jewish law. Hardly one of them had studied it in the familiar traditional manner. Scarcely a vestige of the specific method of Jewish legal thought can be discovered in them or in their works. They were in every respect emancipated and wholly merged in the German culture. It is therefore impossible to see how these men could have acquired the spirit or the method of Jewish law or could even have been influenced by it. Their achievements in the various fields of German law, their share in the advancement of German jurisprudence and in the enhancement of its prestige, their participation in the promotion of law and justice, nationally as well as internationally, sprang directly from nineteenth-century civilization. They were "men of the nineteenth century," meaning that they not only lived during that century but also spiritually belonged to it.[29]

[26] Goldschmidt, *Ein Lebensbild in Briefen*, pp. 432–436; reprinted in Sinzheimer, *Jüdische Klassiker der deutschen Rechtswissenschaft*, pp. 89–92; see also Silving (*supra*, note 4), p. 293, n. 5.

[27] *Universal Jewish Encyclopedia*, VII (1942), 278.

[28] Nussbaum (1877–1964), *Der Polner Ritualmordprozess. Eine kriminal-psychologische Unterscuchung auf aktenmässiger Grundlage. Mit einem Vorwort von Franz von Liszt*. 2nd ed. (Berlin, 1906).

[29] *Cf.* Silving, *l.c.*, p. 295.

The Voluntary American Jewish Community

By PHILIP M. KLUTZNICK
Chicago, Illinois

It is impossible for me to adequately complete this assignment in a few pages. When I undertook it, I believed that it could be the first chapter of a book I want so much to write. Instead it ends up as limited spots of personal history, a bit of personal philosophy and a setting for what, one day, I hope to fill in with a more complete compendium of experiences. If what follows seems to be disconnected, it is due to a much busier period of my life than I anticipated and a set of personal files which need more extensive editing. I am certain that some of my readers will appreciate the delays that are encountered when the papers of yesterday are read again. Both laughter and tears consume so much time that little is left for analyses. This is by way of apology; it is also by way of a promise to myself that I must delve deeper into the many small events that together pattern one of the most trying, moving and exciting periods of modern Jewish history.

Looking backward through a maze of personal experiences covering nearly three generations during which the constant rediscovery of Jewish uniqueness is omnipresent, the realization grows on me that there are severe limitations to this view. The uniqueness of Jewish life, I have seen world over, is complicated by its seeming quick capacity to take on the coloration of the larger society of which it is a part. Perhaps, its power to be itself and at the same time something else is the main source of its regenerative power.

This special quality predestined the American Jewish community to become over-organized and organizationally competitive as well as the marvel of giving of time and resources to causes of every type. There are many aspects of America that we take for granted. Its size and its present wealth is obvious; and its endless physical and human variety is extraordinary. But if I chose the one distinguishing facet of this revolutionary nation, I would opt for its distinctive voluntarism.

There is much talk about the decline in the number of democracies and the corresponding growth of autocracies and state controlled nations. Much of this is political forum oratory. Many states that were called democracies merely have democratic form but not substance. A free land must be free not just constitutionally but in fact. Whether the dictator is a President, Party Secretary or General is of no significance. We tend to confuse form with substance so our mathematics of democratic decline could be faulty.

A world traveler sees few nations that are truly free. The test is not whether the people are free to cast a ballot at an election but rather whether the system under which they live allows them without the consent of government, to act alone or in concert with others as volunteers to act to right a wrong or to achieve a public good. In this sense, there were few nations and now are not many less who qualify to be designated as a democracy or free land.

Parenthetically, lest I be completely misunderstood, painful facts have taught Americans to cooperate with nations whose frontispiece belies their true nature. Nor do I condemn the pragmatic necessity to do so in a world of such diversity that not to do so may leave a few nations lonely. My sole purpose is to set the American Jewish community apart from most in the world because of the special quality of the American Revolution and what it produced. Those who fail to understand American Jewry or to condemn, envy or even frown upon it, must view it against the background not alone of Jewish experience but in even a larger measure against the extraordinary birth, emergence and development of the United States of America.

In this brief paper, an exploration of all of the factors that make us what we are is impossible. For a people like ours, burdened with an endless list of problems and hopes, it is essential to appreciate the special chemistry of America if one is to form a value judgment on the complex multiplicity of Jewish organized life. When my Jewish friends from Israel, Europe or Latin America expect us to be more unified organizationally, they must understand one cannot be anything other than what an environment nourishes.

The most recent study of voluntary giving of time and resources in America was published in late 1975 by the Commission on Private Philanthropy and Public Needs on which I was privileged to serve. This involved one of the most thorough set of research projects ever undertaken in this area. In addition to giving 26 billion in 1973, Americans contributed 6 billion hours of voluntary work to an endless list of institutions and causes. It caused the Commission to introduce its report as follows:

> "Few aspects of American society are more characteristically, more famously American than the nation's array of voluntary organizations and the support in both time and money that is given to them by its citizens. Our country has been decisively different in this regard. Historian Daniel Boorstein observes, 'from the beginning, as the country settled, communities existed before governments were there to care for public needs.' The result, Boorstein says, was that 'voluntary collaborative activities were set up to provide basic social services. . . .' "

When Alexis de Tocqueville first looked on America in the early 1800's, he paid tribute to the unique quality of its voluntarism. He observed that there was nothing to stop Americans who felt keenly about any matter to organize and do something about it, and as he wrote: "Americans are forever forming associations." The Commission reports that they still are.

Since environment came to the front, actually tens of thousands of environmental organizations sprang up in a few years.

To defend duplication and multiplicity may be difficult, but, to end it in America, the land of premier voluntarism, is almost hopeless. Actually, there is some evidence that in over 3 million square miles of territory and about 6 million Jews the competition to serve causes has not been all bad.

We are a proud community that celebrated the tercentenary of the landing of the first Jews in New Amsterdam (New York) in 1953. The ancient tale of the 23 escapees from Brazil when Portugal ousted the Dutch is now a part of American Jewish legendry. The vow exacted by Governor Peter Stuyvesant that they would take care of their own and never be a charge on the community is likewise a part of that history. But, history must have its fables as well as its facts. Nearly all of the 23 left the new world. They were a seed, but only a small speck on the escutcheon of American Jewish beginnings in this land.

It is estimated that there were only 2,500 Jews in the colonies at the time of the American Revolution. While they acquitted themselves well, as the story of Haym Salomon tells us, or even the few recollections of Jewish soldier heroes, they hardly formed a significant portion of the then America.

The early few settlers and those who followed were in large part Sephardim. But, even the latter and more substantial German and Ashkenazi immigration did not number more than 50,000 in the mid-1800's. Yet, the early small numbers organized synagogues and their attributes. Later the voluntarism expanded with other types of societies primarily to help one another in the burgeoning Jewish community. For obviously sentimental and personal reasons, I mention the first fraternal society, the Bundes Bruder, or as we have known it for a very long time, the B'nai B'rith. Created in 1843 it remains the oldest continuous Jewish voluntary association in this and now many other lands.

However, the full impact of American Jewish voluntarism emerged with the largest voluntary emigration of modern history—the trek of nearly 2 million Jews from Eastern Europe to the shores of the new land. The saga is brilliantly recounted in Irving Howes' "World of our Fathers." The reaction to the oppression and deprivation they escaped would naturally motivate the maximum use of the freedom they acquired. One could trace the heavy beginnings of American Jewish voluntarism to this era. Not only did this huge wave of newcomers acquire the liberty and freedom of America but they brought with them a pack of problems, ills and troubles which provided a fertile ground for organizations among themselves to help one another and organizations by others to paternistically help them. Thus began the peak period of American Jewish voluntarism with its greatest underlying motive, the Americanization of Jews. The modern era of American Jewish life arose out of this unusual combination of freedom to organize and the need to adjust to a new and challenging environment.

It is an oversimplification to bridge most of the more than 300 years since the 23 landed in New Amsterdam in a few words, but space demands it. The early Sephardim and their descendents developed voluntary associations to meet their conceived needs. But, the community was small and the new land was itself in its beginnings. The later German and related immigration, while larger even as the land was growing, still represented only another stage of development as the economic and social aspects of the United States emerged into a new scope and depth.

The story oft told of the Sephardim disdain of the new German Jewish immigration is only matched by the attitude of the German Jews towards their Eastern European cousins. There are more modern versions of this progression in many places and specifically several countries in Latin America where there are relatively similar histories of tiers of immigration.

Recently, I visited one such country after an absence of 20 years. In the 1950's, the emphasis was on the Sephardic community, the Ashkenazi community, the Hungarian and even the separate German community representing layers of immigration. Last year, the head of the Jewish Community Center made a little welcoming speech at a luncheon in the Sephardic House. He observed that when he and others first came, they were Jews, but separate. More recently, he said, there is what they call intermarriage—one of sephardic origin marrying one of German origin or of Hungarian origin. Soon he suggested this will disappear and they will all be one family in fact.

When I came on the scene of voluntary Jewish life in Kansas City, Missouri as a lad of 14, 57 years ago, the remnants of this decision was still evident. In this midwest city, we were spared three divisions, but two, Western and Eastern European origin were very clear. The temple was indeed the place reserved for those of Western European origin. It had not yet become the active converter of Litvaks into Reform Jews; the B'nai B'rith had not yet accepted Eastern European leadership either at the top or in the community. It had only begun to accept members who were of Eastern European origin. There was a settlement house which was born out of the tradition of paternal, and sometimes loving, care of the Western European Jews for their uncouth Jewish neighbors from Eastern Europe. There was the beginnings of a YM-YWHA (I edited its little newspaper when I was 17) but it and the charitable functions and activities except for the Workmens' Circle, the Chrevra Kadisha, the societies associated with orthodox synagogues and a struggling Zionist complex, were in the hands of the first comers. This was the Jewish establishment in most Jewish communities in the America of 57 years ago.

The Federation existed in only a few communities. They did not faintly represent the institution that began its upward thrust in the 1930's and became the power house of Jewish life after World War II and the birth of the State of Israel. By then, the primary motivation of Americanizing Jews had changed. With the limitation on immigration imposed in the early 1920's, and with the passage of time, Americanization slowly faded out as the broader participation of the Jew in the total community became the rule rather than the exception. These recent days, only a relatively few Russian Jewish immigrants have reawakened some Americanization activity.

In the earlier days, the few efforts to unite the Jewish community failed at both local and national levels. The famed Louis Marshall effort to establish a Kehillah in New York City foundered. For a short time, the major Jewish organizations compelled by the events of World War I and its aftermath united into the American Jewish Congress, but all but the core led by the potent Rabbi Stephen Wise left the Congress when the pressure was off. Thereafter, Rabbi Wise even created his own seminary, the Jewish Institute of Religion in New York City, to differentiate his commitment from the then non-Zionist, if not anti-Zionist leadership, of Cincinnati's Hebrew Union College. Those were days of struggle between different pasts and different postures which were deeply felt, divisive and at times personal and brutal.

In 1926, when I completed a term as the Grand Aleph Godol of the AZA, the junior B'nai B'rith, I moved to Omaha, Nebraska, the headquarters of this organization to become its first semi-professional employee. I worked part-time for all of $50 a month while I attended law school. There were few trained Jewish club workers or social service specialists who also had Jewish backgrounds in these days. At 19, I lost my amateur standing and became a professional. The next few years were among the most meaningful and decisive of my life. They spanned a significant period in the American Jewish community. I was fortunate to be spending those years stationed in a midwestern "metropolis," the largest city in Nebraska.

I arrived in Omaha as it was dedicating a new and beautiful building exclusively devoted to its Jewish Community Center. As a Kansas Citian who had grown up in a YM-YWHA old mansion, only succeeded in 1924 by a fine building but yet a YM-YWHA, the idea of a Jewish Community Center was new. I had served as chairman of the junior membership campaign for the Kansas City "Y" so I became immediately intrigued by and involved in the activity of the Omaha building. It was for me a "Y" with a different name, but this was not wholly true. It really represented physically the beginning of the movement toward local Jewish unification.

Two years ago, Omaha dedicated a new Jewish Community Center. The cost was 4½ million dollars—roughly ten times the cost, except for inflation, of its 1926 predecessor. My wife and I joined my wife's family in helping to endow a facility in that building in memory of her parents.

Quite recently, the President of today's Omaha Jewish Community Center joined in recognizing the 50th Anniversary of that dedication in 1926. In that connection, the following quotation is pertinent:

> "The Jewish home may have failed, the synagogue and the temple may not maintain their hold, but the Jewish Community Center will not fail; it represents the spirit of the entire Jewish community, and of all phases of Jewish life. The cure for Jewish ills is more Jewishness and Judaism which the Community Center will provide."

These words were uttered by the then executive of the Center in 1926. Some believe them current in 1976–77.

By the time I became a part-time professional in AZA, I had already seen Jewish communities from New York City to Los Angeles and from North Dakota and Minnesota to Mississippi and Louisiana. Generally, I found them as one finds even now, a certain camaraderie and community spirit present in the smaller and middle-size Jewish communities that was absent in the larger and largest. Just recently the Jewish Welfare Board published the results of a study of membership in Jewish Community Centers in the period of 1970 to 1975. A quote is significant:

> "The ratio of Center membership to total Jewish population is close to 50% in smaller Jewish communities. As the size of the community grows, the average number of Center members grows, but not at the same rate. Thus the affiliation ratio drops to 30%—15%—6% respectively in the three largest population categories."

A parenthetic thought occurs to me, time and again, as I remember personal experiences and read these statistics. Much is made these days about the deficiencies in Jewish life which is in part attributed by some to the large numbers of unaffiliated. This problem can never be totally solved. When all of Jewish life was on the precipice of peril in Hitler's days or when the dangerous predicament of Israel exposed all of Jewish life to grevious potentials, there were many who preferred the sidelines. But, certainly, this number could be reduced if we found a way to humanize our institutions by reducing where practical the size of the instrument. Large institutions, synagogues and temples serve their proper roles, but the sheer growth of Chavurah and small fellowships reflect a desire for greater proximity and closely knit institutions.

I am grateful for my youth and young adult days in Kansas City and Omaha for I saw and heard the heart beat and felt the warmth of Jewish experience at first hand. I saw revolutionary change in process and I felt the keenness of organizational competition and even jealousy. I learned to appreciate the importance of all this and even more as today's Jewish community emerged. Not all I saw or heard squared with the idealism and hero worship of youth.

Maybe the absence of prime theater, opera, professional sports and the scholarship of great universities compelled the small communities of the then 10,000 Jewish souls in Omaha and 20,000 or so in Kansas City to make a life of their own. These were not great cosmopolitan communities so the elements of social anti-semitism or exclusion and non-acceptance in the establishment which rules the general community had only rare and token exceptions. Yet, there was much more mingling with the non-Jewish community than in the large centers. Remember the racial compromises that permitted statehood for new applicants? I lived through its modern interpretation in the 1920's. In Kansas City, schools were segregated, in Omaha, they were integrated. This was a difference without much distinction. Racial and ethnic distaste and separatism were the prevailing doctrines in both places. The 1920's were the height of KKK sway as I knew when in my freshman year at the University of Kansas at Lawrence, I was shocked more than once by a burning cross.

The American Jewish Committee, the American Jewish Congress, the Anti-Defamation League of the B'nai B'rith were more concerned with the lampooning of the Jew, the immigrant and the greenhorn than they were with the great issues that were to begin to surface in the 1930's and later to burgeon in the post World War II period. Here, too, there was a division. Generally, the Committee postured the Western European attitude and developed what their competitors called a "sha sha" approach. In political representation, they were held to reflect the "stadtlanes" of Europe and early American Jewish history. The Congress under the militant, Dr. Wise mirrored his openness and call to arms. While, the ADL fell somewhere between because it was responsive to the largest constituency of the three, its sponsor the B'nai B'rith. The sharpness of these differences lost its edge with the later rise of Hitler and the horrors of the Holocaust. Here too, the ideological struggle of real moment concerned the Jewish State and Zionism. When, recently, we were all stunned by the United Nations resolution on Zionism and racism, few remembered words like the following:

> "There is no such things as a Jewish nation or a Hebrew people; the Jewish nation ceased to exist eighteen hundred years ago. There is no Jewish nation now, we are Jews in religion only. Jew, therefore, is the proper name to be applied to us; Israelite is a misnomer, because that is the name of an ancient nation that exists no more; so also is Hebrew a wrong appellation, for if it is the name of the people speaking the Hebrew language, it certainly cannot be applied to the Jews, because the least of them understand, much less speak Hebrew; if it is a race term, it is also a misnomer, because it is very doubtful whether there is one pure stream of blood of an ancient Hebrew flowing through the veins of the Jews today, and Jew alone is the proper appellation of the religion which is named Judaism, not Hebrewism, not Israelitism."

These words were spoken at the 1891 Convention by one of the Deans of Reform Judaism, Rabbi David Philipson, who was ordained in the first class to graduate from Hebrew Union College in 1883. His ire had been aroused by the proposal of some to have a separate Jewish exhibition in the World's Fair in Chicago so he also said:

> "If this is distinctly understood, namely, that we are Jews in religion only, then the whole present agitation as to having a separate Jewish exhibition at the World's Fair at Chicago will be seen to be ill-timed and out of place."

But in 1937, at Columbus, Ohio, the Central Conference adopted "Guiding Principles of Reform Judaism." It was prepared by a small committee on which David Philipson sat. Among other principles, it included these words:

> "In all lands where our people live, they assume and seek to share loyally the full duties and responsibilities of citizenship and to create seats of Jewish knowledge and religion. In the rehabilitation of Palestine, the land hallowed by memories and hopes, we behold the promise of renewed life for many of our brethren. We affirm the obligation of all Jewry to and in its upbuilding a Jewish homeland by endeavoring to make it not only a haven of refuge for the oppressed but also a center of Jewish culture and spiritual life."

During a spirited discussion on this issue which marked a decided turning away from the Pittsburgh Platofrm of 1885, Philipson stated:

> "I am now the only man living who was at the Pittsburgh Conference. I was not in favor of a new Declaration but the Conference wanted it. For the sake of historic continuity, I should like to be the one to move the adoption of this Declaration of Principles."

And finally on June 29, 1946, when the British had arrested members of the Jewish Agency, it was Philipson, as the oldest member of the Conference who expressed not only "horror" at the event but stated that Britain had forfeited all the respect and love which I and many others have had. . . ." The resolution of condemnation was adopted and Dr. Philipson joined Maurice Eisendrath and Felix Levy in presenting the resolution to President Truman.

The saga of change on this issue is not alone in the modern history of our community. While external events made opposition meaningless, it was doubtless the competitiveness of voluntary association that hastened change. By 1937, and certainly before 1946, the conservative Rabbinate was outspoken in its Zionism. The modern orthodox Rabbinate and others were likewise fervently committed. Reform Judaism had been invaded in the

Temple and in the Rabbinate by Litvaks, Polish and Russian Jews. One of its most distinguished sons of that day, Abba Hillel Silver oft time said, that the future of Reform depended on the descendants of the orthodox. He spoke from his own experience.

But it was not on the religious point alone where change was moving at a quickened pace. I have already referred to my B'nai B'rith affiliation. It began in Kansas City as a youth. It matured in the midwestern hotbed of B'nai B'rith, Omaha. I was permitted membership before I became of 21. The great Omaha B'nai B'rith leader was Henry Monsky, the founder of the Youth movement was from Omaha, Sam Beber. Omaha was to provide the 11th and 13th International Presidents of B'nai B'rith—Henry Monsky, the first descendent of Eastern European family to head the B'nai B'rith from 1938 to 1947 and the writer who served the then permissible two terms from 1953–1959. In Omaha it was natural for a young man, having served as President of the local B'nai B'rith lodge to become active in the Jewish National Fund or the Omaha Zionist District. I finished my term as President of B'nai B'rith at 22 and immediately became President of the Zionist District and a few years later Vice-President of the Southwest Region. Yet, the B'nai B'rith itself at the international level was still neutral on the proposition of a national Jewish homeland. Even though it had established a lodge and a library in Jerusalem in 1888, and had established a moshav in the Galilee in 1938, it was sensitive to the possibility of a split in its own ranks between members who were Zionists, some who were non-Zionists and some who still adhered to the early Philipson position.

But, by 1941, President Monsky brought the issue to a head and the B'nai B'rith at its highest level approved the support of the Zionist goal. This enabled Monsky to call for the Pittsburgh Conference out of which grew the American Jewish Conference in 1943. But, even at the first meeting of the Conference in New York City, the American Jewish Committee withdrew over the issue and the Jewish Labor Committee abstained on the vote in favor of a Jewish National home in then Palestine. This was only 35 years ago. But, it was not until the real ravages of Hitler became generally known and partition was approved in November 1947, that it could be said that there was an overwhelming acceptance in America for this simple proposition. The Council for American Judaism continued its dissidence vocally for several years. To this day, it operates primarily a philanthropic fund. The carryover of opposition where it may exist is muted and qualified.

Why do I sketch ever so briefly this bird's eye view of some phases of American Jewish life? I have purposely omitted more detailed reference to the unbelievable pace of change in American Jewish life since the birth of the third commonwealth. Fund raising rose from a voluntary indulgence to a fine art; from 100 million dollar goals to one-half billion and more; from modest bond sales to multi-million dollar sales; from mere fund raising to honors giving, etc., ad nauseum. We already have a young group of leaders who would not think of fund raising in less than multi-million dollar goals or without a man or woman of the year and at least one or more missions to Israel. Our voluntary associations reflect the almost unbelievable changes that have taken place in American Jewish life in two generations and less.

At the outset, I directed attention to the unique feature of Jewish life in its capacity to take on the coloration of its geography while retaining its own special flavor. As we boast of our generosity and activity, we might do well to remember different days.

Today, Jewish communities like Omaha and Kansas City meet multi-million dollar quotas. In 1934, I chaired either the 3rd or 4th united campaign in Omaha. It was called the Omaha Jewish Philanthropies. It was relatively successful in a country emerging from a depression. We raised about $30,000.

It was at this time, in my position as chairman that I first met Henry Montor and a very plainly dressed lady called Goldie Myerson, representing the Pioneer Women. It was difficult in Omaha to get her a hearing before the Budget Committee, but I was so impressed that we managed it. The Yishuv was not the number one favorite then. How times have changed?

During the depression of the 1930's the figure 3 had unusual significance for Jewish life. The B'nai B'rith which now boasts of 500,000 men, women and young people was scraping the bottom of the barrel to total 30,000 male members, a handful of Hillel Foundations and a struggling youth movement. As the nation lived in the nadir of its modern economic experience so did the Jewish community. It was then, however, that the Council of Jewish Federations and Welfare Funds emerged and became the springboard for the present movement of size and influence. It was then also that the seeds were sown for collaboration among the so-called Jewish defense agencies.

All this was really only a day ago in terms of Jewish history. Only recently, I returned to Kansas City to address a few meetings. At one, a contemporary approached me and asked me in that frequently painful experience if I remembered him. As I searched the utmost recesses of my memory, he jogged it by saying: "We went to Cheder together in the old shul at 17th and Paseo" and that was more than 60 years ago and he was a star pupil and I was a dud. My nostrils quivered as recollection brought back the smell of whiskey and the stale tobacco of an ancient with one arm who served as our melamed. We both laughed as we recalled the strength of that arm as it whacked us and our lagging memories. We did not laugh then.

It seems a miracle that this contemporary and I are still able to meet under Jewish auspices. If ever a generation of American Jews had the inducement to break ranks and leave Judaism it was some of us. We lived in two worlds—the world of our grandparents and parents who had brought their old world manners and habits, their synagogues from whence they came, their fine Yiddish and difficult English—and the world of a free America. The latter with its relatively fine schools, not basement cheders; its new way of almost reckless freedom; and its exciting environment of organizations, clubs, fraternities, etc.

Even this brief recitation suggests that Jewish life as I have known it has been frenetically physically active. The forging of instruments to cope with the religious, social, economic and political needs of American Jewry has required much debate, movement, and energy. Yet, Jews cannot be Jews without education and culture as major ingredients. In this area, the mixture of old country culture with modern American methods created clashes and problems. The "teeming masses" of New York City maintained a degree of separatism which the "deserts" of the provinces did not support. In the more densely populated East whether New York, Boston or Philadelphia, permanent institutions such as Dropsie, The Educational Alliance, early YM-YWHA's, in college the Menorah Society represented an unwillingness to leave education and culture to the synagogue and synagogue related institutions.

The early labor movements, and secular societies including the incipient Zionist movement made culture an essential aspect of their purpose. The firebrand lecturer in Yiddish or English was highly esteemed whether at a union meeting, a Zionist society or at a Workmen's Circle meeting. The landsmanschaften of the earlier days and in measure even now, relive the story and the culture of the area from whence they hailed. This experience in many instances entirely blocked out the growth of indigenous American-Jewish educational experience or shared it only for the minimum needs of an American environment. In some instances, in the more populous Jewish communities the, prevalent "Yiddishkeit" delayed adjustment or actually clashed with the idea of a new American-Jewish culture. This was abetted by the continuing if declining, infusion of European personalities which helped stoke the Jewish educational and cultural furnace such as it was before immigration virtually ceased.

Some insight into the rude awakening from early isolation to the growing American-Jewish culture is represented by the story told by Bess Myerson in response to a question put to her in the Touro Synagogue in celebration of the American Bicentennial last year. She was asked how she was at no time aware of anti-semitism around her.

Her own words tell it best. They follow:

"- - - -, I grew up in the Sholom Aleichem apartment houses; I went to Music and Art High School and Hunter College. I went to the Folk Shule and the YIVO Folk Shule, my parents spoke Yiddish, all the people in the building where I lived spoke Yiddish, we celebrated Jewish holidays. We were not religious in the sense of going to synagogue. There was no synagogue in the neighborhood that I was even aware of. But we were rooted in our Jewishness. It wasn't until I became a contestant in the Miss New York City contest, without my parents' approval or knowledge, and subsequently went to Atlantic City, that I discovered the whole world wasn't Jewish. I was so isolated and protected that the first evidence of this was shocking to me.

"I have never told this story in public, and it is a traumatic thing to relate, because I've never explained to Jewish audiences or to anyone what motivates me in terms of my life as a Jew.

"There were three long nights of competition—I went into the first night, then the second night. By the third night, the elimination kept on until there were fifteen girls. A woman who was director of the pageant came from Atlantic City and took me to the back of the theatre and said: 'You really have an extraordinary talent and it's very possible that you might win. If you win the New York City contest, you'll go on to Atlantic City and might become Miss America. You're a great pianist, you might want to have a professional career . . . but the last name of Myerson is so strange. Have you ever thought of changing it?' I said, 'Not really, what would you suggest?' She said, 'Merrick or Meredith.' 'That's fascinating,' I said, 'that's a delightful name, but I don't know that I really would enjoy not having my own name that much, and my name was Bessie for most of my life.'

"Bess Meredith, my God that's really a transition. I said 'no' to myself. I don't think I will. One, I don't think I'll win; two, if I win the only people I want to know about it are the other two hundred families who live at the Sholom Aleichem apartment houses, the kids I went to the Folk Schule with and the girls I graduated Hunter with.

"When I went to Atlantic City, by the third night I was the only Jewish girl there. The press, most of whom were Jewish, encouraged me to be as good as I could. By the second or third night, small groups of people would gather in the hotel I was staying at, at the Brighton Hotel, and spoke to me in Yiddish. They'd wait for me and they would ask do you know what this means?

"In September of 1945 the war had been over for several months and we began to know what happened to our people. At the same time these people in Atlantic City said to me: if you win, you will be the first Jewish Miss America. You'll represent all American womanhood. And after six million Jews dying, wouldn't it be significant if a Jewish girl were selected to represent American womanhood?

"After I won, for the first two months I agreed I would travel around representing American womanhood, and I went to Wilmington, Delaware to do a War Bond tour of the city. When I came back that afternoon I was at the home of a very gracious hostess in a beautiful mansion, and I heard her saying to the pageant director as I was walking down the stairs, 'Oh,

I'm terribly sorry but we cannot have Miss Myerson at the country club reception in her honor. It's a restricted country club and we have never had a Jew in the country club.'

"I packed my bag and I walked out of the house. I was crying, I was young, and I was full of what this opportunity meant to me. I went home and I met a man called Ben Epstein and another called Arnold Forster. I went out all that year—not representing the pageant but the B'nai B'rith Anti-Defamation League and started speaking as a Jew. It didn't make me more Jewish, because I had to be Jewish in order to have the response that I had when the woman said 'change your name.' Changing my name meant changing my identity and denying my Jewishness. But that experience gave me a shock. I didn't know how terrifying it was out there."

In the small centers of Jewish populations, many of which I visited as a young worker in the junior B'nai B'rith, the more customary pattern was one of clash between the modernizing tendencies and the tenacious clinging to old world educational, cultural and religious values and practices. In more instances than I would now like to recount, young men and ladies of my acquaintance would prefer to meet somewhere other than at home where the old world style still prevailed—where Yiddish was the language spoken—where tea meant a glass and cubed sugar—and where yarmulkes and prayer somehow mingled to produce an increasingly unfamiliar atmosphere. But, the change has come rapidly. In less than 70 years, a new educational and cultural style and statistic has emerged.

In 1964, the Jewish Publication Society published "The American Jew—A Reappraisal" edited by Dr. Oscar I. Janowsky. It is a volume to which many distinguished scholars made valuable contributions. While much has happened since then, some of the observations are pertinent even now. Interesting essays on Hebrew letters, Yiddish literature, Jewish awareness in American literature, art and the American Jew, and music and the American Jew collectively demonstrate a remarkable change since the end of the great Eastern European emigration. The intervention of World Wars I and II, the Holocaust and the rebirth of the Israel commonwealth constitute a trilogy of such magnitude as to have compelled massive change not always for the better.

In the earliest periods of Jewish awareness of themselves in the new world, there were a few significant centers of either incipient or mature Jewish educational and cultural efforts. They were New York, of course; its satellities, Philadelphia, and Boston; and the midwest center, Chicago, Los Angeles was still a village and Baltimore while important, ranked with Cleveland and Detroit. There were those beautiful smallish but tasteful communities of Charleston, Savannah, New Orleans and even San Francisco that were more American Jewish than Jewish American.

Alfred Werner wrote in 1964: "It is not surprising that *The American Jew* published in 1942 contained no chapter on the space arts; printing, sculpture and architecture. Two decades ago, there was no longer a dearth of American Jews in all realms of art - - -" "But, the Jewish Community as such, was not yet art conscious."

This, in its way, is an index to an evaluation of many developments in this young Jewish community. We tend to agree with what others think of us, because frequently, we are not aware of what is going on in education, art, culture in which Jewishness or Jews are involved. It is not that I believe that the American Jewish community has reached its proper level of commitment or practice in Jewish education, culture and the arts. It is only that the real evidence indicates progress in the right direction, even with occasional setbacks. Because we live in the forest we cannot see it for the trees. And many who live outside never bother to see the trees or the forest.

Statistics are not conclusive, but they are revealing. Before World War I, there were only two Hebrew Teachers Colleges in the United States—Gratz which was established in Philadelphia in 1895, and the Teachers Institute of the Jewish Theological Seminary in New York in 1909. By 1928, seven additional teachers' colleges were established in New York, Boston, Philadelphia and Chicago. In 1907, Dropsie College for Hebrew and Cognate Learning for graduate study was founded in Philadelphia.

Dr. Janowsky directed attention to two significant surveys of Jewish education—one in 1909 by Mordecai M. Kaplan and Bernard Cronson; the other by Alexander M. Dushkin published in 1918. The former concluded: "1. The demand for Jewish education is comparatively small; 2. small as the demand is the means and equipment which we possess at present are far too inadequate to meet it; 3. wherever the demand is met there is a lack of system or content." Dr. Dushkin's report 11 years later was equally miserable. He estimated that only 23.5% of the 275,000 Jewish children received some Jewish instruction and 37% of that number attended Heder or received instruction at home. The drop-out rate was unbelievable. Most schools lost more than half of their students every year and only 3% reached the highest grade. The conditions outside New York were no better.

By 1964, the enrollment increased from 45,000 to 589,000. The real jump took place after World War II, the Holocaust and the rebirth of Israel. Even though this might be termed education that is a "mile wide and an inch thick" there are even some signs that are encouraging. While recent figures show a decline in enrollment in one day schools, the enrollment in day schools is growing and is approximately 100,000 now. All of which is only a trend.

A notable change has taken place since the disturbances of the 60's. With black studies seeking a place in the sun, Jewish studies and Hebrew have become common items in nearly 400 colleges and universtiies as well as in a growing number of high schools. Certainly availability has grown and with it must come some meaningful results.

In the field of informal education, the trend is also upward. Religious institutions have established camps and other facilities for youth and adults to engage in educational and cultural activities. As early as 1923, the B'nai B'rith established its first Hillel Foundations on college campuses to supplement the more limited Menorah Societies. The YMHA-YWHA movement which provided a variety of shared activities among Jews beginning in the late 19th century emerged into the major Jewish Center program. In its well known post war World II survey headed by Dr. Salo Baron and directed by Dr. Oscar Janowsky, it recommended programs that were Jewishly oriented as the basic justification for the movement. I remember the long debates that resulted in a positive Jewish commitment at a well attended national meeting of the NJWB.

The tendency in the World War II period and the years following the 1948 historic establishment of the State of Israel have found American Jews actively engaged in the pursuit of a culturally and ethnic identity attuned to the freedom of America. We have seen an expansion of theological facilities in New York with the merger of HUC and the Jewish Institute of Religion, the opening on the west coast in Los Angeles of branches of the Hebrew Union College and the Jewish Theological Seminary as well as the initiation of the first Reconstructionist Seminary in Philadelphia. The Hebrew Theological College in Chicago survived the test of post war years and is flourishing again.

The Council of Jewish Federations and Welfare Funds sired the National Foundation for Jewish Culture which struggled its way to a balanced if modest program. Later under the pressure of protest, it gave birth to a short lived but necessary Institute for Jewish Life.

The B'nai B'rith long ago, started its retreats and then enlarged its activity to cover ongoing programs of adult Jewish education as well as its Lecture Bureau and good books. The Synagogue Council created its own Institute of Jewish Policy Planning engaged in research and timely reports of its analyses. Rabbi Yitzhak Greenberg launched his Jewish Conference Center and scholars in residence have become commonplace. Harvard with the earliest of American Jewish studies is engaged in a major $15 million campaign to develop a program in depth to keep scholarships in Judaica alive and productive. Not many miles from Cambridge, sits American Jewry's proud jewel, Brandeis University with its Lown School and a vast variety of interests in Jewish culture. And Yeshiva University, once only a place for training and ordaining rabbis is now a major university with a respected and growing cultural influence.

This is a capsule of a half-century and little more of American Jewry's concern with the mind and with the modern needs for scholarship and learning. It has not attained the acme of quantitative and fiscal advance, but its signs of growth and depth are a far reach from the level and character that prevailed at the turn of the century.

Whenever, I hear loud concern about all of the statistics of assimilation, decline in Jewishness, and Judaism and the hopelessness of the Jewish future I think back and remember so much that I cannot begin to write. If I and so many of my generation who survived two world wars, a holocaust and all the inducements to quit are still around trying to fight today's challenges, then the miracle of Jewish survival still subsists. "Unique" is an overused word, but it seems to have been coined for a small determined folk who persist through one way or another to prick the conscience of the world.

There is one potent lesson in all this that needs to be urged. Whenever there is a great strain in the Jewish world, as indeed there is now, a tendency to over emphasize uniformity or "one voice" grows very tempting. Large majorities resent small numbers who disagree. They either try to overwhelm them, quiet them or ostracize them. This is very understandable and especially so when a dream of the ages, a Jewish state, is in peril. More recently, we have indulged in a new kind of solution—disagree, argue, and differ but keep it quiet and in the family. Do not let the goyim and particularly, the Arab goyim, know that we differ about methods or programs.

Certainly, discretion and care in debate is a good rule normally. It is even a better rule for both sides of a highly emotional difference to use a measure of restraint. But, if the American Zionists of the 1920's had followed the rule of "please do not disturb the neighbors" it is doubtful if the overwhelming acceptance of the State of Israel would have come to pass. Just as the Jewish community of this land refuses to become one neat voice, so is it with the land itself. There is nothing trim and neat about genuine freedom and democracy. It provides the largest room for debate and discussion without penalty. True statesmanship in this free land is not achieved by compelling uniformity; it is best achieved by using the greatest possible force to achieve maximum cooperation even among those who differ.

Through a process oft time painful and full of anguish in our own untidy way, six million American Jews have achieved a large area of cooperation and a sense of commitment within the framework of genuine freedom. Our goals must be to maintain this momentum and improve our cooperative spirit without dampening the spirit of constructive dissent and difference. This is what voluntarism is all about. And this is what gives the required space for creativity, originality and growth.

The Expository Traits of the Targum to Ezekiel

By YEHUDA KOMLOSH
The Dropsie University

THE AIM OF this paper is to dwell on the exegetical methods adopted by the Aramaic Targum attributed to Jonathan ben Uziel to the Book of Ezekiel, and to evaluate its importance from the point of view of the understanding of the Masoretic text.* The Targum to Ezekiel is based on expository principles in the spirit of the tradition and, like all the other targumim, has educational objectives. At the same time, however, many passages and verses have been translated literally without any specific expository intentions.

Importance attaches to the Targum to the Book of Ezekiel from the point of view of the biblical text. It is particularly important in this respect when the Targum is identical with the other translation. The Targum of the Prophets is generally based on our Masoretic text,[1] although at times one traces a deviation from the Masoretic text. These deviations have already been pointed out by David Kimḥi, and in his wake by Yedidyah Norzi in "Minḥat Shay."[2]

Pinkhos Churgin pointed to the translations of several words of the Prophets concerning which he claimed there were changes in version already in the period when doubts existed as to the reading of certain words.[3] Owing, however, to the homiletical nature of the Targum, it is difficult to establish whether the deviation was due to a version that differed from the Masoretic text or to the expository intention of the translator.[4] Each place therefore calls for special examination and evaluation.

In several instances the Targum reflects a more improved vocalisation

* Concise Bibliographical References.

P. Churgin, *Targum Jonathan to the Prophets*, New Haven, 1927. (Churgin)

G. A. Cooke, *A Critical and Exegetical Commentary on the Book of Ezekiel* (I.C.C.), 1937. (Cooke)

C. H. Cornill, *Das Buch des Propheten Ezechiel*, Leipzig, 1886. (Cornill)

W. Eichrodt, *Der Prophet Hezekiel* (*ATD*), Göttingen, 1966. (Eichrodt)

G. Fohrer, *Ezechiel* (*HAT*), Tübingen, 1955. (Fohrer)

H. G. May, *The Book of Ezechiel* (Interpreters Bible, Vol. 6), New York, 1956. (May)

W. Zimmerli, *Ezechiel, Biblischer Kommentar* (*BK*), Neukirchen, 1969. (Zimmerli)

M. Z. Segal, תנ"ך עם פירושים, כרך ב', יחזקאל, תשכ"ך (Segal)

[1] מ"צ סגל, מבוא המקרא 963, p. 4.

[2] Churgin, p. 52 of U. Simon, ספר בר־אילן, 1 (תשכ"ה), 237–191

[3] Churgin, *ibid.*, pp. 62–64.

[4] See Y. Komlosh, *The Bible in the Light of the Aramaic Translations* (Hebrew), Tel Aviv, 1973, p. 63.

than that of the Masoretic text. Thus, for example, in the verse 6:9 the word נשברתי is translated תברית, on the basis of שברתי.[5] This version was commented on by Joseph Kara (12th century) and by his contemporary Eliezer of Beaugency. Rashi on the other hand renders according to the compassion of God נכנעתי אצלם, similarly David Kimḥi, in the pattern of "and it grieved him at his heart (Gen. 6:6)."

In another example עת נשברת (27:34) is rendered כען אתברת (now art thou broken). This is the rendering also of the Septuagint Νῦν συνετρίβης. Vulg.: nunc contrita es. All these three translations are rendered instead of עת – עתה.[6]

The continuation of the verse מימים[7] in the Targum is already a paraphrase, and parts of the sentence are connected to this expression by a subsidiary clause.[8] In the Masoretic text the vocalisation of the city identified as Heliopolis is given as אָוֶן (30:17), whereas the Targum edition of Sperber gives the proper vocalisation of the name as: אוֹן.[9] In the verse, 29:3, concerning Egypt we read: לי יארי ואני עשיתני; this unusual grammatical form[10] is rendered by the Targum without suffix, as if: ואני עשיתי (ואנא כבשית). It should be pointed out, however, that the Targum here based himself on verse 9 in the same chapter, where the reading is: ואני עשיתי and the translation is as above ואנא כבשית.

We shall now quote several translations of verses to which importance attaches from the point of view, of the biblical text.

Among the prophets' visions we read: "והָיְתָה חרפה" (5:15), which the Targum renders "ותהן," namely in the second person singular. This gives ground for the assumption that the text was וְהָיִתָ חרפה, the same as the rendering of the Septuagint καὶ ἔσῃ.[11] We must not, however, overlook the fact that in the continuation of this verse, as well as in the preceding verse, the verbs mostly refer to the second person, and there is also ground to believe, that the Targumist employed the second person with an expository intention in mind, so as to coordinate between the various sections of the verse.

[5] In this form, as translated by Aquila Theodothion Symmachus and the Vulgate, *cf.* Cornill, p. 209, May, p. 97, and Zimmerli, p. 140. We may add that so is also the translation of Peshitta דתברית ללבהון. The text שברתי is confirmed by about 14 MSS of Ezekiel. The modern commentators translate according to שברתי as well, so Fohrer, p. 155 and Eichrodt, p. 92.

[6] *Cf.* May, p. 216.

[7] This word is translated by Sept. ἐν θαλάσσῃ according to the text בימים, and the Vulgate, on the other hand, translates according to the Biblical text "a mari."

[8] דהוית יתבא בגו ימיא.

[9] So is the translation of Aquila Ὠν.

[10] According to the *Hebrew Grammar* of Gesenius-Kautzsch-Cowley (p. 369) either עשיתיו is to be read . . . or עשיתים. The Septuagint translates ἐποίησα αὐτούς (I made them)

Or take another example: in the verse ומלאתי את הריו חלליו (35:8) and I will fill his mountains with his slain. The use of the suffix is not uniform. In the beginning of the verse, the objects are in third person (הריו[12] חלליו) and then in, the second person (גבעותיך וגיאותיך וכל אפיקיך). On the other hand, Targum Jonathan employs the third person throughout, in the meaning of: his hills, his valleys, and all his streams.

Sometimes the deviation in version is based on the reading of a "שׂ" instead of a "שׁ." In connection with the idolator, the Masoretic text reads "והשמותיהו" (14:8) which Targum Jonathan renders "ואשויניה",[13] as though the text read "והשׂמתיהו."

Similarly the expression "חשך" (the day shall withdraw itself) (30:18), which is written with a "שׂ," is translated "חשך" as though it were written with a "shin." This indeed is the version in various manuscripts[14] as well as the rendering of the Septuagint, συσκοτάσει. This is the correct version.

On the basis of the Targum, it is sometimes possible to arrive at conclusions, not only in regard to variations in vocalisation and suffixes, but also in regard to changes in verb roots which deviate from the Masoretic text. Thus, for example, ולא תקבץ is rendered "ולא תתקבר" (29:5).[15]

It must be pointed out, however, that this change may possibly be due to the fact that the verse preceding this expression has the expression לא תאסף and the Targumist chose to render, instead of the synonymous expression, by some expression that approximates to the content of the verse.

Generally Targum Jonathan translates in accordance with the "keri," but there are instances to show that he sometimes translates in accordance with the "ketiv." For example, the verse "ועריך לא תֵישַׁבְנָה" (35:9) is amended by the keri to read "תָשֹׁבְנָה" in the sense of "returning to their former condition." Targum Jonathan, however, translates according to the "ketiv יתיתבן based on the root "ישב." The Septuagint also has the rendering οὐ μὴ κατοικηθῶσιν, thy cities shall not be inhabited and the Vulgate renders it too "non-habitabantur"; and so the Peshitta לא נתיתבן.

It is known that Targum Jonathan sometimes translates in accordance

and so is the translation of verse 9. The Peshitta translates ואנא עבדתה (I made him).

[11] The Peshitta, Vulgate also translate in second person. S. Cornill, p. 129, M. Z. Segal, p. 10.

[12] The Septuagint translates βουνούς σου according to the text הריך. We see here the tendency to adapt the grammatical form according to the word גבעותיך.

[13] The Peshitta translates the root עבד, which corresponds to the word שׂים. The Vulgate also translates in the same manner: "et faciam."

[14] See this word in *BHS, cf.* Cooke, p. 337.

[15] The Septuagint translates οὐ μὴ περισταλῆς from περιστέλλω. This is the usual expression for the preparation of the corpse for the funeral. S. Cornill, p. 365. We may add to the examples brought by Zimmerli, p. 704 (Ben Sira 38:16; The Book of Tobit 12:13), Isa. 58:8, too, where the same root is used by the Septuagint.

with the "Eastern" version.[16] Thus, for example, the word אגרע (5:11) is rendered אקטוף as though it were written אגדע.[17]

Special importance attaches to the Targum from the etymological point of view. We shall not make mention here of the places where the Targum gives a literal translation, but rather the instances where it deviates from the accepted root. At times a word is explained not in accordance with the accepted root but rather in accordance with what approximates to it in form and sound. For example, among the symbolic deeds of the Prophet we read: ואני נתתי לך את שני עונם (4:5), referring to the number of years that the Jewish people shall carry this punishment, whereas the rendering of the Targum is על חד תרין בחוביהון, namely that they shall suffer double punishment for their iniquities, because the Targumist understood the word שני in the sense of משנה,[18] even as we read in Jeremiah: "משנה עונם (16:18)."

The verb תמר (5:6) in the verse ותמר את משפטי (and she hath rebelled against mine ordinances) is rendered ואשניאת, namely "and she hath changed"[19] because Targum Jonathan understood the verb to be derived from the root מור, rather from than from the root מרה, as it is interpreted to be. Rashi and Kimḥi confirm the Targumist's concept in their commentaries.

In the verse מי כצור כדמה (27:32) some interpret the word as being derived from דמם be silenced. This indeed is the rendering of the Vulgate (obmutuit), Targum Jonathan, on the other hand, renders it לית דדמי לה, namely "there is none to compare to her."[20] This indeed is the interpretation given by some modern commentators.[21]

The Prophet complains that his words are regarded (33:32) as "a love song." The Targum, however, does not understand the word עגבים in this sense, but rather in the sense of "עוגב" (musical instrument), and so renders it אבובין. This too was the concept of the LXX ὡς φωνὴ ψαλτηρίου, and the Vulgate: Carmen musicum.[21a]

[16] A. Geiger, *Urschrift*, 1928, pp. 481–490 (Hebrew) 316–322, המקרא ותרגומיו. R. Gordis, *The Biblical Text in the Making*, Philadelphia, 1937, pp. 74 ff.

[17] According to the "Minhat Say" it was written in the text which was used by the Targum אגדע, and so it is also in some MSS. In the dictionary of Elias Levita (מתורגמן) Isnae 1541 (reprint in Israel), the text is אגדע and not אגרע. See the item "קטף." *Cf.* Churgin, p. 62.

[18] The Peshitta translates also according to this meaning: תרין.

[19] This sense is rendered by the Peshitta וחלפת and by Theodothion ἠλλάξαντο from ἀλλάσσω.

[20] This explanation is quoted by P. Joüon, *Biblica* 10 (1929), pp. 306–307, *cf.* Zimmerli p. 633.

[21] See the explanation of Eichrodt, p. 259.

A. Guillaume suggests an Arabic root כדם and renders the verse: who is like Tyre held fast in the midst of the sea? *JTSt.N.S.* 13 (1962) pp. 324–325, but this suggestion has not the necessary evidence.

[21a] *Cf.* Cooke, p. 312.

In other instances the words in the Targum were given an expository etymology in addition to the meaning of the word in Hebrew. The Scroll of a book about which mention is made in the prophet's dedication is written פנים ואחור (2:10), namely on both sides, but Targum Jonathan renders it "from the beginning and the end."[22] The phrase אבני אש (28:16) is interpreted by the Targumist as referring to the people of Israel because he conceived the expression in the sense of עם קדש.[23] Similarly in homiletical fashion is interpreted the word גבעתי in the verse 34:26 as referring to the Temple. Possibly this rendering approximates to the meaning of the verse ונשא מגבעות in Isaiah's exhortation (2:2).

At times a thought that finds expression in a certain verse or in a whole chapter leaves its impression on the Targumist's interpretation of the words. For example, the expression לבז וללעג (36:4) is rendered לחיך וללעיב. Seemingly the Targumist understood the word בז in the sense of בוז, "shame" rather than "prey." This etymology was probably influenced by the word לעג that is close to it.[24]

At times in the etymology of a word one traces the Targumist's intention of removing any trace of anthropomorphism. Thus the verse ואפרס כנפי עליך[25] (16:8) is translated ואגינית במימרי עליכון.

Another characteristic of the Targum is that whenever a word or phrase is repeated in one and the same verse, they receive a different meaning.[25a] Thus, for instance the expression "בדמיך חיי" (16:6), which appears twice, is translated homiletically, the first being ascribed to the blood of circumcision and the second to the blood of sacrifice.[26]

From the lexicographical point of view the Targum is found to have ideas and assumptions of its own. The chapters concerning Tyre serve as examples of such interpretations. Thus, for example, the word "הבנים" (27:15) which is generally understood to mean "ebony" is rendered "טום"[27]

[22] ... מה דהוה מן שירויא ומה דעתיד למהוי בסופא

[23] R'dak follows the explanation of the Targum, that Israel is compared to the stones of fire.

[24] Indeed, בז (prey) is not parallel to לעג and therefore the Targumist translated חיך (derision) according to the text Ps. 123:3; Prov. 18:3; Job 12:5.

[25] It is a symbolic expression of the marriage, see Ruth 3:9; *cf.* Deut. 23:1, and the Targumist wanted to remove the anthropomorphism and the metaphorical expression. This tendency appears in the translation of the Peshitta, too. It translates instead of כנפי — כפי. The translation of the Vulgate is "amictum meum."

[25a] See Isa. 6:3; Jer. 7:4; 22:29.

[26] In this sense the verse is translated by Mathiah b. Heres: נתן להם הקב"ה שתי מצוות, דם פסח ודם מילה שיתעסקו בם כדי שיגאלו. *Mechilta d'Rabbi Ismael*, ed. Horovitz-Rabin, 1931, p. 14. *Cf.* W. Bacher, *Agada der Tannaiten*, I, p. 388; II, p. 96.

[27] Cornill suggests (pp. 132, 342), that the word טום is corrupted from the text תוכיים, but there is no proof in his suggestion.

(pea fowl). Or the word "גמדים"[28] (27:11) is taken to refer to a people which the Targumist identifies with Cappadocians (קפוטקאי) which is generally the rendering of כפתר (see Deut. 2:23; Amos 9:7; Jer. 47:4).

After a textual and etymological analysis we shall choose two traits in the Targum which are the result of expository tendencies characteristic of the Targum: a) the removal of figurative expressions; b) the eschewing of anthropomorphisms.

The tendency of the Aramaic translations is to do away with metaphors and with figurative expressions and instead of the literal translation of the metaphor to render the imputed meaning. Traits of this are found also in the Targum to Ezekiel. Ezekiel's style is replete with figures of speech and metaphors,[29] and the Book contains several chapters of parables and allegories which according to the principles of the Targumist require clear explanation and interpretation.

In two admonitions of an historical-allegorical nature (in chapters 16 and 23), the Targumist sought somewhat to mitigate and moderate the harsh utterances of the Prophet against the people of Israel and to bring them closer to the concept of the people. At times, when a metaphor hints at some event not recorded in history, the Targumist found it proper to interpret it in some other way than is rendered in the Biblical text. Thus, for example, instead of a description of the origins of Israel from foreign origin: "The Amorite was thy father and thy mother was a Hittite" (16:3)[30] —explains the Targum paraphrase in order to avoid the dishonorable expression from the past of Israel. His translation is: "In the merit of your fathers I expell the Amorite before you and destroy the Hittite."

Also in chapter 23 (verse 2) the Targumist interprets the allegory that the two women referred to two countries.[31]

[28] The Septuagint translates φύλακες (watchman) and in this sense the Peshitta also translates: נטרין. Aquila renders two translations: 1.) πυγμαῖοι (dwarfs) 2.) τετελεσμένοι, from the root τελέω which corresponds to the text "וגמרים" (Gen. 10:2; I Chron. 1:5). According to P. Lagarde this is the right text (*cf. Onomasticon*, vol. 2, p. 95; Cornill, p. 348). Cornill himself suggests to read צמרים on the basis of Gen. 10:18. The identification of "גמרים" with "גמדים" was already suggested by R. Hananel (died about 1055/56) see S. Barol, *Menachem ben Simon aus Posquieres u. sein Kommentar zu Jeremia u. Ezekiel*, 1907, p. 52. Symmachus translates: ἀλλὰ καὶ Μῆδοι which corresponds to the text: וגם מדים.

[29] Eichrodt, p. 23.

[30] Some modern scholars see in this verse the historical fact that the prophet refers to the settlement of tribes of Israel in their homeland. (Eissfeldt, *JPOS*, 16 (1936), pp. 286–292). Eichrodt's exaggerated opinion (p. 204) about the prophet's words that the city owed its origin to a Canaanite population of mixed races, is unacceptable. Y. Kaufman rightly rejects this suggestion in his book תולדות האמונה, Vol. 3, book 1, p. 508, that the poetic words of the prophet do not contain historical value (*cf* M. Weiss, המקרא כדמותו, pp. 69–70, 208–209.) I. van Seters, recently, wrote about this verse (*VT*, 22, 1972, p. 80), that the intention is an ideological rather than a historical manner.

[31] תרתין מדינן דאנון כתרתין נשין דבנת אימא חדא הואה. In Isa. 32:9 the expression is translated "tranquil countries."

In the dirge on the leaders of Israel (chap. 19) the parable is translated in accordance with the imputed meanings in that "thy mother a lioness" is the congregation of Israel and her whelps had grown up in the midst of the young lions are kings. Despite the fact that the verses themselves provide ground for the identification of the kings, the Targumist made no attempt here to identify them.[32] On the other hand, elsewhere figurative expressions are explained by historical exemplification. Thus, for example, in the verse 21:31 "the mitre shall be removed" referred, according to the Targum, to Serayah, the High Priest;[33] "the crown taken off" to Zedakiah and the continuation of the verse "that which is low shall be exalted" refers to Gedaliah, the son of Ahikam, who was the governor of the remnant of Israel after the destruction of the Temple. "That which is high abased"—again refers to Zedekiah. "This also shall be no more until he come whose right it is"—(verse 32) is regarded by the Targumist as a hint to the fact that Gedaliah's rule was not long lived and he was killed by Ishmael, the son of Netanya.[34]

It would appear that the Targum here is like a biblical commentary, and although modern scholarship holds views of its own, this exegesis nonetheless points to the Targumists' historical sense.

In Chapter 34 concerning the sheep and the shepherd,[35] the Targumist is given an extensive opportunity of interpreting the allegorical picture as referring to Israel and its leaders. In verse 17: "I judge between cattle and cattle, even the rams and the he-goats," the Targumist interprets it that the Lord judges between man and man and between sinners (חטאיא) and those that are evil (חייביא). Concerning the rams and the he-goats, the Prophet says (verse 21) that they thrust with side and with shoulder and push the weak till the sheep are scattered abroad. The Targumist interprets it as implying that the rich[36] in wickedness and with might push the

[32] The first whelp refers according to the mediaeval Jewish commentators to the king Jehoahaz. This is the opinion of May (163) and Eichrodt, p. 252. The identification of the second whelp is much more difficult. According to May, the second whelp is Jehoiahin (p. 165), but Eichrodt identifies with Zedekiah (p. 254).

[33] II Kings 25:18, 23. Rashi accepts the identification of the Targum with Serayah, but R'dak doesn't agree with this suggestion.

[34] R. Eleazar of Beaugency refers it to Nebuchadnezzar in whose hands was given the judgement of God to fulfill it. On the other hand Malbim refers it to the Messiah. This explanation was accepted by M. Z. Segal and by some other commentators, see A. Bertholet, *Das Buch Hezekiel* (Kurzer Hand-Com.), 1897, p. 114, C. Orelli, *Ezechiel* (Kurgef. Kom.), 1904, p. 87, J. Herrmann, *Ezechiel* (*HAT*), p. 134. A. Ehrlich had objected to this statement, *Mikra ki-Pheschuto*, III, 1901, p. 327.

[35] See about this chapter, W. Brownlee, *HThR* 51 (1958), pp. 191–203, further bibliography of Zimmerli, p. 825, *cf.* J. Vancil, *The Symbolism of the Shepherd in Biblical, Intertestamental and New Testament Material*, dissertion, Dropsie University, 1975, pp. 227 ff.

[36] The Targumist translates שה בריה (verse 20) גבר עתיר.

sufferers aside and in the end cause their being dispersed,[37] namely bring about their exile among the nations.

Many expressions are translated in the accepted spirit of removing any sign of anthropomorphism, so as to preserve the honour of God. Only a few examples out of many can here be quoted.

Concerning the blasphemy of Edom, the Prophet adds: "וה' שם היה" "Whereas the Lord was there" (35:10). Apparently, on account of the extraneous nature of this expression, and as though it were possible to connect God with time and place, the Targumist was beware of rendering this phrase literally and so translated: "וקדם ה' גלין מחשבת לבא" (The cogitations of the heart were revealed to God).

In the Prophet's vision concerning the Lord's return to the Temple, it is written: "And His voice was like the sound of many waters" (43:2). This simile was regarded by the Targumist as anthropomorphic and so his translation reads that this refers not to the voice of God but rather קל מברכי שמיה, to the voice of those that bless the Lord. The Septuagint also alters the figure to read: *φωνὴ τῆς παρεμβολῆς* his voice is like the voice of a company of soldiers.[38] The word *παρεμβολῆ* is used in the Septuagint in the rendering of מחנה אלהים (Gen. 32:3).[39] The rendering of the Targum in Ezekiel is similar to the Septuagint in the tendency to remove the anthropomorphism.

The verse והכרתי ממך צדיק ורשע "I will cut off from thee the righteous and the wicked" (21:8), implying as it were that the Lord makes no differentiations between the righteous and the wicked is rendered with the intention of guarding God's righteousness, in a way to indicate that the Lord will exile the righteous in order to save them when the wicked are cut off. In other words, the Lord does not deal equally with the righteous and the wicked but rather shields the righteous by sending them into exile so as to save them from the misfortunes that are about to come.

The Septuaginta also introduces a change in the text so as to guard God's justice and renders: I will destroy out of thee transgressor and unrighteous (*ἄδικον καὶ ἄνομον*).[40]

The material that we have had the opportunity to deal with here has revealed but a very small part of the properties and traits of the Targum. But possibly it has succeeded in convincing that in Biblical exegesis one has to have consideration also for the Aramaic translations.

[37] The Targumist is clearly hinting here to the exile עד דבדרתון יתהון לביני מדינתא.

[38] G. Hirschler, לתרגום השבעים של ספר יחזקאל in *B. Heller Jubilee Vol.* (ed. by A. Scheiber), 1941, Hebrew section, p. 21.

[39] Hatch and Redpath, *Concordance to the Septuagint*, II, 1897, pp. 1067 ff.

[40] G. Hirschler, *op. cit.*, p. 20.

Human Dignity: From Creation to Constitution—A Philosophy of Human Rights from the Standpoint of Judaism

By MILTON R. KONVITZ
Cornell University, Ithaca, New York

I

THE SCENE IS quite familiar to us. Socrates is in prison under sentence of death. Crito comes to him with the news that Socrates does not really need to die the next day, for his friends can bribe the jail keepers so that he may escape and be taken to Thessaly, where Crito's friends will look after the old man. But Socrates refuses to accept this little scheme and proceeds to explain why. His fellow Athenians, he says, have done an evil thing by handing down an unjust verdict against him, but a good man will not return evil for evil. But why would it be evil for him to escape? Well, Socrates argues, he would be breaking not only the unjust law made in his case by Athens, but the total legal order; and then he proceeds to paint a touching, sentimental picture of what that legal order had done for him: By its terms, his father and mother became legally husband and wife, and when he was born, it was the legal order that made him their son. And it was by reason of the compulsory education laws that he was trained in literature, music, dancing, and gymnastics. He was, therefore, the child and servant of these laws, which are to him like a father and a master. "Would you," Socrates asked on behalf of the Laws, "have any right to strike or abuse or do any other harm to your father or your master, if you had one, because you had been struck or abused by him . . .?" Then Socrates says that the Laws and Government of Athens spoke to him in these terms:

> Has a philosopher like you failed to discover that our country is more to be valued and higher and holier far than mother or father or any ancestor, and more to be regarded in the eyes of the gods and of men of understanding? To be reverenced and humoured in its anger, even more than a father, . . . And when we are punished by her, whether with imprisonment or stripes, the punishment is to be endured in silence; . . . and if he may do no violence to his father or mother, much less may he do violence to his country.[1]

What a far cry is this paean to the State from the substance and tone of John Locke's *Second Treatise of Civil Government* and *A Letter Concerning Tolera-*

[1] Plato, *Crito* 50.

tion; for Locke takes as his fundamental premise the proposition that Adam, the paradigmatic man, was the child of God and not of the State. Indeed, it is men who make the State rather than the State that makes men. Men in the state of nature have children, and the *parents* have the duty to take care of them. This duty includes the education of the child's mind. It is the *parents, and not the State*, that have the power to form the character of their children by bringing them up in a culture and religion of their choice.

Socrates felt overawed when, on the day before his death, he thought of all that he owed Athens; Locke could stand at a distance from the State and take its measure against Adam, the creature of God—a creature that could live a fairly decent, good life *without* the State, though a better, richer and more secure life as a citizen—provided, of course, that he is a citizen of a State that respects him as a creature of God and not as a creature of the State. Locke was able to build this belief into the very structure of his political theory because his building blocks were biblical and not Greek—essentially biblical though admittedly weathered by the forces of many centuries of religious, intellectual, political and economic history.

In this context the letter and spirit of the decision and opinion of the United States Supreme Court in *Pierce v. Society of Sisters of the Holy Name*[2] is illuminating. The State of Oregon in 1928 enacted a statute that prohibited parochial and private schools for children between eight and sixteen years of age. They could attend only public schools. The Supreme Court held the statute invalid. Children, said the Court, are not mere creatures of the State. "The fundamental theory of liberty upon which all governments in this Union repose," said the Court, "excludes any general power of the state to standardize its children by forcing them to accept instruction from public teachers only. The child is not the mere creature of the state; those who nurture him and direct his destiny have the right, coupled with the high duty, to recognize and prepare him for additional obligations." So, too, in 1972, when Wisconsin tried to compel Amish children to attend secondary school up to the age of sixteen, against the religious beliefs of the parents, the Supreme Court held that such compulsion contravened the rights of the parents under the Free Exercise Clause of the First Amendment.[3]

These decisions are fruit of the Lockean tree. They are consequences of a political theory which is founded on biblical conceptions of the nature of man and of the world in which man is born, lives, and dies.

II

The starting point for Locke, as it is for any theory of human rights, is the belief *that man is more than citizen*. It is not merely that man *has* a soul.

[2] 268 U. S. 510 (1925).

[3] Wisconsin v. Yoder, 406 U. S. 205 (1972).

It is that man *is* a soul—a divinely-created being, invested with rights and dignities at birth, subject to God-made laws and ordinances, and responsible to his Maker. He cannot divest himself of his God-given nature as man. The time may come for him to become a citizen of Athens or Rome or Jerusalem, but his citizenship will not be all-absorbing. He will always retain for himself certain rights and liberties, certain powers and dignities—prerogatives which he enjoys as gifts from the Giver of gifts, and which he can never lose.[4]

The idea that certain essential rights and liberties are inseparable from the very conception of *man* has its deepest and most productive roots in many biblical conceptions, as we will see, including the idea of covenant, the idea of man made in the image of God, the belief that every man is free to choose between good and evil, and the idea that the right law is ultimately founded on the righteousness of God and not on the will of any man, even if he be king or judge.

The fifth of our Ten Commandments is to honor one's father and one's mother. There is no commandment in our Bible to honor one's state. But Socrates, and the Greeks generally, would have had a commandment to honor one's state as if it were one's father and mother. For to the Greeks the citizen came before the man.

The Bill of Rights of the United States Constitution mentions only "people." It is people, and not only citizens, who have freedom of religion, freedom of speech and the press, freedom of assembly; security in their persons, houses and papers against unreasonable searches and seizures; the guarantee against excessive bail and against cruel and unusual punishments; and all the other enumerated guarantees. The Thirteenth Amendment against slavery and involuntary servitiude is for the protection of all men, and the Due Process and Equal Protection Clauses of the Fourteenth Amendment are guarantees made for the benefit of "any person."

These provisions share the common presupposition that fundamental rights are not dependent upon any constitution, upon the grant from any ruler or government. The fundamental human rights are provided for in the unwritten constitution of man—a constitution that is beyond the reach of any government or earthly power.

This was essentially the view of Thomas Jefferson and of the Framers of the Constitution and its Bill of Rights. The Constitution was adopted though it had no Bill of Rights because the latter was deemed to be unnecessary for a free society with a government that was to have only delegated powers.

Writing from Paris on December 20, 1787, Jefferson told James Madison that although their political theory made a Bill of Rights technically unnecessary, ". . . a bill of rights is what the people are entitled to against

[4] John Locke, *Second Treatise of Civil Government*, chs. 2, 6, 7, 9.

every government on earth, . . . and what no just government should refuse," nor should its existence be permitted to "rest on inference."[5] Nothing could state more clearly and definitively the basic, most essential concepts of the philosophy of human rights; namely, (1) That man is prior to and always is more than citizen; (2) That men make states, and governments are formed by men to serve men's interests and needs; (3) that governments are formed to enhance men's enjoyment of their basic human rights; that no majority—no government—may deprive any man of his fundamental human rights.

III

The biblical story of Creation has a special significance in our context, for establishing the idea that there is an eternal order that is prior to and independent of man and mankind—an order that is both natural and moral, an order that is divinely ordained and unalterable.

For the same God who created the sun and the moon created Adam and Eve; and just as He was the law-maker for the former, so, too, was He the law-maker for the latter. If God can make the laws that regulate the physical bodies, He can also make the moral laws that should guide the actions of men. All these laws—both physical and moral—are part of the eternal order that was prior to and independent of Adam and Eve, Cain and Abel, and Noah and his sons and daughters. No man, no king or government, can alter the moral order, can repeal or amend the moral law. No king can make the killing of an innocent man anything other than *what it is*—murder. The act has a moral nature, and that is something no man can change. It is from this that we get the notion of a Higher Law—a kind of unwritten constitution for mankind, which no statute, ordinance or judgment may contradict. From it we also get the notion of the Rule of Law—the idea that governance excludes arbitrariness, willfulness, unreasonableness, and that all things, events, and actions are subject to law.

It is this basic biblical postulate—that the moral no less than the physical order of the universe is founded in Creation—that is the burden of the answer out of the whirlwind in Job. He who made the hippopotamus gave him his physical nature, so that he lies under the lotus plants and among the willows of the brook. So, too, the crocodile, whose back is made of rows of shields, whose sneezings flash forth light, and from whose mouth go flaming torches. Can Job understand the thoughts and plans of Him who is their maker? And if he does not understand the physical laws, yet knows that they are operative, why should he doubt the operation of the moral laws, of whose operations he is equally ignorant? A man who does not know

[5] *Life and Selected Writings of Thomas Jefferson*, eds. A. Koch and W. Peden (New York, 1944), 436.

the way to the dwelling of light, who has not entered the storehouses of the snow, who has not commanded the morning since his days began, such a man can be wise only in his own conceit,—and yet he dares to question the ways of God with those who practice iniquity and with those who follow the paths of justice! "Shall a faultfinder contend with the Almighty?" The righteous man may suffer, and he may see the evil flourish, yet he must not doubt the righteousness of God and deny God's justice and power.

> Behold, He will slay me; I have no hope;
> Yet I will defend my ways in His face.
> This will be my salvation,
> That godless man shall not come before Him.[6]

Though the biblical man move in ignorance and darkness as to the ways of God and His moral laws, yet he remains, through all trials and afflictions, the man who trusts his Creator. He trusts God that the sun will rise and set, and that fire will burn and snow will freeze. "I shall never believe," said Einstein, "that God plays dice [or games] with the world. . . . The Lord God is subtle, but malicious He is not." The biblical man of faith believed that God does not play moral tricks; that in the moral realm He is as subtle as in the physical realm, and that in neither realm is He malicious.

What it all comes to is the belief that man is born into a world for which there are preordained moral, no less than physical, laws—moral laws which he may not break with impunity. "Though the mills of God grind slowly, yet they grind exceeding small." And no man, not even the most exalted and powerful king, can change these laws, these ways of God, by a jot or a tittle. Man can therefore never be totally and exclusively a citizen. He can never be subject only to the laws of his state. He is first and always a man, created by God, and a citizen of a world of which God is King and lawmaker. In God's domain, where His law prevails, every man has the dignity that comes from being God's handiwork; all men are equal because they are equally citizens of His city; they are all free because they are all, king and commoner alike, equally subject to the ordered liberty which He has ordained from the beginning of time and for all time.

IV

From the standpoint of Judaism, human rights—just as the Bible itself—must begin with Genesis, with God the Creator. For Judaism, human rights have their "beginning"—their *bereshet*,—their foundation, outside the state, outside any man-made constitution or bill of rights, outside even humanity itself. Their beginning is linked with the beginning of the sun and moon, land and water, day and night.

[6] Job 13:15–16.

There is recorded in the Jerusalem Talmud[7] a disputation between Rabbi Akiba and Ben Azzai as to which is the most fundamental principle of the Torah. Akiba, quoting Leviticus, said: "Thou shalt love thy neighbor as thyself." Ben Azzai, quoting Genesis, said that "This is the book of the generations of Adam" expressed a still greater principle. The full passage cited by Ben Azzai reads as follows: "This is the book of the generations of Adam [man]. When God created man [Adam] He made him in the likeness of God." Ben Azzai's answer is by far the more convincing one, for without it the Love Commandment has no metaphysical base; it stands as a naked assertion of God's will, in no way different from many other commandments. But the text chosen by Ben Azzai goes to the very nature of man; for it says that all men are the children of one father; that just as their father—Adam—was made in the image of God, so each man, a son of Adam, *ben Adam*, is made in God's image; that there is only one human family, that all men are born with equal dignity, that all men are equal. It is on the basis of this principle—this *klal godol*—that God, the maker of Adam, can say to the children of Adam: "Love thy neighbor as thyself."

With the dispute between Akiba and Ben Azzai before him, Hermann Cohen said that the latter was evidently right; for the love of the neighbor is, said Cohen,

> dependent upon God's creation of man, and not upon the subjective feeling with which I love myself or somebody else. "This is the book of the generation of man . . . in the likeness of God made he Him." Upon this principle rests the history of mankind. . . .[8]

One might say that Jewish thought and ethics almost instinctively feel themselves constantly driven back to their sources in God the Creator. Let me cite but one instance that will exemplify this way of thinking and feeling.

When a Jewish court had jurisdiction in capital cases, the law required that the judges charge the witnesses against the accused in the following terms:[9]

> Perhaps what you are about to say is mere conjecture or hearsay, based on secondhand information, on what you heard from a trustworthy person. Perhaps you are unaware that we will in the course of the trial subject you to inquiry and query. Know that capital cases are unlike monetary cases. In a monetary case, one may make restitution and his offense is expiated; but in a capital case (the witness) is accountable for the blood of the man and the blood of his (potential) posterity until the end of time. Thus with respect to Cain it is said

[7] Jer. Tal., Nedarim 9.

[8] Hermann Cohen, *Religion of Reason* (trans. S. Kaplan, New York, 1972), 119.

[9] Text as it appears in Maimonides, Book XIV of Code, *Book of Judges* (Yale Judaica Series) (New Haven, 1949), 34.

"The voice of thy brother's bloods crieth" (Gen. 4:10)—that is, his blood and the blood of his (potential) descendants. For this reason, but a single man was created, to teach us that if any man destroys a single life in the world, Scripture imputes it to him as though he had destroyed the whole world; and if any man preserves one life, Scripture ascribes it to him as though he had preserved the whole world. Furthermore, all human beings are fashioned after the pattern of the first man, yet no two faces are exactly alike. Therefore, every man may well say, "for my sake the world was created." And perhaps you will say, "Why borrow this trouble?" It is said: "He being a witness, whether he hath seen or known, if he do not utter it, then he shall bear his iniquity" (Lev. 5:1). And perhaps you will say, "Why should we incur guilt for the blood of this man?" It is written "And when the wicked perish, there is joy" (Prov. 11:10).

One of the characteristic aspects of Judaism is marked dramatically in the above passage; that is, the inextricable intermixture of metaphysical, ethical and legalistic strands—the way normative thought allows itself to be bitten into by metaphysical principles. Here stands before the court an ordinary man who, in a preliminary inquiry, had qualified to testify as a witness in a case in which another ordinary man is on trial for his life, and the witness and the accused are suddenly transported to the time and place of the very creation of man. The witness is made to feel that it is no ordinary creature who faces life or death, but Adam himself, and the whole of mankind, and the whole of creation, which was made for Adam, who can enjoy creation only as long as he has life. Yet it was not, of course, the judges who cast this terrifying, awesome burden on the witness—they merely reminded him of what God the Creator had done when He fashioned man on the sixth day after all His other work had been accomplished, and fashioned him in His own image.

V

In the second century, in order to establish the absoluteness, newness and uniqueness of the Christian religion, Marcion contended that there were two Gods, the God of the Hebrew Scriptures, who was the Creator and Judge, and the God of the Pauline Epistles, who was the God of love whom Jesus had revealed. The God whom Judaism proclaimed was the inferior God. He was the one who had made the material universe, including man, and He ruled by law and justice. He was the Ruler of the world of matter and bodies; He issued commandments, and judged by works. The Christian God, however, He whom Paul had proclaimed, was the God of pure love, the God of spirit, the God of faith and grace. He had nothing to do with the world of nature but only with the world of spirit; He does not judge, and He delivers only souls. He is not the Messiah of the Hebrew Scriptures, and He will not rescue man from the material world.

In Marcion we can see the Platonic dualism of matter and spirit, the dualism of body and soul which Socrates had taught some four centuries before, a teaching which came to pervade much of Hellenistic thought and religion.

The Christian ecclesiastical leaders who became aware of Marcion's influence repudiated him and condemned Marcionism as heresy. They put him on a level with the Gnostics, whom they severely condemned.

But though condemned, Marcion's teachings affected the bias and tone of Christianity; for though Christianity does not countenance the idea of two Gods, yet it always finds ways to belittle the God of whom Judaism has been the witness. He is the God of the material world, the God of justice, the God of law, the God of rewards and punishment, the God of the past; while the Gospel proclaims the God of pure spirit, of pure love, of pure grace, of pure faith, the God of the future. The dualism of body and soul has remained basic in Christianity, and Pauline antinomianism has remained firmly rooted in the Christian religious consciousness.

But if there is truly—not merely rhetorically—a Judeo-Christian tradition of natural rights and human rights, it must be based on a monism that recognizes the hand of God in matter and body, and in human nature and human beings; that sees the possibility of a reconciliation of law and justice with grace and love; and that hopes for the concord of nature and spirit. But above and underlying all it must be based on the belief that the goodness and wisdom of God the Creator are somehow reflected in Adam whom He fashioned out of the dust of the earth. Only man having this transcendent dignity can be said to have "natural, imprescriptible, and unalienable rights."

It is important to note that the universal elements of Judaism, which clings to the belief in God the Creator, come ahead of the particularistic; that the bonds of humanity come ahead, in the metaphysical order of God's goodness and wisdom, of the special bond or covenant between God and Israel.

Rabbi Josua ben Levi said: "When a man goes on the road, a troup of angels proceed in front of him and proclaim: 'Make way for the image of the Holy One, blessed be he'."[10] And wherever man goes, on whatever road, he has the "unalienable rights" with which "all men . . . are endowed by their Creator."

It is all summed up in the glorious Psalm 8, in which the work of the first day of creation is intimately and indissolubly bound with the work accomplished on the sixth day:

[10] Deut. Rabbah, Reʾeh, iv:4.

When I look at Thy heavens, the work of Thy fingers,
the moon and the stars which Thou hast established;
what is man that Thou art mindful of him,
and the son of man that Thou dost care for him?
Yet Thou hast made him little less than divine,
and dost crown him with glory and honor.
Thou hast given him dominion over the works of Thy hands;
Thou hast put all things under his feet, . . .
O Lord, our Lord,
how majestic is Thy name in all the earth!

The Psalmist does not glorify only those who are bound in the covenant of Abraham. He sings of man, of Adam. It is man, generic man—not the Jewish man, not the white man, but just man, Adam, made, the rabbis taught, of the dust gathered from all parts of the earth, so that no one race might claim that for them alone was the world made—it is undifferentiated, unhyphenated man who was made little less than divine and crowned with glory and honor, and given dominion over all the works of creation.

It is only of man so created and thus endowed that one can say that he has, by virtue only of his birth as man, the fundamental human rights that define and shield his God-given human dignity.

Judaism has never proclaimed that salvation can come only by faith in its teachings or by mere membership in the people of Israel. It has always proclaimed the dignity of MAN, man made in God's image. Thus the rabbis have taught:

> Whence can you know that a Gentile who practices the Torah is equal to the High Priest? Because it says (Lev. 18:5) "which if a man do, he shall live through them." It does not say, "the law of Priests, Levites, Israelites," but "this is the law of man, O Lord God." It does not say, "open the gates and let the Priests and Levites and Israel enter," but it says (Isa. 26:6) "Open the gates that a righteous Gentile may enter." . . . It does not say, "rejoice ye, Priests and Levites and Israelites," but it says, (Ps. 135:4) "Do Good, O Lord, to the good." So, even a Gentile, if he is righteous, is equal to the High Priest.[11]

I realize that this language may sound strange to sophisticated, modern ears. As Carl Becker wrote in 1932, impliedly separating himself from the world of Psalm 8: "What is man that the electron should be mindful of him? Man is but a foundling in the cosmos, abandoned by the forces that created him. Unparented, unassisted and undirected by omniscient or benevolent authority, he must fend for himself, and with the aid of his own limited intelligence, find his way about in an indifferent universe."[12]

[11] Bab. Tal., Ab. Zar. 3a; Sifra 86b; Sanh. 59a; Bab. K. 38a.

[12] Carl L. Becker, *The Heavenly City of the Eighteenth Century Philosophers* (New Haven, 1932), 15.

The values of the Declaration of Independence are just as much expressions of beliefs as are the values of Judaism which I have discussed. The Declaration of Independence and Judaism are alike committed, not to facts but to the resolution to translate certain ideals into facts, to bring the city of God down to this earth, to fulfill the great commandment: "Be ye holy, for I the Lord am holy," i. e., not just to believe in our ideals, but to *live* them.

Sumerian Literature: Recovery and Restoration

By SAMUEL NOAH KRAMER
The University of Pennsylvania

THE MODERN SCHOLAR first became aware, ever so vaguely to be sure, of the possible existence of an ancient Sumerian literature with the appearance of *4R* in 1875,[1] a magnificent pioneering publication of texts from the Ašurbanipal library that included parts of several literary compositions written in both Sumerian and Akkadian, and even a literary catalogue listing the incipits of various types of literary genres. Six years later, in 1881–82, Paul Haupt published his *Akkadische und Sumerische Keilschrifttexte* (*ASKT*), which also included several such bilingual literary works from the Ašurbanipal library, among them a hymn of some length to the goddess Inanna. Fifteen years later, in 1896, George Reisner published his epoch-making *Sumerisch-Babylonische Hymnen und Gebete nach Tontafeln Griechischer Zeit* (*SBH*), consisting of copies of numerous Sumero-Akkadian literary bilinguals, primarily liturgical laments, some of which duplicated pieces published in *4R* and *ASKT*. From these publications it could be inferred that (1) the Sumerian texts, which were usually written above the Akkadian, were the originals, and (2) these Sumerian originals must have been of a considerably earlier date than that of the bilingual tablets inscribed in the first millennium B.C.E.

Moreover, the existence of early Sumerian literary documents was not a matter of mere surmise, for beginning with 1884 there appeared Ernest de Sarzec's *Découvertes en Chaldée*, which included two long, and complex poetic compositions commemorating Gudea's rebuilding of the Eninnu temple, inscribed on two impressive terra-cotta cylinders. However, the compositions inscribed on the Gudea Cylinders differed so materially in both content and form from the Sumerian text of the published bilinguals, that it was difficult to perceive any significant relationship between them.[2] But then, in 1902, appeared *Cuneiform Texts from Babylonian Tablets in the British*

[1] *4R* is the generally accepted abbreviation for the fourth of the five folio volumes of the series *The Cuneiform Inscriptions of Western Asia* that was planned and edited by the "father of Assyriology," Henry Rawlinson, and was published between the years 1851 and 1884. The scholar who copied *4R* was the renowned George Smith; a second edition of the volume with some additions and corrections by Th. G. Pinches was published in 1891.

[2] The most recent and reliable translation of the Gudea Cylinder hymns is found in Adam Falkenstein and Wolfram von Soden's *Sumerische und Akkadische Hymnen und Gebete*, pp. 137–182. A more definitive edition of the text based on Falkenstein's "Nachlass" is now being prepared by his former student Dietz Edzard of the University of Munich.

Museum (*CT*), *XV*, with L. W. King's copies of sixteen well preserved tablets of the Old Babylonian period, inscribed with unilingual Sumerian compositions concerned with various Sumerian deities, some of which were designated by the scribe as *iršemma*,[3] and these were so similar to the published bilinguals of the first millennium that it became reasonably certain that there must have existed a number of Sumerian literary works in the Old Babylonia period which could be taken as their forerunners.

Still these relatively few unilingual compositions with their rather brief lamentful content could hardly be taken as conclusive proof of the existence of a large, complex, and variegated literature. The conviction that this was so grew gradually in the course of the decades that followed, with the accumulation of evidence that derived primarily from three sources: (1) the publication of copies of many of the several thousand Sumerian literary tablets and fragments excavated at Nippur by the University of Pennsylvania between the years 1889 and 1900,[4] that began in 1909 with Hugo Radau's "Miscellaneous Texts from the Temple Library of Nippur,"[5] and continued in one form or another to the present day; (2) the publication of more than three hundred tablets and fragments of unknown provenance from the purchased collections of the Berlin Staatliche Museen, the Louvre, and the British Museum; and (3) the publication of some four hundred tablets and fragments excavated by Henri de Genouillac at Kish and by Leonard Woolley at Ur. Decade by decade, the major publications of Sumerian unilingual texts from the Old Babylonian period may be itemized as follows:

The years 1911–1920 were rich vintage years that saw the publication of twelve volumes concerned with the Sumerian literary documents. Two of these appeared in the very first year of the decade, in 1911, with copies of a score of tablets and fragments from the Nippur collection of the University Museum: (1) D. W. Myhrman's *Babylonian Hymns and Prayers*, which is particularly noteworthy for the inclusion of the upper half of a six-column tablet inscribed with the first half of the myth "Inanna and Enki: the Transfer of the *me* from Eridu to Erech";[6] and (2) Hugo Radau's *Sumerian*

[3] The *iršemma* is a lamentful literary genre usually bemoaning the destruction of a city and its temples or the suffering and death of a deity (especially the demi-god Dumuzi); for full details *cf.* the forthcoming study by Mark Cohen, who has devoted several years of research to this Sumerian literary genre.

[4] These are now located in approximately equal portions in the Istanbul Museum of the Ancient Orient (part of the Istanbul Arkeoloji Müzeler complex) and in the University Museum in Philadelphia.

[5] This important pioneering publication of some of the Sumerian literary documents in the University Museum appeared in the *Hilprecht Anniversary Volume*, pp. 374–457.

[6] This "charter" myth which celebrates the rise of Erech as one of Sumer's great political and religious centers has now been edited and published by Gertrud Farber-Flugge who began the relevant research some years ago in the University Museum, as *Studia Pohl*, *10* (1975).

Hymns and Prayers to the God Nin-ib, consisting of texts revolving about the god Ninurta, including several inscribed with extracts of the *lugal-e* myth.[7]

One year later, in 1912, Heinrich Zimmern published the first volume of *Sumerische Kultlieder aus altbabylonischer Zeit*, with copies and photographs of one hundred tablets and fragments from the tablet collection of the Berlin Staatliche Museen, some of which were large multi-column tablets inscribed with a varied assortment of liturgical laments and dirges, not a few of which revolved about the god Dumuzi.[8] In the very next year, 1913, Zimmern published the second volume of his *Sumerische Kultlieder*, with copies of another hundred or so Sumerian literary pieces, this time mostly fragments. That same year Hugo Radau published thirteen tablets and fragments from the Nippur collection of the University Museum inscribed with a varied assortment of Dumuzi texts in his *Sumerian Hymns and Prayers to the God Dumuzi* 1, and Stephen Langdon published his *Sumerian Liturgies*.

In the following year, 1914, appeared Arno Poebel's superb *Historical and Grammatical Texts*, which actually should have been entitled *Historical, Literary, and Grammatical Texts*, since it includes copies of more than a score Sumerian literary tablets and fragments, among them a large six-column tablet inscribed with the second half of the myth "Inanna and Enki: the Transfer of the *me* from Eridu to Erech" (the first half was inscribed on the fragmentary six-column tablet published by Myhrman three years before), as well as three extracts from the myth "Inanna's Descent to the Nether World" (the Sumerian forerunner of the Akkadian "Ištar's Descent to the Nether World" that had become known to the scholarly world half a century before),[9] not to mention fragments of various other literary genres. And in the very same year, 1914, Stephen Langdon published his *Historical and Religious Texts from the Temple Library of Nippur*, containing copies of more than fifty pieces from the Nippur collection of the Istanbul Museum of the Ancient Orient.

[7] The text of this myth, concerned with the deeds and exploits fo the god Ninurta, has been pieced together from more than one hundred and fifty tablets and fragments by the late E. Bergmann (who spent several years in the University Museum copying the pieces that I had identified), J. J. A. van Dijk, and J. L. Zubizaretta (both of the Biblical Institute, Rome); a definitive edition of the myth is now being prepared by the two last named scholars.

[8] Most of these are written in a phonetic non-historical orthography that obscures the reading and meaning of many of the words and phrases, and it is only in recent years that a breakthrough has been made, at least to some substantive extent, in the translation and interpretation of these important documents. For fuller details *cf.* my *The Sacred Marriage Rite*, p. 158, n. 6, and especially Joachim Krecher's *Sumerische Kultlyrik*.

[9] The myth "Inanna's Descent to the Nether World" has been reconstructed by me over the decades from more than twenty tablets and fragments; for bibliographical details *cf. The Sacred Marriage Rite*, p. 154, n. 3. The conclusion of this myth, which is still only partially preserved, is found on a tablet in the British Museum that was excavated by Leonard Woolley at Ur, and that will be published by me in the near future.

Stephen Langdon dominated the Sumerian literary scene during the remaining years of the decade with his publication in 1915, 1917, and 1919, respectively, of (1) *The Sumerian Epic of Paradise, the Flood, and the Fall of Man*;[10] (2) *Sumerian Liturgical Texts*; (3) *Sumerian Liturgies and Psalma.* Langdon's copies of the tablets and fragments from the Nippur collection of the University Museum are rather shoddy, and his attempted transliterations and translations are quite unreliable. Nevertheless it should be recognized and appreciated that by making available the texts of close to one hundred tablets and fragments, whose contents range over the entire gamut of the Sumerian literary repertoire, Langdon enriched immensely our knowledge of the nature, scope, and significance of Sumerian literature.

Finally, towards the very end of the decade, in 1918, George Barton published his *Miscellaneous Babylonian Inscriptions*, which included copies of eleven tablets and fragments from the Nippur collection of the University Museum. Barton's autographs and translations are even worse than those of Langdon. Nevertheless it is to be acknowledged that he, too, added considerably to the ever growing stock of essential source material. Moreover, he included copies and photographs of a clay cylinder inscribed probably as early as the period of the Dynasty of Akkad with what seems to be a myth of Enlil and Ninḫursag, although most of its contents still remain obscure. What is most significant about this document, however, is that it provided clear evidence for the existence of Sumerian literary works in pre-Gudean days, a surmise that has since been amply corroborated by the archaic Sumerian literary texts excavated recently at *Abu Ṣalabiḫ*, an ancient site northwest of Nippur.[11]

The decade that followed, 1921–1930, was almost as productive as the preceding one; it witnessed the publication of eight volumes containing between them copies of more than two hundred tablets and fragments, representing virtually every Sumerian literary genre: myths, epic tales, hymns, laments, "Sacred Marriage" songs, essays, disputations, proverbs, and precepts. In 1921 appeared *CT, XXXVI,* which included Cyril Gadd's excellent copies of ten well preserved tablets in the British Museum. In 1923 Stephen Langdon again came on the literary scene with a very important publication of texts from the Weld-Blundell collection of the Ashmolean Museum, entitled *Sumerian and Semitic Religious and Historical Texts.* In 1924 Edward Chiera, who played a key role in the restoration of Sumerian literature despite his early and untimely death in 1933, published his

[10] Langdon's rather pretentious title of the composition is quite unjustified — the myth has nothing to do with "the Flood" or "the Fall of Man," and while it does concern a "Paradise-land," the protagonists are not mortals like Adam and Eve, but divine beings; for full details *cf.* my monograph "*Enki and Ninhursag: A Sumerian Paradise Myth.*

[11] *Cf.* now Robert D. Biggs, *Inscriptions from Tell Abu Ṣalabih,* a major and fundamental contribution to the early stages of Sumerian literature.

Sumerian Religious Texts, with elegant copies of fifty-three tablets and fragments in the Istanbul Museum of the Ancient Orient. In 1924–25, Henri de Genouillac published a considerable number of Sumerian literary pieces, mostly quite fragmentary, in his *Première recherche archéologique à Kich*, which gave evidence of the existence of a Sumerian literary repertoire in Kish in northern Sumer similar to that of Nippur in central Sumer. And at the very end of the decade, in 1930, this same scholar published two volumes of *Textes religieux sumériens du Louvre*, containing copies that are by no means as bad as they look at first glance, of ninety-eight tablets and fragments that augmented impressively our stock of fundamental source material.[12]

The decade 1931–40 saw the publication of only two volumes of Sumerian literary texts, Edward Chiera's *Sumerian Epics and Myths* and *Sumerian Texts of Varied Content*, but these contain more than two hundred and fifty pieces, some of which are of very considerable size and immense importance. Chiera had copied them in the University Museum in the 1920's, when he was still a member of the Department of Oriental Studies of the University of Pennsylvania, and later, when he was invited by Henry Breasted to become editor-in-chief of the Assyrian Dictionary Project, it was agreed between them that the Oriental Institute would publish these documents. Chiera's unexpected and premature death left these texts, to which he had devoted much time and labor, "stranded," as it were, and I was invited by the editorial department of the Oriental Institute to prepare them for posthumous publication. It was in the course of trying to understand the contents of these documents and penetrate their meaning, that I became convinced that the restoration, translation, and interpretation of the Sumerian literary works, especially those of any considerable length, would be virtually impossible until many more of the Sumerian literary tablets and fragments lying about in the cupboards of the various museums, and particularly in the Nippur collections of the University Museum and the Museum of the Ancient Orient, were made available to the scholarly world in one form or another. I therefore travelled to Istanbul in 1937, where in the course of the next eighteen months I copied close to two hundred tablets and fragments of wide-ranging literary content. The resulting volume, however, did not appear until 1944, and was the only collection of Sumerian literary texts published in the entire 1941–1950 decade.

The situation improved considerably in the course of the following decade. In 1952 appeared my *Enmerkar and the Lord of Aratta*,[13] and in 1959 Edmund Gordon published the ground-breaking fundamental volume

[12] A very careful and helpful collation of these texts is now being prepared by J. Durand of the École Pratique des Hautes Études, Paris.

[13] This was published as a monograph of the University Museum. A revised and improved edition of this epic tale has been prepared by Sol Cohen, as a dissertation in the Department of Oriental Studies of the University of Pennsylvania (1973).

Sumerian Proverbs;[14] both these works contained copies and photographs of quite a number of tablets and fragments from the Nippur collection of the University Museum and the Museum of the Ancient Orient. In 1957 J. J. A. van Dijk published the second volume of *Tabulae Cuneiformes à F.M.H. Th. de Liagre Böhl*, which included seven important Sumerian literary pieces. But the most impressive contribution of the decade came in 1959 with the publication of *CT XLII*, a volume containing H. H. Figulla's copies of forty-six Sumerian tablets from the British Museum. This publication was doubly welcome to cuneiformists:[15] it marked the revival, under the far-sighted sponsorship of the then Keeper of the Western Asiatic Section of the British Museum and his associate Edmond Sollberger, of the *CT* publications that had lapsed for a quarter of a century, and it gave evidence of the unsuspected existence in the British Museum of a large number of Sumerian literary documents.

The last decade in our chronological sketch, 1961–1970, was the most productive of all. It witnessed the publication of more than a thousand pieces, mostly fragments, to be sure, that brought to light numerous hitherto unknown literary works, and helped to restore many a fragmentary and unintelligible composition. Thus in 1961 and 1967 there appeared Bernhardt and Kramer's *Sumerische literarische Texte aus Nippur*, with copies of more than a hundred tablets and fragments from the Hilprecht Sammlung of the Friedrich-Schiller Universität, Jena.[16] In 1963 and 1966 appeared the first two parts of volume VI of *Ur Excavation Texts*, with Cyril Gadd's copies of over three hundred tablets and fragments excavated at Ur by the joint British Museum-University Museum Expedition conducted by Leonard Woolley in the years 1923–34. And 1969 saw the publication of volume I of *Istanbul Arkeoloji Müzelerinde Bulunan Sumer Edebi Tablet ve Parcalari* (Sumerian Literary Tablets and Fragments in the Archaeological Museum of Istanbul), with copies of some six hundred pieces prepared by Muazziz Cig and

[14] This, too, was published as a monograph of the University Museum. Gordon followed up this study with several additional articles on Mesopotamian proverbs, based primarily on tablets and fragments from the Nippur collections of the University Museum and the Museum of the Ancient Orient.

[15] For a detailed summary of the contents of these tablets, *cf.* my review article in the *Journal of Cuneiform Studies*, vol. 18, pp. 35–48, and for the collation of the texts, *cf. ibid.*, vol. 23, pp. 10–16.

[16] The copies were prepared with my help by Dr. Inez Bernhardt who was in charge of the Hilprecht Sammlung at the time. Dr. Bernhardt, however, is no Sumerologist, and though she had a sharp eye and a good hand for copying, her autographs contained quite a number of errors. These have now been corrected by Claus Wilke's helpful collations published as part 4 of vol. 65 of the *Abhandlungen der Sächischen Akademie der Wissenschaften zu Leipzig*.

Hatice Kizilyay, two Turkish ladies who over the years have contributed much to cuneiform research.[17]

As for the coming decade, 1971–1980, it might well turn out to be even more productive than the preceding. To begin with, the second volume of *Istanbul Arkeoloji Müzelerinde Bulunan Sumer Edebi Tablet ve Parcalari*, consisting of my copies of one hundred and seventy tablets and fragments, is now in the hands of the Türk Tarih Kurumu (The Turkish Historical Commission) and should appear in the very near future. In the British Museum, Aaron Shaffer has now virtually completed the copying of some three hundred fragments that will be published as the third part of volume VI of *Ur Excavation Texts*. In Oxford Oliver Gurney has completed the copying of close to fifty tablets and fragments in the Ashmolean Museum, which will be published as *OECT* (*Oxford Edition of Cuneiform Texts*), *V* probably in November of the year 1976. In the University Museum, Jane Heimerdinger is about to complete the copying of some five hundred small fragments from the 1948–52 excavations of the joint Oriental Institute-University Museum Expedition to Nippur. In the British Museum Edmond Sollberger, now Keeper of its Western Asiatic Section, has identified more than fifty important Sumerian literary pieces, many of them quite well preserved, which I catalogued several years ago, and which will no doubt be copied and published in the not too distant future.[18] The University Museum and the Yale Babylonian Collection still have quite a number of Sumerian literary tablets and fragments, and these will be published under the competent supervision and editorship of Ake Sjöberg and William Hallo, hopefully before the end of the decade.

[17] There are still about two hundred unpublished Sumerian literary pieces, mostly small fragments, in the Istanbul Museum, and it is hoped that these will be copied by some Turkish scholar in the not too distant future.

[18] These British Museum tablets cover the entire range of the Sumerian literary repertoire. Several of them fill gaps in long known compositions, but most of them contain altogether new texts. Among the better preserved and more significant of these are: (1) a myth revolving about the birth of the cursed *elpētu*-rushes, which begins with a passage about the Flood; (2) an elegy in the form of a playlet featuring two protagonists: an unnamed "maid" whose lover has died in a distant land, and her friend and adviser who exhorts her to prepare herself for the imminent arrival of his dead body; (3) a tablet with two hymns to the sun-god Utu, the second of which ends with a remarkable address to the god by his sister Inanna; (4) a tablet that originally contained twelve *iršemma*: three to the storm-god Iškur, two to Enlil, four to his son Ninurta, three to Enki; (5) a long liturgy revolving about the goddess Ninisinna, which includes chants to the gods Enki and Abu; (6) several lamentful compositions concerned with the suffering of the goddesses Inanna and Ninhursag; (7) several fragmentary texts related to the Dumuzi-Inanna cult; (8) a minutely inscribed tablet containing a hymnal prayer to Inanna for the health of Išme-Dagan, a king of Isin who reigned about 1850 B.C.E.; (9) two very small terra cotta cylinders inscribed with literary catalogues listing the incipits of more than a dozen *balag*-songs (that is, songs probably accompanied by the harp).

So much for the publication of the textual source material. As for the restoration, translation, and interpretation of the individual compositions represented by it, these may be said to have begun seriously and fruitfully in the 1930's, and to have continued to make no little headway down to the present day—the interested student can follow their progress over the years in the bibliographical sections of *Orientalia* and the *Archiv für Orientforschung*; in R. Borger's *Handbuch der Keilschriftliteratur*; in the lists of Adam Falkenstein's and Thorkild Jabosens's books, articles, and reviews itemized in the *Heidelberger Studien zum Alten Orient* (1967) and *Toward the Image of Tammuz* (1970); in the Introduction to the various text volumes in which I participated in one way or another;[19] in a number of recent articles by William Hallo, and in Miguel Civil's forthcoming comprehensive catalogue of the published Sumerian literary texts.

This is not the place to go into details; here, very sketchily and *grosso modo*, the contents of the extant Sumerian literary documents may be summarized as follows: twenty myths, nine epic tales, over two hundred hymnal compositions of diverse genre and size, a score or so of liturgical lamentations, some thirty songs and dirges revolving about the Dumuzi-Inanna cult, a dozen disputations and school essays, and another dozen or so collections of proverbs and precepts. All and all, it is not unreasonable to conclude that this immense literary stock, with close to thirty thousand lines of text, mostly in poetic form, provides a fairly representative cross section of the literary repertoire current in Sumer in the Old Babylonian period, although no doubt some surprisingly unexpected genres may still turn up.

Nevertheless, *a priori*, it can be surmised that the Sumerian literary material excavated to date is but a fraction of that which had existed in Sumer, and that many a composition is still lying buried in its tells and ruins. Thus, there are quite a number of unidentifiable compositions of which we have at present only meager and fragmentary extracts. The numerous epithets by which the more important deities are designated imply the existence of at least some relevant tales relating to their origin, none of which have been recovered to date. Here and there in the available documents there are hints of as yet altogether unknown myths, such as the avenging of Enlil by one of the lesser gods, or Enki's struggle with the *kur* and his elevation to the kingship of the *abzu*. Most important of all is the evidence derived from the Old Babylonian literary catalogues prepared by the ancient scribes themselves. Until very recently there were known six Old Babylonian catalogues that between them listed the incipits of over one hundred and fifty Sumerian literary compositions of diverse genres, but the texts of only about sixty of these have been recovered wholly or in part.

[19] *Cf.* also the itemized list of my publications in the recently published *Kramer Anniversary Volume* (vol. 28 of *Alter Orient und Altes Testament*).

In 1975 I published two hitherto unknown Old Babylonian catalogues in the British Museum that were first identified by Edmond Sollberger, and these provided the titles of over one hundred *iršemma* compositions, of which only some ten have been recovered to date.[20] It is obvious therefore that many, if not most, of the Sumerian literary works are still buried underground awaiting the lucky spade of the future excavator.

The Second volume of *Istanbul Arkeoloji Tabletler ve Parcalari*, as well as *OECT V*, have appeared in 1976; the "elegy" mentioned in note 18, appeared in 1977 in the *Finkelstein Memorial Volume*.

[20] For full details *cf. Studia Orientalia, XLIV* (a volume dedicated to Armas Salonen), pp. 141–166.

The Origin of the Synagogue*

By LEO LANDMAN
Yeshiva University

THE SYNAGOGUE IS Judaism's contribution to the area of public worship and its establishment created a unique form of worship. Today, the synagogue provides the central outlet for Jews in their expressions of prayer; yet, its origins are obscure and blurred. Opinions among scholars differ greatly and all kinds of theories concerning the synagogue's inception have been put forth. Following is a brief resume of the more well-known views:

Julius Wellhausen[1] maintained that the synagogue is the outgrowth of the provincial *bamoth*; that is, just as the *bamoth* catered to the spiritual needs of the rural areas, to people who could not visit the Temple in Jerusalem often enough, so the local synagogues provided the people of the outlying areas with a place of worship.

Louis Finkelstein[2] refuted Wellhausen's proposal. He pointed out that:

a. the *bamoth* were set up as rivals to the Temple whereas the synagogue was meant to supplement the Temple service or at least, was an institution apart from Temple worship and not in competition with it. Sacrifices were never a part of the synagogue worship as they were a part of the *bamoth* service.

b. the *bamoth* were constantly being condemned by the prophets, whereas the synagogue was conducted within the spirit of Judaism. Finkelstein concludes that the synagogue stems from the prophetic prayers and institutions. In other words, Finkelstein traced the synagogue to religious gatherings conducted by the prophets. He does not specify which institution sired the synagogue.

* This article was my first attempt at writing in the field of ancient Jewish History under the guidance of our beloved teacher, Dr. Solomon Zeitlin, of blessed memory. Whatever talents I might have developed in this area since this first term paper, I owe to him. He always freely gave of his time to me and was ever ready to discuss whatever issues or academic problems confronted me. I recognize the void his death left in my life and how much I miss him, his warm personality, which he revealed in great measure to his students, and above all, his genuine concern in the academic and personal welfare of those whom he loved. This article is dedicated to his memory.

At the same time, I want to thank my colleague Dr. Sidney B. Hoenig for reading this manuscript and for his valuable suggestions. However, the final responsibility rests upon me alone.

[1] Julius Wellhausen, *Israelitische und Jüdische Geschichte* (Berlin, 1901), pp. 184 ff.; 197.
[2] L. Finkelstein, "The Origin of the Synagogue," *PAAJR* I, 1930, pp. 49–59.

L. Löw[3] connects the term *Beth Am* found in the Prophets[4] with the synagogue. The *Beth Am* was a kind of town-hall wherein the civic affairs of the people were conducted. Afterwards, this institution was slowly converted to a synagogue. The people apparently still called the synagogue by its secular name, *Beth Am*, and the talmudic sages opposed this. The same was true of the Holy Ark which originally was but an ordinary chest in the town-hall and which contained civil and communal documents. The people, instead of referring to it as the *Aron ha-Kodesh*, still called it *arna*. Thus, the sages warned that the *Amme ha-arets* would die "because they call the holy ark a chest and because they call a synagogue *Beth Am*.[5] Finkelstein sort of combines his own views with that of Löw. He stated: "Is there not a possibility that, as prayer gatherings grew in size and importance, they were transferred from private dwellings into specific buildings and frequently into town halls?"[6]

The Talmud[7] dates the origin of the synagogue to the Babylonian exile. As a result, W. Bacher proposed[8] that the synagogue came about as the result of the destruction of the First Temple and, in fact, served as the substitute for the Temple. It filled the religious vacuum created and provided for the spiritual needs of the Jews of Babylon.[9]

Solomon Zeitlin[10] showed, quite convincingly, that the synagogue could not have originated in the pre-Exilic times since the term chosen for the synagogue, *Beth ha-Kenesseth*, never occurred in the pre-Exilic parts of the Bible and furthermore, the Greek term *synagogue* never appeared in the LXX. Had the institution of the synagogue already been in existence during the pre-Exilic days, as is maintained by the scholars previously cited, terms such as בית התפלה, בית ד׳, בית הקהל, בית העדה... and in the Greek the term *Proseuche* should have been utilized.[10a]

Having shown that the origin of the synagogue must be post-Exilic, Zeitlin proceeds to search for and eventually finds a specific model from which the synagogue, as we know it, in time developed. Zeitlin maintained that the Pharisees "stood for the democratization of the institutions of Jewish life and endeavored to bring the Jews into immediate contact with the Temple service."[11] To prove his point, Zeitlin cites the well-known

[3] L. Löw, *Gesammelte Schriften* IV (Szegedin, 1898), pp. 5 ff.; also "Der Synagogale Ritus," *MGWJ* XXXIII, 1884, pp. 97 ff.

[4] Jer. 39:8.

[5] *Shabbath* 32a: בעון שני דברים עמי הארצות מתים על שקורין לארון הקודש ארנא ועל שקורין לבית הכנסת בית עם.

[6] L. Finkelstein, *op. cit.*, p. 50, n. 6.

[7] *Megillah* 29a: ואהי להם למקדש מעט א״ר יצחק אלו בתי כנסיות ובתי מדרשות שבבבל.

[8] W. Bacher, "Synagogue," *JE* XI, p. 619b.

[9] S. Krauss, *Synagogale Altertümer*, 1922, pp. 52–66.

[10] S. Zeitlin, "The Origin of the Synagogue," *PAAJR* II, 1931, pp. 69–81.

dispute of the Sadducees, who maintained that the daily sacrifice should be considered a private sacrifice.[12] This would mean that only those of the aristocratic group, the wealthy, could afford the cost of an animal necessary for the sacrifice. The Pharisees, on the other hand, maintained that the *tamid* should be purchased from communal funds.[13] In this manner, the entire community would be involved. Furthermore, according to Zeitlin, it was the Pharisees who went a step further. They wanted the entire nation to participate in parts of the sacrificial act of the *tamid* and since, practically speaking, not all Israelites could possibly participate, they divided the dwellers of the cities, towns and villages into twenty-four divisions called *ma'amadoth*. However, not even these representatives could always go to the Temple in Jerusalem. They, therefore, assembled in their respective communities and on those days when they were supposed to be in Jerusalem, they recited portions of the Torah related to the sacrifices being offered at that moment in the Temple.

The Mishnah,[14] which mentions the *ma'amadoth*, relates that the *kohanim* and Levites had been divided into twenty-four divisions called the *mishmaroth* and the Mishnah attributes the institution of the *mishmaroth* to the **נביאים הראשונים**, whom the Tosefta[15] identifies as the prophet Samuel and King David. Correspondingly, twenty-four divisions of Israelites were created and, as we have indicated, were called the *ma'amadoth*. This Mishnah does not identify the creators of this latter institution. The Mishnah does, however, state the reason for the institution of the *ma'amadoth*, namely, no offering could be brought unless its donor is represented.[16] As a result, Zeitlin concludes that as long as the Sadducean view prevailed and the *tamid* was an individual offering of a member of the wealthy class, only representation of the priests or Levites was essential. However, once the Pharisees changed this practice and the *tamid* no longer was offered by wealthy individuals but was purchased by communal funds and therefore became an offering brought by all of Israel, it also became necessary to institute communal representation. This change was instituted by the Pharisees when they came into power at the time of the Hasmoneans. True, theoretically speaking, this may have been part of their outlook for many years before the Hasmonean era, perhaps even from the time of the Restoration when the Pharisees came into being. However, practically speaking, they were not able to translate

[10a] *Ibid.*, p. 74.

[11] S. Zeitlin, *History of the Jewish Second Commonwealth* (Philadelphia, 1933). p. 51

[12] *Menahoth* 65a: שהיו אומרים הצדוקים יחיד מביא ומתנדב.

[13] *Ibid.*, שיהיו כולן באין מתרומת הלשכה.

[14] *Ta'anith* 4:1.

[15] T. *Ta'anith* 3:2.

[16] *Ta'anith* 26a: וכי האיך קרבנו של אדם קרב והוא אינו עומד על גבו.

their ideas into practice until the Hasmonean age.[16a] If one accepts Zeitlin's view that it was the Pharisees, in their quest to democratize religion, who instituted the *ma'amadoth*, then the obvious conclusion results; namely, the *ma'amadoth* came into being during the reign of the Hasmoneans. Zeitlin, furthermore, claimed that the synagogue is the outgrowth of the *ma'amadoth*. Private prayer was always part of Judaism. Moses, Hannah, the prophets and Jews in general prayed. The *ma'amadoth*, however, provided the first instance of communal, formal prayer in specific places of worship. Since the *ma'amadoth* arose during the early days of the Hasmonean period, the first kernels that seeded the synagogue were planted during the same period.

F. Landsberger[17] accused Zeitlin of attributing the origin of the synagogue to a secular source just as Löw did, even though Zeitlin dated the beginning of the synagogue to a much later time. He quoted Zeitlin as follows: "The rabbis,' he argues, 'were greatly opposed to the secularization of the synagogue and they even said that the עם הארץ were dying young because they called it the people's house."[18] Landsberger obviously quoted Zeitlin out of context since the latter merely used the phrase while disproving Löw's theory. Zeitlin, quite clearly indicated that the sages would never have given the synagogue the name *Beth Am* since such a name connoted a secular origin and the sages completely opposed any attempt at the secularization of the synagogue. In fact, Zeitlin cited the very source[19] upon which Löw based his theory to disprove the contention. The passage shows precisely how vehemently the sages opposed such a view.

Landsberger, following the interpretation of Isaac Abravanel of the verse in Jeremiah, claimed that the phrase *Beth Am* refers to the Temple itself. After all, it would indeed be strange if the prophet should bemoan the destruction of the *Beth Melekh* and yet make no mention of the destruction of the Temple, the mournful reaction to which must have at least paralleled that of the royal palace. Some scholars have even suggested that the destruction of the Temple was in the original text but through scribal error somehow became deleted.[20]

Landsberger prefers Abravanel's interpretation; namely, that no textual emendation nor scribal error is to be assumed. Rather, the peculiar phrase *Beth Am* refers to the Temple. In response to Zeitlin's criticism that such an appellation for the synagogue cannot be reconciled with the talmudic warning against that very name, Landsberger said that these scholars misread

[16a] See S. Zeitlin, "The Pharisees," *JQR*, 52 (1961), pp. 246 ff.; for a different view, see J. Neusner, *A Life of Yohanan b. Zakkai*, Leiden, 1970, p. 23, and the sources cited there.

[17] F. Landsberger, "The House of the People," *HUCA* XXII, 1949, 149–155.

[18] *Ibid.*, p. 151.

[19] *Shabbath* 32a.

[20] R. H. Graf, *Der Prophet Jeremia* (Leipzig, 1862), p. 465; Heinrich Ewald, *Die Propheten des Alten Bundes* (Göttingen, 1868), p. 30.

the meaning of the rabbinic warning. The rabbis were opposed to the term *Beth Am* not because such a name would emphasize the synagogue's *secular* origin and therefore would be a derisive term not to be used for so laudable an institution as the synagogue. To the contrary, the rabbis warned against the use of *Beth Am* because it was a term that was too holy—reserved for the *Beth ha-Mikdash* alone. The rabbis did rule that "a person may not make a house in the form of the Temple, or a porch (exedra) in the form of the Temple—porch (*'Ulam*), or a court corresponding to the Temple-Court, or a table corresponding to the table (*shulḥan*), or a candlestick corresponding to the menorah."[21] In the same way, the sages may have forbidden the use of the name *Beth Am* for the synagogue since it was reserved for the Temple. Similarly, the word ארנא should not be construed to mean a chest used for public documents but rather as the word normally used for the 'Ark of the Covenant' in the Temple and therefore, forbidden. The term *Aron ha-Kodesh* is a new phrase, not at all connected with any appurtenance of the ancient Temple.

Although Landsberger's interpretation of the rabbinic text is clever, it is not the interpretation our sages gave to it. One cannot invent explanations, ingenious though they may be, when the sages themselves clearly explained the text otherwise. The violation referred to in this rabbinic statement was an entirely different one. The fact is that we must examine the passage in question in its context. The Mishneh stated:[22] R. Gamaliel had images of the phases of the moon on a tablet [hung] on the wall of his upper chamber, and he used to show them to the unlearned and say, "Did it look like this or this?"

The Talmud was curious to know how R. Gamaliel permitted himself to make use of these images. Does not the Torah explicitly forbid their usage, when it is said: "Thou shalt not make these for me,"[23] whereupon the sages conclude—"thou shalt not make the images of my servants,"[24] meaning, one is forbidden to create the images of the heavenly servants among which is included the image of the moon. How, then, did R. Gamaliel allow himself to act contrary to the aforementioned prohibition? Abaye then replied that the prohibition referred only to "servants that may possibly be created."[25] To prove his contention, Abaye cited the baraita with which we are concerned. "A person should not make a house . . ."

[21] *Rosh Hashanah* 24a; ᶜ*Abodah Ẓarah* 43a; *Menahoth* 28b: לא יעשה אדם בית תבנית היכל, אכסדרה תבנית אולם, חצר כנגד עזרה, שלחן כנגד שלחן, מנורה כנגד מנורה

[22] *Rosh Hashanah* 2:6: דמות צורות לבנה היו לו לר׳ גמליאל בטבלא ובכותל בעלייתו שבהן מראה את הדיוטות ואומר הכזה ראית או כזה

[23] Exod. 20:20.

[24] *Rosh Hashanah* 24a: לא תעשון כדמות שמשיי.

[25] *Ibid.*: אמר אביי לא אסרה תורה אלא שמשין שאפשר לעשות כמותן כדתניא לא יעשה אדם בית תבנית היכל . . .

Thus, we see that this entire talmudic passage tells us that traditionally there were two interpretations of the biblical verse לא תעשון אתי. First, it was assumed to mean that it prohibits the making of those heavenly bodies that serve God. However, it became quite obvious that R. Gamaliel by his own actions proved this interpretation to be incorrect. The second and conclusive interpretation had nothing at all to do with images. It claimed that here the Torah forbade the making "for your own use such items normally used by Me"; that is, used for God in the Temple. The prohibition obviously refers to the making of items such as are enumerated in the baraita; namely, house, exedra, menorah, etc. The ark was not named since the Second Temple did not contain one.[26] Consequently, the name of the Temple, be it *Beth Am* or otherwise, cannot be considered within this prohibition since the prohibition refers only to items to be manufactured. "Thou shalt not make" cannot apply to a name. The fact was that after the destruction of the Temple there were many who attempted to imitate as closely as possible the procedure of the Temple. Others, who attempted to refrain from using such items as salt, oil, etc. because these items were formerly used as part of the sacrificial services, were deemed to be in error.[27] Apparently, it was not prohibited to imitate aspects of the Temple procedures, unless such imitation involved the manufacture of appurtenances similar to the ones used in the Temple. Landsberger's theory, intriguing though it may be, is not borne out by the sages themselves.[28] What, then, was the origin of the synagogue?

We agree with Zeitlin that the synagogue is definitely the outgrowth of the institution of the *ma'amadoth*. However, we disagree with Zeitlin con-

[26] See David Rappaport, *Mikdash Dovid* (Jerusalem, 1969), 2, p. 12, s. v., *keli shareth*, who cited Joseph Babbad, *Minhat Hinukh* #95, p. 103b, c . . . : שהקשה אמאי לא קתני ארון תבנית ארון. Three responses are given. See especially ובבית השני לא היה ארון כידוע. Also, *ibid.*, p. 103c: גם ארון אסור לעשות כמו היכל דוגמת היכל. ואפשר דארון הוא הוא עם כרובים כלי אחד וא"כ כרובים בלא"ה אסור לעשות כמבואר במצות לא תעשון אתי. וארון בלא כרובים אין איסור ואפשר דמותר. See also, Moses Schreiber, *Hatam Sofer*, *Y. D.*, 236.

[27] T. *Sotah* 15:11. Additional instances of tannaitic attempts to continue the ceremonial practices of the Temple may be found in *ᶜEduyyoth* 8:6: א"ר יהושע שמעתי שמקריבין אעפ"י שאין בית . . . T. *Maᶜaser Sheni* 1:13; *Taᶜanith* 2:1. See also, S. B. Hoenig, "Temple Synagogue," *JQR* LIV (Oct., 1963), 124–7.

[28] It is interesting to note that Maimonides prohibits the making of such items but includes the prohibition in the one that requires awe for the Temple; i. e., under the concept of ומקדשי תיראו. He does not refer to the verse לא תעשון אתי. See *Beth ha-Behira* VII, 10. Apparently, Maimonides rejected the interpretation of this verse rendered by Abaye and accepted the original one. Accordingly, Maimonides ruled in *Abodath Kokhabim* III, 11: וכן אסור לצור דמות חמה ולבנה כוכבים ומזלות ומלאכים שנא' לא תעשון אתי לא תעשון כדמות שמשיי המשמשין לפני במרום . . . Joseph Babbad, *op. cit.*, #39, sees the obvious problem created by Maimonides. והנה הר"מ כאן בלאו זה לא כתב כלל ד"ז דלא יעשה בית תבנית היכל וכו' אך בפ"ז מהל' בית הבחירה במ"ע של יראת המקדש כתב ד"ז דלא יעשה תבנית מקדש . . . ובאמת מנ"ל הא? ובסוגיות אלו משמע דתבנית מקדש עוברים בלאו זה? Babbad responds that Maimonides accepted Abaye's statement as a provisional one only.

cerning the dating of the *ma'amadoth*. We believe that they originated immediately after the Exile, probably at the time of Haggai, Zecharia and Malachi. Consequently, we believe, that the synagogue's first traces are to be found during this period of the Restoration.[29]

Some basic questions must first be resolved. First, why did the dispute of the Pharisees and the Sadducees revolve merely around the *tamid*? After all, there were many other communal sacrifices which were funded by the community? The Mishnah[30] cites, "What was done with the appropriation? They bought therewith the daily burnt-offering, and the additional burnt-offering . . . and all the other public offerings." However, we find no dispute regarding these offerings. The Sadducees did not maintain that any of these other offerings should be funded privately, by individuals. It is not reasonable to assume that the dispute centered around the *tamid*, merely because it was a daily sacrifice while the others were offered less frequently. It is true that the *tamid* assumed great importance in Jewish life of that era, as is evidenced by the many instances that the conquerors of Judea forbade the practice of the *tamid*. Most likely it became synonymous with the Temple worship. Nevertheless, this would not have kept the Sadducees from insisting that individuals should be the only ones to be permitted to offer the *musaf* or the other public sacrifices. Prof. Zeitlin, in a conversation held several years ago, argued that the term *tamid* was a *terminus technicus* which included all sacrifices that were public offerings. When the Sadducees and Pharisees argued about the *tamid*, it was not limited to the daily sacrifice alone but in reality involved all public sacrifices. The Mishnah, however, contradicts this view.[31] If, indeed, the word *tamid* had been a technical

At the conclusion, however, the association is rejected since this association between **תבנית מקדש** and silver idols (**אלהי כסף**) is a tenuous one.

The explanation we offered in the text would solve this problem as well. The negative command of **לא תעשון אתי** includes the making of **תבנית מקדש** only when the Temple was in existence. It is for this reason that Maimonides rejects it in *ᶜAbodath Kokhabim*. However, **יראת המקדש** is possible even after the destruction of the Temple. Thus, Maimonides ruled in *Beth ha-Behira* and derived it from *Yevamoth* 6b: **ואין לי אלא בזמן שבהמ"ק קיים בזמן שאין בהמ"ק קיים מניין? ת"ל את שבתותי תשמורו ומקדשי תיראו מה שמירה האמורה בשבת לעולם אף מורא האמורה במקדש לעולם**. The difficulty with this explanation is that Maimonides failed to make such a distinction. The prohibition is obviously only to "create" Temple paraphernalia. There is no interdict against a name. A similar distinction was made by Babbad, *op. cit.*: **והנה מלשון הר"מ כאן והרה"ה מבואר דהלאו הוא העשייה דאם עשה עובר בלאו ואפילו עשאו לאחרים מ"מ העושה עובר בלאו כמו העושה מלאכה בשבת דהתורה חייבה רק העושה אבל בלא עשאו בידים . . .** True, the distinction arrived at is one between a manufacturer of such items and one who engages another to make them, but the essential point is that the manufacture of such items is consequent.

29 We confirm the talmudic statement and those of Bacher and others. However, we arrive at this conclusion for different reasons.

30 *Sheqalim* 4:1: **התרומה מה היו עושין בה? לוקחין בה תמידין ומוספין . . . וכל קרבנות הצבור.**

31 *Ibid.*

term signifying all public sacrifices, the Mishnah would not have enumerated the *tamid*, the *musaf* and all other communal sacrifices. The term *tamid* alone would have sufficed, especially in the connection it is used by the Mishnah. Zeitlin's response was that this Mishnah was of later origin when the term *tamid* was no longer understood in its technical sense. However, Zeitlin was unable to prove this last contention.

If we assume that the dispute of the Sadducees and Pharisees revolved only around the *tamid*, an assumption which will be shown to be borne out by the sources, then we must conclude that the Sadducees agreed that all other public sacrifices were to be funded by the community while the *tamid* alone came from private funds. The Sadducees, who acknowledged only the Written Law, based their view upon the biblical injunction[32] "The one lamb shalt thou offer in the morning," the singular indicating the need for an individual to be its donor. However, if everyone agreed that all other communal sacrifices were funded by the community, we may ask, where was the people's representation for these public offerings? The Sadducees did not deny the principle of representation.[33] They only said that as far as the *tamid* was concerned, since an individual donated it, the rest of the people do not require representation. Therefore, the institution of the *ma'amadoth* encompassed not only the *tamid*, but the *musaf* and the other communal offerings also.[34] The fact is that the *ma'amadoth* existed from the time of the Restoration and all the Pharisees did during the Hasmonean period was to rule that the *tamid*, like all communal sacrifices, was also to be funded by the community. With this change, the community required representation for the *tamid* as well. Thus, the *ma'amadoth* were expanded to include the *tamid* also.

The Mishnaic statement[35] כל יום שיש בו הלל אין מעמד בשחרית which obviously refers to *Hanukkah* and to the early Hasmonean period might be cited to show that the *ma'amadoth* were substituted, as Zeitlin maintained, during this period. First of all, during the Temple days only the Hallel recited with the pascal lamb offering is recorded. All other references to Hallel are of the post-destruction period. Secondly, it is of interest to compare this Mishnah with the Tosefta which states[36] "Eight *mishmaroth* were instituted by Moses for the *kohanim* and eight for the Levites. When David and Samuel, the Seer arose, they made it twenty-four *mishmaroth* for the

[32] Num. 28:4: וכבש אחד תעשה בבקר.

[33] *Menahoth* 65a.

[34] Even though the Mishnah *Ta^canith* 4:1, which states that the *musaf* cancels the *ma^camadoth*, refers only to those representatives who went to Jerusalem and who did not have ample time to recite the required readings, those who assembled in their own individual communities and who were not pressed for time, continued to recite these readings.

[35] *Ta^canith* 26a.

[36] T. *Ta^canit* 3:2: ח' משמורות תקן משה לכהונה וח' ללוים. משעמד דוד ושמואל הרואה עשאום כ"ד משמורות כהונה וכ"ד משמרות לויי'.

priesthood and twenty-four *mishmaroth* for the Levites . . ." While the Mishnah merely refers to the נביאים הראשונים as the innovators of the *mishmaroth*, the Tosefta clearly mentions King David and Samuel, the prophet by name. Though the Tosefta continues to deal with instances when the *ma'amadoth* were not to be recited because of lack of time, it does not mention the point found in the Mishnah; namely, the time of *Hanukkah*, when *hallel* is recited, yet no קרבן מוסף was offered. Why was this omitted?

It is quite clear that the Tosefta by stating עמדו נביאים שבירושלים וקבעו שם כ"ד מעמדות כנגד כ"ד משמרות כהוניה ולויי' "the prophets of Jerusalem arose and established twenty-four *ma'amadoth* to parallel the twenty-four priestly and Levitic *mishmaroth*," attributes the origin of the *ma'amadoth* to the period *prior* to the Hasmoneans when prophecy still reigned. We suggest this referred to the post-Exilic period. Consequently, the Tosefta could not mention the *hallel* of *Ḥanukkah* which was as yet non-existent. The Mishnah does not at all deal with the origin of the *ma'amadoth*. Therefore, the נביאים שבירושלים are not included. The Mishnah discusses the halakhic details as they pertained to their day. By then, *Ḥanukkah* was established and the principle that when time is short, the *ma'amadoth* are to be cancelled was extended to include *Ḥanukkah* as well.

Lastly, as Zeitlin pointed out,[37] the term כנס is first found in the Book of Esther,[38] in the post-Exilic period. When the Jews returned to Judea they were scattered in various towns and villages. When problems arose they summoned all the people from the surrounding areas to gather in places of assembly. Those who participated were called בני הכנסת. The head was called ראש הכנסת. The overseer of the religious needs of the community was called חזן הכנסת.[39] When a permanent place of assembly was designated, it became known as the *Beth ha-Kenesseth*. In any case, it was at the time of the post-Exilic period that the term and the institution began.

[37] S. Zeitlin, *op. cit.*, p. 75.

[38] Esther 4:16.

[39] L. Landman, *The Cantor: An Historic Perspective* (New York, 1972).

An Approach to Hebrew Poetry through the Masoretic Accents

By WILLIAM SANFORD LaSOR
Fuller Theological Seminary, Pasadena, California

Purpose and *Method*

THE *purpose* OF THIS work is to approach the study of poetry in the Hebrew Bible by observing the accents which were supplied by the Masoretes. It may be stated frankly at the outset that the study was undertaken with no preconceived notions. I set out neither to prove nor to disprove any theory. I was not even certain that when I finished an intial study I would have any heuristic results. Now I feel certain that this is a productive method of study, and I present it to my fellow scholars for further study and refinement.

To the best of my knowledge, this approach has not previously been attempted, although I am fully aware that countless articles have been published in places that are not known to me. I questioned a number of other scholars, and received the same answer from each one: they did not know of anything published along this line. I should indeed be most happy to know of other studies, if there are any, if for no other reason than to see how our methodologies compare.

My *method* is quite pedestrian. I simply cut up a photocopy of a Letteris Bible and pasted it up, carefully following the accents. Each line (or in some cases, where the line was too long, it included a runover) ended with a major pausal accent. After the heavy disjunctive accents I left a larger space (about three extra letters or ems), and after the lesser disjunctives I left a smaller space (about one extra letter or em). Although there were places where my feeling for the structure of Hebrew poetry might have suggested a different division, I strictly resisted every temptation to impose my theories on the Masoretic pattern. This was to be—and I trust that it succeeded in being—a study of the Masoretic indicators of how the passage was traditionally broken up into smaller segments at the time when the accents were added. The paste-ups have been supplied along with this article, and are reproduced photographically in the form in which I prepared them.

The Masoretic Accents

The question must be answered, Why did I turn to the Masoretic accents? The Masoretes, as we all know, lived long after the time of the composition of the poetic passages. In fact, they lived long after the time where there was a unified liturgical service among the Jewish people, as the existence of an Eastern, as well as a Western Masorah indicates. Other questions might be added to this primary question. For example, it may be asked, Why use the Letteris Bible? Why not the Leningrad manuscript of the Ben Asher Text, or Kittel's *Biblia Hebraica*? Why was the Eastern Masorah not consulted? My replies are simple, and I believe they are satisfactory.

The Masoretic heritage. I began with the conviction that there was a long-standing tradition of how the sacred Scriptures were read, including both the pronunciation and the division of a passage into the component units or meaningful word-groups. This conviction was based on thirty years of reading and teaching Biblical Hebrew, in the course of which I carefully studied the phonetic and phonemic regularity (and some irregularities) of the Masoretic points, and noted the close relationship between the syntax and the Masoretic accents. The regularity of the points and accents convinces me that the addition of these marks was not a matter of whim or caprice, but the recording of a tradition that could be analyzed and reduced to a number of linguistic laws.[1] At the same time, the irregularities indicated that the Masoretes were not simply inventing a system and imposing it on an almost meaningless text consisting of nothing but consonants. The Masoretes may have invented the points and the accents, but they did this in order to preserve a living tradition which was in danger of passing away.

It is precisely in liturgical passages that tradition is strongest. Poetry can be memorized more easily than prose, even when the meanings of some of the words and figures of speech are not known. Nursery rhymes stay with us all our life. So do prayers, Psalms, and hymns that we learned in childhood. The elements of formal worship from the Prayer Book or the Passover Haggadah can be readily recalled and recited with great accuracy. Among the Jewish people, the liturgical passages from the Hebrew Bible formed an important part of such tradition. Therefore it is most reasonable to assume that the Masoretic accents preserve that tradition with great reliability.[2]

I used the Letteris Bible, frankly, because it was available in a large, clear form, which made it easier to cut up and rearrange. The accents in the Kittel text are not as clear, and the plethora of critical marks distracts greatly from the accents. Moreover, the Kittel text, as I shall show in this

[1] The results of my work can be seen in my *Hebrew Handbook*, which appeared in 1951, passed through several revisions, and is now about to appear in an enlarged two-volume work to be entitled *Handbook of Biblical Hebrew*, to be published by Eerdmans.

[2] The cavalier emendation of the text, particularly in poetic passages, is to be resisted. It seems to assume that at some point nothing was left but a meaningless pile of consonants which were rearranged, possibly prior to the Masoretes, and then given a new set of meanings by Masoretic pointing and accentuation. It fails to take into account the long persistence of liturgical forms.

article, regroups words often with disregard for the accents, and this regrouping would have to be undone for our study. My study of several different Hebrew Bibles convinced me that there was nothing to be gained in an initial study, and something to be lost, if I used anything other than the Letteris.[3]

However, if this approach to the study of Hebrew poetry commends itself, it certainly would be in order to compare the results of the study with similar studies in the Ben Asher text, in the Eastern Masorah, and in any other tradition. If similar strophic divisions are indicated in both the Eastern and Western M^e^soroth, then we must conclude that there was indeed an ancient tradition that underlay these later traditions. I have not attempted such a study in this present work, but I would welcome such a study by scholars familiar with the Eastern tradition.

The system of accents. In conversations with other teachers of Biblical Hebrew I have found that some are not familiar with the Masoretic accents, and some think that they are only of liturgical value. I therefore feel that some description of them, at least as I have used them in this study, is in order.[4]

The accents or punctuation (to be distinguished from the vocalization or vowel points) are marks added to the consonantal text, both supralinear and infralinear, that serve at least three purposes: (1) they generally indicate the stressed (or accented) syllable; (2) they indicate musical notation for chanting the text; and (3) they break up the text into meaningful segments, much as we use marks of punctuation. For the study of Hebrew poetry, only the first and third uses are relevant,[5] and for our present study, the third, or division of the text, is the most significant.

There are upwards of twenty different accent-marks, each of which is named, and the names sometimes are indicative of the values of the respective accents. These accents are divided into two principal categories, the *conjunctive* and the *disjunctive* accents. We are usually told that there is a second system of accents used in the books of Psalms, Proverbs, and Job, but I have not found the differences to be great enough to cause any serious problems. What I say here generally applies to the entire Hebrew Bible.

[3] The Letteris Bible is a printed edition of the Ben Ḥayyim text edited by Meir Halevi Letteris. My copy was printed in Austria before World War II. Every copy of Letteris that I have seen, regardless of size, appears to be a photographic reproduction from the same original.

[4] A concise presentation can be found in *Gesenius' Hebrew Grammar* (edited and enlarged by E. Kautzsch, 2d Eng. ed. by A. E. Cowley; Oxford: Clarendon Press, 1910), § 15. Remarks in § 16*c–i* are also helpful. At times I differ from Gesenius in the order of rank of the accents. For bibliography, *cf. Ges.* § 15*a*.

[5] Perhaps this statement only serves to show my ignorance of the value of musical notation, and another scholar, who knows the accents as musical notes, may provide valuable insights into the study of Hebrew poetry.

Conjunctive accents join the word on which they are found to the following word; disjunctive accents separate the word on which they appear from the following word. As a general, rule, the accent is placed over or under the consonant which (with its vowel and sometimes a following consonant) bears the stress-accent. In some instances, an accent is "prepositive," in which case it is placed on the first letter of the word, or "postpositive," in which case it is placed on the last letter of the word. In some cases, a prepositive or postpositive is repeated on the accented syllable. A word joined to the following word with *maqqēp̱* does not usually have an accent-sign.[6]

The *conjunctive accents*, as we have said, join words together. Two, three, or more words may be conjoined into a phrase or clause by conjunctive accents. The most common conjunctive accents are: *mûnaḥ* ◌֣, *mêr*^{e}*ḵā* ◌֥, *m*^{e}*huppāḵ* (or *mahpāḵ*) ◌֤, and *ʿazlā* ◌֨. As a general rule, the shape of the accent indicates that it is conjunctive by pointing toward the following word. There are notable exceptions to this rule.

The *disjunctive accents* separate words, thus marking the end of a clause or a sentence, or indicating a slight pause between words, sometimes, it seems, simply for effect. There does not seem to be any satisfactory way of equating disjunctive accents with our modern system of punctuation marks (as, for example, to say that the *ʾaṯnāḥ* is "like a semi-colon"). Disjunctive accents may be divided into *pausal* and *nonpausal* accents, the difference indicated by the terms depending on whether an accent commonly requires a pausal form of the word which bears it. However, there are many exceptions to this difference, quite often indicated by a marginal masorah, and I see no value in retaining it for this study. There is value, however, in noting the primary disjunctives (which are pausal almost without exception), the secondary disjunctives (which are sometimes pausal, and more often not), and the lesser or weaker disjunctives.

The strongest disjunctive is, of course, the *sillûq* ◌ֽ, which occurs regularly before the *sôp̱ pāsûq* (or end of the sentence). In our study of poetic passages, it always ends a line. Next to the *sillûq* is the *ʾaṯnāḥ* ◌֑, except in Psalms, Proverbs, and Job, where *ʿôlê w*^{e}*yôrēḏ* ◌֫◌֥ often outranks it.[7] If both of these accents occur in a verse, I have divided it into three lines. Gesenius ranks *s*^{e}*ḡôltā* ◌֒ and *šalšéleṯ* ׀◌֓ above *zâqēp̱ gāḏôl* ◌֕, *zâqēp̱ qāṭôn* ◌֔, *ṭip̱ḥā* ◌֖, and *r*^{e}*ḇîaʿ* ◌֗. In my reading I have found *r*^{e}*ḇîaʿ* to be the strongest of the secondary disjunctives, sometimes replacing *ʾaṯnāḥ* in shorter verses, and *zâqēp̱ qāṭôn* is almost as strong. On the other hand, *zâqēp̱ gāḏôl* ◌֕ seems

[6] This is by no means to be considered as an exhaustive presentation. I am selecting those factors which I have found to be significant for this study and simplifying as much as possible for the person who is not familiar with the accents.

[7] When *ʾaṯnāḥ* follows *ʿôlê w*^{e}*yôrēḏ* it sometimes does not have the pausal form. This will be noted in the marginal masorah.

to be a rather weak disjunctive, often standing on *nomina regentia* in construct annexion. Among the weaker disjunctives, the most common appears to be *ṭip̄ḥā* (or *ṭarḥā*) ֖.[8]

As a general rule, the disjunctive accents either are vertical or point away from the following word. There are, however, notable exceptions to this rule which must be carefully observed, otherwise the separation of the elements in the verse will be obscured. Note that *pašṭā* ֙ (postpositive), *y^{e}ṯîḇ* ֚ (prepositive), *l^{e}garmēh* |֣, *m^{e}huppāḵ l^{e}garmēh* |֤, and *ʿazlā l^{e}garmēh* |֨ are all disjunctive.[9]

Those who are familiar with the very detailed studies of the masoretic accents and their sequence will perhaps criticize my great oversimplification of this discussion. I have deliberately avoided elaborate theories, seeking to work inductively from the texts and to establish some semblance of a system therefrom. I believe this preliminary step has been achieved in this article, and I welcome further studies that would draw upon established theories of accents for whatever light they might throw upon this approach to poetry. From the simple to the complex seemed to me to be the better method. So, then, let us turn to several passages.

An Analysis of Several Poetic Passages

Psalm 119:1–8. I selected this passage because the acrostic structure of Psalm 119 places the strophic structure beyond doubt. Each verse (referring to the modern verse-division and numbering, not to the poetic verses) is a distich, marked by beginning with a word with initial *ʾālep̱* and ending with *sillûq* and *sôp̱ pāsûq*. (See page 340.)

In almost every instance, the distich is divided into two parts by *ʾaṯnāḥ*. Verses 4 and 5, however, are divided by *r^{e}ḇîaʿ*. In each case the second part is closely connected to the first part, in fact, forming a single statement.

Verse 2 is clearly synonymous parallelism,

Blessed (are) those who keep his testimonies,
  With a whole heart they seek him.

[8] It should be noted that in a few cases, accents which appear to be the same have different names and serve different functions. Anyone undertaking the study of poetry using the method I am suggesting should carefully note every detail of Gesenius' explanation, and then make an inductive study of several passages. For example, note that *ʿazlā* ֨ is *con*junctive, whereas *pašṭā* ֙ is postpositive and *dis*junctive.

[9] The vertical line |, according to *Ges.* § 15*f*, n. 2, is not to be confused with *pāsēq*. It seems, however, that it is often used to insert a slight pause where the accent otherwise would be conjunctive.

Verse 3 is antithetic parallelism:

Indeed, they have not done iniquity;
  In his ways they have walked.

But verses 4 and 5 do not seem to have a clear parallelism:

Thou, thou hast commanded thy precepts
  To guard exceedingly.
My wish! Let my ways be established
  To keep thy statutes!

This structure, where the second stich completes the first, is sufficiently common in the Hebrew Bible that it should cause no consternation.

Lamentations 1:1–8. The second selection likewise is an alphabetic acrostic, hence the original lines are clearly marked. Because of the length and structure of each numbered verse, I would prefer to use the term "distich," and refer to each half of the verse as a "stich." In fact, this should be standardized terminology, in my opinion. Careful comparison of the structure as indicated by the accents with the structure of a translation (such as RSV or JB) is strongly recommended. (See page 341.)

The stichs of verse 1 are divided into three parts each, indicated in each case by *r*^{e}*ḇî*^{a}ᶜ and *zâqēp̱ qāṭôn*. Verse 2 has the same division for the first stich, but the second stich (after the *ʾatnāḥ*) is divided into only two parts, indicated by *zâqēp̱ qāṭôn*. Verse 5, on the other hand, has no strong disjunctives in either stich. The stichs of verse 6 are divided into two and three parts, respectively, whereas verse 7 is divided into four and four parts, and verse 8 is divided into two and two parts. We would be hard pressed, indeed, to establish any semblance of the *qinah* meter (3 + 2) on this portion of Lamentations![10] Because the masoretic divisions of this passage differ so markedly from the printed translations which I have seen, I venture to include a translation, for which I claim no literary excellence but only division that follows the accents.

How she sits alone,| the city full of people,| she has become like a widow!
  She was great among the nations,| princess among the cities,| she has become a vassal!
She weeps in the night,| and her tears (are) on her cheek;| she has no comforter among all her friends.

[10] The unusual form *rabbā́ṯî*, which occurs twice in verse 1, is usually identified as a construct with *-î* (*Ges.* § 90*k*, *l*). The accent shift is explained as due to *nāsôg ʾāḥôr* (*Ges.* § 90*l*), but this will explain neither the second occurrence, *rabbā́ṯî baggôyîm*, nor the following *śārā́ṯî bamm*^{e}*ḏînôṯ*.

All her companions have dealt treacherously with her; | they have become her enemies.
Judah has gone into exile because of affliction and the magnitude of her work; | she dwells among the nations; | she has found no rest.
All her pursuers have overtaken her amidst her distress.
The roads of Zion are mourning | from lack of any to come in to the appointed feasts; | all her gates are desolate; | her priests are groaning.
Her maidens are afflicted and she—it is bitter to her.
Her foes have become chief; | her enemies prosper, | for YHWH has afflicted her on account of the multitude of her transgressions.
Her children have gone captive before the foe.
There has gone forth[11] from the daughter of Zion all her glory.
Her princes have been; | [12] like harts they have found no pasture, | and they have gone without strength before the pursuer.
Jerusalem remembers: | days of her affliction and her wanderings, | all her beloved (things), | which were from days of yore.
When her people fell into the hand of the foe, | and she had no helper; | her foes saw her; | they laughed on account of her annihilation.
Jerusalem indeed has sinned; | therefore she has become unclean.
All who honored her have come to despise her, | for they have seen her nakedness. | She, too, groans, and she turns away.

Job 3:2–10. I have selected this passage because it includes *ʿôlê w^{e}yôrēḏ* and because there are several tristichs or division of the verse into three parts. Verse 2 is a "prose cliché." In my opinion, such clichés regularly belong outside the poetic structure. It would be possible to consider verse 3 a tristich, divided by *ʾatnāḥ* and *r^{e}ḇî^{ac}*, as indicated in RSV, but elsewhere in the passage the tristichs are indicated by *ʿôlê w^{e}yôrēḏ* and *ʾatnāḥ* (see verses 4, 6, 9). Note that *ʿôlê w^{e}yôrēḏ* is indicated by ◌֥֫ over the same word when the stress accent is on the ultima, but by ◌֥ ◌֫ when the stress accent is on the penult thus requiring that the other accent be placed on the preceding word, as can be seen by comparing verse 9 with verses 4 and 6. In verse 5a *pâzēr* ◌֡ is a minor disjunctive. In verses 6a and 9a *ṣinnôr* (*zarqā*) ◌֮ serves as the principal disjunctive before *ʿôlê w^{e}yôrēḏ*, whereas the "little" *r^{e}ḇî^{ac}* serves the same purpose in verse 4a. In my reading I have not found the so-called *r^{e}ḇî^{ac} qāṭôn*, which precedes *ʿôlê w^{e}yôrēḏ*, to be any weaker disjunctive than the regular *r^{e}ḇî^{ac}* (*r^{e}ḇî^{ac} gāḏôl*), which occurs in verse 9c, or the *r^{e}ḇî^{ac} mugrāš* ◌֗◌֜, which occurs in verses 6c and 8b. All seem to be of the same relative disjunctive strength. I present the passage without translation, since RSV, with little change, is a satisfactory rendition. (See page 342.)

[11] The *wâw* seems to make little sense; was it used only to fit the acrostic?

[12] The strong disjunctive (*r^{e}ḇi^{ac}*) makes the reading "they have become like harts" impossible. I therefore take *hāyû* in the sense of "existed, were, but are no longer."

Psalm 92. I have included Psalm 92 because it provides further opportunity to observe the accents in the books called *tᵉʾām* (*tᵉhillîm*, *ʾiyyôb*, *mišlê*, or Psalms, Job, and Proverbs). The verse numbering follows the Hebrew Bible rather than the English Bible. Verse 1 is a prose cliché. I have assumed that my readers are fully aware of *méteg* ֽ, which occurs only on syllables with secondary accent (as in 3b, 5b, 6a, etc.) and in other usages which have no bearing on our present study.[13] The *dᵉḥî* (*ṭip̄ḥā*), prepositive, occurs in verses 4a, 7a, 8a, 13a, 14a, 15a, and 16a—in all cases, except 8a, on the first word or word-group in the verse. We find *rᵉḇîaᶜ mugrāš* in verses 3b, 6b, 7b, 10b, 11b, 12b, and 16b, in every case serving as the principal disjunctive of the stich and before *sillûq*. (See page 343.)

Of particular interest are verses 8 and 10, for these are usually divided into tristichs, as in RSV. Verse 10 is particularly significant, since it is closely parallelled by a passage in Ugaritic Text 68:

ht ibk bᶜlm	Lo, thine enemies, O Baal,
ht ibk tmḫṣ	Lo, thine enemies thou shalt smite,
ht tṣmt ṣrtk	Lo, thou shalt destroy thy foes!
	(68:8–9)

It would, of course, be possible to break Psalm 92:10 into a similar tristich:

For behold, thine enemies, YHWH,
For behold, thine enemies shall perish;
They shall be scattered, all doers of iniquity.

However, verse 10, like verse 8, has only *ʾaṯnāḥ* as the major disjunctive, and *rᵉḇîaᶜ* as the principal disjunctive prior to the *ʾaṯnāḥ*. In verse 10, moreover, *rᵉḇîaᶜ* also divides the second stich preceding *sillûq*. I have therefore resisted the temptation to divide these verses into tristichs. Verse 8 may be rendered as follows:

When the wicked sprout like grass, and all doers of iniquity
flourish,
(It is) for them to be destroyed for ever and ever.

Exodus 15:1b–18. Having examined a few clearly poetic passages, we now turn to passages that are often identified as poetry even though they occur in prose works. The first is the Song of Moses. (See page 344.)

It is apparent to me that the masoretic divisions of the text closely follow the poetic structure, even though they indicate distichs several places where RSV divides the verses as tristichs. Of these, verses 8, 11, and 17 divide the first stich with *zâqēp̄ qāṭôn*; these verses could be read as tristichs. Verse 15, however, is divided into three parts in the first stich, with two occurrences

[13] For fuller discussion, *cf. Ges.* § 16*c-i*.

of *zâqēp̄ qāṭôn* before the *ʾatnāḥ*, and verse 9 is structured in a completely different manner than RSV. I would render it as follows:

> Said the enemy: "I will pursue, I will overtake, I will divide the spoil;
> My soul shall take its fill of them; | I will draw my sword; | my hand shall dispossess them."

For the rest of the passage, RSV closely follows the masoretic division.

It is perhaps of value to compare the masoretic division with that of *Biblia Hebraica* (*BH*^{3}). *BH*^{3} divides verse 8 into two parts, closely following the masoretic division, even though this is generally not so in the rest of the passage. Verse 9 in *BH*^{3} is divided in a way similar to that of RSV (see above). Verse 11b is joined with 12. Verse 15 closely follows the masoretic division, and verse 17b is joined with verse 18. We produce the passage as printed in *BH*^{3}. (See page 345.)

Numbers 24:15–19. In this passage I would put verse 15a (to the *ʾatnāḥ*) outside the poetic structure, but the masoretic accents do not seem to support this. Otherwise the division is not remarkable, except for verse 17 where the second part (after the *ʾatnāḥ*) is divided into four parts with *r*^{e}*ḇî*^{a}ʿ, *zâqēp̄ qāṭôn*, and *zâqēp̄ qāṭôn*. Without emending the text, it can be rendered

> I see him, but not now; | I behold him, but not nearby;
> There shall go forth a star from Jacob, | and there shall arise a scepter from Israel; | and he shall smite the corners of Moab, | and he shall crush all the sons of Sheth.

The entire passage is found on page 346.

Deuteronomy 32:15–19. In the Letteris Bible Deuteronomy 32 is set in two columns, with space down the middle of the page. I feel certain that there is a tradition behind this arrangement, but I do not know it. The division seems to follow faithfully the masoretic division of the verses into shorter portions, but there does not appear to be any attempt either to fit the arrangement to the logical (or poetical) structure or to place the primary disjunctives (*ʾatnāḥ* and *sillûq*) at line-end. The passage as printed in the Letteris Bible is as on page 347.

Divided according to the accents the passage is as on page 348.

Judges 5:1–31. I have selected this long passage for two particular reasons. For one thing, its antiquity is generally admitted. More important, it gives us a good opportunity to observe the accents in a long and graphic passage, and to get something of the feeling of Hebrew poetry when it is free from modern theories of versification, rhythm, meter, and the like. The impression I get—and I say this not to urge agreement, but simply to to express my feelings—is that there is great variety and flexibility in the poetic structure. The stichs vary in length from two words (*bārᵉḵû* YHWH, 2b and 9b) to four portions of two to four words each (4a, 11a, and 30a).

Contrast, for example, the following passages. Verses 4–5 portray movement:

YHWH,| when you went forth from Seir, when you marched from the field of Edom,| earth trembled,| even heaven dripped,
Even clouds dripped water!
Mountains departed (?) from before YHWH—
This Sinai!—| from before YHWH the God of Israel

Verses 6–7, on the other hand, are more lethargic:

In the days of Shamgar ben-Anath, in the days of Jael,| journeys ceased,
And those that did walk the roads,| they went by roundabout journeys.
Peasantry ceased in Israel, it ceased!
Until you arose, Deborah,| you arose a mother, in Israel.

Or contrast the structure of verse 22 with verse 23:

Then hammered the hooves of the horse,
From the driving, driving of the mighty.
"Curse Merom!"| said the angel of YHWH; "Curse terribly its inhabitants,
Because they didn't come to the aid of YHWH,| to the aid of YHWH against the mighty!"

These last two stichs we would prefer to divide according to the obvious parallelism, but that is not the way the masoretic accents indicate, and the result is a sweeping feeling, contrasted with the staccato effect of the preceding verse. Verses 26–27 offer yet one more chance to observe the strong contrast in style:

Her (left) hand to the peg she placed, and her right hand to the workmen's hammer,
And she struck Sisera, she crushed his head,| she both pierced and passed through his temple.
Between her feet | he bent, he fell, he lay;
Between her feet he bent, he fell;| where he bent, there he fell destroyed.

The entire passage is on pages 349–50.

The Kittel Bible. Before we close our study, it may be helpful to analyze a few passages as printed in the third edition of *Biblica Hebraica*. It should be understood at the outset that by selecting passages where this methodology seems to prove useful I am not making a blanket condemnation of the Kittel Bible. At many points the poetic structure as printed is reasonably in agreement with the masoretic accents. However, this is not always the case, and there are, in fact, some passages where I find little to support Kittel's division.

In Genesis 16:11–12 it appears that the editor is attempting a structure consisting of alternating stichs, the first of which contains two short and one long portion, and the second stich consisting of a single long portion. The accents, however, divide verse 11 into a single unit to the ʾatnāḥ, followed by two units which are divided by *zâqēp̄ qāṭôn*. Verse 12, on the other hand, has three units before the *ʾatnāḥ*, and one after it. I am not convinced that this passage is poetry. The passage is on page 351.

Genesis 17:1b–5 is another passage that indicates that the editor is attempting to divide the stichs into units or "feet." In most cases, there is no major disjunctive, and in some cases (e. g. 4a and 5b) the editor has disregarded conjunctive accents. In 5a, there is not only the disregard of conjunctives, but what is far more objectionable, an *ʾatnāḥ* is ignored. The resulting division *BH*³ comes out as follows:

And it shall not be called | any more thy name | Abram, but it shall be | thy name Abraham,
For father of a multitude of | nations I have appointed you.

Once again, I question whether the passage is poetic, and I am unable to accept the Kittel division. The passage as printed in Kittel is on page 352.

Genesis 35:10b–12 likewise illustrates the disregard of accents and the imposition of a theory of metrics in the Kittel text. The clause *lôʾ-yiqqārēʾ šimḵā ʿôḏ yaʿăqôḇ* is clearly a unit, both in syntax and in masoretic accents. It belongs with the following *kî ʾim* clause. Verse 12, divided according to the accents, would read somewhat as follows:

And the land | which I have given to Abraham and to Isaac, I would give to you; || and to your seed after you I will give the land.

I see no evidence of poetic structure in this passage. It is reproduced on page 353 as it appears in *BH*³.

Conclusions

In a preliminary study such as this, conclusions are at best premature. Nevertheless, there are certain indications that may be pointed out that will guide further study and may lead to firm conclusions.

Validity of the accents. From this study I believe I have demonstrated that the masoretic accents are a valid division of the biblical text. While they are not infallible, still they can be disregarded only with great care. Even in places where a disjunctive accent seems to break into a phrase or clause, we should attempt to hold to the division, for in Biblical Hebrew, as in other Semitic languages, there is widespread use of the "nominal" sentence, that is, a sentence constructed with a noun or noun-clause as subject, and a verbal clause as predicate. Such constructions are often indicated by *r^{e}ḇî^{ac}* on the first or second word of the verse. This suggests that a correlation of the study of accents with the study of Hebrew syntax may be profitable.

The Nature of Hebrew Poetry. The masoretic accents, I believe I have demonstrated, indicate a kind of poetic structure in passages that are clearly poetic. Lest this seem to be an *argumentum in circuitu*, I hasten to say that the principle of parallelism (*parallelismus membrorum*) in Hebrew poetry is well established and widely accepted. We do not fully understand some of the types of parallelism, particularly those where the second stich completes the first but can hardly be called "parallel" with it. Nevertheless, we have long passages, both in Hebrew and in Ugaritic, where parallelism is clearly demonstrable. In such passages, as we have shown, the masoretic accents indicate in general an awareness of this structure.

When we attempt, however, to impose on Hebrew poetry any theories from our western thought, we run into difficulties. Certainly there is no indication of "meter" or "feet" in the accent system. This seems to hold, whether we are thinking in terms of a rigid system of scansion (such as dactylic ⏑– or anapestic ⏑⏑–), or in more general terms of a regularity of the number of units in a stich regardless of the number of heavy accents. When I began this study, I attempted to construct some such system of units, but it soon became obvious that nothing of the sort could be derived from the accents. Theories of 2 + 2 or 3 + 2 "feet" simply will not hold up, to judge from the accents.

This is precisely what we have found in studies of Ugaritic poetry. Granted the vowels are lacking, but there is no system of vocalizing Ugaritic poetry that will provide uniformity of the feet in a sequence of stichs. It seems, then, that Semitic poetry in general and Hebrew poetry in particular had much more flexibility than we know in Greek, Latin, or even English poetry (excepting free verse). Stichs may be quite short (sometimes a single word) or quite long (including three or four units each of which consists of several words). A distich may consist of a short stich followed by a long stich, or just the opposite, or they may be of approximately equal length. Tristichs may be interspersed with distichs almost at random, it would seem. The mood or feeling which is conveyed would appear to be more significant than the rhythm—or perhaps we should say that the rhythm is established in an emotional, rather than a mathematical, manner.

For over a quarter-century I have been trying to teach students to read Hebrew meaningfully, and to do this I have stressed attention to the accents.

I recommend this to my fellow teachers. Along the way, I came to have an appreciation of Hebrew poetry when read according to the accents, which in turn led to the study which I have presented here. It is my hope that other scholars will pursue this method and enlarge upon it, to the enrichment of all who study the Hebrew Bible.

1 אַשְׁרֵ֥י תְמִֽימֵי־דָ֑רֶךְ
הַ֝הֹלְכִ֗ים בְּתוֹרַ֥ת יְהוָֽה׃
2 אַ֭שְׁרֵי נֹצְרֵ֣י עֵדֹתָ֑יו
בְּכָל־לֵ֥ב יִדְרְשֽׁוּהוּ׃
3 אַ֭ף לֹא־פָעֲל֣וּ עַוְלָ֑ה
בִּדְרָכָ֥יו הָלָֽכוּ׃
4 אַ֭תָּה צִוִּ֥יתָה פִקֻּדֶ֗יךָ
לִשְׁמֹ֥ר מְאֹֽד׃
5 אַ֭חֲלַי יִכֹּ֣נוּ דְרָכָ֑י
לִ֝שְׁמֹ֗ר חֻקֶּֽיךָ׃
6 אָ֥ז לֹא־אֵב֑וֹשׁ
בְּ֝הַבִּיטִ֗י אֶל־כָּל־מִצְוֺתֶֽיךָ׃
7 א֭וֹדְךָ בְּיֹ֣שֶׁר לֵבָ֑ב
בְּ֝לָמְדִ֗י מִשְׁפְּטֵ֥י צִדְקֶֽךָ׃
8 אֶת־חֻקֶּ֥יךָ אֶשְׁמֹ֑ר
אַל־תַּעַזְבֵ֥נִי עַד־מְאֹֽד׃

1 אֵיכָה ׀ יָשְׁבָה בָדָד הָעִיר רַבָּתִי עָם הָיְתָה כְּאַלְמָנָה
רַבָּתִי בַגּוֹיִם שָׂרָתִי בַּמְּדִינוֹת הָיְתָה לָמַס׃
2 בָּכוֹ תִבְכֶּה בַּלַּיְלָה וְדִמְעָתָהּ עַל לֶחֱיָהּ אֵין־לָהּ מְנַחֵם מִכָּל־אֹהֲבֶיהָ
כָּל־רֵעֶיהָ בָּגְדוּ בָהּ הָיוּ לָהּ לְאֹיְבִים׃
3 גָּלְתָה יְהוּדָה מֵעֹנִי וּמֵרֹב עֲבֹדָה הִיא יָשְׁבָה בַגּוֹיִם לֹא מָצְאָה מָנוֹחַ
כָּל־רֹדְפֶיהָ הִשִּׂיגוּהָ בֵּין הַמְּצָרִים׃
4 דַּרְכֵי צִיּוֹן אֲבֵלוֹת מִבְּלִי בָּאֵי מוֹעֵד כָּל־שְׁעָרֶיהָ שׁוֹמֵמִין כֹּהֲנֶיהָ נֶאֱנָחִים
בְּתוּלֹתֶיהָ נּוּגוֹת וְהִיא מַר־לָהּ׃
5 הָיוּ צָרֶיהָ לְרֹאשׁ אֹיְבֶיהָ שָׁלוּ כִּי־יְהוָה הוֹגָהּ עַל־רֹב פְּשָׁעֶיהָ
עוֹלָלֶיהָ הָלְכוּ שְׁבִי לִפְנֵי־צָר׃
6 וַיֵּצֵא מִן־בַּת־צִיּוֹן כָּל־הֲדָרָהּ
הָיוּ שָׂרֶיהָ כְּאַיָּלִים לֹא־מָצְאוּ מִרְעֶה
7 זָכְרָה יְרוּשָׁלִַם יְמֵי עָנְיָהּ וּמְרוּדֶיהָ כֹּל מַחֲמֻדֶיהָ אֲשֶׁר הָיוּ מִימֵי קֶדֶם
בִּנְפֹל עַמָּהּ בְּיַד־צָר וְאֵין עוֹזֵר לָהּ רָאוּהָ צָרִים שָׂחֲקוּ עַל־מִשְׁבַּתֶּהָ׃
8 חֵטְא חָטְאָה יְרוּשָׁלִַם עַל־כֵּן לְנִידָה הָיָתָה
כָּל־מְכַבְּדֶיהָ הִזִּילוּהָ כִּי־רָאוּ עֶרְוָתָהּ גַּם־הִיא נֶאֶנְחָה וַתָּשָׁב אָחוֹר׃

2 וַיַּ֥עַן אִיּ֗וֹב וַיֹּאמַֽר׃
3 יֹ֣אבַד י֭וֹם אִוָּ֣לֶד בּ֑וֹ
וְהַלַּ֥יְלָה אָ֝מַ֗ר הֹ֣רָה גָֽבֶר׃
4 הַיּ֥וֹם הַה֗וּא יְֽהִ֫י־חֹ֥שֶׁךְ
אַֽל־יִדְרְשֵׁ֣הוּ אֱל֣וֹהַּ מִמָּ֑עַל
וְאַל־תּוֹפַ֖ע עָלָ֣יו נְהָרָֽה׃
5 יִגְאָלֻ֣הוּ חֹ֣שֶׁךְ וְ֭צַלְמָוֶת תִּשְׁכָּן־עָלָ֣יו עֲנָנָ֑ה
יְ֝בַעֲתֻ֗הוּ כִּֽמְרִ֥ירֵי יֽוֹם׃
6 הַלַּ֥יְלָה הַה֗וּא יִקָּחֵ֥הוּ אֹ֥פֶל
אַל־יִ֭חַדְּ בִּימֵ֣י שָׁנָ֑ה
בְּמִסְפַּ֥ר יְ֝רָחִ֗ים אַל־יָבֹֽא׃
7 הִנֵּ֣ה הַלַּ֣יְלָה הַ֭הוּא יְהִ֣י גַלְמ֑וּד
אַל־תָּב֖וֹא רְנָנָ֣ה בֽוֹ׃
8 יִקְּבֻ֥הוּ אֹרְרֵי־י֑וֹם
הָ֝עֲתִידִ֗ים עֹרֵ֥ר לִוְיָתָֽן׃
9 יֶחְשְׁכוּ֮ כּוֹכְבֵ֪י נִ֫שְׁפּ֥וֹ
יְקַו־לְא֥וֹר וָאַ֑יִן
וְאַל־יִ֝רְאֶ֗ה בְּעַפְעַפֵּי־שָֽׁחַר׃
10 כִּ֤י לֹ֣א סָ֭גַר דַּלְתֵ֣י בִטְנִ֑י
וַיַּסְתֵּ֥ר עָ֝מָ֗ל מֵעֵינָֽי׃

מִזְמֹ֥ר שִׁ֗יר לְי֣וֹם הַשַּׁבָּֽת׃ 1

ט֗וֹב לְהֹד֥וֹת לַיהוָ֑ה 2
וּלְזַמֵּ֖ר לְשִׁמְךָ֣ עֶלְיֽוֹן׃

לְהַגִּ֣יד בַּבֹּ֣קֶר חַסְדֶּ֑ךָ 3
וֶאֱמ֥וּנָתְךָ֗ בַּלֵּילֽוֹת׃

עֲלֵי־עָשׂ֥וֹר וַעֲלֵי־נָ֑בֶל 4
עֲלֵ֖י הִגָּי֣וֹן בְּכִנּֽוֹר׃

כִּ֤י שִׂמַּחְתַּ֣נִי יְהוָ֣ה בְּפָעֳלֶ֑ךָ 5
בְּֽמַעֲשֵׂ֖י יָדֶ֣יךָ אֲרַנֵּֽן׃

מַה־גָּדְל֣וּ מַעֲשֶׂ֣יךָ יְהוָ֑ה 6
מְ֝אֹ֗ד עָמְק֥וּ מַחְשְׁבֹתֶֽיךָ׃

אִֽישׁ־בַּ֭עַר לֹ֣א יֵדָ֑ע 7
וּ֝כְסִ֗יל לֹא־יָבִ֥ין אֶת־זֹֽאת׃

בִּפְרֹ֤חַ רְשָׁעִ֨ים ׀ כְּמ֥וֹ עֵ֗שֶׂב וַ֭יָּצִיצוּ כָּל־פֹּ֣עֲלֵי אָ֑וֶן 8
לְהִשָּׁמְדָ֥ם עֲדֵי־עַֽד׃

וְאַתָּ֥ה מָר֗וֹם לְעֹלָ֥ם יְהוָֽה׃ 9

כִּ֤י הִנֵּ֪ה אֹיְבֶ֡יךָ ׀ יְֽהוָ֗ה כִּֽי־הִנֵּ֣ה אֹיְבֶ֣יךָ יֹאבֵ֑דוּ 10
יִ֝תְפָּרְד֗וּ כָּל־פֹּ֥עֲלֵי אָֽוֶן׃

וַתָּ֤רֶם כִּרְאֵ֣ים קַרְנִ֑י 11
בַּ֝לֹּתִ֗י בְּשֶׁ֣מֶן רַעֲנָֽן׃

וַתַּבֵּ֥ט עֵינִ֗י בְּשׁ֫וּרָ֥י 12
בַּקָּמִ֖ים עָלַ֥י מְרֵעִ֗ים תִּשְׁמַ֥עְנָה אָזְנָֽי׃

צַ֭דִּיק כַּתָּמָ֣ר יִפְרָ֑ח 13
כְּאֶ֖רֶז בַּלְּבָנ֣וֹן יִשְׂגֶּֽה׃

שְׁ֭תוּלִים בְּבֵ֣ית יְהוָ֑ה 14
בְּחַצְר֖וֹת אֱלֹהֵ֣ינוּ יַפְרִֽיחוּ׃

ע֭וֹד יְנוּב֣וּן בְּשֵׂיבָ֑ה 15
דְּשֵׁנִ֖ים וְֽרַעֲנַנִּ֣ים יִהְיֽוּ׃

לְ֭הַגִּיד כִּֽי־יָשָׁ֣ר יְהוָ֑ה 16
צ֝וּרִ֗י וְֽלֹא־עַוְלָ֥תָה בּֽוֹ׃

1 אָשִׁירָה לַיהוָה כִּי־גָאֹה גָּאָה
סוּס וְרֹכְבוֹ רָמָה בַיָּם׃
2 עָזִּי וְזִמְרָת יָהּ וַיְהִי־לִי לִישׁוּעָה
זֶה אֵלִי וְאַנְוֵהוּ אֱלֹהֵי אָבִי וַאֲרֹמְמֶנְהוּ׃
3 יְהוָה אִישׁ מִלְחָמָה
יְהוָה שְׁמוֹ׃
4 מַרְכְּבֹת פַּרְעֹה וְחֵילוֹ יָרָה בַיָּם
וּמִבְחַר שָׁלִשָׁיו טֻבְּעוּ בְיַם־סוּף׃
5 תְּהֹמֹת יְכַסְיֻמוּ
יָרְדוּ בִמְצוֹלֹת כְּמוֹ־אָבֶן׃
6 יְמִינְךָ יְהוָה נֶאְדָּרִי בַּכֹּחַ
יְמִינְךָ יְהוָה תִּרְעַץ אוֹיֵב׃
7 וּבְרֹב גְּאוֹנְךָ תַּהֲרֹס קָמֶיךָ
תְּשַׁלַּח חֲרֹנְךָ יֹאכְלֵמוֹ כַּקַּשׁ׃
8 וּבְרוּחַ אַפֶּיךָ נֶעֶרְמוּ־מַיִם נִצְּבוּ כְמוֹ־נֵד נֹזְלִים
קָפְאוּ תְהֹמֹת בְּלֶב־יָם׃
9 אָמַר אוֹיֵב אֶרְדֹּף אַשִּׂיג אֲחַלֵּק שָׁלָל
תִּמְלָאֵמוֹ נַפְשִׁי אָרִיק חַרְבִּי תּוֹרִישֵׁמוֹ יָדִי׃
10 נָשַׁפְתָּ בְרוּחֲךָ כִּסָּמוֹ יָם
צָלְלוּ כַּעוֹפֶרֶת בְּמַיִם אַדִּירִים׃
11 מִי־כָמֹכָה בָּאֵלִם יְהוָה כָּמֹכָה נֶאְדָּר בַּקֹּדֶשׁ
נוֹרָא תְהִלֹּת עֹשֵׂה פֶלֶא׃
12 נָטִיתָ יְמִינְךָ תִּבְלָעֵמוֹ אָרֶץ׃
13 נָחִיתָ בְחַסְדְּךָ עַם־זוּ גָּאָלְתָּ
נֵהַלְתָּ בְעָזְּךָ אֶל־נְוֵה קָדְשֶׁךָ׃
14 שָׁמְעוּ עַמִּים יִרְגָּזוּן
חִיל אָחַז יֹשְׁבֵי פְּלָשֶׁת׃
15 אָז נִבְהֲלוּ אַלּוּפֵי אֱדוֹם אֵילֵי מוֹאָב יֹאחֲזֵמוֹ רָעַד
נָמֹגוּ כֹּל יֹשְׁבֵי כְנָעַן׃
16 תִּפֹּל עֲלֵיהֶם אֵימָתָה וָפַחַד בִּגְדֹל זְרוֹעֲךָ יִדְּמוּ כָּאָבֶן
עַד־יַעֲבֹר עַמְּךָ יְהוָה עַד־יַעֲבֹר עַם־זוּ קָנִיתָ׃
17 תְּבִאֵמוֹ וְתִטָּעֵמוֹ בְּהַר נַחֲלָתְךָ מָכוֹן לְשִׁבְתְּךָ פָּעַלְתָּ יְהוָה
מִקְּדָשׁ אֲדֹנָי כּוֹנְנוּ יָדֶיךָ׃
18 יְהוָה ׀ יִמְלֹךְ לְעֹלָם וָעֶד׃

1 אָשִׁירָה לַיהוָה כִּי־גָאֹה גָּאָה סוּס וְרֹכְבוֹ רָמָה בַיָּם׃
2 עָזִּי וְזִמְרָת יָהּ וַיְהִי־לִי לִישׁוּעָה
זֶה אֵלִי וְאַנְוֵהוּ אֱלֹהֵי אָבִי וַאֲרֹמְמֶנְהוּ׃
3 יְהוָה אִישׁ מִלְחָמָה יְהוָה שְׁמוֹ׃
4 מַרְכְּבֹת פַּרְעֹה וְחֵילוֹ יָרָה בַיָּם וּמִבְחַר שָׁלִשָׁיו טֻבְּעוּ בְיַם־סוּף׃
5 תְּהֹמֹת יְכַסְיֻמוּ יָרְדוּ בִמְצוֹלֹת כְּמוֹ־אָבֶן׃
6 יְמִינְךָ יְהוָה נֶאְדָּרִי בַּכֹּחַ יְמִינְךָ יְהוָה תִּרְעַץ אוֹיֵב׃
7 וּבְרֹב גְּאוֹנְךָ תַּהֲרֹס קָמֶיךָ תְּשַׁלַּח חֲרֹנְךָ יֹאכְלֵמוֹ כַּקַּשׁ׃
8 וּבְרוּחַ אַפֶּיךָ נֶעֶרְמוּ מַיִם נִצְּבוּ כְמוֹ־נֵד נֹזְלִים
קָפְאוּ תְהֹמֹת בְּלֶב־יָם׃
9 אָמַר אוֹיֵב אֶרְדֹּף אַשִּׂיג אֲחַלֵּק שָׁלָל תִּמְלָאֵמוֹ נַפְשִׁי
אָרִיק חַרְבִּי תּוֹרִישֵׁמוֹ יָדִי׃
10 נָשַׁפְתָּ בְרוּחֲךָ כִּסָּמוֹ יָם צָלְלוּ כַּעוֹפֶרֶת בְּמַיִם אַדִּירִים׃
11 מִי־כָמֹכָה בָּאֵלִם יְהוָה מִי כָּמֹכָה נֶאְדָּר בַּקֹּדֶשׁ
נוֹרָא תְהִלֹּת עֹשֵׂה פֶלֶא׃ 12 נָטִיתָ יְמִינְךָ תִּבְלָעֵמוֹ אָרֶץ׃
13 נָחִיתָ בְחַסְדְּךָ עַם־זוּ גָּאָלְתָּ נֵהַלְתָּ בְעָזְּךָ אֶל־נְוֵה קָדְשֶׁךָ׃
14 שָׁמְעוּ עַמִּים יִרְגָּזוּן חִיל אָחַז יֹשְׁבֵי פְּלָשֶׁת׃
15 אָז נִבְהֲלוּ אַלּוּפֵי אֱדוֹם אֵילֵי מוֹאָב יֹאחֲזֵמוֹ רָעַד
נָמֹגוּ כֹּל יֹשְׁבֵי כְנָעַן׃
16 תִּפֹּל עֲלֵיהֶם אֵימָתָה וָפַחַד בִּגְדֹל זְרוֹעֲךָ יִדְּמוּ כָּאָבֶן
עַד־יַעֲבֹר עַמְּךָ יְהוָה עַד־יַעֲבֹר עַם־זוּ קָנִיתָ׃
17 תְּבִאֵמוֹ וְתִטָּעֵמוֹ בְּהַר נַחֲלָתְךָ מָכוֹן לְשִׁבְתְּךָ פָּעַלְתָּ יְהוָה
מִקְּדָשׁ אֲדֹנָי כּוֹנְנוּ יָדֶיךָ׃ 18 יְהוָה יִמְלֹךְ לְעֹלָם וָעֶד׃

27 [a] 𝔐 נִסְעִים ‖ 28 [a] 𝔊𝔖 וְאֶת־כָּל ‖ 31 [a] 𝔊 בֵּאלֹהִים ‖ Cp 15, 1 [a] 𝔊 לֵאלֹהִים ‖ [β] Vers ‖ לְנִי 𝔖 [β] ‖ 𝔊 cf ,עֹז 𝔖 [a] 2 ‖ וְרֹכֵב 𝔊𝔙𝔏𝔖[h] [δ] ‖ id 21 ,(crrp) גוי 𝔐 [7] ‖ אשרו 𝔐 ;נָשִׁירָה ‖ 3 [a] 𝔐 גִּבּוֹר בְּמִי, 𝔊 συντρίβων ‖ 5 [a] 𝔐 יְכַסְמוּ; cf 𝔊 ἐκάλυψεν αὐτούς ‖ 6 [a] 𝔊𝔖 plur ‖ 7 [a] 𝔊 קָמִים ‖ 9 [a] 𝔊 אֲמַלֵּא 𝔙 ,תְּמַלֵּא 𝔖 ,תְּבַלְּעֵמוֹ ‖ [b] 𝔊 κυριεύσει (= תּוֹרִישׁ?) ‖ (אוֹיִבֶיךָ 𝔖) ‖ 10 [a] 𝔐 נְשַׁבְתָּ ‖ 11 [a] 𝔐 נֶאְדְּרִי ‖ [β] 𝔊𝔖[h] בַּקְּדֹשִׁים.

Cp 15, 2 [a] l frt c 3MSS 𝔐𝔙 וְזִמְרָתִי (𝔊 וְסִתְרָתִי) ‖ [b] dl c 𝔐 ‖ [c] prps וְאַרְנְהוּ ‖ 4 [a] dl mtr cs ? ‖ [b] l frt c 𝔖𝔊[A] טֻבַּע.

15 וַיִּשָּׂא מְשָׁלוֹ וַיֹּאמַר
נְאֻם בִּלְעָם בְּנוֹ בְעֹר   וּנְאֻם הַגֶּבֶר שְׁתֻם הָעָיִן׃
16 נְאֻם שֹׁמֵעַ אִמְרֵי־אֵל   וְיֹדֵעַ דַּעַת עֶלְיוֹן
מַחֲזֵה שַׁדַּי יֶחֱזֶה   נֹפֵל וּגְלוּי עֵינָיִם׃
17 אֶרְאֶנּוּ וְלֹא עַתָּה   אֲשׁוּרֶנּוּ וְלֹא קָרוֹב
דָּרַךְ כּוֹכָב מִיַּעֲקֹב   וְקָם שֵׁבֶט מִיִּשְׂרָאֵל
וּמָחַץ פַּאֲתֵי מוֹאָב   וְקַרְקַר כָּל־בְּנֵי־שֵׁת׃
18 וְהָיָה אֱדוֹם יְרֵשָׁה   וְהָיָה יְרֵשָׁה שֵׂעִיר אֹיְבָיו
וְיִשְׂרָאֵל עֹשֶׂה חָיִל׃
19 וְיֵרְדְּ מִיַּעֲקֹב
וְהֶאֱבִיד שָׂרִיד מֵעִיר׃

טו וַיִּשְׁמַן יְשֻׁרוּן וַיִּבְעָט
שָׁמַנְתָּ עָבִיתָ כָּשִׂיתָ
וַיִּטֹּשׁ אֱלוֹהַּ עָשָׂהוּ
וַיְנַבֵּל צוּר יְשֻׁעָתוֹ׃
16 יַקְנִאֻהוּ בְּזָרִים
בְּתוֹעֵבֹת יַכְעִיסֻהוּ׃
17 יִזְבְּחוּ לַשֵּׁדִים לֹא אֱלֹהַּ
אֱלֹהִים לֹא יְדָעוּם
חֲדָשִׁים מִקָּרֹב בָּאוּ
לֹא שְׂעָרוּם אֲבֹתֵיכֶם׃
18 צוּר יְלָדְךָ תֶּשִׁי
וַתִּשְׁכַּח אֵל מְחֹלְלֶךָ׃

15 וַיִּשְׁמַן יְשֻׁרוּן וַיִּבְעָט   שָׁמַנְתָּ עָבִיתָ כָּשִׂיתָ
וַיִּטֹּשׁ אֱלוֹהַ עָשָׂהוּ   וַיְנַבֵּל צוּר יְשֻׁעָתוֹ׃
16 יַקְנִאֻהוּ בְּזָרִים
בְּתוֹעֵבֹת יַכְעִיסֻהוּ׃
17 יִזְבְּחוּ לַשֵּׁדִים לֹא אֱלֹהַּ   אֱלֹהִים לֹא יְדָעוּם
חֲדָשִׁים מִקָּרֹב בָּאוּ   לֹא שְׂעָרוּם אֲבֹתֵיכֶם׃
18 צוּר יְלָדְךָ תֶּשִׁי
וַתִּשְׁכַּח אֵל מְחֹלְלֶךָ׃

1 וַתָּשַׁר דְּבוֹרָה וּבָרָק בֶּן־אֲבִינֹעַם בַּיּוֹם הַהוּא לֵאמֹר׃
2 בִּפְרֹעַ פְּרָעוֹת בְּיִשְׂרָאֵל בְּהִתְנַדֵּב עָם
בָּרְכוּ יְהוָה׃
3 שִׁמְעוּ מְלָכִים הַאֲזִינוּ רֹזְנִים
אָנֹכִי לַיהוָה אָנֹכִי אָשִׁירָה אֲזַמֵּר לַיהוָה אֱלֹהֵי יִשְׂרָאֵל׃
4 יְהוָה בְּצֵאתְךָ מִשֵּׂעִיר בְּצַעְדְּךָ מִשְּׂדֵה אֱדוֹם
אֶרֶץ רָעָשָׁה גַּם־שָׁמַיִם נָטָפוּ
גַּם־עָבִים נָטְפוּ מָיִם׃
5 הָרִים נָזְלוּ מִפְּנֵי יְהוָה
זֶה סִינַי מִפְּנֵי יְהוָה אֱלֹהֵי יִשְׂרָאֵל׃
6 בִּימֵי שַׁמְגַּר בֶּן־עֲנָת בִּימֵי יָעֵל חָדְלוּ אֳרָחוֹת
וְהֹלְכֵי נְתִיבוֹת יֵלְכוּ אֳרָחוֹת עֲקַלְקַלּוֹת׃
7 חָדְלוּ פְרָזוֹן בְּיִשְׂרָאֵל חָדֵלּוּ
עַד שַׁקַּמְתִּי דְּבוֹרָה שַׁקַּמְתִּי אֵם בְּיִשְׂרָאֵל׃
8 יִבְחַר אֱלֹהִים חֲדָשִׁים אָז לָחֶם שְׁעָרִים
מָגֵן אִם־יֵרָאֶה וָרֹמַח בְּאַרְבָּעִים אֶלֶף בְּיִשְׂרָאֵל׃
9 לִבִּי לְחוֹקְקֵי יִשְׂרָאֵל הַמִּתְנַדְּבִים בָּעָם
בָּרְכוּ יְהוָה׃
10 רֹכְבֵי אֲתֹנוֹת צְחֹרוֹת יֹשְׁבֵי עַל־מִדִּין וְהֹלְכֵי עַל־דֶּרֶךְ שִׂיחוּ׃
11 מִקּוֹל מְחַצְצִים בֵּין מַשְׁאַבִּים שָׁם יְתַנּוּ צִדְקוֹת יְהוָה
צִדְקֹת פִּרְזוֹנוֹ בְּיִשְׂרָאֵל
אָז יָרְדוּ לַשְּׁעָרִים עַם־יְהוָה׃
12 עוּרִי עוּרִי דְּבוֹרָה עוּרִי עוּרִי דַּבְּרִי־שִׁיר
קוּם בָּרָק וּשֲׁבֵה שֶׁבְיְךָ בֶּן־אֲבִינֹעַם׃
13 אָז יְרַד שָׂרִיד לְאַדִּירִים עָם
יְהוָה יְרַד־לִי בַּגִּבּוֹרִים׃
14 מִנִּי אֶפְרַיִם שָׁרְשָׁם בַּעֲמָלֵק אַחֲרֶיךָ בִנְיָמִין בַּעֲמָמֶיךָ
מִנִּי מָכִיר יָרְדוּ מְחֹקְקִים וּמִזְּבוּלֻן מֹשְׁכִים בְּשֵׁבֶט סֹפֵר׃
15 וְשָׂרַי בְּיִשָּׂשכָר עִם־דְּבֹרָה וְיִשָּׂשכָר כֵּן בָּרָק בָּעֵמֶק שֻׁלַּח בְּרַגְלָיו
בִּפְלַגּוֹת רְאוּבֵן גְּדֹלִים חִקְקֵי־לֵב׃
16 לָמָּה יָשַׁבְתָּ בֵּין הַמִּשְׁפְּתַיִם לִשְׁמֹעַ שְׁרִקוֹת עֲדָרִים
לִפְלַגּוֹת רְאוּבֵן גְּדוֹלִים חִקְרֵי־לֵב׃
17 גִּלְעָד בְּעֵבֶר הַיַּרְדֵּן שָׁכֵן וְדָן לָמָּה יָגוּר אֳנִיּוֹת
אָשֵׁר יָשַׁב לְחוֹף יַמִּים וְעַל־מִפְרָצָיו יִשְׁכּוֹן׃
18 זְבֻלוּן עַם חֵרֵף נַפְשׁוֹ לָמוּת וְנַפְתָּלִי
עַל מְרוֹמֵי שָׂדֶה׃

19 בָּאוּ מְלָכִים נִלְחָמוּ   אָז נִלְחֲמוּ מַלְכֵי כְנַעַן   בְּתַעְנַךְ עַל־מֵי מְגִדּוֹ
בֶּצַע כֶּסֶף לֹא לָקָחוּ׃
20 מִן־שָׁמַיִם נִלְחָמוּ
הַכּוֹכָבִים מִמְּסִלּוֹתָם   נִלְחֲמוּ עִם סִיסְרָא׃
21 נַחַל קִישׁוֹן גְּרָפָם   נַחַל קְדוּמִים נַחַל קִישׁוֹן
תִּדְרְכִי נַפְשִׁי עֹז׃
22 אָז הָלְמוּ עִקְּבֵי־סוּס
מִדַּהֲרוֹת דַּהֲרוֹת אַבִּירָיו׃
23 אוֹרוּ מֵרוֹז אָמַר מַלְאַךְ יְהוָה   אֹרוּ אָרוֹר יֹשְׁבֶיהָ
כִּי לֹא־בָאוּ לְעֶזְרַת יְהוָה   לְעֶזְרַת יְהוָה בַּגִּבּוֹרִים׃
24 תְּבֹרַךְ מִנָּשִׁים   יָעֵל אֵשֶׁת חֶבֶר הַקֵּינִי
מִנָּשִׁים בָּאֹהֶל תְּבֹרָךְ׃
25 מַיִם שָׁאַל חָלָב נָתָנָה
בְּסֵפֶל אַדִּירִים הִקְרִיבָה חֶמְאָה׃
26 יָדָהּ לַיָּתֵד תִּשְׁלַחְנָה   וִימִינָהּ לְהַלְמוּת עֲמֵלִים
וְהָלְמָה סִיסְרָא מָחֲקָה רֹאשׁוֹ   וּמָחֲצָה וְחָלְפָה רַקָּתוֹ׃
27 בֵּין רַגְלֶיהָ   כָּרַע נָפַל שָׁכָב
בֵּין רַגְלֶיהָ כָּרַע נָפָל   בַּאֲשֶׁר כָּרַע   שָׁם נָפַל שָׁדוּד׃
28 בְּעַד הַחַלּוֹן נִשְׁקְפָה וַתְּיַבֵּב אֵם סִיסְרָא בְּעַד הָאֶשְׁנָב
מַדּוּעַ   בֹּשֵׁשׁ רִכְבּוֹ לָבוֹא   מַדּוּעַ אֶחֱרוּ   פַּעֲמֵי מַרְכְּבוֹתָיו׃
29 חַכְמוֹת שָׂרוֹתֶיהָ תַּעֲנֶינָּה
אַף־הִיא תָּשִׁיב אֲמָרֶיהָ לָהּ׃
30 הֲלֹא יִמְצְאוּ יְחַלְּקוּ שָׁלָל   רַחַם רַחֲמָתַיִם לְרֹאשׁ גֶּבֶר
שְׁלַל צְבָעִים לְסִיסְרָא   שְׁלַל צְבָעִים רִקְמָה
צֶבַע רִקְמָתַיִם לְצַוְּארֵי שָׁלָל׃
31 כֵּן יֹאבְדוּ כָל־אוֹיְבֶיךָ יְהוָה   וְאֹהֲבָיו כְּצֵאת הַשֶּׁמֶשׁ בִּגְבֻרָתוֹ
וַתִּשְׁקֹט הָאָרֶץ אַרְבָּעִים שָׁנָה׃

הִנָּךְ הָרָה וְיֹלַדְתְּ[a] בֵּן וְקָרָאת שְׁמוֹ יִשְׁמָעֵאל
כִּי־שָׁמַע יְהוָה[b] אֶל־עָנְיֵךְ[a]׃
12 וְהוּא יִהְיֶה פֶּרֶא אָדָם יָדוֹ בַכֹּל | וְיַד כֹּל בּוֹ
וְעַל־פְּנֵי כָל־אֶחָיו יִשְׁכֹּן׃

אני־אל שדי התהלך לפני והיה תמים׃

2 ואתנה בריתי ביני ובינך וארבה אותך במאד מאד׃ — ל̇ יו מל בליש י

3 ויפל אברם על־פניו וידבר אתו אלהים לאמר׃

4 אני הנה בריתי אתך והיית לאב המון גוים׃ — ל̇

5 ולא־יקרא עוד את־שמך אברם והיה שמך אברהם — ג מ̇שק̇ כל

כי אב־המון גוים נתתיך׃

כא שִׁמְךָ יַעֲקֹב לֹא־יִקָּרֵא שִׁמְךָ
עוֹד יַעֲקֹב כִּי אִם־יִשְׂרָאֵל יִהְיֶה שְׁמֶךָ
וַיִּקְרָא אֶת־שְׁמוֹ יִשְׂרָאֵל׃ 11 וַיֹּאמֶר לוֹ אֱלֹהִים
ל ל אֲנִי אֵל שַׁדַּי פְּרֵה וּרְבֵה גּוֹי וּקְהַל גּוֹיִם יִהְיֶה מִמֶּךָּ
ל ד וּמְלָכִים מֵחֲלָצֶיךָ יֵצֵאוּ׃
ה וכל את השמים ואת הארץ רבות ל 12 וְאֶת־הָאָרֶץ אֲשֶׁר נָתַתִּי לְאַבְרָהָם וּלְיִצְחָק לְךָ אֶתְּנֶנָּה
וּלְזַרְעֲךָ אַחֲרֶיךָ אֶתֵּן אֶת־הָאָרֶץ׃

On Midrashic Sources for Byzantine Palestine

By ISRAEL D. LERNER
Board of Jewish Education, New York

IT IS UNDERSTANDABLE that leading Jewish historians would wish to include Midrashic references in their studies of Byzantine Palestine. That era and area in general are stricken with a paucity of good primary sources. To be sure, Christian Patristic literature is noteworthy, written by a good number of theologians who were deeply involved in unraveling Jewish ties to the Holy Land and apocalyptic scripture. But precisely because of its tendentious proclivities, it alone cannot offer a satisfactory historical perspective of the Jewish community in Palestine circa 415 C.E.–636 C.E. The first date marks the removal of the last Nasi, the sixth Rabban Gamliel, by Theodosius II, and the second date is that of the conquest of most of Palestine by the Caliph Omar. For our purposes, we discount the brief Persian hiatus (614–629 C.E.). Now while the Byzantine era may be said to have started before, nevertheless, Byzantine rule minus vestiges of Jewish self-government, is encompassed by that period. And so, if we desire to include Jewish sources, we are in need of the Midrash, for the redaction of the Jerusalem Talmud in 400 C.E. precluded relating its references to occurrences of subsequent years, and the Babylonian Talmud, still in the process of being written and assembled at the time, had the disadvantage of being evolved in another geographical-political environment.

However, do the Midrashim transcend all these difficulties? The difference of opinion as to the dates of the various Midrashim is well-known, with times stretching from the early Talmudic period into the Gaonic one. Even among proponents who favor a later date for most, there are those who assign to such period the process of editing rather than that of creative authorship.[1]

In this respect the chronological primacy of בראשית רבה among all the Rabbot has been well established. Despite Isaac Hirsh Weiss' speculations[2] that it may or may not have antedated the Jerusalem Talmud, Professor Solomon Zeitlin associates it with the parameter of events of the third century.[3] Also איכה רבתי belongs to that period since eschatology and consolation were themes which touched and reached the deeply felt

[1] See אייזיק הירש ווייס, דור דור ודורשיו. ברלין, תרפ"ד. חלק ג', pp. 252 ff. *Cf.* יהודה דוד אייזענשטיין, אוצר מדרשים. חלק שני, ניו־יורק, תרע"ה, pp. 504 ff.

[2] Weiss, *op. cit.*

[3] Solomon Zeitlin, "Midrash: A Historical Study," *Jewish Quarterly Review*, Volume XLIV, No. 1 (July 1953), pages 21–36, *passim.*

emotional needs of Jews after the tragedy of destruction and a failed revolution. Likewise it is conceded that the פסיקתא דרב כהנא is of early vintage and was already redacted in the period of the Jerusalem Talmud.[4]

It is therefore worthy of inquiry as to how historically valid are some passages from these Midrashim, chosen by a number of leading historians as sources for Byzantine Palestine of the 5th and 6th centuries. Roman Palestine—yes. The era of Constantine and his immediate successors—yes. However, the closing centuries of Byzantine rule with their persecutions and curtailment of Jewish spiritual creativity is another matter. One can argue, of course, that later interpolations parallel chronologically later events. One can always argue that; for if the codification of the Bible and the Talmud did not escape such allegations, then the Midrashim whose period is less fixed, cannot hope to do so. But we must be aware at least that the chronology and content of the passages quoted do not truly coincide with the period and events discussed.

We refer to such outstanding historians who encompass in their works the whole range of Jewish history as Salo Wittmayer Baron, but more particularly to an historian of the calibre of Samuel Klein (1886–1940), a truly authoritative scholar in the field of post-Roman Palestinian studies,[5] indeed the first professor for the subject at the Hebrew University.[6]

Baron[7] in discussing Palestinian Jewry's irredentist strength and aspirations "to the days of Heraclius and beyond"[8] points out dependence on a two world system, i. e. the rivalry between Rome and Persia. In connection with this he quotes the Midrash: "When you see empires fighting one another watch for the footsteps of the Messiah."[9] Now this saying is by Rabbi Elazar Bar Avina. He certainly did not live in the time of Heraclius since he is quoted also in the Babylonian Talmud.[10] He belonged to the fourth generation of Palestinian Amoraim. This places him at the latest in the fourth century. Of course, in all likelihood Professor Baron did not intend to have the particular quotation illustrate a specific event at a specific time. Rather it was intended to illuminate ongoing Jewish thinking and reactions to a fluid situation of war and imperialistic rivalries which spilled over from one century into the next. But that is precisely our contention, viz. that a number of Midrashic sources which are applied to a certain era are not applicable specifically. They mesh well with introductory or background material, but do not supply factual material for the text.

[4] Note the introduction of שלמה באבער to the פסיקתא דרב כהנא Lyck, 1868, page IV.

[5] See his תולדות הישוב היהודי בארץ־ישראל, תל־אביב, תש"י.

[6] His appointment to the post was in 1924.

[7] Salo Wittmayer Baron, *A Social and Religious History of the Jews*, Philadelphia, 1952. Volume II, Part 24, page 214.

[8] Heraclius (575–642).

[9] Genesis Rabbah XLII, No. 4.

[10] יבמות סג.

Klein who brings to his work[11] an array of impeccable sources, many of them primary, is even more hard put to link Midrashic quotations with a chain of events. He quotes[12] from the commentary of Hieronymus[13] (on Zechariah 12:3) that there is a long-standing custom in Judaea, for boys in the villages and towns to test their prowess by raising heavy round stones to the knee, hip, shoulder and head. For this type of gymnastic activity, an indication of remaining physical vitality within Jewish life, Klein finds a Midrashic source in a parable offered by Rabbi Yudan: "As a strong person who grapples with a heavy quarried stone, and a passerby sees him and says to him: perfect your strength, increase your strength . . ."[14] The difficulties of correlating this passage with the era under discussion are obvious. Hieronymus speaks of an old custom, hoary if you will, and the **פסיקתא** and **ר' יודן**[15] cannot be wrenched out of their era and placed forcibly in the later period which Klein states in his introduction is the era he set out to study, namely that of post Nesiut. Rabbi Yudan was a fourth century Palestinian Amora and as for the Pesikta its dates were discussed above. Yet Klein is not guilty of an anachronism. He is very much aware of the place and time when events were staged and of the persona involved. However, having set out to depict the later era and the events enacted therein, and perforce seeing the emptiness of his stage, he fills it with props and people of a preceding scene. Close enough. It is legitimate, for this way of life may very well have continued beyond its original setting. But again we are at a loss for a solid artifact, for something clearly and uniquely belonging to those mist-shrouded centuries under discussion.

The same is true with an **איכה רבתי** reference to a ruler of **פליסטיני**, and a **בראשית רבה** reference to **פיניקיה, ערביה ופליסטיני** as indicating the political divisions and provincial administration introduced by Byzantium.[16] The name **פליסטיני** supplanted Judaea, and this is supposedly indicative of the changes concomitant with the abolishment of the Nesiut. It is even of interest, or should be, not only to the historian but to the political analyst who may wish to make a contribution to Israel's informational services of today. Except for one thing. The name Palestine was already used in Vespasian's day in the first century, and its exclusive usage to suppress the legitimate name of Judaea is a fourth century phenomenon rather than a fifth or sixth one according to Klein himself!"[17]

Or when our historian quotes briefly the Midrash on Psalms: "When

[11] *Op. cit.* See note 5.

[12] *Ibid.*, page 18.

[13] Died circa 420.

[14] *Op. cit.*—**פסיקתא דרב כהנא. פסקא כ"ו.**

[15] For **ר' יודן** and his sayings see, e. g., Jerusalem Talmud, **תענית פ"ג ה"א, מגילה פ"א ה"ד, כתובות פ"ד ה"ד.**

[16] Klein, pages 10–11.

[17] *Ibid.*

we went up (on) the festivals to see thy face (Jerusalem), we and our children in such a great throng that nations were struck dumb in our presence . . . that is as long as the Temple was standing the nations were struck dumb in my presence. But now I am struck dumb in theirs . . ."[18]

Klein correlates this with the description rendered by Hieronymus who as indicated earlier died early in the fifth century. This again aids us not in our quest. "Buber's arguments for the provenance of Midrash Tehillim from Palestine and for its comparative antiquity are on the whole correct . . ."[19] But more than that. Whatever the dates involved may be, this Midrashic passage is as valid for the beginning of the Byzantine era as for its close. It fails to express uniquely a point in time.

We can truly sympathize with the plight of our historians when we see a meticulous Genizah scholar as Jacob Mann founder on the same problematic centuries, clutching at a weak reed indeed.

In publishing "The Book of Deeds,"[20] Mann wrote: "To a certain extent there are reflected in these passages the life of Jews in the Land of Israel . . . in a very obscure period from the redaction of the Jerusalem Talmud to the Arab conquest."[21] To exemplify he quotes one deed, i. e., one of the laws emanating from the high court of the Yeshiva of Tiberias:[22] "A non-Jew who enters upon litigation under Jewish law is to be judged under Jewish law without any reference to Gentile law . . . except that he should not be judged in a roundabout[23] fashion lest it cause desecration of the Name, but all this should be done upon writing a 'קופרוסימא' concerning the judgment sought."

Mann identifies the term קופרוסימא with קומפרומיסין, or pre-trial contractual agreements between litigants involving procedural and judgmental aspects of the case.[24] This explanation quoting רבי יוחנן, a first generation Amora, hardly sheds light directly on the dark age under consideration. As for the involvement of non-Jews in Jewish courts, such involvement too was well known in the Talmudic period to require elucidation. Other laws and dicta in this work hardly break new ground and are even more in the mainstream of Jewish Halakhah of the centuries.

Are we then to conclude that we ought to forego traditional ancient Jewish sources for Byzantine Palestine in the 5th and 6th centuries? Not

[18] Klein. Note 2 on page 14. For fuller quotation see original מדרש תהלים מ"ב, *passim*, or the translation: *The Midrash on Psalms*. William G. Braude. Yale University Press, New Haven 1959.

[19] "Some Midrashic Genizah Fragments," Jacob Mann. Hebrew Union College Annual, Volume XIV, Cincinnati, 1939. Pages 305–306.

[20] "ספר המעשים לבני ארץ־ישראל," יעקב מאן. תרביץ, שנה א', ספר ג'. ירושלים, תר"ץ.

[21] Page 5.

[22] The original case is found in the manuscript: Cambridge T-S 10 F4.

[23] I. e., unfair.

[24] ושטרי בירורין רבי יוחנן אמר קומפרומיסין. ירושלמי: מועד קטן, פרק ג', הלכה ג'.

at all. A specific reference such as one found in **סדר עולם זוטא** is valuable.[25] "In the four hundred and sixteenth year after the destruction of the Temple[26] the world[27] existed without a king[28] . . . and Mar Zutra, the son of Mar Zutra, left for the Land and they placed him at the head of the school." Later, the year four hundred and fifty two after the Temple's destruction[29] is mentioned in connection with four hundred Jewish troops who fought the Persian army in one of the intermittent wars plaguing both the Persian and the Byzantine empires.

In **ספר אליהו** ascribed to a later century[30] an additional allusion to this period may be found provided that we accept Yehudah Ibn Shmuel's interpretation of the vague statements and reject that of Samuel Krauss.[31] It speaks of Persian-Roman wars. "The last Persian king shall go against Rome for the three years in succession until he spreads his dominion during a twelve-month period." Ibn Shmuel affixes this to the Persian emperor, Khosrow II, no one earlier, and his conquest of Damascus in 613 and Jerusalem in 614. However Khosrow's wars against Byzantium lasted over a longer period, and Krauss' identification of the "last Persian king" with Artaxerxes who founded the Sassanid dynasty in 226 C.E., and fought against Alexander Severus, may also fit the description.

Be that as it may, the Midrashim are by and large historical only in depicting Israel's striving for spiritual continuity, for maintaining its bonds with past tradition and ongoing faith. They were little concerned with political, military or economic events except insofar as they lent themselves to Messianic stirrings, to moral lessons and telling parables. They are valuable for an understanding of how our people continued to live in that dark age sustained as they were by that past which seemed to be a more desirable one than the reality of their present, and by future hopes yet to be realized. They, the Midrashim, are meta-historical, even as Israel's existence appears at times to be.

[25] סדר עולם זוטא השלם, עורך: הרב משה יאיר ווינשטאק. ירושלים, תשי"ז. פרק תשיעי י"ח, דף קכ"ח, ופרק עשירי ב', דף קל"ג.

[26] 486 C.E.

[27] I. e., The Land of Israel.

[28] Head of a Yeshiva.

[29] 522 C.E.

[30] "מדרשי גאולה," עורך, יהודה אבן־שמואל. מוסד ביאליק, ירושלים–תל אביב, חשי"ד דף 32.

[31] *Jewish Quarterly Review*. Old Series, Vol. XIV. 1902, page 359.

The Ascension of Enoch and Elijah
A Tenth Century Karaite Interpretation

By LEON NEMOY
The Dropsie University

THE ASCENSION OF a human being to heaven, temporarily during his lifetime or permanently, after his death or bypassing death, is a motif common to the ancient tradition of several religions.[1] In Jewish thought this motif goes back to the Bible, where Enoch and Elijah are said to have been permanently translated to heaven without first having to undergo corporeal death.[2] In both cases Scripture uses indirect and rather enigmatic language, in the case of Enoch, *And Enoch walked with God, and he was not* (ואיננו), *for God took him* (Gen. 5:24), and in the case of Elijah, *And Elijah went up by a whirlwind into heaven* (II Kings 2:11). The statement about Enoch was particularly puzzling by reason of its mystifying phraseology. It was only natural that this motif aroused the curiosity of thoughtful individuals who sought to explain it in the light of either fanciful imagination or pure reason. Since the early Karaite savants prided themselves on their adherence to rational speculation (Arabic *naẓar*) and on their opposition to mysticism (which they identified with crude superstition), they found two answers to the puzzle of ascension. Some of them denied bodily ascension altogether[3]—a person must go through corporeal death before his spiritual self can be translated to heaven—and cited Scriptural statements about the mortality of all mankind and physiological reasons for the impossibility of a human body traversing the space between earth and heaven without being con-

[1] In general, see the extensive article "Assumption and ascension" in Hastings' *Encyclopedia of Religion and Ethics*, II, 151–157. In Christian theology the principal example is the ascension of the Virgin Mary after her death, commemorated by the Feast of the Assumption (August 15) and recently declared part of the official Roman Catholic dogma. In Islam the prophet Idrīs (Koran 19:57–58: *We raised him up to a high place*) is usually identified with Enoch (Aḥnūkh; Bayḍāwī's commentary, ed. Fleischer, I, 583), occasionally with Elijah; see Georges Vajda's article in the *Encyclopedia of Islam*, 2nd ed., III, 1030–31. Elijah (Arabic Ilyās) is likewise mentioned in the Koran (6:85, 37:123); see *ibid.*, III, 1156. Both articles supply extensive bibliographies of the subjects.

[2] For a retelling of the copious Rabbinic legends on the ascension of Enoch see Louis Ginzberg's *The Legends of the Jews*, I, 130–140. For a selection of the pertinent original texts see M. M. Kasher, תורה שלמה, II (Jerusalem, 1929), 358–360; Shimon Kasher, פשוטו של מקרא, I (Jerusalem, 1963), 244–246. On the ascension of Elijah see Ginzberg, IV, 200–202.

[3] The eminent fourteenth century Karaite savant Aaron the Younger ben Elijah (*Keter Tōrāh*, Eupatoria, 1866–67, I, 32 b) offers an involved explanation of the Biblical *and he was not*, but seems to incline to the idea that Enoch did actually die first (אפשר שיהיה ענין מיתה) before his soul ascended to heaven.

sumed in transit. Others, without denying the literal meaning of the Scriptural evidences of human mortality, asserted that the cases of Enoch and Elijah were exceptions from the general natural rule, willed and ordained by God.

Among the adherents of the latter view was one of the ablest minds in tenth century Karaite thought, Abū Yūsuf Yaᶜqūb al-Qirqisānī, who devotes to ascension a special chapter in his monumental Arabic code of Karaite law entitled *Kitāb al-anwār wal-marāqib* ("Book of Lights and Watchtowers," composed, or completed, in the year 937; henceforth KA), which is here translated. Unfortunately the text of the chapter is incomplete, there being a lacuna at the end of the first section and at the beginning of the second section of the chapter. But the preserved context seems to indicate that the lacuna, while regrettable, dealt with relatively secondary matters, namely arguments in support of al-Qirqisānī's assertion that rejection of ascension *in corpore humano* "leads to negation of prophecies and denial of miracles."

As the reader will perceive, al-Qirqisānī's argument is twofold. First, Scripture often employs sweeping generalizations in cases where exceptions from the rule, sometimes numerous, are patently in existence, and this applies to the statements of universal human mortality—God can, and does, save from corporeal death whomsoever He wishes, and, we are to conclude, God can also preserve this blessed individual's earthly shell from destruction on its perilous journey from earth to heaven. Secondly, once the individual has arrived at the gates of the celestial sphere, God strips him of this base shell and clothes him with a heavenly body which can endure the fiery heat of the journey through that sphere; and when the individual finally reaches the apogee of heaven, he once more sheds his heavenly shell and becomes pure spirit, like unto angels.

A similar procedure, in reverse order, applies to angels who are sent by God on a mission earthward. Pure spirits as they are, they don a heavenly body which they cover with an earthly shell upon arrival on earth. Having, in this earthly guise, accomplished their mission, they return to heaven, shedding their earthly vessel, and upon arriving at their angelic abode, shed their heavenly body as well and revert to their original purely spiritual form.

Whatever the merits or demerits of this theory of assumption, it displays the characteristic trait of the author's mind—his devotion to logical thinking and direct rational argument. The more reason for us to continue to hope that his only work so far discovered, his code of law, may some day be joined by his other works, particularly by his commentary on Genesis, which, judging from references in his code, was an equally monumental and highly interesting opus.

CHAPTER 25[4]

Against those who assert that Enoch and Elijah did not ascend bodily to heaven

(1) We have already stated, in discussing the differences current among our coreligionists, that some of them, who are adherents of rational speculation, assert that Enoch and Elijah—peace be upon them—did not ascend bodily to heaven,[5] since the human intellect (*al-ʿuqūl*) regards this as an impossibility and Scripture itself brands it as false (*yubṭiluhu*).

According to them, this is the rational proof of its impossibility: As a person increases his distance from the earth by rising aloft, he is subjected to steadily increasing cold, until eventually the cold becomes so intense that the (human) body cannot endure it and (forthwith) perishes. But this view leads to negation of prophecies and denial of miracles, and he who holds such a view is compelled to disavow the story of . . .

(2) . . . [They refer to such Scriptural verses as] *All are of the dust, and all return to dust* (Eccles. 3:20); *What man is he that liveth and shall not see death?* (Ps. 89:49); *For that is the end of all men* (Eccles. 7:2); *His breath goeth forth, he returneth to his dust* (Ps. 146:4); (*For I know that Thou wilt bring me to death, and*) *to the house appointed for all living* (Job 30:23); *All flesh shall perish together* (Job 34:15), and similar verses. Now while these verses are indeed outwardly of general application, yet it cannot be denied that one, or two, or more of them admit of exceptions, for Scripture does occasionally employ generalizations from which there are in fact a considerable number of exceptions. For example, *And the land was filled with them* (Exod. 1:7); *And all countries came into Egypt* (Gen. 41:57); *Yea, all Israel have transgressed Thy law* (Dan. 9:11),[6] and many other similar passages, whose number can hardly be computed. This being so, such verses as *What man is he that liveth and shall not see death?* and its like (must be understood to) mean "with the exception of those individuals concerning whom Scripture states that they did not die," that is to say, these two (Enoch and Elijah).

There is another possible explanation, namely that the aforecited verse means "What man is he that liveth (past death) without God reviving him?", since the verse goes on to say *that shall deliver his* (*own*) *soul from the power of the grave, selah?* (Ps. 89:49), meaning that no man can himself save his own

[4] From the third Discourse of KA; ed. Nemoy, III, 338–339.

[5] "Some schismatics of Baghdad assert that both Enoch and Elijah died, and could not possibly have bodily ascended to heaven" (KA, I, 19, 5; ed. Nemoy, I, 62,18–63, 1).

[6] Each statement is obviously exaggerated: some Israelites, however few, did not transgress the law; surely not every country in the then known world was afflicted with famine; the earth was not literally chock-full with human beings.

person and deliver it from the power of the grave, but God can indeed revive him and deliver him from death.

(3) Having thus expressed our view that Enoch and Elijah had ascended bodily to heaven, we must now explain how they did so. We say therefore that each one of them reached heaven in his (earthly) body, but once he arrived there, God stripped him of this body and clothed him with a more noble body. For his former body was terrestrial and coarse, [liable to perish] in the heat of the celestial sphere; not so his latter noble body. Then, after he reached the apogee of the heavenly sphere, God divested him of all corporeality, and he became a purely spiritual substance (*jawharan mujarradan rūḥānīyan*).

This is similar to what God does with angels, when He wishes to send one of them down to earth. Namely, He clothes him with a noble heavenly body, and then encases this heavenly body in an earthly body, in which (outer) form the angel descends to earth and is sent to whichsoever (earthly) person he is sent to. Having delivered his message, the angel is then divested of his earthly body, rises in his heavenly body heavenward, and having arrived there, is stripped also of his heavenly body and rejoins the world of pure reason (*khalaṣa ilā ᶜālam al-ᶜaql*).

Conversational Uses of the Root *Dabhar* in Neo-Biblical Hebrew.

By DAVID PATTERSON
Oriental Institute, Oxford, England

IT MAY, PERHAPS, seem curious that throughout the long period of post-biblical Hebrew literature, comprising two millennia, the most deliberate and sustained attempt to write in the language and style of the Hebrew Bible began in the last decades of the eighteenth century and continued throughout most of the nineteenth, spanning a hundred years approximately, from the time of the French Revolution onwards. This surge of neo-Biblical literature appeared first in Germany, where it was comparatively short-lived. The centre of activity then gradually shifted eastwards, and by the middle of the nineteenth century the literature had struck deep roots among the much more populous Jewish communities of the Russian Pale of Settlement.

A second feature of the literature is equally noteworthy. In contrast to almost all prior strata of Hebrew literature, it is avowedly and unashamedly secular. Whereas the vast majority of all previous Hebrew writing is religiously motivated, and reflects the view of a universe tinged with the divine, the new literature pointed towards the secular reader, and was, indeed, regarded by many as a key to the gates leading to the world beyond the ghetto. A product of the movement of enlightenment, known in its Jewish aspect as *Haskalah*, its exponents, the *Maskilim* were convinced of the need for a radical change in Jewish education in order to attain the coveted goal of emancipation.

The mental climate of Western Europe in the last quarter of the eighteenth century, with its emphasis on the rights of man and its pleas for religious tolerance, seemed to herald a new era of Jewish-Gentile relations. The long nightmare of the ghetto, the centuries of humiliation and oppression seemed about to end, as the sweet dawn of reason appeared along the horizon. All that was needed now, or so at least it seemed to the *Maskilim*, was for the Jews to change their image by means of a process of self-improvement, and their entry into the glittering world beyond the ghetto would be both welcome and assured.

In the light of hindsight, this Jewish self-delusion concerning emancipation and enlightenment which persisted stubbornly from the French Revolution well into the Hitler era, and in many cases even beyond, seems pathetically and tragically absurd. For the *Maskilim*, however, no task could seem more necessary and urgent than a reform of Jewish education. The old system which was devoted almost exclusively to the study of traditional texts, with the main emphasis on Rabbinic literature, required drastic modification in order to introduce the Jewish child, however cursorily, to the range of secular subjects designed to facilitate entry into the outside world. Hence, the time available for Talmudic study had to be curtailed drastically in order to make room for a little geography, history, science, mathematics, and even the rudiments of the language of the country in which the child was living!

At this point it is pertinent to recall that the vernacular language of the vast majority of Ashkenazic Jews in Europe, with whom this paper is concerned, was Yiddish. In spite of a considerable literature dating back several hundred years, Yiddish writing prior to the second half of the nineteenth century merited scant esteem, and was considered mainly fit for women. For men the reading of Yiddish was regarded as a sign of an inadequate Hebrew education and bore something of a slur; although in view of the obscurities of much of the Hebrew writing of the time, the number of male readers of Yiddish may well have been much greater than is usually supposed. Most educated men regarded Yiddish literature with some disdain. Indeed, such leading exponents of enlightenment as Moses Mendelssohn and his disciples were openly contemptuous of Yiddish, which they referred to disparagingly as Jewish-German or simply Jargon. The hybrid nature of Yiddish, with its Germanic, Slavonic and Hebraic elements became the particular target for their scorn—a somewhat illogical attitude in view of their undisguised admiration for such equally hybrid languages as English and French! With a similar lack of logic they dismissed Yiddish as a language without a grammar, perhaps because its rules did not conform with those of German which they prized so highly. But certainly, for the early advocates of literature as the means of Jewish self-improvement, Yiddish was clearly a non-starter.

Hebrew, on the other hand, and particularly Biblical Hebrew, enjoyed a prestige among the *Maskilim* bordering on veneration. It was the holy tongue, the repository and treasure house of the religion, law, history and literature of the Jewish people, its pride and glory. Virtually every Jewish boy learned Hebrew from the age of four, or even earlier, and the world of the Bible, and the stories of the Patriarchs often seemed more real and certainly more colourful than the contemporary environment.[1] Hebrew was not only the language of heaven, but for most Jews the only literary language. If the advocates of enlightenment were to attempt a reform of Jewish education, the first and most natural literary medium must, of course, be Hebrew. But what kind of Hebrew? The answer to this question favoured by most *Maskilim* determined the course of Hebrew literature for almost a

[1] *Cf.* D. Patterson, "Some Aspects of the Transference of Hebrew Literature from Eastern Europe to *Eretz Israel*" in *Sefer Meir*, Jerusalem, In Press.

century. In order to understand what seems in retrospect a somewhat curious choice, some consideration must be given to the underlying aims.

For the exponents of enlightenment, Jewish self-improvement signified the abandonment of traits acquired by centuries of ghetto life. They were particularly anxious to stimulate the aesthetic and emotional aspects of personality, which they believed had suffered atrophy behind cramped walls and cut off from contact with nature and its beauty. They were concerned with sensibility and refinement in manners, dress and above all speech. Perhaps because of the disdain with which they viewed their own vernacular, Yiddish, they constantly advocated for Hebrew a purity of expression and a fastidious use of language, which—ironically—was employed solely by the characters in their own stories and novels![2] Their obsession with rhetoric was bolstered by a passionate interest in Hebrew grammar—regarded by their orthodox opponents as anathema. They firmly subscribed to the view that aesthetic refinement would raise the general level of ethics, and as loyal supporters of enlightenment they naturally revered reason and wisdom. Finally, intent on bolstering Jewish self-respect, they conjured up the glories of the Jewish past.

All such considerations pointed—or so it seemed—towards the Hebrew of the Bible. Reacting against the Rabbinic Hebrew of their day, which was considered crude, crabbed and ungrammatical, they decided to imitate the language and style of Biblical Hebrew. Their choice may have been strengthened by the knowledge that the Gentile world which they aspired to enter, while holding the Rabbinic in light, albeit untutored regard, revered the Bible in equal if not greater measure than the *Maskilim* themselves.[3] As the fountainhead of Hebrew, the language of the Bible was considered pure and unalloyed, and the closest attention was devoted to its grammar, syntax, vocabulary, style and idiom. Strangely, however, no serious attempt appears to have been made to recognize the various linguistic strata in the Bible, which span a period of not less than a millennium.[4] Biblical Hebrew seems to have been regarded as a self-contained, harmonious unity. Anything in the Bible was ripe for imitation and adaptation, and great ingenuity was displayed in scouring and utilising its linguistic resources in a brave if largely unsuccessful attempt to meet the demands of modern expression. The splendid poetry, ethics and wisdom of the Bible, its rootedness in nature, its sense of grandeur and dominion all seemed

[2] *Cf.* D. Patterson, *Abraham Mapu*, London, 1964, pp. 88 ff., and *The Hebrew Novel in Czarist Russia*, Edinburgh, 1964, pp. 74 ff.

[3] For the impact of Biblical Hebrew on eighteenth century European literature see, e. g., R. P. Lessenich, *Dichtungsgeschmack und Althebräische Bibelpoesie in 18. Jahrhundert*, Köln, 1967.

[4] *Cf.*, e. g., J. Barr, "Hebrew Lexicography" in *Studies in Semitic Lexicography*, Quaderni di Semitistica, n. 2, University of Firenze, 1973.

admirably suited to stimulate the Jewish self-improvement which the *Maskilim* so fervently desired.

Once convinced of the overriding claims of Biblical Hebrew, the *Maskilim* proceeded to compose a considerable body of literature in that medium, most of which falls beyond the scope of this paper. Of more immediate concern is their attempt to produce conversation in a series of stories and novels, using mainly if not exclusively Biblical idiom. The examination of their efforts to introduce convincing dialogue is all the more interesting in view of the emphasis which they placed upon refined speech and felicitous expression. Inevitably, the results are often highflown and artificial, almost a parody of what the writers hoped to achieve. In one respect at least, however, these attemps at conversation deserve serious attention. They constitute a bridge-stage between Biblical and modern idiom. By going back to the Hebrew of the Bible for the raw material of dialogue, the *Maskilim* began at the point where—so far as conversation is concerned—the Hebrew Bible left off. In that respect their work reflects the *potential* of Biblical Hebrew, and a study of their techniques is essential, if Hebrew is to be regarded as a continuous thread. After all, they are the only people to have made a prolonged and systematic attempt along such lines.

Admittedly, the predilection for Biblical Hebrew offered certain advantages. Biblical narrative, and conversation, is brief, succinct and often tantalising, and may exert a powerful dramatic effect. It can be forceful and grand in manner, and the familiar words exercise a vast authority. It contains subtle and ironic elements of prime importance for simulated speech. On the other hand, the total vocabulary and range of subject matter of the Bible are severely restricted when measured against the intricate patterns of modern society.

In consequence, resort had to be made to all kinds of clumsy circumlocution (with the occasional help of a post-Biblical term) for even the commonest of objects—a cigarette, for example, is rendered as "leaves of bitter herbs in a paper robe,"[5] and similar examples abound. Moreover, the conversational elements comprise only a small proportion of the Biblical text, so that narrative style had to be transformed into dialogue, often with considerable stress and strain.[6] The problem was aggravated by the narrative techniques of Biblical Hebrew, which present a relentless series of events in their time sequence, with scant speculation or psychological analysis,

[5] In P. Smolenskin, *Ha-Yerushah* (The Inheritance) Petersburg, 1898 (first published in Vienna, 1878–84), pt. 1, p. 181. See D. Patterson, *The Hebrew Novel in Czarist Russia*, *op. cit.*, p. 104, and *cf. idem*, "Some Linguistic Aspects of the Nineteenth Century Hebrew Novel" in the *Journal of Semitic Studies*, Vol. 7, No. 2, 1962.

[6] For a study of colloquial elements in Biblical Hebrew see, e. g., I. Lande, *Formelhafte Wendungen der Umgangsprache im Alten Testament*, Leiden, 1949.

[7] P. Smolenskin, *Ha-Toʿeh be-Darkhei ha-Ḥayyim*, Warsaw, 1905 (first published 1868–

Nineteenth Century Hebrew Novel	*Literal Translation*	*Idiomatic Equivalent*	*Modern Hebrew Usage*
[7] טוב הדבר	The word (or thing) is good	All right	בסדר
[8] יהי כדבריך	Let it be as your words	All right then	בסדר גמור
[9] לו יהי כדבריך	May it be as your words	I hope you're right	הלואי
[10] כדבריך כן הוא	It is just as your words	Just as you say	נכון מאד
[11] צדקת בדבריך	You are right in your words	You're right	אתה צודק
[12] שקר הדבר	The word is a lie	It's a lie	שקר!
[13] שקר הוא דובר	He speaks a lie	He's lying	הוא משקר
[14] טוב הדבר, אני אעשה כדבריך	The word (or thing) is good, I shall do as your words.	All right, I'll do as you say	בסדר, אעשה כך
[15] דבריך טובים אבל לא נכונים	Your words are good but not firmly established.	That's all very well, but it's not the point.	יפה אבל לא נכון
[16] מי דבר כאלה באזניך?	Who said (words) like these in your ears?	Who told you that?	מי אמר לך את זאת?
[17] דבר, אך מהר לכלות דבריך	Speak, but hurry to finish your words	Come to the point	בקצור?
[18] דבריך נשגבים מבינתי	Your words are too lofty for my understanding	I don't comprehend	אני לא מבין
[19] מה ירמזו דבריך?	What do your words indicate?	What are you getting at?	למה אתה מתכון?
[20] כדבריך אדונינו נעשה	According to your words, our master, shall we do.	We shall do as you say, sir.	נפעל לפי ההוראות [שלך]
[21] מישרים דברו שפתיך	Your lips have spoken right things.	You're perfectly right	אין כמוך
[22] הואיל נא לבאר דבריך	Be so good as to explain your words	Please explain	אולי תסביר את הענין עוד הפעם
[23] חי נפשי, כי צדק מאד בדבריו	My soul lives, for he is very right in his words	Bless my soul, he's right	כל הכבוד

and with little resort to extraneous detail. For the purpose of dialogue, such attributes are of very doubtful value.

In order to illustrate the problems which faced the Hebrew novelists of the nineteenth century in their attempt to create idiomatic and convincing dialogue in neo-Biblical Hebrew, the above examples drawn from a single root *Dabhar* may prove instructive, particularly when compared with the modern equivalents in current speech.

It will be seen that while some of the phrases employed by the 19th Century novelists are fairly neat, most seem clumsy, and the overall impression remains that in the light of more modern idiom too many words are used in the majority of cases. The very tentative question which the examples might appear to raise, therefore, is whether Biblical Hebrew was ever an adequate vehicle of conversation.[24]

70), pt. 2, p. 152.

8 *Ibid.*, p. 125.

9 *Ibid.*, p. 68.

10 *Ibid.*, p. 119.

11 *Ibid.*, p. 90.

12 *Ibid.*, p. 214.

13 *Ibid.*, pt. 3, p. 223.

14 R. A. Braudes, *Shetei ha-Ḳeṣawoth*, Warsaw, 1888, pt. 1, p. 32.

15 S. J. Abramowitz, *Ha-ʾAbhoth we-ha-Banim*, Odessa, 1868, p. 29.

16 P. Smolenskin, *Gaʿon we-Shebher*, Warsaw, 1905 (first published in 1874), p. 202.

17 *Ibid.*, p. 99.

18 P. Smolenskin, *Ha-Yerushah*, *op. cit.*, pt. 2, p. 113.

19 S. J. Abramowitz, *op. cit.*, p. 8.

20 P. Smolenskin, *Ha-Toʿeh be-Darkhei ha-Ḥayyim*, *op. cit.*, pt. 3, p. 209.

21 *Ibid.*, pt. 2, p. 98.

22 S. J. Abramowitz, *op. cit.*, p. 18.

23 P. Smolenskin, *Ha-Toʿeh be-Darkhei ha-Ḥayyim*, *op. cit.*, pt. 2, p. 297.

24 The difficulty of making conversation in Biblical Hebrew is clearly illustrated in a footnote by Dr. S. Haramati in his book *Mapu: Teacher of Hebrew*, Jerusalem, 1972, p. 62 in which he writes: "I had personal experience of this problem during the years 1970–1972 when a new approach to the teaching of Biblical Hebrew for children from the age of eight (in the U.S.A.) was developed at the 'Centre for Jewish Education in the Diaspora' (in the Hebrew University). A text for instruction was planned in the form of conversations on subjects of everyday life in the period of the Bible. It was exceedingly difficult for us to find writers in Israel who could measure up to this assignment."

Theocentricity in Jewish Law

By EMANUEL RACKMAN
Bar-Ilan University

The study of ancient legal systems helps us to understand many Biblical and Talmudic texts. The Jews of antiquity had contact with other peoples and civilizations and inevitably there were reciprocal influences. Sometimes what was foreign they adopted while, at other times, there was unmistakable rejection. However, from the point of view of the philosopher and theologian the more important concern is what were the uniquely Jewish components and how they derived from the unique faith that the Jews embraced. This paper will suggest how the Covenant affected the rules of law. One has reason to doubt that the legal rules and principles could have been the same were it not for the theocentricity of the system.

I

Professor Jacob I. Talmon wrote in his essay "Uniqueness and Universality of Jewish History" that when political theorists of the West spoke of Oriental despotism they meant that "the Orient did not know the problem of the legitimacy of power. Power to them was a datum, or fact of nature, an elemental amoral force to be taken for granted like sunshine and rain, storm and plague. It need not always be tyrannical and malign, it might be as benign as one could wish. But it is given, it is there, and we have to bow to it."[1]

It was the Jewish people who were obsessed with the notion of the legitimacy of power. And this obsession had its roots in the idea that they had but one sovereign—God alone. Because of this, Professor Talmon argues, mature Christian civilizations differed from other civilizations in that in Christendom there always was tension between Church and State. Elsewhere "there was no example of it in antiquity, and none . . . in Islam or the Eastern Asiatic civilizations. And this ingredient is substantially Jewish." Because Jews constituted a people committed to transcendental laws and aims with God alone as the ultimate source of law and values, all authority that is exercised by one person over another had to be legitimatized by resort to the Book. "It is not enough that the law is promulgated by the authority which is recognized to have power to legislate. King, Parliament, the sovereign people, even pope and council, must at all time exhibit their credentials in the face of divine or natural law. Natural law, is of course, of hellenistic and Roman provenance.

[1] See "The Unique and the Universal" (George Braziller, New York, 1966), pp. 64–90.

Yet it is fair to say that without its being amalgamated with divine law, it would have failed to become the great formative influence that it did."

Josephus understood well this uniqueness of Judaism and defined a "theocracy" as a state in which God and God alone is sovereign. It is not a state in which a pope or priests are sovereign. Nor is it a state in which spiritual and temporal authorities hold equal sway—as in the historic Gelasian conception of two swords. But it is a state in which all authority exercised by one human being over another is delegated by God and, therefore, when challenged one must prove by resort to the Written or Oral Law that God did, in fact, delegate the power sought to be exercised. And it is because God alone is sovereign that Judaism is a "theocracy." As in the case of so many other attributes of God we cannot say positively what His sovereignty is. We know better what it negates. It means that no one else is sovereign. Only the ultimate Creator—He who is responsible for the "being" of everything—is sovereign. All created things have their place in that order which He ordained but none can exercise more power than He permitted. Indeed, it is precisely because Judaism was theocratic in the sense that it recognized only God's sovereignty that Judaism was able to inspire so much democratic thought.

II

God—the only Sovereign—transmitted a Law, under which all derivative authority is exercised. No one—not kings, not priests, not rabbis, not majorities, not aristocracies—can exercise any authority which is inconsistent with the Law, and even the power to interpret the Law is as diffuse as all other forms of authority. This is the meaning of the sovereignty of God. And this was a revolutionary conception that Judaism brought to the world. It was revolutionary because kings in ancient times were god-kings. Either they themselves were deities or they descended drectly from deities. It was, therefore, no accident, as Samson Raphael Hirsh once said, that when the Torah began to tell us about the life of Moses it started with a simple sentence telling us that our greatest prophet was a man, born of a man and a woman, and by implication not from the gods. This was a new note—a new approach. An unseen God was sovereign and no one else.

That no one other than God was sovereign, however, meant more than simply a limitation on man's pretentiousness. It meant that every man was subject to God's Law. No matter what a man's status, he was subject to what God had willed. Never before and never since was the sovereignty of law so placed above the sovereignty of man. Indeed, only in the light of this theocratic principle can one understand the Biblical verses pertaining to kingship.

The Bible, in Deuteronomy, speaks of the appointment of a king in Israel.[2] Is such appointment mandatory or is it only permitted? Abarbanel—

[2] 17:15.

with justifiable hatred of the monarchy of Spain—held the latter view.[3] He regarded Nimrod as the progenitor of all that was despicable in a human sovereign. Moreover, he held that Samuel was justly critical of the people's desire to have a king. Maimonides, however, regarded the appointment of a king as mandatory.[4] Why did Samuel then deem the request for a king a flouting of God's will?

A careful reading of the text in Samuel[5] reveals that he was objecting to the fact that his people wanted a king who was the Lawgiver—as kings served in non-Jewish societies. They said "Give us a king to judge us as among all peoples." They completely misunderstood the unique role of a king in Judaism for in Deuteronomy the verses dealing with a king are separate and distinct from the verses dealing with the judicial and legislative powers with regard to which the king enjoys no special prerogatives. The king, moreover, was to cause a copy of the Law to be written for his constant guidance—to such an extent was his office only a creature of the Law! However, in their gradual reversion to idolatry the Hebrews clamored for a king in pagan terms. That is why Samuel warned them about the consequences. They would have a king above the Law. Samuel deemed this a rejection of the prophet. God told him that it was not a rejection of the prophet but rather a rejection of God—the only Lawgiver. Nonetheless, they could have what they wanted. Prophets, however, would do the anointing—prophets would make the selection, and the people's voice was expressed through the elders of the Sanhedrin.

It is important to bear in mind that the denial to the monarch of the role of lawgiver and the retention of that role for God alone, which is the essence of theocracy, had economic as well as political significance. The appointment of the king was not to take place until after the promised land had been conquered and divided among the Jews. No king could ever maintain—as was the case in all feudal societies—that land was acquired from the monarch. Land was acquired, according to the Torah, from God, and the entire system of land tenure, its alienation and its redemption, was ordained by God whose ultimate ownership Jews could never forget. And to corroborate this point, one might cite a coincidence Martin Buber noticed that only in two instances in Torah are the conquest and division of the land prerequisites for the performance of the Mitzvot described. These two instances are the appointment of a king and the law of Bikurim—the law of the first fruits.[6] Each year, with the first fruit of his land, the Jew was to go to the city where the king ruled and then and there, thank God for the land which God—not the king—had

[3] For a brief summary of his view see R. Lerner, "Moses Maimonides," in *History of Political Philosophy*, ed. Strauss and Crofsey (Rand McNally: Chicago), 1963, p. 194.

[4] M.T., Hilhot Melahim, 1:1.

[5] I Sam. 8:5–22.

[6] Deut. 26:1.

given him. If any Jewish king should ever indulge himself the illusion that the land was his, and that it is he who dispensed it to his subjects, then the Torah ordained that once each year, in his own capital, the Jews would give their first fruits to the priest and recite a paragraph of Scripture which described exactly how and when God had made the gift of the land to them. Indeed, the language of that text seems to emphasize the fact that every Jew received his land directly from God—and not even via forbears. This also precluded the establishment of a feudal system—the land was not received from a King. Thus did Jewish theocracy deal a death blow to feudalism.

The institution of the Sabbatical year was to make both kings and subjects recognize "man's temporal tenancy of God's creation." One might also cite the ceremony of "Hakhel"[7] as another magnificent illustration of the Torah's intent that kings and subjects shall ever be aware of the ultimate sovereignty of the law. At the conclusion of the Sabbatical year—again in the king's capital—the text of the original covenant was read to all men, women and children. In the face of the verses of Deuteronomy what king could ever hold himself out as lawgiver?

III

To all of this a functional or—realist—jurist would offer the rejoinder, "But even if the law is sovereign, it is man who must promulgate it, interpret it, or legislate with regard to it, and aren't these men in the final analysis, the lawgivers?" This challenge must be met, for otherwise the phrase "sovereignty of law" becomes only a pious mouthing of a meaningless concept. Judaism is almost congenitally practical, rather than theoretical. Philosophical principles are far less important than behavior patterns. Is the sovereignty of law, then, only a mirage since God's law, once given, is forever the responsibility of men who thereafter must decree what is lawful and unlawful?

Judaism meets this challenge in two ways. Both ways were far more highly developed in Judaism than in any other human society. First, the law-making power was so diffused among priests and elders, prophets and people, sages and scholars, rabbis and saints, that it was virtually impossible to pinpoint who had the ultimate authority in Jewish jurisprudence. Yet all the debates of these participants in the unfolding of God's will had to revolve around what it was that God had ordained. The many who shared the authority had to exercise it with erudition, but also with a prayer that they had discovered God's will and that those who were expected to obey would recognize it as such. Consequently, the second way emerged—all Jews themselves had to be expert in God's law. How else might they participate in the authority if they were not themselves students of Torah? Beginning with Moses, the command was given to teach the law. Nay, Abraham was chosen

[7] *Ibid.*, 31:12.

because God recognized that he would teach the law to his posterity. Thus authority wss diffused among a numerous and learned people. Judaism became an exoteric religion instead of an esoteric one.

Indeed it was because man is created in the divine image, and Jews in particular had entered into a covenant with their Creator, that the lawmaking process even in a theocracy involves man, and many of them. Many different groups enjoyed what one might call jurisdiction in different areas. The priests, over whose election the people had minimum control, had a minimum voice in the legislative and judicial process. Even the prophet's role was minimal. The rabbis—the doctors of the law—had, by far, the more powerful voice but their authority emanated from colleagues with the approval of the people who enjoyed some kind of unwritten veto over their ultimate selection. The community or the populace was thus very powerful. But that did not make Judaism a "democracy." The theocracy was democratic insofar as the people played so dominant a role in the preservation of the law. But the voice of the people was not the voice of God. What the people were expected to do was themselves to act as God had willed that they act. (Would that majorities and mobs would act today with this awareness of their responsibility to God in every political, social, and economic situation!)

IV

However, it was not only by diffusing the lawmaking authority among many that Judaism safeguarded God's ultimate sovereignty as lawgiver. What was more important was the extent to which legal education made every Jew aware of his duties in that theocracy. Judge Moshe Silberg of the Supreme Court of Israel has pointed out that in Jewish law the emphasis was always on an individual's duties rather than on the rights of other persons against him.[8] This duty-orientation of Jewish law made Jews seek out how they should behave before committing sin, rather than how they should right or mitigate wrongs already committed. This concern for righteousness makes of the sovereignty of law a truly potent force in the life of the community. Even a functional jurist must reckon with it. For especially among Jews, ideas had great force. A people that could martyr itself for a God no one ever saw is a people to whom the sovereignty of law could be a very real thing.

That universal legal education might make for the sovereignty of law rather than the sovereignty of men is an insight captured by Plato in his "Laws." In modern times, a Russian jurist, Petrashitsky, articulated it.[9] In-

[8] See his *Talmudic Law and the Modern State* (trans. Bokser) (Burning Bush Press: New York), 1973, pp. 66–70.

[9] See E. N. Cahn, *The Sense of Injustice* (New York University Press: New York), 1949, p. 105.

deed, it was not only fathomed by the Bible but articulated by it in a score of different texts beginning with the first commandments regarding the Passover and ending with Moses' final peroration to his people prior to his death.

Yet, even the fact that in Jewish law the focus of attention is on duties rather than rights is a consequence of its theocentricity. It is true that whenever there is a duty, someone has a right to expect the performance of that duty. One without the other is inconceivable. Right and duty are correlatives. But what counts is where one places the accent. In modern society the accent is on rights—rights against government, rights against teachers and parents, even the right to die. In classical Hebrew one rarely finds the word for "right"—Zechut—but one encounters the word for duty—Mitzvah—almost everywhere. What preoccupied the rabbis were duties of the body and of the heart, to man and God, to others and to the self—even duties to live and make live.

What must have prompted this concern for the duty rather than for right is the fact that the lawgiver was God and it was unthinkable that against Him a subject would have rights. To Him there are only duties and even though He enters into covenants and obligates Himself to the performance of obligations, man is rarely presumptuous enough to make demands upon Him.

V

Theocentricity accounts not only for the diffusion of authority but also precipitates a separation between spiritual power and temporal power and this ultimately creates the permanent tension between Church and State—between the champions of what ought to be and the executors of what is. The former retain only moral force; the latter have virtually limitless power.

And this separation is of ancient origin. Moses himself, pursuant to God's command, divided even the succession to himself. Priestly power was given to his brother Aaron and the executive power was given to Joshua—of another tribe. Even Augustine recognized that the Bible did not approve of the merging of the spiritual and temporal authorities but diffused power.

The Rabbis before him were also aware of it when they frowned upon the Maccabees who arrogated unto themselves kingship and priesthood. Thus it appears that theocentric character of Jewish law made not only for the sovereignty of law but also for the separation of Church and State.

Milford Q. Sibley, in his "Political Ideas and Ideologies" writes: "throughout most of their political experience and speculation, Hebrew thinkers repudiate the notion that the priestly and royal functions should be exercised by one man. No doubt this separation of functions is in part to be attributed to the very ambivalence with which Hebrews tended to look at kingship. It is also possibly rooted in a feeling that the priesthood must be independent of direct royal control if it is to be a critic of kingly government."[10]

Professor Sibley also cites the view that the early Jewish experience and theory of the independence of the religious community is the foundation for the very conception of "church" which played so important a role in western civilization and made possible its continuing juxtaposition to state in the democratization of the west. Who among the prophets and the priests, the saints and the sages, were the dominant factor in attaining the result is not our concern. What matters is that the theocentricity of Jewish law—the insistence that God is the one and only Sovereign—is responsible for the basic tenets that the legitimacy of the exercise of authority must always be questioned; that to prevent the unlawful seizure of power, sovereignty must be diffused; and that to insure the possibility of challenging authority the temporal and spiritual powers must be kept separate from each other.

VI

Judicial review was the inevitable consequence of commitment to these tenets. The Bible itself did not instruct the courts to block the unlawful exercise of power by those to whom some of it was delegated. But they did have the power to protect slaves against masters, debtors against creditors, the weak against the strong, and they similarly undertook to prevent the abuse of power by kings. Precisely this happened in the United States. The federal constitution failed to specify what might be done if the executive or legislative branches of the Government did that which was unconstitutional. And Justice Marshall in the historic case of *Marbury v. Madison* made up for the deficiency.

One may call it a "usurper" by the Supreme Court but for many it does appear to come within the purview of the judicial function. The Sanhedrin did the same thousands of years earlier and as reported in the Talmud, and as subsequently codified by Maimonides, a person to whom a king gave a mandate which was in violation of the Torah might disobey the monarch with impunity.[11] He could defend himself against the charge of treason by charging that the king's command exceeded his authority.

More recently the problem appears in Jewish legal literature in reverse. If a king gives an unconstitutional command, and the subject obeys and commits the wrong, is he liable or can he defend himself by claiming that he did what he did in response to higher authority?[12]

[10] (Harper & Row: New York), 1970, p. 20.

[11] M.T., *ibid.*, 3:4.

[12] See A. Kirschenbaum, "A Cog In The Wheel," *Israel Yearbook on Human Rights* (Tel Aviv University: 1974), Vol. 4, 168–193; and A. Enker, שנתון המשפט העברי, רצח מתוך הכרח וצורך במשפט עברי, (Hebrew University: 1975), Vol. 2, 154–174.

The theocentricity of Jewish law was responsible for the principle that in the commission of a crime, only the person committing the crime pays the penalty and not the person who plotted it or even paid the criminal to execute it. The principal in such a case is not the criminal because the agent was not forced to heed him. He could have exercised his own free will and he should have obeyed the ultimate Principal—God Himself! Is the same rule applicable when the principal is the King or a Commanding officer in war? Are commands from such powerful people coercive by their very nature? Whatever the answer, one realizes that the factor of theocentricity is still at work. Presently the problem is one of international law as evidenced by the Nurnberg trials.

The Talmud also records, in several different versions, how kings defied the Sanhedrin and refused to be accountable to the judiciary.[13] Pagan conceptions of kingship had been at work and that led to the conclusion that when such conceptions prevail—as happened in the case of the kings of Israel in antiquity as distinguished from the kings of Judah—then kings are ineligible to judge or be judged.[14] They are removed beyond the system of justice that has God's approval. Sad it is that offending monarchs should not be subject to law but when this happens, they too shall be disqualified to be judges lest they corrupt the system altogether.

VII

While theocentricity was, on the one hand, a liberalizing force insofar as it relieved man of subjection to excessive human authority, it also was a restricting force—it subjected man to more duties vis-à-vis his fellowman. The very fact that God created man in His image gave rise to many legal and ethical norms which are basic in Judaism.

Thus the Rabbis debated which was the more fundamental precept in Judaism—the requirement that man love his neighbor as himself or the dogma that God created man in His likeness.[15] The latter was deemed far more consequential. For, argued the Rabbis, there are persons who do not hesitate to demean themselves and if they subscribe only to the commandment that the love of oneself is the measure of one's love for one's neighbor, the neighbor may not fare so well. But if one must always bear in mind that one's fellow man is divine, then no matter how badly one treats one's own person, one may not do so to another—that other is to be respected as God is.

That man was endowed with the divine image meant also that every murder was deicide. Even suicide was deicide. The human body was God's and its spirit as well. To destroy either was an attack on Him. The famous

[13] BT. Sanhedrin, 19a.
[14] *Ibid.*
[15] Breshit Rabba, 24:7.

Talmudic rule that no human being may incriminate himself before a court of law—a rule much more extensive than that contained in American constitutions—was understood by Maimonides to be a derivative of the law against self-destruction.[16] Alas, there are people who in their distress seek their own end and confessing to a crime may be a way of achieving the goal. Jewish law, therefore, would not tolerate it to happen.

Similarly, the manipulation or exploitation of another human being was immoral—it was like exploiting God. From this point of view, Martin Buber's important caveats regarding the exploitation of one's fellow-man have not only Aggadic but also Halachic roots. Rabbinic attitudes toward human slavery are discussed in many places but one discussion is worthy of special mention here—the status of the person who is half-slave and half-free.

If one of two owners of a slave emancipates him, then thereafter the slave is bound to serve the other owner only half time. For that reason the school of Hillel said that he should work for the master Sundays, Tuesdays and Thursdays, and for himself on the remaining days. However, the school of Shammai objected. "You have provided for the master but you have not provided for the slave. A free woman he cannot marry because he is half slave and a slave woman he cannot marry because he is half free." The final solution which was unanimously accepted was that the court orders the master to emancipate him and as a free man he works and indemnifies the master for his financial loss.[17]

Jewish law would not tolerate a condition in which the slave could not fulfill himself as a human being and relate to a woman and establish a family with her. The rights of the owner had to yield to this humane consideration. Recognition must be given to the needs and drives with which God endowed man.

Similarly, the Torah explicitly prohibited a farmer to muzzle an ox at the time of the threshing of the wheat.[18] The Rabbis so interpreted another verse of the Torah that the same principle was applicable to a man working in the field.[19] As he harvested his employer's crop he could eat to his heart's content from all that he reaped. It would be the sheerest cruelty to muzzle the employee and make him feel doubly punished that he is not the field's owner and though he does the work he cannot partake of the fruit!

VIII

The dogma that man is created by God in His image also proscribed man's rights vis-à-vis himself. If the body and its spirit are God's creation,

[16] M.T. Hilhot Sanhedrin, 18:6.

[17] Mishnah, Gittin 4:4.

[18] Deut. 25:4.

[19] B.T. Baba Mezia, 87a, ff.

then man is certainly not the sole arbiter as to what is to be done with them. That suicide was deicide has already been noted. But there were also restrictions on the abuse of one's person. Self-mutilation was prohibited.[20] Even in mourning one was to avoid excesses in the expression of one's grief.

The presently prevailing view that a woman's body is hers to do with as she pleases, and that, therefore, she alone may decide whether she wants an abortion, is not an authentic Jewish view. The notion that a foetus is like a limb of its mother's body was known and accepted in Jewish law, but not to justify its destruction. In Jewish law no person may inflict injury upon oneself. In the final analysis even our bodies belong to God, Who permits us to enjoy them only in accordance with His will and He does not will our misuse of them. The practice of abortion was prohibited for both Jews and non-Jews. It is part of the Naohide laws.[21]

A notable exception to the general rule that self-mutilation is prohibited is the Covenantal rite of circumcision. Perhaps it was appropriate that such a rite be chosen as the one evidencing religious commitment because no other assault upon the body was countenanced and the one act permitted would always suggest its special meaning. Of course, if one's health or survival required surgery it was to be performed. God had given an overriding commandment that one was to live by the Law and not perish because of it. This would also apply to an abortion for reasons of health.

To such an extent was the body regarded as God's and its mutilation prohibited but for exceptional circumstances that even after one's death the Rabbis prohibited mutilation of the body by others. They ruled that no one may derive a benefit from the use or misuse of a cadavre.[22] This rule gave rise to the problem of post-mortem examinations in hospitals in Israel and elsewhere. Again in the interest of the health of humans the prohibition yields but the principle is firmly established—the body of man and his spirit belong to God and only in accordance with His will are they to be treated. They are a bailment from Him and the bailees must ultimately render an account to the Bailor. This is not only a premise in the Aggadah; it is also basic in the Halacha.

IX

The impact of theocentricity on Jewish law is most easily discerned in the rules pertaining to charity. Like other legal systems Jewish law wrestled with the problem of promises—when they would be enforceable. Since courts do not compel promisors to keep their word under all circumstances, it was necessary to fashion criteria and Anglo-American law developed the doctrine of consideration while continental systems searched for causa. The one type of

[20] *Ibid.*, Baba Kama, 91b.
[21] *Ibid.*, Sanhedrin, 57b.
[22] *Ibid.*, Arachin, 7a and b.

promise that Anglo-American courts found especially difficult to enforce were promises to charity. In such cases the promisee gives nothing in return and in many situations the beneficiary never had a prior relationship to the benefactor. Thus the magic ingredient of either consideration or causa is not present. Yet in Jewish law promises to the poor or to the temple were the easiest to enforce. Why?

All such promises were deemed executed and not executory. They required no fulfillment because they were fulfilled as soon as they were uttered. Since God was the trustee of the poor, the promise was in effect to Him and since His is the earth and all that is therein, He was in possession of the promisor's assets as soon as the promise was expressed. Indeed, if only it could be proved, the mere thought of a gift to the poor would be enforceable because God also knows the thoughts of man.

The legal maxim which gave expression to this unusual rule was אמירתו לגבוה כמסירתו להדיוט—the mere utterance of a gift to God is the equivalent of a delivery to an ordinary mortal.[23]

Less explicit but equally unique was the impact of theocentricity on the right to privacy and the protection of one's home against search and seizure. The right to privacy probably had its conception in the Jewish emphasis on privacy in sexual intercourse. The story of Adam and Eve in the Garden of Eden accounts for the sense of shame with regard to genital organs and a cherished Midrash makes it appear that the non-Jewish prophet Bilaam was impressed by the fact that already in his day Jews pitched their tents so that their entrances did not face each other. Families even in the wilderness of Sinai cherished privacy. Furthermore, the insistence in Jewish law that when men and women count days of uncleanness before qualifying for sundry privileges in temple service, it is they that do the counting on their honor—without the verification of disinterested witnesses—gave support to the notion that the condition of one's body is one's own inviolable area of concern.[24]

It comes as no surprise, therefore, that thousands of years before other legal systems became preoccupied with the right to privacy, Jewish law—in the Talmud and Codes—devoted hundreds of folios to the theme.[25] The right, which first applied to one's person and one's residence was subsequently expanded to include one's court (where one stored assets) and one's garden—even to one's mail and trade secrets. The Bible also precluded creditors from entering the home of the debtor to seize property in payment of the debt and the Rabbis extended the rule to preclude even the sheriff from doing it.[26]

From a philosophical point of view, the creation of man in God's image

[23] *Ibid.*, Kiddushin, 28b.

[24] *Ibid.*, Ketubot, 72a.

[25] *Ibid.*, Baba Batra, beginning with 2a. See *Talmudic Encyclopedia*, Vol. VIII, pp. 659–702.

[26] B.T. Baba Mezia, 113a.

also makes for the right to privacy. In Neo-Platonic discourse God is the most lonely of all that is and religion is the flight of one who is lonely to the One Who is most alone. It would be unthinkable to invade the privacy of that flight. Indeed, Jewish mystics—unlike other mystics—rarely, if ever, described their mystical experiences. And they were thus secretive about them not only because such experiences are generally ineffable but also because they are so personal and private.

Jewish ideas about God affected the development of Jewish legal ideals and rules. The secularization of Jewish law, however, may affect them adversely. The danger ought not be ignored.

Apocalypse and Philo

By SAMUEL SANDMEL
Hebrew Union College—Jewish Institute of Religion, Cincinnati

GENESIS 15:12 TELLS THAT a deep sleep (*tardēmah*) befell Abraham, in the course of which the deity disclosed to him the future enslavement of his descendants in a land not theirs and their later redemption after 400 years. It is not at all surprising that Gen. 15:12 is the basis for the pseudepigraphic work, the Apocalypse of Abraham. In this book, Abraham rises to heaven, as in the Hekalot literature later sages did, accompanied by an angel named Jehoiēl. To Abraham the sights of the seven heavens, those of Hell, and of the Garden of Eden, were disclosed, as was the history of both the past and the present. Abraham saw the eschatological punishment of the wicked heathēn nations, and the Elect Messiah who, on God's sounding the trumpet, would gather Israel from among the nations.

While Christian interpolations are believed discernible, the Apocalypse of Abraham[1] is ordinarily deemed to be a Jewish book stemming from within the first Christian century. Hence, it is neither the earliest nor the latest apocalypse. One may express the judgment that for the most part, the Apocalypse of Abraham is devoid of significant uniqueness; it is a stock apocalypse, coming from the time when an abundance of such books were in circulation.

If the dates usually given for Philo of Alexandria are right, namely, 25–20 B.C.E.—40–45 A.C.E., then his dates place him within the period of the writing, and the reading, of apocalypses. He gives a great deal of attention to Genesis 15, and to the *tardēmah* matter, though in his unique way. But there is nothing directly apocalyptic in Philo. Can we explain why? Will an exposition of Philo's exegesis enable us to see whatever latent similarities relate him to apocalyptic, if only negatively?

Though Philo cites passages from Genesis 15 throughout his corpus of writings, the most focused and thorough use of the chapter is in his treatise, based on verses 2–18,[2] *Who is the Heir to Divine Things?*. In my opinion, this

[1] See "Abraham, Apocalypse of," *Interpreter's Bible Dictionary*, I, p. 21. A comparable though different work, "The Testament of Abraham" (*ibid.*), is not based on Genesis 15, but on the visions granted Abraham before his death.

[2] A brief summary of the verses emphasizing Septuagintal aspects, may be useful:

LXX Gen. 15:2 reads: "And Abram said, Lord God, what wilt thou give me, seeing I go childless, and the steward (MT. *ben mesheq*) of my house is this Eliezer of Damascus . . . And, behold the word of the Lord came unto him, saying, This one shall not be thine heir, but he that shall come forth out of thine own bowels shall be thine heir" (v. 4). Thereupon (v. 8) Abraham asked how he would "know"; the deity enjoined on him to take animals and birds which Abraham "divided into two." The birds—here LXX deviates from MT—

treatise is simultaneously the most profound and complex of all Philo's writings, and in it, so it seems to me, there is more personal self-revelation of Philo than elsewhere.

The treatise can be understood only in the light of Philo's total approach to Scripture. Here the following brief summary may be useful to the non-Philonist. Philo's exegetical device is allegory. He allegorizes verbs, nouns, adjectives, incidents. More especially, he allegorizes the names of biblical characters, reaching his allegorical definitions on the supposed meaning of the name in Hebrew; thus, Abram means "lofty father" (*ab*, "father"; *ram*, "lofty"). As Abram, the patriarch was born in Ur into an environment of astrology, a pursuit that entails having the eyes rove the lofty heavens. When Abram left Ur, he was leaving astrology; he progressed even further by learning. Abraham for Philo is the ancestor who reached perfection by what he learned. Accordingly, everything that Scripture tells about Abraham is related to the progress which a gifted learner makes as he moves toward his attainment of perfection.[3] But there is this additional overtone: Philo assumes, or implies, or states that all who can progress by learning are kindred to Abraham. Hence his Abraham is at times the historic patriarch, at times Philo himself, and at times his gifted reader. Accordingly, in describing the progress of Abraham, Philo discusses general aspects of progress.[4] *Who is Heir* deals preeminently with the progressing mind near and at the end of the process of progressing.[5]

Bound in the treatise as he is by the Scriptural reading, Philo expends a good many words on the import of verse 8, "How shall I know?" Do these words imply that some doubt existed in Abraham? In this context Philo asserts that it reflects only curiosity.[6]

But to our point: Gen. 15:12 in the Hebrew tells that a *tardēmah* ("deep sleep"?) fell upon Abraham; in the LXX, "at sunset, an *ecstasis* fell upon Abraham and, behold, great dark terror falls on him." Ecstasy exists in

came down to the divided pieces, and Abraham "sat with them"; LXX reads *vayesheb ᵓitam* rather than the MT *vayashev otam*; see on this latter my *Philo's Place in Judaism*, p. 149, note 228.

[3] Progress in Philo is the advance in a person whereby he is able to rise above his bondage to his body, the seat of sin and passion, to the point where his soul comes into union with the divine. In babyhood one is bound to the body for mere survival; one can reasonably progress through adolescence (the age of vice) into maturity, the stage where the higher mind has gained release from the imprisonment in the body in the premature years. See below note 7.

[4] Thus his treatise *On Mating for the Sake of Erudition*, about Abraham and Hagar, allegorically describes the progressing man through learning the encyclical studies. The treatise moves on to discuss the educational value of the encyclica, equivalent to our liberal arts, and also their limitation. The goal of learning is to get to Sarah, who is true philosophy, which in effect is Judaism.

[5] Philo contrasts the mature Abraham (see note 2) with Eliezer, mentioned in Gen.

four types: delusion, consternation, passivity, prophecy.[7] It is the last, prophecy, which here concerns us.

The ecstasy of the prophet is, according to Philo, completely silent. Prophecy is granted to every worthy man, but no prophet himself pronounces any word. Rather, God speaks through the prophet (*Heres* 259 ff.).

Deceptively, Philo tells us that it is good to hear what kind of predictions were made in the passage. But thereafter he gives us absolutely no predictions at all! The sentence, that Abraham's seed would be a stranger in a country not its own for four hundred years (Gen. 15:13), becomes Philo's ordinary allegory. He tells us that a wicked man inhabits his body as his own land, intending to reside there, and not simply to sojourn. The passions which are "not its own" are "strangers; obstacles to understanding." Numbering four, the passions, strong as "hundred" implies, have great power, and "entail a grievous slavery on their subjects." It is, however, God's will to weaken that strength (i. e., "judging the nation," Gen. 15:14), for it is God's practice to lighten the evil inherent in men. Strict and thorough education ("the stock," LXX Gen. 15:14) enables the soul to resist the evils arising from the passions.

That Abraham would "depart to thy fathers nourished with peace, in a goodly old age" (Gen. 15:15) is an allusion to the perfect among men, nourished in freedom from war and slavery. The good man does not die, but "departs," since the soul, fully purified, is "unquenchable and immortal," and journeys to heaven, without meeting "dissolution and corruption, which death appears to bring." "Thy fathers" may either be the sun, moon, and stars, or the archetypal ideas, or else the four elements (earth, water, air, and fire) into which everything "that has come into being is duly resolved," though, preferably, the soul returns to the "fifth essence," the ether (*Heres* 268–283). The "return" of the "fourth generation" (Gen. 15:16) speaks of the restoration of the soul.[8] The incomplete sin of the

15:2, a contrast between a mind which treats the senses as a servant, and a mind which treats them as a master; *Heres* 40–62; *cf. Philo's Place in Judaism*, pp. 151, where it is noted that in LXX Masek (Heb. mēsheq) is treated as if a proper name.

[6] *Cf. Philo's Place*, p. 171 and note 323. The divine words of Gen. 15:9, "take for Me," are the proof that no sense of doubt is implied in 15:8. See *Heres* 90 ff. and 129.

[7] Each type of *ecstasis* is illustrated by biblical passages containing some form of the word *ecstasis*; the first type is dealt with in *Heres* 249–250; the second in 251–256; the third in 257; and the fourth, elaborately, in 258–265.

[8] Philo speaks of four "generations" of the soul. The first is from birth through seven years, when the soul has as yet received no impression of either good or evil. In the second generation, that after childhood, the soul associates with evil, both by initiative and through the actions of others (proved by Gen. 8:21). In the third, the soul is as if on a sickbed, tended by philosophy, a healing art, and by "sound and salutary reasonings." In the fourth, power and vigor grow in the soul, which is "immovably established in all virtues" (*Heres* 293–299).

Amorites (allegorically, "talkers") is the period of time in which the plausible fallacies of the fluent are as yet unrefuted (*Heres*, 284–306).

Every worthy man receives prophecy, and in a number of passages Philo classifies himself with the prophets, the "members of God's family."[9] In no passage that I can recall does Philo ever venture any prediction. Rather, for him a prophet is a philosophical mystic who has achieved union with God. His citations from the biblical prophetic literature seem to be ten from Isaiah, six from Jeremiah, two from Hosea, and one each from Ezekiel, Obadiah, and Zechariah. But in none of these passages is there any focus on prediction and fulfillment. The latter are, to repeat, absent from Philo. Accordingly, the contrast between the apocalyptic of the *Apocalypse of Abraham* and Philo's mysticism could not be sharper.

Is Philo disinterested in apocalyptic? Is it the case that he was unacquainted with this genre of literature? Was he acquainted with its flamboyance, its unrestrained dramatic and colorful figures of speech, and so scornful of these, that, rationalist that he was, he rejected the whole enterprise? Or, is it that his rationalism leads him only to appear to accept the idea of predictions, but always to understand these, or apocalypses he may have known, in his idiosyncratic, allegorical way? I suspect that since Scripture on the literal level contains predictions, Philo gave some lip-service to Scriptural prophetic prediction. I doubt that he gave more than lip-service.

A bent for apocalypse would seem to be something which Philo, with condescending tolerance, relegates to the "crowd," the literalists whom he repeatedly scorns. It is clear that he himself will have nothing to do with it. For the elite, so one can infer, apocalyptic was too base to take seriously.

And yet Philo's assertion that in prophecy there is utterance, though on the part of God and not the prophet himself, can seem almost to be a verification and validation of prophetic prediction. But while one encounters the prophet in Philo, he encounters virtually no prophecy.

I wish I knew more precisely how to account for the anomaly that Philo's belonging to the age of apocalyptists did not prompt him into revelations or an affirmative relationship to it, even respecting himself. Figures such as Philo, so we read, are ordinarily best understood as reflective of their age[10] and environment; hence it is striking that respecting prediction, Philo is so at variance with trends of his time.

[9] For the Philonic reference, see *Philo's Place in Judaism*, pp. 177–178, note 347, 182–185; 186; 202. Briefly, the prophet is a member of God's family. He rises above all corporeality. He himself remains silent, but the deity speaks through the prophet's vocal capacities.

[10] He is at variance with Paul, as in II Cor. 12:1–10. If Scholem (*Jewish Gnosticism, Merkabah Mysticism, and Talmudic Tradition*) is right in ascribing Merkabah mysticism to the first or second Christian century (see *Philo's Place in Judaism*^{2}, pp. xii–xiii), then Philo is at variance with it too.

Perhaps he is a clue to the procedure by later figures, whether gnostics or medieval philosophers, who in various ways so dealt with many phenomena in Scripture that their literal import tends to disappear. Can we infer that even beyond Philo the man, he presents an instance of a process destined to be repeated on the part of subsequent philosophical minds?

The Divine Title *ʾabhîr yaʿăqôbh*

By NAHUM M. SARNA
Brandeis University

One of the distinguishing characteristics of the Book of Genesis is the high concentration of rare or unique divine titles to be found there. One such is אֲבִיר יעקב (Gen. 49:24) which is exceptional in that it appears in a poetic text and again occurs elsewhere four times (Isa. 49:26; 60:16; Ps. 132:2, 5).[1] It further shows up in the variant form אֲבִיר ישראל (Isa. 1:24).[2] Two problems present themselves, one morphological, the other semantic. The first relates to the fact that אֲבִיר is invariably found in the *status constructus* and that another form אַבִּיר exists as well, so that the relationship between the variants has to be established; the second involves the interpretation of the epithet itself.

The attempts to reconstruct the putative absolute singular form have yielded three defensible suggestions, each of which has its proponent(s).

The first possibility is אָבִיר*. As a *qĕṭîl* form, it would follow the pattern of such nouns as בְּדִיל (Num. 31:22), גְּבִיר (Gen. 27:29), כְּסִיל (Ps. 49:11), כְּפִיר (Judg. 14:5), and, with initial guttural, חֲזִיר (Lev. 11:7), חֲנִית (I Sam. 13:19) and חֲסִין (Ps. 89:9). This is the understanding of Judah ibn Balʿam (d.c. 1090)[3] and is given as a possible alternative explanation by Jonah ibn Janakh (c. 985–c. 1040).[4] Ben-Yehuda lists אָבִיר as a separate entry in his *Thesaurus*, though not without some hesitation.[5]

[1] H-J. Kraus, *Psalmen* [Biblischer Kommentar Altes Testament XV/2] (1960), p. 884, mistakenly includes Ps. 78:25; *cf.* his comment to that passage, I, p. 545.

[2] IQIsa.[a] has a lacuna after צבאות, but the reading ישראל is found also in the Greek, Vulg. and Pesh. A. Alt, "Der Gott der Väter," *Kleine Schriften*, I (Múnich, 1953), pp. 19ff. (=*Essays in Old Testament History and Religion*, translated by R. A. Wilson, New York, 1968, p. 32), simply explains the variant as due to the later identification of Jacob with Israel. On the other hand, G. B. Gray, *Isaiah* [I.C.C.], Edinburgh, 1912, p. 34, notes approvingly that Budde and Marti omit the epithet here as a later insertion (see on this further below, n. 53). A. B. Ehrlich, *Randglossen zur Hebräischen Bibel*, Leipzig, 1908, I, p. 251, merely remarks on the rarity of the combination. S. Mowinckel, *The Psalms in Israel's Worship* (translated by D. R. Ap-Thomas), Oxford, 1962, I, p. 100, n. 57, strangely cites "*ʾabbîr yiśrāʾel*" (sic!) as occurring in Ps. 132:2, 5. L. F. Hartman in *Encyclopaedia Judaica* (1971), vol. 7, col. 681, suggests that בורא ישראל in Isa. 43:15 should be read אביר ישראל. The fact of the matter is that ישראל in Isa. 1:24 is conditioned by the fossilized epithet ה' צבאות אלהי ישראל (*cf.* Isa. 21:10; 37:16) which never appears with a יעקב variant. Therefore, it is doubtful that an independent epithet אביר ישראל ever existed.

[3] Commentary to Isa. 1:24, reprinted in *Commentaries on the Book of Isaiah*, Jerusalem, 5731/1971. II, p. 21.

[4] *Sefer HaShorashim*, ed. W. Bacher, Berlin, 1896, p. 11.

[5] E. Ben Yehuda, *Thesaurus*, I, p. 23 and n. 1.

Another option is אָבִיר*. This would follow the well attested *qāṭîl* pattern which yields the construct form *qĕṭîl* such as appears in קְצִיר (Gen. 30:14) < קָצִיר (Gen. 8:22), בְּצִיר (Judg. 8:2) < בָּצִיר (Lev. 26:5), פְּקִיד (Neh. 11:14) < פָּקִיד (II Kings 25:19), and with initial guttural[6] חֲצִיר (II Kings 19:26) < חָצִיר (I Kings 18:5). This suggestion has enjoyed wide popularity. Jonah ibn Janakh,[7] followed apparently by Solomon ibn Parchon,[8] embraced it, and modern lexicographers have by and large concurred.[9]

The third explanation derives אֲבִיר from an original אַבִּיר, a *qaṭṭîl* form, by analogy with the sing. constr. form פְּרִיץ (Isa. 35:9) < פָּרִיץ = *parrîṣ* (Ezek˙ 18:10; Ps. 17:9), the absolute form being determined by פָּרִיצִים = *parrîṣîm* (Jer. 7:11; Ezek. 7:22) > פָּרִיצֵי *parrîṣê* (Dan. 11:14). This theory was advanced by J. Barth,[10] but found no support and is explicitly rejected by some lexica.[11]

Whatever be the hypothetical absolute form of אֲבִיר, there exists well-nigh[12] scholarly unanimity that the received vocalization is artificial, the product of a later pietistic, dogmatic alteration of an original אַבִּיר made for the purpose of distinguishing the sacred usage of the word as a divine epithet from its secular meaning.[13] The authors of this "emendation" have

[6] No *qāṭîl* noun with initial *ʾaleph* exists in both sing. abs. and const. forms, but clearly belonging to this class are אָסִיר (Ps. 79:11), pl. אֲסִירִים, אֲסִירֵי (Gen. 39:22, 20); אָצִיל*, אֲצִילֵי (Exod. 24:11) and אָפִיק*, אֲפִיק (Job 6:15; *cf.* 12:21; II Sam. 22:16).

[7] *Op. cit.*, p. 11.

[8] *Makbereth He-Arukh*, ed. S. G. Stern, Pressburg, 1844, s. v. אבר.

[9] So the biblical Hebrew dictionaries of Brown, Driver and Briggs, Gesenius-Buhl (1962) and Baumgartner-Koehler (1967). B. Luther, *ZAW*, 21 (1901), p. 72, states that, "*Im massoretischen Text wird punkiert* אָבִיר" (sic!). S. R. Driver, *The Book of Genesis*, 1904, p. 409; W. F. Albright, *The Vocalization of the Egyptian Syllabic Orthography* [American Oriental Series 5], New Haven, 1934, p. 33, III A.1; A. S. Kapelrud in *Theologisches Wörterbuch zum Alten Testament*, eds. G. J. Botterweck u. H. Ringgren, Stuttgart, 1970, I, p. 43 (= *Theological Dictionary of the Old Testament*, translated by J. T. Willis, Grand Rapids, 1974, I, p. 42), all presuppose אָבִיר*.

[10] Nominalbildung in dem Semitischen Sprachen, Leipzig, 1889, pp. 51 f. §35.

[11] E. g., Gesenius-Buhl; *cf.* Gesenius' Hebrew Grammar, ed. Kautzsch-Cowley, Oxford, 1910, p. 234, § 84ᵇ, f. 25.

[12] As far as I can ascertain, only M. Haran in *Oz leDavid* [Hebrew], Jerusalem, 1964, p. 59, n. 39 among modern scholars has suggested that the received vocalization may well, be original.

[13] In addition to the authors cited in n. 9 above, this view has been espoused by T. K. Cheyne, *The Prophecies of Isaiah*, New York, 1886, II, p. 136; A. B. Ehrlich, *Die Psalmen*, Berlin, 1905, p. 344; C. A. Briggs, *Psalms* [ICC], Edinburgh, 1907, II, p. 473; J. Skinner, *Genesis* [ICC], 2nd ed., Edinburgh, 1930, p. 531; H. Gunkel, *Genesis*, 3rd. ed., Göttingen, 1910 [reprint, 1964], p. 486. Strangely confused is Th. J. Meek, *Hebrew Origins*, New York, 1960, p. 138, n. 60, to whom "the vocalization *ʾabbîr* (sic!), "mighty one," is clearly an artificial one for *ʾābîr*, "bull." The same theory is repeated on p. 140 which mentions "the term *ʾābîr*, "bull" (later vocalized *ʾabbîr*, "mighty one," when the bull cult fell into disrepute), as an appellative of deity."

variously been identified as "the Soferim,"[14] "the Rabbis"[15] and "the Massoretes,"[16] although most scholars have been content merely to record the phenomenon without specifying its initiators.

As to the motivation for the separation of the sacred and secular usages, a wide consensus maintains that it is because אַבִּיר means "a bull." Opinion is divided, however, as to whether the divine epithet denoted the actual representation of YHWH as a bull, or whether it simply employed the bull image as a literary figure, or whether it was merely the connotative theriomorphism that supposedly evoked the opposition of pietists.

The father of the literalist school was K. Budde[17] who was convinced that YHWH was pictured as a bull-god in the Hebrew Bible. If it be asserted that bull-worship, where attested, is designated by עגל,[18] and not אַבִּיר, the answer is, according to this scholar, that the latter term carried a more noble sound than the former which was redolent of scorn and derision.[19] To the anticipated challenge that the biblical use of אביר as an appellative of God is surprisingly sparse in contrast to the allegedly widespread cult of the bull, Budde responded that the received Hebrew text had been tampered with and the originally more frequent usages excised or emended. He thereupon cavalierly proceeded to "restore" אביר in many places where the present text has אפוד[20] or ארון.[21]

Budde's singular methodology did not find much support, but the notion that the epithet אביר יעקב testifies to the one-time existence of bull-worship in Israel, or that it conjured up bovine attributes, persisted. Thus Skinner, while not certain as to whether the epithet is really a survival of the bull-worship of Bethel and Dan, is nevertheless sure that אֲבִיר is intended to avoid an association of ideas with אַבִּיר "bull," the idolatrous emblem of YHWH in Northern Israel.[22] Gunkel translates the phrase in question *Stier*

[14] Ben Yehuda, *op. cit.*, I, p. 23, s. v., אֲבִיר.

[15] Gunkel, *op. cit.*, p. 486.

[16] So Ehrlich, Briggs, Skinner, *op. cit.*, n. 13 above, Kapelrud, *op. cit.*, n. 9, above.

[17] *ZAW*, 39 (1921), pp. 1–42. L. Waterman, *AJSL*, XXXI (1915), 229–255, without mentioning אביר יעקב had expressed his conviction that the bull-cult of YHWH in Israel "was widespread and deep-seated, and the most prominent interpreter" of YHWH throughout the period from the Judges to the eighth century prophets.

[18] So Exod. ch. 32; Deut. 9:16, 21; I Kings 12:28, 32; II Kings 10:29; 17:16; Hos. 8:5 f.; 10:5; 13:2; Ps. 106:19; II Chron. 11:15; 13:8. It should be noted that the syncretistic pr. n. עגליו in the Samaria Ostraca No. 41, further proves that it is עגל, not אביר that is redolent of the bull cult.

[19] Budde, *op. cit.*, p. 38. Of course, there is no warranty for this notion. Heb. עגל is "a bullock of two or three years, just at the prime of life" (W. F. Albright, *From the Stone Age to Christianity*, 2nd. ed., New York, 1957, p. 300), and as such was particularly desirable for sacrifice.

[20] Viz., Judg. 8:27; 17:5; 18:14; I Sam. 14:3; 21:10; 23:9.

[21] E. g., I Sam. 14:18.

[22] *Op. cit.*

Jacobs which, he says, is "*ein Nachklang des Stiersymbols*."[23] This is based on the view of G. Hoffmann.[24] B. Luther asserted that, "*Der 'Stier Jakobs' ist der Stier der Jakob gehört, das Kultobject, in dem der Gott Jakob verehrt wird . . .*"[25] On the other hand, Alt has scoffed at "the mania amongst modern scholars for seeing bulls everywhere" which "has led several of them to suggest without very convincing reasons" a meaning "the Bull(-god) of Jacob."[26] Kapelrud appears to share Alt's view, but he attributes the non-dagheshed form אֲבִיר to the Massoretes who "clearly heard in the word *ʾabyr* (*sic!*) the idea of "bull," and who possibly had in mind I Kings 12:25–33." He says that it cannot be determined "whether they also were thinking of the Canaanite Bull cult, but probably they were not."[27] Kapelrud does not inform us how the Massoretes, who labored between the 6th–8th centuries C.E., might have obtained a knowledge of ancient Canaanite religion. Be that as it may, it is largely under the influence of Ugaritic literature that the association of YHWH with a bull has been revived.

The Canaanite supreme god El frequently bears the designation "bull." This symbol has been taken by M. Pope to signify his procreative powers.[28] Albright has noted that the title carries the idea of precedence and strength,[29] an aspect of the epithet that has also been stressed by Eissfeldt.[30] P. D. Miller has effectively demonstrated that El in Ugarit is not a fertility god and that the primary characteristic of bull imagery is strength and belligerence whether in Ugaritic or in Hebrew.[31]

Now the equation: Ug. "El the bull" = Heb אֲבִיר יַעֲקֹב is taken for granted by many scholars, and the earlier interpretation of Gen. 49:24 as "Bull of Jacob" seems, at first sight, to be reinforced by the Ugaritic texts, though opinion differs as to whether the Hebrew title is a carry over from Canaan or is indigenous to Israel and belongs to the original patriarchal El cult.[32] The problem is, however, that the Ugaritic term in question is not

[23] *Op. cit. Cf.* E. Meyer, *Die Israeliten und Ihre Nachbarstämme*, Halle, 1906, pp. 283–285.

[24] *ZAW*, 3 (1883), 124.

[25] *Op. cit.*, pp. 72 f. Skinner, *op. cit.*, p. 531, note, finds the idea that Jacob was the deity originally worshipped in the bull to be "perhaps too adventurous."

[26] *Op. cit.*

[27] *Op. cit.*

[28] *El in the Ugaritic Texts*, Leiden, 1955 [Suppl VT II], pp. 35–42. *Cf.* A. S. Kapelrud, *Baal in the Ras Shamra Texts*, Copenhagen, 1952, pp. 21, 68, 97.

[29] W. F. Albright, *Archaeology and the Religion of Israel*, 5th ed., New York, 1968, p. 145; *Yahweh and the Gods of Canaan*, New York, 1968, p. 120.

[30] O. Eissfeldt, *El im Ugaritischen Pantheon*, Berlin, 1951, p. 56; *Kleine Schriften*, Tübingen, 1966, III, pp. 481–485; IV, p. 85. *Cf.* Mowinckel, *op. cit.*; B. Vawter, *CBQ*, 17 (1955), p. 11; M. Dahood, *Biblica*. 40^2 (1959), p. 1006; N. C. Habel, *Yahweh v. Baal*, New York, 1964, p. 48, n. 11; U. Oldenburg, *The Conflict between El and Baal in Canaanite Religion*, Leiden, 1969, p. 174.

[31] *HTR*, 60 (1967), pp. 411–431, esp. pp. 418–422.

[32] *Cf.* F. M. Cross, *Canaanite Myth and Hebrew Epic*, Cambridge, 1973, pp. 4 (n. 6), 15, 244.

ʾ*ibr* but *ṯr* which corresponds to Heb. שׁוֹר, "ox." It is this that is the title of El and it remains to be explained—which it never has—why Israel should not have carried over the Canaanite epithet intact. The question is the more pertinent since שׁוֹר is a frequent Hebrew word and one actually used in connection with the wilderness calf worship in Ps. 106:20,

> "They exchanged their glory
> for the image of a bull (שׁוֹר) that
> feeds on grass."

The Hebrew equivalent of Ug. *ṯr il* should have been שׁוֹר אֵל a phrase that N. H. Tur-Sinai[33] brilliantly postulated to be embedded in the consonantal text of Hos. 8:6 מִי שֹׁר אֵל=מישראל. This reading seems to have been adopted by *NEB*. "For what sort of a god is this bull?" Tur-Sinai[34] himself categorically rejected the association of אביר with a bull and tried to show that, in fact, none of its usages need be so understood.

Conscious, perhaps, of the weakness of connecting El with the Hebrew appellative, some scholars have claimed that the prototype was Baal who, it is asserted, is connected with Ug. *ỉbr*, the equivalent of Heb. אביר. Thus, Mowinckel tells us that "Baal is called the 'bull,' *ỉbr* in the Ugaritic texts, the hump-backed bull, the bison."[35] Vawter writes that "Ugar. *ibr*, which always means "bull,"[36] is associated in 75:I:32; :II:55 f.; 76:III:21 with Baal and his offspring."[37] What is the evidence? Ug. text 75:I:30–33 reads:

> (30) *bhm qrnm* (31) *km. ṯrm. wgbṯt* (32) *km. ỉbrm*
> (33) *wbhm. pn. bʿl*

The reference is to the birth of gods who have "on them horns like bulls and humps like buffaloes and on them is the face of Baal." The text actually tells us nothing about the bull character of Baal. Ug. text 75:II:55 f. merely

[33] *Halashon VeHaSefer*, III, Jerusalem, 1955, p. 47; ʾ*Encyclopedia Miqra*ʾ*ith*, I, col. 31. Pope, *op. cit.*, p. 35, is dubious about this reading, but Miller, *op. cit.*, p. 422, n. 46 seems to endorse it.

[34] *ZAW*, 39 (1921), 296–300; *HaLashon VeHaSefer*, *op. cit.*, pp. 39–47. Tur-Sinai based his philological argument on the suggestion of S. D. Luzzatto, *Commentary to Isaiah* [Hebrew], Padua, 1867, p. 40, deriving the term from אֶבְרָה "a wing." Whereas Luzzato saw in the latter the idea of protection (*Cf.* Ps. 91:4), Tur-Sinai understood the underlying idea to be "elevation, exaltation."

[35] *Op. cit.*, p. 100, n. 57. Incidentally, ʾ*abbîr* is there cited in place of the correct ʾ*ăbhîr*. A. S. Kapelrud, *The Ras Shamra Discoveries and the O.T.*, translated by G. W. Anderson, 1963, p. 39, also claims that Baal is referred to as a bull.

[36] *Cf.* J. Gray, *The Krt Text in the Literature of Ras Shamra*, Leiden, 1964, p. 49. It should be noted that H. L. Ginsberg, *The Legend of King Keret*, New Haven, 1946, pp. 16, 39, prefers to render *ỉbr* in KRT, l. 120, "stallion;" so *ANET*, p. 144. Actually, the word is not common in Ugaritic. In text 51: 7:55 f. it is more likely the equivalent of Heb. אֵבֶר "wing" (*cf. ANET*, p. 135).

[37] Vawter, *op. cit.*

informs us that "Baal fell like a bull (*ṯr*), Hadd collapsed like a buffalo (*ỉbr*)." The precise context is obscure because the text is broken, but the image again tells us nothing about Baal's nature or representation, only about the manner in which he collapsed. Text 76:III:21 (36 f.) indeed informs us that Baal sired a "buffalo" (*ỉbr*), "a wild bull" (*rʾum*), but once again, the context is unknown due to the fragmentary state of the text. If there is evidence for Baal having the character of a bull, it can hardly rest on the literary evidence.[38] There is certainly no basis for the claim that Baal actually bears the title *ỉbr*.

How is ʾ*BR* used in Semitic languages? Albright has noted that ʾ*a-bi-ir-ya* (=ʾ*abîr*) was borrowed from Canaanite by the Egyptians of the New Empire as a word for "stallion."[39] This is the precise meaning of Heb. אַבִּירִים in Judg. 5:22 and Jer. 8:16. In both texts the term appears in synonymous parallelism with סוּסִים "horses." The same meaning certainly applies also in Jer. 47:3 and seems to be most appropriate in Jer. 50:11 as well. Hence, אַבִּיר can hardly be said unequivocally to signify "bull." Furthermore, in several passages the term is used of humans, certainly in Ps. 76:6 where אַבִּירֵי־לֵב "stout-hearted," is synonymous with אַנְשֵׁי־חַיִל "warriors," and in Lam. 1:15 where אַבִּירַי parallels בַּחוּרָי "young men." The same is most likely true also in Ps. 78:25 לחם אבירים,[40] I Sam. 21:8 אביר הרעים[41] and

[38] *Cf.* P. W. Miller, *HTR*, *op. cit.*, p. 419; A. S. Kapelrud, *Baal*, *op. cit.*, pp. 20 f., 52, 62 f., 93. T. H. Gaster, *Thespis*, 2nd. ed., New York, 1961, p. 172, notes that S. Arabian inscriptions record the title *Ṯ-r-bʿl*, "Bull Baal." Significantly, it is *ṯr*, not ʾ*br*, that is used.

[39] *The Vocalization*, *op. cit.*, p. 33, III.A.1; p. 52, X1.B1; *BASOR*, 62 (1936), p. 30.

[40] *Cf.* *NJPS*, "a hero's meal:" *RSV* and *NEB* render, "bread of angels," based on G. Ἄρτον ἀγγέλων; so Rashi, *cf.* Targ. Certain it is that אַבִּירִים here has no connotation of bulls or any other theriomorphic association.

[41] This is the only non-poetic usage of אַבִּיר. C. D. Ginsburg, *The Massorah*, London, 1905 [Ktav reprint: New York, 1975], IV, p. 24, § 69, points out that in some mss. the punctuation is אֲבִיר followed in the *editio princeps* of Soncino, 1488. The Aleppo Codex reads אַבִּיר (courtesy of Prof. M. Goshen-Gottstein). The Greek reads νέμων τὰς ἡμιόνους, "herdsman of the mules," apparently based on a Hebrew *Vorlage* / רועה הפרדים העירים. S. R. Driver, *Notes on the Hebrew Text . . . Samuel*, 2nd. ed., Oxford, 1913, p. 176 retains אַבִּיר but favors the emendation of Graetz רָצִים for רֹעִים. This is rejected by M. H. Segal, *Sifrê Shemuel*, Jerusalem, 1956, *ad loc.*, on the grounds that Doeg was not a runner as is clear from the narrative in I Sam. 22:17 ff. He suggests that אַבִּיר in this context may be an Edomite title. A. B. Ehrlich, *Randglossen*, III, p. 243, emends אַבִּיר to אַדִּיר (*cf.* Judg. 5:25). P. D. Miller, *Ugarit-Forschungen*, 2 (1970), p. 180 and n. 18, recognizes here the phenomenon of animal name designation for high officials. N. H. Tur-Sinai, *ZAW*, 39 (1921), p. 300, also finds no difficulty in the phrase. He takes אַבִּיר in the sense of "officer," drawing attention to the parallel רעה — אביר in Gen. 49:24 and the epithet with. האדון in Isa. 1:24. The same point is made by M. Haran, *op. cit.*, who also suggests that I Sam. 21:8 should be vocalized אֲבִיר, a reading which, indeed, enjoys some support, as noted above.

Isa. 46:12 אבירי לב.[42] In only a minority of cases[43] does אַבִּיר unambiguously refer to animals, probably "bulls:" Isa. 34:7; Ps. 22:13; 50:13; 68:31 and apparently also in Jer. 46:15.[44]

Now it is possible, of course, that in those texts in which אביר is applied to humans we may be witnessing a phenomenon attested in Ugaritic, the use of animal names as designations for warriors, high officials or dignitaries.[45] Even if this be the case it would only prove that אביר had early become metaphorically stereotyped and that, therefore, when used of God, could hardly have had cultic associations.[46]

Turning to the use of the term in Akkadian, we find the noun *abāru*,[47] "strength," applied to kings and gods. Sargon is described as *gamir dunni u abāri* "consummate in power and strength." The title *bēl abāri*, "endowed with strength," is an epithet of the gods Nergal, Tammuz and Ninurta.[48] This has particular relevance for the Hebrew divine appellative אֲבִיר יעקב. One wonders why this cannot simply mean "The strong One of Jacob," which is exactly the way it is rendered in the ancient versions.

Thus, the Targumim have תקיפ(א) for all occurrences. The Greek has *δυνάστου* in Gen. 49:24, *ἰσχυοντες* in Isa. 1:24, *ἰσχύος* in Isa. 49:26; similarly, Vulg. has *potentis* in Gen. 49:24 and *fortis* in the Isaiah passages.[49] It is worth noting that the Hebrew of Ben Sira uses אביר as "mighty one"[50] and in Rabbinic Hebrew there is the phrase אביר שבאבירים, "the mostly highly esteemed,"[51] as opposed to קל שבקלים "the least esteemed," as well as, remarkably, even a verbal form אִיבֵּר[52] "to strengthen," "harden."

[42] Behind the Greek *οἱ ἀπολωλεκόντες τὴν καρδίαν* seems to be אֹבְדֵי לב a reading adopted by J. L. McKenzie, *Second Isaiah* [Anchor Bible], New York, 1968, p. 86. 1QIsa^a = MT.

[43] Isa. 10:13; Job 24:22; 34:20 are all obscure.

[44] Heb. מדוע נסחף אביריך is rendered by *NJPS*, "Why are stalwarts swept away?" The translators give no alternate translation, not even their "emendation yields" footnote. *NEB*, so J. Bright, *Jeremiah* [Anchor Bible], New York, 1965, p. 303, accepts the Greek which bisects נסחף, taking the second syllable as "Apis," the sacred bull of the Egyptians and reading אבירך sing., the latter supported by several Heb. mss.

[45] P. D. Miller, *Ugarit-Forschungen*, *op. cit.*, pp. 177–186, esp. p. 180.

[46] Incidentally, the figurative use of animal imagery with God in poetic texts is not necessarily objectionable. Witness II Sam. 22:3 = Ps. 18:3 קרן ישעי, lit., "the horn of my salvation," clearly deriving from bull imagery. Similarly, God roars like a lion (Jer. 25:30; Joel 4:16; Amos 1:2).

[47] *CAD*, *A*/1, p. 38.

[48] *Ibid.* K. Tallqvist, *Akkadische Götterepitheta*, Helsingfors, 1938, pp. 40, 395, 427.

[49] In Isa. 60:16; Ps. 132:2, 5, G. has simply Θεός; Vulg. has *Deus* in the latter passage.

[50] Ed. M. H. Segal, Jerusalem, 1953, p. 288; *cf.* R. H. Charles, *The Apocrypha and Pseudepigrapha*, Oxford, 1913, I, p. 474, and notes m-m.

[51] Rosh Hashanah 25^b; Yer. Rosh Hashanah II:9, 58^b; Koheleth Rabbah I:8 (to 1:4).

[52] Sanhedrin 109^b שאיבר עצמו; var. שאיבר לבו.

To sum up, the primary meaning of אביר is "strong one," whether applied to humans or animals. There is no warranty for the widespread belief that the dagheshed form ever conjured up in Hebrew the specific image of a bull in all its bovine qualities much less as a cultic object. For this reason the non-dagheshed form is not an artificial dogmatic creation.

The implausibility of the emendation theory is further strengthened by the employment of the divine epithet on the part of First and Second Isaiah. The earlier prophet lived at a time when, supposedly, the so-called "bull" association of אביר was still part of the living language and when the influence of paganism on Israel was still strong. It is hardly conceivable that he would have used an appellative redolent of the grossest pagan associations.[53] Equally incomprehensible would be the two-fold use by Second Isaiah whose uncompromising monotheism and anti-pagan rhetoric rule out any possibility of insensitivity to אביר if that term invoked bull-cult imagery.

For all the afore-going reasons, the distinction between the sacred epithet אֲבִיר יעקב and the secular dagheshed form cannot be the artificial product of late pietism. Rather, the two forms existed side by side from the beginning.

[53] Budde (*op. cit.*, n. 2 above) regarded the presence of the divine appellative in Isa. 1:24 as a late intrusion. Is it because it interfered with his theory?

An Unknown Responsum of David Ibn Abi Zimra

By A. SCHEIBER
Budapest, Hungary

A COMPREHENSIVE WORK on David Ibn Abi Zimra's life and works appeared some years ago.[1] He has continued to interest scholars since.[2]

His responsa show how considerable was the respect he enjoyed even outside Israel.[3] "With this Rabbi the *Responsa* literature of the Sephardim reached its peak."[4]

We have already published one of his responsa in the Kaufmann Collection.[5] Not long ago a sizeable volume of his Responsa was published by J. Z. Sopher.[6]

There is in the library of the Jewish Theological Seminary of Budapest a manuscript collection containing for the most part the responsa of rabbis of the Balkan region. It bears some kinship with the volume in the library of the Hebrew University once described by S. Assaf.[7]

In this Collection may be found an unknown Responsum of David Ibn Abi Zimra (pp. 183–191). As so often, it describes an event in Saloniki. The signature is identical with that shown by D. Tamar.[8]

The Responsum includes the following authors or works:

ס' האגודה	קולון
אפרים	ראב"ד
יוסף הלוי ן' מיגאש	רא"ש
יעקב בן אשר	ריא"ף (רי"ף)
יצחק הלבן	ריטב"א
ירוחם	רינב"ר
ישעיה מיטרני	רמב"ם
מאיר (מרוטנבורג)	רשב"א
מרדכי	רש"י

[1] I. M. Goldman, *The Life and Times of Rabbi David Ibn Abi Zimra* (New York, 1970.)

[2] H. Bentov, *Shalem. Studies in the History of the Jews in Eretz-Israel*. I. Ed. J. Hacker (Jerusalem, 1974), p. 215; H. Z. (J. W.) Hirschberg, *Salo Wittmayer Baron Jubilee Volume*. II (New York-London, 1974), p. 577; D. Tamar, *Tarbiz* XLIII (1974), pp. 235–236; A. David, *ibid.*, XLI (1971/72), pp. 325–329.

[3] E. Silberschlag, *From Renaissance to Renaissance* (New York, 1973), p. 47.

[4] H. J. Zimmels, *The Sephardi Heritage*. Ed. R. D. Barnett (London, 1971), p. 396.

[5] M. Benayahu–A. Scheiber, *Sefunot* VI (1962), pp. 125–134.

[6] **ספר שו"ת הרדב"ז מכתב יד** (Bne Brak, 1975).

[7] S. Assaf, *D. Yellin Jubilee Volume* (Jerusalem, 1935), pp. 221–237.

[8] D. Tamar, *Sinai* XL (1975), Nos. 1–2, pp. 66–71.

נמקי יוסף	ר״ת
סמ״ג	תוספות
עטור	ס׳ התרומות

In the following the text of the Responsum is given.

[183] **מעשה** היה בשאלוניק ראובן הוציא שטר חוב על שמעון וכתו׳
כלשון הזה וכדי ליפות כח ראובן נכנס לוי ערב קבלן ופרען בעד כל
הסך הנז׳ באופן שכשיגיע הזמן הנז׳ יוכל ראובן הנז׳ לגבות חובו מאי זה
מהם שירצה תחלה כדין ערב קבלן ופרען המשתעבד בשעת מתן
מעות ועתה ראובן הביא את לוי לב״ד ותובע ממנו תחלה ולוי השיבו
הנה אני לא יצאתי ערב אלא כשלא תוכל לגבות משמעון הלוה והרי
שמעון לפניך ויש לו נכסים ידועים וקרקעות ואם לא תוכל לגבות
חובך אז הנני מוכן לפרוע ע״כ. ונשאלה שאלה זו לפני אחד מחכמי
העיר והשיב ז״ל

תשובה הן זה בא לפני אני הצעיר הבא על החתום ועם היות
ששבח לאל נתפשרו ולא הוצרכו לעמוד בגזרתי מ״מ להיות אמרתי
שהדין היה לו. ואולי יחשדני שומע. והייתי בעיניו כמתעתע. שוגג או
פושע. ראיתי לכתוב בקוצר מאי זה טעם אמרתי מה שאמרתי ומה
ראיתי על ככה שלכאורה נראה שיכול ראובן לתבוע תחלה מלוי
משני טעמים הא׳ כי רבו הפוסקי׳ האומרים כי כאשר התנה המלוה
שיוכל לגבות חובו ממי שירצה מהם תחלה שתנאו קיים. גם מטעם אחר
שנכנס לוי ערב קבלן וכו׳ וקי״ל כחכמים דקבלן יש למלוה לגבות
ממנו חובו אפי׳ לא התנה לגבות ממנו תחלה כפי דעת רוב הפוסקים
קמאי ובתראי כ״ש בנדון דידן שכתו׳ קבלן גם תנאי כנז׳. אמנם נר׳ לע״ד
כי עכ״ז הדין עם לוי הערב כי מספיקא לא מפקי׳ ממונא ויכול לומ׳
קים לי כהראב״ד והנמשכים אחריו שכתבו שאפי׳ התנה בפי׳ שיגבה
ממי שירצה תחלה אם יש נכסים ידועים ללוה יגבה ממנו תחלה ויתבענו
[184] לדין וטעם זה דקים לי וכו׳ כת׳ מהררי׳ קולון״ ז״ל שמועיל אפי׳
להחזיק כמה שתפס אחר שנולד הספק כמו שכתב בשורש קסא וז״ל
ודאי גבי ממונא מצי למימ׳ המוחזק קים לי כחד מרבוותא ואע״ג שכנגדו
חלוק עלי עד ופשיטא דכה״ג לא הוה מצי למימ׳ קים לי כדברי היחיד
ודלא ככל חכמי ישראל ואפי׳ תפס מפקי׳ מיניה וכו׳ משמע דאי לא הוי
יחיד מצי למימ׳ קים לי כי הני אע״ג דיש רבים כנגדם וא״כ כ״ש וק״ו
בנדון דידן דעדיף טפי שמוחזק בממונו מעולם שיועיל לו זה הטעם ומה
גם עתה שכת׳ בנמקי יוסף וז״ל והסכימו האחרונים ז״ל דלענין ערב
אפי׳ התנה בפי׳ ע״מ שאגבה מן הערב תחלה אם יש לו נכסים ללוה לא
יגבה מן הערב. וגדולה מזו כת׳ בשם הרשב״א ז״ל שאפי׳ בירר בתוך
התנאי ואמ׳ ואפי׳ יהיו נכסים ידועים ללוה אני מתנה שאגבה מן הערב
תחלה אם ארצה דלא מהני דפטומי מלי נינהו ובזה כת׳ אלא שיש מן
האחרונים שחלקו בזה מ״מ משמע שהסכמת האחרוני׳ שאפי׳ כשהתנה
מאי זה מהם שארצה אגבה תחלה ולא בירר בתוך תנאו ואפי׳ יהיו
נכסים ידועים ללוה אם יש נכסים ללוה יגבה מן הלוה תחלה. ולזה
הדעת מסכים ר״ת לע״ד כי התוספות בפר׳ גט פשוט מביאים דבריו

ומחלקים דיני ערב לה׳ חלקים א׳ ערב סתם דלא אתני. ב׳ אי אתני
ממי שארצה וכו׳ ואין נכסי׳ ללוה. ג׳ אי אית ליה נכסים ללוה אפי׳
אתני כפרע מן הלוה תחלה. ד׳ קבלן דהיינו תן לו ואני נותן. ה׳ נושא
ונותן ביד. ואם איתא כסברת ר״ת לחלק בין אמ׳ ללא אמ׳ שיתא הוו.
וכן תמצא במרדכי אלו הה׳ חלקים. א״כ נר׳ כי גם ר״ת מסברת האומרים
דכל שאינו קבלן אפי׳ התנה וכו׳ אם יש נכסים ללוה אינו גובה מן
הערב תחלה. וא״כ ברור הוא דבזה זכינו לדין כי ראוי לפסוק
הלכה// כבתראי ואין צורך להאריך בזה עכ״ל החכם הפוסק כטעם [185]
הראשון. ושאלת ממני אם יש לסמוך על טעם זה או על פסק זה או לא.
תשובה איני רואה לסמוך לא על הטעם ולא על הפסק מהטעמים
שאכתוב בע״ה. ואיברא שאם אמׂ לו מכל מי שארצה אני נפרע תחלה
יש מחלוקת בין הפוסקי׳ דאיכא מאן דסבר דאם יֶש נכסים ללוה
אין נפרע מָן הערב תחלה אבל קבלן גמור כגון דאמׂ לו תן לו ואני
נותן או שאמׂ לו תן לו ואני קבלן לכ״ע כפרע ממי שירצה תחלה אעפ״י
שיש נכסים ללוה דהא מתרצי׳ לה למתני׳ דפר׳ גט פשוט ואמרי׳
חסורי מחסרא והכי קתני המלוה את חבירו ע״י ערב וכו׳ וקבלן
אעפ״י שיש נכסים ללוה נפׂרע מן הקבלן. רשב״ג אומ׳ אם יש נכסי׳ ללוה
אחד זה ואחד זה וכו׳ וליתה לדרשב״ג דאמ׳ רבה בר אבוה א״ר
יוחנן כל מקום ששנה רשב״ג במשנתינו הלכה כמותו חוץ מערב וצידן
וראיה אחרונה. וכי תימא דאיירי בדאמ׳ ליה ע״מ שאפרע ממי שארצה
הא ליתא דא״כ ליכא מידי בין ערב לקבלן לרשב״ג. ותו מדקאמ׳ ליה
קבלן משמע דלא אמ׳ אלא תן לו ואני אתן או תן לו ואני קבלן כסתם
קבלן. עוד צריך שתדע דאם אמ׳ לו הלוהו ואני קבלן אי בעיא לן בגמ׳
אי הוי לשון קבלנות או לשון ערבות ואיפליגו בה אמוראי ורבוותא
הריא״ף ז״ל פסק שהוא לשון ערבות אבל רבוותא קמאי פסקו הלכתא
כרב הונא דאמ׳ לשון קבלנות הוא. והשתא ניחזי נדון דידן למאן דמיא
אי דומה לערֻבות או לקבלנות. ואומ׳ אני דודאי לשון קבלנות הוא
דמסתברא דאמׂ ליה בלשון המועיל כגון תן לו ואני נותן או תן לו ואני
קבלן והסופר לא כת׳ הלשון אלא הענין. וכי תימ׳ דילמא הכי קאמ׳
ליה הלוהו ואני קבלן והוי פלוגתא וקי״ל דיד בעל השטר על התחתונה.
[186] י״ל כיון דהוי// ספיקא במלתא דתליא בפלוגתא לא אמרי׳ יד בעל
השטר על התחתונה דהבו דלא לוסיף עלה. ותו דכיון דאמ׳ ליה ערב
קבלן ופרען הוי כאלו אמ׳ ליה קבלן גמור. וכת׳ הרשב״א ז״ל שאם
אמ׳ לו קבלן גמור דנין אותו כקבלן וכל שהודה שהוא קבלן גמור
סתמא דמלתא קבלן כדיני׳ הוא וכך אמ׳ לו תן לו ואני נותן. וכענין זה
כתו׳ בתוספות ע״כ. אף בנדון דידן נמי כיון דאמ׳ קבלן ופרען סתמא
כדיני׳ קאמ׳ דאי למימרא דאם לא נמצאו נכסים ללוה שאז יגבה מן
הקבלן. במלת קבלן הוה סגי אלא להכי כת׳ לו ופרען לענין שיפרע
ממי שירצה תחלה. ותו דכת׳ ליה בהדיא ע״מ שאגבה מאי זה מהם
שארצה תחלה. ואע״ג דאיכא כמה גדולים דפסקו דאפי׳ הכי אם יש
נכסים ללוה לא יפרע מן הערב תחלה ה״מ היכא דלא אמ׳ ליה לשון
קבלנות אלא בלשון ערבו׳ אבל היכא דאמ׳ ליה ערב קבלן ופרען
וע״מ שאפרע ממי שארצה תחלה כנדון דידן כ״ע מודו דהוי קבלן.

ותו כיון דהתנה עמו בפי׳ ע״מ שאפרע ממי שארצה אמאי כת׳ לו קבלן
אלא ודאי כדין קבלן גמור קאמ׳. ועוד אני אומ׳ דעד כאן לא קאמ׳
מהררי׳ קולון בשם המרדכי דמצי למימ׳ קים לי כפלו׳ להחזיק הממון
בידו אלא היכא דלא קבלו עליהם לדון כפלו׳ פוסק או שלא נהגו
לדון כאחד מן הפוסקים אבל היכא לפסוק כדעת הרמב״ם ז״ל כי
אתרין או כדעת הרא״ש ז״ל כי אתרייכו לא מצי למימ׳ קים לי כפלוני
שהרי כל השטרות וכל ההלואות לדעת אותו פוסק נעשו והוי כאלו
קבלוהו עליהם שאין לסופר לכתו׳ את השטר לדעת כל הפוסקים
מפורסמים או בלתי מפורסמים וכיון דהרמב״ם והרא״ש ורי׳ בנו ז״ל
וכל אותם שאנו רגילים לפסוק כמותם כתבו דאפי׳ יש נכסים ללוה
גובה מן הערב תחלה מפקי׳ ממונא אפומיהו דאי לא תימ׳ הכי לא שבקת
[187] חיי לכל בריה דאפי׳ שהוא // חכם גדול לא תקיף ידיעתו לכל הפוסקים
כי איפשר שיש פוסק אחד שהוא לא ראה ויאמ׳ בעל הדין קים לי כאותו
פוסק אלא ודאי כיון שנעשה השטר לדעת אותו פוסק שנהגו לפסוק
כמותו תו לא מצי אידך למימ׳ קים לי כפוסק אחר. ודוק כי זה טעם
נכון לבטל פסק זה כ״ש בהצטרפות שאר הטעמים. עוד אני אומ׳ דלא
אמרי׳ דמצי למימ׳ קים לי כפלוני פוסק אלא היכא שהם אחד כנגד
אחד או שנים כנגד שנים אלא שהדיין אשר בא לפניו המעשה סובר כחד
מיניהו אז מצי אידך למימ׳ תביא ראיה שאין הלכה כפלו׳ ותוציא
ממני. אבל כשיחיד חולק על רבים או רבים כנגד מרובי׳ לא אמרה
אדם מעולם דא״כ בטלת מה שכתו׳ בתורה אחרי רבים להטות וקרא
איירי בין לאפוקי ממונא בין לאוקומי ממונא וכן לענין דיני נפשות אפי׳
שרבו המחייבים יאמ׳ קים לי כאותם הפוטרין. וג׳ שישבו לדין נמי שנים
חייבו ואחד פוטר יאמר זה קים לי כזה הפוטר תביאו ראיה שאין הדין
כמותו ותוציאו ממני ונמצא שאין שום דין יבוא לידי גמר. ואלו דברים
של טעם הם אינם צריכין ראיה. אבל כדי שיתברר לך אכתו׳ מה
שכת׳ המרדכי בשם הר׳ שמואל ז״ל דאם יתפוס החתן המוציא מחבירו
עליו הראיה שאמ׳ קים לי כרש״י ז״ל. והרי אתה רואה שהוא מחלוקת
רש״י ור״ת דלדעת רש״י מן הנשואין גובה ולדעת ר״ת אינו גובה הכל
והרי רש״י ור״ת יחיד כנגד יחיד הוא ורש״י יותר מפורסם מר״ת ומשום
הכי מצי למימ׳ קים לי כרש״י. וכ״ש דראביה בשם רי׳ הלבן פסק דגובה
הכל. ומה שדקדק החכם הפוסק מלשונו של מהרי׳ קולון שכת׳ ופשיטא
דבכה״ג לא הוה מצי למימ׳ קים לי כדברי היחיד ודלא ככל חכמי
ישראל וכו׳ משמע דאי לא הוי יחיד מצי למימ׳ קים לי כי הני אע״ג
[188] דיש רבים כנגדם ע״כ. ונ״ל כי זו שגגה היא // דמה לי אחד כנגד רבים
ומה לי שנים כנגד עשרה זה ודאי הלכת׳ בלא טעמא. ומה שכת׳ מהררי׳
קולון ז״ל הוא מפני שרצה ללמוד הדין מכ״ש והמעשה כך היה יחיד
כנגד כל חכמי ישראל ולפי׳ כת׳ כן אבל לא למידק מדבריו כאשר
דקדק זה החכם ודברי׳ פשוטי׳ הם לא היה כדאי לכותבן ולא להשיב
עליהם. ואחר שבררנו דאזלי׳ בתר רובא ולא מצי למימ׳ קים לי
כמיעוטא וכ״ש אם הרוב הם אותם שאנו רגילים לפסוק כמותם. צריך
אני לכתו׳ לך בעלי סברא זו ובעלי סברא זו כדי שתראה עד היכן
הגיע כח זה הפסוק. רבי׳ יוסף הלוי ן׳ מיגאש ז״ל וכן נר׳ דעת רבו הריא״ף

ז"ל דמסתמא אזיל בשטת רביה. ותו כיון שלא פירש סמך על הכלל
כל תנאי שבממון תנאו קיים. וכן מסתברא לי שכל פוסק שלא יזכיר
הן זה בהדיא דעתו לסמוך על הכלל עד שיפרש סברתו. הרמב"ם ז"ל
הרא"ש ז"ל רי' בנו רבי' ירוחם רבי' ישעיה מיטרני ז"ל. ומדברי ר"ת
והתוספות והמרדכי אין ראיה ברורה לגלות סברתם כי מה שכת'
הפוסק הזה ממה שמנו ה' דיני ערבות ואם איתא שיתא הוו לאו כלום
הוא דאנן לאו מתורת ערבות אתינן עלה אלא מתורת תנאי שבממון
דכל תנאי שבממון תנאו קיים. וכן כת' הרא"ש ז"ל בפסקיו וז"ל ואם אמ'
המלוה ממי שארצה אפרע תחלה כל תנאי שבממון קיים ואפי' יש
נכסים ללוה יפרע מן הערב ע"כ. ואדרבא נ"ל שהם בעלי סברא זו
חדא דכיון דלא פירשו מסתמא סומכים על הכלל. ותו שהרא"ש ז"ל
ברוב המקומות אזיל בשטת התוספות. ותו דהרשב"א ז"ל לא סייע
סברתו אלא מדברי הראב"ד ז"ל שכת' וכן מצאתי להראב"ד בספר
ההשגות. ואם היה כן דעת התוספות או דעת ר"ת כאשר כת' בעל הפסק
היה הרשב"א ז"ל מסתייע מהם כנגד כל גאוני עולם אלא ודאי לא מצא
[189] זולת // הראב"ד ז"ל. ובעלי הסברא האחרת לא ראיתי זולת הראב"ד
והרשב"א ז"ל. ומה שכת' נמקי יוסף וכבר הסכימו האחרונים וכו' לא
ידעתי מי הם האחרונים אשר הסכימו בזה אבל דרכו לקראו אחרונים
הריטב"א והרינב"ר והן לו יהי כדבריו סמי הני מקמי כל הני רבוות'
דכתיבנא לעיל. חדא דרבים נינהו ותו דעליהם נהגו לסמוך ככל
גלילות ישראל. ומפני שראיתי בעל הפסק הזה סמך על מהרי' קולון ז"ל
טרחתי למצוא לבטל דבריו ממקום שבא. וז"ל בשורש קפ"ג ואע"ג שכת'
ר' אשר שרבי' אפרים ז"ל דחה הראיה וגם גאון אחר שהביא הוא
ואיפשר שחולקין גם על עיקר הדין יהיה כן סמינהו מקמי כולהו רברבי
קמאי ובתראי שהבאתי לעיל וכל דיינא דלא דנין* כהאי דינא לאו
דיינא הוא וזה פשוט שאם אין לכמה"ר שלמה ממה לפרוע ויהיה לכמה"ר
אברהם לפרוע שודאי יכולין ליפרע מכמה"ר אברהם מדין ערב.
וכדכתי' לעיל ע"כ. ולדעת הפוסק הזה אמאי יפרע כמה"ר אברהם
הערב לימ' קים לי כר' אפרים וכאותו גאון. עוד כת' ונחזור לעיקר
הדין דאם יש נכסים וכו' אין להוציא חלק המגיע לכמה"ר שלמה
מכמה"ר אברהם מאחר שרבו גם הפוסקים שאמרו וכו' וגם מן האחרוני'
כגון רבי' מאיר וספר האגודה וכו'. מכל הני טעמי נר' לע"ד שראוי
שלא לחייב לכמה"ר אברהם בחלק המגיע לאחיו כמה"ר שלמה אם יש
לכה"ר שלמה ממה לפרוע עכ"ל. ולדעת הפוסק הזה אמאי איצטרכי'
לכל הלין טעמי תיפוק לי דמצי למימ' קים לי כהנך רבני' אלא ודאי
לא אמרי' הכי היכא דהם מועטים במקום רבים וכ"ש אם הם מפורסמי'
יותר ופשוט הוא. ולענין הטעם השני כת' החכם הפוסק וז"ל אומ' אני כי
אעפ"י שכת' ר"ת בשם ר"י ז"ל כי אעפ"י דקבלן לא הוי אלא כשאמ'
למלוה תן לו וכו' מ"מ אם כתו' בשטר ונעשה קבלן מסתמ' בלשון
המועיל קאמ' וכן הביא הסמ"ג וכן הסכים הרא"ש ז"ל אמנם נר' שהפוספים

---

* בכ"י דאין (בטעות).

[190] שלא // הביאו דין זה כמו הריא"ף והרמב"ם ז"ל מסתמא אית לן למימ' דלא סברי הכי שהרי הרמב"ם ז"ל כת' אי זהו ערב ואי זהו קבלן אמ' לו תן לו ואני נותן זהו קבלן א"כ נר' שנוכל לומ' שאעפ"י שכתו' בשטר נכנס קבלן שלא אמ' לו אלא לשון שאינו מועיל לקבלנות כמו הלוהו ואני קבלן וכיוצא בו ע"כ. ראה גם ראה אתה המעיין כמה הוא תוקע עצמו לדבר הלכה עד שמשים מחלוקת בין הפוסקים מאומדן דעתא כי הרא"ש על הרוב הולך בשטת הריא"ף ז"ל או התוספות והסמ"ג בשטת הרמב"ם ז"ל והוא רוצה שיהיו חלוקים להפיק זממו אשר זמם בתחלה ויצא מפיו דלוי פטור מהערבות ועל כיוצא בזה שנינו שגגת תלמוד עולה זדון וכן היו פתח דברו.

עוד כת' וכן כת' בעל העטור וז"ל הילכך בעי למיכתב בשטרא לישנא דקבלנות דאמ' ליה הב ליה ואני קבלן הב ליה ואנא יהיבנא ואי לא כתי' בשטרא הכי אלא קבלן סתמא א"נ לישנא דמשמע הכי והכי אמרי' דילמא הלוהו ואני קבלן קאמ' ואית ליה דין ערבות ולזה הסכים בעל התרומות וז"ל ואחר אשר פסק הריא"ף ז"ל דאפי' תן לו ואני קבלן לשון ערבות זה אינו מוסכם בעי למיכת' בשטרא שאני אמרתי לו תן לו ואני נותן לך ואי כתי' בשטרא ערב קבלן סתם אמרי' יד בעל השטר על התחתונה ונאמ' אולי תן לו ואני קבלן רצה לומ' שהוא כמו ערב הילכך לא הוי אלא ערב בלבד ע"כ. א"כ אחר שהרב בעל העטור ובעל התרומות סברי דאמרי' יד בעל השטר על התחתונה ואיפשר שכן היא סברת שאר הפוסקים שלא הביאו דברי ר"י וכמו שנר' קצת מלשון הרשב"א ז"ל שכתן וז"ל יש מי שאומ' שאם כת' בשטר ונעשיתי לו קבלן גמור שכל שנעשה קבלן גמור סתמא כך אמ' לו תן לו ואני נותן נר' מלשונו שרוב הפוסקי' לא ס"ל הכי מ"מ אפי' לא יהיו אלא בעל העטור
[191] ובעל התרומות מספיק // להחזיק מה שבידו ע"כ. ואני אומ' שכל מה שכת' הוא בטל מהטעמי' שכתבתי למעלה. עוד כת' וז"ל וכ"ש דבנדון דידן לפי דעתי כ"ע מודו דלאו קבלן גמור הוא מדכת' קבלן ופרען ובקבלן גמור הס כי לא להזכיר בו ענין פרעון כלל וכמו שכתו' בפר' גט פשוט במרדכי וז"ל וקבלן היינו תן לו ואני נותן. א"נ בלעז כל שאינו מזכיר לא לשון הלואה ולא לשון פרעון א"כ נר' דבנדון דידן כ"ע מודו דלא אמרי' מסתמא וכו' כ"ש שכפי האמת כל אלו הלשונות נראה לע"ד שכותבים הסופרים כעור הממשש ובלי ספק שראוי לדקדק ולעיין קודם שנוציא ממון מספק כי זה כלל גדול וכו' ועל כן אמרתי שמה שגזרתי היה דרך נכונה וכו' ואני אומ' אין זה דרך נכונה כלל אלא מוציאין מלוי מה שיצא עליו ערב קבלן. ומה שכת' הס כי לא להזכיר בו ענין פרעון אינו נכון כלל כי לא אמרו כן אלא כשלא הזכיר לשון קבלן וכגון דאמ' לו הלוהו ואני פורע או שאמ' לו בלשון לעז אי יו טידיביראי* כמו שכתבו התוספות ז"ל אבל אם אמ' לו ואני קבלן ופרען כ"ש שיפה את כחו ועשה אותו קבלן גמור לענין שאפי' יהיו נכסים ללוה יפרע ממי שירצה תחלה לדעת כ"ע. ולפי' אני אומ' דאין ראוי לסמוך על פסק

* ייט"י דיברא"י (ב"ב קע"ג, ע"ב, ד"ה חסורי).

זה חדא שהוא לשון קבלנות גמורה שהרי כת׳ קבלן ופרען. ועוד שכת׳ לו שאגבה מכל מי שארצה תחלה. ועוד שחזר לבסוף וכת׳ כדין קבלן ופרען ומשמע לעפויי מלתא אתי. הילכך קבלן גמור הוי. ותו דאפי׳ שלא היה קבלן כיון שהתנה עמו שיפרע ממי שירצה תחלה תנאי שבממון הוא ותנאו קיים לדעת רוב הפוסקים שאנו רגילין לסמוך עליהם ולא מצי לוי למימ׳ קים לי כהראב״ד והרשב״א ז״ל ומפקי׳ מיניה. והנר׳ לע״ד כתבתי.

/ דוד ן׳ אבי זמרה /

Altaras in Russia: The Failure of a Scheme

By SIMON R. SCHWARZFUCHS
Jerusalem, Israel

ALTARAS' TRAVEL TO Russia and Poland during the summer of 1846 is a well known episode in the long history of attempts to improve the lot of the Jews of Eastern Europe. This Aleppo-born son of a Jerusalem rabbi had settled in 1806, at the age of 20, in the French city of Marseille. He became a ship builder there and one of the most important merchants who dealt with the Levant. His devotion to Jewish affairs was unabated: he became chairman of the local consistory, while also serving as head of the Marseille Chamber of Commerce. He had become very rich and wanted to help his brethren in different countries. His excellent reputation and his numerous acquaintances brought him an invitation in 1842 from the French authorities to visit Algeria, which had been conquered, although not completely, by French troops. The French authorities wanted him and his colleague, the young lawyer Joseph Cohen, to study the situation of the Algerian Jewish communities and to make suggestions about the ways to reorganize them and to bring them nearer to the French model. Their joint report served later as the working paper which became the basis of recommendations by the special committee appointed by the Ministry of War and which brought about a complete reorganization of Algerian Jewry along the French consistorial system.[1]

In 1846 Altaras arrived in Russia. Contemporary reports relate that he intended to settle about 40,000 Jewish families from Russia and Poland in Algeria, and that he was ready to pay great sums in order to get permission to take these families out of Russia. The Rothschild family had assured him of their support and he himself was ready to devote his considerable wealth to this aim. The French Minister of Foreign Affairs had recommended him to the French consul in Saint Petersburg and to the Russian government. The latter had first requested a sum of 60 rubles for each emigrant, but had later relented and agreed to give the emigration permit free of charge. Altaras then left Saint Petersburg and visited Warsaw, where he intended to meet with candidates for emigration and settlement in Algeria. It was there, in October 1846, that he suddenly decided to return to France,

[1] See Z. Szajkowski, *The struggle for Jewish emancipation in Algeria after the French occupation, Historia Judaica*, XVIII, 1956, pp. 27–40 (Jews and the French revolutions of 1789, 1830 and 1948, N. Y., 1970, pp. 1119–1132) and M. Rosenstock, *The Establishment of the consistorial system in Algeria*, Jewish Social Studies, XVIII, 1956, pp. 41–54.

without any explanation. The Altaras settlement plan of Russian and Polish Jewish families had suddenly come to an end, precisely when it would have seemed that its success was at last possible. Altaras never explained why he had changed his mind. At any rate no explanation has reached us.[2]

It is therefore not very surprising that the major historians of Eastern European Jewry should have asked why Altaras had to give up his plan. Some, like Dubnow[3] or S. Gintzburg[4] had to admit their ignorance, while others, like B. Weinryb[5] guessed that this change in Altaras' plan was a consequence of a change of policy by the French colonial government, which had preferred a military settlement in Algeria and had thus discouraged a civilian attempt to colonize Algeria, of which the Jews could eventually have been a part. Hitherto unknown documents enable us today to give the answer to this riddle.[6]

It must be asked first who was responsible for Altaras' plan and how it came into being. There can be no doubt that during his Algerian trip in 1842 he was very impressed by the Arab emigration from North Africa. In the first months of the occupation the French authorities returned to the Turkish Empire the Turkish population of Algiers: civil servants and members of the military. Thus Altaras writes at the beginning of his as yet unpublished report on the Jews of Algeria:

> "Un fait signalé par les plus remarquables écrivains qui ont parlé de la question d'Afrique et dont nous avons pu vérifier l'exactitude, c'est l'émigration des familles indigénes; tous les Arabes que leur fortune met en position de s'expatrier vont grossir de leur nombre les populations du Maroc ou de Tunis, enlevant ainsi à l'industrie locale, qui consiste surtout en objets de luxe, de précieux débouchés. Quant aux familles pauvres que notre contact a réduites à une misère encore plus grande, elles revienment à la vie des peuplades nomades, et se joignent aux Kabyles vagabonds ou aux Arabes du désert."

The sight of the largely unpopulated Turkish-Arabic districts of Algeria's major towns surely impressed him, as it probably must have impressed

[2] See M. A. Gintzburg, *Debir*, II, 1861, pp. 116–118, 122–127 (letters 59, 61–63); *Leket Amarim* (supplement to *Hamelitz*), 1889, pp. 81–86; Bulletin de l'A.I.U., 2e série, n° 23, 1898, pp. 43–45; S. Gintzburg, *Historische Werke* (Yiddish), II, N. Y., 1937, pp. 203–219; Y. Klausner, *Historiah shel ha-sifrut ha-ivrit ha-hadashah*[2], Jerusalem, 1953, p. 138, 152–3; B. Weinryb, *Quel fut le but du voyage d'Altaras en Russie? Revue des Études Juives*, XCIV, 1933, pp. 172–178; S. M. Dubnow, *History of the Jews in Russia and Poland*[2], II, Philadelphia, 1946, p. 69.

[3] Dubnow, *loc. cit.*, p. 69.

[4] S. Gintzburg, *loc. cit.*, p. 219.

[5] Weinryb, *loc. cit.*, pp. 175–176.

[6] These documents belong to the files of the former French Ministry of Religion, (now in the Archives Nationales, F 19. 11146. (Jerusalem Central Archives microfilm).

another French traveler in Algeria: Albert Cohn, the Rothschilds' representative in Jewish affairs, who visited Algeria in 1845.[7] Very probably he knew about Altaras' efforts on behalf of Algerian Jewry and had seen the unpopulated cities of Algeria as well.

It is therefore all the more remarkable that, in a letter which he sent to the editor of the Parisian monthly Archives Israélites de France, he should have reported on the audience which Louis Philippe, King of the Frenchmen, had granted him on the preceding 10th of February 1846. He had conveyed to the King the gratitude of the North-African Jewish communities, and the King had shown great interest in their welfare. Towards the end of the audience, Albert Cohn reports:

> "S.M. me demanda ensuite quel était l'état des Juifs en Allemagne, en Pologne, dans tous les pays enfin où une fausse politique les prive encore des droits les plus précieux. J'osai demander à S.M. si peut être au milieu de circonstances fâcheuses, la France et l'Algerie ne seraient point ouvertes à un grand nombre de ces malheureux qui viendraient chercher là-bas une patrie et le respect de leur foi. "Vous savez, et vous pouvez le dire, me répondit le Roi, que des obstacles à rien de pareil ne seront jamais suscités ni de moi, ni du côté de mon gouvernement."[8]

It would have been impossible for Albert Cohn to have brought up such a proposal to the King without the knowledge or the assent of his employer, the Rothschild family. On the other hand, did he suggest the settlement of Russian Jews in Algeria as his own plan or did Altaras discuss it with him beforehand? It is quite probable that Altaras had the idea first,[9] but there is no doubt that it was brought up with the full agreement of the House of Rothschild. Anyway, things could now move rather quickly.

Alerted by Albert Cohn as it would seem, Altaras turned to the prefect of the Bouches du Rhône department in Marseille in order to get his recommendation. The prefect transmitted to the Secretary of State a letter from Altaras, and this minister saw fit to send it to the Minister of War, who was in charge of Algerian affairs, in order to get his opinion on the matter. The letter was sent on the 27th of May, and was probably received the same day. The minister asked that the matter be looked into right away and one of the members of his ministry added the next day—May 28th—a handwritten note in which he remarked that some of the French governors and generals in Algeria had requested the expulsion of the Jews from the country! He added that to recruit Jews in Europe would be an unwise

[7] See Isidore Loeb, *Biographie d'Albert Cohn*, Paris, 1878, pp. 132–133.

[8] A.I.F., VII, 1846, pp. 188–190.

[9] According to the Ministry of War's letter published here, Altaras had already mentioned the idea two years earlier, that is, in 1844! (Document B).

political measure towards the Moslems, and an imprudent one as far as colonisation was concerned![10] Despite this rather abrupt opinion, it would seem that the matter was not decided right away. It was only on the 19th of June that the answer to the Ministry of War was written and signed.[11] By that time, as will be shown, Altaras, who seems to have received letters of recommendation from another branch of government, was already on his way to Russia. According to press reports, he was in Nuremberg on the 27th of July,[12] in Berlin on the 4th of August,[13] and somewhat later in Saint Petersburg, where he tried to meet the Tsar and members of his government! Reassured as to the possible success of the mission he had undertaken, he traveled to Warsaw in order to begin the implementation of his plan. He arrived there on the 15th of September[14] and wrote an official letter to the Russian governor, in which he asked for his help to expedite the matter, while mentioning that he had been given assurances that the Tsar would be favorably disposed towards his plan.[15]

On the 15th of October he was already back in Paris,[16] and no further mention was made of his scheme, although the Tsar's positive answer was finally given on the 19th of October.[17] What, then, had happened between the 15th of September and the 5th—10th of October[18] which had compelled him to give up his plan? It would seem that the contents of the Minister of War's letter to the Minister of Foreign Affairs had finally reached him.

The Minister of War had written his colleague that he very much respected Altaras personally and had the highest opinion of his good will and zeal. On the other hand, he was of the opinion that the immigration of European Jews into Algeria would be of no advantage whatsoever. The colonisation of Algeria requires an agricultural population: the Jews are

[10] See Document A.

[11] See Document B.

[12] *Allgemeine Zeitung des Judentums*, 1846, p. 479.

[13] A.I.F., VII, p. 711, where it is also mentioned that Altaras had sent to the Berlin Gazette of August 4th a letter denying that he had been entrusted an official mission by the French government in order to bring about the emigration of the Polish Jews to Algeria.

[14] According to the *Orient*. 1846, p. 330. It is possible that he arrived a few days earlier.

[15] See Weinryb, *loc. cit.*, p. 177. The letter was also published by S. Gintzburg, *loc.* cit., pp. 304–305.

[16] *Univers Israélite*, III, 1846, p. 130. The same journal sees him in Frankfrut on the 15th of September (p. 124) which is obviously impossible. Altaras had been in Frankfurt at the beginning of his voyage. He had met Montefiore there.

[17] See Weinryb, *op. cit.*, p. 174. According to the documents published here, Altaras did indeed plan—contrary to Weinryb's contention—a mass emigration from Russia.

[18] He was in Paris on the 15th of October. He must then have left Warsaw 5 to 10 days before.

not known to possess the disposition necessary to agriculture. Moreover, one has to keep in mind that the Moslems will be opposed to the increase of a population they despise. This would cause very great difficulties—therefore Altaras' proposition must be rejected. In a first draft of this letter, the language was much stronger and rather offensive to the Jews.[19] Although there seems to have been a slight hesitation on the minister's side, the answer was categoric, and Altaras could but draw the necessary conclusions when he heard of it. The interest of French colonisation in Algeria required a pacific relationship with the Arabs after the conquest, and therefore made the presence of a great number of Jews undesirable.

But why did Altaras hear of this decision only in Warsaw? It would seem that bureaucratic practices, Altaras' constant traveling, and perhaps also the heat of the summer prevented the Minister of War's letter from being brought to Altaras' attention in due time. When the minister gave his answer on June 19th he sent it to the Minister of Foreign Affairs, who had to send its content to the prefect of Marseille in order to enable him to inform Altaras of its content. All these steps took some time and we know that Altaras was already on his way to Russia during the second part of the month of July: would it then be impossible for him to have remained ignorant of the Minister of War's answer during the first part of the Russian trip? A report sent by the French chargé d'affaires in Saint Petersburg, which was received in Paris shortly before the 26th of September, tells about Altaras' meetings in the Russian capital,[20] but seems to be completely unaware of the now official French attitude towards Altaras' plan. If the French representative knew nothing about the matter, this fact would then confirm the probability that Altaras had not yet received any information about the change of attitude in Paris. The minute he heard of it, he could only return to Paris and Marseille, and give up the plan which was condemned not by Russian intransigence but by the French decision to placate the Arabs of Algeria.

Documents

A

Letter from the Minister of Foreign Affairs to the Minister of War.

Paris, le 27 mai 1846.

Monsieur et cher collègue

M. le préfet des Bouches du Rhône vient de me transmettre en l'accompagnant des témoignages les plus honorables pour son auteur la lettre ci-jointe de M. Jacques Altaras, ancien négociant et président du consistoire

[19] See document B.
[20] See document C.

israélite de Marseille qui se propose de se rendre en Allemagne et en Russie dans le but de déterminer un grand nombre de ses coreligionaires à aller s'établir en Algérie et qui sollicite à cet effet des lettres d'introduction auprès des agens du gouvernement du Roi à l'étranger.

Avant de recommander M. Altaras à nos agens diplomatiques, je vous prie, Monsieur et cher collègue, de vouloir bien examiner sa demande et de me faire savoir si vous pensez que ses démarches méritent encouragement. Je vous serai obligé de me renvoyer sa lettre lorsque vous en aurez pris connaissance. (1)

Agréez, Monsieur et cher collègue, l'assurance de ma haute consideration,

Pour le ministre et par autorisation,
Le Conseiller d'Etat, directeur,
Em. Desages.

1) The following remarks were added to the letter:
Direction de l'Algérie. Examiner la question dont il s'agit et répondre à M. le ministre des Affaires étrangères.

Le ministre.

J'ai entendu plusieurs des gouverneurs et généraux de l'Algérie exprimer le voeu qu' on expulsât les Juifs de l'Algérie. Il serait aussi impolitique vis à vis des Musulmans qu' imprudent pour la colonisation de recruter en Europe des Juifs pour l'Algérie. Il faut se refuser absolument à une pareille novation. 28 mai.

Signature illisible.

B

Letter of the Minister of War to the Minister of Foreign Affairs (final draft)

Paris, le 19 juin 1846.

Monsieur et cher collègue.

Vous m'avez fait l'honneur de me transmettre en communication le 27 mai derrier une lettre de M. Altaras, président du Consistoire israélite de Marseille, par laquelle il annonce être dans l'intention de se rendre en Allemagne et en Russie afin de déterminer un grand nombre de ses coreligionaires à se rendre en Algérie.

Vous me priez en même temps de vous faire connaître si dans ma pensée il y a lieu d'encourager les démarches que M. Altaras se propose de faire et de lui donner à cet effet des lettres d'introduction auprés des agents du gouvernement du Roi à l'étranger.

Sans aucun doute, le but de M. Altaras est louable et c'est pour moi une nouvelle preuve du concours efficace qu'il a toujours prêté à mon departement dans l'oeuvre de regénération entreprise à l'égard de ses coréligionaires de l'Algérie; mais je ne puis croire qu'il resultât un avantage quelconque pour nous de l'immigration d'israélites européens dans ce pays.

La population, en effet, que le gouvernement cherche autant que possible à appeler en Afrique est une population agricole qui puisse se vouer aux travaux de la colonisation; or le caractère de la nation juive ne comporte pas les qualités particulières que réclame la culture.

D'ailleur, Monsieur et cher collègue, il me paraîtrait impolitique vis à vis des Musulmans de jeter au milieu d'eux une population qu'ils méprisent. Je ne saurais douter qu'il ne résultât pour nous d'une immigration de cette nature de très graves difficultes de la part des indigénes professant l'Islamisme qui ne sauraient point reconnaitre dans, cette mesure la pensée civilisatrice de la France et verraient avec déplaisir une semblable population s'établir au milieu d'eux. (1)

Je pense donc qu'il n'y a pas lieu de satisfaire à la demande de M. Altaras dont j'ai l'honneur de vous renvoyer la lettre. (2)

Recevez, Monsieur et cher collègue, la nouvelle assurance de mes sentimens de haute considération et de sincére attachement.

Le Pair de France
Ministre secrétaire d'Etat de la guerre.

1) This paragraph reads as follows in a first draft which was crossed out:

D'ailleurs, Monsieur et cher collègue, le peuple israélite en Allemagne et en Pologne est en général corrompu, vivant au jour le jour du produit de l'usure et de la débauche, et le gouvernement doit formellement s'opposer au recrutement d'une population semblable pour l'Algérie.

Je n'ignore pas toutefois que M. Altaras a fait, il y a deux ans, connaître à mon ministre qu'il existe en Russie des population israélites agricoles, mais alors même que cette assertion serait fondée, je ne saurais favoriser le passage de ces population en Algérie qu' avec une très grande circonscription (!), car il serait à craindre qu'à la faveur de pareilles immigrations il ne s'introduisît en Afrique un grand nombre d'individus sans moyens avoués d'éxistence dont il serait bien difficile de constater, au milieu d' un pays étranger, les connaisances en agriculture.

Il me paraitrait donc convenable, Monsieur et cher collège, que vous voulussiez bien inviter M. Altaras à vous faire connaître quelle classe d'individus il a désiré attirer en Algérie.

Vous serez alors bien plus à même de statuer sur la demande de M. Altaras, et si je venais à être consulté de nouveau par vous à cet égard je pourrais vous exprimer une opinion beaucoup plus explicite.

J'ai l'honneur de vous renvoyer sous ce pli la lettre de M. Altaras.

2) This letter seems to have disappeared from the file.

C

Letter from the Ministry of Foreign Affairs to the Minister of War.

Paris, le 26 septembre 1846.

Monsieur et cher collègue,

Le chargé d'affaires du Roi à Saint Petersbourg m'informe que M. Altaras, président du Tribunal de commerce de Marseille, et qui poursuit le projet de former en Algérie une colonie de Juifs polonais, a fait dernièrement le voyage de Saint Petersbourg afin d'obtenir pour son projet l'agrément du gouvernement impérial. Il a été très bien recu par Mr. de Nesselrode,[1] et par Mr. Petoffoki, ministre de l'intérieur, qui ont parlé favorablement de lui à l'Empereur et ont obtenu l'entier assentiment de Sa Majesté, Mr. Altaras est parti pour Varsovie, muni de recommandation, officielles pour le prince Paskevitch.[2]

Je m'empresse de vous transmettre cette information qui m'a paru de nature à intéresser le Département de la Guerre.

Agréez, Monsieur et cher collège, l'assurance de ma haute considération,[3]

Pour le ministre et par autorisation,
Le maitre des requêtes et directeur[4]
L. de Vieil Castel

[1] Minister of Foreign Affairs.

[2] Vice King of Poland.

[3] Letter received on September 27th and acknowledged on October 8th.

[4] At the direction politique.

"Realia As Portrayed By Rashi: A Description of Medieval Household Utensils"

By ESRA SHERESHEVSKY
Temple University

THE IMPORTANCE OF Rashi's commentary for the history of French culture and civilization was emphasized in a previous article, entitled "Some Aspects of Everyday Life in Rashi's Times," which appeared in the *Jewish Quarterly Review*, Volume LXV, No. 2 of January 1975. It was proved by a substantial number of examples culled from Rashi's commentary on Bible and Talmud, as well as from some of his responsa. The passages there cited dealt primarily with human behavior, the clothes worn by men and women, and the latters' jewelry. For the sake of elucidating the text and interpreting Bible and Talmud in terms of his time, Rashi drew on all areas of human life. Thanks to his detailed description of many phenomena and realia of his time, we are allowed to glimpse into the life of Rashi's days reflecting the civilization and environment in which he lived.

It would be presumptuous to enlist the term "technology" for a century as remote as the eleventh. It seems, however, that mankind have always understood how to make the maximum use of the available resources and, combined with their intelligence and the forces of nature, to invent implements and processes which made life easier and more comfortable by speeding up certain operations. Rashi, the great teacher, gifted with remarkable pedagogical and psychological insight, uses the phenomena of his contemporary life as one of his interpretive techniques to bring the meaning and intricacies of Bible and Talmud closer to the student of his time. With this end in view he describes technical matters, contemporary machinery and tools, many professions and workshops of his century which he could have known only by actually witnessing them, as we find them described nowhere else, certainly not in the rabbinic literature preceding Rashi. Rashi's knowledge of such details also attests to the harmony in which Jews lived with their gentile neighbors; this is also borne out by the responsa literature stemming from that time.

Liquid matter, being one of the most common elements, has properties easily employed by man and, therefore, also open to man's observation and description. The Champagne province with its capital Troyes, being an area in which viniculture was predominant and many Jews being owners of vineyards,[1] offered Rashi many opportunities to observe the ways wine was

[1] *Tᶜshuvot Hachmei Ẓarfat veᵓLother*, ed. by Yoel Hakohen Miller, 13,92,95.

handled. The decanting of wine from barrel to barrel was done by syphoning (*Djofee*—*διαφύσσω*: to drink out entirely). "Wine is transferred from one vat to another by means of two pipes cut obliquely. These obliquely cut ends are attached to one another. The end of one pipe is put into the one—the full—vat and one draws some wine by mouth suction via the other, the free end, of the second pipe. The mouth is then removed from the pipe and the wine flows freely by itself."[2] On another occasion Rashi illustrates this process in greater detail, stating that the two slanting ends are to be affixed to one another, while the other ends point downwards. One of these ends ought to reach the full vat and, as soon as the mouth suction is successful, an empty vat is to be placed beneath the flowing wine and thus the wine is transferred from vat to vat.[3] Rashi seems to have drawn an actual illustration of this implement.[4] The copyist, however, apparently ignored the drawing and omitted it. It, therefore, does not appear in our texts. The oblique cutting of the piping was necessary as, obviously, the use of rubber was not known at that time, nor was apparently any other elastic material available to produce bent piping.[5] Another implement (*the Araq*), used for storing liquid, "was made of metal and had a very narrow opening. Its bottom was perforated by very fine holes. As long as the upper opening was plugged, the liquid did not escape through the perforation at its lower part, but when the plugging was removed the liquid left the vessel drop by drop."[6]

Water was used for weighing purposes. There existed water scales "which had measuring lines and other signs marked on a container to be filled with water. Marks indicated how high the water had to rise for a pound of meat—as tested beforehand."[7] It seems that the product to be weighed was actually placed in the water to establish its weight by means of its water displacement. For measuring liquid a large earthen vessel was employed with protruding markings (*Shnatoth*) looking like little nuts signifying the various quantities. The markings were painted with lime so as to be white

[2] ʿEruvin 104a. מעלין יין מחבית לחבית ע"י שני קנים החתוכים באלכסון ומניח ראשון המשופעים זה כנגד זה ונותן אחד מן הקנים בחבית ומוצץ בפיו בראש הקנה האחר מעט מן היין אליו ומסלקו משם והיין יוצא כולו מאליו.

[3] ʿAvodah Zarah 72b. חותכין שני קנים בשיפוע ומדביקין ראשיהן מלמעלה ושניהן פונים למטה "כזה" ומניחין אחד מן הראשון בחבית מלאה עד שמגיע לשוליה, וראש קנה השני נותן בפיו ומוצץ מעט עד שעולה היין ושומטו מפיו ומניח חבית ריקנית כנגד הקילוח, ויין עולה מאליו כולו מחבית לחבית.

[4] "כזה".

[5] Descriptions of this implement differing from that of Rashi are offered by R. Hannanel *ad loc.*, and by R. Zadok Gaon (brought in *Ginzei Jerushalajim*, I, p. 6).

[6] ʿEruvin 104a. כלי הוא ופיו צר ושל מתכת הוא ומנוקב בתחתיתו נקבים נקבים דקין וממלא מים וסותם פיו העליון וכל זמן שפיו סתום אין המים יוצאין בנקבים התחתונים וכשרוצה נוטל פקק העליון והמים יוצאין בנקבים טיף אחר טיף.

[7] Bezah 28a. מאזני מים יש לו שנתות וסימנים בכלי ונותנין בו מים והסימנים מודיעין אותו כמה המים עולים למעלה בשביל ליטרא בשר שכבר שיערו בכך.

and visible.[8] There were also weighing machines. Some of them consisted of a pole to which a horizontal rod and tongue were affixed and at the ends of the rod chains were holding the scales.[9] Wood, wax and copper were weighed on wooden scales.[10] Expert butchers needed no scales at all. They knew to assess the weight of meat in one hand against the weight held in the other hand.[11] Gold and silversmiths used small scales.[12] Heavy metal loads were apparently lifted by means of magnets which were known to Rashi as the stone "that lifts metal without touching it."[13]

They had glass vessels shaped in a way that when filled with water, they would concentrate the rays of the sun. "A vessel made of glass and being hot is filled with water and exposed to the heat of the sun. The glass then produces a flame which ignites chaff brought near to it."[14] Likewise, the exploitation of water energy was known in Rashi's time as he mentions the wheel of a water mill.[15]

Often a number of people could drink simultaneously from the same container by means of a wide and large vessel (*Knishkanin*) from the side of which two or three pipings branched out turned upwards to the height of the vessel. When this container was filled with wine, all the pipe branches filled at the same time and a number of people could drink from it simultaneously.[16] The problem of hygiene was evidently non-existent.

Hot water was kept warm in an implement that reminds us very much of the samovar (*Muliar*—*μιλιάριον*). It was a vessel that had attached to it at its side a small container in which coal was burning so that the water in the large container next to it was kept hot.[17] There seem, however, to have been other techniques to preserve the heat of warm water. Ovens had two compartments. "In the empty one, which is next to the coal compartment, water is kept." Although this technique is in principle similar to the samovar type system, the difference lies in that "the partition in the oven

[8] Shabbath 80b. כלי חרס גדול ויש בו בליטות בליטות כמין אגוזים קטנים, עד כאן לסאה עד כאן לסאתים וסדין אותו בסיד כדי שיהיו לבנות ונכרות.

[9] Shabbath 60a. והערסה הוא עץ ארוך שהקנה שקורין ייש"א והלשון תחוב בו והשלשלות קבועות בקנה וכולן העץ ארוך מעמידן שהוא פליי"ל ששתי כפות המאזנים תלויות בב' ראשין.

[10] *Ibid.* מאזנים גדולות לשקול צמר ושעוה ונחושת, והן של עץ.

[11] Bezah 28a. טבח אומן שיודע לכוון משקל כנגד משקל בידיו לאחוז הליטרא בידו אחת והבשר בידו אחרת ולכוין .... כיון דאומן הוא בכך אורחיה הכי.

[12] Bava Bathra 89a. מאזנים של כסף וזהב קטנות הן.

[13] Sanhedrin 107b. מגבהית מתכת בלא נגיעה.

[14] Bezah 33a. נותנים מים בכלי זכוכית לבנה ונותנו בחמה כשהשמש חם מאד והזכוכית מוציאה שלהבת ומביאין נעורת ומגיעים בזכוכית והיא בוערת.

[15] Sukkah 36b. כמין קרשים כעין גלגל של ריחיים של מים.

[16] ᶜAvodah Zarah 72b. כלי רחב ויש לו שני קנין או שלושה יוצאין מצדו ונמשכין ועולין כנגד גובהן כשנותנין יין בפיו מתמלאין כל הקנים ויכולין כמה בני אדם לשתות בו ביחד.

[17] Shabbath 41a. כלי שיש בית קבול קטן אצל דופנו מבחוץ מחובר לו ונותן שם גחלים והמים בקיבולו הגדול.

between the two compartments is very thick and as the oven is heated constantly, the heat of the partition warms the water even if there is no coal in the other compartment."[18] A third way was to have (*Bei-Dudei*—a vessel within a vessel), "a large double-bottomed kettle and having placed coal in between the two bottoms, the water is kept warm in the upper part."[19]

It seems that the same principle was applied to the bathhouse. There were holes through which hot air and water were directed subterraneously to the bath house,[20] as a fire was burnt outside and underneath the bath house.[21] There were also facilities for a "Turkish bath" where one stood or sat in the bath house without pouring water over the body, but just to warm up and sweat.[22] The floor of the bath house was made of stones.[23] It may be that even a kind of shower bath was known where the water dropped downwards and people washed on top of planks.[24]

To prepare clothing for pressing a copper vessel (*Oochla*) was used which was perforated with tiny holes like a sieve. The laundryman sprinkled water through this implement onto the clothing.[25] Clothes were perfumed by means of a laundry chair consisting of a large board perforated by many holes under which perfume was placed. The clothing on top of this board absorbed the fragrance through these holes.[26] The perfuming process was probably necessary to dissipate the odor of the detergent function of dog excrements which were admixed with the rain water in which clothing was laundered.[27] Clothing was pressed between two long and heavy boards (*Makhbesh*). The upper one was lowered onto the lower one by means of pegs which were pushed into staggered holes in the four poles at the four corners of the boards. The space in between the boards could be regulated by up and down moving boards which were kept steady by means of the pegs.[28] Folds in new garments remained longer than those of old garments as the new material was hard and did not crease.[29]

18 *Ibid.* חלל יש בכירה אצל חללה שהגחלים בו ומים נתונים בחללה השני . . . . . מיהו כירה דופנה עב והאור תדיר בתוכה כל ימות החול ודופנה חם מאד ומוסיף הבל במים אעפ״י שגרופה מן הגחלים.

19 *Ibid.* יורה גדולה עושין לה שתי שוליים ונותנין גחלים בין שניהם והמים על העליונים.

20 Shabbath 29a. נקבים שהמים באים דרך שם למרחץ.

21 Shabbath 40a. שהאור ניסקת מבחוץ מתחתיו.

22 *Ibid.* עומד או יושב בבית המרחץ ואינו נותן מים עליו והוא מתחמם ומזיע.

23 Shabbath 151b. המרחץ רצפת אבנים הוא.

24 ᶜAvodah Zarah 16a. בקרקע היו עשויין עמוקין מאד והמים נופלים מתחת ואנשים רוחצים מלמעלה ע״ג נסרים.

25 Shabbath 123b. כלי נחושת העשוי כנפה נקבים נקבים והוא של כובסים ונותן על הבגדים ומזלף בו המים עליהן.

26 Shabbath 88b. מאספים עליו את הבגדים והוא דף ארוכה ומנוקבת נקבים הרבה ומניח המוגמר תחתיה והכלים מתגמרים דרך הנקבים.

27 Bava Bathra 17a. . . . . ומי גשמים מתכנסין בה לכבס בגדיהם . . . ששורין את הבגדים יום או יומיים בצואת כלבים.

28 Shabbath 141a. שני לווחות ארוכים וכבדים וסודרין בגדים על התחתון ומורידין

The proliferation of gadgets is not a sign of modern times only. The multifarious forms and nuances apparent in man's power of invention shows itself in many of Rashi's descriptions. It is astounding that Rashi, despite his complete absorbtion in the rabbinic text, had the astuteness and patience to observe and differentiate among them. A large variety of needles mentioned, each one for a special purpose and profession, is perhaps an indication that this tiny gadget is one of the most important instruments to extend the limits set by nature, be it by wear and tear, or simply by the creation. The small needle (*Mahat shel Yad*) was used for sewing clothing[30] and the very finest of needles (*M. Sidqith*) to mend the minutest slit in the garment.[31] A big, coarse needle was used by the sack makers.[32] Saddlers used an awl (*M. D'ushkafa*) having sharpened ends which cut the threads at the seams.[33] A double needle (*M. D'Talmiutha*) made stitches resembling the furrows made by the plough on the field.[34] Rashi describes also the needle used for tatooing. First the person who wants a tatoo writes onto his flesh with a chemical or with red paint. Then he tatoos his flesh with a needle or a knife. The color oozes in between the skin and the flesh, and is permanently visible.[35] Needles were manufactured by stretching copper or iron wire through holes of different sizes. As this was a rather noiseless profession it could be performed during night time.[35a] They were mostly manufactured by coppersmiths.[35b]

A similar variety of knives found their description in Rashi's commentary. Households used ordinary small knives for the cutting of bread, meat, and other food. These knives were in frequent use.[36] Some of them had hornlike ornaments on their blunt part.[37] Butchers had various kinds of knives. A large one was for the most part unsuitable for slaughtering, but just for

העליון עליו וכובשים את הבגדים על יתידות, שיש עמודים קבועים מנוקבים בארבע זויותיה ועולה ויורד בעמודים וכפי מה שהוא רוצה לכבוש מורידה, ותוחב יתד בנקב העמוד ואינה יכולה לעלות.

29 Shabbath 113a. ישנים קיפולן מתקנן יותר מן החדשים שהחדשים קשין מאליהן ואין ממהרין לקמוט.

30 Sanhedrin 84b, Shabbath 122b. מחט של יד הוא מחט קטנה שתופרין בה בגדים.

31 ᶜEruvin 53a, Megillah 19a. מחט שתופרין בה סדקי בגדים והוא דק ביותר. מחט שלנו שהיא דקה ותופרין בה סדקי בגדים.

32 Shabbath 122b. מחט גדולה שתופרין בה שקים, מחט גסה.

33 Ḥullin 31a. מרצע הרצענין שפיותיו חדודין וחותכין חוטי התפר.

34 Berakhoth 63a ....שהתפירות עשויות שורות שורות כתלמי מענה; Qiddushin 82b. מחט תלמיית שהתפירות עשויות תלמים תלמים שורות שורות כתלמי מחרשה.

35 Makkoth 21a. כותב תחילה על בשרו בסם או בסיקרא ואח'כ מקעקע הבשר במחט או בסכין ונכנס הצבע בין העור ולבשר ונראה בו כל הימים.

35a Bava Meziᶜaʾ 83b. רדד, מותח חוטי נחושת וברזל לעשות מחטין, ואומנותן בלילה לפי שמושכין בכלי אומנותו בנקבים דקים, זה דק מזה, ואין קולו נשמע בלילה.

35b Ḥullin 30b. .....כעין שעושין צורפי נחושת חוטין שעושין מהן מחטין

36 Shabbath 123b. וסכין קטן שחותכין בו לחם ובשר ואוכלין דהני תדירין בתשמיש.

37 Ḥullin 31a. רגילין היו לעשות כמין קרניים לאזמילין לנוי על גביהן.

cutting the meat and breaking the bones.[38] It resembled a hatchet. Some were double headed with one head being similar to the cutting tool of the saddler.[39] Another one was used in the meatmarket as a meat slicer.[40] A saw-like knife with many teeth and cutting fast is likened to those knives employed by comb manufacturers.[41] An unusual combination described by Rashi is the knife with a smooth edge on the one side of the blade and a notched one on the other.[42] Toothed knives were of two kinds. Some had their teeth bent in one direction, others in the opposite direction. If one tested with a fingernail from the grip towards the top, the fingernail was caught by those teeth pointing towards the top of the knife; and if he tested in the opposite direction, the nail was caught by those pointing towards the grip.[43] Rashi describes a number of "professional knives": the saw for cutting wood which is similar to a knife full of notches,[44] the knife of the saddlers,[45] and a smaller knife for cutting dried figs,[46] and a curved knife for reaping figs.[47] Finally, we also find a brief description of the razor (*Shaḥor*) which removes hair[48] and the pair of scissors with two blades which can be separated from each other.[49] Scissors were primarily used for cutting woolen garments.[50]

Rashi acquaints us also with a variety of household gadgets which are in many ways similar to those of our times. Flour was sifted in a doubled-up piece of material (*Nifvata*), well woven and tied together at the top looking like a bag.[51] Legumes were stored in small bags (*Gulki*).[52] They were sifted in a utensil (*Kanon*) which was wide at the top and had at its other end a short spoutlike opening. The legumes were put into the upper wide opening,

38 Pesaḥim 70a. קופיץ, סכין גדול הוא ורובן אינן לשחיטה אלא לחתוך בשר ולשבירת עצמות.

39 Bezah 31a. סתם קופיץ הוא סכין של קצבים, דומה לקרדומות שלנו שאינם כלי אומן, ויש שעושין בו שני ראשים והשני דומה קצת לקרדום של האוכפות.

40 Shabbath 123b. סכין של בית המקולין שהקצבין מקצבין בו בשר.

41 ᶜArakhin 23b. סכין שיש בו פגימות וחותך מהר כעין שיש לעושי מסרקות.

42 Ḥullin 15b. . . . ויש לה שתי פיות האחת חלקה כסכין והאחת יש בה פגימות.

43 Ḥullin 17a. . . . פגימותיה מכוונות לעומקן ויש לפגם שני עוקצים, כשאתה מוליך צפורנך מסוף הסכין לראשה צפורנך חוגרת בעוקץ של צד הראש וכשאתה בודק מראשה לסופה צפורנך חוגרת בעוקץ של סופה.

44 Shabbath 157a, 123b. המסר הגדול. מגרה שהיא לאומנין לקוץ בו עצים . . . שהוא עשוי כסכין מלא פגימות.

45 Shabbath 123b. חרבא דאושכפי, סכין של רצענין.

46 *Ibid.* מקצע, איזמל שמחתכין בו דבלה.

47 Nedarim 61b. מכפילין, הסכינים שקצצו בהם תאנים ומצניעין אותם.

48 Bezah 35b. השחור, תער על שם שמשחיר את השער.

49 *Ibid.* והזוג של מספרים, יש להן שני סכינין להכי מקרי זוג ויש להן חליות ופורקין אותם זה מזה.

50 ᶜAvodah Zarah 75b. זוגא דסרבלא, מספרים שגוזזין בהן בגדי צמר.

51 Sukkah 20b. נפוותא, לנפות בהן הקמח כמות שהן נותנין עליו קמח וכופלין אותן וקושרין בראש הכפל כעין בויט״ל שלנו.

52 Bezah 23b. גולקי, כעין שקים שנותנים בהם קטניות ופירות דקין.

the implement was shaken firmly and the legumes—being round—rolled through the spout while the chaff remained in the upper part.[53] There were, however, also sieves made of metal.[54] Wine was kept in vats[55] which were covered with a special piece of cloth (*Prunka*).[56] A ladle was used to draw the wine from the vat.[57] The filling of bottles was done with a funnel, wide on top and having a small and short opening at its bottom. It was placed into the small opening of the customer's bottle into which the wine was poured from the measure.[58] A pitcher made of glass was used for the washing of hands.[59]

The kitchen utensils used by Rashi are not as specialized as those of our times, but they met well the needs of the household. Brooms were made of palm twigs, probably most suitable for sandy floors.[60] Ashes were removed from the stoves with small shovels. These shovels looked like pot lids with a handle made of thin metal.[61] They were also used to separate figs sticking to their clusters.[62] A similar implement was used to scrape bread loaves from the floor of the oven.[63] Handles of the utensils were attached to the metal parts by a peg penetrating the metal part thus fastening the handle.[64] A special grass was known[65] as cleanser and polishing material, while wooden utensils were polished with the rough skin of a fish[66] which served the same purpose as our sand paper. Food was kept warm in a hay box[67] after having been cooked on a tripod.[68] The froth was skimmed off from

[53] Bezah 12b. קנון, כלי הוא, ראשו אחד רחב והשני עשוי כעין מרזב קצר ונותן קטניות בתוך הרחב ומנענע, והאוכל מתגלגל דרך המרזב, והפסולת נשאר בכלי.

[54] Bezah 23b. משום כלי קבול.... גזרו טומאה על כברה.... ושלנו שהוא של מתכת...

[55] Shabbath 88a. גיגית, קובא שמטילין בה שכר.

[56] Shabbath 48a. פרונקא, בגד העשוי לפרוס על הגיגית.

[57] *Ibid.* נטלא, כלי ששואבין בו יין מן הכובא.

[58] ʿAvodah Zarah 72a. משפך, מלמעלה פיו רחב ומלמטה נקב קצר ומושיבין אותו על פי צלוחית של לוקחין שפיהן צר ושופכין היין מן המידה לתוכו והוא יורד לתוך הצלוחית.

[59] Ḥullin 107a. של זכוכית קרוי נטלא, והיתה מוצנעת לשער בו כלי של כל איש ואיש שמתקנו ליטול ידיו.

[60] Shabbath 124b. של תמרה, כעין שלנו לכבד את הבית דאסור משום אשויי גומות.

[61] Exod. 27:3. יעים, כתרגומו מגרפות שנוטל בהן הדשן והן כמין כסוי קדרה של מתכת דק ויש לו בית יד.

[62] Ḥagigah 20a. ומגרפה...., כלי ברזל הוא... שגורפין בו אפר הכירה וגם מבדילין בו תאנים המודבקות זו בזו.

[63] Shabbath 117b. מרדה, כלי שרודין בו הפת ומפרידין אותו מכותל התנור שנדבק בה. Taʿanith 75a. מרדה, פל"א בלעז על שם שרודין בהפת מן התנור.

[64] Shabbath 102b. שיפתא, יתד קטן שתוחבו בתוך בית יד של מרא בהיותו בנקב הברזל להדקו שלא יצא.

[65] Ḥullin 25a. לשוף, לשפשף בדבר המחליקן ומצחצחן כמו שעושין בעשב שקורין אשפריי"ל.

[66] *Ibid.* להטיח בטונס, דג הוא... ושפין בעורו כלי עץ להחליק.

[67] Shabbath 34a. טומנין את החמין, נותנים בקופה של מוכין להיות חומם משתמר בהם.

[68] Shabbath 78a. פטפוט, רגל למקום מושב הכור שהיו מושיבין על כן העשוי לכך כגון טרפיי"ד לשפות הקדירה.

the boiling pot with a ladle.[69] A pan was placed underneath broiling geese to catch the fat.[70] Firewood was stacked for the various seasons in the yard behind the house.[71] Spices were pounded with a pestle and meat was cut on a special meat board.[72]

Three kinds of writing material are described by Rashi: a kind of paper made of grass, probably papyrus;[73] parchment on which pens made a noise sounding like "ken-ken";[74] and finally wax tablets on which one wrote with a slate pencil.[75] It seems also that a kind of paper clip (*Atbi*) was known in the form of a stick with a notch at its top into which the pages were squeezed.[76] Lines were drawn with a special ruler.[77] Scribes used a piece of steel with one end split into two like a pen.[78] Letters, like anything else that had to be securely closed, were sealed by means of a seal ring.[79]

Interesting are the extended or composite rods mentioned in various connections. Painters who whitewashed and painted homes carried with them composite rods topped with a rag which was dipped into a lime solution with which they whitewashed the house. The lower part of the house could only be painted with a very short rod but the upper parts were painted by placing one rod on top of another.[80] These rods which could be lengthened by placing part into part were well known.[81] Coppersmiths and weavers going from town to town for their work carried with them rods which could be taken apart.[82]

[69] Shabbath 123b. זוהמא לסטרון, כף גדולה שמסלקין בו זוהמא של קדרה.

[70] Ḥullin 111b. דוגי, שנותנין כלי לקבל השומן כדרך שאנו עושין לאווזין והוא נקרא בי דוגי בלשון ארמי.

[71] Shabbath 157a. אלא לא בעצים שבמוקצה, שהניחם ברחבה שאחורי ביתו והקצם לימות הסתיו. מוקצה רחבה שאחורי בתים שהקצה אחורי ביתו להכניס שם דבר לאוצר.

[72] II Chron. 24:14. עלה, כלי שרת והעלות – שטושי"ל בלשון אשכנז הוא שכותשין את הבשמים בכתשת . . . ויש אומרים והעלות אלו הנסרים שחותכין עליהם בשר.

[73] Shabbath 78a ניר, מעשבים עושים אותו.

[74] Giṭṭin 6a. קן קן קולמוסא, תיקון הקולמוס . . . כשחותכין אותו ומחליקין אותו. ולי נראה קול הקולמוס כשהוא כותב וקול היריעה, שהוא נשמע כמי שאומר קן־קן, ואית דגרסי קל־קולמוסא.

[75] Ezek. 9:2. קסת קסת סופר, פנקס, הם לוחות שמחופין בשעוה וחורטין בם בעט.

[76] Shabbath 98b. . . . ולי נראה פ׳ דאטבי כמו אטבא דספרי האמור במנחות (32) והוא טלואון בלעז שמבקע מקל אחד בראשו ונושך בו דפי הקונטרוס.

[77] Shabbath 11b. בקיסם שבאזנו, קיסם ארוך ושוה כעין סרגלא שמשרטטין בה ספרים שקורין ויר"א בלעז ובו משוין את הנסרים כדרך נגרים שלנו משווים בנטיית קו.

[78] Sukkah 32a המנק, ברזל של סופרים שיש לו שני ראשים וראשו אחד מפוצל.

[79] Shabbath 57a. חותם, צורה לחתום בה איגרת או כל דבר סגור.

[80] Shabbath 47a. קנה של סיידין, הטחין ומלבנין הבית בסיד יש להן קנים של פרקים ונותן מטלית בראשה ושורין בסיד המחוי וטח את הבית וכשהוא טח מלמטה אי אפשר לו אלא מקנה קצר וכשהוא הולך ומגביה מוסיף קנה על קנה ומאריכו.

[81] Sukkah 4b. . . . . לבוד – סניף, אשפוטי"ץ בלעז, דבר שמאריכין אותו על ידי סניפין כדי לסנוף חקק על חקק.

[82] Shabbath 47a. צורפי נחושת או גרדיים והולכים מעיר לער למלאכתן ונושאין עמהן מטות של פרקים.

Tools described by Rashi include the hammer with its various properties, evoking sparks from iron,[83] smashing rocks into many particles,[84] and as the large implement made of iron and to be used for structures of iron.[85] With the hammer any size ring was widened[86] and material was stretched and expanded.[87] The hammer beat was also a signal that the work was finished and was about to glide off the anvil by its last stroke.[88] Goldsmiths used smooth hammers to flatten the gold plates.[89] The plane (*R'hitni*) is described as consisting of two parts, the one of wood and the other of iron inserted into it with which the width of boards was levelled and smoothed.[90] The saw is illustrated as a blade full of teeth which may have many directions.[91] We also find the description of a kind of telescope or looking glass. It is a hollow rod through which one sees better if it is short, but if long, one cannot see very far.[92] A time keeper indicated the hours of the day in the form of steps made opposite the sun so that the shadow thrown by the sun lets people know what the time of day was.[93]

The wealth of the realia described by Rashi in his commentaries and the multicolorness of the mode of his description show us how well acquainted he was with all aspects and areas of his contemporary life. His commentaries are indeed a most valuable source for the history of French culture and civilization.

83 Shabbath 21b. גץ, ניצוץ . . . . הוצאת מן הברזל כשהפטיש מכה עליו.

84 Shabbath 88b. מה פטיש, מתחלק הסלע על ידו לכמה ניצוצות.

85 Shabbath 102b. מעצד, אף הוא כמו קורנס גדול של ברזל לבנין של ברזל.

86 Shabbath 52b. הכה בפטיש עד שנתפשט ונתרחב הנקב סביב סביב.

87 Ḥullin 25b. להקיש קורנס, שיש בו פחיתות ופושטן בקורנס.

88 Shabbath 73a. מכה בפטיש היא גמר מלאכה שכן אומן מכה בקורנוס על הסדן להחליקו בגמר מלאכה.

89 Shabbath 123a. קורנס של זהבים, צריך שיהא חלק לרדד טסין.

90 Shabbath 97a. שני גווני כלים של עץ וברזל חד נעוץ בתוכו ובהן משוה פני רוחב הקרש ומחליקה.

91 Bezah 31a. מגרה, שיג״ה (Saege) כעין סכין מלאה פגימות וממהר לקוץ בו עצים וכלי אומן הוא.

המסר הגדול, מגירה שהיא לאומנין לקוץ בו עצים . . . שהוא עשוי כסכין מלא פגימות.

92 ᶜEruvin 43b. שפופרת, קנה חלול וכשהוא ארוך אין צופין בו מרחוק, וכשהוא קצר צופין בו יותר.

93 Isa. 38:8; *cf.* II Kings 20:10. צל מעלות. כמין מדרגות עשויות כנגד החמה לבחון בהן שעות היום, כעין אורלוגין שעושין האומנין.

"By A Prophet The Lord Brought Up Israel Out of Egypt"

By DANIEL JEREMY SILVER
The Temple, Cleveland, Ohio

I SHALL FOREVER be grateful to Dr. Zeitlin for long mornings spent in his Drake Hotel apartment. There were books everywhere and learning. During the first years we talked about my thesis on the Maimonidean controversy for which he was advisor and referee. Later we talked of many things, including my interest in the treatment accorded to Moses by our tradition.

Dr. Zeitlin guided me to Artapanus and through Josephus. He helped me to recognize the richness of the midrashic materials on Moses which circulated during Hellenistic times. Out of these talks came my paper on "Moses and the Hungry Birds" (*JQR*, Vol. 64, pp. 123–153) in which I suggested *inter alia* that Moses had been worshipped as an intercessor by some among the para-military Judean clans who came down to Egypt with the Persians and the Ptolemies.

The more I reflected on the profusion of such Hellenistic embellishments the more I became conscious of the marked contrast between the number and nature of these eulogistic traditions, and the diffidence of the Torah biography and of the conventional references to Moses in the other canonized books. Surely, numerous stories about Moses must have circulated in pre-exilic times. The Hellenistic midrash had not sprung up full-blown. Yet, the Torah editors were remarkably parsimonious in providing details of Moses' life. Why? The more I pondered this question the more it became apparent that not only had the Torah narrative kept a tight rein on legendary embellishments of Moses' biography, but that the editors had reshaped popular history to reduce Moses' leadership role. Why? The nature of the Biblical material makes any explanation necessarily highly conjectural; but, I believe, the attempt is worth making and I gratefully dedicate this piece to my revered teacher.

* * * * * * * *

Rudolf Kittel belonged to a distinguished generation of German scholars who, around the turn of the century, elaborated and refined the then current text critical approach to the Hebrew Bible. Late in his career, in 1925 to be exact, Kittel published a popular book, *Great Men and Movements in Israel*, in which he outlined what had happened in Biblical times as these events had been reconstructed by the scholars of his generation. Though designed for a non-professional audience, the book was highly praised by scholars and continued to attract attention.* Thirty years later Emil Kraeling would describe it as "a noble book."[1] Ten years ago Theodor H. Gaster felt it useful to prepare critical notes to a reprint edition.[2]

Kittel organized his history around the biographies of Old Testament personages. He began with Moses. Why did he begin with Moses rather than with Abraham? Kittel did not consider it possible to disentangle the real Abraham from the patriarchal legends; yet, with Moses he felt on more solid ground. Indeed, Kittel not only was prepared to differentiate fact from legendary addition in the Biblical account of Moses; but to provide a physical description of the man: "the tall and powerful frame, the well-poised head, the sharp penetrating eyes of the leader, of the victor of man over obstacles, the firm hand of the ruler ever alert and faithful to his duty. . . ."[3]

All this is pure invention. The Bible tells us a good deal about various events in Moses' life but no line of Bible text provides a physical description of the man.[4] We do not know if he was tall or short, thin or fat, dark skinned or light; whether, in fact, he had what might be considered a commanding presence. Kittel simply projected his own image of the hero on to a man whom he believed to have been heroic. This process is no more scholarly than the research behind all those illustrated books of Bible stories which fill popular libraries in which Moses always is presented as tall, dark, well-muscled and prepossessing. Paid illustrators can be forgiven; after all, they have to provide features; but scholars should know better. Kittel here had ceased to be a critical scholar and had become a creative writer and artful propagandist. As Gaster has shown, Kittel reveals here his political life as a passionate German nationalist, part of that generation of post World War I revanchists who clamored for a noble leader, a *fuehrer*, who would lift the Reich from the bourgeois tawdriness of the Weimar Republic to glory.[5] This side of the Holocaust it seems particularly grotesque to find Moses recast as one of Wagner's Teutonic heroes, but our argument is not simply with Kittel's politics or even with his preconception that heroes come with a six foot frame, blue eyes and blonde hair. Our question goes to Kittel's conception of Moses as a man of affairs and political skill. Kittel stands for many scholars and populists who have written that the Bible presents a Moses who

* I am grateful to Peter Machinist of Arizona State University who read this paper carefully and whose criticisms were most helpful. Needless to say, he is in no way responsible for the thesis or any mistakes which remain.

[1] Kraeling, Emil, *The Old Testament Since the Reformation*, Harper & Row, N. Y. C. 1955, p. 298.

[2] Kittel, Rudolf, *Great Men and Moments in Israel*, Ktav, N. Y. C., 1968.

[3] Kittel, p. 19.

[4] Exod. 4:10. "I have never been a man of words . . . I am slow of speech and slow of tongue" seems to be conventional hyperbole, not an actual physical description.

[5] Kittel, pp. XVI–XVII.

is larger than life, dynamic, a man of imposing will, brave and daring.[6] The image of Moses as Seigfried shocks everyone, but the image of Moses as a leader of men and a hero does not; though well it should. I suggest that the received text reflects a conscious effort not to present Moses in this guise and that his portrait reflects some of the central religious forces at work at the heart of the Torah enterprise.

In common usage, we use the term hero to denote either a man of great courage and initiative or the chief character in a saga or chronicle. Kittel has no doubt that Moses is a hero in both senses of the word:

> From earliest times in Israel, generation after generation has told the story of the great man who, even before the Israelites could be called a nation, led them from Egypt, the house of bondage, into freedom and a new life. He broke the Egyptian yoke, led his hosts into the desert where he gave them the God whom they afterwards worshipped, gave them the code of laws of their God, and finally led them through the desert to the land which they had learned to look upon as their own. Through all the ages Moses has been honored as the helper in need, the leader, the founder of the nation, but most revered as the messenger of the new God and His laws.[7]

Kittel assumed that Moses was the central figure in the pivotal events chronicled in Exodus-Deuteronomy and that as the central figure in these happenings his will and ability made happen what did happen. My reading suggests that the Torah presents Moses as an obedient servitor rather than as a man of initiative, as a holy man rather than as a practical man of affairs.

[6] The list of such works is legion. I cite only one writer, Elias Auerbach, an exile from the Reich Kittel's Fuehrer built:

> The superiority of (Moses) his spirit was so immense that it would not have been surprising if he had immediately been raised up as a god-man. At no time did he succumb to this temptation! And in addition he had to have all the ability of a statesman and army commander; he had to be able to assume the leadership of a people and to deal with the pressing dangers of every hour; he needed infallible judgment and the ability to make prompt decisions. He had to give the right command at the right moment. He required never-flagging power of will to carry things through, and the ability to probe into the smallest details in order to make possible their execution. He was unfeeling to the point of cruelty in order to break opposition and annihilate opponents. But he was not cruel; on the contrary he was just; violent in anger and "full of jealousy" when some principle was to be guarded and deviations from the novel way had to be averted. In addition he had infinite patience and forbearance with the weakest of the weak who indeed were no giants as he was. A tireless teacher who by example and instruction so filled a new generation with his ideas that they endured after his death. And yet he was so close to the heart of the simplest one that all trusted his judgment and saw in him the father to whom they could come with all their trials, troubles and disagreements. He "bore the burden of the people." He had to provide food and water. He had to give guidance on the way and provide security; he had to "stem the careless selfishness of the people and within his community enforce subordination" etc. Auerbach, Elias, *Moses*, Wayne University Press, Detroit, 1975, pp. 215–6.

[7] Kittel, p. 19.

For our purposes let us put aside the much-debated question of the historicity of Moses. Lacking extra Biblical confirmation any search for the historical Moses begins in conjecture and ends in uncertainty. I have no doubt that Moses lived and played a major role in some of the events with which the received text associates him, but the biography of the man is beyond reconstruction. Why do I come down for the historicity of Moses? As I shall show, the text makes a conscious effort to diminish his role and it seems to me unlikely that editors would invent someone whose presence in the narrative would cause them embarrassment. No one deliberately creates problems for himself.

I want to concentrate on Kittel's other assumption, the typically modern assumption born out of recent research into the pious literary conventions of Near Eastern writing and out of our inbred humanism; that however the Exodus and the Covenant may have been perceived and reported by the Israelites, these events can only have been human achievements, and that since the received tradition gives Moses pride of place in those stories he was, in fact, the actual liberator and lawgiver.

Is this assumption faithful to the Torah's version of these events? I invite you to reread the Exodus-Numbers narratives which deal with Moses. Read carefully; but, for the moment, pay more attention to the narrative of the received text than to all you know about its various strata. Pay particular attention to those paragraphs which describe Moses after he assumes a public role and go right through to the end of the first telling of these events in the book of Numbers.[8] Notice that nowhere does the received text suggest that Moses broke Pharaoh's will: "the Lord struck down all the first-born in the land of Egypt" (Exod. 12:29); "That very day the Lord led the Israelites from the land of Egypt, troop by troop" (Exod. 12:15); or that Moses led his people in the wilderness, "The Lord went before them in a pillar of cloud by day to guide them along the way, and in a pillar of fire by night . . ." (Exod. 13:20); or that Moses presented to them the God whom they afterwards worshipped, "the Lord called to him (Moses) from the mountain saying, 'thus shall you say to the house of Jacob . . . if you obey Me faithfully and keep My covenant you shall be My treasured possession among all the peoples' " (Exod. 19:35). Always it is God who is the liberator and leader: "the Lord continued: 'I have come down to rescue them from the Egyptians, and bring them out of the land to a good and spacious land, a land flowing with milk and honey, the home of the Canaanites . . . (Exod. 3:8).

More often than not Moses is pictured as a trustworthy ambassador carrying out the royal will. Moses makes no move to return to Egypt until God

[8] Most private scenes occur in chapters 1–3 of Exodus and precede Moses' commissioning, but not all (*cf.* Num. 10:29 ff.). Interestingly, almost all such material is assigned to the older strata of the received tradition.

orders him to go. His mission in Egypt is to carry God's message and to announce God's miracles. He has no latitude to act on his own. It is not Moses' skill as a diplomat, but the forceful logic of God's plagues which persuade Pharaoh. When faced with a difficult decision Moses retires to the Tent of Meeting to consult God. Moses does not determine the daily line of march; he humbly follows the lead of God. Moses does not lead the army in battle. It is God who determines which of the neighboring people are to be attacked and with which negotiations are to be entered. Moses does not provision the people. God provides manna and quail. Moses does not make law, he repeats law which God makes known to him. When Moses' authority is challenged God defends him.

In his public role Moses carries with him the staff which announced his role as God's ambassador and which was the agency through which God's power manifested itself. This rod, which began life as a mundane shepherd's tool, had been transformed at Moses' commissioning by God's word into a staff of power and served ever after as an unmistakable sign that the bearer was not an ordinary man but God's agent. When God wishes to display His power He orders Moses to lift the rod or cast it down. When, on God's command, the staff is held high the armies of Israel are victorious. When, at God's command, it is held over the rock, water gushes forth from the rock. The rod's power is God's, not Moses'. It is the staff which signals that Moses is *eved adonai*, God's servant or agent (Deut. 34:5). No other figure in the prophetic tradition is provided by God with a similar badge of office. Moses is pictured as the foremost among God's emissaries, as first among those designated God's man, *ish ha-elohim.*[9]

Moses is depicted as agent, not as principal; as holy man not as political activist.[10] Indeed, one can come away from a reading of the Exodus-Numbers narrative convinced that more often than not Moses is depicted as a puppet being manipulated from above. That most readers push away any such impression testifies to the central role of Moses in the living religious traditions and to the fact that we come to Moses' public

[9] Deut. 33:1, Josh. 14:6, Ps. 90:1. *ish-ha-elohim* refers to a divine messenger (Judg. 13:8) or prophet (I Sam. 2:27, 9:6 etc.) who brings God's words to an individual. Though both labels, *ish-ha-elohim* and *eved-adonai*, in relation to Moses occur in the Torah only in the concluding chapters of Deuteronomy, these sections are assigned to earlier strata *ish-ha-elohim* (E) and *Eved Adonia* (J), and were conventional terms during Israelite times.

[10] As in all areas of Biblical interpretation there are exceptions. Most exceptions appear in the J stratum: Moses on his own offers a sacrifice before ascending Sinai (Exod. 24:4); welcomes the prophetic powers of Eldad and Medad (Num. 11:26 ff.); sends diplomatic messages to the king of Edom (Num. 20:14 ff.); and negotiates with Reuben and Gad (Numbers 32). Consistency was not the hallmark of the editing process; (*cf.* Exod. 32:19 ff., Exod. 36:2 ff., Exod. 37:43); but the impression is inescapable that there was a concerted effort to present Moses as agent, not actor. The intercession texts will be discussed later.

career after a number of incidents from his early life in which Moses does seem to have a will and personality of his own. Moses is his own creature when he strikes down a taskmaster and when he interferes in a quarrel between two Hebrew slaves (Exod. 2:11–12). Moses is his own master in the lovely pastoral by the well when he protects the daughters of Jethro from the local bully boys (Exod. 2:16–21). Presumedly, he acted on his own while tending Jethro's flock (Exod. 3:1). There was no need to force theology upon biography in these domestic scenes; but once Moses has turned aside to see the flaming bush and is commissioned there is evidence that the editors have gone well beyond the requirements of conventional piety in shaping the text so as to define Moses' role as merely God's agent. "Come I will send you to Pharaoh" (Exod. 3:10), "and the Lord called Moses to the top of the mountain and Moses went up" (Exod. 19:20) . . . "The Lord said to Moses: 'Carve two tablets of stone like the first,' . . . so Moses carved two tablets of stone like the first" (Exod. 34:1, 4). Moses says as much: "The Lord sent me to do all these things. They are not of my own devising" (Num. 16:28).

Behind the received text lies a perception of Moses as holy man. Holy men lead by the word rather than by the whip. People do their bidding out of fear of unseen consequences rather than out of fear of their police. The text never suggests that Moses had either police or troops at his disposal. When nobles challenge his authority Moses has no recourse than to turn to God. When his own family challenges his authority, God comes to Moses' aid and the text underscores Moses' lack of authority and his non-political nature: "Now Moses was a very humble man, more so than any other man on earth" (Num. 12:3). When Moses requires lieutenants he must ask for volunteers: "Whoever is for the Lord, come here" (Exod. 33:26). Moses is not present at Israel's battles as a general, but as the shaman who brings God's power: "Whenever Moses held up his hand (with the rod of God in it) Israel prevailed; but whenever he let down his hand, Amalek prevailed" (Exod. 17:11). As was the custom of shamans and holy men in many societies, Moses lived apart. His tent was set up ". . . at some distance from the camp . . . whenever Moses went out to the Tent, all the people would rise and stand each at the entrance to his tent" (Exod. 33:7–8). It is believed that God visits the holy man in that tent set apart (Exod. 33:10). When he is or has been with God his face seems radiant (Exod. 34:27). The sense of mystery seems to have been deliberately heightened. Moses veils his face after he has been with God, but only then (Exod. 34:29).

The received account in Exodus-Numbers seems at times to go out of its way to diminish Moses' private virtues in order to contrast these to the power which emanated from him during his public career when God's puissance flowed through him. This is particularly evident in some of the pre-commissioning scenes where Moses is allowed to appear as his own master. Take the description of his attack on an Egyptian taskmaster. "He saw the Egyptian beating a Hebrew, one of his kinsmen. He turned this way and that and seeing no one about he struck down the Egyptian and hid him in the sand" (Exod. 2:11–12). When the next day Moses discovers that the matter is known, the text reports that Moses was frightened and that he fled. Heroes do not strike down unsuspecting victims, work desperately to hide all traces of their deed, and flee into the night. Heroes proclaim their defiance and attack their enemies openly. A hero may prudently retire before a superior force, but he does not flee in panic. If he retires from the field it is to fight another day. Moses flees out of fear and there is no talk of returning to the fray. After the stabbing of the taskmaster, Moses is never again pictured with a weapon in his hands. The long pastoral in Midian is set against the continuing suffering of the Hebrews in Egypt; yet, nowhere is it suggested that Moses gave the slaves much thought. The Torah does not report any move on Moses' part to aid the slaves; out of sight seems to have been out of mind, until God orders him to go. When God orders Moses to return, the saga suggests that far from being eager to accept this chance to be of service, Moses repeatedly attempted to excuse himself: "Please, O Lord, make someone else your agent" (Exod. 4:13).

Once you finish the book of Numbers pause a moment to clear your head and turn to the book of Deuteronomy. Here the theme of Moses as the courtier-agent and obedient messenger is not as consistently developed. The very form of the book suggests this change of emphasis. Deuteronomy is presented as several valedictory speeches shaped by Moses. In these speeches Moses asserts, *inter alia*, that he, on his own initiative, had been responsible for the organization of the judicial system, the appointment of the spies, the choice of cities of refuge and the division of land among the tribes. Moses seems to be the organizer of the great ceremony of covenant affirmation (Deut. 27:11 ff.). But even in this tradition Moses' accomplishments remain modest and he is pictured most frequently as God's trustworthy agent. God determines the line of march. God "scouts the place where you are to encamp" (Deut. 1:32). God determines which kings shall be treated with and which engaged in battle. God is responsible for military victories. The law is from God and reported without change or addition. God punishes the people when they delay entering the Promised Land. The point is made forceably that the costly defeat at Hormah occurred not because Moses had stayed in the camp but because God had not gone out with the host (Deut. 1:42 ff.). In his initial speech Moses reminds the people that God has "carried the tribes as a Father carries his son, all the way that you traveled until you came to this place" (Deut. 1:31).

In Deuteronomy Moses is both agent and actor, but God is the chief actor. For reasons which can only be guessed at the editors did not feel the need to drain Moses' biography of all evidence of initiative and power.

Recently Moshe Weinfeld and others have emphasized various wisdom elements in Deuteronomy. Is this willingness to give some due to Moses, the man, a product of the fact that Deuteronomy was shaped in circles influenced by a "humanistic" tradition?[11] Perhaps, but Deuteronomy's "humanism" must not be overemphasized. When all is said and done liberation and law are God's achievements and His alone. "This day I begin to put the dread and fear of you upon the peoples everywhere under heaven so that they shall tremble and quake because of you whenever they hear you mentioned" (Deut. 2:24). The familiar eulogy a Deuteronomist editor added to his scroll by way of conclusion praises not a heroic leader or a royal figure but a prophet-agent "whom the Lord singled out, face to face, for the various signs and portents the Lord sent him to display in the land of Egypt, against Pharaoh and all his courtiers and his whole country, and for all the great might and awesome power that God displayed before all Israel" (Deut. 34:10–11). It is God who makes the exodus possible, not Moses. It is God who legislates and leads, not Moses. The portrait offered neither assigns to Moses primacy of place nor attributes to Moses the power of political office or the virtues of personal initiative or military skill. If these be the attributes of a hero, it must be said that Moses is not presented as hero. If these be the attributes of a man of affairs, it must be said that Moses is not presented as a power broker. It is his faithfulness and loyalty that is praised rather than his initiative or daring.

I know of no other national saga in which the founding father is treated with so little sense of his own presence. Generally, such recitals tell of wise leaders who promulgate just laws and who lead their armies to brilliant victory, albeit with the help of the gods. Moses never straps on a sword or rides out to battle in a war chariot. Moses is never pictured as enthroned. He is often depicted prostrate before God at the entrance to the Tent of Meeting (Num. 20:6). When challenged, powerful kings quickly dispatch those who dare to rebel. When Dathan and Abiran refuse Moses' summons he can only plead to God for help (Num. 16:12–15). Kings establish dynasties. Moses' sons fade from view.[12] The all wise leaders of saga make provision for the nation's future before their death. When Moses is informed that he is about to die he can only petition God: "Let the Lord . . . appoint someone over the community . . . so that the Lord's community may not be like sheep that have no shepherd" (Num. 27:15–17). Kings promulgate law. Moses is a secretary who transcribes the law God dictates to him.

[11] The current debate on the extent of the "humanism" of the wisdom literature may well force us to make other guesses to explain the Deuteronomic treatment of Moses, *cf.* Crenshaw, James ed., *Studies in Ancient Israelite Wisdom*, Ktav, N. Y. C., 1976.

[12] The mosaic lineage of the priest Gershom (Judg. 18:30) remains conjectural and has no parallel in the Torah narrative.

This treatment of Moses was deliberate. As their literature reveals, the Israelites enjoyed heroic saga as well as any other people. We have parts of such a saga in the Deuteronomic version of Israel's most famous king, David. The comparison of the Moses and the David material is revealing. Moses is never physically described. Young David is "ruddy, and withal of beautiful eyes, and goodly to look upon" (I Sam. 16:12). In one version the young David is already "a mighty man of valour, and a man of war, and prudent in affairs and a comely person" (I Sam. 16:18). In another version the young David is an inexperienced shepherd (I Sam. 16:11). In both versions he becomes a fearless warrior who has many killings to his fame and a brilliant field commander who remains in the field for a good part of his life and who returns to combat even when he has been crowned.

In the David epic the sense of God's control of events is present but attenuated. The text is full of the expressions of conventional piety, "and David waxed greater and greater for the Lord was with him" (II Sam. 5:10), but the story is essentially stock aretology, the tale of a hero who is a daring soldier, a man of overwhelming ambition, even great lust; a capable political organizer and manipulator and a larger than life figure whose virtues and vices are outsized. Samuel anoints David in the name of God and tells David to return to private life. God commissions Moses directly; and thereafter, Moses has no private life. As king, David rules by fiat. He breaks new ceremonial ground by his acts (II Sam. 6, II Sam. 12). Moses is pictured as unwilling or unable to act except in response to specific instructions from God. David takes advice from a variety of counselors and makes his own decision. Generally, Moses accepts advice only from God. David is a master strategist as well as trained soldier. Moses never leads Israel's troops or plans strategy. David must hire court prophets like Nathan to know God's will. God speaks directly to Moses who is not only his agent but his prophet. When Absalom rebels against David, the king sends mercenaries to put down the uprising. When Korah rebels, Moses throws himself prostrate and God has the earth swallow up the opposition. When David sins, his are the sins of ambition, cruelty, lust and power. When Moses sins he stands guilty of not having followed with absolute fidelity a ritual instruction about the handling of God's rod. Moses is married before his public career begins and as far as the Torah is concerned that is the end of his sexual interests. David's love affairs are amply described and unceasing.

The image of Moses as the obedient emissary of God, whose authority is charismatic rather than the authority of office, is too consistent to permit the possibility that it was drawn haphazardly. The force behind this image seems to reflect some of the strongest and most consistent elements of the emerging Biblical faith, particularly faith in the redeemer God. Certainly it does not seem to be the result of a revisionist decision, such as we have seen in recent years in China and Russia, to discredit a once powerful leader whose policies are now denounced. One has only to reread the eulogy with which Deuteronomy concludes to recognize the respect in which Moses con tinued to be held.

Introductions to the Bible conventionally describe the material in Genesis-Kings as sacred history. As Von Rad has pointed out, the term is misleading if it suggests a national literature whose purpose was limited to that of chronicle detailing God's original redemption and His up-till-now providential care of Israel.[13] The Torah emerged from liturgical materials which served not simply as a record, but as an evocation. The recital was significant because it called forth God's presence and power. The recital of the original redemption summoned God's redeeming power into the here and now.

This assumption is suggested both by what we know of the Israelite cult, particularly such covenant renewal ceremonies as is described in Joshua 24; and by the special interest in history reflected in what remains of the literature. In other West Asian cultures history seems to have been an occasional interest with attention focused on court related materials; dynastic lists and military campaigns; and cult related materials: evidence of a shrine's legitimacy and antiquity. In ancient Israel history emerges as a central and critical component of the religious culture. Why? Certainly the Israelites believed that their history served to prove God's choice of Israel and to vindicate God's fidelity to His part of the covenant bargain.[14] This is certainly true, but not a complete explanation. In Israel history was turned into liturgy as an outgrowth of certain assumptions about the power of a recital of God's redemptive acts. "The Israelites came to a historical way of thinking, and then to historical writing, by way of their belief in the sovereignty of God in history."[15] In one sense these histories are no more than a particular form of praise of God. Song and psalms of praise were not simply pious exercises, but power laden acts designed to evoke an existential display of God's redemptive might. Certainly some of Israel's early songs lift up God's power in the hope of stimulating God's continuing care. The Song of the Sea says it clearly: "I will sing to the Lord for He has triumphed gloriously . . . He is become my salvation . . . In Your strength You guide them (Your people) to Your holy abode. The peoples hear, they tremble . . . (Exod. 15). Deborah's song has a similar purpose. She is to "utter a song" (Judg. 5:12) that the power of the Lord may go forth. The liturgical recita-

[13] Von Rad, Gerhard, *The Problem of the Hexatuch*, McGraw Hill, N. Y. C., 1965, pp. 3 ff.

[14] Burrows, Millar, "Ancient Israel" in *The Idea of History in the Ancient Near East* R. Denton, Ed., Yale University Press, 1953, pp. 99–131; Von Rad, Gerhard, The Beginnings of Historical Writing in Ancient Israel, Von Rad, *Studies*, pp. 166–204.

[15] Von Rad, "Historical Writings," p. 170.

tion of redemptions past—song—clearly was deemed effective in calling forth God's power.[16]

There are significant reasons to believe that the narrative of Exodus-Numbers and perhaps also Deuteronomy reflect the interests of such liturgists and are an outgrowth of familiar formulae of praise whose public recitation had the forces of confirming the covenant, of affirming the God who had delivered the nation from bondage and of summoning the God who would deliver them from present dangers.

What little we know about Israelite rites suggests that they included public recitals of God's saving acts—history, apparently organized not only to educate the people about the significance of the founding events, but to please the King of kings by rehearsing His victories in well turned phrases, much as oriental courtiers offer an emperor their salaams in the expectation that such courtesies and panegyrics will open his ears and soften his heart to their requests. The Middle-Eastern courtier made no attempt to limit his praise and was careful to list all of the royal accomplishments and to associate no one else with the king's victories. Power belonged to the king alone and not to his viceroy or general.

For example, Deuteronomy contains this early Passover form:

> When, in time to come, your son asks you, "What means the exhortation, laws, and rules which the Lord our God has enjoined upon you?" you shall say to your son, "We were slaves to Pharoah in Egypt and the Lord freed us from Egypt with a mighty hand. The Lord wrought before our eyes marvelous and destructive signs and portents in Egypt, against Pharaoh and all his household; and us He freed from there, that He might take us and give us the land that He had promised on oath to our fathers. Then the Lord commanded for us to observe all these laws, to revere the Lord our God, for our lasting good and for our survival, as is now the case. It will be, therefore, to our merit before the Lord our God to observe faithfully this whole instruction, as He has commanded us" (Deut. 6:20–25).

The Israelite understood that the purpose of this Passover exercise was to gain merit, to have some hope of immediate benefit. God alone is praised. Moses is not mentioned. Deuteronomy also contains a formula recited when farmers brought to a shrine the first fruits of their harvest. A priest takes the offering and the faithful are told to recite:

[16] In the ancient Middle East worship was dominated by concern for ritual precision. Every act and chant had its power laden function. The priestly histories describe the function of the Temple singers with the verb נבא (I Chron. 25:1 ff.) a post-exilic recollection of the power of song to evoke the presence of God.

> My father was a fugitive Aramean . . . The Egyptians dealt harshly with us . . . We called unto the Lord . . . and the Lord heard our plea and saw our plight . . . The Lord freed us from Egypt by a mighty hand, by an outstretched arm and awesome power, and by signs and by portends. He brought us to this place, and gave us this land . . . wherefore I now bring its first fruits of the soil which you, O Lord, have given me (Deut. 26:5–10).

The purpose of this exercise is a practical one "so that you may enjoy all the bounty that the Lord your God has bestowed upon you and your household" (Deut. 26:11). Moses is not mentioned. God and God alone is praised. Psalm 135, generally credited as a pre-exilic piece composed for and sung during shrine worship, lifts up a similar picture of the God's saving acts.

> I know that the Lord is great . . .
> He it was who smote the first born of Egypt
> both of man and of beast
> Who in thy midst, O Egypt
> Sent signs and wonders
> Against Pharaoh and all his servants
> Who smote many waters
> and slew mighty kings . . .
> And gave their Lord as a heritage
> A heritage to his people
> Thy name, O Lord, endures forever
> Thy renown, O Lord, throughout all ages
> For the Lord will vindicate his people
> and have compassion on his servants (Ps. 135:5, 8–14).

Again, God and God alone is praised. Again, Moses is not mentioned. Again, the praise is preface to petition and a help in that direction. Such liturgies emphasized faith in a God whose power is revealed in history and encouraged humble submission to a God who controls providentially the fate of the nation(s). Moses is missing from these recitations, though he does appear in a recital attributed to Joshua (Josh. 24:2–13). Here the text makes it clear that Moses is merely a useful agent: "I sent Moses and Aaron, and I plagued Egypt . . . afterward I brought you out . . ." (Josh. 24:5). Such liturgies lifted up the form which emerged as Torah and set the limits which shaped the presentation of Moses. Had Moses been associated with events other than the critical beginnings of the national history when God's display of His power established His claim over Israel and His promise to Israel, he might have been drawn along quite different lines.

It is now impossible to recover the original elements in the popular Israelite biography of Moses or when and how these elements were reshaped into the figure of God's holy man known to us from the received tradition. What is clear is that the received text reflects the concerns of liturgists and priests rather than of the folk. Moses' treatment reflects an orthodox concern to magnify God's power and declare Him, Redeemer.[17]

I do not claim that the present Torah narrative was ever used liturgically, though parts of it certainly were; but that it was shaped by familiar liturgical attitudes and formed with the thought that its text would have practical effect. The Torah narrative is a statement of faith, proof of the redeeming power of God and a raising up of God, a lifting up of the promise of the redemption yet to come. Interest in this form reflects a time of uncertainty and trauma. A sovereign people, secure in the possessions in its land, will present a commemorative pageant on the Fourth of July. An unsettled people will not be satisfied with pageants dedicated to the glories of yesteryear. Pageant must lead to promise. Moses could not help against the Moabites or the Philistines, but God could; so by song and recitation they affirmed the God who had redeemed and evoked a new display of His redemptive powers. Washington and Valley Forge read Moses and Kadesh Barnea—dim in significance and God's mighty hand and outstretched arm come center stage. The leader recedes and the miraculous staff comes to the fore.

The cradle legend apart, the Moses who is presented to us in the Torah is not fashioned on an imperial model nor is he given the usual attributes of a hero. Moses' courage is not that of the battlefield nor his skill that of the decisive leader; rather his image reflects the attributes of the holy man. His skill is that of the prophet and his courage rests on his willingness to intercede to protect his people from an angry God. Late in the seventh pre-Christian century God announced through Jeremiah a severe drought. Jeremiah relayed the oracle in an artfully composed diatribe in which the prophet underlined the rightness of God's act. The drought is deserved. The nation's sins were so black that not even a man of proven prayer power could intercede effectively with God on the nation's behalf. "Then God said to me: 'even were Moses and Samuel to stand before Me, I would still have no sympathy for his people. Pass them out of my sight. Let them go.' " (Jer. 15:1). The role of intercessor is archaic and modern readers often fail to notice Moses in this role, yet, it is a role in which he is frequently described. A few incidents will stand for many. When the people fashioned

[17] Those few psalms which mention Moses (77:21, 99:6, 103:7, 105:26, 106:18, 23, 32) laud him as God's agent and underscore that he was the servant and not the master. "Thou dist lead Thy people like a flock by the hand of Moses and Aaron" (77:21). "He sent Moses His servant and Aaron whom He had chosen" (105:26).

the Golden Calf, God bitterly condemns the nation. Moses is told that this stiff-necked, faithless motley of ex-slaves will be eliminated. God will fashion for Himself another nation out of Moses' family. At this critical juncture Moses steps out of his role as obedient courtier and becomes the heroic minister who risks his life to change the imperial mind. " 'Let not your anger blaze forth against your people' . . . and the Lord renounced the punishment He had planned to bring upon His people" (Exod. 32:10–14). A year later, at the Kadesh Barnea camp, when the spies so frighten the council with their report of the well-defended Canaanite cities that the elders refuse to obey God's order for an immediate attack, God again pronounces the nation's death sentence. Again Moses intercedes: "Let my Lord's forebearance be great . . . pardon, I pray, the iniquity of this people according to your great kindness, as you have forgiven this people ever since Egypt" (Num. 14:13–20). Moses is described as a well-known intercessor who was frequently approached for this service:

> They set out from Mount Hor by the road to the Sea of Reeds to skirt the land of Edom. But the people grew restive on the journey, and the people spoke against God and against Moses, "Why did you make us leave Egypt to die in the wilderness? There is no bread and no water, and we have come to loathe this miserable food." The Lord sent seraph serpents among the people. They bit the people and many of the Israelites died. The people came to Moses and said "We sinned by speaking against the Lord and against you. Intercede with the Lord to take away the serpents from us!" And Moses interceded for the people (Num. 21:4–6).

An intercessor might petition his God to act for someone's benefit or against an enemy. We are shown Moses interceding with God, asking Him to turn away from the offering of certain rebels (Num. 16:15). In most of the reported cases Moses' intercession met with success; but not always. When Miriam badmouthed Moses because of his marriage to a Cushite woman God punished her with "snow white scales," presumedly leprosy; then "Moses called out unto the Lord, saying 'O Lord, pray heal her' " (Num. 12:13), but God refused an immediate reprieve and Miriam suffered for a week before she was cured. The role of the intercessor belongs to the image of the holy man and the prophet, not to the practical man of affairs.

Theoretically, the independent power of a prayermaster is incompatible with a faith which emphasizes God's control of history and God's *hesed*, His covenant loyalty. If God is just and dependable what reason or right would anyone have to intercede with Him? But the evidence is clear that Moses is presented as an idealized type of a familiar class of holy men who interceded for individuals or the community and who were venerated and feared for their success in this role.

A peculiar and special meaning of heroism among the Israelites is suggested by this aspect of the Moses tradition. It was a risky business to be courtier to a pharaoh or an Assyrian emperor or to the King of kings. The courtier who tries to change the royal mind draws the sultan's attention to himself, sometimes with unwanted results. "The wrath of a king is as messengers of death" (Prov. 16:14). When Moses interceded with God after the sin of the Golden Calf he knew that his life was on the line. "If you will forgive their sins, well and good; but if not, erase me from the record you have written" (Exod. 32:32).

The mindset of the Israelite was markedly different from ours; but man is by nature a pragmatic beast, and in every age men have turned to faith to secure prosperity and security. Today we tinker with political structures or we turn to the laboratory or the research institute for answers. We operate with the assumption 'can do.' The Israelite operated with the assumption 'only God can do.' The Israelites looked to God to rectify the insecurity of his society. Change came slowly, if at all. All experience seemed to confirm the observation that God, not man, controlled history. Naturally, it was to his interest to discover how he could persuade God to his benefit. The Israelite faith insisted that God based His decisions on a published covenant to which He had committed himself. Fidelity to the covenant was taught as the key to security; but since no nation or individual is that constant in his actions, it was desirable that there be extra covenantal means of winning God's favor. A special hero emerges; the person who could effectively plead with God when the nation or individual failed in his duty, which is to say, whenever evil befell man or people.

If what I am describing smacks suspiciously of the later Christian cult of saints, so be it. The similarities are real. To be sure, apologists can marshal an impressive array of rabbinic texts which prohibit praying to any save God. "If trouble comes to a person, let him not cry to Michael or Gabriel, but let him cry unto Me" (P. T. Ber. 9:12); but the evidence is overwhelming that throughout their history the Jewish people did consult holy men. The last chapter of a second century B.C.E. apocalypse, *The Testament of Moses*, features a scene in which Moses announces his impending death. Joshua, the chosen successor, immediately prostrates himself, openly grieving. What is his chief concern? "Who shall pray for them"[18] which is to say 'how will the tribes survive without having available a proven intercessor?' To this pious writer it was not Moses' competence as leader which would be missed, but the proven power of Moses' prayer. In early rabbinic times the popular faith knew of *Tzaddikm* whose lives had been so exemplary that they had built up with God a deposit of merits which they could draw on when necessary. Throughout Jewish history the Torah's report of Moses' life provided the popular faith with its model of such an intercessor.

[18] Testament 11:11 *cf.* also 12:6.

How did a holy man prove that he is holy? He spoke God's words. He announced God's redeeming acts. He cured illness. He pleaded with God for rain. He performed ritual and oracular acts which were expected of him. He brought the symbols of God to the battlefield. Moses' role as prophet was the unique and ultimate proof of his holiness. In exilic and post-exilic times the emphasis seems to shift from prophet-intercessor to prophet-mediator. By then the idea that a unique covenant relationship bound Israel and God was commonly accepted as was the idea that the terms of the covenant had been announced by Moses. Several versions of this critical event existed: the law had been given on the mountain of revelation; the law had been given on the mountain and during the remaining years of the wilderness trek; the law had been given at various times to Moses who published it at a great covenant ceremony just before his death. The inconsistencies in the Exodus-Numbers and Deuteronomy narratives reflect an imperfect amalgam of these traditions; but, clearly, the thrust of piety and tradition operated over the centuries to ascribe all law deemed covenant to the mediation of Moses. By post-exilic time the identification of Israel's oracular law with the rule mediated by Moses was conventional and uncontested. The law is given "through the hand of Moses" (I Chron. 6:34, 15:15, 22:13; II Chron. 33:8, 34:14). Outside a few mentions of Moses for genealogical purposes (I Chron. 23:14–15, 26:14) and two references to Moses as builder of the desert tabernacle (I Chron. 21:29; II Chron. 1:3); post-exilic priestly writings make no reference to Moses except to identify him with the law that he had mediated: "The Torah of God which was given through the agency of Moses" (Neh. 10:30), the Torah of Moses (Exod. 3:2; Neh. 8:14, 9:14; II Chron. 23:18, 30:11), the book of Moses (Ezek. 6:18; Neh. 13:12; I Chron. 35:12), the book of the Torah of Moses (Neh. 8:1), the commandments of Moses (II Chron. 8:13), the Torah in the book of Moses (II Chron. 25:4). The single reference to Moses in post-exilic prophecy appears in the concluding piety of the scroll of Malachi and indicates simply: "Remember the law of Moses, my servant, which I commanded unto him in Horeb for all Israel" (3:22).

The law is not by Moses but delivered by Moses. Moses is not lawgiver but prophet-mediator of God's law. When Near Eastern emperors promulgated basic law, law often similar in style and even substance to the Biblical rules, the king is described as having been ordered by Shamash or another god to issue the rule; but there is no attempt to hide the king's initiative and authority in the matter. Shamash reveals abstract justice to the king. The king translates the divine abstraction 'justice' into discrete rules. He claims to make his law conform to justice; but the law is his.[19] The Biblical

[19] Greenberg, Moshe, "Some Postulates of Biblical Criminal Law," in *The Jewish Expression*, ed. Goldin, Judah, Bantam, N. Y. C., 1970, p. 21.

law is God's and God's alone. Moses does not write a law book based on his own feelings or research, but receives the law from God and repeats the law to the tribes or writes it down for posterity as if he were a stenographer taking God's dictation. The interest is not in the man but in the message.

Moses, as presented to us by the Torah text, is an exception to the rule that the legends of great men grow through the centuries. If anything, the received text diminishes Moses' role. He is *ish-ha-elohim* God's man, and not his own man; *eved adonai* God's faithful servitor, not a powerful leader in his own right. Moses is emissary of God's word, not a royal figure. It is best to think of the Moses of the received text as having been drawn after the model of Near Eastern holy men and prophets. His is not the heroism of the sagas but the heroism of the charismatic. He is presented to us not as a leader of men but as the servant of God.

From earliest times in Israel, generation after generation has told the story of the great God who . . .

Le Psaume VIII commenté par Salmōn b. Yerūḥīm

By GEORGES VAJDA
Université de la Sorbonne Nouvelle Paris III

LES VICISSITUDES QUI sont le lot de l'ancienne littérature karaïte n'ont pas épargné Salmōn b. Yerūḥīm bien que la connaissance que nous avons de son oeuvre soit relativement moins imparfaite que l'information sur celle de plusieurs de ses aînés ou cadets.[1] La partie non explorée de ses écrits demeure néanmoins très considérable et l'exploitation de ce qui en est présentement accessible voire publié laisse encore beaucoup à désirer. Nous n'en donnerons pour exemple que son volumineux commentaire sur les Psaumes dont une partie avait été imprimée, avec une annotation réduite à peu de choses près à l'identification des citations bibliques, d'après un seul manuscrit dont l'éditeur possédait un photostat depuis de longues années. Parue en 1956,[2] cette publication partielle n'a pas été continuée. L'éditeur, qui ne fournit pas, outre la cote, IIe collection Firkovic 1345, le moindre détail sur le document sur lequel il a travaillé, semble avoir ignoré que la Bibliothèque d'État de Leningrad possédait encore une autre copie du même ouvrage. L'auteur de ces lignes eut la bonne fortune d'obtenir des microfilms de l'un et de l'autre manuscrit; celui que M. Marwick s'était procuré dès 1939 (nous le désignerons par le sigle A) contient la traduction et le commentaire des quatre-vingt-neuf premiers psaumes; l'autre (cote 1345 (II), sigle B) ne va pas au-delà de Ps. LXXII. La bibliothèque de Leningrad détient sans doute un ou plusieurs exemplaires du commentaire complet, mais nous ne possédons aucun renseignement sur ce point.

Il nous semble peu utile de tenter une description détaillée des deux documents sur la base de microfilms, d'exécution parfaite du reste (et agrandis par les soins du service photographique de l'Institut de Recherche et d'Histoire des Textes). Voici seulement un très bref signalement de l'un et de l'autre (notons d'entrée de jeu que la plus récente des deux copies ne dépend point de l'autre).

Le manuscrit A est acéphale; il en manque un ou deux feuillets (le premier conservé est d'ailleurs rapporté, d'une main autre et d'une mise en page différente de celles de la suite), et on relève plusieurs lacunes et

[1] Il suffit de renvoyer ici à Z. ANKORI, *Karaites in Byzantium*, New York, 1959, p. 164, n. 298, et à G. VAJDA, *Deux commentaires karaïtes sur l'Ecclésiaste*, Leyde, 1971, p. 8.

[2] *The Arabic Commentary of Salmon ben Yeruham the Karaite on the Book of Psalms, Chapters 42–47. Edited from the unique manuscript in the State Public Library in Leningrad by Lawrence MARWICK*. Philadelphia, The Dropsie College, 1956.

feuillets détériorés dans le reste. Il fut transcrit à Damas par Isaac b. Samuel b. Joseph b. Samuel b. Joseph, dit RWGK (?), qui date son travail de l'an 1703 de l'ère d'Alexandre correspondant à 793 de l'hégire (9 décembre 1390—28 novembre 1391; en fait l'an 1703 de l'ère des *šṭārōt* (ou Séleucides) correspond à 1391-2 de l'ère chrétienne).

Le manuscrit B n'est pas signé, mais porte la date de rajab 921 de l'hégire (11 août—9 septembre 1515).

Notre propos est de présenter ici le commentaire du Psaume VIII.[3] Dans ce texte, Salmōn ne dédaigne pas de recourir, en dépit de son attitude généralement anti-intellectualiste, à la dialectique du *Kalām*, et l'on y trouve aussi quelques détails non sans intérêt, d'ordre exégétique et idéologique.

Après avoir rappelé une interprétation assez incolore du terme technique *gittīt*[4] et précisé, selon sa méthode constamment suivie dans ce commentaire, la connexion de ce psaume avec le précédent, Salmōn passe à la traduction[5] et à l'exégèse du texte.

Ce psaume est, d'un bout à l'autre, de louange (*tamjīd*, "glorification").

(Vs. 2) *Seigneur, notre Maître* (*sayyidnā*), *combien majestueux*[6] *est ton Nom dans toute la terre*, [*toi*] *qui as placé ta splendeur* (*bahāka*) *sur le ciel. YHWH* *ᵓadōnēnū* connote la profession de la souveraineté [divine] (*iqrār bil-rubūbiyya*) et [l'idée] que c'est à partir des traces de son oeuvre (*ᵓāṯār ṣanᶜatih*) que l'on conclut (*yastadill*) au Créateur, puissant et majestueux. L'écrivain inspiré déclare dans le même sens (Job XXXVII, 23): *Šadday lōᵓ meṣāᵓnūhū saggīᵓ kōaḥ*; il veut dire [l'Être] Suffisant [à soi-même], nous ne l'appréhendons pas en son essence (*lam najidhū wajda ḏāt*), c'est-à-dire nous n'en avons pas de connaissance directe (*lam nušāhidhū*); cependant nous savons qu'il est *saggīᵓ kōaḥ*, immensément puissant (*ᶜaẓīm al-qudra*); l'immensité de sa puissance est connue à partir des marques imprimées par son oeuvre (*taᵓṯīr al-ṣanᶜa*)[7] sur le ciel et la terre, ainsi que par l'agencement et la composition (*tartīb wa-taᵓlīf*) de l'homme.

[3] Ms. A, fol. 38ᵛ–41, suivant la foliotation marquée dans la bibliothèque de Leningrad sur le coin supérieur gauche; ms B, fol. 54–58ᵛ, foliotation de l'agrandissement du microfilm.

[4] "*gittīt* est, dit-on (*qālū*), un instrument de musique comme *tōf*, *māḥōl*, *minīm* et *ᶜugāb*"; pour d'autres explications laissant plus de place à l'imagination, on peut voir le karaïte contemporain David b. Abraham al-Fāsī, *Jāmiᶜ al-alfāẓ*, éd. Skoss, I, 355, 10–15, ainsi que Saadia, éd. Y. Ḳāfaḥ, Jérusalem, 1966, p. 64, et Yefet b. ᶜElī, éd. J. J. L. Bargès, Paris, 1861, p. 11.

[5] Traduction délibérément servile, qui ne recule pas devant le barbarisme; afin de donner une idée de la méthode de l'exégète, nous n'hésiterons pas à calquer ces transpositions littérales.

[6] A *ajzar*, litt. "surabondant"; B *aᶜẓam*; dans sa singularité, la leçon de A parait plus

Tout cela est évoqué dans ce psaume, et d'abord le ciel. En disant *ᵓašer tenāh hōdkā*, [le Psalmiste] exprime l'idée que l'homme a le sentiment de la splendeur et de la magnificence (*bahāᵓ*, *bahja*) [de Dieu], lorsqu'il voit le ciel, substance pure, solidement établi par la puissance du Miséricordieux, alors qu'il n'a ni fondements ni piliers. [L'homme] acquiert alors la certitude (*taḥaqqaqa*) que le ciel est créé.

C'est à cette idée que fit allusion Salomon lorsque les deux hommes, Itīᵓēl et Ūkal lui demandèrent des éclaircissements (*tibyān*) sur l'adventicité (*ḥidaṯ*) du monde. Il leur dit (Prov. XXX, 4): *Qui est monté au ciel et en est descendu?* Autrement dit: le ciel que voici a inéluctablement besoin d'un agent qui l'a confectionné (*ṣāniᶜ ṣanaᶜahā*). Or de deux choses l'une: ou bien le ciel s'est produit lui-même ou bien c'est un producteur qui l'a produit (*muḥdiṯ ᵓaḥdaṯahā*). Admettre la première branche de l'alternative nous place devant un nouveau dilemme: le ciel s'est produit soit avant soit après qu'il ait existé. La première solution est absurde, car le moyen pour ce qui n'est pas de l'ordre de l'existence (*laysa min al-wujūd*) de produire ou d'agir! Direz-vous qu'il s'est produit une fois existant? C'est admettre nécessairement qu'il n'a rien fait puisqu'il était déjà existant. Si vous dites que c'est un autre qui l'a produit, informez-moi: *Qui est monté au ciel et en est descendu?* Quelle est la créature qui a gravi le ciel, l'a arrangé, agencé et confectionné sous la forme que nous lui voyons, puis en est descendu? On conclura donc nécessairement que c'est un être incréé qui l'a produit et oeuvré par sa puissance et son unicité, et ce [n']est [autre que] le Seigneur,[8] ainsi que le proclame l'Écriture (Is. XLIV, 24): *Tout seul, j'étends le ciel* et (Ps. CXXXVI, 5): [*Louez*] *Celui qui fait le ciel avec intelligence*, et on en dira autant quant aux autres créatures.

(Vs. 3) *De la bouche des enfants et des nourrissons tu as fondé la force en face de tes ennemis afin que tu mettes à néant* (*tuᶜaṭṭil*) *l'ennemi et le vindicatif.* [Par ces paroles, le Psalmiste] entend ce que les créatures[9] discernent de la

authentique; B semble l'avoir banalisée, peut-être sous l'influence de la version de Saadia; David b. Abraham, *Jāmiᶜ* I, 35, 55, traduit par *jalīl*, de même Yefet.

[7] Nous dirions: le monde visible porte la marque de fabrique de son producteur. Noter que dans sa traduction et commentaire, *in loc.*, Saadia va (éd. Y. Ḳāfaḥ, Jérusalem, s.d., p. 183 *sq.*) moins loin: Dieu n'est pas inconnaissable; c'est seulement la connaissance exhaustive de ses attributs qui est refusée à l'homme (*cf.* également l'introduction à son commentaire sur le *Livre de la Création*).

[8] Le commentaire de Saadia à ce verset des *Proverbes*, éd. J. Derenbourg et M. Lambert, Paris, 1894, p. 185 (pas de parallèles dans *Amānāt* et *Tafsīr Kitāb al-Mabādiᵓ*) est, différemment, une mise en garde contre l'excessive curiosité en matière de cosmologie et de physique; voir aussi *Deux commentaires*, p. 131, n. 2.

[9] Les hommes.

puissance de Dieu, en considérant[10] le langage (*nuṭq*) révélateur[11] de la raison. En effet, l'être humain commence par être un "petit" (*ṭifl*), dépourvu de langage (*ʾabkam*, *ʾakhras*) ne parlant ni ne s'exprimant. Puis, par la puissance de Dieu, sa langue est déliée, et alors il parle et s'exprime. L'Écriture dit à ce propos (Is. LVII, 19): [*Dieu*] *crée le fruit des lèvres.*

L'auteur veut mettre en évidence le passage de l'homme d'un état à un autre, chacun de ses états étant une merveille. Il commence par être une goutte [de sperme] déversée dans la matrice comme du lait liquide (*al-laban al-rajrāj*); ensuite cette goutte se caille comme le fromage et devient, os, veines (nerfs), cartilages et [finit par] se mouvoir grâce au souffle de vie (*nasamat al-ḥayāt*), ainsi que le proclame (Job X, 10–12, cité en abrégé): *Ne m'as-tu pas versé comme du lait . . . de peau et de chair tu me vêtis . . . de la vie tu m'accordas la grâce.* En évoquant la "grâce" (*ḥesed*), l'auteur veut désigner la faveur (*faḍl*) que Dieu témoigne à l'être humain alors que celui-ci est dans le sein de sa mère: don, à la fois, de la vie et de la nourriture. [Le Psalmiste CXXXIX, 15] dit à ce sujet: *quand j'étais fait dans le secret.* Puis, étonnante merveille, sa sortie de la matrice, lieu pourtant étroit, comme le dit (encore le Psalmiste XXII, 10): *c'est toi qui m'as tiré de la matrice.* Ensuite la section du cordon ombilical, sans souffrance ni douleur pour l'enfant ni pour la mère, ce que relève (le Psalmiste LXXI, 6): *c'est toi qui me détaches du ventre de ma mère.*[12] L'homme une fois né, son Seigneur pourvoit à sa subsistance afin de le diriger vers Lui: (Ps. XXII, 10) *tu m'as confié aux mamelles de ma mère.* Au stade suivant, son corps et ses membres deviennent forts si bien qu'il est capable de s'asseoir, après quoi Dieu, par sa puissance, lui donne le langage et le transfère successivement de l'état de nourrisson (*ṭufūliyya*) à l'enfance (*ṣabwa*), à l'adolescence (*ḥadāṯa*),

[10] Litt. "par."

[11] Traduction conjecturale. Les deux manuscrits portent *ʾLMBTR*, qui représente l'article défini plus un participe de deuxième ou de quatrième forme, mais les dérivés des racines *BTR*, *BTHR* ne donnent pas de sens plausible dans le contexte. On pourrait penser à une altération paléographiquement concevable, en supposant un archétype en caractères arabes, de *ʾLMᶜBR*, *al-muᶜabbir*, qui conviendrait fort bien (ainsi, dans un développement beaucoup plus abondant, mais parallèle quant au fond, chez Baḥyē Ibn Paqūda, *Hidāya*, éd. Yahuda, p. 113, 10–11 = Ḳāfaḥ, p. 116, 9: *al-nuṭq . . . alladhī yuᶜabbir bihi ᶜammā fī nafsihi wa-ḍamīrih*), mais la construction fait difficulté (*lil-ᶜaql*, au lieu de *ᶜan al-ᶜaql*); cette difficulté serait moins grave sinon éliminée avec certitude en supposant une leçon primitive *ʾLMTRJM*, *al-mutarjim* (Baḥyē qualifie dans la suite la langue de *turjumān al-nafs*), mais plus malaisée à justifier paléographiquement. Au sujet des altérations qui pourraient s'expliquer par des erreurs survenues lors de la transcription des textes judéo-arabes en *nasẖī* en caractères hébraïques, voir le récent article de M. Leon NEMOY, "The Factor of Script in the Textual Criticism of Judaeo-Arabic Manuscripts," *JQR*, LXVI (1975/76), pp. 148–159.

[12] A partir d'ici, le texte est imparfaitement conservé dans A.

à la vigueur de la jeunesse (*quwwat al-shabāb*), à l'âge mûr (*kuhūla*), enfin à la décrépitude et la faiblesse (*haram, ḍuʿf*).

Tout cela est un indice qu'il existe un être qui dirige et gouverne (*musayyir, mudabbir*) l'homme, selon la parole de Job (XIX, 27): *Je vois Dieu à partir de ma chair.*[13]

L'homme ne disposerait-il que de la démonstration fournie par ses organes corporels et l'ordonnance déterminée par la sagesse de chacun de ceux-ci (*dalālat al-aʿḍāʾ alladhi* [!] *fī jismih wa-kayfa kull wāḥid minhā limaʿnā ḥikamī wa-sabab yaḍtarr ilayh*) qu'il y trouverait la pleine certitude qu'il a un Créateur sage, puissant dont le Nom est béni.

On comprend à présent le verset. C'est à partir du témoignage délivré par[14] la parole des enfants au sein et le changement de leurs états que tu as fondé la force de l'argument et des preuves (*ḥujja, barāhīn*) de ton unité et de ta souveraineté (*tawḥīd, rubūbiyya*). Et la suite du verset signifie: réduire à néant l'argument de tout ennemi et éliminer toute doctrine mensongère (*madhhab kadhib*). Par "vindicatif," il faut entendre les doctrines de tous les ennemis d'Israël.[15]

(Vs. 4) *Quand je regarde tes cieux, oeuvres de tes doigts, la lune et les astres auxquels tu as donné être et figure* (*kawwanta wahayyaʾta*).

[Le Psalmiste] évoque de nouveau le ciel afin de mentionner les marques qu'il porte de l'oeuvre [divine]; c'est l'idée que met en évidence l'expression *oeuvre de tes doigts;* [le mot] "doigts"[16] désigne la puissance; il n'est pas qualification de Dieu par un membre. Que la création du ciel ne s'opéra point par une intervention corporelle,[17] ressort avec clarté de (Ps. XXXIII, 6): *Par la parole du Seigneur furent faits les cieux.* Nous savons dès lors de science certaine (*yaqīn*) qu'il ne faut pas entendre littéralement (*ʿalā ẓāhir al-lafẓ*) l'expression "oeuvre de tes doigts." L'Écriture veut évoquer ces oeuvres [divines] particulièrement subtiles que sont les étoiles fixes et les planètes, de même qu'elle emploie "doigt" en parlant (dans Ex. XXXI, 18) de l'écriture des 'Tables'

[13] Au sujet de l'emploi fait de ce verset dans les spéculations cosmologiques et anthropologiques, *cf.* les références groupées par A. ALTMANN, *Studies in Religious Philosophy and Mysticism*, Londres, 1969, pp. 3–4. A propos des âges successifs qui jalonnent la vie de l'homme, *cf.* l'ouvrage récent de Dimitri GUTAS, *Greek Wisdom Literature in Arabic Translation* (American Oriental Series, 60), New Haven, pp. 227–231. Les divisions rapportées par deux auteurs musulmans du Xe siècle, al-ʿĀmirī (*ṣabī, šābb, kahl, šaykh*) et al-Tawḥīdī (*ḥadātha, šabāb, šaykhūkha*) diffèrent de celles données dans notre texte.

[14] *Mimmā yušāhad min*; le verbe arabe connote le témoignage et l'expérience concrète immédiate.

[15] Apès cette phrase, les deux manuscrits divergent; *cf.* ci-après, n. 29.

[16] Le copiste de B (le passage n'est pas conservé dans A) a écrit par distraction *al-aʿmāl* au lieu de *al-ʿawāmil.*

[17] Litt. "n'est ni une saisie (*baṭš*) ni un membre (*jāriḥa*)."

écrites par le doigt de Dieu; le but de ces évocations est d'amener les hommes à réfléchir aux oeuvres divines dont la contemplation les fera conclure à [l'existence de] leur Artisan, que son Nom soit béni.[18] L'Écriture recommande dans le même sens (Is. XL, 26): *levez les yeux en haut et voyez qui a créé ces êtres.*

(Vs. 5) *Qu'est-ce que l'homme pour que tu te souviennes de lui et qu'est (donc) le fils d'Adam pour que tu le distingues?* Autrement dit: à l'homme qui commence[19] dans la poussière et qui finit dans la poussière, tu as octroyé une haute valeur (*ja*ʿ*alta lahū miqdār jalīl*), par la raison, le discernement, la station droite, la crainte qu'il inspire, la dignité et la beauté, comme le souligne la suite:

(Vs. 6) *Tu l'as fait inférieur de peu aux anges et [l'as couronné] de gloire et de beauté.* Son infériorité par rapport aux anges tient à ce qu'il meurt et se nourrit. [Mais] c'est l'homme seul, à l'exclusion des anges, qui est qualifié des dons en question, et c'est ce que l'Écriture[20] désigne par le terme de *kābōd*. De même, seul l'homme parmi les êtres de la terre entend la parole de Dieu,[21] ainsi que le dirent nos pères (Deut. V, 21): *Voici que le Seigneur notre Dieu nous a fait voir sa gloire.*[22] Et [ce privilège] trouve son application dans (*yunṣaraf ilā*) la crainte devant Adam et sa race, inspirée par Dieu à tous les animaux comme cela a été proclamé à l'époque de Noé (Gen. IX, 2): *La crainte et l'effroi [que vous inspirez] s'imposeront à tous les animaux de la terre et à tous les oiseaux des cieux*). Bien que les bêtes féroces soient hostiles à l'homme,[23] elles le redoutent jusqu'au moment où Dieu lui retire sa protection et le leur livre, comme il est dit (I Rois XIII, 26): *le Seigneur l'a livré au lion qui l'a broyé*[24] *et mis à mort.* La même idée est énoncée dans la suite du texte:

(Vs. 7) *Tu lui donnes la domination sur l'oeuvre de tes mains*, et dans la Tora (Gen. I, 28): *ayez autorité sur les poissons de la mer . . .* et (I, 26): *qu'ils aient autorité sur les poissons de la mer . . .*[25]

[18] La rédaction de cette phrase est gauche, mais l'enseignement, d'ailleurs banal à l'époque, que le commentateur veut tirer des textes, est clair.

[19] Prend origine.

[20] *dawarān al-kitāb*; l'emploi, insolite, de *dawarān* "rotation," s'explique peut-être par la locution *dāra l-kalām* (*cf.* l'emploi similaire de "tournure" en français, *Wendung* en allemand, *giro* en italien et en espagnol).

[21] Le copiste a écrit *kl* ʾ*l*ʾ*mh*, en deux mots, au lieu de *kl*ʾ*mh* (*kalāmahū*).

[22] La citation s'arrête ici, mais la suite est également pertinente: *et sa grandeur, nous avons entendu sa voix du milieu du feu.*

[23] La construction de la phrase est incorrecte, à moins que le texte ne soit altéré, mais le sens est clair.

[24] *Lapsus* du copiste, *wyšmrhw* au lieu de *wyšbrhw*.

(Vs. 9) *Oiseau[x] du ciel et poissons de la mer [ce qui] passe les chemins des mers.* Dans la Tora, les versets (Gen. I, 26 et 28) qui proclament la domination de l'homme sur les animaux se présentent suivant le déroulement de la création: poissons créés le cinquième jour, bétail, etc., le sixième. Ici, les êtres sont énumérés dans l'ordre inverse, suivant leur proximité par rapport à l'homme qui vit au sein de la civilisation. Dans la Tora (Gen. I, 26), la mention de la terre est insérée dans l'énumération: *et sur toute la terre*, [addition] qui évoque l'intelligence octroyée par Dieu à l'homme, grâce à laquelle celui-ci réalise les grandes constructions,[26] laboure le sol et l'ensemence de diverses sortes de graines et de plantes et en extrait des métaux comme l'or, l'argent, le fer et le cuivre. L'expression *qui passe les chemins des mers* que l'on trouve ici fait allusion à la construction[27] des bateaux et des barques qui permettent [à l'homme] de passer d'une rive à l'autre, ainsi que des grands navires (*darāmīn*) qui peuvent contenir une très grosse quantité de marchandises et qui peuvent servir à la navigation au long cours. Et[28] Dieu a gratifié l'homme de la sagesse par laquelle celui-ci s'entend à fabriquer des nacelles en papyrus qui lui assurent la traversée sans naufrage dans les parcours semés de rochers, comme il est dit (Is. XVIII, 2): *des nacelles de papyrus sur la face des eaux. Tous* (au vs. 8) désigne les autres animaux non spécifiés ici.

(Vs. 10) *Seigneur, notre Maître*, etc. La fin de ce psaume reprend, à l'instar de beaucoup d'autres, son commencement: évocation [donc] de la puissance immense, proclamation de l'unité, et louange du Miséricordieux.

APPENDICE[29]

Dans le manuscrit A, le verso du fol. 40 présente des anomalies. Il commence (dans le commentaire de vs. 3) par *al-ṭifl* qui correspond à B 55^{v}, pu., mais après le sixième mot (*yaqūl*), la suite du texte, jusqu'aux trois premiers mots de vs. 4 cités en hébreu (C = B, fin de 56^{r}), est écrite sur

[25] Le reste du commentaire du vs. 7 et celui du vs. 8 sont purement philologiques: "*mᶜsy* est écrit avec un *yod*, c'est pourquoi j'ai traduit par *oeuvres* (*afᶜāl*) et non par *oeuvre* (*fiᶜl*) puisque le mot ne se termine pas par un *hé* (vs. 8) [à propos du mot *ṣōneh*] il s'agit de l'ensemble du petit et du gros bétail, animaux domestiques comme sauvages; le mot *ṣnh* se retrouve dans *lṣnᵓkm* (Nomb. XXXII, 24), tandis que *ṣᵓnkm* (Ex. X, 24 et ailleurs) se rattache à *ṣᵓn*."

[26] Litt. "les palais, les forteresses et les citadelles (*al-quṣūr wal-ḥuṣūn wal-qilāᶜ*).

[27] Litt. "constructeur" (*ṣāniᶜ*, calquant le participe *ᶜōbēr* de l'hébreu). La syntaxe de cette phrase, en elle-même limpide de sens, est de nouveau fort lâche.

[28] A partir d'ici, nous retrouvons la concordance entre A et B.

[29] *Cf.* ci-dessus, n. 15.

les marges (le copiste a marqué l'addition par un signe de renvoi): d'abord à droite, verticalement, puis en bas, enfin en haut, tête-bêche par rapport au corps du texte. Du fragment qui couvre le reste de la page et qui n'a pas de correspondant dans B, seule une partie (lig. 11, avant-dernier mot—lig. 15, fin de page) se rapporte clairement au psaume commenté (vs. 7); ce qui précède est une démonstration, fondée sur Ps. CXLVIII, du caractère créé des anges, au même titre que des corps célestes et terrestres. Quant à ce qui subsiste du commentaire de vs. 7, en voici la traduction.

> *Tu lui confères la domination sur les oeuvres de tes mains, tu as placé toute chose sous ses pieds*, conséquence de la crainte [révérentielle éprouvée à son égard][30] dont tu l'as gratifié, ainsi qu'il est dit (au verset précédent): *de gloire et de beauté tu l'as couronné. Kābōd* s'applique à la prophétie[31] parce que la lumière que la nation [d'Israël] appelle *shekīnāh* n'est manifestée par Dieu à aucune des créatures terrestres . . . (fin du fragment).

[30] *hayba.*
[31] Litt. "notion de la prophétie."

A Biblical Echo of Mesopotamian Royal Rhetoric

By NAHUM M. WALDMAN
The Dropsie University

NUMEROUS WRITERS HAVE pointed out the influence of Mesopotamian royal inscriptions upon the idiom of the Bible. Themes such as the election of the king by the gods, their endorsement and support for him, his role as shepherd and liberator, and his achievements as builder of temples and palaces have been discerned in the Bible and in Aramaic royal inscriptions, based ultimately upon Sumerian and Akkadian royal inscriptions.[1] The goal of this study is to demonstrate a specific parallel between the Mesopotamian royal inscriptions and the Bible, that relating to the theme of the journey through impossible terrain, desert and mountain, and the opening, by the king, of paths never before trodden.

The following abbreviations will be used:

AfO—*Archiv für Orientforschung*.

AKA—L. W. King, *The Annals of the Kings of Assyria* (London, 1902).

ANET—J. Pritchard, ed., *Ancient Near Eastern Texts Relating to the Old Testament*, 3rd edition with supplement (Princeton, 1969).

ARI—A. K. Grayson, *Assyrian Royal Inscriptions*, vols. 1 and 2 (Wiesbaden, 1972, 1974).

CAD—*The Assyrian Dictionary of the Oriental Institute of the University of Chicago* (Chicago, 1956 ff.).

CT—*Cuneiform Texts from Babylonian Tablets in the British Museum* (London, 1896 ff.). (New Haven, 1957).

EMRT—W. W. Hallo, *Early Mesopotamian Royal Titles*, American Oriental Series 43 (New Haven, 1957).

IAK—E. Ebeling, B. Meissner, and E. F. Weidner, *Die Inschriften der altassyrische Könige, Altorientalisch Bibliothek* (Leipzig, 1926).

JAOS *Journal of the American Oriental Society*.

JNES—*Journal of Near Eastern Studies*.

OIP 2—D. D. Luckenbill, *The Annals of Sennacherib, Oriental Institute Publications*, 2 (Chicago, 1924).

4 R—H. Rawlinson, *The Cuneiform Inscriptions of Western Asia* (London, 1860–1909), vol. 4.

RISA—G. A. Barton, *The Royal Inscriptions of Sumer and Akkad* (New Haven, 1929).

UET—C. J. Gadd and L. Legrain, *Ur Excavations, Texts*, 1, *Royal Inscriptions* (Philadelphia and London, 1928).

UMPBS 15—L. Legrain, *Royal Inscriptions and Fragments from Nippur and Babylon, The Museum of the University of Pennsylvania, Publications of the Babylonian Section*, 15 (Philadelphia, 1926).

WHJP 1—*World History of the Jewish People*, vol. 1, *The Dawn of Civilization*, ed. E. A. Speiser (Rutgers University Press, 1964).

[1] See S. Paul, "Deutero-Isaiah and Cuneiform Royal Inscriptions," *JAOS* 88 (1968), 180–6, and the literature cited there, pp. 181–2, nn. 2–5; *WHJP* 1, 120; H. Tawil, "The

Naram Sin (2291–2255), king of Agade, claims: *ḫarran*^{ki} *sua šar in šarrī manāma lā illik Naram-*^{il}*Sîn šar Agade*^{ki} *illikma*, "that journey, no king among the kings had marched, Naram Sin, the king of Agade, marched."[2] Hammurabi, king of Babylon (1792–1750), summing up his achievements on behalf of his people in the Epilogue to the Code, says: *ašrī šulmim ešteʾišināšim pušqi waštūtim upetti nūram ušēṣināšim*, "I sought out peaceful regions for them, I overcame grievous difficulties (lit.: I opened difficult and impenetrable places), I caused light to rise on them."[3]

The theme is widespread in Assyrian inscriptions and is more developed. Tukulti-Ninurta I (1244–1208), king of Assyria, claims: *ḫuršāni bērūti ašar lā mēteqi ša šarru jāʾumma arḫatēšunu lā idû ina līt kiššūtīja šūturti ētettiqma*, "with my surpassingly strong might I frequently traversed impassable mountains, the paths of which no other king knew."[4] The kings also reported how their men hacked through the mountains with tools, such as the *akkullu*; for example: *šadê dannūti kiṣir šapšaqī ša šarru jāʾumma arḫatēšunu lā idû ina līt kiššūtija šūturti ītettiqma ḫuršānīšunu ina akkullāt erî lûpeṣṣid arḫatēšunu lā pitāte ušpilkīma*, "with my surpassingly strong might I frequently traversed mighty mountains (and) extremely difficult ranges, the paths of which no other king knew; I cut into their mountains with copper picks and widened their impassable paths."[5] The same king, boasting of a remarkable feat of engineering, reports that he cut through certain distant mountains as straight as a string (*kīma qê lûšelliṭ*) in order to clear a path for a life-supporting stream.[6] Similarly, Ashurnasirpal II (883–859) claims: *šadû ina kallabāte parzilli akkis ina akkullī erî aqqur*, I hacked the rock with iron hatchets, cut through (it) with bronze picks."[7]

Mountains are no problem to Sennaherib (704–681), who boasts: *qirib ḫuršāni zaqrūti eqil namraṣi ina sīsî arkabma narkabat šēpāja ina tikkāte ušašši ašru šupšuqu ina šēpāja rīmāniš attagiš*, "in the midst of the high mountains

End of the Hadad Inscription in the Light of Akkadian," *JNES* 32 (1973), 477–82; *idem*, "Some Literary Elements in the Opening Sections of the Hadad, Zakir, and the Nerab II Inscriptions in the Light of East and West Semitic Royal Inscriptions," *Orientalia* 43 (1974), 40–65; R. Brauner, "The Old Aramaic *Zakir A* Inscription and Comparative Semitic Lexicography," *Gratz College Annual*, ed. by I. D. Passow and S. T. Lachs, vol. 4 (Philadelphia, 1975), 9–27; *EMRT*.

2 *UET* 1, 72, #274, II, 3–10.

3 *Epilogue, Code of Hammurabi*, Col. XLVII (Rs. XXIV), 17–21; *ANET*, 177–8.

4 E. Weidner, *Die Inschriften Tukulti-Ninurtas I und seiner Nachfolger*, *AfO Beiheft* 12 (Graz, 1959), 12, #5, 33–38; *ARI*, 1, #715.

5 Weidner, *AfO Beiheft* 12, 27, #16, 40–45; *ARI*, 1, #773. Other examples of this theme are rather numerous among other kings, as well, see, for example, *ARI*, 1 #530 (Shalmaneser I); *ARI* 2, ##13, 16, 21, 30 (Tiglath Pileser I); *ibid.*, #216 (Ashur-bel-kala); *ibid.*, ##468 (Tukulti-Ninurta II); *ibid.*, ##539, 544, 562, 568 (Ashur-nasir-apli II); *cf.* the corresponding Akkadian passages in *AKA* and *IAK*.

6 Weidner, *AfO Beiheft* 12, 30, 17, 13 f.

7 *AKA*, 230, r. 12, cited in *CAD A/1*, 276b.

I rode on horseback where the terrain was difficult and had my chariot drawn up with ropes; where it became too steep, I clambered up on foot like the wild ox."[8] The theme of the unopened path and untravelled road recurs in this king's inscriptions: *urḫī lā pitūti ṭūdī pašqūti ša lapān šadê marṣūti ullânuʾa qiribšun mamman lā illikū šarrānu pānî mahrûti*, "before my day none of the kings who lived before me had travelled the unblazed trails and wearisome paths which stretch along these rugged mountains."[9]

Ashurbanipal (668–631) is most poetic in describing the difficulties of the passage through the mountains and the desert: *nār Idiglat u nār Purattu ina mīlīšina gabšī šalmeš lū ēbirū irdû urḫī ruqûti ētillû ḫuršāni šaqûti iḫtalpū* ^is^*qištē*^mes^ *ša ṣululšina rapšū birīt iṣē*^mes^ *rabûti*^mes^ *giṣṣī* ^is^*amurdinnē*^mes^ *ḫarrān eṭṭeṭ ētettiqū šalmeš madbar ašar ṣummê kalkalti ša iṣṣurū šamê lā išaʾû qiribšu purīmē*^mes^ *ṣabāti*^mes^ *lā irteʾû ina libbi*, "they (my army) safely crossed the Tigris and the Euphrates at the time of their highest flood; they took (lit.: followed) a path (leading to) far away regions. They ascended high mountain chains, winding their way through woods full of shadow, proceeding safely upon a thorny road between high trees and *sidra*-shrubs full of spines . . . they marched forward through the desert where parching thirst is at home, where there are not even birds in the sky and wherein neither wild donkeys (nor) gazelles pasture."[10]

The last passage bears comparison with Jer. 2:2:

לכתך אחרי במדבר בארץ לא זרועה

"how thou wentest after me in the wilderness, in a land that was not sown," and with Jer. 2:6:

ולא אמרו איה ה' המעלה אתנו מארץ מצרים המוליך אתנו במדבר בארץ
ערבה ושוחה בארץ ציה וצלמות בארץ לא עבר בה איש ולא ישב אדם שם

"neither said they: 'where is the Lord that brought us up out of the land of Egypt, that led us through the wilderness, through a land of deserts and pits, through a land of drought and the shadow of death, through a land that no man passed through, and where no man dwelt."[11]

In several passages in Second Isaiah the command is given to clear a path and to pave a road for the triumphal procession of God and his people, e. g., 40:3–4:

קול קורא במדבר פנו דרך ה' ישרו בערבה מסלה לאלהינו

[8] *OIP* 2, 26, col. I, 68–71.

[9] *Ibid.*, 37, col. IV, 15–17.

[10] M. Streck, *Assurbanipal und die letzten assyrischen Könige*, *Vorderasiatische Bibliothek* 7 (Leipzig, 1916), 2, 70, 79–90; *ANET*, 299; on *halāpu*, "wind, slink," see *CAD Ḫ*, 35.

[11] For a discussion of many parallels in language between Deuteronomy, Jeremiah, and Mesopotamian literature, see M. Weinfeld, *Deuteronomy and the Deuteronomic School* (Oxford: Clarendon Press, 1972), 59–157, 320–65.

"Hark, one calleth: clear ye in the wilderness the way of the Lord, make straight in the desert a highway for our God," 57:14:

ואמר סלו סלו פנו דרך הרימו מכשול מדרך עמי

"and he will say, 'cast ye up, cast ye up, clear the way, take up the stumbling-block out of the way of my people," and 62:10:

עברו עברו בשערים פנו דרך העם סלו סלו המסלה סקלו מאבן

"Go through, go through the gates, clear ye the way of the people; cast up, cast up the highway, gather out the stones."

A hint of the theme of solemn and triumphant procession is given by the use of the verse *aštamdiḫ*, from *šadāḫu*, "march in procession," in an inscription of Sennacherib: *anāku kīma rīmi ekdi panuššun aṣbat ḫurrī naḫallī nadbak šadî mēlê marṣūti ina kussî aštamdiḫ ašar ana kussî šupšuqu ina šēpāja aštaḫiṭ*, "I, like a strong wild ox, went before them; gullies, mountain torrents and waterfalls, dangerous cliffs I surmounted in my sedan chair. Where it was too steep for my chair, I advanced (lit.: leapt) on foot."[12] The verb *šadāḫu* is used in an inscription of Nebuchadrezzar II: *bābu šuātum ana aṣê u nīribi ša apli bēl ilāni* [il]*Nabû ša išaddiḫa ana qirib Babili*[ki] *unammir kīma ūm* (sic!), "this gate, for the departure and entering of the son of the lord of the gods, Nabu, who comes in procession into Babylon, I made shine like the day."[13]

It is important to consider these themes in Second Isaiah in the context of other themes, some of which also derive from Mesopotamian royal rhetoric. We have noted above that Tukulti-Ninurta reports on his cutting through the mountains in order to make a passage for the nourishing waters. Similarly, Sennacherib relates the following: *ana berâte šummuḫi ultu pāṭi* [al]*Kisiri mūlâ mušpālum ina akkulāte aḫra ušēšir pattu mê*[mes] *šunūte ṣīr tamīrti*

[12] *OIP* 2, 36, col. IV, 2–5. *Cf.* Cyrus Cylinder, *VAB* 3, 4, 24.

[13] *UMPBS* 15, 39, col. I, 73–75. The influence of the Babylonian "Sacred Way" and literature connected with it upon the imagery of Second Isaiah has been recognized, *cf.* J. L. McKenzie, S. J., *Anchor Bible*, *Second Isaiah* (New York, 1968), 10, 12, in connection with Isa. 35:8. It might be observed, however, that this "Sacred Way" is not mainly within a city, as was the processional road of Babylon, but leads through the wilderness to it. The context of Isa. 35:1–10, accepting the common ascription of the chapter to Second Isaiah, is that of the wilderness, with streams being opened in the desert. See the continuation of this study for Mesopotamian parallels. On the theme of the "Sacred Way" see also F. Stummer, "Einige keilschriftliche Parallelen zu Jes. 40–66," *JBL* 45 (1926), 171–89; C. Westermann, *Isaiah 40–66, A Commentary* (Philadelphia, 1969), 38–9; A. Moortgart, *The Art of Ancient Mesopotamia* (London and New York: Phaidon, 1969), 161–2, Pls. 290, 291; H. W. F. Saggs, *The Greatness That Was Babylon* (New York: Mentor, 1968), 367. In connection with this theme, it is of interest to compare Isa. 54:12 and 60:18, which speak of richly decorated gates and gates with triumphant names. On the writing of the last word quoted from the inscription, *u-um* in the text, see the discussion on final vowels in Neo-Babylonian in D. B. Weisberg, *Guild Structure and Political Allegiance in Early Achaemenid Mesopotamia*, *Yale Near Eastern Researches*, 1 (New Haven and London, 1967), 106–111.

Ninua[ki] *ukīnamma qirib ṣippāte šâtina ušaḫbiba atappîš*, "to increase the productiveness of the cultivable (lit.: low-lying) fields, from the border of the city of Kisiri, through the high and low ground I dug with pickaxes, I ran a canal; those waters I brought across the plain (around) Nineveh and made them flow through the orchards in irrigation ditches"[14] and *aššu mālak mê*[mes] *šunūti šadê*[mes] *marṣūti ašri pašqūti ina akkullāte ušattirma muṣûšun ušēšira ana tamīrti Ninua*[ki], "to (give) these waters a course (through) the steep mountains, I cut through the difficult places with pickaxes and directed their outflow on to the plain of Nineveh."[15]

It cannot be denied that the biblical narrative of the wandering of the Israelites through the desert has also inspired the imagery of Second Isaiah,[16] but this does not rule out the Mesopotamian influence. It may be suggested that the motifs of supplying water and providing straight roads are to be subsumed under the more general theme of the shepherd and provider, e. g., [d]li.bi.it Ištar síb.búr.na nibru[ki] engar.zi urí[ki].ma, "Lipit-Ishtar, the humble shepherd of Nippur, the just irrigator of Ur,"[17] warad.[d]Sîn ú.a urí[ki].ma...síb.nig.si.sá ukù.dagal.la.na ú.sal ne.in.nàd.a, "Warad-Sin, nourisher of Ur . . . the shepherd of righteousness, who makes his widespread people to lie down in peace,"[18] *Hammurabi rēʾûm nibīt* [d]*Enlil anāku mukammer nuḫšim u ṭuḫdim*, "Hammurabi, the shepherd called by Enlil am I, the one who makes affluence and plenty abound,"[19] and *ilū rabûtum ibbûninnīma anākuma rēʾûm mušallimum ša ḫaṭṭašu išarat ṣillī ṭābum ana ālīja tariṣ ina utlīja nišī māt Sumerîm u Akkadîm ukīl*, "the great gods called me, so I became the beneficent shepherd whose scepter is righteous; my benign shadow is spread over my city. In my bosom I carried the peoples of the land of Sumer and Akkad."[20]

14 *OIP* 2, 114, col. VIII, 25–30.

15 *Ibid.*, 114–5, 36–38.

16 On the Exodus theme in Second Isaiah, see J. L. McKenzie, *Anchor Bible*, *Second Isaiah*, 11–12, 57. *Cf.* Exod. 17:1–7; Pss. 78:16; 105:41.

17 *UET* 1, 91, #295, 1–5; *RISA*, 307.

18 *UET* 1, 35, #128, 6–14; *EMRT*, 147–9; on ú.sal = *aburru*, "pasture," see *CAD/A1*, 90b–92a; compare *haṭṭašu el kiššat nišī šutēšuri māssu aburriš šurbuṣi*, "so that he may lead his people aright with his staff, let his country lie in safe pastures," *4 R* 12:19 f., and *ša ina šulum šiberšu irteʾu aburriš māssu*," "(Tukulti-Ninurta) who keeps his land on safe pastures under the salutary rule of his staff, "E. Weidner, *AfO Beiheft*, 12, 26, #16, 7, both cited in *CAD A/1*, 90b, 91b. Compare the biblical passages Gen. 48:15, Deut. 8:2 ff., Isa. 14:30, 40:11, Ezek. 34:15, Zeph. 2:7, Ps. 23:1 and 80:2. Akkadian *ušallu*, derived from Sumerian ú.sal, has the meaning "meadow" and "flooded land," *cf. kima ūri mithurat ušallu*, "the landscape (covered by the flood) was as level as a flat roof," *Gilgameš* XI:134; *ANET*, 94. Syriac *ʾwslʾ* is derived from the Akkadian, S. Kaufman, *The Akkadian Influences on Aramaic*, *Assyriological Studies*, 19 (Chicago and London, 1974), 110.

19 *Code of Hammurabi*, *Prologue*, I, 50–56; *ANET*, 164.

20 *Code of Hammurabi*, *Epilogue*, XLVII (Rs. XXIV), 40–52; *ANET*, 178. Compare Isa. 40:11. In connection with the themes of the shepherd and the straight path, we should

The themes we have found in the inscriptions were carried down to the Neo-Babylonian period, thus providing the link with Second Isaiah, e. g., *šarrru ša ina milki šadlam itellû šadîm bīrūtim ittabalakkatu ḫuršāni zaqrūtim*, "the king who, with his great skill, climbed many remote mountains and crossed many high peaks" (Nabunaʾid, 555–539),[21] *ilNabû-kudurrī-uṣur šar Babiliki rubâm naʾadam migir ilMarduk iššakku ṣiri narām ilNabû rēʾûm kīnim ṣābit uruḫ šulum ša ilŠamaš u ilRammān*, "Nebuchadnezzar, king of Babylon, the exalted prince, the favorite of Marduk, the exalted prince, the favorite of Marduk, the high chief priest beloved of Nabu, the faithful shepherd, who follows the path of peace of Shamash and Ramman."[22] Nebuchadnezzar also claims: "What no former king had done (I achieved); I cut through steep mountains, I split rocks, opened passages."[23]

The motifs of the shepherd, the providing of food and water, the straight path through the mountains, and the release from darkness are all conjoined in Isa. 49:9–11:

לאמר לאסורים צאו לאשר בחשך הגלו על דרכים ירעו ובכל שפיים מרעיתם; לא ירעבו ולא יצמאו ולא יכם שרב ושמש כי מרחמם ינהגם ועל מבועי מים ינהלם: ושמתי כל הרי לדרך ומסלתי ירמון:

"Saying to the prisoners: 'go forth'; to them that are in darkness 'show yourselves'; they shall feed in the ways, and in all high hills shall be their pastures; they shall not hunger nor thirst, neither shall the heat nor sun smite them, for he that hath compassion on them will lead them, even by springs of water will be guide them; and I will make all my mountains a way, and my highways shall be raised on high."[24]

The passage from the Epilogue to the Code of Hammurabi, cited above (see note 3) also combines the motifs of seeking a peaceful place (the shepherd motif), opening difficult places, and causing light to shine on the people.

Other biblical verses which relate to the passage through mountains are Jer. 31:9(8), and Zech. 4:7. If the reading of *LXX* and *1QIsa*[a] be accepted, Isa. 45:2, might also be included. In the Masoretic version it reads והדורים אישר, "I will make the crooked places straight," but the variants indicate *והררים, "I will make the mountains straight."[25]

Finally, in connection with the theme of God's overcoming the moun-

consider the Akkadian idiom *mātam/nišī šutēšurum*, "to guide aright the land/people," e. g., *mušūšer ammi*, "who guides the people aright," *Code of Hammurabi*, *Prologue*, IV, 54; *ANET* 165, and *ana šutēšur nišī*, "to guide the people aright," *Code*, V, 14, and *ANET*, *ibid.* Compare a similar idiom in Hebrew, Pss. 5:9, 27:11, 143:10, Prov. 3:6, 4:11.

[21] *CT* 37, 5, i, 13 f., cited in *CAD B*, 208a.

[22] *UMPBS* 15, 37, col. I, 1–4; *uruh šulum* invites comparison with Isa. 40:3, 59:8.

[23] *ANET*, 307.

[24] The theme of releasing those who are in darkness is fully treated in Paul, *JAOS* 88, 182. Compare *ša in bīt ṣibitti nadû tukallam nūr*, "you (Marduk) liberate (lit.: show light to)

tains, it is of interest to compare the talmudic legend which relates that the ark, called also the chariot (I Chron. 28:18), levelled the mountains before the triumphant march of the Israelites through the desert.[26]

In summary, we can add one more example to the existing store of borrowings adapted to the God of Israel, a reasonable application of the principle that "the Torah speaks in the language of men."

him who has been thrown into prison," *AfO* 19, 66:8; *CAD B*, 157b, cited by Paul, *op. cit.*, 182, n. 21.

[25] A. Rahlfs, ed., *Septuaginta* (Stuttgart, 1935), 2, 627, reading: καὶ ὄρη ὁμαλιῶ; R. Kittel, *Biblia Hebraica*, 3rd ed. (Stuttgart, 1937, repr. 1959), 671; E. Y. Kutscher, **הלשון והרקע הלשוני של מגילת ישעיהו השלמה ממגילות ים המלח** (Jerusalem, 1959), 168–9.

[26] *TB Berakot* 54a–b; *Midr. Tanhuma*, *Hukkat*, 20. Variants of this legend have flames emanating from the ark, destroying enemies (*Midr. Numb. R.* 5:1), or exterminating snakes and scorpions (*Deut. R.* 7:10); L. Ginzberg, *Legends of the Jews*, vol. 3 (Philadelphia, 1911), 157; *ibid.*, vol. 6 (Philadelphia, 1928), 116; *cf. Tosefta Sotah*, 4:2, on the pillar of cloud.

Ariel, "City of God"

By RONALD YOUNGBLOOD
Wheaton College Graduate School, Wheaton, Illinois

THE NAME "ARIEL" (MT *ʾryʾl*), used four times by Isaiah in reference to Jerusalem (Isa. 29:1 [twice]; 29:2a; 29:7), remains an enigma to modern scholars. "Lion of God" and "(Altar-)Hearth of God" are the two major (and most obvious) interpretations of the name usually cited in the commentaries. While the latter is preferred by most commentators[1] (primarily on the basis of Isa. 29:2b, 6c; 31:9; Ezek. 43:15 f.), it is typically done so with something less than absolute conviction; and the former is not without its supporters as well.[2] But because of the difficulty of choosing between the two options, some commentators simply cite both without making a decision on the matter.[3]

Other interpretations have also been proposed, though without attracting large numbers of adherents. The meaning "Belonging to God, Possession of God" has been suggested tentatively by making appeal to Ugaritic *ʾary*, "kinsman, dependent."[4] "Light of God" is another proposal that has been put forth (comparing Hebrew *ʾôr*/*ʾûr*), but only as a possibility.[5] A third suggestion has been strongly urged: to relate Ariel to Akkadian *Arallu*/*Arallû*, "underworld," Egyptian *ʾi-ir-ʾi-ra*, "warrior, hero," and II Sam. 23:20, understanding the word to mean "Hero" in Isa. 29:1 and 29:2a and "denizen of the underworld, shade" in 29:2b.[6] "Sign of God"[7] is only one of a number of other proposals to have been suggested in recent years. But the problem of the meaning of Isaiah's "Ariel" is far from being solved, and a scholarly consensus on the subject seems as remote as ever.

This paper, therefore, will attempt to point the way toward a solution.

[1] *Cf.*, e. g., N. H. Snaith, *Notes on the Hebrew Text of Isaiah: Chapters XXVIII–XXXII* (London: Epworth, 1945), p. 26.

[2] *Cf.*, e. g., *The Jerusalem Bible* (Garden City: Doubleday, 1966), p. 1187, fn. a.

[3] *Cf.*, e. g., G. A. Smith, *The Book of Isaiah* (rev. ed.; New York: Harper, 1927), I, p. 215. See also *ASV* mg. at Isa. 29:1.

[4] E. J. Young, *The Book of Isaiah* (Grand Rapids: Eerdmans, 1969), II, p. 305, fn. 1.

[5] W. C. Kaiser in M. C. Tenney, ed., *The Zondervan Pictorial Encyclopedia of the Bible* (Grand Rapids: Zondervan, 1975), 1, p. 301.

[6] W. F. Albright, *Archaeology and the Religion of Israel*[4] (Baltimore: Johns Hopkins, 1956), p. 151; p. 218, fn. 86. For the same etymology with a radically different interpretation, see F. L. Moriarty in R. E. Brown, J. A. Fitzmyer and R. E. Murphy, eds., *The Jerome Biblical Commentary* (Englewood Cliffs: Prentice-Hall, 1968), I, p. 278. Albright emphatically denies that the first element in *ʾryʾl* "means etymologically 'hearth' " (*op. cit.*, p. 218, fn. 85).

[7] A. Penna in R. C. Fuller, ed., *A New Catholic Commentary on Holy Scripture* (London: Nelson, 1969), p. 586.

As its title indicates, I would propose that *ᵓrᵓl in Isa. 29:1, 2a and 7 means "City of God." While such a suggestion is by no means brand new,[8] I shall try to bring some hitherto unnoticed evidence to bear on the question while at the same time recycling and refurbishing other tantalizing data scattered here and there throughout the scholarly literature on Ariel and related subjects.

Perhaps the best place to begin would be to remind ourselves of a well-known fact: The discovery of the Dead Sea scrolls has made the vocalization of *ᵓrᵓl in Isa. 29:1 ff. more uncertain than ever. While MT reads *ᵓărîᵓēl* (*ᵓryᵓl*) throughout, 1QIsa[a] reads *ᵓrwᵓl* throughout.[9] Such a consonantal structure would lead to a conventionalized spelling of "Aruel," "Uruel," or the like.

The Ariel/Aruel pair, demonstrating the interchange of *y* and *w*, is not without parallels elsewhere. The Sumerian logogram for the city of Ur can be transcribed (and therefore, presumably, pronounced) as either URÌ.UNU(G)^{KI} or URÙ.UNU(G)^{KI}.[10] The place called "Peniel" in Gen. 32:30 is called "Penuel" in the very next verse; and whereas it appears in the form *Per-nu-al* as Number 53 in the Pharaoh Shishak's list of conquered cities, it is spelled *Panili* in late Assyrian records.[11] The proper nouns Jeriel (a descendant of Issachar, according to I Chron. 7:2) and Jeruel (a part of the wilderness of Judah mentioned in II Chron. 20:16) are surely variants of each other. The Aramaic form of "Jerusalem" is *Yᵉrûšlem/Yᵉrûšlēm*, while its Syriac counterpart is *ᵓÛrišlem*.

This latter pair raises again the intriguing question, noted often by lexicographers and commentators,[12] of whether the initial two syllables of "Ariel" and "Jerusalem" were originally identical. The earliest known attestation of "Jerusalem" comes from the last half of the third millennium B.C.E., the period of the *fluorit* of Ebla (modern Tell Mardikh), which is currently undergoing excavation. There Jerusalem was called *Urusalima*,[13] equated by the Ebla excavation's epigrapher, G. Pettinato, with "Salim, the city of Melchizedech."[14] In Egyptian execration texts from the nine-

[8] *Cf.*, e. g., J. Hastings, ed., *Dictionary of the Bible* (rev. ed. by F. C. Grant and H. H. Rowley; New York: Scribner's, 1963), p. 52, where it is mentioned briefly and then rejected—but for insufficient reason, as I shall argue.

[9] Unfortunately, although portions of Isa. 29:1 ff. are extant in 1QIsa[b], not one of the five occurrences of "Ariel" has survived in that MS. In any event, it is very difficult (though not "impossible," as claimed by S. Loewinger in *VT* 4 [1954], p. 156) to distinguish between *wāw* and *yôd* in 1QIsa[b].

[10] *Cf.* W. F. Albright and T. O. Lambdin in *CAH*², Vol. I, Chp. IV, p. 30.

[11] S. Cohen in *IDB* K–Q, p. 727.

[12] *Cf.*, e. g., T. K. Cheyne in *Encyclopaedia Biblica* (New York: Macmillan, 1899), I, pp. 298 f.

[13] *Cf.* W. S. LaSor in *Christianity Today* 20/25 (1976), p. 49; see also *Newsweek*, November 15, 1976, p. 82.

[14] G. Pettinato, *BA* 39/2 (1976), p. 46.

teenth century B.C.E. we find the spelling *Urušalimum*, written *ꜣwšꜣmm*.[15] The Amarna letters of the fourteenth century refer to Jerusalem as *Urusalim*, written *Ú-ru-sa-lim*,[16] while the eighth-century Assyrian ruler Sennacherib calls it *Ursalimmu* (*Ur-sa-li-im-mu*)[17] which, incidentally, exhibits the inevitable loss of the short *u*-vowel (a phenomenon reflected also in Nabataean *ᵓÛršālîm*).

The *uru*-prefix of these forms is obviously the same as the *yᵉrû*-prefix in the Hebrew/Aramaic forms of the name "Jerusalem," a fact recognized long ago.[18] The initial phoneme of the name has been handled variously throughout its history: zero-element or *ᵓāleph* in Akkadian cuneiform and Egyptian hieroglyphics as well as in Nabataean, Syriac and Arabic; *yôd* in Hebrew and Aramaic; smooth breathing mark in LXX (reflected in the spelling "Ierosalem" in early editions of KJV); rough breathing mark in Josephus and in New Testament Greek (reflected in the spelling "Hierusalem" in early editions of KJV).

The meaning of the first half of the word "Jerusalem" is still a matter of considerable debate.[19] While it may be somewhat hasty to assume an etymological relationship between the Akkadian *uru*-prefix and Hebrew *ᶜîr*, "city,"[20] or even between *ᶜîr* and Sumerian *URU*, "city,"[21] it is surely not too daring to propose that *Urusalim* was popularly understood to mean "City of (the god) Salim" by (incorrectly?) equating the *uru*-prefix with Sumerian *URU*.[22] A possible parallel in this connection is the Latin word for "Byblos," *Alcobile*, which we are perhaps to understand as an attempt to represent *āl Gubli*, "City of Byblos" (*ālu* means "city" in Akkadian).

Most modern scholars assume that the Salem of Gen. 14:18 is the Salem of Ps. 76:3 (2 English) and is, therefore, Jerusalem.[23] The latter equation was made, in fact, already in 1QapGen. 22:13[24] as well as by Josephus.[25]

[15] W. F. Albright, *BASOR* 83 (1941), p. 34.

[16] *EA* 287:25, 46, 61, 63; 289:14, 29; 290:15.

[17] D. D. Luckenbill, *The Annals of Sennacherib* (*OIP* II; Chicago: University of Chicago Press, 1924), col. iii 15, 28, 40.

[18] M. Jastrow in *JBL* 11/1 (1892), p. 105.

[19] For a convenient summary *cf.* P. Winter in *NTS* 3 (1956–57), p. 140, fn. 1.

[20] As P. Winter seems to do; *cf. ibid.*, pp. 139 f., fn. 1.

[21] Although such a relationship is commonly taken for granted; *cf.*, e. g., *KB*, p. 701.

[22] *Cf.* G. A. Cooke, *The Book of Joshua* (Cambridge: Cambridge University Press, 1918), p. 84; M. Jastrow, *loc. cit.*

[23] E. g., J. J. M. Roberts, *JBL* 92/3 (1973), p. 331; E. Jacob, *Theology of the Old Testament* (New York: Harper, 1958), p. 47, fn. 2; H. Renckens, *The Religion of Israel* (New York: Sheed and Ward, 1966), p. 156; Y. Aharoni, *The Macmillan Bible Atlas* (New York: Macmillan, 1968), p. 27.

[24] See J. A. Fitzmyer, *The Genesis Apocryphon of Qumran Cave I. A Commentary* (Rome: Pontifical Biblical Institute, 1966), p. 64.

[25] *Ant.* 1.10.2; 7.3.2; *J. W.* 6.10.1.

There may even be a reference to this shortened form of "Jerusalem" in Ezra 4:7, where *bišlām* perhaps means "against Jerusalem"[26] and thus corresponds to the phrase *ʿal-Yᵉrûšlem* in the following verse.

Salim/Salem/Shalem is a well-known deity in the west-Semitic pantheon; his name is attested at Ugarit and elsewhere. It is quite likely that he is the god after whom Jerusalem was named and that he was worshiped there in the pre-Israelite period. El Elyon, "God Most High," was also worshiped in Jerusalem at least as early as Melchizedek's time (Gen. 14:18–22),[27] but it is not necessary to assume, with I. Engnell[28] and others,[29] that El (Elyon) and Shalem are virtually to be equated. It is enough to affirm that both were known in ancient Jerusalem and that El (Elyon), at least, was worshiped there. And perhaps it would not be amiss at this point to assert that Abram recognized in Melchizedek the makings of a believer in the one true God by identifying Melchizedek's "God Most High" with "Yahweh" (Gen. 14:22).[30]

In any event, if the first two syllables of "Ariel" were originally written "Uru-" (as 1QIsaᵃ leads us to believe), and if "Jerusalem" originally meant "City of S(h)alem" (as seems quite likely), there is no longer any compelling reason to reject the translation "City of God" for "Ariel" ("*Uruel"). In fact, one of the Amarna letters adds another bit of evidence to strengthen this interpretation.

EA 252, written by a ruler of Shechem, is a Canaanite document with the thinnest of Akkadian veneers and has therefore been studied intensively. A phrase in lines 29 f., *URU i-li*, was rendered "the town and my god" by W. F. Albright in conformity and in context with lines 12 f., *URU ù i-li*, which he had rendered "the city as well as my god."[31] Later, apparently observing the omission of the conjunction *ù* in lines 29 f., he revised his translation there to read "city of god," adding that the phrase "may well refer to the temenos (sacred enclosure) of Shechem, excavated by Sellin and Wright. . . ."[32] F. M. Cross has reminded us of "three liturgical epithets in the Patriarchal narratives . . . : ʾEl god of Israel-Jacob (Shechem), ʾEl ʿÔlām (Beersheba), and ʾEl [ʿElyôn], Creator of Heaven and Earth (Jerusalem)."[33] If Albright's latter translation of *URU ili* is correct (even

[26] *Cf. The Jerusalem Bible*, p. 573, fn. k.

[27] *Cf.* J. A. Sanders in *JBL* 88/2 (1969), p. 283, fn. 17; F. M. Cross in *HTR* 55 (1962), p. 244; H. Renckens, *op. cit.*, p. 156; E. Jacob, *op. cit.*, p. 47, fn. 2; J. J. M. Roberts, *loc. cit.*

[28] See the judicious discussion in E. Jacob, *op. cit.*, pp. 45–48.

[29] E. g., H. Gaubert, *Abraham, Loved by God* (New York: Hastings House, 1968), p. 110.

[30] See further R. Youngblood, *The Heart of the Old Testament* (Grand Rapids: Baker, 1971), p. 30; E. Jacob, *op. cit.*, p. 47, fn. 2; J. J. M. Roberts, *JBL* 92/3 (1973), p. 340.

[31] *ANET*², p. 486.

[32] W. F. Albright in *CAH*², Vol. II, Chp. XX, p. 19; *cf.* also *Yahweh and the Gods of Canaan* (Garden City: Doubleday, 1968), p. 195.

[33] F. M. Cross in *HTR* 55 (1962), p. 244.

allowing for the conventional Akkadian normalization *āl ili*—which, however, would by no means be automatic in a Canaanite letter), and in the light of Cross' observation that El was the patron deity of both Shechem and Jerusalem, the **Uruel* of Isaiah 29 could easily mean "City of God" with reference to Jerusalem or, at least, to its sacred precinct, the temple area.

Does this analysis imply that "altar-hearth" is an erroneous translation of **ʾrʾl* everywhere in Isaiah 29? Not at all. I would argue that 1QIsa^a correctly reads *ʾrwʾl* in Isa. 29:1 (twice), 2a and 7, but that MT correctly reads *ʾryʾl* in 29:2b[34] and that *ʾryʾl* there means "altar-hearth." Ezek. 43:15 f. exhibits the word **ʾrʾl*[35] three times with that meaning—each time, incidentally, preceded by the definite article, making it highly unlikely that the word is a two-part construct phrase containing the element *ʾēl*. Line 12 of the Mesha Stele includes the expression *ʾrʾl dwdh*, which probably means "altar-hearth[36] of his beloved" or the like.

It is highly likely, then, that 1QIsa^a leveled out all five occurrences of our word to *ʾrwʾl* and that MT leveled them all out to *ʾryʾl*. By doing so, both recensions missed the paronomasia[37] intended in Isa. 29:1 f., which I will not try to reproduce in this rendering:

> Woe to you, City of God, City of God,
> the town where David settled!
> Add year to year;
> let the cycle of feasts continue.
> But I will afflict the City of God;
> there will be mourning and lamenting,
> and she will be like an altar-hearth to me.

[34] It is just barely possible that 1QIsa^a reads *ʾryʾl* in Isa. 29:2b as well, since the *wāw* in *ʾrwʾl* there is more ambiguous than in the other four occurrences of the word in Isaiah 29; see especially the photographs by J. C. Trever in F. M. Cross *et al.*, eds., *Scrolls from Qumrân Cave I* (Jerusalem: AIAR and Shrine of the Book, 1972), pp. 60 f. In any event, those responsible for transcribing 1QIsa^a 29:1–7 into modern Hebrew characters in the *editio princeps* had their own difficulties in distinguishing between *w* and *y* in *ʾrw/yʾl*; at first they read *yôd* in all five occurrences, and then later they lengthened the tail of the *yôd* (with ink) in all five places to make each look like a *wāw* (see M. Burrows, ed., *The Dead Sea Scrolls of St. Mark's Monastery* [second printing; New Haven: *ASOR*, 1950], I, Plate XXIII, left-hand page)!

[35] See *BH*^{3} for details.

[36] So, for example, E. Ullendorff in D. Winton Thomas, ed., *Documents from Old Testament Times* (New York: Harper, 1958), p. 197. "Hero" has also been suggested, comparing such passages as II Sam. 23:20 (=I Chron. 11:22) and Isa. 33:7. On the basis of certain Mari texts, W. F. Albright proposed the rendering "Arel (or Oriel), its chieftain" for the complete phrase *ʾrʾl dwdh* (*ANET*^{2}, p. 320). But the meaning "chieftain" for the word *dwd* has been shown to rest on rather shaky foundations; *cf.* especially H. Tadmor in *JNES* 17 (1958), pp. 129–141.

[37] *Cf.* independently T. K. Cheyne, *loc. cit.*

If *ʾrʾl does indeed mean "City of God" four times in Isaiah 29, it joins a number of other Biblical phrases with the same or similar meaning. In Ps. 46:5 (4 English), 48:2, 9 (1, 8 English) and 87:3 we find *ʿyr (h)ʾlhym*, "city of God"; 101:8 and Isa. 60:14, *ʿyr Yhwh*, "city of Yahweh"; Ps. 48:9, *ʿyr Yhwh ṣbʾwt*, "city of Yahweh of hosts"; Jer. 31:38, *hʿyr l-Yhwh*, "the city of Yahweh";[38] Heb. 12:22, *polei Theou zōntos*, "city of the living God"; Rev. 3:12, *tēs poleōs tou Theou mou*, "the city of my God."

It is of more than passing interest that "city of God" or its equivalent throughout the Bible always refers to Jerusalem, whether in history or in the eschaton. Portions of the prayer in Daniel 9 seem to bridge history and eschatology in their references to Jerusalem as "your city" (9:16, 19) and "the city that is called by your name" (9:18). Augustine, Bishop of Hippo in the fifth century C.E., was inspired by the Biblical phraseology mentioned above to write his great philosophy of history, *De civitate Dei*, the essence of which one writer relates to the entire "community of God's people."[39] That Paolo Soleri, the Italian-born architect currently engaged in building the ultramodern city of Arcosanti in the Arizona desert, should use the term *Civitate Dei* of his visionary project in the final chapter of his book, *Matter Becoming Spirit*,[40] is impressive testimony to the enduring attraction and value of a great Biblical concept.

[38] *The Jerusalem Bible*, p. 1304; J. Bright, *Jeremiah* (Garden City: Doubleday, 1965), p. 278—but *cf.* the note on p. 283.

[39] M. Dods, tr. and ed., *The City of God* (New York: Hafner, 1948), p. xi.

[40] See *Newsweek*, August 16, 1976, pp. 78 f.